THE SECRET WAR AGAINST THE JEWS

THE SECRET WAR AGAINST THE JEWS

HOW WESTERN ESPIONAGE BETRAYED THE JEWISH PEOPLE

John Loftus *and* Mark Aarons

St. Martin's Griffin
New York

 For information, address St. Martin's Press, 175 Fifth Avenue, New York, N.Y. 10010.

Design by Michael Mendelsohn of MM Design 2000, Inc.

CAST OF HISTORICAL FIGURES SHOWN ON THE JACKET (LEFT TO RIGHT):

Top: Queen Elizabeth II, Joseph Stalin, Dwight Eisenhower, Charles De Gaulle, John F. Kennedy, William Casey, Pope Pius XII

Bottom: Franklin D. Roosevelt, T. E. Lawrence, George Bush, Winston Churchill, Oliver North, Margaret Thatcher, J. Edgar Hoover

Library of Congress Cataloging-in-Publication Data

Loftus, John.
Secret war against the Jews / John Loftus and Mark Aarons.
p. cm.
ISBN 0-312-15648-0
1. United States—Foreign relations—Israel. 2. Israel—Foreign relations—United States. 3. Espionage, American—Israel. 4. United States. Central Intelligence Agency. I. Aarons, Mark. II. Title.
E183.8.17L63 1994
327.7305694—dc20 93-44058
CIP

10 9 8 7 6 5

To the "Old Spies,"

the hundreds of men and women
from the secret intelligence services
on both sides of the old Iron Curtain
who trusted us

Whatsoever ye shall do
unto the least of men . . .
So shall ye do
also unto me

—Jesus of Nazareth, called by the Romans
"King of the Jews," circa A.D. 32

Fuck the Jews . . .
they won't
vote for us anyway.

—The Honorable James Baker, Secretary of State,
United States of America, circa A.D. 1992

CONTENTS

ACKNOWLEDGMENTS

During the last twelve years, the authors asked more than 500 former intelligence officers to tell us about every hostile operation they had carried out against the Jews. In describing the complex covert links between oil, Jews, and espionage, the subjects of our interviews revealed as much about the secret history of the Western governments as they did about Israel. The recollections of these "old spies," buttressed by extensive archival research, provide a new and shocking insight into the dark corners of the twentieth century.

In attempting an oral history of this size and scope, undoubtedly errors have crept into the manuscript. We had to make judgments about which sources were credible, which stories were newsworthy, and which material could be synthesized into a readable form. The errors are ours alone. Those who wish to correct, comment, or criticize our efforts can write to John Loftus at PO Box 13075, Main Post Office, St. Petersburg, FL, 33733, USA, or Mark Aarons at PO Box 120 Rozelle, NSW, 2039, Australia.

By the very nature of the sources on whom we have relied so heavily for much of this book, we cannot list those who have been invaluable in telling the story of the secret espionage war against the Jews. While we would have liked to thank publicly hundreds of men and women who served in the international intelligence community, their well-being depends on anonymity. They know who they are and that they have our gratitude.

Some of the "old spies" now can be named because they are no longer alive. These include men such as Dan Harkins, formerly of U.S. Naval Intelligence, and John McIntyre, formerly with the U.S. Army's Counter Intelligence Corps (CIC). A few have volunteered to come forward and allow themselves to be identified, including William Gowen, also a former CIC officer, who generously shared his original research on James Jesus Angleton's Vessel forgeries and several other issues that we have dealt with in this book.

Several other scholars and researchers have shared their information and documents with us, among them Peggy Robohm and Rachel Verdon. We are particularly grateful to the members of the Shnadow family who shared their memories of Sol Shnadow with us. Although the Government of Israel did not cooperate with this book, we appreciate the many members of the American and Israeli Jewish community who volunteered to be interviewed.

Additionally, a number of people have read early drafts of the manuscript and provided criticism, feedback, and corrections, including Bob Weis, Manny Winston, and others who do not wish to be identified. We especially thank Peter Wertheim for reading every chapter of the book at every stage and providing hundreds of helpful comments, corrections, and pointers that have greatly enriched and improved the book.

Finally, many other people gave us support of many kinds without which we would never have been able to complete our work. Among these are Susan and Meg Loftus, Robyn Ravlich, Julia Gaythwaite, Martha Gaythwaite and John Tebbetts, John and Dixie Francey, Mark and Pat Spudie, Dave Butler, Fran Lonsdale, Fred and Dorothy Harrison, Donna Cornetta, Anne and Jack Walker, Greg Hart, Walter and Edie Loebenberg, Paul and Murray Martin, Carol and Rick Sanders, Ron and Cindy Benedetti, Lisa Allison, and David Basta, Danielle DiCosmo, Robert Klarnet, Stan Correy, Liam Hogan, Marty Clark, and Steve Goldman.

We would also like to thank the staff of the Central Security Facility in Fort Meade, Maryland, John Taylor and the staff of the U.S. National Archives, as well as the Tampa Bay Holocaust Museum and Educational Center for their many contributions. Sadly, our friend and secretary, Mrs. Patricia Desroches, died just before the book was finished.

Last, but by no means least, we thank our agent, Reid Boates, and the staff of St. Martin's Press, and especially our editor, Robert Weil, his assistant, Rebecca Koh, and Bert Yaeger, production editor, for their professional assistance in getting *The Secret War Against the Jews* from a few ideas on a couple of pages to final form. They helped us keep this volume readable and to a manageable size. Had we inserted every footnote and supporting reference, the book would be twice its present length. Research, like a work of art, is never completed, only abandoned.

John Loftus and Mark Aarons
August 1994

INTRODUCTION

THE SECRET WAR AGAINST THE JEWS

The major powers of the world have repeatedly planned covert operations to bring about the partial or total destruction of Israel. Long before there even was a Jewish state in Palestine, Western spies already were out to wreck the Zionist dream. The savage extent of the secret wars against the Jews will horrify the Western public. This chapter of espionage history, beginning in the 1920s, and continuing to the present day, has never been revealed before.

Half a world away from Israel, a sleepy suburban community hides one of the secret entrances to the underworld of espionage. Most, but not all, of the classified archives of the U.S. government are in Suitland, Maryland, just outside Washington, D.C. The Suitland complex contains several restricted access buildings, including the one where Jonathan Pollard worked for Naval Intelligence, before he was discovered to be an Israeli spy.

Across from the Naval Intelligence facility with its geodesic radar domes is a one-story brick warehouse, built as a storage annex for the National Archives. This is where the government's secrets are buried, literally. Only the top floor shows aboveground. It is a long, low building, about the length of a football field, surrounded by wide, well-mowed grassy fields that yield no clue of what lies beneath.

Anyone can visit the top floor of the facility. It is open to the public. There is even a shuttle out to the Suitland annex from downtown Washington. The gray government van stops halfway between the White House and the Capitol on the corner of the imposing main Archives building on Pennsylvania Avenue, in front of the motto carved in stone: "What is past is prologue."

It is chilling to be reminded that history really does repeat itself. The National Archives hold the records of the Indian wars, the American Revolution, the War of 1812, the Civil War, the Spanish-American War, World War I, World War II, Korea, and Vietnam. Most of these records are held in storage at Suitland. The original documents lie in humble gray boxes, on row after row of dark metal shelves. Here are the orders of generals and rosters of immigrants. Here are the files of American diplomacy and foreign policy.

The Suitland vaults also contain the records of American espionage and covert action, the kind of foreign policy that the history books are not meant to mention. Beneath the public reading rooms on the first floor is another world. It is entered from a locked elevator that can be operated only with a coded security card.

In the underworld below, one-third of modern history is still classified. Here are the captured files of the Third Reich, some of which are still secret half a century later. Here are records of the British secret service, which no unprivileged British or American citizens are allowed to see. There are levels and levels of hidden nuances, layers of secrets. After the journey down, the elevator doors open onto a long, wide underground street stretching off into the distance, dimly lit by ceiling lights fifty feet overhead.

On either side of the cement street are tall, thick, blast-proof doors, the kind you see in old-fashioned banks. Some of the heavy steel doors are open. Small squares of bright light spill out onto the street from the entrances to the vaults. There are about twenty of these enormous storage caverns, each approximately an acre in size. It is like the last scene from the movie *Raiders of the Lost Ark*.

The aisles of the vaults stretch hundreds of feet away into the darkness. From the aisles, rows and rows of shelves stacked with classified files reach two stories up to the ceiling. The workers scurry about pushing giant stepladders on wheels as they retrieve the old documents from their slumber.

As you come out of the elevator, the number-six vault on the left belongs to the National Archives. Just inside the door to this top-secret room are several plain wooden tables, a small office, and several rows of filing cabinets. Only a few people from the National Archives staff work here. The rest are teams of retired spies or reserve officers from one of the military intelligence agencies on their annual tour of duty. They are reviewing the old classified files, page by page, to see what can be handed over to the Archives staff and passed upstairs into the public domain. It is a slow process, and the reviewers are a little behind in their work. "About a half century to be exact," said the escort. "They're still at the beginning of World War II."

What makes matters worse is that even after the intelligence files are declassified, there are few archivists to index them. After Ronald Reagan became president in 1981, the budget of the U.S. National Archives was cut to the bone, allegedly in the interests of economy. Some grumble that it is in the interest of government secrecy. Without an index, locating a declassified file is like searching for a needle in a haystack. The Archives are the perfect place to bury a scandal.

The Archives staff cannot wander down the underground street into the rest of the vaults. Those are still the private property of other government agencies: the State Department, Naval Intelligence, the army, and so on. A chain-link fence with a locked gate blocks off the rest of the street beyond vault six. It takes more than a mere top-secret clearance to get through that gate.

A top-secret clearance is good only for American files. You need a "COSMIC clearance" to see the top-secret records from NATO countries and a code word clearance for each security compartment you want to access above top secret. There is one compartment for satellite intelligence, another for electronic espionage, another for cryptography, and so on. Each compartment has its own subset of secret access words, known only to the initiated.

It is also essential to obtain a special "Q" clearance from the Atomic Energy Commission. Many embarrassing records have been intentionally misfiled down in vault two in the special security cage for nuclear warfare documents. Hiding documents in another agency's vault is the intelligence equivalent of putting a soul in limbo. Files can be lost in this underground graveyard until Judgment Day, or so it is hoped.

Why aren't the records just destroyed? Shredding is not always an option. Each copy of a top-secret document is accounted for on a security log. Shredding would require filling out a "document destruction form" and fielding a lot of questions from the Archives staff. Even if an agency obtained permission to shred one of its own files, it could not hope to retrieve all the copies that previously had been distributed to other agencies. Asking another agency to return a file is a guarantee that someone will read it and make a copy first. Losing records in the vaults with a little judicious misfiling is much simpler. It happens all the time.

A record may disappear from the official files but still be known to the "institutional memory." The retired intelligence officers remember where a lot of the bodies are buried, and some of them can be quite helpful. A few years ago there was a public scandal when French intelligence accused the U.S. State Department of protecting Klaus Barbie, the notorious Nazi war criminal. The State Department issued the usual denials, but then the French released a memo quoting State Department file numbers on the Barbie case. The State Department said that it could not find the files and knew nothing about Barbie.

Our source recalled that the State Department had hidden a lot of its secret correspondence over in the army vault, with the records for the Military Government of Germany. He found the "missing" Barbie files and passed the word to one of the authors, who promptly telephoned his former colleagues in the Justice Department. The State Department was not amused and retaliated by blaming Army intelligence for protecting Barbie.

Our source, who had been in Army intelligence, was not amused himself. He knew that it was the State Department's intelligence group which was at fault for hiring Nazis like Klaus Barbie. The old spy and his friends told us precisely which State Department files to request from the vaults for declassification under the Freedom of Information Act. It is easy to find a needle in a haystack, if you have the help of a magnet. The result was our last book, *Unholy Trinity,* a history of Nazi smuggling by the Vatican, the State Department, and the British secret service.[1]

It seems that little has changed in the State Department for the last fifty years. We told one of our sources about our proposed dedication to this book. He laughed and said, "Did Baker really say 'Fuck the Jews,' or was it just *attributed* to him by the press?" Although there is some dispute about the exact wording, the secretary of state's vulgarism has been confirmed by two reporters from different sources who were present when he said it.[2] Nor was it the first such outburst. When Baker was being sworn in, one of the White House aides commented humorously that every American secretary of state had left office hating the Israelis. Baker is supposed to have joked: "What if one started that way?"[3]

"I hadn't heard that story," said our source. "That's pretty funny." That depends on whether one is the butt of the joke or not. The Israelis were not laughing. Secretary Baker was, in theory at least, a neutral umpire in the 1992 peace negotiations between Israel and the Palestinians. Yet he seemed to have a bit of a bias.

In fact, Baker's personal investments in oil interests were so extensive that he may have been violating federal conflict-of-interest law by having any influence on Middle East policy.[4] In 1990 President Bush asked the attorney general to grant Baker a secret waiver from the statute.[5] It may be no coincidence that rapid progress toward peace was achieved in the six months immediately following Baker's departure from office.

In 1993 Jews and Arabs finally found themselves looking across the bargaining table without outside onlookers. For the first time in seventy years, Jews and Arabs met on a level playing field, without the help of "neutral" arbitration from one or another of the superpowers. To the chagrin of many Western diplomats, the citizens of the Middle East appeared capable of solving their own problems without anyone's help. Perhaps all they needed was to be left alone.

The main thesis of this book is that the secret bias of Western governments against the Jews was and is the single largest obstacle to peace in the Middle East. We present a shameful history of racism, greed, and secret betrayal that is so sickening that it will be difficult for many Western readers to accept. On the other hand, our evidence is particularly hard to ignore.

This book presents the point of view of non-Jews, most of whom are retired intelligence officers. These "old spies" plotted against Israel and the Zionist movement that built the Jewish homeland. Most of the hundreds of intelligence officers we interviewed over the last decade were trained to regard Jews, and hence Israel, as hostile targets. Their input does not require that this book be hostile to the Jewish people.

Indeed, many of our sources regret their past hostility to the Jews and, in speaking out, were motivated, at least in part, to make amends and clear the air. The classified information they provided, and which is presented here for the first time, is far more damaging to those leaders of Western countries who have purported to be Israel's friends and allies than it is to our sources.

The espionage professionals whose stories are told here for the first time served with both the civilian and military branches of the far-flung intelligence communities on both sides of the Cold War. They include the services of most countries in the Western alliance and several from the old Soviet bloc. Many are now retired, others work as university professors, lawyers, and businessmen.

The international intelligence community is fairly small—perhaps fewer than 50,000 people really count. They all seem to know each other or at least *of* each other. In many ways, it is an intellectually incestuous community, even nepotistic. One introduction in the United States can lead to several generations of intelligence officers, especially among the families who worked on CIA covert operations. The spouses of spies seem to have the best memories and the most developed sense of humor. They often take what their husbands or wives did for a living with a large grain of salt.

British spies are the best educated and the most wittily incisive of American foibles. Two of the brightest people we met were women from the British intelligence services. Their male counterparts in the Secret Intelligence Service, or MI6, the counterintelligence service, MI5, and the Ministry of Defense were a bit dull by comparison. This may explain why Britain is now the only nation to have a woman, Stella Rimington, in charge of an intelligence service.

The Russians, on the other hand, are predominantly male, more affable, and almost as corrupt as the British. Our impression is that the civilian KGB has consisted of lip-service Communist yuppies and politicians' children, while the military GRU has benefited by recruiting the less well connected on the basis of intellectual merit and fanatical devotion. Still, for several generations, the Soviet communists ran the best intelligence operations in the world. No one else came close. The Russians do not want to talk about the past, but they often are frightened by the future. In the next generation, they see their economy run by leftist dilettantes or ex-KGB incompetents and the government controlled by nationalistic right-wingers from the GRU, the worst of all possible combinations. Our Russian sources thought it a waste of time to talk about past Soviet transgressions against Jews when the rise of Russian fascism is staring them in the face.

The only ones worse to interview than the Russians are the code breakers. The former officers of the U.S. National Security Agency (NSA) and the British Government Communications Headquarters (GCHQ) are hopeless. Having been inundated with daily mountains of trivial information, they are conditioned against any belief in reasoned analysis. They are the cynics of the intelligence community. One former NSA officer, now a partner in a prominent Boston law firm, stated that an agency that dumps forty tons of intercepts in the trash everyday has no time to understand anything.

FBI types are fun to watch a football game with, but their eyes glaze over when asked to explain a knotty contradiction in a twenty-year-old intelligence report. Their job was to report every rumor as potential fact and not to think about how the pieces of the puzzle fit together. Perhaps our opinion was biased by a classified Justice Department study reporting that a sample of FBI databases revealed a 50 percent error rate. The FBI compounded the confusion by sending deliberately misleading files to the CIA. To be fair, the CIA men and women present themselves as corporate professionals, but after a few drinks they candidly admit that they often don't have a clue either.

Far and away our favorite interviews were with former members of the U.S. Army Counter Intelligence Corps (CIC). Recruited for their high IQs, CIC folk seem to love the game of analysis, the hunt for the layer beneath the layer. Although their agency fell out of political favor long ago after a contretemps involving a security check on Eleanor Roosevelt's lover, the CIC has a tradition of stubborn honesty, diligent research, and meticulous file indexing. Because of these traits, the CIC has earned the enmity of most of the American intelligence community. No one is more despised around Washington than someone who insists on telling the truth and can back it up with good files.

Not that the CIC types were all Boy Scouts. For example, the late John McIntyre of Quincy, Massachusetts, was a hilariously funny man who survived numerous trips behind the Iron Curtain when all the other American agents had been betrayed by Soviet moles inside Western intelligence. McIntyre threw away his officially issued phony passport and, without telling anyone in the U.S. government, built an international network of Communist border guards who thought they were part of his black-market liquor business.

Neither the CIA nor Army intelligence ever suspected that on his weekends off, McIntyre drove up and down the border delivering bottles of scotch from the American military store to his Communist "employees" who warned him whenever the KGB was closing in. McIntyre's choirboy looks and amazing success as a border-crosser enabled him to escape the wrath of his superiors for such pranks as dropping his trousers and "mooning" General Reinhard Gehlen, Hitler's former intelligence chief who was then working for the CIA.

Not all of the tales are funny. William Gowen, a former CIC agent, discovered from the authors' last book that he had been falsely portrayed in U.S. intelligence records as a man who smuggled Nazi war criminals to the United States. His reputation had been defamed, his career sidetracked, in a vicious forty-year campaign to mislead congressional investigators and make him the secret scapegoat for others' misdeeds. Gowen was a victim in the secret war against the Jews, and we are glad to help him clear his reputation in this book. We also are grateful for his assistance with document location and for his introduction to other sources.

We are indebted to many, many others whom we cannot name, but whose efforts were equally valuable. Over the years, they have approached us on the lecture circuit, at airports and at intelligence seminars. A few are welded in our memory. There was the middle-age businessman who wept as he described his previous work as a professional assassin. The daughter of a senior CIA official who wanted to know why her father committed suicide. The elderly Jew who knew what Western intelligence had done to Israel but begged us not to write about it for the sake of future relations between Israeli intelligence and its Western counterparts.

All of the "old spies" have some amazing stories to tell. Convincing them to talk, even off the record, is not an easy task. There is a tendency among former intelligence officers to clam up when approaching the borders of their clandestine history, as if they were approaching a checkpoint at the old Iron Curtain. When you ask them exactly what they did during the Cold War, most give you the same look, a sudden aversion of the eyes, upward and away from the subject.

The sad part is they want to talk, especially the retired spies who were present for the birth of Israel. They want to tell someone about the secret world in which they once lived. Not that it was exciting or glamorous, far from it. Most of the business of the intelligence community is boring, pedantic scholarship—the cross-checking of gossip and exacting fact. Not the kind of "facts-are-stubborn-things" that politicians say for sound bites, but real facts. Secrets of state, the kind that politicians want to hide from the voters.

Most often the truth is suppressed for legitimate reasons of national security. All too frequently, though, lies are told to secure a politician's reelection. With respect to the Middle East, our governments do not want their own citizens to know that a covert double standard has applied to the Jews, and so they have lied to us for half a century. But there is one group of citizens whom the politicians cannot deceive or, at least, not for long.

Spies are in the truth business, and truth is an acquired taste. In its undiluted form, truth is an acid. Sooner or later it burns those who handle it. The "old spies" keep their leaders' ugly secrets bottled up within them, and it hurts. You can see the pain of knowing what really happened burning inside them. Although they want to denounce these deceptions to their fellow citizens, they preserve with painful silence the lies told by their superiors.

Unlike the rest of us, the citizens of the international intelligence community are not free to criticize the shortcomings of their own governments. They are bound by rules, strict rules: contracts of secrecy cast in stone. Their job is to make history and then bury it. Silence is what they get paid for. Continued silence keeps the pension checks coming.

Not that they are mercenaries. The men and women of the intelligence profession are, on the whole, honorable people. They believe in constitutional government, free speech, and human rights, which is to say they are vastly superior to their political masters. Most of them now also realize that there was nothing noble or honorable in their role in the secret war against the Jews.

In fact, most of the former intelligence officers whom we have met and interviewed in the last decade are more decent, more intelligent, and more dedicated to democracy than many of the citizens they serve. It is a pity that such bright, capable people were given tasks that included some despicable things. It is a tragedy that the public does not know what they did. Perhaps they did their jobs too well. Omission from history is the hallmark of success in covert operations. On the other hand, George Orwell said that omission is the most powerful form of lie, and it is the duty of historians to ensure that omissions do not creep into the history books.

The little rubber stamp marked TOP SECRET is both a powerful sword and a shield. In time of war, secrecy may be the keystone of victory. In time of peace, classification too often is the cornerstone of cover-up. Doctors may bury their mistakes, but politicians hide them in the intelligence vaults under a shroud of national security. The former intelligence officers who provided the information for this book agree that there are some secrets that should not be kept. Political deceptions based on self-interest, not national interest, fall within this category. A leadership that recklessly lies to its own people commits a crime against democracy. The best method of deception is to prevent public access by improperly classifying the records of political misconduct.

A few of the sources we talked to admitted that sometimes they were guilty accomplices. Their complicity of silence was essential to continued illegal conduct by their own governments. The conflict between what the state said in public and what it did in private drove many to acts of desperation. Some became defectors, particularly from former Communist countries where the discrepancy between truth and lies was greatest. Some became whistle-blowers and today endure the opprobrium of their colleagues for breaking the pact. Most are self-condemned to the worst alternative of all. They live in Dante's Inferno, in the Seventh Circle of Hell, the place reserved for those who had the ability to prevent evil but did nothing.

For the honest spy, there are no easy choices. Truth can burn politicians, but it also can burn "sources and methods." There is more to these words than the bureaucratic jargon of the intelligence community. To a spy, sources are human beings who provide information—the truth, it is hoped—usually about mutual enemies, often about their own country, frequently at the risk of their own lives. These people are treasured and should be. Good sources can win wars or prevent them. The "old spies" believe that so few good sources are available now because so many have been burned before.

Eyewitnesses are the only alternative to archives, but asking a spy to become a source is a historian's nightmare. To intelligence officers, a historian is simply a reporter with a book contract, and they hate reporters. At best, the intelligence community regards members of the press as naive simpletons, endowed with a constitutional privilege to do damage: loose cannons with a license to leak. On the other hand, governments should not be allowed to classify their crimes to hide them from journalists and their readers.

During the last ten years we have been approached by many people from the Western intelligence services. They wanted to confide some of their secrets. Their conditions for sharing information were severe. In most, but not all, cases, the first requirement was total anonymity. All discussions were subject to the attorney-client privilege of confidentiality in a jurisdiction that prohibits disclosure of a client's identity without explicit consent. Due to this privilege we were able to submit portions of this book to the intelligence community for prepublication review, without identifying which of their former employees had provided information to us. While the CIA review board suggested a few helpful changes, it is not responsible for the contents of this book.

Nor should any inference be drawn that this book is supported, or endorsed, by the government of Israel, several of whose officials privately expressed their desire that it not be written. To be perfectly blunt, it is hard to believe that what we say will make their intelligence liaison relationships worse than they already are. Telling the truth might even help. The same goes for the governments of what was once the Union of Soviet Socialist Republics and the "People's Democracies." Our only responsibility is accurately to publish the information that was given to us by concerned individuals acting out of conscience and outside official channels.

It is not easy for a responsible journalist to find a middle ground between the public's right to know and the government's legitimate need for secrecy. As a rule, the "old spies" regard journalists as being only a cut above politicians, who, they agree, leak more secrets than anyone else. The Reagan administration is a classic case. In the aftermath of a terrorist bombing in West Germany, one White House official insisted that the Libyan government was responsible for the attack. When asked for proof at a press conference, he boasted that United States intelligence had monitored Gadhafi's secret cable traffic.

A groan went up among the wiretappers of the National Security Agency who were watching. He had revealed one of the few secret advantages the U.S. government possessed. After the press conference, Libya quickly changed its outdated, easily intercepted, cable-coding equipment to one of the more modern, virtually unbreakable systems.

It is an article of faith among the intelligence community that politicians deliberately leak classified information when it favors them but scream "national security" when they want to conceal their mistakes and, more particularly, their crimes. The "old spies" hate politicians as much as they hate being called "old spies." On the other hand, they have their own derisive vocabulary. Those who serve in the field call their desk-bound colleagues "anal-ists." In turn, the intelligence analysts describe field agents as "spooks," when they are not calling them something worse.

"Intelligence officer" is the preferred designation, but then garbagemen prefer to be called "sanitation engineers." In this book, we frequently describe our intelligence sources generically as the "old spies." Spying is what they did. This book is about those who spied on Israel.

"No, it isn't," said one of our sources. "It's not about us. It's about hypocrisy." He is correct. This is not an indictment of those men and women from the intelligence community who were merely the foot soldiers in the generals' secret wars against the Jews. This book is the shameful record of those politicians around the world who made these policies and then kept them secret from their own citizens for decades. Most of us do not know that our own Western governments have launched a secret war against Israel. If the "old spies" are right, and we think they are, even Israel's government does not know everything that has been and still is being done to it.

In a larger sense, this book is about more than the betrayal of one nation. Israel is simply a good example of a bad example. Many groups have been the victims of international double-dealing, although few have suffered from it as much as the Jews. We could have written, for example, about the Western governments' complicity in the ongoing genocide of East Timor, a tiny island nation of Catholics being murdered by Moslems for the sake of Western oil profits. It is a silent siege, a secret war that is too rarely mentioned in the press. But then, neither was the Holocaust at the time. East Timor has much in common with Israel.[6] Crimes against Jews are just not news, certainly not big news. Moslem crimes against minorities almost never make the press.

There is much good to be said about the Western media. As much as television is criticized, the fact remains that many people know much more about the world around them than did their grandparents. On the other hand, our intelligence sources say that of six recent scandals—Watergate, debategate, Irangate, Contragate, Iraqgate, and the savings and loans scandal—the Western media succeeded in only one investigation. Moreover, the press got Nixon only because someone in the intelligence community spoon-fed them the story.

The almost unanimous conclusion among the people we interviewed is that the American press has been unwilling to commit sufficient resources to develop its own expertise in intelligence matters and has simply abandoned any pretense of long-term investigations. Television news has been particularly derelict in documenting the longer, more complex stories. Dan Rather, one of the most prominent American anchormen, recently admitted to a group of broadcasters: "We should all be ashamed."

The intelligence community thinks even less of congressional investigations. Somehow we must find a way to strike a better balance between the need for secrecy in intelligence operations and the necessity for oversight by democratic institutions. For the last seventy years, neither Congress nor Parliament has been inclined to exercise its responsibilities in a responsible and effective manner.

The result of this combined negligence of the media and public institutions has been shameful indeed. It does not matter whether we are talking about the savings and loan scandal, or the arms race, or the intelligence wars against Israel. The fact remains that our politicians have developed the cover-up into an art form. We simply do not know what our civil servants are ordered to do, because their political masters have classified the truth about their activities. Sometimes, although we are reluctant to admit it, we do elect crooks to high office. Crooked politicians and the intelligence services make a dangerous combination.

Classified crime is the hardest to prosecute, even before the bar of history. We were a little reluctant to attempt to probe into those dark corners where oil and espionage mix. Even with the help of so many sources of information, the subject matter is so complex that we wondered how it could be organized into a readable form. One intelligence officer turned art teacher suggested a useful approach.

He displayed a color slide of an abstract sculpture. The piece was over six feet tall, of metal branches all intertwined. There were harsh angles, jagged pieces, fire-scored surfaces. It was, to all appearances, a random column of ugliness. Hardly the model for a book. "Don't look at the sculpture itself," our friend advised. "Look at the holes." Inside the twisted sculpture was an orderly pattern of smooth ovals, arranged in perfect balance, making sense of the whole.

That became the intellectual model for this book. Known history is like the visible surface of the sculpture, a series of harsh, twisted, seemingly unconnected branches. The hidden parts of history, the covert sides, are more orderly and rational, but can be seen and understood only if you are told where to look. The holes in history are what make sense of the thing. The hidden motives, secret agendas, classified purposes: All these tell the *why* of human events. In order to understand the *what* of modern Israel and its context in the harsh, twisted annals of the Middle East, it is necessary to identify the holes in the history books. The holes are the unwritten history of covert operations, the classified omissions that make up *The Secret War Against the Jews*.

Our sources suggested that if we wanted to write the previously omitted history of the Middle East, we should begin at the beginning, pointing out all the classified holes along the way. That, in undiluted form, would be a bit much for the reader to digest. For a start, including everything that the hundreds of "old spies" have told us over the years would have made the book too unwieldy. Each chapter therefore is based on the claims of the four or five sources who were most directly involved in the events under discussion. To help chart the way, each chapter begins with a capsule of the known history of the period, followed by a summary of our intelligence sources' list of omissions. Then we present our research evidence to support or rebut their allegations.

There are, we admit, some deficiencies in this approach. For a start, there is a great danger in relying on interviews from anonymous sources, especially when they are intelligence officers who are professionally trained in spreading propaganda and deception. A further problem is that much of what the "old spies" have to say about Israel has never been published before and cannot be absolutely corroborated, even from declassified files. We have made every effort to cross-check our sources against each other. That the former intelligence officers we interviewed agree with each others' stories is not, of course, a guarantee that their recollections are accurate.

We do not know for certain if our sources have told us the truth, only that they want us to believe it is the truth. Much of their information can be verified from existing archives and historical works, which are cited in the text, but even this cannot ensure that we have not been misled in other ways. You may not be convinced that the spies' version is true in all respects, but at least you may be convinced that much of what has hitherto been accepted history is either false or, at best, seriously deficient. Our only claim for this book is that it is an accurate account of how many spies view the West's conduct toward Israel. This is their story, their book, and a very different look at history.

But is it true? We have taken great pains, particularly in the most controversial modern sections, to document extensively our sources' allegations with concrete facts. Corroboration has been obtained from such diverse sources as Oliver North's diary, hundreds of volumes of congressional investigations, and thousands of declassified files.

Our goal was to present oral history in the context of the documents of the period, giving readers enough information to judge the facts for themselves. We believe we have made a convincing case that at least 80 percent of what the "old spies" say can be confirmed through open sources. That is a remarkable claim for the power of independent research, because less than 10 percent of their material has been officially declassified. It is amazing how much secret information is sitting in a public archive or library, once someone tells you where to look.

On the other hand, we hope you will find this account anything but a boring, academic treatise. It is a lively tale of espionage told by interesting and unusually informed people who wanted to contribute their institutional memory to the pool of public knowledge. One of the primary purposes of this book is to introduce the public to the world of classified operations, without endangering lives or exposing networks. Except for the ubiquitous genre of the spy novel, most readers are not even aware that this other world exists. It is your history too. You are entitled to know the weaknesses of your own intelligence services so that defects may be corrected. Where intelligence agencies are concerned, secrecy is the guarantee of short-term efficiency. In the long run, it is democracy that decides whether our secret services have done more harm than good.

To make it easier for you to decide for yourselves, we have divided our chronology of what has hitherto been omitted from history into three parts. The first part, "The Age of Bigotry," covers the period from the end of World War I to just after the end of World War II. Its purpose is to show the reader how our modern spy scandals have evolved naturally, and inevitably, from what went on before. It begins with the biographies of the first Western spies who betrayed the Jews because of their racial bigotry.

The middle part, "The Age of Greed," covers the postwar era up through the Nixon administration. This section of the book traces the transition from crude bigotry to a sophisticated form of insider trading, using government intelligence to further corporate policy, especially the interests of the giant oil companies. This resulted in secret aid to the Arabs during their wars with Israel.

The final part of this book traces the West's war against the Jews in the modern era, what we call "The Age of Stupidity." From the CIA's sabotage of Jimmy Carter's presidency, through the twelve long years of Presidents Reagan and Bush, the secret betrayal of Israel was the touchstone of the men who made their incredible profits from the Arabs. In a series of shocking revelations, our sources allege that the Reagan administration set up Israel as the scapegoat for the Iran-Contra scandal, while the White House bought guns from a PLO terrorist and wiretapped American Jews.

There are many books about espionage *by* Israel, most of which have been extremely negative. The Jews are popularly portrayed as having a siege mentality: paranoids with yarmulkes—insufferable, ungrateful, and untrusting. Why, for example, would Israel recruit Jonathan Pollard to spy on the United States? Don't they know that Americans are on their side? The American people may be so inclined, but their government has fluctuated between reckless indifference and secret hostility, a hostility that has manifested itself over the decades as covert action.

Although Secretary Baker was probably joking when he said "Fuck the Jews," some people feel that he was summarizing the State Department's policy toward Israel for the last seventy-five years. If the "old spies" are right, the U.S. policy was lenient compared to that of the British, French, Japanese, Soviets, and Germans. In fact, all the great nations have treated the Jews as expendable assets, obstacles to the secure supply of Arab oil.

This book is the history of Western espionage *against* Israel. It is the other side of the coin or, perhaps more appropriately, a look at the underside of a rock. The spies have a view of the world that we rarely see. Although we are loath to admit it, perhaps it is a glimpse of the world as it really is and as it has been throughout this century.

THE SECRET WAR AGAINST THE JEWS

PART I

THE AGE OF BIGOTRY

1920–1947

For more than twenty centuries, the Jewish people, more than any other segment of humanity, have been persecuted, uprooted, and annihilated. It is true that many other ethnic and religious groups have suffered grievously at the hands of tyrants, but there was a crucial difference.

More Africans were killed in the era of slavery, but there was no determined intent to eradicate the entire Negro race. A higher percentage of Armenians perished in the Turkish genocide before World War I, but the main intent was to deport them, not extinguish their genetic pool. Stalin, Mao, Pol Pot, and Suharto murdered millions of their own citizens, but the motive for those crimes was political power, not racial animus.

In each of these cases, the genocide was intended to serve a deeper purpose—the conquest of territory, the acquisition of wealth, the enlargement of political power, or the achieving of an ideological objective. In contrast, the genocide of the Jewish people was not intended to be a means to an end. It was not attempted in order to achieve a more fundamental purpose. It *was* the fundamental purpose. This is what makes the Nazi Holocaust unique in human history.

The most persistent explanation for the hatred of the Jews by some Christians and Moslems is that they refused to accept Jesus and were punished for pursuing their own faith. Yet close to a majority of Jews in Nazi Germany either were agnostic or had been converted to Christianity for several generations. People who had never set foot in a synagogue and who were physically indistinguishable from others in the Aryan genetic pool found themselves loaded into boxcars and taken to death camps. Religious affiliation, on its own, cannot be ascribed as the source of prejudice.

Nearly 75 percent of Jews in Israel today are secular, but that does not prevent them from being hated by people of other religions. Ironically, Jesus was an observant Jewish rabbi, and Muhammed honored Jewish religious traditions. The Koran reveres both Christian and Jewish prophets, and the Judeo-Christian tradition is considered the philosophical fundament of Western civilization.

According to both Jewish and Arab traditions, the nomad patriarch Abraham crossed into Canaan, or what became Palestine, and had two sons, one who became the father of Jacob, the founder of the Hebrew tribes, the other of whom became the progenitor of the Arabs. The early Semitic tribes can be distinguished racially and ethnically only by drawing on pedantic analysis of several subdivisions. Basically they originated from the same cultural and racial source. In language, culture, and habits, the Hebrew and non-Hebrew Canaanite tribes were virtually indistinguishable.

What made the cousins differ was literacy. Like the Arabs, the early Hebrew nomads were caught in a semiarid pastureland between two large warring kingdoms, Egypt, based on the Nile, and the powerful Mesopotamian cultures, which grew in the lush soil across the Euphrates. As the armies traveled back and forth, the nomads of Canaan became the most conquered people on earth.

Caught in the cross-fire of geography, the Hebrews quickly absorbed the strengths of their captors' various cultures in order to preserve their own. They adopted a crude form of alphabet similar to Assyrian cuneiform, but written like Egyptian hieroglyphs, from right to left. What made the Jews unique to all other early cultures was that literacy became an obligation for the masses.

The Hebrew nomads used writing to share survival skills among the tribes of kinsmen. For example, using the same wooden bowls for milk and meat products is a bad idea, as in the hot desert climate of their homeland, unhealthy bacteria will proliferate. This fact was the beginning of the kosher tradition, the first written public health code in the world, which appears in the Hebrew Bible, or Torah.

Literacy also allowed the Jews to develop a unifying sense of their own history and destiny. Thirteen different versions of Noah's flood developed in the ancient Middle East, but the Jewish one became part of Western civilization. Much of the early Hebrew tradition is recorded in the first five books of the Hebrew Bible. Undoubtedly it was the ancestors of the Jews who wrote the enduring history of this land. The ability to read was recognized by the Hebrews as such an important survival trait that it received the force of religious law. Almost a century before Jesus was even born, every Jewish village was required to have a teacher to train young men to read religious scripture.

Thus, eighteen centuries ahead of the rest of the world, the Jews had compulsory public education. This early religious commitment to literacy was the secret of continuing Jewish success and the source of consistent envy. For the next two thousand years, Jews were the only literate nomads on the face of the earth.

Even after the Romans smashed the central temple of Jerusalem and evicted most of the population of the region, the Jews could carry their religious traditions with them into exile. Wherever they were scattered, Jews could reproduce their culture because their children read the same Torah. All of their rituals were recorded, all their proud history written down. Nothing was lost.

Education was one of the principal reasons why the early Christians hated the Jews and the early Moslems respected them. In a purely social sense, Jews almost always came out better in comparison. For instance, a Jewish farmer would constantly outproduce a nearby Christian one simply because of the knowledge that literacy gives regarding planting cycles, fertilization, and crop production. The early Christian solution was to ban Jews from agrarian pursuits and force them into urban occupations.

The Moslems were different. Muhammed admired the Jews so much that he wanted to make Jerusalem the center of his religion. He recognized both Jewish and Christian prophets, and added the literacy requirement for the study of the Koran. Muhammed treated the Jews with a modicum of tolerance that put the Christian attitude to shame.

During the Christian Dark Ages, the literate religions of Moslems and Jews were having a Golden Age. The very words for algebra, magazines, and medicine all came from Arab scholars who worked in close harmony with Jews, particularly in Spain. To be sure, there was prejudice and discrimination, such as forcing Jews to wear distinctive clothing, and sometimes more serious abuse, but by and large the Moslem world treated its Jewish neighbors fairly decently.

The flower of Judeo-Moslem cooperation was crushed in the aftermath of the Crusades. In response to Western militarism, Arab leaders modified the semipacifist Moslem religion and by the eighteenth century, had transformed it into a warrior's code of domination over non-Moslem subjects and discrimination against the Jews. The era of tolerance and respect for education was over. The Moslem dark ages had begun. Harsh religious interpretations became an instrument of tribal loyalty and unity.

In the early part of the twentieth century, the Saudi Arabian king Ibn Saud used the extremist Wahhabi sect as the logical political extension of religion to prop up a tribal dictatorship. It was natural that the isolationist Wahhabi culture would feel threatened by the European Jews who were then starting to move into Palestine. In a bit of revisionism, Ibn Saud placed more emphasis on that part of the Koran that reflected Muhammed's anger toward the Jews, not his respect.

The Moslem tradition was artificially rolled back to the ninth century. The gentle Moslem religion was, and continues to be, perverted into an instrument of war, hatred, xenophobia, and, above all, ignorance. Where once, during the Christian Dark Ages, the Arab universities were the glory of the world, today the literacy requirement is kept to a minimum for the masses. Almost half the population of Saudi Arabia, Syria, Iraq, and Iran cannot even read the Koran. The reason for this blasphemy is, we submit, political. Too much public education might threaten dynastic control.

In comparison, the literacy rate in Israel, among Jews and Arabs alike, is more than 92 percent. The Jewish immigrants were, and are, a persistent threat to Arab backwardness and the luxurious lifestyle consequently enjoyed by the Arab dictators and their kin. Among other faults, the Jews who arrived in Palestine in the first decades of this century wanted to build public universities open to all residents. A literate Palestinian Arab community might taint the neighboring Arab population and spread the contagion of education, democracy, and human rights to challenge the feudal monarchs.

Education, democracy, and human rights, of course, are anathema to a dictator. Whoever opposed Jewish plans for Palestine was the natural ally of the Arab ruling classes. The Middle East was fertile ground for hatred. The first third of the twentieth century marked the dawn of the Age of Bigotry and the twilight of British influence in the Arab world.

The accepted British view of history is that England played a charitable role toward Jews in the first half of this century. It was England that gave Zionism, the movement to revive a Jewish state, its first political nourishment. It was England that lobbied the League of Nations for a mandate to govern the new colony of Palestine, England that appointed a Jew to oversee the mandate, England that tried to help the Zionists in the face of American indifference, England that condemned Hitler's racism. All of that is true, as far as it goes.

But what happens in public is not always a reflection of the clandestine policies of governments. The truth is that the British intelligence service undermined such noble notions. The first third of this book develops the thesis that bigotry, even more than economic advantage or geopolitical strategy, was the primary motive for early covert operations against the Jews. This period, stretching from the end of World War I to just after the end of World War II, was characterized by three very evil men: Jack Philby, a British spy; Ibn Saud, his Arab protégé; and Allen Dulles, an American spy and Wall Street lawyer specializing in international finance.

The racist nature of their secret war against Zionism does not appear in history books for a simple reason. Jack Philby later was paid by Western oil companies to write pro-Arab propaganda disguised as history. Ibn Saud is remembered as the glorious Arab leader who unified Saudi Arabia and led the richest oil region in the world into partnership with the West. Philby, if he is remembered at all, has the reputation of a scholarly British Arabist overshadowed by his son, Kim, the infamous Soviet double agent.

Jack Philby has become an obscure footnote to the history of the Cold War. But his legacy was far from minor. He is one of the lesser-known but most influential persons in the modern history of the Middle East, the renegade British intelligence agent who plucked an obscure terrorist out of the desert and helped to make him the king of Saudi Arabia. Ibn Saud was very much his creation. Philby stole the information from British intelligence files that engineered Saudi control over the holiest shrines of the Moslem world.

Jack Philby and Ibn Saud betrayed the British Empire and made the American oil companies economic masters of the region. The man who helped them do it was Allen Dulles, an American spy who had befriended Philby while he was coordinating American intelligence gathering in the Middle East in the first half of the 1920s.

Between them, these three men built the very foundations of the modern Middle East. They were the architects of the oil weapon, the instigators of war, the manipulators of history. More important, Philby's and Ibn Saud's political and philosophical allegiance was to Nazi Germany, while much of Dulles's profits came from the same source.

United by their hatred of Jews, they waged an unremitting campaign against the Zionists and, after 1948, against Israel. They fought their secret war in silence, sabotaging peace conferences, funding terrorist groups, betraying all who stood in their way. The truth of what they did has never been told before. It is an ugly story.

Jack Philby's intelligence role has been classified for many years. One after another, the Western nations were induced to abandon their façade of support for Zionism and acquiesce to his demand to abandon the Jewish state. It was Philby who represented the Arab point of view in the Western capitals and who subtly sabotaged the Zionist aspirations at the Palestinian partition conferences, while pretending to befriend the Jewish leaders.

Jack Philby was Ibn Saud's proxy in the secret war to stop Zionist immigration before World War II. Philby led the campaign to play the Nazis, the British, and the Americans against each other. He created the oil weapon as an instrument of foreign policy and made presidents and prime ministers bend to his will. He designed the Arab ultimatum: no Jews in Palestine, or no oil for the West.

It was Allen Dulles who delivered on the blackmail by threatening Western oil supplies at the most desperate stage of World War II. While paying lip service to their promises to partition Palestine into Arab and Zionist states, the West, especially the British, slowly strangled the birth of a Jewish homeland through restricted immigration, revised interpretations, and an endless series of committees to study the future of Palestine. At a critical point in history, Jack Philby held the keys to Palestine in his hand. The gates were closed to the 6 million Jews who fell victim to the Nazis.

After the Holocaust, Philby rewrote history to paint himself and Ibn Saud in a favorable light. The Allied intelligence services went along with the fraud, lest the public learn that their own governments were accomplices before the fact of genocide. Philby's and Dulles's oil blackmail had helped to tip the scales of history, by blocking the only viable escape route for Europe's persecuted Jews—the route to Palestine.

It is too easy to blame a couple of bigots for the consequences of the Holocaust. Many others in the English and American establishments played their part. But Philby and Dulles were the archetypical upper-crust anti-Semites and dominant figures in the early wars against the Jews. What kind of men were they? What kind of times produced such extraordinarily talented, and successful, bigots as these?

CHAPTER 1

PHILBY OF ARABIA

Three decades before the state of Israel was even born, there were British spies on the job, dedicated to the destruction of the Zionist dream. One made it his life's work. Harry St. John Bridger Philby was no ordinary spy but a professional nonconformist and dissembler. He manufactured so many contradictory sides to his character that even his real controllers were never sure where his true loyalties lay. A self-confessed fanatic, irascible and cantankerous, he was among the first, and most effective, of those who spied on the Zionists.

Remarkably, he has escaped the major attention devoted to his famous Communist double-agent son, Harold Adrian Russell Philby, or "Kim" as he was known. Certainly Kim was more notorious, particularly after his fellow double agents, Guy Burgess and Donald Maclean, fled to Moscow in 1951, and his own defection from British intelligence and flight behind the Iron Curtain in 1963. But in many ways, Kim was but a shadow of his father, St. John Philby—"Jack" to his friends.

Although there were earlier spies on the Zionists, none was more effective or more zealous than Jack Philby. He was the original inventor of the modern intelligence network that carried on the secret war against the Jews. It is now over three decades since he sat up in his bed in Beirut, muttered "I am bored" to his son, Kim, and died. But the anti-Semitic stranglehold he helped his close friend, Allen Dulles, put on U.S. policy in the Middle East endured right through to George Bush's White House in the 1990s.

Much of history is biography. This chapter examines the early life of Jack Philby, the secret founder of Saudi Arabia. The untold story of Philby's life is one of the biggest holes in the history of the Middle East. The allegations made by our sources in the intelligence community are as follows:

- Philby was dismissed from the British civil service and recruited by the British secret service, MI6, because of his sexual misconduct.

- Jack Philby used his intelligence assignment in the Middle East to take revenge on the British government and secretly joined forces with a fanatical Arab sect led by Ibn Saud, the man he helped make the king of Saudi Arabia.
- Philby proved his loyalty by passing Ibn Saud the intelligence information that ensured military victory for the House of Saud against Arab leaders supported by the British government.
- Jack Philby's sexual politics and example of betrayal had a formative impact on his son, Kim, who secretly became a Communist agent while at college.
- Kim Philby, who later became the most important Communist mole in the British secret service, was originally recruited by Moscow to spy on his father and Ibn Saud.

If these allegations are correct, they are indeed the missing links in the history of Middle Eastern espionage and explain how the Kingdom of Saudi Arabia succeeded in breaking British control of the area. None of this information has ever been reported before, and it is worthwhile to consider whether evidence exists to support our sources' allegations.

Jack was a child of England's empire, a minor civil servant in the espionage hothouse of India. He was born in Ceylon, now Sri Lanka, into a traditional Christian and politically conservative family. Like his son, Kim, after him, Jack left Trinity College, Cambridge, as a rebel, having discarded the family's establishment views. As he proclaimed in his autobiography, he became "something of a fanatic" and "the first Socialist to enter the Indian Civil Service." Before too long he had scandalized the establishment by becoming an anti-imperialist in the age of Rudyard Kipling.[1] Like his well-known contemporary, T. E. Lawrence, Philby "went native."

Despite his own claims to have sided with the native colonials, most contemporary scholars have seen Jack as the typical British imperial agent in India and then later in the Middle East.[2] He was also a noted Arabist, explorer, and gifted linguist, who spoke several Indian and Middle Eastern tongues fluently. According to the scholars, this gave Philby the opportunity to pose as an ally to the "natives" while actually subverting them.

Philby's job in the Indian civil service soon brought him into contact with the subterranean world of espionage. Kipling wrote of the "great game" between the Russian bear and the British lion, with Indian colonials as pawns. Philby was so caught up in the romance of espionage that he nicknamed his son after Kipling's spy character, Kim. But this prophetic sobriquet was not the origin of Kim's dislike of his father. Other sons have lived with worse names and survived. There was another special reason for Kim's hatred.

According to two British intelligence officers we spoke to, Jack had raped Kim's mother.[3] Young Kim was a bastard. It was all hushed up, of course. A young British woman of good family did not admit that her virtue had been tarnished, even forcibly. However, when it was discovered that the woman was pregnant, a marriage was quickly arranged in September 1910. According to the rumors, Kim was born on January 1, 1911, not 1912, as officially recorded. With the help of Jack's colleagues in the civil service, an altered birth certificate was planted in the hospital files on the next New Year's day, when the regular staff members were drunk or off duty.[4]

There is some circumstantial evidence to support our sources' account that a forced marriage had taken place. Junior officers in India were prohibited from marrying for three to five years, and Philby had been in the country for only a little more than eighteen months. Although one historian, perhaps inadvertently, listed Kim's birth date as 1911, the rape rumors have never been verified.[5] One of the few people who must have known the truth was Bernard Montgomery, Philby's distant cousin and later deputy commander-in-chief of the Allied armies during World War II. "Monty" stood up for Jack at the wedding as best man and later, to his deep regret, vouched for young Kim for his first employment in British intelligence. On the other hand, Montgomery may have only felt sympathy for the boy. Philby was not the ideal father.

Whether Philby was a rapist or not, he had certainly blotted his copybook with the British authorities in India, who noted only that he mixed too much with the "native element." It should be recorded that Philby himself had dark features, and it was widely gossiped that his wife, Dora, had some "colored" or Indian blood.[6] While at Cambridge, one of Jack's friends was Jawaharlal Nehru, later prime minister of India. Philby had hopes of a permanent career with the Indian civil service. It was not to be.

Shortly after his marriage, Philby was labeled an incompetent by the civil service and banned from further promotion. Nothing was ever written about the alleged rape. The official charge was that he had allowed a Moslem to be publicly handcuffed to a member of the untouchable Hindu caste. While officially Philby was only banned temporarily from holding certain positions in the bureaucracy, his Indian career was at an end, despite his success with the civil service language examinations.

It was at this point, in 1915, that our sources say that Philby switched from the civil service to the secret service. According to his own account, he received an appointment as head of the finance branch of the British administration in Baghdad during World War I.[7] Others say he was actually in charge of the intelligence department's secret financial records. That would be interesting, if true, as it would indicate that Philby may have had access to the British list of paid Arab informants, a priceless asset to men such as Ibn Saud.

There is no doubt that Jack Philby was lying about his job with military finance. He was working for the secret service and was assigned to the army only for cover. Both British intelligence officers we interviewed on Jack Philby's remarkable career agree with the version of British historian Anthony Cave Brown.[8] Jack Philby had been inducted into the secret world of British intelligence and became "a pendant of the British military intelligence service in Arabia, which was a term invented to conceal the existence of the secret service."[9]

Jack Philby began a bizarre espionage career that was exceeded only by the strangeness of his personal life. According to a retired official from the British Foreign and Commonwealth Office, Jack Philby was a sexual profligate, an adherent of the old Arab proverb: "For children, a woman; for pleasure, a boy; but for sheer ecstasy, a melon."[10] Our sources suspect that, as a young man, Philby had had a number of bisexual adventures in the British public school system, which endeared him forever to the homosexual network within the aristocracy of the empire. Such youthful dalliances were widely tolerated, despite the public prudishness of post-Victorian England.

In fact, one of our sources, a U.S. Army Counter Intelligence Corps (CIC) agent who went to school in England with several young men who later entered the British secret service, states that homosexuals were favored for recruitment by MI6. Before World War II, the upper ranks of the intelligence service were, he asserts, dominated by openly gay men. Bisexuality was seen as an asset for a British spy, as it offered unlimited opportunity for blackmail.[11]

In contrast, the Americans were, at least officially, homophobic. Gay men and women were driven from the ranks of the intelligence and diplomatic services, regardless of their loyalty and probity. This may have had more to do with the fact that the director of the Federal Bureau of Investigation (FBI), J. Edgar Hoover, was himself filled with self-hatred and fear that his own homosexuality would be discovered.[12]

During the 1950s it was Jack's son, Kim, who received most of the scrutiny, as he was suspected of being Guy Burgess's lover and of warning him to flee to Moscow to avoid arrest as a spy. However, when Kim fled to Moscow in 1963, Jack's sexual proclivities became the subject of security interest when intriguing similarities between father and son were discovered. Both British and American intelligence began to dig back into ancient history.

During the 1960s British intelligence tore itself apart as it tried to retrace the lovers' links that led Kim Philby and his friends to become

Communist spies. The embarrassing debacle of the Cambridge spy ring revealed a homosexual network that seemed to stretch back for decades. The investigations uncovered the fact that earlier homosexual alliances had provided an easy entry for the young Red spies into the heart of the empire's intelligence services. Kim Philby was known to be a secret homosexual and Communist. Was the father one as well? The answer is yes, and no.

There are some indications that Philby, Sr., was a manic depressive, filled with wild bursts of genius and energy, followed by long periods of dark depression. Postmortem psychoanalysis employed by Western intelligence questioned whether Jack's divided nature began with his failure to resolve his bisexuality and ended with the betrayal of his country. In this sense, father and son were very much alike, although they came to different ends.

Jack liked sex well enough, with either gender, but was never a witting Communist agent. He did briefly embrace the Soviets at the height of the Cold War, but it was just another persona behind which to camouflage his real work of vengeance against the British. His closest friends did recognize that Philby was a supreme egotist, an adrenaline addict, and a chameleon. Even those who knew him best, though, had no idea what game he really was playing.

In order to unravel the knot of conflicting allegations, it is vital to retrace Jack Philby's espionage career from the beginning. If you want to know the son, study the father. In November 1915, when Jack transferred from India to the Middle East, he sent his wife and Kim off to live in England, as his father had done to his mother and him before. The parallels did not end there. Jack insisted that his son undertake exactly the same education as he had himself. Kim was packed off to Westminster and then Trinity College, Cambridge, just as Jack had been before him.

Alone in the Middle East, Philby, Sr., pursued his real love, the adventure of espionage. Before long he got "his first taste of the intrigue which went on in the bazaars of Baghdad."[13] It also was his first taste of the powerful adrenaline that comes with spying. As one account of Philby's early spy work reported, he was even involved in plotting the capture and assassination of two of the most effective German agents in the Middle East.[14]

There are unconfirmed reports that Philby also directed an agent network out of Baghdad, inside the Moslem territories of the Soviet Union. Another source stated that his first network was out of India into Kazakhstan and Afghanistan.[15] Philby became infatuated with the world of secrets. He began to disguise himself as a native. Years later an experienced Arab intelligence agent noted that Philby could easily have passed as a bedouin, except that his by then hardened and blackened feet were still not dirty enough. His cover improved over the years, to the point that he was able to infiltrate a Comintern meeting.

In an age of gifted amateurs, Philby had chosen to become a professional spy. The problem was, he could not decide which side to work for. His first field controller was probably Gertrude Bell of the British Military Intelligence Department, who worked with Lawrence of Arabia (T. E. Lawrence). From Bell, Philby learned the finer points of the art of espionage.[16] Before long, however, they were on different sides in the complex world of competing Arab rulers and pretenders. It did not really matter, since Philby's loyalty to the empire had already died.

Philby may have begun the process of "going native" in India, but he ended up transferring his loyalties to the Arabs. In a way, it did not matter which ethnic group he joined. If he had been assigned to Belfast, Philby would have joined the IRA. All that mattered was that his new allies were as different as possible from the stultifying British bureaucrats who had ended his career.

The Arabs were certainly different. For one thing, they were far more tolerant of sexual peccadilloes. Word began to reach the drawing rooms of London that Philby had abandoned his family and was becoming a bit of a rake. For appearances' sake, he would return to England from time to time, where he would impregnate Kim's mother even as he bragged to her about his Arab mistresses. Young Kim later admitted that his father treated his mother abominably. The more repulsively he was regarded by society, the more Philby turned to the Arabs. While Jack was becoming a legend as an Arabist, young Kim had developed a permanent stutter.

For Jack, the deciding issue behind his secret break with England was political, not sexual. After Iraq, Philby was assigned to promote Arab revolutions against Germany's Turkish ally in the Middle East. His resentment over the Indian experience apparently accompanied him, and he soon fell out with his superiors.

The trouble was that Philby believed in his intelligence assignment and could never forgive the duplicity of his own government. He thought that Britain had genuinely promised the Arabs independence in return for their support against the Germans and their Ottoman ally. As a result of such naïveté, British Military Intelligence agents such as Philby and Lawrence had promised their favored Arabs the sun and the moon. Unfortunately, the British government had little faith that the Arabs either would, or could, deliver on the field of battle.

Within a year after Philby's arrival in the Middle East, the British ignored the promises made to the Arabs that they would receive self-determination and political independence. Instead, the secret Sykes-Picot agreement of 1916 divided the Arab world into French and British spheres of influence. Even worse, that deal was altered the following year, when the British government issued a private letter to Lord Rothschild, a leader of the Jewish community in England.

The Balfour Declaration of 1917 promised that Palestine would be "a national home" for the Jews. Not *the* national home, only *a* national home. The absence of the definitive article left the British some wiggle-room on this promise as well, to say nothing of ambiguities about whether London intended that there should ever be a sovereign Jewish state throughout the entire territory of Palestine. They intended to let only a few Jews immigrate, few enough so that they would always be a powerless minority in an Arab state. Jack Philby thought that any Jews would be too many.

According to our source from the Foreign and Commonwealth Office, the only reason that the British even made the Balfour Declaration was for foreign propaganda purposes, not for domestic consumption.[17] The bigots of British intelligence believed that the Jews controlled the American press and that gaining the support of American Jews was the key to obtaining the commitment of the U.S. government to send more than token forces after it entered World War I.[18]

Laughable as it may seem to us today, some of the senior officials of British intelligence actually believed that they could tip American public opinion in favor of a genuine military commitment by dangling a bit of bait before the noses of American press barons. In fact, there were only two Jewish families of any significance among American publishers and their influence was hardly enough to swing a local election.[19]

The truth is that the support of American Jews was unnecessary. The American military commitment was well under way even before the Balfour Declaration was published. Still, it was an article of faith among some British leaders, such as Winston Churchill, that the declaration was the price England paid to the Jews to ensure the full commitment of the United States to the war.[20]

One British source alleges that Jack Philby was himself partly responsible for the declaration. He and Lawrence had sent several intelligence estimates predicting that the Ottoman army would move across Palestine and threaten British holdings in Egypt. The files of the British Public Record Office confirm that British Military Intelligence had sent a barrage of doom-and-gloom warnings from the Middle East, in order to bolster support for their pet Arab causes.[21] Philby and Lawrence may have hoped that such reports would lead the British government to make an open declaration of support for Arab self-determination; however, they had the opposite effect.

The British government believed, with some justification, that Philby,

Lawrence, Bell, and their ilk were crackpots. By then Churchill had considerable experience of the fighting qualities of the Turks and was skeptical regarding the abilities of the Arab guerrillas.[22] By then, the British government had formed quite a positive view of the pro-Allied Palestinian Jews, who had developed "secret plans to capture Jerusalem when the Turks retreated" and "offered to set up a spy network for the British" to monitor enemy troop movements.[23] The small but vibrant Jewish community in Britain also was playing an important role in the war effort.

The ambiguous promise of a Jewish homeland in Palestine had little effect in terms of the United States' commitment to the war effort. It did, however, have a major effect on Jack Philby. From that moment on, he would never trust his own government again. The Balfour Declaration, according to Philby, was "an act of betrayal for whose parallel, the shekels and the kiss and all the rest of it, we have to go back to the garden of Gethsemane."[24] To put it bluntly, the declaration made Philby realize that Palestine was an unimportant square on the British chessboard and that the Arabs were merely pawns to be pushed around at will. To Philby, however, Palestine was the site of the third holiest shrine in Islam and the Arabs were noble princes.

In autumn 1917 he was given charge of the operation that was to determine the rest of his life. He was sent on a supposedly minor political mission to Ibn Saud.[25] The major game was being played by Lawrence of Arabia. In a secret memorandum to the Foreign Office, Lawrence urged that the British employ Sharif Hussein as a useful puppet head of a Moslem nation, but united only on paper. The Arabs would "remain in a state of political mosaic, a tissue of small jealous principalities, incapable of cohesion."[26]

While Hussein was fighting the Turks for the British, Ibn Saud, the young chieftain of the ultra-conservative Wahhabi sect, was sending terrorist raids against him. Philby was supposed to pressure Ibn Saud's dissidents back into line.[27] Instead, it was the beginning of a long and mutually beneficial relationship, which ultimately set Philby against any policy of his own government that conflicted with Ibn Saud's best interests.

None of the published histories explains why Philby embraced Ibn Saud with such intensity or why the equally fanatical king responded with such enthusiasm. According to the versions of several former intelligence officers, Philby and Ibn Saud shared a common hatred of the Jews. When Philby learned of the Balfour Declaration, he took it as a personal affront and made a number of inquiries among his associates in British intelligence.[28] He then informed Ibn Saud that they had both been betrayed by England and turned over classified information from the British secret service, including the fact that there would be no Arab nation, only another colonial jewel in the crown.

Both British sources we talked to on this point say that it was Philby's disclosure of London's secret intelligence policies that convinced Ibn Saud to trust him.[29] After all, he had committed treason by revealing classified information during wartime. There also were stories that Philby had become enamored of, and perhaps entrapped by, the sexual favors the king bestowed upon him. Both men believed themselves brothers in betrayal and devoted opponents of British imperial policy in the Middle East. Together they would work to end British colonial rule, especially the policy of a Jewish homeland in the Moslem world.

This meeting with Ibn Saud in 1917 was the seed from which grew Philby's treachery to his country and his bitter hatred for the Jews and their undeserved "national home" in Palestine. From that time onward, Philby was Ibn Saud's private ally in the secret and increasingly vicious war against Zionism.[30]

For Jack Philby, his relationship with Ibn Saud was just another manifestation of his own fanaticism. They became further bonded through their mutual dedication to the fanatical and brutal Moslem Wahhabi sect.[31] In the eyes of the educated Jews of Britain, the Wahhabis were barbarians, the wellspring of Arab anti-Semitism in its purest form. The American public should not have been surprised during Operation Desert Storm in 1991, when the Saudis refused to permit American soldiers to hold Jewish prayer services before going off to fight in defense of Saudi Arabia. They were simply being consistent with their anti-Jewish Wahhabi traditions.

Philby knew them well. Such fanatics were of Jack's mold, and he warmly embraced his new friends. It would not be long before he could begin his work for them, and they could begin to reward him. First, they helped insinuate him more closely in the secret service. As soon as the war was over, his Arab friends helped Philby obtain a major intelligence coup. In 1919, disguised as an Arab, he "infiltrated the Communist International's First Congress of the Asian People at Baku."[32]

From the point of view of the secret service, Philby was clearly a spy to be reckoned with. He had found a back door into the Bolsheviks at a most opportune time. While Sidney Reilly and other British agents were coming to naught in their assault on Moscow, Philby had attended a Comintern meeting. What the British did not recognize was that Philby had begun to associate the Jews of the Comintern with the Jewish bankers in Britain, who influenced imperial policy in Palestine.

It seems odd in hindsight, but it was an article of faith among the right-wing officers who dominated the secret service that all Jews were secretly Communists, even the bankers. One of the Rothschilds finally had to appeal to the prime minister to absolve him of charges that he was a secret Communist agent.[33] He was ultimately cleared. In the early part of this century, a history of anti-Semitism was not a hindrance to employment with the British secret service; it was more often an asset.

It seems to have been so in Philby's case. According to several intelligence officers we spoke to, Philby's dislike of the Jews was among the factors that led to his rapid advancement in the service.[34] By the time Philby returned to London in 1920, he was already the secret service's first spy against the Jews—a counterweight against the Foreign Office's tendency to be soft on Zionism. In this mission, he collaborated with Lawrence of Arabia to wrest control of Middle East policy from the "pernicious grasp" of the Foreign Office.[35]

By the summer of 1921, Philby's disdain of British policy came out in the open. He was fired because of his "fanatical nature" and his "personal bias" in favor of the Arabs.[36] Lawrence saved Philby's career by arranging a transfer. The men were bitter enemies on most points, but they shared a common dislike for the Jews and their Zionist dreams. In November 1921 Lawrence and the secret service engineered Philby's appointment as chief British representative in Amman, Transjordan. As chief representative, Philby was technically a British diplomat sent to advise what is now the nation of Jordan; in fact, he was the Secret Service head for the entire area, including what is now Israel.

Philby and Lawrence discussed the situation and "agreed on some immediate topics." In particular, Palestine must be an independent Arab nation, to "a degree that would place it out of bounds to Jewish settlement." Clearly, Philby, Lawrence, and the secret service were pursuing a different line from the Foreign Office. Unfortunately for Jack, the Jews proved to be as stubborn as mules and as prolific as the trees they planted. He was not the first to have that experience.

There have always been Jews living in Palestine. During Roman times they numbered in the millions, before they were dispersed by force around the Mediterranean basin. By the nineteenth century there were perhaps 50,000 left, principally in the holy city of Jerusalem, where they formed a slight majority from about 1800 onward. The Arabs called them "the dead ones" and treated them execrably. Jews who wished to pray at the Wailing Wall were forced to enter through the dung gate of the old city, used for the dumping of human waste. In the latter part of the nineteenth century, German Jews prevailed upon the kaiser to ameliorate their condition.

When the kaiser arrived in Palestine, he was disgusted with the condition of the country. The Palestinian Arabs had let the old Roman aqueducts fall to ruin. The Ottoman Empire had stripped the forests for lumber and firewood. The ultimate ecological curse was the ubiquitous herds of black goats. For nearly two thousand years since the Diaspora of the Jews, Arabs had allowed the black goats to graze unfenced across Palestine. They had eaten the grass down to its roots, and the topsoil had eroded and blown away. The biblical land of milk and honey had become a dust bowl.

When the kaiser arrived in Jerusalem, he was met by a contingent of German Jews. He surveyed the barren landscape and, according to the legend, mopped his brow and asked: "Why is there no shade?" The Jews explained that they could not plant any trees because they did not own the land, the Arabs did. The kaiser rejoined: "Whoever plants the trees will own the land."

This apocryphal story was the bane of Philby's existence. After it was formed in 1902, the Jewish National Fund (JNF) increased efforts to purchase land from the Arabs and plant trees. Although today it is considered one of the leading environmental agencies in Israel, indeed in the world, the JNF's original motives were not entirely ecological. Under Ottoman law, land had to be planted or farmed in order to retain ownership.

During the late 1800s Jews purchased obscure tracts of swampland at exorbitant prices from the Arabs. The huge malarial swamps of northern Israel were drained, and trees were planted to reclaim the marsh for farmland. Many of the pioneers died of malaria, but the trees they planted kept the land in Jewish ownership.

On this tiny wedge of territory, so uninhabitable that the Arabs did not want it, the Jews built the first modern base of settlement. The second wave of immigration came just before World War I. By the 1930s there were hundreds of thousands of Jews in Palestine. He was determined that there should not be any more. This unofficial British policy had the enthusiastic support of the Palestinian Arabs.[37]

During the early 1920s, Philby and his secret service colleagues did everything they could to undercut Zionist immigration. Philby's secret service station organized anti-Jewish propaganda in Palestine. To be fair, he was merely carrying out a policy organized by his predecessors to stir up the Arabs against the Jews.[38] According to several of our sources, Great Britain was the first modern country to use its intelligence service to organize terrorist acts against the Jews.[39] A large number of Jewish settlers lost their lives from the early 1920s on, but their heroic resistance had an opposite effect from that intended by the secret service.

A public relations backlash developed. Instead of caving in and canceling the Balfour Declaration, the Colonial Office appointed a Jew, Sir Herbert Samuel, as British High Commissioner of Palestine. The new

Jewish governor soon became Philby's nemesis. Soon after his arrival, a war for Palestine broke out between Sir Samuel's friends in the Foreign Office and Philby's friends in the secret service. British intelligence agents sponsored waves of Arab terrorism, protests, and propaganda that began to wear down the Foreign Office's resolve toward the Jews. By 1922 London began to waver in its support for a Jewish homeland by declaring that Balfour had only used the word "a," not "the" in relation to Palestine.[40] The anti-Semites already had achieved a major victory over the Zionists in 1920–21, when the first partition of Palestine had given the Golan Heights to the French colony of Syria, and all territories east of the Jordan had been incorporated into Transjordan and closed to Jewish settlement.

At the end of 1922 Jack accompanied Abdullah Hussein of Transjordan to London and held extensive meetings with all those involved in the Palestine question. It was on this trip that Philby began his relations with a number of the top Zionist leaders, among them Dr. Chaim Weizmann.[41] For the next two decades, Philby courted Weizmann, pretending to be his ally in order to subvert his movement.

Philby had a major coup on this visit, one that would greatly assist his anti-Zionist crusade for years to come. After tough negotiations, an agreement was reached that included Britain's promise of independence for Transjordan. This promise directly resulted in the formation of the Arab Legion, perhaps the crowning achievement of Philby's years in Amman. At last there was a force to fight the Jews.

In May 1923 under Philby's watchful and proud eye, an elaborate celebration was held in Amman to mark the independence arrangements that had been made in London and to formally launch the Arab Legion. It turned out to be another bitter watershed for Philby. The whole occasion was spoiled for him because the Jewish high commissioner, Viscount Samuel, had deeply insulted him. It was a sin of omission: "Samuel's speech made no reference to him or his work. Samuel's silence rankled with Philby for weeks."[42] The whole event, meant to be a high point in his career, merely increased Philby's loathing for both Britain and the Jews.

Worse still, the British were letting boatloads of Jews into Palestine. It may only have been a trickle, but it was more than he could stand. In January 1924 Philby resigned as chief British representative in Transjordan, after a series of disagreements with the viscount. He explained his decision to one of his friends: "I have resigned this job for many, very many reasons; the chief of them is that I can no longer go on working with the present High Commissioner who, being a Zionist Jew, cannot hold the scales even between Zionist and Arab interests."[43]

Philby's bigotry toward the Zionists and his own government had boiled over. There was more than a little coincidence in the timing of his resignation from his official position in Amman. According to several versions provided by our former intelligence sources, Philby had been secretly aiding Ibn Saud's campaign against his rival, Sharif Hussein, wherever he could for some years past.[44] Now Ibn Saud's final assault on Mecca, which the sharif controlled, would make Philby's position untenable in Transjordan, where Hussein's son Abdullah ruled under Philby's less than supportive eye.

Shortly after Jack resigned from his post as adviser to the Hussein monarchy, Ibn Saud also deserted the flock and began to call for the overthrow of the British puppets. In retaliation, Britain cut off its longstanding subsidy to Ibn Saud, who then felt no further constraints in attacking his archenemy. Philby allegedly played his part in Hussein's defeat by handing over a great deal of intelligence to Ibn Saud, which proved crucial to his successful campaign. Ibn Saud's victory does seem inordinately swift.[45] Thus was the Kingdom of Saudi Arabia founded by a renegade British spy. It was time for Ibn Saud to reward his most valued secret agent.

Ibn Saud immediately and publicly recognized the value of Philby's espionage contribution by assigning his loyal friend to take care of the details of the coronation. By then Philby was a completely free agent, having formally resigned as a British civil servant, "to serve my country after my own fashion."[46] He did not, however, resign from the secret service. It foolishly continued to pay him for another five years.

Between 1925 and 1930 Philby played a double agent for both the British and the Arabs. He moved to Saudi Arabia to become the confidential adviser to Ibn Saud. After arranging the king's coronation, he became his financial adviser. "Ibn Saud took a special interest in Philby."[47] So did other Arab fanatics.

In 1929 Philby visited Jerusalem, where he formed a lasting friendship with the viciously anti-Jewish grand mufti (religious leader) Haj Amin al Husseini.[48] Soon after Philby took the final step in "going Arab": He converted to Islam and took up his right officially to use the royal concubines.[49] Ibn Saud had used the inducement that, if Philby became a Moslem, he could have four wives.[50] Before he could take his pleasure with them, however, Jack had to recover from the mandatory circumcision, an extremely painful and traumatic operation for a man of forty-five. Such was the level of fanaticism Jack allegedly felt for his adopted country and religion.

There also were much more materialistic gifts, including a house and a job "as Saud's go-between in most business negotiations—with appropriate commissions."[51] Others said that Philby had "no particularly strong religious convictions" and that he converted to Islam "in order to facilitate his business dealings." Indeed, there were many among Saudi Arabia's merchants who "assumed the Englishman's motive for converting was to advance the interests of the various commercial agencies he had acquired, from Ford cars to Marconi wireless sets."[52] The insults apparently did not disturb Jack's peace of mind:

> From the moment of his conversion, Abdullah Philby became able to participate fully in the camaraderie of the Sa'udi court, to lounge with [Ibn Saud] in his house at Mecca looking down from its balcony into the courtyard of the Grand Mosque below, to share the long Ramadhan nights of feasting and gossip, to test out the slave girls . . . and to become a fully fledged member of that knot of boon companions, half Privy Council, half gang of chums, who went everywhere with [Ibn Saud], chatting, laughing and arguing, discussing politics one minute, playing practical jokes the next.[53]

The scandal certainly shocked London, most of all young Kim, who was just starting at Cambridge while his father was off to Mecca and the pleasures of Arabian concubines. To make things worse for the son, the father praised Islam for its "absence of the unjust stigma of bastardy" and declared his open allegiance to the Arab political cause. The secret service quickly dropped him from the payroll. It was now clear that he had gone over to the other side, even though many at Ibn Saud's court believed he was, in fact, "a British spy in our midst . . . promoting British imperialist interests in this country."[54]

It was a turning point in his son's life. Kim's father was now the most talked about lunatic in London. Kim was determined to have his revenge. Everything his father was for, he was against. Everything his father was against, he was for. Kim was already an intellectual Marxist, and like his father he had dabbled in homosexuality while still just a youth. Despite his own admission that he "buggered and was buggered" at school, Kim was determined to be heterosexual. He fled to Austria to put his intellectual revolutionary ideals into practice in the looming war between the working class and fascism. There he married the first woman who was kind to him, who happened to be a Jew.[55]

At the time, Kim actually wanted openly to join the British Communist party. His association with the Austrian Reds, not to mention his marriage to Litzi, a well-known Jewish Communist, completely blew his cover. For a brief while, Kim played an important role for the Austrian left, as a secret courier. Among those who knew about Kim's Vienna adventures was a Zionist named Teddy Kollek, who later became mayor of Jerusalem after a most interesting intelligence career.

Fifteen years later, when Kollek saw Kim again at the Central Intelligency Agency (CIA), he warned the Americans about his leftist past, but no one believed him. By then Kim's cover as a closet Fascist was too complete. During the intervening years the Soviet Union had gone to great lengths to conceal Kim's true affiliations. They had risked the life of a key agent inside MI5 by pulling every derogatory reference from his file.

What made the Soviets take such a risk? The reason is quite simple. They desperately needed Kim to collect information on Ibn Saud through his father. They even tried, unsuccessfully, to get Kim a job as the court tutor for Ibn Saud's children. As John Costello and Oleg Tsarev discovered recently in the KGB files, the Soviets gave Kim the code name of "Synok," Russian for "Sonny." The Soviets had a long file on Jack Philby, and when they began the process of recruiting Kim in mid-1934, his father was seen as an important target.

Over the years the son provided some interesting material to the Soviet secret service on developments in Saudi Arabia, especially on British military activities and preparations, including plans for an air force base. Indeed, the Soviets were so interested in Philby, Sr., that they psychoanalyzed his son as suffering from acute repression, as a result of Jack being "an ambitious tyrant" who "wanted to make a great man out of his son."[56]

It was the perfect opportunity to begin to place Kim at the side of Jack. They were an incongruous pair. The son was also a fanatic and a chameleon, a Communist who posed as a Fascist, while the father was a Fascist who pretended to be a Moslem. Between them they nearly strangled the state of Israel in its infancy.

Most espionage historians have ignored the father and focused on the younger Philby. But Jack's espionage career outlasted his son's and had a far greater impact on the Jews, as we shall see in the following chapters. Through his connections with the great anti-Zionist American corporations, Jack Philby was the central figure in building a coalition of powerful forces dedicated to destroying the Jews' national homeland in Palestine.[57]

But something happened in the late 1930s that made Kim far more important to the Soviet secret service than it had previously realized. Kim had already started the process of dropping his left-wing connections and making up to his father. But if Kim could get even closer to Jack again, he would be of priceless help to the Soviets. The Soviet intelligence service was interested in something very specific: Kim's father was helping his American friends sell oil to the Nazis through Spain. Germany was getting its war machine ready to attack Stalin, and Jack Philby was selling Hitler the fuel.

CHAPTER 2

THE SORCERER OF OIL

The history books describe the rise of fascism as the most important event of the 1920s. They were wrong. The Nazis would have remained a minor political party, and Germany would have remained a cash-starved country, weaponless and powerless, but for a massive influx of outside investment capital. Our intelligence sources believe that the most important event of this period was the alliance between American oil companies and Saudi Arabia. It was the indispensable precondition for war and the Nazi Holocaust.

The history books do not even mention the secret partnership of Ibn Saud, Jack Philby, and Allen Dulles. Together they were the secret source of oil, wealth, and international influence that worked behind the scenes to put Hitler onto the world stage. These men, who fueled the Nazi war machine in the 1930s, were the same ones who sabotaged the Jews' last, best hope of an escape route to Palestine. The partners in oil, our sources allege, were profoundly evil men who bore substantial responsibility for the Holocaust but escaped the judgment of history.

These are serious charges indeed. In the next two chapters we review the evidence at length. In this chapter we examine the following allegations concerning the origins of this secret alliance:

- Jack Philby recruited Allen Dulles in the 1920s, first as his agent to influence American policy against the Jewish homeland and then as his secret partner in the development of Saudi Arabian oil.
- With Dulles's help, Philby ensured the economic and political survival of Ibn Saud by creating a partnership with American oil companies, allied against British interests, and in favor of Nazi Germany.
- Philby worked with Nazi intelligence to sabotage international efforts to create a Jewish homeland.

According to our sources, when it came to spying on the Zionists, Jack Philby had American partners in crime. Not just any Americans, but the Dulles brothers, Allen and John Foster, two of the most powerful men in the world. Their mother's brother was Secretary of State Robert Lansing, founder of the State Department's first centralized intelligence unit. John Foster Dulles went on to become U.S. Secretary of State, while his brother Allen became head of the CIA during the Eisenhower administration.

At the turn of the twentieth century, anti-Semitism was a popular philosophy among the upper-class, Ivy League students who were attracted to the U.S. diplomatic service. Robert Kaplan, in his book *The Arabists,* captures the culture of a society in which anti-Semitism was an accepted, even unconscious, part of everyday life for the American establishment.[1] As a result, it is not hyperbole to say that the State Department had a fair number of bigots on its payroll. It was not unusual to find references to "oily Jews" in official diplomatic reports of both the United States and Britain.

The Dulles family had a mixed record in this regard. Foster claimed that he had many Jewish friends and even had Jewish law partners. But when their sister fell in love with a Jew, the family talked her out of such a disastrous alliance. Foster later reported that his sister had become "a devoted Hitlerite." Her Jewish fiancé had committed suicide. Foster hid his donations to pro-Nazi isolationists under his wife's name, while currying favor with German clients. Allen's record toward the Nazis is equally ambivalent, at least according to the accepted histories.[2]

A number of the "old spies" insisted the Dulles brothers were unmitigated charlatans who believed in nothing but making money.[3] Their crooked relationship with Jack Philby went back to at least 1921. When Philby was made the secret service's head of intelligence for Transjordan that year, he met his American counterpart, Allen Dulles, who was then stationed in Istanbul. From there Dulles had run networks across the Middle East and had accumulated a surprising amount of information on the potential oil wealth of Arabia—to say nothing about the potential sticking point of Zionist aspirations.

Most of our sources say that Philby was one of Dulles's sources and in fact was the man who jump-started Allen's career by feeding him timely bits of information. He also had a profound influence on Allen's views concerning a Jewish homeland in Palestine. After Istanbul, it was onward and upward for Allen Dulles: "His reputation as an observer solidified, and he returned to Washington to head up the Near East Division from 1922 to 1926. He analyzed Kemal Ataturk and masterminded U.S. bargaining moves at Lausanne, met most of the emerging Arab leaders, and fell into an acquaintanceship with the influential Zionist Chaim Weizmann which started him musing earlier than most Americans about the utility of a realized Jewish homeland."[4] Dulles reported that the utility of a Jewish state was zero. It would do nothing but complicate the entry of

American oil companies into the region. This was just what the State Department wanted to hear, and it was exactly the line that Philby was preaching. His new friend Dulles shared his own view of their common "friend" Weizmann, and his Zionist dreams.

From 1922 on, while Philby was running Britain's spy operations in Transjordan, Allen was back in Washington reporting on him as head of Middle Eastern affairs for the State Department. Dulles visited Palestine and, allegedly with Philby's help, had a private audience with Abdullah of Transjordan. Dulles wrote papers on Palestine and Arabian affairs that gathered dust back in Washington. American policy toward Zionism was already set, at least among Dulles's colleagues in the State Department. The Jews were an obstacle to the smooth flow of Arab oil.

Philby and Dulles were more than kindred spirits, they had once worked for the same master. Dulles had been easy prey for recruitment by the British secret service, for he had a penchant for sleeping with the wrong kind of women. According to several British sources, Dulles was first recruited by the British during World War I in Bern, Switzerland.[5] He fell victim to a honey trap set up by a female spy who worked for the Austrians. She traded her sexual favors to Dulles, and other Americans, in return for a job in the American Legation's secret code room. As an enemy agent, she was perfectly positioned to pass British and American secrets to her Austrian employers. British intelligence had its own spies in Switzerland and traced the leak back to Dulles's mistress. According to one published version of the story, Dulles helped the British secret service to arrest his mistress with incriminating documents in her possession.[6]

The story is true, according to the former intelligence officers we asked about it, except that there was no prearrangement with British intelligence.[7] They grabbed young Allen and his mistress and caught her in possession of his coded files. The implications were grim. The British played good cop/bad cop, with the heavy accusing Allen and his mistress of selling Allied secrets to the enemy in time of war. Allen swore that he knew nothing about her treason and readily agreed to be "helpful" to the British if they preserved his neck, not to mention his career.

From then on, he was in the bag. He became the first, if not the only, American slavishly to follow British foreign policy directives for Central Europe and the Middle East.[8] After his Swiss fiasco, Allen is supposed to have helped the British torpedo Woodrow Wilson's peace positions at Versailles. If the story of the Swiss mistress is true, it certainly did not dissuade Allen from further sexual adventures, in spite of the obvious security risks. According to former CIA director General Walter Bedell Smith, within a year of being transferred to France, Allen had fallen in love with a whore and had set her up in an apartment in Paris.[9] Such scandals are not the sort of thing upon which a diplomatic reputation is built.

When Dulles was posted to the hinterlands of Istanbul, it was up to British intelligence to salvage his career. Philby briefed him repeatedly. Suddenly young Allen was a fountain of information and was called back to Washington to report on Arab affairs. It was a crucial time for Palestine.

After the 1921 partition of Palestine, Jack Philby had helped direct the anti-Jewish terror from his base in Transjordan. But mobs were not enough to stem the tide of Jewish immigration. In 1923, Philby set to work creating the Arab Legion, an armed force under British direction, ready for the (eventual) battle against the Zionist interlopers. Still, the Jews kept coming. In 1924 Philby switched sides. Ibn Saud's forces captured Mecca and Medina by force in 1924 and 1925. Ibn Saud became king in 1926, with Philby as his trusted confidential adviser.

At that point, Allen Dulles suddenly resigned from the State Department as chief of the Middle East Division. Like Philby, he found private intelligence work to be more profitable. Far more profitable, especially once he and his brother worked out how to make huge sums from doing business with the Saudis and his new friend, Jack Philby. As the key player involved in introducing American oil money into the country, Philby used Dulles's contacts to give Ibn Saud the financial resources eventually to expel British influence. We shall examine more of Dulles's role in the next chapter, but for now we turn our attention back to Jack.

Philby's part in the Saudi Arabian oil story was a covert act of treachery against Britain's interests. As early as 1922, he already had found the key factor in controlling future Western policy toward the Middle East: "The real crux is oil."[10]

The genesis of Philby's creation of the Saudi oil weapon started in the late 1920s, when the U.S. giant, Gulf Oil, began exploration in Bahrain.[11] Soon after Gulf turned its Bahrain interests over to Standard Oil of California (Socal) and pursued its own interest in Kuwait. In response, the British government invoked agreements it had made with Kuwait and Bahrain "that oil development should be entrusted only to British concerns," effectively blocking Gulf and Socal from developing their concessions.[12]

The Americans did not take this lying down. Gulf and Socal exerted incredible pressure in Washington to reverse the position. It was the beginning of the long U.S. campaign to replace Britain and dominate Middle Eastern oil. A "rather nasty series of negotiations" followed between London and Washington, and the British reluctantly backed off.[13] In May 1932 oil was discovered in Bahrain, unleashing far-reaching implications for the entire region, especially on the nearby Saudi Arabian mainland.

That year Ibn Saud had consolidated his rule and proclaimed the modern nation of Saudi Arabia, which he now ruled without opposition. But the onset of the Depression had caused him considerable financial hardship. Unable to pay the usual bribes to the disparate tribes that make up the country, Ibn Saud's grip seemed in danger of slipping. Enter "the sorcerer's apprentice of Saudi oil," Jack Philby.[14] In his autobiography, Philby credits himself as the man who sparked Saudi Arabia's oil hunt. Skeptics believe "we only have Philby's word that he was the master puppeteer pulling every string in the discovery of Sa'udi oil."[15] In fact, however, Jack did play the decisive role.

During one of his frequent intimate conversations with Ibn Saud in late 1930, the king expressed his despair at the state of his treasury. Philby, always the master of calculated eloquence, quoted the king's favorite passage from the Koran: "For verily God doth not change the state of a people unless they change themselves." Jack then persuaded his financially desperate friend to embark on the search for oil.[16]

Philby had planted the seed that grew into the giant Arabian-American Oil Company (Aramco). Through the enormous international power of Aramco, Philby would continue his war on Zion, even from his grave. In 1931 he introduced the king to the American philanthropist Charles Crane, who lent Ibn Saud the famous mining engineer Karl Twitchell "to investigate the mineral prospects of Arabia."[17]

In spite of his financial straits, Ibn Saud at first remained reluctant to grant concessions to foreigners, but Twitchell's encouraging reports of oil potential in the east of the country "made Ibn Saud, on consideration, less adverse to foreign investment in his kingdom." When Philby told him the price he could expect, to say nothing of longer-term profits, the king was converted. By now official British attitudes toward Philby were extremely hostile, but even the imperial bureaucrats did not dream of the treachery that Jack was planning.[18]

Under the cover of his position as adviser to Ibn Saud, Jack arranged an oil concession with Standard Oil of California. Twitchell had observed how influential Philby was in royal circles. He recommended Jack to Socal, and Philby met Frank Loomis, a Socal vice president and former senior U.S. State Department official, over lunch at Simpson's in the Strand. Only he knew Ibn Saud's terms, and he told Loomis in a most direct manner: What the king "wanted for his oil concession was cash on the nail."[19]

It was the kind of talk that Californian oil companies understood. A few weeks later Socal asked Philby to be its go-between to Ibn Saud to "ascertain the conditions on which the King might be prepared to grant a concession." Negotiations began in January 1933, with the arrival in Saudi Arabia of Socal's representative, Lloyd Hamilton.[20]

Philby was in his element, especially as he secretly stood to make a small fortune if he played the game well. Like Kim after him, Jack excelled at playing a double game. After his meeting with Loomis, "Philby promptly passed on to his old friends in the British oil business the news that the Americans had their eyes on an Arabian oil concession." Philby claimed to his friends in Anglo-Persian Oil that he was a free agent and not committed to Socal, but would help anyone interested in oil exploration in Saudi Arabia.[21]

As a result of Jack's mischievous work, the Iraq Petroleum Company—which was dominated by Anglo-Persian—sent former British government official Stephen Longrigg to negotiate on its behalf with Ibn Saud and his finance minister, Abdullah Suleiman. "Between this cast of characters Philby himself scurried about with delighted self-importance."[22] At first he played the field, to stimulate competition among the oil companies, but while bidding through his friends at Anglo-Persian for a contract as their agent, Jack slyly accepted Socal's offer.

Longrigg firmly believed that Jack was his man, but Philby agreed to Socal's terms of $1,000 a month for six months, to be followed by another $10,000 if Socal got the concession. As a bonus, he would receive a further $25,000 if commercial exploitation followed, plus U.S. 50 cents for every ton of oil exported up to another $25,000. Jack kept the deal secret and went on dealing with Longrigg as if nothing had happened.[23] While secretly on Socal's payroll, Philby manipulated the final outcome: "Though others were growing frustrated by the pace of negotiations, Philby, who delighted in being a mystery man, was glorying in his multiple roles—working as a paid agent for Socal, acting as an adviser to the Saudis . . . serving as Longrigg's confidant, and casually dropping in conversation with the various oil men what the King had said to him on their most recent auto ride up to Mecca."[24]

As non-Moslems the chief British and American negotiators were trapped in Jidda, while due to his standing as a Moslem adviser of the king's court, Philby could travel to Mecca. On his return from the holy city he would drop "mysterious hints, [to] coax out higher bids and generally impart to the proceedings an atmosphere of tension which the facts did not justify."[25]

Eventually the deal was done in late May 1933. It was very satisfactory, given the state of the king's treasury. In return for a sixty-year concession, Ibn Saud would receive an immediate £30,000 loan against royalties, plus an immediate payment of £5,000 in advance as the first year's royalty, all in gold. This would be followed by further substantial loans and royalties.[26] It was chickenfeed, compared to the billions that would eventually go to Saudi Arabia's coffers thanks to Jack Philby.

There was a general air of jubilation, except among the British. Philby was inordinately pleased at having shafted the empire and knew he had pulled off something much bigger than an oil deal. By introducing an American oil company, Jack had successfully and permanently changed "the whole Middle Eastern balance of power."[27]

On the other hand, both the king and Socal were extremely grateful to Philby for his role in negotiating the deal. Jack had more than justified the king's loyalty, in the face of serious charges at his own court that Philby really was a British imperialist spy. He had averted financial disaster for the kingdom, and Ibn Saud would do everything he asked to further their common fight against the Jews.

Similarly, Socal would help Philby, and not just with financial rewards, although there were plenty of them. In July 1933 Socal showed its appreciation by hiring Philby permanently at a salary of £1,000 a year.[28] The big rewards came five years later, in March 1938, after oil was struck, and Socal declared it was going into commercial production. Soon after Philby received the first of two payments of $25,000.[29]

Not content with his success as a duplicitous go-between, Jack became indispensable to Socal's operations, regularly traveling to the remote exploration sites, while Socal's "administrative headquarters had been established in Jidda, in a tall building with multiple balconies and its own electric generating plant. The landlord was none other than H. St. John B. Philby."[30] It was another nice little money earner for good old Jack, the first and arguably most important of the United States' spies on the Jews.

As will be seen, Jack Philby did more, much more, for U.S. oil companies than obtain the Saudi oil concession. He taught them how to interpret Ibn Saud and his court. The Americans quickly learned that a good dose of old-fashioned anti-Semitism did not go astray in Jidda. Not that the Arabian-American Oil Company lacked in hatred for the Jews. Far from it. That was another common bond with Jack. More than anything, though, he gave the oil men the means to guide, if not control, the mysterious potentates of Arabia.[31]

On the eve of World War II, Socal had its first successes in Saudi Arabia. By then Socal had already taken in its second partner, the Texas Oil Company (Texaco). After the war, Socony Vacuum (Mobil) joined the Saudi club, as did the Rockefeller-dominated Standard Oil of New Jersey.

Before the war Standard of New Jersey had forged a synthetic oil and rubber cartel with the Nazi-controlled I. G. Farben, prompting official claims of treason in the United States, especially after the country joined the conflict in 1941.[32] The New Jersey oil company was not the only U.S. corporation working with the industrial conglomerate Farben and the Nazis, however. As will be seen, Jack Philby had ties to the entire network through his friend Allen Dulles. But it was Jack who showed his American friends how to set up their own anti-Jewish network in the Middle East.

Jack Philby shared another thing in common with many of his friends in the American oil companies which later formed Aramco. As discussed in the next chapter, like Jack, there were a number of oil executives, particularly in Standard of New Jersey and Texaco, who were ardent supporters of fascism. The first sign came in Spain. The Spanish Civil War was a testing ground for the coming conflict between Germany and the Soviet Union. Jack Philby had convinced Ibn Saud to join the winning side, the side of fascism. After the civil war, "neutral" Spain would become the oil pipeline to the Third Reich. The Arabs and Americans would get rich. Philby also was negotiating for German support to keep the British out of the Middle East. The Germans, he claimed, knew how to treat the Jews.

Several of the "old spies" insist that St. John Philby met Adolf Eichmann during the mid-1930s, when he was on a fact-finding tour of the Middle East.[33] Before becoming Hitler's chief executioner of the Jews, Eichmann held himself out as Germany's expert on Palestine. It was the sort of exaggeration that greatly irritated the German Foreign Office.

In fact, his tour was an unequivocal disaster, and Eichmann was hurriedly shipped home after a series of diplomatic contretemps. Both Western and Israeli historians continue to downplay Eichmann's expertise, pointing out his minimal grasp of Hebrew, not to mention his overweening sense of self-importance. Yet our sources say that Eichmann had some influence on the course of events, although not the type that he intended. It was he who gave Jack Philby the germ of an idea: Ransom the Jews for profit.[34]

In the early days of the Third Reich, there was no formal plan for genocide—only the outlines of anti-Semitic philosophy spelled out in *Mein Kampf*. Hitler was content to make living conditions so deplorable in Germany that the Jews would choose to emigrate, leaving all their wealth behind. Eichmann played a minor role in enriching the SS treasury with expropriated Jewish property. It was this genius for organized theft, not any burning desire for the destruction of the Jewish race, that endeared him to his superiors. The more Jews who could be forced to emigrate, the more money Eichmann produced.

In the beginning, it was a simple task. Despite all the propaganda about Jews running the country, there were, in fact, only half a million in all of Germany. The larger problem of the huge Jewish populations of occupied Eastern Europe had not yet arisen. The Jews of Germany and Austria were all Eichmann could handle, for the moment.

After 1934 most of those with money or influence wanted to emigrate, but few countries would take in more than a handful. In order to keep the "cash cow" working, Eichmann had to find someplace for the Jews to go. His original idea was to send them all to Palestine. However, his tentative explorations were a disaster. The last thing the Arabs wanted was more Jews.

Eichmann was replaced on the Middle Eastern scene by a far more skilled intelligence officer, Otto von Bolschwing. Before World War II von Bolschwing set up an import-export business in Palestine as a cover for his espionage initiatives. He was an educated man from a good family and an enthusiastic supporter of Hitler. After the war von Bolschwing became one of Allen Dulles's senior agents in the CIA.[35]

Dulles helped von Bolschwing emigrate to California, where he established a business association with Helen van Damm, later Ronald Reagan's ambassador to Austria. In later years, his business went bankrupt and he was forced to surrender his American citizenship on the grounds that he was a Nazi war criminal. He was just the sort of fellow to get along well with Jack Philby. He hated Jews.

In the 1930s Otto von Bolschwing was a realist. He knew full well that the Moslem bigots would never accept even a token immigration of Jews to Palestine. Philby agreed. After more than a decade of anti-Zionist propaganda, quietly supervised by the British secret service, the climate was hardly receptive toward a homeland for the Jews in the Middle East. Still, there was profit to be made in the attempt.

In any future war, von Bolschwing said, the support of the Moslem world was essential to Hitler's plans. Not to mention that Philby and Ibn Saud could make a healthy profit by secretly ensuring Germany's supply of oil. Hitler would guarantee that the Moslems received favored status. Indeed, they later had their own SS division, raised, ironically, from among the Bosnian-Moslem population subjected to "ethnic cleansing" by the Serbs and Croats fifty years later.

The SS division was personally blessed by Philby's old friend, the grand mufti of Jerusalem. The mufti had been Hitler's honored guest and was even taken on guided tours of the Nazi death camps. Hitler promised that when Germany won the war, he would guarantee that the Arab states would be free of British colonial domination. They would be independent states, and full allies with the Third Reich. All of Philby's dreams could come to pass. All that was needed was a little push.

Von Bolschwing's proposition was simple. Philby should encourage British support for Zionist emigration schemes, penetrate the secret negotiations, and then leak them to the press, with the certain knowledge of the popular discontent that would result among Moslems. The Arab backlash to a new British-Zionist initiative might not drive the region into the arms of the Third Reich, but it would certainly keep the oil-producing Arabs "neutral," but actually tilting toward the Nazis.

It was no secret that Ibn Saul had more than a little sympathy for the German position on the Zionist issue. His extreme anti-Jewish feelings were made clear to a British diplomat in 1937. The king said his "hatred for the Jews" stemmed from "their persecution and rejection" of Christ and "their subsequent rejection" of Muhammed. Ibn Saud added that "for a Muslim to kill a Jew [in war], or for him to be killed by a Jew, ensures him an immediate entry in Heaven and into the august presence of God Almighty."[36]

According to several of our sources, this was one of the aspects of Islam that most appealed to Philby. He had all sorts of schemes that could aid the Nazis, who meant business when it came to the Jews. Our sources say Jack obtained the king's permission to become a double agent for the Third Reich, publicly helping the Jews, privately aiding the Nazis, always making a profit for the House of Saud and, naturally, himself.[37] The scheme appealed to Philby's clandestine nature. The more he worked to link Britain and Zionism publicly, the more damage he could do to the empire's position in the Middle East.

A great deal of circumstantial evidence supports this version of Philby as an anti-Zionist double agent given to us by the "old spies." For more than a decade Philby had opposed any scheme to increase Jewish emigration. Suddenly, in 1937, he opened extensive negotiations with the Zionist leader David Ben-Gurion about a plan to allow unlimited Jewish immigration into a greater Palestine under Ibn Saud's protection.[38] Shortly thereafter he went a lot further to "help" the Zionist cause.

In July of that year, the Arab world was horrified at Philby's support of the Peel Report, in which Britain proposed to partition Palestine. Philby even turned his well-honed propaganda skills to the partition cause in a series of newspaper articles. This caused Ibn Saud a lot of trouble at court, and he had to repudiate Philby's views publicly.[39]

In fact, the king and Jack were playing a nasty little game with the Jews. Despite their "disagreement" over the partition plan, in early 1939 Ibn Saud sent Philby to London to be on hand for the Palestine Round Table Conference. It does seem rather strange that the king would send someone whose views conflicted so clearly with his own. Apparently Philby's true mission was sabotage.

In order to set all sides against each other, Philby developed his own plan on the Palestine question, which he put to British officials as well as to the Jews and Arabs. In February 1939 he had a secret lunch with Weizmann and Ben-Gurion, and introduced the Zionist leaders to Fuad Hamza, Ibn Saud's long-time foreign affairs official. Philby offered the Zionists substantial Jewish immigration into Palestine if they would support the country coming under Saudi domination.[40]

Weizmann was blamed when the "secret" plan was leaked to the press, and there was no further progress. As will be seen, all of Philby's schemes with the Zionists had a suspicious habit of coming to nothing. There is a definite pattern of sabotage, with the Zionists as "fall guys" every time. Amazingly, the Zionists stuck by Philby for nearly five critical years, while he treated the game as an auction.

It was not by chance that one of Philby's first moves after World War II began was to court the Zionists. On September 29, 1939, Jack met Professor Lewis Namier, a Zionist from Manchester University, and told him that Ibn Saud would reject German overtures if he received money and armaments from other quarters. It was a none-too-subtle demand.

Naturally, Namier concluded that Philby wanted to arrange a Jewish loan for the king. He promptly set up a luncheon meeting at the Athenaeum between Philby, Weizmann, and Moshe Shertok (later Sharett), the head of the political department of the Jewish Agency, which had been established by the League of Nations in the 1920s to represent Jewish interests under Britain's mandate in Palestine. It was the start of a bribe-for-Palestine scheme: Philby wanted £20 million, in return for which "the whole of Palestine should be left to the Jews."[41]

According to Philby, the Zionist leadership promptly accepted the plan at another lunch at the Athenaeum in early October 1939, at which his son, Kim, by then a well-established Soviet agent, was also present.[42] Naturally, Kim was feeding a great deal of intelligence to Moscow about his father's schemes.

It should have been obvious that such terms would never be acceptable to the Arab world. Still, on the eve of the Holocaust, the Jewish leaders were desperate to find a safe haven. Weizmann promised to seek President Roosevelt's support for the scheme, as he was soon going to the United States. Philby hurried back to Saudi Arabia to consult with Ibn Saud.

It is extraordinary that there is only one biography devoted to Jack Philby. Elizabeth Monroe, in her 1973 book *Philby of Arabia*, simply did not have enough facts about his game. She thought it was Jack's stubborn streak, his "unshakeable faith in his own ability to influence the course of events," that pushed him to yet one more round of negotiations with the Zionists. On the other hand, she was right to question "the long survival of the Zionist trust in his capacity to mediate."[43] The Jews still did not realize that Philby's job was to sabotage their enterprise. The £20 million ransom offer was a fraud, but that was not discovered for several years.

Philby discussed the scheme with Ibn Saud in January 1940, but the king allegedly instructed him that on no account was he to tell anyone else about it. Strangely, Philby willfully ignored this directive and leaked news of the deal to members of the royal entourage. His "indiscretion" had a devastating effect on the negotiations. Ibn Saud was not alone among royal Jew-haters. Jack's leak enabled the "King's Syrian and Palestinian courtiers to drum up opposition to a deal with the Jews."[44]

Philby deliberately had destroyed the plan. All he had to do now was string out Weizmann and keep the other parties from knowing the whole truth. He succeeded for much longer than even he thought possible. Weizmann pursued the futile ransom dream that Philby had concocted for the next few years. His discussions with Roosevelt "remained theoretical," but in March 1942 Weizmann met with Churchill before visiting Roosevelt once more.

Churchill told Weizmann that he wanted to make Ibn Saud "boss of bosses" in the Arab world, "provided he settles with you." Weizmann treated this as explicit approval of Philby's scheme, but this soon turned out to be yet another mirage.[45] Ibn Saud had no intention of making any settlement with Weizmann, or any other Jew, despite Philby's claims. In a very short time the Western leaders would discover Philby's fraud for themselves.

In 1943 the Holocaust was in full operation, but in April of that year in Bermuda, a conference of British and American officials formally decided that nothing should be done about it. They "ruled out all plans for mass rescue." The British Foreign Office and the U.S. State Department were both afraid that the Third Reich would be quite willing, indeed eager, to stop the gas chambers, empty the concentration camps, and let hundreds of thousands, if not millions, of Jewish survivors emigrate to freedom in the West. The Foreign Office "revealed in confidence" to the State Department its fear that Hitler might permit a mass exodus. If approaches to Germany to release Jews were "pressed too much that is exactly what might happen."[46]

The bigoted reality behind the Secret Report of the Easter 1943 Bermuda Conference was that not a single Allied nation wanted to let the Jews settle in its country. The unspoken consensus was that it was better to let Hitler handle them than arrange a mass evacuation to the United States, England, or Canada. In short, the Jews were expendable to the war effort.[47] Only after the war was it confirmed that a rescue operation to the Nazi concentration camps could have been successful. "Marshal of the RAF Sir Arthur 'Bomber' Harris declared afterwards that a rescue plan was 'perfectly feasible, but I was never asked to undertake it.' "[48]

No one campaigned to rescue the Jews because the leaders of the Western nations had deliberately withheld the truth about the Holocaust from their own citizens. After verification by each of the Allied intelligence services, the body counts of murdered Jews were quietly classified as early as September 1941.

If cynicism and hypocrisy ruled in London and Washington about the fate of the Jews, caution was the word when it came to upsetting the Arabs. President Roosevelt was personally sympathetic to a Jewish homeland in Palestine. Emotion was fine, but convincing the Arabs was another thing. Both sides were pressuring the president to take a role in shaping Palestine's future, but he had to be even-handed and especially careful not to offend the Saudi king, who had placed his trust in an American oil company.

A few months after the Bermuda Conference, Roosevelt sent a moderately worded message to Ibn Saud. He promised to consult both Arabs and Jews about the future of Palestine. Privately the president encouraged Weizmann by indicating that both he and Churchill might attend a conference of all the parties. Weizmann suggested to Roosevelt that Ibn Saud should be softened up by an envoy the king trusted. His first suggestion was Jack Philby, and his second was the American Arabist Colonel Harold Hoskins.

Weizmann inadvertently had hit on Philby's weak spot: An outsider would discover the ruse that he and Ibn Saud were involved in. Roosevelt did send Hoskins, who quickly discovered Jack's game. In August 1943 Hoskins held detailed discussions with Ibn Saud, and in no time at all he worked out that the king had no intention of meeting Weizmann to discuss Jack's deal. This flatly contradicted Philby's previous representation that the king supported the ransom-for-Palestine proposal.

In their discussions, Ibn Saud exploded into a rage and told Hoskins that he "hated Weizmann personally because the latter had impugned his character by offering a bribe of £20 million if he would accept Arab settlers from Palestine."[49] Hoskins had discovered the truth and quickly reported it to Roosevelt. As a result, Philby had to abandon his whole fraudulent scheme.

Several of the former intelligence officers we interviewed believe that Philby and Ibn Saud had stage-managed the whole affair.[50] They claim that Ibn Saud planned Philby's leak to the king's court precisely to sabotage the scheme. It was a perfect cover. The king could explain that domestic pressures were very great and hide himself behind his mock affront at being offered a bribe by a Jew.

Amazing as it seems, even after the Hoskins mission Weizmann continued to push Jack's scheme to ransom Palestine for the Jews in a letter he wrote to the U.S. State Department, urging that "Mr. Philby's scheme offers an approach which should not be abandoned without further exploration."[51]

Jack's operation had been a triumph. From von Bolschwing's point of view in Berlin, it also was a huge success. The Nazis had a field day spreading propaganda in the Middle East that the war was being fought at the instigation of the Jews to provide themselves with a homeland at the expense of the Arabs. The net result of Philby's pretense at pro-Zionism was a major backlash against Britain and the Jews in the Arab world.

The truth is that Philby's "pro-Zionism" was simply a ploy in his intelligence service to the Third Reich. How the Zionists could deal with him in light of his very public pro-Fascist sentiments remains something of a mystery. Throughout the entire four years of the ransom scheme between 1939 and 1943, the Zionists were aware of Jack's admiration for the Nazis. He even stood as a candidate for an unabashed pro-Fascist party in the British election of 1939.[52]

Quite a few in Britain agreed with Philby. Edward Windsor, during his brief regency, had emphatically stated that Britain had no business in interfering in the Third Reich's internal affairs "*re* Jews, or *re* anything else."[53] Senior members of the British aristocracy openly called for an alliance with Hitler against the godless Bolsheviks.

Jack certainly was busy promoting the Nazi cause around this time. It was not just a case of eccentric grumblings. He led the secret negotiations on his favorite subject—Ibn Saud's oil. A number of our sources say that Philby was also drawn to the Nazis for profit.[54] Having sabotaged the Zionists' negotiations, he and the Saudis now wanted something from the Germans: money. During the late 1930s Philby held a series of secret talks with the Germans on behalf of the Saudi government.

The discussions, which took place largely in Spain, were designed to ensure that Nazi Germany would have sufficient supplies of oil in the event of war. Even if a worldwide embargo was imposed, the oil would be shipped from "neutral" Saudi Arabia to "neutral" Spain. The fascist dictator of Spain, General Francisco Franco, was offered a cut for each transshipment, with payments through the Bank of Spain. As Franco was then dependent on Germany's help during the closing stages of the Spanish Civil War, he was more than glad to participate in the negotiations.[55]

It did not take long for word of Philby's Spanish-Saudi-Nazi oil negotiations to reach Joseph Stalin. The Soviet Union had penetrated German intelligence fairly thoroughly, and the Soviets had more than a passing interest in the outcome of the Spanish Civil War. If Philby succeeded, Saudi oil would fuel the Nazi war machine and enable it to launch the eastward march against the Communists.

Stalin's military advisers were aghast at the prospect of an unlimited supply of cheap Arabian oil sailing across the Mediterranean. If Hitler attacked the Soviet Union, the international community would do nothing but cluck their tongues, while sympathetically supporting the Spanish shield of neutrality that protected the transshipment of Saudi oil to Hitler. Even if the Soviet Union declared war on the Spanish or the Saudis, the Soviet naval presence in the Mediterranean was minimal. Its fleet was harbored in the often-frozen Baltic Sea. Soviet warships had no safe warm-water outlets.

The progress of Jack Philby's Spanish negotiations became a matter of Soviet national interest. At all costs, Stalin had to have an agent inside to keep him informed. The Soviet secret service already had such an agent in place to keep them apprised of Jack's dirty oil deals with Hitler—Philby's own son, Kim. After recruiting him in the mid-1930s, Soviet intelligence had told him to dump his Jewish wife, sever his leftist connections, join a Fascist club, and make up to his father as the prodigal son who had admitted his youthful errors.

His father, apparently desperate to have his son succeed, fell for the story. On May 20, 1937, Jack arranged with an old school chum for young Kim to become special war correspondent for *The Times,* covering Franco's war in Spain. It was not the last time that Jack would unwittingly help Kim's penetration mission for the Soviets.

Because of his father's clout, Kim was the favorite of the right-wing set in Spain. General Franco even gave him a medal. According to our sources, Jack was so delighted by Kim's newfound fondness for fascism that he fully confided in him the news that a secret pact between Ibn Saud and Hitler was about to be concluded. Kim promptly reported this to his Soviet controllers, who told him to inform the British and see what happened.[56]

When Kim's shocking report reached London, it was never published in *The Times.* The right-wing faction in control of the secret service thought it might be a splendid development. Our British intelligence sources agree it was the deputy of the secret service Sir Stewart Menzies himself who quietly encouraged the idea of an all-out war between Germany and the Soviet Union, while Britain sat quietly on the sidelines.[57] In fact, there were some in the secret service who endorsed Jack Philby's oil negotiations as a way to help Germany without officially involving the British government. Kim was told to keep his mouth shut and keep the reports flowing.

British tolerance of the Saudi oil initiative was apparently the last straw for the Soviets, who even then were negotiating a peace treaty with Britain. To the utter shock of the British secret service, Germany concluded a nonaggression pact with the Soviet Union in August 1939. Now it appeared that it would be Stalin who sat on the sidelines while Hitler turned west against Europe. Suddenly shipping Saudi oil through neutral Spain to Germany did not seem like such a good idea. Jack Philby never knew it, but it was his own son who turned in the evidence against him.[58] As soon as the father set foot on British soil, he was clapped in jail.

Jack Philby's dalliance with fascism could not have escaped the Zionists' notice. In 1940, while the ransom-for-Palestine negotiations were still in their infancy, Philby was detained under Regulation 18b, the section dealing with potential Nazi sympathizers, who could present a danger to the war effort. The official reason for his detention was that he had told Ibn Saud that Britain would do badly in the war, "and that the King would be wise to withdraw his sterling investments to a safer place."[59]

The accepted story is that it was the British class system which helped poor old Jack in his hour of need.[60] After only four months, the detention order was revoked unconditionally. It is not known precisely who arranged for St. John Philby to be released. It may well have been one of his many establishment friends in the senior ranks of the British secret service, such as Valentine ("Vee Vee") Vivian, then MI6's deputy chief.[61] Or it may have been David Footman, head of Section I (Political).[62]

Despite having been sacked from the secret service almost a decade earlier, and despite his unsavory role in obtaining the Saudi oil deal for the Americans, Philby could still move freely in MI6 circles, even at a time when he was considered a potential traitor. Then again, perhaps his easy access was actually because of his pro-Fascist sympathies.

In any event, the son was only too happy to take advantage of the entrée that his father provided to the British establishment. Kim used Jack to push his career in the British secret service. In 1940 Kim visited France as a war correspondent, where he further enhanced his growing reputation. After his return his father "began taking his now rather distinguished son on a tour of his still prolific establishment contacts."[63]

A few months later, Vivian made the mistake of recruiting Kim. His father's pro-Nazi proclivities were no bar to "Vee Vee," who

> invited St John, just out of detention, and Kim to lunch. As he later told Patrick Seale of *The Observer,* "When Kim went out to the lavatory, I asked St John about him. 'He was a bit of a communist at Cambridge, wasn't he,' I enquired. 'Oh, that was all schoolboy nonsense,' St John replied. 'He's a reformed character now.' " Vivian accepted St John's assessment of Kim's political past and told [his subordinate] to go ahead and engage him.[64]

The father's old-time spy connections had helped launch the son's infamous espionage career. Ironically, Kim's job was to keep an eye on his father for both the Soviet and British secret services. In order to protect Kim, the British spread the story that Ibn Saud tipped them off so they were able to detain Philby, Sr., under Section 18b, but it does seem odd that the king would inform on his own confidential adviser and close friend.

It seems stranger still that the British never said anything about the king's double dealings with the Germans. Even Churchill lavished "extravagant praise" on Ibn Saud at war's end in 1945.[65] What seems downright bizarre is that the British would let Philby out of jail and allow him to roam around proselytizing for the Nazis.

Jack was certainly stubborn on the issue of support for fascism, and the Zionists could not have missed it. His internment had meant nothing to Philby. As will be seen, he had cut a deal to keep himself out of prison as a Nazi sympathizer. He was free to continue his pro-Axis propaganda. In October 1941, while the Weizmann–Churchill–Roosevelt–Ibn Saud negotiations were still under way, he wrote to *The Manchester Guardian* on the subject of his old friend, the pro-Nazi Grand Mufti of Jerusalem.

The mufti was then visiting Hitler in Berlin to discuss their common fight against a Jewish homeland in Palestine. In his defense, Jack described the mufti as "a good enough fellow if properly handled." Such public utterances could not go unchallenged, and prominent Zionists took strong issue with Philby's benign views.[66] The Jews did not know the half of it. Jack Philby was no lone wolf. There was more to Jack's oil deals than anyone knew. His American connections were impeccable.

CHAPTER 3

THE PIRATES OF WALL STREET

The history books have been kind to Allen Dulles, perhaps because he, like Jack Philby, wrote several of them. He is remembered as a kind, grandfatherly type, the man who directed much of the intelligence war against Adolf Hitler and then professionalized the CIA. His affectionate nickname was the "Great White Case Officer," and many remember him fondly as a key figure of the Eisenhower administration and a great public servant.

The truth, according to our sources, is quite different. They describe Allen Dulles as one of the worst traitors in American history, an economic version of Benedict Arnold. He was the man who sold his country out for money, blackmailed presidents, and helped to fund Hitler. Our sources say that there was a secret side to Allen Dulles that has never made it into the history books. In this chapter we examine in detail the evidence concerning the following allegations:

- In the 1930s Dulles established an interlocking financial network among major Nazi corporations, American oil men, and Saudi Arabia.
- Dulles led a team of American and British investors that funded the early Nazi party and continued to do business with the Third Reich throughout World War II.
- During the war Dulles's client Standard Oil blackmailed the Allies with the threat of withholding oil, procured bribes for Ibn Saud, and coerced extortionate oil price increases for their own benefit.
- At the end of the war and immediately afterward, Dulles evaded Allied surveillance and directed the smuggling of Nazi money back to his Western clients.

We first turn to Dulles's creation of international financial networks for the benefit of the Nazis. In the beginning, moving money into the Third Reich was quite legal. Lawyers saw to that. And Allen and his brother John Foster were not just any lawyers. They were international finance specialists for the powerful Wall Street law firm of Sullivan & Cromwell. The firm has known its share of controversy.

Before the United States had a formal intelligence service, it had Sullivan & Cromwell. According to some accounts, this firm helped organize the seizure of land for the Panama Canal. Later it represented the French government, several titans of British industry, and more important for this story, most of the leading banks of prewar Nazi Germany.

The 1930s were not the first time that one of the Dulles boys had represented German money. During and after World War I, Foster tried desperately to keep Kaiser Wilhelm II's assets from being seized by the U.S. Alien Property Custodian. As a member of the U.S. War Trade Board, Foster had good sources of information. German bribes went all the way to the attorney general.

In defending the crooked attorney general, Harry Daugherty, his trial counsel pointed out that there was a bigger crook behind the bribery scandal: the lawyer John Foster Dulles, who "strutted about the Peace Conference promoting himself as [Secretary of State] 'Lansing's nephew' while 'carrying a bag'—looking for a bribe—misdirecting his client, and comporting himself overall as a man who should be disbarred."[1]

Unfortunately, Foster was allowed to continue the practice of law. As a reward for his services, he became the representative of several major German companies, such as I. G. Farben, which owned huge blocks of stock in American oil companies. Farben later became infamous as the holder of the patent for the poison gas used at Auschwitz and for working thousands of Jews to death as slave laborers. Foster's dream was to make the world one big monopoly, controlled by his German and American clients.

In 1934 Dulles helped draft the agreements establishing the international cartels, joint ventures, and market-sharing among the Belgians, the British Imperial Chemical Industries, and I. G. Farben. As discussed in Chapter 2, it was agreements such as that signed by the Rockefeller-controlled Standard Oil Company of New Jersey with Farben that helped the Third Reich to gain such important advances in the development of synthetic rubber and gasoline. In return, Farben became a shareholder in the New Jersey oil company second only to John D., Jr., himself.[2]

Sullivan & Cromwell seemed to have connections everywhere. It was the original revolving door between the government and Wall Street. As we explain in Chapter 10, after World War II the revolving door became a way of life for the men who populated the oil companies and the espionage world. By the time the team of Ronald Reagan and George Bush took over the White House in 1981, it was impossible to tell where private interests ended and public duties began and ended.

Allen Dulles had joined Sullivan & Cromwell after quitting the State Department in 1926. His brother Foster had previously served with State

Department intelligence. Allen was on the board of a leading German bank. Foster was a director of I. G. Farben. They dealt in millions and traded with nations as equals. In fact, they taught many of the twentieth-century robber barons how to rob.

The Dulles brothers were the ones who convinced American businessmen to avoid U.S. government regulation by investing in Germany. It began with the Versailles Treaty, in which they played no small role. After World War I the defeated German government promised to pay war reparations to the Allies in gold, but Germany had no gold. It had to borrow the gold from Sullivan & Cromwell's clients in the United States. Nearly 70 percent of the money that flowed into Germany during the 1930s came from investors in the United States, many of them Sullivan & Cromwell clients.

Some of the biggest American financial houses, such as Morgan et Cie and Chase, also invested heavily in Germany after World War I. In return for their gold, the American clients received bonds and promissory notes backed by shares of stock in Swiss holding companies that owned stock in German banks. These banks in turn owned the stock of major German corporations, which in turn owned some of the most valuable industrial patents in the world.

In fact, the German bankers had almost created a worldwide high-tech monopoly. American companies, such as Du Pont and General Motors, were more than willing to swap gold for patent rights, at bargain basement prices. There was even talk of setting up a worldwide patent cartel in Germany, so that the American investors could escape the strictures of the U.S. antitrust laws. It was a heady time. When the price of the mark stabilized and the German economy started to revive during the 1930s, the profits were enormous.

The Dulles brothers looked like geniuses. Their "Dawes Plan" of recycling U.S. gold so that Germany could meet its international reparations payments, while rebuilding its domestic industry, was a stunning success, at least for a while. Under the plan, the United States lent Germany the money to pay Britain and France their war reparations. In turn, Britain and France repaid the United States. As the biographer of the Dulles family, Leonard Mosley, has noted: "Financially speaking, it was a mad sort of merry-go-round, but it gave the statesmen a breathing space."[3]

Perhaps it was only a coincidence, but it also made for big profits for the brothers' clients. The German economy began to boom while the United States was in the early years of the Depression. That was hardly surprising, since so much desperately needed American capital had been shunted off to Dulles clients in Germany.

These German clients were mostly not Nazis, at least not originally.

Most were conservative Catholic monarchists who believed in the traditions of the kaiser, Prussian nobility, and the honor of the German officer corps. They hated the chaotic liberals who ruled the Weimar Republic. Most of their money went into moderate or center-right political parties. Contrary to popular belief, only a fairly minuscule amount of money was given by the German industrialists to the radical right in the 1920s. A few businessmen, such as Fritz Thyssen, financed Hitler's beer hall putsch of 1923, but Thyssen came to regret it bitterly.

To the business community, Hitler was just another hired dog-on-a-leash to keep the left at bay. From the industrialists' point of a view, the Nazis were just not worth funding. They preferred the aristocratic Franz von Papen. The early Nazi party obtained most of its funding from small contributions from party members. It was enough to get Hitler started. To everyone's surprise, he obtained a significant percentage of the vote in the 1930 elections. The truth is that Hitler was a self-made politician with genuine popular appeal to the far right.

If Hitler wanted a bigger share of the vote in 1933, he had to go after a much bigger source of funding. In January 1932 Hitler met in Düsseldorf with a group of twenty-five German industrialists. This was the turning point for the Nazi party. Without sufficient funding, they would go down to defeat in 1933 as a lunatic fringe. With heavy financial backing, the Nazis could win a sufficiently substantial minority to obtain a share of power in the government coalition.

Hitler told the industrialists what they wanted to hear. If they helped the Nazis increase their vote in 1933, it would be the last election they would ever have to worry about. There would be no more elections, no more problems with unions, no more antibusiness liberals. When asked how he would handle inflation, he replied "with concentration camps." Hitler would solve unemployment by throwing out the Jews. His words brought the house down. The industrialists immediately pledged 3 million marks.[4]

Perhaps 3 million marks was small change, but it is an axiom among politicians that the early donations are the most valuable. The members of the Düsseldorf Industrial Club in 1932 gave Hitler small but significant contributions when he needed them the most. Among the contributors was the manager of Giesche, Germany's largest zinc producer. His company was a client of Allen Dulles. So was another 1932 contributor, I. G. Farben.

Before 1932, the Nazis had conducted a vicious propaganda campaign against Farben "as an exploitative tool" of "money-mighty Jews."[5] In June 1932 two I. G. Farben officials met secretly with Hitler at his home in Munich to try to end the campaign.[6] A deal was struck: In return for election donations, Hitler halted the campaign and promised to keep tariff protection after he won power. A sigh of relief went up at the Standard Oil Company of New Jersey, which stood to lose millions if Hitler kept his word and dismantled its partner.

Following Hitler's triumph and consolidation, I. G. Farben led the way among the German corporate world, adapting itself to the Nazi ideology and purging itself of "undesirable" (i.e., Jewish) elements. "By 1937–38 it was no longer an independent company but rather an industrial arm of the German state, and fully Nazified."[7] Allen Dulles was pleased. With clients like Farben, there were megaprofits to be made all round—provided, of course, that one was prepared to abandon the Jews.

Dulles found himself in a dilemma, as he also represented a Jew. Not just any Jew, but Sigmund Warburg, one of the leading financiers of Hamburg. Although Warburg believed that the Nazis were people he could do business with, he was driven out of Germany shortly after the 1933 election and took refuge in New York. Still, business was business, and Dulles continued to develop his German ties while representing Warburg.

The left wing of the Nazi party did not particularly relish Hitler's new American ties. Gregor Strasser, leader of the left Nazis, launched a propaganda attack to discredit Hitler. Strasser's attack was a clever piece of forgery, a book supposedly written by Dulles's Jewish client Warburg and published in Holland in 1933, shortly after the businessman had fled Germany.

It purported to describe three conversations Warburg had with Hitler at the request of American financiers, the Bank of England, and Western oil firms to facilitate payments to the Nazi party. Warburg allegedly lamented being a "cowardly instrument" of his American banking colleagues and regretted financing Hitler. The Führer apparently retaliated against the forgery by arranging for the publisher and translator to be murdered. The Nazis suppressed all copies of the book, but the damage was done. Although there was hardly a word of truth in it, it came too close for comfort for the Dulles brothers.

Hitler's financial wizard, Hjalmar Schacht, was indeed getting money from his good friend Montagu Norman at the Bank of England, as well as from Dulles brothers' clients Giesche and Farben.[8] In fact, Schacht was on the verge of arranging a secret cartel arrangement among German, British, and American investors, which would make the Farben–Standard of New Jersey oil deal look small time indeed. The last thing the investors wanted was publicity. Strasser's phony Warburg book was the last straw.

Hitler paid a high price for power. In order to obtain continued funding from the conservative bankers, he had to get rid of the leftists in his own party. One historian claims that Hitler's bloody purge of the SA in

1934 was a plot by the German army, heavy industry, and banking interests, linked with American capital against the German electrochemical industry, the Farben corporation, and the Deutsche Bank.[9]

That would be interesting, if true, as it would mean that Dulles had clients on both sides of the Nazi faction fight. But then, so did the British. The British secret service had been running joint anti-Communist operations with German Military Intelligence since the late 1920s. Lord Rothermere, the English press baron, was one of Hitler's most vocal and generous supporters. Throughout the 1920s and well into the 1930s, Britain's Imperial Chemical Industries scrambled for a piece of the German chemical trade. In order to please the conservative Western financiers, Hitler ordered a massacre of the leftist members of his party.

The Western investors may have been satisfied with the bloody results of the Night of the Long Knives, but it should be recalled that Hitler was not the first choice of any of the businessmen. Himmler, it has been alleged, was I. G. Farben's second, or compromise, choice, once Gregor Strasser was eliminated.[10] Foster Dulles, as a member of the board of I. G. Farben, seems to have had little difficulty in getting along with whoever was in charge. Some of our sources insist that both Dulles brothers made substantial but indirect contributions to the Nazi party as the price of continued influence inside the new German order.

At least one historian, R. Harris Smith, has disputed the claim that the Dulles boys were soft on Hitler, pointing out that the German office of Sullivan & Cromwell was closed down after 1934.[11] But this did not prevent the Dulles brothers from pursuing secret profits from their Nazi friends. They simply shifted their businesses to front men, and in fact, their profits increased substantially as Germany marched along the road toward the rearmament boom of 1938.

At first, the big winners were the British investors in Germany. Although they had not backed the Nazis in the beginning, in the early 1930s they made up for it with a vengeance. France and England fell over each other to finance Hitler's industrial base, even as they despised Hitler himself.[12] The American and British investors were all surprised when Hitler broke his leash and seized political power from the Catholic Center Party's Chancellor Franz von Papen. Now it was Hitler's turn to put the leash on Dulles's German clients.

For example, Allen Dulles represented the American multinational Anaconda Copper, which had purchased stock in the German Giesche conglomerate. One of Giesche's companies was the largest zinc producer in Germany, with important holdings in Poland. As security for its investment capital, Anaconda controlled 51 percent of Giesche's interests in Polish Silesia.[13] So far, so good for Dulles.

Giesche, like many other German firms, had helped fund the nascent Nazi party in the early 1930s and was on good terms with the government. After Germany invaded Poland in 1939, the manager of Giesche was summoned by Luftwaffe chief Herman Göring and told that the Nazis would take over his operation because of the foreign ownership. "To sever its incriminating American tie, Giesche bought out Anaconda's Polish interests with the help of Swiss banks."[14]

It should not be a surprise that the Dulles brothers and their friends also represented the helpful Swiss banks, which "loaned" the buy-back money to their German clients. As collateral, the Swiss banks received stock in German banks that now controlled, on paper at least, the holdings of the major German corporations.

The net effect was to use Swiss bank secrecy as a shield to prevent Hitler from realizing that the American and British investors still pulled the strings behind the scenes. In fact, it was Hitler's bank disclosure law of 1933 that forced a flood of German money over the border into Switzerland. In 1934 the Swiss made disclosure of bank accounts a crime.

Some historians believe that the Swiss shield law had a more nefarious purpose than protecting American-owned businesses from Hitler. The Swiss bank laws also kept the Dulles brothers' clients away from the prying eyes of the American Justice Department with its strict laws against monopolies, trusts, and cartels. Apart from being illegal, helping the Nazi cartels dominate world trade was against U.S. foreign policy. Although the United States was not at war with Germany in 1939, it took a dim view of "neutral" American businessmen who acted in favor of the Third Reich.

Still, for two heady years the Dulles clients had the best of both worlds. Between September 1939 and December 1941, American investors structured their multinational holdings to legally make a profit on both sides of the war. As along as the United States remained officially neutral, such conduct was technically legal, or at least offered a plausible defense. John Foster Dulles remained on the board of I. G. Farben. His brother Allen remained on the board of the Schröder. Bank, along with a scar-faced representative of the SS.

The situation was a little more awkward for some British investors, who were receiving royalties through Switzerland from German industry for the manufacture of war munitions to be used against Britain. When Britain declared war in 1939, American businessmen rushed to Germany to fill the investment vacuum. Henry Ford sent copies of his anti-Semitic tracts to Hitler, who handed them out to guests at Berchtesgaden. Other companies, such as General Motors and Du Pont, which had longstanding relationships with the Third Reich, began to question their involvement.

The British investors were in a quandary. They had seen the war coming but, as one wit put it, "it is very hard to emigrate with a steel mill." Hitler had their money. They did not want to give it up, and so a few of Britain's finest found a discreet way to commit treason. They hired the Wallenberg family of Sweden to launder their money for them.

The Wallenbergs just happened to run Sweden's largest commercial bank during World War II. According to the Dutch authors Gerard Aalders and Cees Wiebes, the bank "helped Nazi Germany dispose of gold and jewels stripped from murdered Jews," and "the Wallenberg brothers also acted as front men to disguise foreign subsidiaries of German companies associated with Adolf Hitler's regime." The authors "traced accounts that the Wallenbergs helped establish as covers for subsidiaries of Bosch, IG Farben, Krupp and other German corporations to avoid having their assets confiscated by Allied governments. They wrote that under a secret agreement the German corporations would have the right to repurchase the companies once the war was over."[15]

Not all the family was involved. At least one of their cousins, Raoul, was so anti-Nazi that he rebeled against the family and tried to help the Jews of Hungary to escape. His relatives, though, were bankers who worked for the British secret service. Although the Dutch authors did not know it, the Wallenberg brothers, Jacob and Marcus, were couriers for Sir Stewart Menzies, better known as "C," the mysterious head of MI6.[16] In contrast to the American intelligence services, which were a lawyers' club. The British had bankers as spies. The Wallenbergs were couriers between British intelligence and the German generals, who were feebly trying to overthrow Hitler and restore the monarchy, with the backing of the Dulles brothers' German clients.[17]

The spy work against Hitler gave the Wallenbergs a convenient cover to continue their very profitable business relationship with the industrialists of the Third Reich. Even Pope Pius XII, who as the Vatican's nuncio in Germany in the 1920s had once funded Hitler, had a hand in the businessmen's coup plotting. The ubiquitous Wallenbergs even went to work for the Dulleses' American clients. Perhaps they would have succeeded in killing Hitler had they paid more attention to conspiracy and less to their profits.

A classic example of moral ambiguity is the case of the Czech gold. After Hitler conquered Czechoslovakia, the Bank of England simply transferred ownership of its Czech gold deposits to him. While it caused a bit of an uproar in Parliament, the bankers prevailed. At all costs, they wanted to avoid a repeat of the debacle of the early 1930s when the central banks of Europe fought against each other. International banking stability was more important than the mere inconvenience of war. The Bank of International Settlements in Switzerland and, to a lesser extent, the Vatican Bank in Rome were created in part to avoid the international currency blockades imposed by the warring powers.

While the British had to use third-party agents, or "cut-outs" like the Wallenbergs to continue their trade with Germany, the United States was still a neutral country. During the "phony war" of 1940 when both sides made little aggressive movement, British intelligence watched with chagrin as American competitors moved into their Axis markets. U.S. oil flowed to Germany, Spain, and Italy, while German marks and captured gold continued to pile up in Switzerland.

To put it simply, in 1940 there was a three-way deal. Jack Philby represented the Saudi sellers of oil, Allen Dulles represented the Nazi buyers such as I. G. Farben, while John Foster Dulles represented the German bankers and Spanish financiers.[18]

On paper, the Texas Oil Company (Texaco) was the principal supplier of Franco's oil during the Spanish Civil War. In addition, Texaco had become partners with Socal, which controlled Saudi oil through Jack Philby. The result of this union was Caltex, which was largely the making of James Forrestal. As will be seen in Chapter 7, Forrestal served as secretary of the Navy and later U.S. defense secretary. He played a key role in shaping U.S. oil policy after the war, until paranoid anti-Semitism brought about his premature demise as a political leader. In the 1930s Forrestal was head of the New York investment bank Dillon, Read. He was an ally of the Dulles brothers and a member of the Wall Street financial mafia.

In early 1936 Forrestal brought Socal and Texaco together and, with the help of Dillon, Read vice president Paul Nitze, drew up the scheme to pool the assets of the two companies "East of Suez."[19] The result was that after 1940, when the deal was formalized, Caltex became the parent company of Aramco, the Arabian-American Oil Company.[20]

The wheel was beginning to return to where it had been before 1911, when the U.S. Supreme Court had broken up the Rockefeller's oil cartel, Standard Oil. The result of the breakup had been a sometimes genuine and sometimes even fierce competition between the various independent companies that had once been Standard Oil. Aramco eventually would reunite two of the most important component companies, Standard of California and Standard of New Jersey, which still was dominated by the Rockefellers, in the form of John D. Rockefeller, Jr. The two companies had more in common than oil and greed. They both did business with the Nazis, acting as if they hated the Jews.[21]

They also had a common shareholder: I. G. Farben. The Dulles brothers' client, Hermann Schmitz, president of American I. G., owned stock in both Socal and Standard of New Jersey.[22] American I. G. later changed its name to General Aniline and Film (GAF), and Forrestal was recruited to the board of the new front company. In fact, GAF's stock in Socal and Standard was effectively controlled by its parent company, I. G. Farben.

When the dust settled on the complex web of paperwork, Dulles's Nazi client, I. G. Farben, had Forrestal on its payroll, while Forrestal's American client, Caltex, had the Saudi oil. The man who held the deal together on the ground was Jack Philby. Through his client, Ibn Saud, a cozy deal could be done to get the Third Reich's hands on Saudi Arabian oil and make lots of money for Dulles's and Forrestal's clients. Ibn Saud was in turn secretly in partnership with the Nazis, who financed his clandestine war against the Zionists in Palestine.

The whole arrangement worked well until the United States joined the war in 1941. Then it began to unravel through the Rockefeller end of the oil business. Standard of New Jersey's relationship with Farben had not gone unnoticed in Washington. As previously discussed, next to the Rockefellers, I. G. Farben owned the largest share of stock in Standard Oil of New Jersey. Among other things, Standard had provided Farben with its synthetic rubber patents and technical knowledge, while Farben had kept its patents to itself, under the strict instructions of the Nazi government. For the United States, "the results were calamitous," especially after Pearl Harbor.[23] Standard's deal with the Nazis looked awfully like treason.

Senator Harry Truman certainly thought so when he read Standard's 1939 letter renewing its agreement, which made it clear that the Rockefellers' company was prepared to work with the Nazis whether their own government was at war with the Third Reich or not. Truman's Senate Committee on the National Defense was outraged and began to probe into the whole scandalous arrangement, much to the discomfort of John D. Rockefeller, Jr. Suddenly, however, the whole matter was dropped.[24]

There was a reason for Rockefeller's escape: blackmail. According to the former intelligence officers we interviewed on this point, the blackmail was simple and powerful: The Dulles brothers had one of their clients threaten to interrupt the U.S. oil supply during wartime. Besides the late U.S. Supreme Court Justice Arthur Goldberg, three other members of the U.S. intelligence community insist that Allen Dulles was personally behind the threat to cut off Saudi supplies to a nation already suffering gasoline rationing.[25] There is evidence to corroborate much of what they allege, including the direct participation of an American oil company in the scheme.

On February 27, 1942, Thurman Arnold, the assistant attorney general of the United States, stormed into the offices of Standard of New Jersey at 30 Rockefeller Plaza in New York and outlined the charges of acting against the best interests of their own government. Arnold demanded fines totaling $1.5 million and control of the Nazi patents. In response, the Standard executives made it clear that the entire U.S. war effort was fueled by their oil and it could be stopped. Arnold could do nothing but accept the fact of the blackmail.[26]

The American government had no choice but to go along if it wanted oil to win the war. One Standard executive paid $1,000, or a quarter of one week's salary, for having betrayed the nation. No matter what they did during the war, Dulles's and Forrestal's clients could get away with anything as long as they controlled the Arabian oil wells. That point was driven home by Socal just as the Allied forces were preparing for the invasion of Normandy. The company demanded profit margins of 250 to 300 percent on production costs for each barrel of Saudi oil sold to the American government.[27] The U.S. government had no choice; it gave Socal its price increase.

It was bad enough that U.S. companies could extort such huge profits from the government, while continuing to make profits on the other side of the war. Apparently under duress, President Roosevelt also was forced to appoint Dulles's oil cronies to the very boards that were charged with oversight of such misconduct. Burton Hersh, in his powerful work *The Old Boys: The American Elite and the Origins of the CIA,* describes an instance where I. G. Farben was concerned that the U.S. Alien Property Custodian might seize the assets of its U.S. subsidiary, General Aniline and Film. Dulles had nothing to worry about, as he had his Wall Street friends on both sides of the dispute:

> James Forrestal was registered as Vice President of General Aniline—[controlled by] the Farben management. . . . The Alien Property Custodian, Leo Crowley, *was on the payroll* of the New York J. Henry Schroeder Bank, General Aniline's depository, where Foster and Allen Dulles both sat as board members. Foster arranged an appointment for himself as special legal counsel for the Alien Property Custodian while simultaneously representing [another Farben subsidiary] *against* the custodian.[28]

Forrestal, it should be noted, had been taken on board by President Roosevelt as his special assistant in 1940 and then promoted to undersecretary of the navy, a key post for U.S. government oil interests. No wonder British intelligence went wild over the Dulleses' machinations to protect Farben's interests.

A lengthy British intelligence report of covert activities against the Nazi-American connection was finally released to the press in 1989. It is a marvelously cynical document, replete with instances of subtle British manipulation of the American press during World War II.[29] One of the first targets of the British secret service was Gerhard Alois Westrick, the front man for Sullivan & Cromwell's former German clients. Westrick remained Allen Dulles's personal client before and after the war.

Westrick was also a German intelligence agent and in close contact with the pro-Hitler oil man Torkild Rieber, a Norwegian-American who was the president of Texaco as well as Socal's partner in Saudi oil and one of Forrestal's clients. Rieber was among the first Americans to start shipping oil to Franco in the Spanish Civil War. President Roosevelt ordered his activities stopped, but Rieber got around this by making a deal with Mussolini's Fascists to ship the oil via Italy to Germany.[30]

State Department archives show that on August 2, 1940, a Texaco employee denounced Rieber as one of Hitler's secret representatives in the United States. In addition, according to the employee, most of Texaco's leadership was "pro-Nazi and openly boasts of it as well as being willing to do all within its power to injure the English and help the Germans."[31] Texaco, like several of the other U.S. oil companies, was selling oil to the Axis via international cut-outs. Things became a little too embarrassing, especially when the press started picking up the story. Still, the company might have gotten away with it, except that Rieber dismissed the problem by simply saying that he "considered it good business."[32]

In the wake of the scandal, Texaco's head, James Moffett, "found it wise public relations" to sack Rieber as chairman "because of his Nazi associations." In a letter to the president of Standard of California, Moffett expressed "sadness over the Rieber episode," but assured his partner in Saudi oil that "there has been no repercussion upon our business throughout the British Empire."[33] The British oil men were very understanding. Profits came before politics, not to mention, the war effort.

Unfortunately, there were some patriots among the British establishment. One faction of British intelligence exposed Westrick's shady activities to their "agents and subagents" among American journalists. It was only the opening shot in the British propaganda war. The next British target was I. G. Farben itself. This was a bit too close to home for the Dulles brothers, as one sat on the board of directors and the other handled Farben's litigation up until 1942.

As the British intelligence file shows, the Dulles boys wasted no time in pressuring the British to call off their pet dogs in the American press. Here is the classified British version of how they were blackmailed into silence: "Dulles and a colleague expressed their desire to have our [British] propaganda action in the U.S.A., as far as I. G. Farben is concerned, discontinued. Their explanation of this was that, in their opinion, this might involve large American companies like Standard Oil of New Jersey, etc., thereby *perhaps impairing the war effort*." (Emphasis added.)[34]

To put it bluntly, Dulles was personally threatening to cut off Britain's supply of oil during the war if the British persisted with their exposé of the American oil connection to I. G. Farben. Dulles had now used the oil blackmail tactic on both sides of the Atlantic, with the same outcome. London and Washington bit their tongues.

The British were more than a little hypocritical in pointing the finger of blame at the American connection. They had their own Farben scandal. Imperial Chemical Industries (ICI) was partners with Farben on several deals. Allen Dulles himself had drawn up the paperwork to bring ICI and Farben into a Nazi chemical cartel. The dominating force of the Nazi-controlled Schröder Bank was Baron Bruno Schröder, whose headquarters were in London. As one of the bankers put it: "The British government had a good attitude toward British banks abroad. British banks in Paris did big business during the occupation."[35] Similarly, the Bank of England continued its association with the Nazi-dominated Bank of International Settlements in Switzerland.

In fact, British financial institutions continued to move Nazi money all through the war, when it suited their own clients' purposes. According to a U.S. congressional investigation, Herman Abs, the president of the Deutsche Bank, used an "old school tie" in Britain to arrange for Nazi money to continue to flow through American cut-outs during the war.[36]

Abs had many friends in Britain. One friend, Lord Hartley Shawcross, was Britain's attorney general and in charge of the Nuremberg Nazi war crimes investigations. At this time U.S. intelligence had prepared a 300-page report on Abs's alleged war crimes, including financing the construction of the I. G. Farben plant at Auschwitz. According to Walter Rockler, one of the American prosecutors at Nuremberg, there was a "sudden lack of interest" and funding for the Deutsche Bank prosecution dried up.[37]

Abs, released from internment, renewed Shawcross's acquaintance. Shortly after the case was dropped, Abs resurfaced as an economics adviser for the British in their zone of Germany. It should be noted that during Shawcross's term of office, virtually all British prosecutions of Nazis petered out for lack of funding.[38] As we said in *Unholy Trinity*, Shawcross, perhaps unknowingly, then joined Abs in an organization that lobbied for the return of German assets impounded by the Allies.

Forty years later Showcross led the fight in the House of Lords against legislation to reopen British prosecutions of Nazi war criminals. In a bizarre statement in Parliament, Shawcross blamed the Jews for Britain's failure to prosecute Nazis after World War II.[39]

If the British seem overly defensive, it should be recalled that their American ally had had more than enough Nazi scandals of its own, particularly in the Middle East. By war's end Washington had replaced London as Ibn Saud's closest ally and protector.

Allen Dulles and his friend Jack Philby had collaborated to bring it all about. Philby was no mere Fascist propagandist and did much more than make speeches and write fanatical newspaper articles. Jack was deeply involved in a number of traitorous games with the Nazis. The Zionists could be excused for missing this part of Jack's life. Unlike his other activities, he tried to keep the Saudi-Nazi connection a deep secret.

According to sources on both sides of the Atlantic, it was Philby who advised Ibn Saud energetically to court Nazi Germany in the months before the war.[40] The relationship was mutually beneficial. As one U.S. intelligence study found, the Nazis "recognized that King Ibn Saud's help was essential for renewing the fight against the British and the Jews in Palestine." The Germans proposed that a new government should be formed in Palestine, under the control of Jack's old friend, the Grand Mufti of Jerusalem. Further, "Jews who had settled in Palestine after the First World War would not be allowed to remain."[41]

In January 1939 Saudi Arabia established diplomatic relations with the Third Reich, and Ibn Saud confided to the Germans that at heart he "hated the English." In the following months he concluded arms deals with Germany and signed a friendship and trade treaty with Japan. Philby was pleased, especially as Ibn Saud concealed his secret dealings with the Axis from both the British and Americans.[42]

The Nazis also were pleased with the progress they had made with the king. They sent their best Middle East agent, Fritz Grobba, to meet with Ibn Saud, and even promised to obtain for him the most prestigious position in the Moslem world, the caliphate.[43] The Saudi–Third Reich connection flourished, with their main link being their mutual hatred for the Jews. The Nazis even promised to supply Ibn Saud with weapons, ammunition, and an armaments factory, and, according to some accounts, gave him bribes during most of World War II.[44]

The king had many reasons for his secret arms deals with Berlin. The primary purpose "was to increase the flow of weapons which [Ibn Saud] had secretly been sending to the Arabs fighting in Palestine," in order to "check the Zionist influx that had followed the Balfour Declaration." Although he later claimed to be genuinely horrified by the Nazis' Final Solution, Ibn Saud's attitude toward the Jews was extreme, even by Arab standards. They were "a race accursed by God, according to His Holy Book, and destined to final destruction and eternal damnation."[45]

The king's Nazi arms deals were not the end of Philby's war on the Jews. According to some of our sources, Philby had cut yet another deal to keep himself out of prison in Britain as a Nazi sympathizer. Saudi Arabia would stay neutral in the war in return for a bribe. In effect, the king would get paid to pump no oil for either side.[46]

Two years after the Nazis had begun their secret bribes to Ibn Saud, the same shakedown was used on the Americans. In June 1941, just six months before the Americans entered the war, one of Ibn Saud's American front men, James Moffett of Caltex, went to President Roosevelt for a bribe. To guarantee that Saudi Arabia's oil would not fall into enemy hands, the American government had to hand over $6 million a year to Ibn Saud.[47]

As already discussed, Moffett had been forced, reluctantly, to rid his company of the notorious Nazi agent Torkild Rieber, under threat of a public scandal. Moffett's covert pro-Hitler stance was now transformed into blackmail of the president. But Roosevelt was not such a simpleton. He turned the matter over to the British. They promptly resumed their subsidy to Ibn Saud, so that he would not sell oil to either side. Suddenly all the Saudi wells were capped temporarily with cement, ostensibly to keep them out of Nazi hands in case Rommel won the battle for North Africa. The Allies might suffer, but at least Hitler would not get the Saudi oil. Or so it seemed.

A few months later, after Hitler declared war on the United States, President Roosevelt established a Bureau of Economic Warfare. The Middle East section brought up numerous complaints that the American Caltex subsidiary involved in Saudi Arabian oil was still shipping oil to the enemy.[48] The Saudi-Nazi scandal just would not die.

Not surprisingly, Dulles's cronies in the State Department dragged out the Nazi oil investigation for more than a year. By late 1942 the Dulles brothers had a solution. They used their old friend and investor Secretary of the Navy James Forrestal for the brassiest sales pitch of all time. If the United States wanted to ensure Caltex's loyalty during the war, it should buy it.[49] Roosevelt thought he already had. The president had surreptitiously increased American lend-lease payments to Churchill, in order to fund under-the-table British subsidies to the King of Saudi Arabia.[50]

That, Dulles's friends said, was the problem. With the secret help of U.S. money, the British were getting entirely too much influence in Saudi Arabia. There was a real risk that the British might even assassinate Ibn Saud and install an oil puppet of their own. The secret U.S. subsidy should be stopped, and the American government should become an investor in Caltex's Saudi oil operations; it was a matter of the highest national interest.

Texaco's James Moffett went once more "to his friend President Roosevelt" and warned that if the bribe money for Ibn Saud was not coughed up, "this independent kingdom, and perhaps with it the entire Arab world, will be thrown into chaos."[51] Moffett seemed to have learned a thing or two about blackmail from Dulles: "As an added inducement for the President's advisers, he pledged annual delivery for the next five years of $6 million worth of petroleum to the United States armed forces at very low prices. The exact nature of this last feature of the proposal subsequently became a subject of great debate and was a contributing factor leading to a federal suit against the major overseas corporations."[52] In the meantime, the president was exactly where Moffett and the others wanted him. In light of the leverage that Dulles, Philby, Moffett, and the rest of the U.S. oil companies now had over the war effort, it did not take long before they obtained the desired result. In December 1942 Washington dumped the London subsidies and outbid Hitler for Ibn Saud's loyalty. The new U.S. policy was exactly what Dulles's stooges had advocated: "the development of Saudi Arabian petroleum resources should be viewed in the light of the broad national interest."[53]

Roosevelt never could get congressional approval for an official U.S. government investment in what soon evolved into Aramco. He did the next best thing. Saudi Arabia became the only neutral nation approved for generous lend-lease terms, despite Ibn Saud's notoriously close links with Hitler. Doing so actually required a major policy back-flip, but the president pushed it through.

In February 1943 Washington granted Ibn Saud his bribe. Roosevelt wrote to the Lend-Lease Administration, declaring that "the defense of Saudi Arabia is vital to the defense of the United States." Much more generous U.S. funding soon replaced London's "subsidy."[54] The British Empire was out, and over the next four years Ibn Saud received $100 million.

Dulles and Philby and their progeny, Aramco, had won. Before long, the State Department effectively had resigned "the conduct of American relations with Saudi Arabia into the company's keeping." Ibn Saud, not slow in seeing which way the wind was blowing, decided that there were political as well as financial rewards in abandoning the last pretense of support for Britain.[55] Naturally, this suited the American oil companies.

Not to mention Jack Philby. For their part, the British could not help but wonder how it had all happened. The British Foreign Office bureaucrats in charge of Middle Eastern affairs predictably concluded that the Jews were to blame and that Britain's previous assistance to the Zionists had poisoned relations with Ibn Saud.[56] They did not know it, but Philby and the Dulles brothers had been their nemesis all along. Ibn Saud had no intention of ever letting a single Jew emigrate to Palestine. President Roosevelt discovered this for himself, but too late.

In February 1945, just before he died, President Roosevelt personally met Ibn Saud. He attempted to enlist the king's support for the Zionist solution, but Ibn Saud firmly rejected the idea, instead suggesting that the Allies should give "them and their descendants the choicest lands and homes of the Germans who oppressed them" or that the Allied countries take in the Jews themselves.[57]

The king's vehement opposition to Jewish migration was a bit of a shock to Roosevelt, who was strongly sympathetic to the Zionist cause. Yet none of the Western nations was ever prepared to take more than a handful of the Holocaust survivors. As one book showed, the Canadian policy was "none is too many." The king seemed to recognize this, and he reminded Roosevelt that Palestine had already taken "its fair share of refugees from Europe."

Suddenly the president's sympathy for the Jews was wavering. He told Ibn Saud that "he would do nothing to assist the Jews against the Arabs and would make no move hostile to the Arab people." Roosevelt's new policy was to be neutral, but neutral in favor of the Arabs.[58] It was an uncomfortable lesson for the ailing president. The choice seemed clear enough. The United States could help the Jews found their home in Palestine, or it could have Saudi Arabia's oil as the engine room for postwar dominance. It seemed to Roosevelt that he could not have both. He chose oil.

The Dulles-Philby team had finally succeeded in pushing London out of Saudi Arabia and gaining the whip hand in Washington. By now oil companies were virtually running U.S. relations with Saudi Arabia, and the Zionists were all but checkmated. The Dulles-Philby team had covered up the Nazi oil scandal as well as Ibn Saud's blackmail of the president. The cover-up endured for a long time.

It could not last forever. Before his death, former Supreme Court Justice Arthur Goldberg granted one of the authors an interview.[59] Justice Goldberg had served in U.S. intelligence during World War II. Although he said little in public, he had collected information on the Dulles boys' activities over the years. His verdict was blunt. "The Dulles brothers were traitors." They had betrayed their country, by giving aid and comfort to the enemy in time of war.

What Justice Goldberg never understood is how the Dulles brothers got away with burying the truth for so long. The answer is simple, and cynical. The foxes volunteered to guard the henhouse. After the Americans and British caved in to Standard Oil's threats, Allen Dulles offered to help the Allied war effort by coordinating U.S. intelligence in Switzerland.

The intelligence services were not the only part of the government penetrated by Hitler's American bagmen. Dulles's clients and colleagues virtually dominated the war production effort. Liberals in the administration could not understand why Roosevelt and Treasury Secretary Henry Morgenthau would allow the pirates of Wall Street access to such sensitive posts, especially when so many of them had known ties to the German war effort.

The official version is that their business contacts in Germany provided a steady flow of intelligence, which was crucial to the Allies. There is some truth in that, but not much. The Nazis quickly exposed most of Allen's clients, who ended up spending the war with him in Lugano, Switzerland, hatching plots to recover their assets no matter who won. As we documented in our previous book, *Unholy Trinity,* Dulles's primary effort was to work with the Vatican to overthrow Hitler and restore the pro-business monarchists.

Failing that, toward the end of the war, the Vatican appealed to Dulles to arrange for the surrender of SS General Karl Wolff's German forces in Italy without destroying the vital northern Italian industrial base around Milan. Dulles himself wrote a book praising his own efforts in Operation Sunrise, the code name for the secret surrender negotiations. This was considered the capstone of Dulles's achievements during the war.

Buried in the U.S. National Archives is a scathing top-secret analysis by Judge Musmano, later one of the team at the Nuremberg war crimes trials. The Musmano report examined all the documents and included interviews with the captured German participants. It concluded that General Wolff led Dulles on, gaining promises of immunity for war crimes, while delaying any actual surrender until the day Hitler committed suicide.[60]

When confronted after the war, Dulles denied that any promises of immunity were given but insisted that the Allies had a "moral obligation" to protect Nazi peace negotiators, like Wolff. Although he had commanded one of the SS mobile killing units on the Eastern Front that had murdered 300,000 people, mainly Jews, Wolff ended up as a witness for the prosecution at Nuremberg. The other war criminals among his close circle were shipped to North Africa and quietly released.

The Communist version of the "Wolff affair" was even worse. In 1988 the Soviet paper *Pravda* cited Allen Dulles's deals in Switzerland as the beginning of the Cold War:

> The German command would have handed Austria and some other "territories" over to the USA and Britain. Had everything snowballed as planned, the capitulation of the Wehrmacht grouping in Italy would have been followed by the opening up of the entire Western front to the Anglo-American forces while maintaining and stepping up resistance against the Red Army's offensive.
>
> It can be added that the "Wolff Affair", more correctly the "Wolff-Dulles Affair", was the largest operation against F. Roosevelt and his course, an operation launched while the president was still alive. . . .[61]

The most embarrassing part of the *Pravda* account is that it correctly quotes top-secret U.S. intelligence documents as its source. More intriguing, Soviet radio broadcasts hinted that they had "other documents" proving that Allen Dulles betrayed Allied plans at Yalta to the Germans. This may be a reference to documents collected by Noel Field, the Communist agent working with Dulles in Switzerland. It should be noted that British intelligence already suspected Dulles's partner in crime, Jack Philby, of having switched to the Communist side.

It is not impossible that Dulles and Philby passed information to the Soviets. Yet if they did so, their motives were personal profit rather than to assist Stalin. The most likely explanation for the leaks were the numerous Soviet moles in British intelligence. Still, the *Pravda* propagandists had a point. Allen Dulles was acting behind Roosevelt's back in his schemes to unite Axis and Allied forces against the Soviets. Moreover, Allen had shown a marked propensity for aiding Axis business interests at the expense of his own country. Why didn't Roosevelt do something? How could the Dulles brothers get away with it for so long?

Roosevelt and the British had laid a trap for them as far back as 1939. As soon as the war was over, they would have their revenge. There is an old saying on Wall Street: "You can make money as a bull or a bear, but you cannot make money as a pig." The piggish Dulles brothers had made too many quick profits and far too many enemies. Although the Dulleses thought they had covered their trail with layer after layer of banks and holding companies, it was not quite enough.

President Roosevelt's liberal supporters could never understand why he allowed Dulles and the pirates of Wall Street into so many important positions. Nor could they believe that their "New Deal" president would allow them to get away with their criminal profiteering, especially when the nation was at war with fascism. Was Roosevelt acting in ignorance, or merely from recognition that Dulles and his cronies were too powerful?

In fact, the president knew exactly what Allen Dulles and his clients were up to with the Nazis. He was reading their mail and transcripts of their conferences and telephone conversations. One chapter of the Ultra files of the British codebreakers has never been published before. Prior to the United States' entry into the war, Roosevelt permitted British intelligence to wiretap American targets.

According to our sources in the intelligence community, the area of coverage included a good bit of the New York financial district, several floors of Rockefeller Plaza, part of the RCA Building, two prominent clubs, and various shipping firms.[62] The wiretaps were crude: microphones linked by hard wire to a machine that cut phonograph records. The scope of coverage was spotty due to the limits of staff and technology, but the results more than justified the effort.

The wiretap unit reported to Sir William Stephenson, a Canadian electronics genius better known by his code name, "Intrepid." From his headquarters in the Rockefeller building, Stephenson's job was to identify U.S. companies that were aiding the Nazis. The information was leaked to FBI director J. Edgar Hoover, but he frequently failed to take aggressive action.

Before the United States officially declared war in 1941, Stephenson's "Purchasing Office" was able to identify the web of Nazi-American financial ties. The wiretaps were illegal, of course, and could never be used in court. Still, they permitted the British to take measures of their own to staunch the flow of American support to Hitler.[63] During World War II the British assassinated some American citizens who collaborated with the Nazis. In at least one case, it appears that British intelligence murdered an American businessman, William Rhodes Davis, who was supplying Hitler with oil through Mexico. Davis's offices were on the fifty-fourth floor of the Rockefeller building, which made him an easy target. The official explanation for Davis's death was a "heart seizure," but Stephenson's biographer hints at "foul play" and links it directly to Stephenson's operations.[64]

Other cases never made it into the history books: bankers who suddenly committed suicide, dockworkers found shot, lawyers who disappeared. The murders faded into the background of New York. Hoover watched Stephenson like a hawk but could never catch the British hit squad. Without hard evidence, Roosevelt shrugged his shoulders at Hoover's complaints.

In fact, according to a number of the sources we spoke to, Roosevelt was also using the British wiretap team to dig up dirt on his political opponents.[65] Prior to the 1940 election, the Third Reich made a concerted effort to intervene in American politics. Seven U.S. senators and thirteen congressmen received campaign contributions. Much of the "isolationist" wing of Congress was bought and paid for in Berlin. Senator Burton Wheeler was so pro-Hitler that he sent Nazi propaganda through the mail, using his congressional franking privilege. He was intended to be the next president. The Nazis had more money than sense if they thought Wheeler could win a national election.[66]

Up until the 1940 election, Hoover spent more time spying on the British than he did on Nazi agents. He was fence sitting—neutral in favor of the Nazis. According to our sources, the isolationists had promised Hoover the job of attorney general once Roosevelt was out.[67] It was a prize Hoover hungered for.

None of our sources would admit how they obtained information on Hoover's private conversations, but one worked for the National Security

Agency, which intercepts and monitors electronic communications, and another had served at the NSA in a liaison capacity.[68] We were unable to confirm our suspicion that the NSA's predecessors had wiretapped Hoover's private office in the main Justice Department building, but it was not unusual for such things to occur.

Years before, Hoover had run his own wiretapping program on American politicians, until a young assistant attorney general named Bill Donovan ordered him to stop. Donovan went on to become Roosevelt's intelligence adviser and head of the Office of Strategic Services during the war. Hoover hated them both.

But when Roosevelt was reelected to a third term in 1940, after a bruising contest with the isolationists in both parties, Hoover scurried to mend fences and cover himself. Suddenly he offered to provide Roosevelt with FBI wiretaps of American politicians and Nazi sympathizers. The problem was, Hoover did not know who they were. Incredibly, the FBI had spent so much energy spying on the left that it had no central index of right-wing radicals. The FBI was forced to beg one of the leading Jewish organizations, the Anti-Defamation League, for its records of suspected Fascists in the United States.[69]

British intelligence, of course, had better files, but were not about to share the fruits of its wiretap records with Hoover. The British feared that some of the right-wing extremists in the FBI would leak the story to the press and force the wiretap operation to shut down. Roosevelt and Stephenson had bigger fish to try.

Several months before the United States declared war, Bill Donovan invited Allen Dulles to head up the New York branch of the Office of the Coordinator of Information (COI), President Roosevelt's new intelligence agency and the precursor to the Office of Strategic Services (OSS). Its primary mission was to collect information against the Nazis and their collaborators. In other words, Dulles was asked to inform on his own clients in New York. FDR's wife, Eleanor, objected to the president that, as Dulles was allied with the Schröder Bank, he was himself likely to be connected with the very Nazis he was supposed to be hunting.[70]

What Eleanor could not have known was that hiring Dulles had been FDR's idea in the first place. The president knew that Allen Dulles's clients included most of the camouflaged financial entities for Nazi-American interests. Despite this, Roosevelt had approved his selection as head of the COI Manhattan branch because he wanted Dulles where the British wiretappers could keep an eye on him. Dulles was appointed in October 1941 and moved into the twenty-fifth floor of 30 Rockefeller Plaza.[71]

One floor below Dulles was Stephenson's wiretap shop. Inside Dulles's operation was one of Roosevelt's spies, Arthur Goldberg, who was later appointed to the Supreme Court of the United States. Before his death, Justice Goldberg confirmed to one of the authors that Dulles's appointment was a setup. As already discussed, he insisted that the Dulles brothers were traitors. The problem was collecting the evidence.

By the time he joined the COI, Allen had already covered his tracks. As the general counsel for the Schröder Bank, he had made sure that all of the American investors in Nazi Germany were shielded. By late 1941 the base of operations had shifted to Switzerland. After a year with the New York intelligence branch, Dulles asked to be transferred to Bern. Donovan, now head of the OSS, offered him a more prestigious post in London, but Dulles insisted on Switzerland.[72]

The motive was simple. Dulles could not move his clients' money from the United States because Roosevelt had frozen all Swiss bank accounts on the grounds that they contained disguised Nazi assets. Dulles had to go to Switzerland if he wanted to control the purse strings.

Roosevelt was giving Dulles enough rope to hang himself. From Stephenson's Manhattan wiretaps, it was known that Dulles was continuing to work with his German business clients, who wanted to remove Hitler and install a puppet of their own who would make peace with the West while forging an alliance against Stalin. It was to be a kinder, gentler Third Reich, favorably disposed to American financial interests. To this end, Dulles had entered into negotiations with conservative members of German intelligence under Admiral Wilhelm Canaris. It was business as usual.[73]

Dulles's private courier was not someone who would be readily suspected as a German agent. Gero von Gaevernitz had a Jewish mother. Still, that did not prevent him from working for the Nazi industrialists.[74] According to several of the "old spies" we spoke to on this point, agreeing to Dulles's request for a posting to Switzerland was another setup.[75] British code breakers targeted Allen Dulles's secret communications net between Switzerland and Germany. They wiretapped the American consulate and Gaevernitz's home but found nothing. Then they discovered how the clever Dulles stayed in contact with the Nazis.

We have confirmed that one land line constantly linked German intelligence headquarters and Dulles's counterpart in Swiss intelligence. This and other telegraph lines to Switzerland were tapped by Allied code breakers. Their reports were forwarded to the U.S. Treasury Department's secret service, without the knowledge of Dulles's cronies in the other agencies.[76]

According to a senior U.S. counterintelligence agent, German intelligence also had mounted its own code-breaking operation against Dulles under the cover of the Luftfahrtforschüngsamt, the radio and telegraph research institute of the Nazi air force.[77] Published sources confirmed that such an organization did exist and that it did break Allen Dulles's OSS codes for communicating back to the United States.[78]

These German records were captured at the end of the war and were added to the Dulles files. They too have never been released to the public. Only a handful of people, including Justice Goldberg, knew that they once existed. A former officer of the NSA also remembered the tapes of the Swiss wiretaps and believes that they are still stored in the NSA vaults at Fort Meade.[79]

The wiretap evidence against Dulles originally was collected by a special section of Operation Safehaven, the U.S. Treasury Department's effort to trace the movement of stolen Nazi booty toward the end of the war. Roosevelt and Treasury Secretary Henry Morgenthau had set up Dulles by giving him the one assignment—intelligence chief in Switzerland—where he would be most tempted to aid his German clients with their money laundering.

Dulles was not the only target. Joseph Kennedy was sent as ambassador to London partly because Roosevelt knew that the British had bugged his embassy and could monitor his financial and diplomatic deals with the Nazis. Nelson Rockefeller had been given a similar intelligence post in South America, where he blindly ignored the pro-Nazi affiliations of his own companies. The foxes were guarding the henhouses, but Roosevelt's wolves were waiting in the dark, and watching.[80]

All through the war, Roosevelt had reluctantly caved in to British demands that the Jewish issue be ignored, that the concentration camp victims must be expendable to the war effort. But the one issue upon which Roosevelt was unyielding was his insistence that after the war, the German bankers must stand in the dock at the Nuremberg war crimes trial. This is confirmed by the top-secret White House–Justice Department correspondence files.[81]

The plan was to wait until Abs, Krupp, Flick, and the rest of the industrialists were charged. Then Morgenthau would unleash the wiretap evidence showing that the Nazis had hidden their stolen assets in Switzerland, with the help of Allen Dulles. The whole scandal of Western aid to the Germany economy would unravel. All the slights of the Standard Oil blackmail would be avenged.

The sudden release of the Safehaven intercepts would force a public outcry to bring treason charges against those British and American businessmen who aided the enemy in time of war. The targets included not only the Dulles brothers, but Forrestal and major industrialists, such as Henry Ford.[82] From a prosecutor's point of view, indicting the German bankers first was a brilliant strategy. To save themselves, Herman Abs and

Hjalmar Schacht would have to reveal the whole history of their sordid dealings with companies such as Ford Motor.

Despite the shields of Swiss banking laws and the layers of corporations that Dulles had erected, he had never anticipated that the Swiss bank codes and cables would ever become public knowledge. Roosevelt and Morgenthau would have hanged him and all his colleagues, forever breaking the power of the pirates of international finance. It was a glorious dream. Yet the scheme completely fell apart because someone tipped off Dulles that he was under surveillance.

Several historians have suggested that Roosevelt did not trust his own Justice Department and tried to isolate his own attorney general from the most sensitive communications. It is possible that through lawyers at the Justice Department Dulles found out about the wiretap scheme. Some of the "old spies" say that the most likely source of the leak, however, was Vice President Henry Wallace, who constantly shared information with his brother-in-law, the Swiss minister in Washington during the war.[83]

Wallace gave many details of his secret meetings with Roosevelt to the Swiss diplomat.[84] Unfortunately, giving information to the Swiss was almost the same as handing it directly to the Nazis, who had recruited the head of the Swiss secret service.[85] Up to January 1944, German intelligence continued to read the most sensitive war plans of the Roosevelt administration.

Exactly what Wallace leaked to his Swiss brother-in-law is open to speculation. However, apparently Wallace was one of the few insiders who knew of Roosevelt's scheme to entrap Dulles and the American industrialists. As Washington journalist I. F. Stone recalled, Vice President Wallace acted as the front man for Roosevelt, fending off inquiries from liberal cabinet members and the press about the number of pro-Fascist businessmen Roosevelt had appointed to high positions.[86]

It is plausible that Wallace was fully briefed on the true purpose of Operation Safehaven and shared these tidbits with his Swiss brother-in-law as well. This, according to several of our sources in the intelligence community, was the real reason Roosevelt dropped Wallace, the second most popular man in the United States, and replaced him with Harry Truman in the 1944 presidential election.[87] Many historians have recorded that it was Wallace's leftist leanings that cost him his job, together with the campaign run by Forrestal and other right-wing Democrats such as oil man Edwin Pauley, who later went into business with George Bush. The "old spies" are adamant that it really was the leak to his brother-in-law that cost Wallace the vice presidency. But it did have a side benefit for the pirates of Wall Street. It saved Allen Dulles's neck.

Dulles must have had a near stroke when his German colleagues suggested that they were all targets of Morgenthau's wiretap system. He wasted no time in damage control. In January 1944, Dulles himself closed down the pipeline by warning both sides that their secret messages had been intercepted.[88] The real problem was that the Allies might still be able to monitor Dulles's Swiss transactions, at the very moment that he was trying to move Nazi assets out of the path of the Soviets.

We now know that Dulles attempted to use one of his assistants, Gero von Gaevernitz, as a cut-out, or secret courier, but he had long been under surveillance. Both Dulles and von Gaevernitz were later charged by the Operation Safehaven team with laundering the assets of the Nazi Bank of Hungary to Switzerland under the guise of a series of movie companies.[89] Although Dulles filed an angry report denying everything, the surviving correspondence proves at least that he was a target of Operation Safehaven.[90]

Because he learned about the Safehaven intercepts so quickly, Dulles knew that there was no smoking gun against him. His work for the Nazis *prior* to the war was not illegal, let alone treasonous. His wartime communications with the Nazis, although highly embarrassing, could be excused as an exercise in deception or as part of his intrigues to overthrow Hitler. Although many of his wartime actions were unauthorized, they were not criminal.

What was criminal was the way that Dulles was trying to help the German industrialists get their money out at the end of the war. After the Nazis' 1943 defeat at Stalingrad, various Nazi businessmen realized they were on the losing side and made plans to evacuate their wealth. The Peron government in Argentina was receiving the Nazi flight capital with open arms, and Dulles helped it hide the money. This was more than a violation of the Trading with the Enemy Act; giving aid and comfort to the enemy in time of war was treason. Once again, however, Allen Dulles was one step ahead of his pursuers.

After the Nazis tipped him off that the Allies had broken the Swiss codes, Dulles carefully shifted the scope of his money laundering from Switzerland to the Central Bank of Belgium. According to our sources, a small but significant part of the Nazi gold stocks found its way there. By prearrangement, the bankers of Belgium, Luxembourg, and Liechtenstein would refuse every postwar demand by the Allies to open their banking files. Apparently, the Allied invasion of Normandy in June 1944 moved too quickly to permit Dulles to ship the rest of the Nazi gold to Belgium. The bulk of the Western investors' capital was still at risk.[91]

How did he move the remaining Nazi money out of Germany? Simply depositing it in Switzerland would have been easy, but it might eventually be traced by the web of wiretaps or, worse, by an American seizure of

Swiss bank records. As mentioned, Swiss bank accounts in the United States had already been seized and were still frozen by the U.S. government. What happened to the rest of Hitler's money?

The Guinness Book of Records lists the missing Reichsbank treasure as the greatest unsolved bank robbery in history. Where did it go? The British journalists Ian Sayer and Douglas Botting, authors of *Nazi Gold,* trace the gold movements in the last days of the war to the vicinity of Garmisch-Partenkirchen on the German-Austrian border.[92]

A senior U.S. counterintelligence agent, who knew several of the original German sources for *Nazi Gold,* says that the authors were deliberately misled on a number of points. According to our source, the bulk of the treasure was simply shipped a very short distance across Austria and through the Brenner Pass into Italy. Dulles's contacts were waiting at the Vatican. The German-Vatican connection was how Allen Dulles and the Nazi industrialists planned to get away with it.[93]

And they did. Except that the Jews were watching.

CHAPTER 4

THE MUTINEERS

Most of the histories of World War II, at least those written by members of the Allied countries, focus on the military struggle against Adolf Hitler and tend to conclude their analysis at the end of the war. There had been clearly defined enemies and a clear-cut victory. The bad guys had surrendered unconditionally, virtue had triumphed. The West, and Americans in particular, turned inward and busied themselves with converting a wartime economy into a consumer's paradise. It was all that simple.

Only a few historians have looked closely at the record of Americans who stayed behind to administer the conquered Axis countries. These new consuls of the West secured the victory of the Allied armies by leading the Fascist nations back on the path toward democracy and away from communism. These kindly conquering heros included General Lucius Clay, the commander of occupied Germany; General Douglas MacArthur, the ruler of conquered Japan; and perhaps the most colorful of them all, Lieutenant James Jesus Angleton, the de facto head of American intelligence in postwar Italy.

Angleton was unique. This low-ranking Office of Strategic Services officer has been widely praised for his work in saving Italy from the Communists in those few heady years after Mussolini's fall. Angleton rebuilt the Italian intelligence services, purged the Reds from government, and obtained American subsidies for the election of freedom-loving Italian politicians. Here too victory was seen as complete.

Angleton went on to a long and colorful career in the CIA. His nickname was "Mother," and tending his prized orchid collection was only one of his eccentricities. Although he later came to controversy, most historians say that it was Angleton's work as chief of CIA counterintelligence that kept Communists from American shores during the Cold War. At Angleton's retirement, President Gerald Ford bestowed upon him the highest decoration that an American intelligence officer can receive. Israelis widely regarded Angleton as their best friend in the United States.

Our sources say that it was not that simple. History books tend to omit the fact that the men who carried out the Holocaust largely went unpunished for their war crimes, an example that haunts us today in Bosnia-Hercegovina. Moreover, the vast bulk of the wealth of the Nazi empire quietly disappeared before the end of World War II, only to reappear within a decade in the hands of the same men who financed Hitler's war against the Jews. Allen Dulles's clients were not defeated, only inconvenienced. This substantial reversal of the Allied victory, our sources say, was engineered by Dulles through his corrupt protégés, James Jesus Angelton and his Fascist father, Hugh Angleton.

The son was not a hero of postwar intelligence but a villain. According to our sources, James Angleton laundered Nazi money, built a Vatican escape route for the fugitives of the Third Reich, and defrauded two U.S. presidents with utterly fictitious intelligence reports that helped twist American policy in the Middle East. Instead of being a friend of Israel, James Jesus Angelton was a vicious enemy of the Jews, kept under Israeli control only by the threat of blackmail. In the end, he went mad.

The sordid story of Angleton's secret life was, our sources insist, so shocking that the cover-up lasted nearly half a century. That the truth about the CIA's use of Nazis remained buried so long is attributed to the efforts of men like Allen Dulles and CIA director George Bush, who later gave Angleton access to his files (which he subsequently destroyed). They were the ones who ensured that the holes in the history books remained hidden in the secret vaults. We examine these controversies in detail, starting in this chapter with a review of the following allegations:

- Allen Dulles recruited the Angletons, father and son, as the key links in his network for smuggling German agents and Nazi money through the Vatican and out of Italy.
- James Angleton deceived two U.S. presidents by fabricating secret information, supposedly obtained from Vatican intelligence.
- The result of the Dulles-Angleton cover-up was the concealment of various Western financial transactions and negotiations with the Nazis during the war and a skewing of U.S. policy afterward.

Since completing our last book, *Unholy Trinity,* we have been contacted by several colleagues of the Angletons, who provided eyewitness accounts of the activities and operations of this bizarre father-and-son team.[1] Before World War II Hugh Angleton was an American Fascist living in Italy. As a businessman and seller of cash registers during the Mussolini regime, Hugh was quick to adopt the local Fascist parlance. On more than one occasion he praised the efficiency of Italian "corporatism" and denounced President Roosevelt as a "socialist." British author Tom Mangold briefly mentions some of Hugh Angleton's diatribes, but passes the subject over.[2]

It is a pity, because Mangold's otherwise excellent biography of Hugh's son misses the main thread of the Angleton mystery. One former CIA officer, who knew both father and son, told us that Hugh Angleton and Allen Dulles first met in the 1930s when Dulles took a short side trip from Switzerland to Milan. The metropolis of Milan is the northern outpost of Italian industry, not far from the Swiss city of Lugano, where Dulles and many of his German clients spent much of the war.

According to our sources, Hugh Angleton had long been a business agent for Allen Dulles. Hugh was not just another American expatriate trying to make a fast dollar in prewar Italy. He was a powerful financial broker with important connections, the European representative of National Cash Register (NCR). It is not generally known that NCR's board of directors included a former member of Sullivan & Cromwell, Allen Dulles's Wall Street firm of lawyers.[3]

Long before the war, Hugh had made all the right connections with the Italian Fascists as well as the right-wingers in the State Department. They all believed that business in Fascist Italy was good for American interests. According to the version later spread around by his son, Hugh was actually using his position in Italian financial and industrial circles to collect intelligence on important military matters that would benefit the United States in the event of war with Germany and Italy.[4]

There is no doubt that Hugh established a far-flung espionage network throughout Europe. Equally, there is no indication that it aided the U.S. government prior to World War II. No evidence in any intelligence service supports the younger Angleton's contention that his father was an "unofficial spy" for the Americans.

The only way in which Hugh's work could have benefited the United States was if the country had stayed neutral in the war and continued to sell arms and equipment to both sides. If that had happened, Angleton would have been a multimillionaire. When both Hitler and Mussolini declared war on the United States, however, Angleton was crushed financially as all his investments were in enemy hands.

Like Dulles's clients, he wanted his money back. Like Dulles, Hugh offered his services to the OSS. Hugh had close friends in the Fascist hierarchy, including a fellow Mason who was a high official in Mussolini's Interior Ministry. Such a contact was too good to ignore, and Angleton was promoted rapidly in U.S. intelligence. He became the second in command to Colonel Clifton Carter, the OSS commander in Italy at the end of World War II.[5]

Hugh Angleton's rise to power was, in part, an accident of geography. He lived in Milan for many years and made more than a few friends there before the war. It was Hugh Angleton who allegedly introduced Giovanni Battista Montini to Michele Sindona, a prewar banker in Milan. Sindona was the corrupt financier who later became the adviser to the Vatican Bank.[6] Montini, who was Vatican Undersecretary of State during the war, later became Pope Paul VI.

There is some circumstantial evidence that Hugh Angleton also introduced both of these friends to Dulles. Both Sindona and Montini allegedly became sources for the CIA after the war, with Hugh's son, James Jesus Angleton, as their case handler. Several historians agree with our sources on this point, although, as we shall see, the Vatican has gone to considerable lengths to deny the allegations.

One of James Angleton's enemies, of whom he had many, insists that his father served as a minor point of contact and occasional courier for secret financial transactions between the Vatican and Nazi Germany. That the Vatican encouraged such investments and even donated money to Hitler himself cannot be denied. A German nun, Sister Pascalina, was present at the creation. In the early 1920s she was the housekeeper for Archbishop of the Vatican-Nazi connection. Eugenio Pacelli, then the papal nuncio in Munich. Sister Pascalina vividly recalls receiving Adolf Hitler late one night and watching the archbishop give Hitler a large amount of Church money.[7]

Sister Pascalina had absolutely no motive to discredit Archbishop Pacelli. She was his greatest admirer and remained his faithful servant all her life, even after he became Pope Pius XII. Her story has the ring of truth, all the more powerful because it admits the worst blunder of Pacelli's career. It was Pacelli who later convinced the Vatican to invest millions of dollars in the rising German economy, money from the Vatican's land settlement with Mussolini that ended the Pope's claim of sovereignty over territory outside the walls of Vatican City. It was Pacelli who negotiated the Concordat with Hitler's Germany and then had to deal with the consequences of his own mistakes when he became pope on the eve of World War II.

The Vatican and the Dulles brothers had the same problem. Once their money was in Hitler's hands, how would they get it back? One ex-CIA officer whom we interviewed insisted that it was Hugh Angleton who personally arranged for the Nazi gold to be trucked to Italy and that it was his son, James Jesus, who later blocked every investigation into his father's criminal collaboration with Dulles's smuggling system. Our source claimed to have seen the trucks full of unmarked crates transported from Germany.[8]

Our sources claim that Dulles and his colleagues exerted a great deal of influence to ensure that Western investments in Nazi Germany were not seized by the Allies as reparations for the Jews. After all, much of

"Hitler's gold" had originally belonged to the bankers in London and New York.

A slightly different version was suggested to the authors by a former colonel in U.S. Military Intelligence who specialized in tracing enemy assets.[9] He claimed that only a tiny portion of the Reichsbank's gold ingots actually reached the Vatican Bank, while the rest was held in cooperative banks in Belgium, Liechtenstein, and especially Switzerland. Contrary to popular belief, it was not necessary physically to move all the gold out of Switzerland, just the bearer certificates, the bonds, and the foreign currency caches.

As long as the gold was physically outside Germany in a "friendly" country, Dulles could move its *ownership* out of Europe simply by transferring the paperwork from bank to bank. The ownership transfers could not be done by telegraph, as they were wiretapped by the Allies. In order to ensure absolute secrecy in moving the foreign currency and the ownership documents out of Switzerland, Dulles used couriers—not just any couriers, but special agents of the Vatican who had diplomatic immunity to move back and forth across both Nazi and Allied lines.

The colonel claimed that Dulles's courier network was run by a Maronite priest on behalf of the Vatican. He transported the Nazis' gold certificates to banks in Japanese-controlled territory in Manchuria (Manchukuo), and the Japanese then delivered a new set of documents through Vatican couriers to the Central Banks of Belgium, Liechtenstein, and Luxembourg. The Japanese and the Germans both exchanged their gold "loans" for new certificates of ownership by adjustments at the Nazi-dominated Bank of International Settlements in Switzerland, of which they were both members.

We have uncovered some circumstantial evidence to corroborate the colonel's accusations. Research into Vatican records has confirmed that a Catholic priest named Cikota was the treasurer of the Maronite order in Rome but was suddenly transferred to Harbin, Manchukuo, where he became apostolic exarch for the Byzantine Catholics.[10] A top-secret interrogation of a White Russian Nazi by General George Patton's intelligence chief names a Bishop Cikota as a "Nazi agent" inside the Vatican. Princess Magdelona Radziwill is named in the same intelligence files as the corresponding Nazi agent in Switzerland.[11] Her relative, Prince Radziwill, later surfaced as a petitioner to retrieve the wartime German assets of Dulles's clients that had been seized in the United States.

Bishop Cikota was not the only senior church official involved in such money-laundering schemes for the Nazis and their rogue friends in Western intelligence. While researching for our previous book, a number of instances of such joint schemes came to light. The Vatican's *eminence grise* for Balkan intelligence, the Bosnian-Croat priest Krunoslav Draganović, was involved in transporting large quantities of Nazi booty, especially gold bullion, from Austria to the safety of the Holy See with the help of the Dulles-Angleton clique in Rome. Some of the booty was transported in truck convoys run by British troops. Other shipments were carried in U.S. Army jeeps provided to Father Draganović so that he could conduct "pastoral visits" on behalf of the Vatican.[12]

Another ardent Nazi propagandist and agent, Slovenian bishop Gregory Rožman, was sent to Bern with the help of Dulles's friends in U.S. intelligence. Declassified U.S. intelligence files confirm that Bishop Rožman was suspected of trying to arrange the transfer of huge quantities of Nazi-controlled gold and Western currency that had been discreetly secreted in Swiss banks during the war. For a few months the Allies prevented Rožman from gaining access to this treasure, but then the way was mysteriously cleared. In fact, the Dulles-Vatican connection had fixed it, and before too long the bishop obtained the loot for his Nazi friends, who were hiding in Argentina.[13]

Such instances turned out to be only the tip of a huge iceberg. It has long been acknowledged that it was Allen Dulles who tipped off General Patton about the buried German treasure that lay in the path of the U.S. Third Army. Patton explicitly urged General Eisenhower to conceal as much of the gold as possible, but his advice was refused.

Our sources claim that Dulles and his colleagues exerted a great deal of influence to ensure that Western investments in Nazi Germany were not seized by the Allies as reparations for the Jews. After all, much of "Hitler's gold" had originally belonged to the bankers in London and New York. The movement of captured Nazi loot went underground. Several U.S. officers have confided to us that a great deal of money, gems, currency, and artwork was in fact never turned over to the Allies.[14] One officer provided an affidavit that he and his source entered a huge vault filled with stolen Nazi treasure.[15] Not one trace of this particular hoard's existence appears in subsequent U.S. files.

In the cause of anticommunism, and to retrieve its own investments in Germany, the Vatican agreed to become part of Dulles's smuggling window, through which the Nazis and their treasure could be moved to safety. When the U.S. Army followed up on leads connecting Dulles's Swiss bank operation to the Vatican, the entire investigation was scrubbed by Dulles's friends in the State Department and by his protégé in Rome, a young intelligence officer with the good Catholic name of James Jesus Angleton.[16]

The irony is that it was Hugh Angleton, not his son James, who was supposed to be Dulles's liaison on the Italian side. Hugh was assigned to

X-2, the OSS counterintelligence branch, and in the fall of 1943 he arrived back in Italy hoping to make contact with his Fascist friends in Rome. Unfortunately, his plans were disrupted. Hugh had his leg shattered when he was blown out of his jeep.[17] After a slow recuperation, he was dropped from X-2, assigned to General Clark's intelligence staff, and consigned to the minor task of war crimes investigations. Now it was up to his son to make contact with Hugh's friends in Fascist intelligence and open the smuggling window over the Brenner Pass from Austria.

James Angleton always claimed that joining X-2 was his own idea and that he had not received any help from his father's contacts. The son claimed that in the summer of 1943, he was a bored corporal assigned to the army's Italian desk in Washington and asked to be transferred overseas.[18] It was a lie. According to a recently declassified OSS memo of September 25, 1943, Hugh Angleton approached James Murphy, the head of X-2, to pull the strings.

Murphy's friend Norman Pearson then wrote to the army: "I would greatly appreciate it if you could get provisional security for Corporal James Angleton, in order that he may commence OSS school on Monday. His father is with this branch, and was with OSS previously."[19] A few months after his father's jeep accident, young Jim had finished his OSS training and was on his way to the Italian desk at X-2 in London. After a brief time he became head of the desk. In October 1944 he was posted to Italy as commander of Special Counterintelligence Unit Z (SCI-Z), a joint British-American unit.

James Angleton's big break came in early 1945, when he was appointed head of X-2 for Italy and became "the only non-Briton in Italy cleared to share the intelligence secrets of Top Secret Ultra, the British breakthrough in cracking wartime German military ciphers."[20] According to several of the former intelligence officers we interviewed, the reason the British took young Angleton under their wing was that he was the only American in X-2, now that his disabled father had been reassigned, who could be trusted with their dirty little secret. The British secret service was working with Allen Dulles to save as much of the Third Reich's money as possible from the Soviets.[21]

Even during the war, MI6 had worked with the Vatican against the Soviet Union, trying to organize a coup to topple Hitler and negotiate a separate peace. Their goal was to enlist Germany as their ally against Stalin. To put it crudely, a small minority of intelligence officers in Britain and the United States had committed mutiny. Behind the back of Roosevelt, and later Truman, and with a wink from Churchill, a clique of Western officers tried to betray the West's alliance with Stalin and snatch a partial German victory from the ashes of defeat. A smaller minority of this minority were people like Hugh Angleton and the Dulles brothers, who were interested primarily in saving their Nazi investments from Allied seizure.

Most of the men, and the few women, involved did not participate in the mutiny for money. They were "true believers" who saw communism, not fascism, as the overriding menace of the time and did what they thought was necessary to save the Western Allies from the "naïveté" of their leaders. The mutineers knew they were acting in complete violation of the "unconditional surrender" policy that Roosevelt and Churchill had announced. Their negotiations with the Nazis had to be kept in the strictest secrecy. Only one intelligence service could cross both Axis and Allied lines with relative impunity: the Vatican's.

As we documented in our previous book, the Vatican was indeed involved in clandestine negotiations for an Axis-Allied pact against the Soviet Union. Before D-Day in Normandy, the Vatican's peace feelers were regarded as innocent but ineffective. In fact, just before the invasion, Allied intelligence had used the Vatican's secret intelligence networks to mislead the Nazis into withdrawing three key divisions from France to put down a nonexistent uprising in the Balkans.

After Normandy, the window of opportunity for a negotiated peace narrowed considerably. Soviet troops were advancing from the east, American troops from the west. Outside Germany itself, the last Nazi stronghold was part of Austria and northern Italy. Dulles and the Vatican engaged in frantic efforts to arrange for a separate peace that would let the German army hold the line against the oncoming Soviets.

At that point, the "old spies" claim, James Angleton warned the Vatican that its codes had been compromised.[22] Angleton later admitted that he had tipped off the Vatican, but claimed that it was because one of their code clerks was selling information to the Communists.

Our sources say that Angleton had another motive for leaking the information: He had to ensure the security of Vatican communications. It was critical that the real purpose of Dulles's Operation Sunrise negotiations with General Karl Wolff be hidden from the American president. At that moment, the pope was attempting to negotiate simultaneous peace pacts with Germany and Japan and to unite all sides against the Soviet Union.

Dulles's Nazi counterpart, SS general Karl Wolff, had approached Hitler on April 18, 1945, and announced that "I am happy to be able to report to you, my Fuehrer, that I have succeeded in opening doors through Mr. Allen Dulles to the President, Prime Minister Churchill, and Field Marshall Alexander."[23] The truth is that Dulles had been lying through his teeth and was acting without anyone's authority. When Hitler lost hope in the deal and committed suicide, Allen had to protect the remaining Nazi negotiators, and himself, from Allied investigators.

Dulles and the Vatican were trying to change history and ensure the defeat of the Soviet Union, not the Axis nations. But their "peace negotiations" were directly undermining Allied policy and indirectly encouraging Hitler to keep fighting while the negotiations continued. Meanwhile, Allied soldiers were being killed while the Nazis' generals desperately fought for time for Dulles to negotiate on their behalf. As the number of Allied casualties mounted, Dulles's promises of a secret deal stiffened the German resolve to hold on for just a little longer until Dulles could arrange a united Axis-Allied front against the Soviet Union. It was one of the most shameful secrets of the war.

There is evidence that the creation of a Japanese-Anglo-Fascist alliance against the Soviet Union was originally a British idea. On November 13, 1939, Lord Cadogan had received the first such proposal, when the foreign secretary, Lord Halifax suggested taking over Hitler's Anti-Comintern Pact and joining Italy, Japan, and Spain in an alliance against Germany. "Cadogan found the idea 'attractive' and passed it to Sir Percy Lorraine, British Ambassador in Rome, for development."[24]

The Vatican encouraged the idea and discussions went forward in Spain with the British ambassador, Sir Samuel Hoare, until 1942. At that time the new SS intelligence head, Walter Schellenberg, had begun his campaign to replace Admiral Canaris of the Abwehr (German Military Intelligence) in handling the secret negotiations. In addition to the British and Vatican team, the SS spy chief was in touch with Dulles's business partner Karl Lindemann, the chief of Standard Oil of New Jersey's German subsidiary, and with Fritz Klein, a good friend of both the Dulles brothers.[25]

According to SS records, captured by the Soviet and U.S. armies, the secret Nazi negotiations continued throughout the war. Schellenberg sent Prince Max von Hohenlohe of the SS as his personal emissary to Dulles. They held a series of talks, culminating in a final discussion on April 3, 1943. Dulles emphasized that German industry must be preserved and a *cordon sanitaire* established against the Soviets.[26]

Hohenlohe took copious notes. His record of the Dulles negotiations was released by the Soviets after the war, but no one believed it. In his history of the OSS, published in the early 1970s, R. Harris Smith quoted a U.S. intelligence officer "that the original German documents were significantly 'altered' by the Soviets before release as part of their 'disinformation' campaign."[27] Given their damaging contents, there was a lot at stake here for Dulles, and the authenticity of the documents had to be questioned—especially after the Communists translated them and had them published worldwide.

However, recently a British copy of the Hohenlohe-Dulles papers surfaced "from the files of a reliable source in England via Professor Klaus von Klemperer, professor of history at Smith College."[28] The author who reported the independent confirmation was attacked as unreliable. However, several of our sources agreed that the memos were genuine, and that a further disinformation campaign had been instigated. Finally, in 1993, the authenticity of the documents was confirmed when they were found in the U.S. Archives.[29]

There were many good reasons why Dulles's friends would want to discredit the Hohenlohe documents as Soviet forgeries. For a start, Dulles made no secret of his hatred for the Jews or his contempt for the British and "peppered his conversation with anti-semitic and anglophobic remarks."[30] He said that he was "sick and tired of listening to stories of . . . prejudiced Jews" and "added that it would be unbearable for any decent European to think that the Jews might return someday."[31]

Dulles also insisted that Karl Lindemann, the German manager of the Rockefeller-controlled Standard Oil company, would be a useful future contact, but that he preferred to meet with Fritz Spitzi, the Nazi agent who had handled the original discussion in Spain with the British and Americans. According to Hohenlohe's report to the SS, Dulles knew all about the secret British initiative of Sir Samuel Hoare in Spain.[32]

This was a key disclosure. It showed that Dulles was fully informed of the secret British-Nazi negotiations to end the war that were being conducted without Churchill's knowledge. From 1939 to 1942, Sir Samuel Hoare, the British ambassador to Madrid, represented a small but highly influential group of mutinous British officials (the so-called Halifax faction) that wanted to make a pact with the Nazis. Other supporters of the British-Nazi alliance were the editor of *The Times,* the Astor family, and the head of the British civil service.

The negotiations were illegal, of course, and flatly contrary to Churchill's orders. Among the British conspirators named in the Nazi documents were former Prime Minister Neville Chamberlain; Foreign Secretary Lord Halifax, later Churchill's ambassador to Washington; and Sir John Simon, the man who interrogated Rudolf Hess. Hess, one of Hitler's closest aides, took it upon himself to advance the secret peace negotiations by parachuting into England during the middle of the war. Hess insisted that he was pursuing a secret British initiative to enter into an alliance against the Soviet Union. His statements were dismissed as the ravings of a madman, and he spent the rest of his life in Spandau prison for war crimes. Our sources say that Hess had told an embarrassing truth.

The names of two other British mutineers were so sensitive that disclosure would have caused an uproar in London. One was Admiral Hugh Sinclair, the former head of the British secret service. The other was Edward Windsor, the former king of England.[33] As will be seen in Chapter 5, our sources insist that Windsor had been a willing tool of Nazi intelligence and a key player in the efforts to bring about an Anglo-Nazi pact against the Soviets. Anthony Cave Brown, a respected British historian, has reported independent corroboration that there was an attempt to bring about a secret alliance between England and Nazi Germany.[34]

Another piece of dramatic evidence confirms our sources' account of the secret Western negotiations with Japan through the Vatican, which were taking place at the same time. At first our research was blocked. During the 1980s, most of the Magic intercepts of Japanese secret cables were declassified and released to the U.S. National Archives. Examining the classified Japanese reports of their wartime discussions with the Vatican was vital to our research. Yet every reference to the Vatican—and only the Vatican—has been blacked out by government censors. Apparently, some secrets are so sensitive that they are still classified *fifty years* after the war is over.

How were we to confirm the central part of our sources' thesis that the Vatican was acting as a secret negotiator with the Nazis and the Japanese to stop the war before a complete Allied victory? It turns out that there is a complete and uncensored set of the Vatican cables available to the public, if you know where to look.

One former intelligence officer who had served in the OSS knew about the censored Magic intercepts. He left the U.S. National Archives and flew to Japan where, as he suspected, the Japanese had declassified their half of the correspondence.[35] The intercepts confirm what the "old spies" said. The Vatican was deeply involved in Japanese negotiations and was desperately trying to stop the fighting before a total Allied victory left the Red Army in control of Catholic Central Europe.

The key to the Vatican's initiative was absolute secrecy. Nothing about the negotiations with the Nazis must leak back to the Allied governments until the deal had been cut. Because James Jesus Angleton was the only American in Italy with Ultra clearances, he was the only American who knew that the British had penetrated the Vatican's codes even partially. For years the British and Americans had been reading the German half of the Vatican correspondence almost without interruption. Toward the end of the war, the British and the Communists had been able to break the Vatican's half because they were buying the cables from one of the Vatican's code clerks.

The Vatican was appalled when Angelton revealed that their codes were broken, especially when he pointed out that the pope's good-faith peace efforts were used to mislead the Nazis about D-Day. The Vatican wanted to change all its codes at once. Angleton and British intelligence had a better idea.

The British secret service had not told anyone else in the American government that it had recently broken several of the Vatican codes. Years later Angleton would insist to historians that there "was no Ultra traffic relating directly to the Vatican."[36] Instead, the British had let the Americans think that they had a human agent inside the Vatican itself. In return for sharing the fruits from this fictitious Vatican spy, General Donovan of the OSS had agreed to have the American code breakers concentrate on other areas. The only Vatican material the Americans obtained directly was what appeared from the decoded German or Italian intercepts.[37]

The last thing Dulles and his British friends wanted to do was to make the Americans suspicious. If the Vatican suddenly changed all its cipher systems, the American code breakers might begin to focus their attention on Rome's cable traffic. It was essential to keep the Vatican's lines of communication open to the Nazis and the Japanese while there was still a chance to negotiate a truce. To this end, the British Ultra team would give the Vatican an additional code system that was truly unbreakable, while feeding the Americans a steady stream of artificial "Vatican" intelligence so that Donovan would not become suspicious.[38]

As long as the Americans believed that there was a British spy inside the Vatican who would hand over the uncoded material, they would not try to break the codes themselves. In the meantime, the British would feed their ally only the information that Dulles wanted them to know. Angleton and the British could twist the Vatican's prestigious intelligence reports to suit their own interests. They could feed Roosevelt false information, mixed with a large number of real Vatican cables that could be cross-checked against other broken codes.

It was an ingenious scheme, but misleading the president of the United States imposed serious risks. It was better to have a cover story. For security's sake, the British wanted to plant two fictitious sources in the Vatican: one for the British and one for the Americans. Each would partly corroborate the other's information. Most important, one would be the "fall guy" in case the scam was ever discovered.

Montini's fellow Vatican undersecretary of state, Monsignor Domenico Tardini, agreed to the British suggestion for a cover story, as it seemed to offer the Vatican protection as well.[39] Tardini had just the fall guy in mind: Virgilio Scattolini, a pornographer who supposedly had seen the light of God and obtained a job on the Vatican newspaper, *L'Osservatore Romano*. Before the war he had peddled Vatican gossip, partly fictitious, to American newspapers. It was a small step to promote him to master forger of Vatican intelligence, from which he would earn good commissions from the various intelligence agencies to which he supplied it.[40]

If the Vatican material was ever discovered to be fraudulent, Angleton would step in, denounce Scattolini as a con man, and reveal that the *real* Vatican source was one of Scattolini's friends in the Vatican code room. Angleton would confirm from this *other* source—the unnamed British spy in the Vatican—that much of Scattolini's information had been true to begin with but that Scattolini had added a gloss of his own invention. The secret British "source" would then continue supplying Angleton the phony Vatican traffic, with the Americans even more convinced that the telegrams were genuine.

And that is exactly what happened. Right after D-Day, Scattolini was brought on board under the code name "Vessel." He played his part to the hilt. According to the version that Angelton gave to the distinguished Yale historian Robin Winks, the Scattolini-Vessel scandal began before Angleton even arrived in Rome, when a Vatican source began to provide high-level information on Japan to the OSS Secret Intelligence chief, Vincent Scamporino.[41]

In fact, the British, with Tardini's help, had primed Vessel with real information that they knew the Americans could verify easily. It was no coincidence that Vessel started with Japanese information. The U.S. Army had a secret radio intercept station in the North African desert, where, because of unusual atmospheric conditions, they were able to listen to the coded radio traffic from the Japanese ambassador in Berlin. Since the Japanese were still using the same diplomatic code that the Americans had broken at Pearl Harbor, Ambassador Oshima's messages, including his reports on the Vatican's peace efforts, could be deciphered.

The Magic intercepts, as these Japanese message intercepts were known, seemed to match Vessel's story. Once Vessel's bona fides were proved, the British fed the Americans some false information: The Japanese were willing to stop fighting the Americans and attack the Soviet Union, if the Vatican could convince the Germans to do the same. The pope had not wanted to get involved, but more and more Vessel reported that the Axis powers were begging him to have the war called off before the Soviets conquered all of Europe. The Vessel material caused a firestorm in Washington and was delivered right to President Roosevelt's desk.[42]

As the British mutineers grew more and more desperate to make peace with the Germans, the Vessel material grew more and more bold. Scamporino, Vessel's first contact in the OSS, had returned to Washington. He suspected that the Japanese material, in particular, was some kind of deception. To cover himself Angleton, who by now had arrived in Italy, went on record as saying that although Vessel's sources checked out against Magic, he was still a little suspicious.

Around February 1945 the conspirators made a blunder, one that would be fully understood only half a century later by one of the "old spies." Because of the historical importance of the whole Vessel affair, this source has decided to go public. His name is William E. Gowen. He was a special agent with the U.S. Army's Counter Intelligence Corps in Rome. His father, Franklin Gowen assisted Myron Taylor, who was serving as Roosevelt's, and then Truman's, personal representative to Pope Pius XII. William Gowen knew James Jesus Angleton personally, as well as senior officers of Italian and British intelligence. His sources are impeccable.

In the last three years Gowen has conducted extensive research in Italy and the United States. He flatly accuses Angleton of fabricating the entire Vessel/Vatican file from beginning to end in a deliberate attempt to mislead the president of the United States. His charges are contained in a letter he wrote to the director of the CIA on November 18, 1992.[43]

According to Gowen, Angleton had coerced Scattolini and his assistant, Setaccioli, into translating the Italian-language versions of the fake Vessel material under threat of execution as alleged German spies. The originals of the Vatican messages were actually written in English by Angleton personally. The whole operation was done from "Angleton's OSS office in Rome at 59 Via Sicilia."

After translation, and some useful suggestions from the con men, the documents were "transmitted almost immediately to Allied military headquarters in Caserta, Italy, and to Washington, where Donovan and Cheston passed many of them, with covering notes, directly to the White House, for President Roosevelt." One day Angleton made a clumsy mistake and included a detail that was proven uncontestably false:

> In February 1945, a "flap" developed when Myron C. Taylor, who had been mentioned in one of the reports [as attending a meeting on a certain date], repeatedly denied its veracity. . . . Undeterred, Angleton continued producing the Scattolini reports, each and every one false. Cheston and others kept accepting them and forwarding them, including to President Roosevelt.

How did Angleton get away with continuing this deception? When Myron Taylor inadvertently blew the Vessel operation, the British tipped off Angleton that a storm was coming and that it was time to drop the first Vessel scapegoat overboard. An American investigation was under way.

Angleton was ready to play his part. He claimed that he was always suspicious of Vessel and that through his own agent, Filippe Setaccioli, had identified Scattolini as a con man in the employ of British intelligence. The British were using Scattolini as a red herring to protect the identity of the real source of the information, a Vatican code clerk whom Scattolini had befriended. Angleton's bottom line was that Vessel was false, but the Vatican's peace initiatives with the Axis were genuine.

The British refused to confirm or deny the story, which made the Americans more convinced than ever that their ally had a valuable Vatican source. Angleton got credit not only for quietly solving the Vessel mystery, but for identifying and recruiting the same British secret source who had provided Scattolini with so much genuine information. However, Angleton said that his "source" insisted that he must tell no one, not even the president, of his identity. Complete confidentiality was the price for continued cooperation by the Vatican spy.

For years afterward various CIA officials in Italy would complain about Angleton's refusal to turn over his key agent in the Vatican.[44] From time to time Angleton would brag about how he solved the Vessel case and would drop various hints about the identity of his "secret source." Robin Winks, who interviewed Angleton extensively, credits Angleton with having a "personal contact" not only in the Vatican code room but within the church hierarchy itself. Winks reported that Angleton's supersource was none other than Bishop Montini, then undersecretary of state at the Vatican.[45] At least one other historian confirms that Montini was the Vatican agent involved in the Vessel affair.[46]

If Montini was Angleton's source in Vatican City, he was not the only prelate involved in the Vessel scandal. Throughout his career, Angleton claimed that he had been the first one to uncover Scattolini, but William Gowen tells it differently: "In March, 1945 . . . Mr. Taylor became alarmed, and discussed one or more of these reports privately with Pope Pius XII, who was equally disturbed, as the reports presumed to describe verbatim his own private conversations within an hour or two after engaging in them in the Papal Study, with senior Vatican officials, including Mons. Giovanni Battista Montini . . ." One of our sources in the intelligence community told us that Montini's colleague at the Vatican Secretariat of State, Monsignor Domenico Tardini, was immediately alerted to help throw the Vessel scapegoat overboard in order to preserve the credibility of the Vatican's peace initiative.[47] It appears that the Vatican had a cover story ready and waiting. Within a few hours of Myron Taylor's inquiry to the pope, Tardini had completed his "investigation" into a matter that had eluded Allied intelligence for months.[48] It was time for Tardini to use Vessel as the fall guy.

Pius XII immediately arranged for Tardini to meet with Taylor's assistant, who was William Gowen's father, Franklin. Tardini gave Gowen, Sr., a full report on the "wholly fraudulent activities of Scattolini and Setaccioli, citing them by name and discussing their backgrounds." As a result, Taylor wrote a detailed report to President Truman, but what neither Taylor nor Gowen knew is that Angleton's version reached Washington first. Angleton told his story about the British using Vessel to hide a secret source in the code room. According to several of the "old spies" we spoke to on this point, the tale had credibility because much of Vessel's story matched the Japanese Magic decrypts.[49]

William Gowen did not realize that Angleton had simply traded Vessel for another fictitious source, his unnamed secret agent in the Vatican. But Gowen did discover that, for some reason, Washington allowed the scam to continue even after Taylor's warning. To his amazement, the reports continued unabated even after Angleton was transferred back to Washington.

We disagree with William Gowen on only one point. Not all of the Vatican material was fraudulent. Angleton's "new and improved" post-Vessel material contained not only actual secret cable traffic, but the Vatican's secret cables exactly matched the information decoded from the intercepted Japanese and German cables.

Unless much of the information was accurate and independently verified from other broken enemy codes, no one in Washington would have continued to believe it for three years after Taylor exposed Vessel. Nor do we think that other CIA employees, such as Raymond Rocca, Angleton's successor in Rome, were aware of the fraud. The more likely explanation is that the willing cooperation of the Vatican and the code-breaking skills of British intelligence kept the scam going for several more years.

After the war was over, why would they bother? For $30 million. The phony Vatican cables convinced Roosevelt's successor in the White House that Italy was in danger of going Communist. Between 1947 and 1948, tens of millions of American dollars were laundered through the Vatican, as handouts for local Christian Democrat and Socialist politicians.[50]

With the help of Angleton's phony cables, his friends not only had an influence on U.S. foreign policy, they also could enjoy the benefits of the American taxpayers' unwitting largesse. The more Vessel warned that the Communists were taking over, the more money the Americans poured into the coffers of the Italian right. The game might have gone on forever if the Communists had not pulled the plug. William Gowen remembers how it all came to an end:

> Finally, in early April 1948, the Vatican became aware that two books of Scattolini reports had been published in Italian by a Communist publisher in Northern Italy, one on relations between Italy and the Vatican,

> the other on relations between the Vatican and other countries. Scattolini's name was not mentioned, but the publisher's note referred to the hundreds of reports included in the two books as genuine Vatican documents and reports on meetings inside the Vatican.

The books were dismissed as Communist propaganda. Then, in 1992, Gowen got suspicious. He compared the "phony" Italian propaganda books against the "genuine" secret cipher intercepts that Angleton had continued to send to Washington. Unlike Angleton, who spoke a crude form of pidgin Italian, Gowen was fluent in several languages:

> What is immediately striking is that many of the [Communist] reports . . . are direct Italian translations of English-language texts transmitted by Angleton . . . Major Eugenio Piccardo (whom I had known well), chief of the Rome intelligence unit of the Carabinieri, arrested Scattolini in Rome on April 9th. The arrest was immediately announced to the press, as were Scattolini's statements that the "reports" included in the two books were all his and that all the "reports" were false, having been invented by him. (Angleton, who by then had already returned to the US, was never mentioned.)
>
> After a July trial in Rome . . . the court sentenced Scattolini on July 23rd to a little over seven months in prison . . . which would have been much longer, the Court stated, had Scattolini not immediately tried to make amends by . . . proclaiming the wholly fraudulent character of the reports. . . .[51]

When Gowen reviewed the trial transcripts, he did find evidence that the whole thing was a stage show. Instead of mentioning the Angleton-Vessel connection, Piccardo told the court that the U.S. Army was the agency to blame: "In his statement to the Court, which is part of the record, Major Piccardo asserted that all Scattolini's reports had been typed up and produced in the (U.S. Army's) CIC office at via Sicilia 59." Gowen was more than a little angry. That was his own address:

> The CIC, my unit, which had previously had offices in that building as had Angleton's OSS/CIG [Central Intelligence Group] unit, had never been involved in any way with Scattolini or Setaccioli, but Piccardo obviously had to "save Angleton" (whom he had known) by accounting somehow for the fact that the reports had been produced in the building at via Sicilia 59. . . . By the time of the trial, moreover, the building had long been evacuated by US units.

Gowen did not discover until 1992 that he, and the army's CIC, had been set up as Angleton's American fall guys. The truth is that no one in the U.S. Army knew what was going on. In fact, Angleton was sending his phony reports to army intelligence in Caserta, Italy, which promptly filed them as highly reliable and kept them in the system for the next forty years.

When the authors obtained some secret army documents under the Freedom of Information Act and cited them in our previous book, the Vatican issued a press release correctly identifying them as Scattolini forgeries. To this day, the embarrassed U.S. Army has no idea how Angleton planted so many phony documents on them.

The army was not the only victim. Recently the authors received a tipoff that the CIA had just declassified a very sensitive collection of Vatican cables and released them to the National Archives. The CIA's "Rome JVX" file is part of the huge collection of Angleton's X-2 unit dossiers and contains hundreds of decoded secret cables. In at least one case, it includes the citation of the original Vatican telegram ciphers.

It looked as if Angleton did have a secret source, after all. But after Mr. Gowen's information, we hired our own researcher in Italy to match the CIA file against the Scattolini trial records. Gowen was right. The CIA documents were all forgeries. In 1992 we attempted to confront Raymond Rocca with this information, but he slammed the phone down.[52]

If authentic, the JVX file would have been dynamite, confirming the pope's personal involvement in secret anti-Communist intelligence operations behind the Iron Curtain as well as in Italy itself. The file includes many supposedly detailed reports of Pius XII's conversations with Montini, Tardini, and senior officials of the Jesuit and Dominican orders as well as with Christian Democrat leaders such as Alcide de Gasperi.

The reports also purport to show that the pope had made a deal with the British to side with London against the Jews in Palestine. The Zionist homeland was said to be part of Soviet expansion in the Middle East. Another of the phony JVX reports detailed the Patriarch of Jerusalem's intelligence: The Soviets were using the West's support for the Zionist cause to stir up the Arabs of Palestine.[53]

None of it was true, of course. All the reports are Angleton forgeries. What is true is that Britain was reneging on the promise of a Jewish homeland in Palestine. As will be seen in Chapter 7, London had some influential allies in Washington, and Moscow was exploiting the situation for its own ends. As we documented in our previous book, the Vatican was indeed involved in covert anti-Communist operations behind the Iron Curtain, utilizing former Nazis. The truth was bad enough, without the JVX forgeries.

No wonder Special CIC agent William Gowen was angry when he discovered that he and his colleagues had been secretly blamed all these years for the Vessel scandal. In his recent letter to the CIA, Gowen made some telling points:

> In effect, Angleton first in the OSS, then in the CIG [Central Intelligence Group] and finally in the CIA produced hundreds of completely false reports for more than three years, while stationed in Rome. For this service, he was commended, promoted and decorated, but was never investigated and condemned as was Scattolini. In fact, of the two, Angleton was the more responsible for this gross fraud, and was therefore, far more guilty. . . . he had shamelessly conned the very organization that by legislation has responsibility for distinguishing useful intelligence from trash.

When the authors of this book discovered that the JVX reports were forgeries, the U.S. Archives conducted an investigation. To its credit, the CIA admitted that its Rome X-2 files are bogus. The Archives placed a warning notice on the JVX file so that future historians will not be misled.

Of course, it was years too late to tell President Truman that he had been the victim of a con game. President Truman, a neophyte at foreign policy, was a captive of his advisers, including Dulles's allies, such as Secretary of the Navy James Forrestal and California oil man Edwin Pauley. Henry Morgenthau's plans for the postwar elimination of the German industrial base were derided as mindless Jewish vengeance by some of the same Americans who had built the Nazi industrial machine in the first place. Misled by his own advisers into believing that a revived German war industry was a necessary defense against the Soviet Union, Truman quickly accepted Morgenthau's resignation as secretary of the treasury.

Although he knew very little about their history, culture, or religion, Truman liked Jews, but he didn't like Morgenthau. When he succeeded to the presidency in April 1945, Truman neither knew nor understood Roosevelt's plans for Operation Safehaven, just as he was kept in the dark about the atomic bomb.

There was one Roosevelt foreign policy, though, that Truman understood only too well. He was shocked to discover that his predecessor had tried to lock the U.S. government into a pro-Arab policy in Palestine. In February 1945 Roosevelt gave oral assurances to King Ibn Saud that the United States would not "assist the Jews against the Arabs." In effect, it was a policy of "neutrality," but one decidedly in favor of the Arabs. One week before he died, FDR had repeated his pledge to Ibn Saud, promising in writing that it was issued "in my capacity as Chief of the Executive Branch of this Government."[54] The Dulles brothers, Forrestal, and the others thought they had the "Jew-loving" Truman boxed in by Roosevelt's written guarantees to Ibn Saud. One of the first memos sent by the State Department to the new president warned Truman that he must never allow the Jews to have their own country, because a Jewish state in "Palestine would become a Communist puppet within three years."[55]

To the utter dismay of the pirates of Wall Street and their friends in the Truman administration, the new president dismissed these scare tactics. Worse, he reversed the commitments that Roosevelt had made to Ibn Saud. Truman had more regard for the probable influence of the American Jewish community on his reelection prospects than he did for the anti-Semites of the State Department.

Six months into his presidency, Truman assembled his top Middle East advisers, who were deeply concerned at the Arabs' hostility toward the new president's pro-Zionist tilt. As hard as they tried, they could not bring him around. Harry Truman did not want to be a one-term, unelected president. He wanted to win the 1948 election and claim the mantle in his own right. Even in 1945 Truman knew there might be just enough Jews in the United States to tip the 1948 election, while Arabs were a negligible electoral quantity.[56] Roosevelt's policy of neutrality in favor of the Arabs was dead, at least as far as the new president was concerned.

As will be seen in later chapters, the Dulles brothers, James Forrestal, and their supporters were determined to defeat Truman at the polls in 1948 unless he changed his support for the Jewish homeland. With the Nazi scandals safely buried with Roosevelt, the Dulles clique presented themselves as patriots who had served their country in time of war. They were deserving of top appointments in the postwar world. Through sheer ignorance, Truman allowed Dulles's cronies to infiltrate the occupation of Germany, Italy, and Austria.

Dulles and some of his friends volunteered for postwar service with the government not out of patriotism but of necessity. They had to be in positions of power to suppress the evidence of their own dealings with the Nazis. The Safehaven investigation was quickly stripped from Treasury, where Morgenthau's supporters were still influential, and turned over to the State Department. There Dulles's friends shredded the index to the interlocking corporations and blocked further investigations.[57]

Dulles had this goal in mind: Not a single American businessman was ever going to be convicted of treason for helping the Nazis. None ever was, despite the evidence. According to one of our sources in the intelligence community, the U.S. Army Counter Intelligence Corps had two large "Civilian Internment Centers" in Occupied Germany, code named "Ashcan" and "Dustbin."[58] The CIC had identified and captured a large number of U.S. citizens who had stayed in Germany and aided the Third Reich all through World War II. The evidence of their treason was overwhelming. The captured German records were horribly incriminating.

Yet Victor Wohreheide, the young Justice Department attorney responsible for preparing the treason trials, suddenly ordered the prisoners' release. All of the Nazi collaborators were allowed to return to the United

States and reclaim their citizenship. At the same time, another Justice Department attorney, O. John Rogge, who dared to make a speech about Nazi collaborators in the United States was quickly fired.[59] However, the attorney who buried the treason cases was later promoted to special assistant attorney general.

Dulles and his Nazi clients had won. The proof is in the bottom line. Forty years after World War II, *Fortune* magazine published a list of the hundred richest men in the world.[60] There were no Jews on the list. The great fortunes of the Rothschilds and Warburgs had been diminished to insignificance by the Depression, the Nazis, and World War II.

Near the top of the list were several multibillionaires who had been prominent members of Hitler's inner circle. A few even had served time in Allied prisons as Nazi war criminals, but they all were released quickly. The bottom line is that the Nazi businessmen survived the war with their fortunes intact and rebuilt their industrial empires to become the richest men in the world. Dulles's clients got away with it. President Roosevelt's dream of putting the Nazis' moneymen on trial died with him.

If the American cover-up was bad, the British were worse. The British authorities in Germany ordered the U.S. Army to release all of the VIP British Nazis and hand over the evidence against them. Even before Roosevelt's death, Churchill had already begun to withdraw from his commitment to prosecute Nazis. As Chapter 5 shows, too many royal skeletons in the Nazi closet might be exposed. Too many British industries might be seized as Nazi fronts. Too many upper-class collaborators might have to be prosecuted. The Germans were defeated, and the Soviets were now the enemy.

Funding for British war crimes investigations suddenly dried up. Nazi bankers such as Herman Abs were released from prison to work as economic advisers in the British zone of Germany. The history of British "efforts" to punish Nazis after the war is aptly summarized in Tom Bower's book, *The Pledge Betrayed.*

The French were even worse than the British. They simply pretended that there had never been any French-Nazi collaboration and ignored the issue, which continues to haunt French society. As late as 1993, elderly French collaborators were being charged with Nazi war crimes. Like the French, the Austrians claimed that they had all been victims of the Third Reich, despite the fact that there was a higher percentage of card-carrying Nazis in Austria than in Germany itself. Allen Dulles's son-in-law, Fritz Molden, gave a wildly erroneous security clearance to known Nazi collaborator Kurt Waldheim. He was not the only Nazi to be cleared by Allied intelligence.

The pattern was repeated all over the remnants of the Third Reich.

Despite direct orders from President Truman and General Eisenhower, I. G. Farben, the citadel of the Nazi industrialists, was never dismantled. Dulles's clients demanded, and received, Allied compensation for bomb damage to their factories in Germany. Only a few of the top Nazis were executed. Most of the rest were released from prison within a few years. Others, like Dulles's old SS friend General Karl Wolff, who had run the killing machinery, would go virtually unpunished.[61] No one ever investigated the Nazi sympathizers in Western intelligence who had made it all possible.

Some, like James Jesus Angleton, had built their intelligence careers on fraud. He became the CIA's expert on the Vatican. Although he didn't know it yet, Angleton's takeover of the Vatican desk of U.S. intelligence also would force him to take over the Israeli desk a few years later. The Soviets and the Zionists were both watching the Vessel scam and waiting for the opportunity to ensnare young James Jesus.

CHAPTER 5

THE SEEDS OF BLACKMAIL

The popular notion of the birth of Israel is romantic. The United Nations, dominated by the sympathetic Western democracies, voted to create the first Jewish state in two thousand years. Pioneer settlers fought arm in arm with Auschwitz survivors to defeat the Arabs and build a country. The whole world applauded as justice triumphed over armed force.

On the contrary, however, our sources in the intelligence community say that the UN vote was a fluke. The Western countries were, in fact, greatly antagonistic to a Jewish nation. Only through blackmail did the Zionists obtain the swing votes needed to create their state. To understand the force of this blackmail, one needs to know the scandals that the opponents of Israel were trying to conceal.

In Chapter 7 we discuss the precise details of how the Zionist leader, David Ben-Gurion, used blackmail to obtain the UN vote in favor of Israel. It is, however, essential first to understand exactly what has been hidden from history for so long by those who were blackmailed. In this chapter we address the following allegations:

- The British secret service and members of the royal family concealed a series of wartime negotiations with the Nazis to bring about an Anglo-German alliance against the Soviet Union.
- Allen Dulles and his protégé, James Angleton, concealed the manner in which Vatican intelligence was used to deceive two U.S. presidents through the Vessel fraud.
- Even forty years after World War II, the Republican National Committee under George Bush recruited Dulles's Nazi agents for Republican party election campaigns.
- Each of the Nazi cover-ups, separately and together, contributed significantly to the success of key Soviet agents in Western intelligence.

One of the Nazis' problems was that they were overly meticulous. They kept extensive files, some of which were intensely embarrassing to the victorious Allies. When the Americans captured a set of German records containing correspondence with the British royal family, the British demanded that they be delivered to their agents. British MI5 agent Anthony Blunt was dispatched to bring the records back to London.

Lord Cadogan personally carried the documents to Buckingham Palace. In his own diary, Cadogan recorded that on October 25, 1945, the "King fussed about Duke of Windsor file & captured German documents."[1] There was good reason for King George to fuss. Here was evidence that his brother, the former king, Edward VIII, had been a Nazi agent and traitor.

One of the sources interviewed on this point was an American who actually had read the Windsor file before handing it over to the British.[2] According to this "old spy," the Nazi records confirmed that the former king was not just sympathetic to Hitler. Edward VIII had encouraged Hitler to seize Czechoslovakia, occupy Alsace, and persecute the Jews. After he was forced to abdicate, and while an officer in the British army during wartime, Windsor passed on to the Nazis secret military information—classified information—on British and French defenses in France. There was no doubt, at least in this source's judgment, that Edward Windsor was one of the British traitors who worked hand in hand with Nazi agents.

A mountain of evidence supports this source. During World War II the FBI secretly wiretapped some of Windsor's communications with the British mutineers in New York and issued a top-secret report to the attorney general. FBI director Hoover was convinced that Windsor was so dangerous a Nazi agent that he insisted that the former king, then residing in the Bahamas, be imprisoned for the duration of the war.[3]

The postwar top-secret interrogation by American intelligence of the Third Reich's foreign minister, Joachim Ribbentrop, also confirmed Windsor's Nazi sympathies.[4] There is no doubt that, technically, the king was a traitor: He gave aid and comfort to the enemy in time of war. However, many of our sources, particularly the British ones, insist that Edward was a bit too dim to comprehend the significance of his actions and that he was only a pawn in the Nazis' game to obtain a royal quisling.[5]

However, all of our sources, on both sides of the Atlantic, reluctantly agree that burying the Windsor investigation had serious repercussions for Western intelligence. The consensus is that it was King George's wife, Elizabeth (queen consort, mother of the present queen), who insisted that none of the royal mutineers ever be exposed. Several other members of the British royal family also had secretly sided with their German cousins during the war. It was, to be kind, an enormous mess, and Elizabeth pressured King George to control the damage at all costs.

Our sources offer some corroboration for Elizabeth's role in the cover-up. After the war, one small-time British traitor, John Amery, was arrested in Italy. There was no way to hide Amery's background. He had broadcast Nazi propaganda from Germany during the war. John Amery knew it all, from Windsor's treason to his own father's duplicitous role in Churchill's cabinet. For the good of the royal family, he was asked to plead guilty and avoid a public scandal. After Amery's execution, King George VI and Queen Elizabeth had the Amery family to Buckingham Palace and sympathized with their guests about the loss of their son.[6]

With Amery dead and the Windsor letters returned to England, Elizabeth believed that she had the family's Nazi scandal under control. All of the British secret service agents who participated in the cover-up received her special favor. The problem was that Elizabeth's (and later Queen Elizabeth II's) damage control operation created a new disaster for Western intelligence.

In protecting Edward Windsor, our sources among the "old spies" say that the British secret service was really protecting itself from investigation, not just the royal family. When Sir Stewart Menzies succeeded Admiral Sinclair as chief of the British secret service in 1939, he continued his predecessor's negotiations for a separate peace with the Third Reich. It was Menzies who authorized the Vatican back-channel to Spain and then to Dulles in Switzerland. It was Menzies who concocted the Vessel scam to hide the Axis-Vatican communications from the Americans. It was Menzies who ordered British troops to help the Vatican truck the Nazi treasure into hiding.

It was Menzies who gave Nazi intelligence chief, Walter Schellenberg and the other Nazi negotiators sanctuary in Britain after the war, and requested the Americans to let the British VIPs out of the internment centers for Nazi collaborators. Menzies also authorized Kim Philby to recruit ex-Nazis as agents and smuggle them through the Vatican to South America and to several Middle Eastern countries, notably Egypt and Syria. Menzies oversaw the program to employ fugitive Fascists as British mercenaries in Eastern Europe.

In fact, it was Menzies's own unauthorized, illegal Nazi contacts that gave Philby and the other Soviet agents the open door to infiltrate Western intelligence. And when the Americans tried to expose Philby and the others as Communists, it was Menzies who blocked the investigations to protect himself.

One of the great ironies of twentieth-century espionage history is that the right-wing head of the British secret service, Sir Stewart Menzies, handed the Communists the key to Britain's secrets on a royal platter. The British Communist party and its front groups could never have done it. Moscow penetrated MI6 from its blind side, on the far right.

Menzies had hand-picked the British agents to carry out the Windsor cover-up because of their known Fascist sympathies. For example, Colonel Charles "Dickie" Ellis, a senior SIS officer and liaison to OSS during the war, had more than just right-wing leanings. He later confessed that he was a paid double agent for the Nazis. Instead of being prosecuted after the war when his treason was discovered, he received a new job in the secret service archives, purging embarrassing secrets from the records.[7]

The reason for putting an admitted Nazi traitor back on the payroll was simple. Ellis had, before the war, wiretapped the Windsor-Ribbentrop conversations in which King Edward promised Hitler his secret support. Even though Ellis was a confessed traitor and Nazi agent, he could never be touched because of what he knew about the royal family's secret deals with Hitler.

According to several former intelligence officers we interviewed, one of those personally protected by Elizabeth was Anthony Blunt, the man who actually retrieved the Windsor file from American custody and passed it on through Cadogan to the king. He was appointed as the Royal Surveyor of Pictures, although there is some dispute as to whether he received the honor before or after he fetched the royal records.[8]

Another was Roger Hollis, the MI5 agent in charge of spying on Nazi agents in Britain. Hollis buried all traces of the royals' Nazi connection and was later promoted to head of Britain's counterintelligence agency, MI5. Years later, when Blunt was discovered to be a Soviet spy, a horrified Hollis rushed to warn Queen Elizabeth II that Blunt could not be subjected to any searching investigation. The queen had no choice but to continue her mother's cover-up. Not only was Blunt given complete immunity from prosecution, he retained his job at the palace. Years later Margaret Thatcher continued the cover-up by repeating misleading information to Parliament as to the extent of harm done by Soviet agents posing as British Fascists. Thatcher herself appears to have been misled by British intelligence.

According to most of the "old spies," the one man whom both queens, mother and daughter, dreaded most of all was Kim Philby.[9] It is another irony that the Fascist veneer of Moscow's top agent, Kim Philby, was provided by his own father, who cleared his son for service in MI6. Through their blinkered dependence on the recommendations of a pro-Fascist, but nonetheless establishment, agent, the British mutineers gave Moscow the means to promote Jack Philby's Communist double-agent son to a position where he was the keeper of the royal family's Nazi secret.

After spying on his father's Spanish oil deals, Kim had become head of MI6's Iberian desk. He knew all about the Windsor machinations in Spain and British ambassador Samuel Hoare's negotiations with the Nazis in Madrid in the early 1940s. He had served as the unofficial channel of communication between the mutineers in London and the Nazis in Spain. As the son of his Fascist father, Kim was entrusted with securing the Vatican communication links and keeping the Americans away from the secret British negotiations with the Nazis.

After Churchill became suspicious, it was Philby who suggested that Hohenlohe switch the site of negotiations from Spain to Switzerland. It was Philby who opened the secret channel of communication through the Vatican. Several of our sources were in a position to know the true identity of the master forger of the Vatican cables. According to them, Kim Philby was Vessel.[10]

The "old spies" have more than allegations, they have evidence. Just before the Vessel signals began to emanate from the Vatican, Philby's espionage jurisdiction was suddenly expanded to include North Africa and Italy. He had access to the American Magic decrypts from North Africa as well as the British reports from the Vatican. Philby was one of the few intelligence officers in the Mediterranean theater with legitimate access to all of the information necessary to forge the entire series of Vessel communications.[11]

These sources believe Angleton was nothing more than a courier for Kim Philby's secret service operations in Italy. Dulles was merely an echo, providing corroboration for Vessel with reports from his Nazi sources in Germany. No wonder Angleton later hated Philby with such venom. It wasn't just that Philby had completely fooled Angleton when he came to Washington after the war as British liaison to the CIA. He knew the secret of Angleton's Vatican forgeries.

There is some historical evidence that the Soviet secret service could have used Philby as a stalking horse, to sound out Western reaction to a separate peace with the Nazis. Stalin was afraid that the West would do to him what he had done to them: make an alliance with Hitler, as he had done when he had betrayed the Western powers with the Molotov-Ribbentrop Non-Aggression Pact in 1939. A Western alliance with Hitler was a logical extension of the initiative begun by King Edward, before he was forced to abdicate.

Philby must have known the entire history. He had been briefed on the Windsor letters by Blunt, had helped Hollis to cover up the domestic scandal, and personally blocked an investigation into Ellis's Nazi collaboration.[12] Moreover, Philby was the only Soviet agent privy to both KGB (civilian intelligence) and GRU (military intelligence) operations to penetrate Western intelligence.

In many ways, Vessel was a propaganda platform that conformed to Philby's pseudo-Fascist mission for MI6 while serving as an early warning device for Moscow. Through Vessel, Philby funneled information to the White House about the necessity to negotiate an alliance with the Nazis against the Soviets, while having the blame for the Nazi initiative fall on the Vatican rather than on himself and Dulles.

From 1944 to 1947 Philby used Vessel to float right-wing balloons to the White House and ascertain the probable Western response to Soviet moves. Where, as in Italy and Austria, the West intended to meet a Communist coup with military force, the Soviets backed off. In places such as Czechoslovakia, Albania, and Poland, where the reaction to the Vessel material indicated the Western response would be weak, the Communists took over. Philby also used the Vatican's cable traffic to encourage the postwar use of Catholic Fascists from Eastern Europe as Western-sponsored "freedom fighters" behind the Iron Curtain. Many of Philby's "Fascist" agents later turned out to be Communist moles.[13]

In 1948, just before Philby was transferred to Washington, he pulled the plug on Vessel and made sure that a complete copy of the "secret Vatican cables" fell into the hands of the Italian Communists for publication. It was an effective means to test Angleton's and Dulles's ability to stifle American inquiries. When Angleton succeeded in blaming Scattolini in Italy and the CIC in Washington, Philby knew the secret was safe on the American side.[14]

Philby never had to worry about any British investigation. His knowledge of the royal scandal alone would guarantee that he would never face prosecution in London and, in fact, was the key to his ongoing success as a Communist double agent inside British intelligence. Nor is there any doubt that Menzies protected Philby and his friends from investigation, although he strongly suspected they were Communists. The reason was simple: They had hidden the worst scandal in the history of the royal family. By quietly pensioning off Philby and the other Communist moles, Menzies had spared his country the horror of a public prosecution of their former king.

Even before the war was over, the British secret service suspected that Philby and his friends were security risks and had placed most of the Cambridge net under surveillance long before Philby, Burgess, and Maclean were posted to Washington as British intelligence liaison and diplomats. The British never warned the CIA or the FBI about their suspicions, however, because they wanted to keep everything under wraps. If Menzies had told the Americans the truth, the FBI would have canceled the security clearances for Burgess and his housemate, Philby, immediately. Untold damage might have been averted. After being posted to Washington, however, Philby was allowed to pillage the CIA and FBI of their secrets for another two years.

As a result of Menzies's concern for the royal family, millions of people behind the Iron Curtain were condemned to communism as Philby betrayed every Allied intelligence net. In the first stages of the Korean War, the Communists knew every U.S. military secret in advance. Based on Philby's information that President Truman would not use the atomic bomb in Korea, the Chinese army invaded and thousands of American soldiers died. Their widows and families deserve to know that the British had gambled with American lives on their assumption that Kim Philby was not really a Communist.

With that much blood on their hands, it is not surprising that the British secret service and, to a lesser extent, the royal family elected to continue the cover-up. When Blunt was finally unmasked in 1964, he received immunity and kept his job. So did Ellis. Both Burgess and Maclean were warned in advance to flee to the Soviet Union. So was Philby. British counterintelligence officer Peter Wright, who tried to uncover the Communist moles, has stated point blank that his superiors conferred with Buckingham Palace and then restricted the scope of his investigations.[15]

The British cover-up lasted well into the 1960s, long after Kim Philby had been forced out of the secret service and into exile in Lebanon. Just as the Americans were getting ready to arrest Philby, the CIA learned, to its horror, that, contrary to all agreements, the British secret service had approached Kim, warned him that new evidence of his treason had surfaced, and then left him alone to escape from Lebanon to Russia. As we shall see in Chapter 11, the CIA had learned this from its operative, an American "oil consultant," who had wiretapped Philby's Beirut apartment and recorded the warning from MI6.

One person who had been with the CIA prayed that Philby would never talk: Allen Dulles. Prior to Philby's defection to Moscow in 1963, President Kennedy had forced Dulles to resign as director of the CIA. Dulles knew that Philby was a Communist, but burying the British end of the scandal also meant burying his own role in the mutiny. Philby was one of the few people left who knew what Dulles had done.

In 1945, with Roosevelt dead, Operation Safehaven stifled, Truman ignorant, and Menzies cooperating, Dulles thought that he had gotten away with his schemes with the Nazis. Soon after the Safehaven inquiry into his own Nazi money smuggling was buried, Allen Dulles resigned from the OSS and returned to New York to do what he did best: move money illegally for his clients. One of the first names on his client list was a "personal matter" for Thomas McKittrick, the head of the previously Nazi-dominated Bank of International Settlements (BIS) in Switzerland.

The BIS had overseen the transfer of Nazi assets to Switzerland. After the war, the Nazis moved the money via the Vatican to Argentina.

Dulles represented a staggering array of Argentine corporate and political entities before and after the war.[16] President Juan Peron and his family were ardent Catholics and violently anti-Communist, as were many Argentines. In fact, Peron was decidedly pro-Fascist and Argentina was the only South American country that continued relations with the Third Reich well into the war. The Argentine economy boomed with the massive postwar transfer of Nazi flight capital.

This time, there was no one peering over Dulles's shoulder to monitor his money laundering. J. Edgar Hoover had taken care of that. Hoover had obtained a copy of General William Donovan's proposal for a postwar centralized intelligence service and leaked the top-secret dossier to the archconservative *Chicago Tribune*. The newspaper quickly denounced the scheme as an American Gestapo. Truman, bewildered at the harsh press criticism, not only canceled plans for an expanded service, he scrapped the OSS.

To his horror, William Donovan saw the massive OSS political files carted off to the State Department and the Pentagon. Most of the staff quit. No one was monitoring anything anymore, except perhaps the Communists. Dulles lost no time in taking the disgruntled Donovan under his wing. The "old spies" say that Dulles did not have to try very hard to convince Donovan that Truman was an idiot and that the only hope for the revival of an American intelligence service was to end the Democratic party's stranglehold on the White House in the 1948 election.[17]

In the meantime, Dulles and Donovan agreed that every effort must be made to sabotage the Truman liberals and quietly prepare for the Cold War. To this end, Dulles convinced Donovan to serve on the board of a company that would help rebuild the German economy as a bulwark against communism. Dulles assured his old boss that there were a large number of wealthy South American investors, especially in Argentina, who were willing to help rebuild Germany.

Although Donovan did not know it, Dulles had conned him into serving as the front man for the Nazi money launderers. He and Sir William Stephenson from British intelligence joined the board of directors of the World Commerce Corporation, with Allen Dulles, naturally, as their lawyer. The Nazi money flowed in a great circle—out of the Third Reich, through the Vatican, to Argentina, and back to "democratic" West Germany. The source of the miraculous West German economic revival in the 1950s was the same money that had been stolen in the 1940s.[18]

One of our sources, Daniel Harkins, stumbled across part of the money laundering in 1945. Harkins had volunteered to work as a double agent for Naval Intelligence before World War II. He posed as a Nazi ring leader in Detroit and even had his picture published in a newspaper giving the Nazi salute. He was promptly invited to Berlin to meet the leading members of Hitler's cabinet. Hitler did not know it, but Harkins's work helped close down the Nazi Bund operation in the United States.

After wartime service as a naval officer, Harkins was posted to the Allied occupation government in Germany. Although he was genuinely anti-Nazi, Harkins loved and respected the German people who had to survive in the ashes of the bombed-out Third Reich. To Harkins's horror, his German sources revealed that the big Nazis had gotten their money out before the war was over.[19]

Through Switzerland, the SS had purchased stock in American corporations and laundered their money through the unknowing Chase and the Corn Exchange Bank. Even worse, the W. R. Grace corporation was using its Pan Am clippers to fly Nazi gems, currency, and bonds to South America. Harkins had discovered a small part of the Dulles money-laundering machine. Before he could find out any more, however, he was suddenly transferred to the State Department, where the Dulles clique could keep an eye on him. To his surprise, he was then reassigned to the outposts of Southeast Asia.

True to form, the intrepid Harkins later stumbled across another of Dulles's machinations in Thailand. He and another whistle-blower informed Congress. Harkins was suddenly fired and sent back to the United States on the next ship. "Whistle-blowers," Harkins mused, "get bruised lips." Until the day he died in 1991, Harkins tried to discover why his security clearance was revoked, his career tarnished, and his reputation smeared by anonymous "derogatory information" in State Department files. As we shall see, this was standard treatment for anyone who came too close to the truth about Allen Dulles's activities.

Dulles's own negligence was to blame for a large part of his security problem. It was one thing to launder Nazi money; it was quite another to smuggle the Nazis themselves. People talk too much, while money sits quietly in a vault. Dulles's problem was that he had intermingled the money-laundering network with his secret Vatican-Nazi negotiations. The money window to the Vatican had become entwined with his Operation Sunrise negotiations to end the war while German troops were still in place in Austria and Italy.

In our last book, *Unholy Trinity,* we documented at some length the Vatican's role in smuggling Nazis out of Italy after the war. The research for that book led us to investigate the Zionist connection further. To understand the origins of the modern Israeli state, one must understand what the Zionists discovered about the network that was smuggling the murderers of their people to safety in the West, the Middle East, and South America. *Unholy Trinity* presents a detailed account; here is a brief recap of how the Vatican's Nazi-smuggling operation worked.

At first, only a handful of Germans, such as Karl Wolff and the other Operation Sunrise negotiators whom Angleton had hidden, were smuggled to safety. Then, after the British had sent to the Vatican other Nazi VIPs, such as Ustashi leader Ante Pavelić, the mass murderer of Croatia, for safekeeping, the smuggling program expanded willy-nilly. By the end of 1946, the crush of escaping Nazis became so large that the Vatican's top agent in the "refugee" network, Father Draganović, was commissioned full time to arrange documents and transportation to Argentina and other South American countries.

By 1947 the Vatican "Ratline," as it was called by U.S. intelligence, was the single largest smuggling route for Nazi war criminals. Nearly all the major war criminals, from Adolf Eichmann to Pavelić, ended up following Dulles's money route from the Vatican to Argentina. The lower-level Nazis wound up in a variety of countries, including Syria, Egypt, the United States, Britain, Canada, and Australia, although several big-time criminals emigrated to those countries too.[20] For years Angleton and Dulles worked to hide the massive smuggling network at Draganović's headquarters, San Girolamo, in Rome, from the prying eyes of the U.S. Army's Counter Intelligence Corps.

By mid-1947 Dulles's cronies in the State Department had gotten careless about security and had involved themselves directly with the illegal British smuggling network. Behind President Truman's back, a series of top-secret messages, beginning with cable FAN-757, had been communicated through military channels to the British. In the cables, the State Department actually agreed in writing to use the Vatican to smuggle Nazis out of Italy to Argentina, before they could be identified as wanted war criminals.

The deal disgusted even such staunch conservatives as John Moors Cabot, the U.S. ambassador to Belgrade. He knew a good deal about what Ante Pavelić's Croatian "freedom fighters" had done during the war and promptly fired off a cable in response to the FAN-757 deal, protesting that "we are conniving with Vatican and Argentina to get guilty people to haven in latter country."[21]

After our book on the Vatican was published, William Gowen, who had served with the army's CIC, volunteered several corrections and much additional material about the Bosnian-Croatian Father Draganović, who ran the smuggling operation for his superior in the Vatican, Undersecretary of State Giovanni Montini. Gowen states that Draganović came to his office and introduced himself as an agent of British intelligence. Gowen said that since Draganović had such high-level connections with British intelligence, he had no need of American contacts.

At that time, Gowen's unit, the CIC, was interested in catching Nazis. Draganović's wartime boss was Ante Pavelić, the Fascist leader of Croatia and one of the most wanted war criminals of World War II. In 1946 the CIC began an investigation, code-named "Operation Circle," to explore the murky ties between the Vatican and fugitive Nazis.

In 1947 the CIC confirmed that Pavelić was living in the Vatican and being driven around Rome in a car with Vatican diplomatic plates. In order to find out what was going on, Gowen questioned a friendly contact who worked Father Draganovic's office. The contact volunteered to show the office files to Gowen, including the "nominal roll" of all persons staying in Draganović's headquarters in the Croatian complex of San Girolamo. Gowen insists that his contact had perfectly legal access to the files. The operation to obtain the files was extremely sensitive as San Girolamo enjoyed Vatican diplomatic status, even though it was outside the Vatican's territorial boundaries.

One evening in mid-1947 the contact brought the San Girolamo files to Gowen's CIC office. "It was a huge thing, hundreds of pages, a stack twelve to fourteen inches high." Gowen recalled that it took most of the night for someone to copy the Vatican files for the CIC office, which then returned them to San Girolamo.

Gowen had made one of the biggest intelligence coups in the history of Nazi hunters, but he did not know it. He could not read the Vatican files because they were in Croatian. Gowen wrote a one-sentence report and forwarded the files to someone who did. Robert Mudd was a CIC special agent in Naples, in southern Italy, where the Bagnoli camp for Croatian refugees was located. Mudd had been investigating the backwater area of Croatian Nazis, who operated their intelligence networks under cover of the refugee camps.

When the Vatican files arrived on Mudd's desk, he had no trouble reading them. Gowen recalled that "Mudd told me almost immediately that something like twelve to eighteen of the Croatian war criminals were on the list." They were living in San Girolamo, under Vatican protection. The "nominal roll" was sensational, because it revealed not just the false identities provided to the fugitive war criminals by the Vatican but their real names. Gowen informed both the CIC and the man upstairs in the Rome headquarters of U.S. intelligence, James Angleton. For a brief period after the war, the CIC, OSS, and British Intelligence all used the same building supposedly to facilitate the sharing of information about Nazi war criminals.

Although Mudd had studied only the Vatican files for Croatian war criminals, Gowen recalled that there were many German names on the list. What Gowen did not know was that British intelligence, on the third floor of the building, was working with Angleton on the second floor to hide the Nazis from the CIC on the first floor. Gowen's contact obtained the Vatican files in the same month, June 1947, that the FAN-757 agreement was concluded. Gowen had in hand hundreds of pages of incriminating evidence that could expose the entire scandal.

With more than a year and a half to go before the next presidential election, it was still too early to let the Nazis out of the closet. Angleton had to buy time. All the polls showed that the likely Republican candidate, Governor Thomas Dewey of New York, would easily defeat Truman. Allen Dulles was handling Dewey's campaign in New York and at the same time recruiting like-minded agents for his proposed new intelligence service inside the State Department, where liberals could not interfere. If the cover-up could hold on for just eighteen months, the Dulles brothers would be back in the saddle in Washington.

If President Truman learned about the back-channel deals, the scandal might cost the Republicans the 1948 election, not to mention landing Dulles and his friends in jail for violating federal laws. The Trading with the Enemy Act was still in force, as were General Eisenhower's orders to arrest fugitive war criminals. If Gowen continued his investigation, Truman would be in a position to blanket the State Department with felony warrants.

The British-Angleton team rushed to control the damage. The first thing was to get the Vatican files back from the CIC. According to several former State Department sources we spoke to on this point, Robert Mudd was quickly invited to make a career move.[22] In return for the Vatican files, Mudd was hired by the State Department and shipped off to a prestigious assignment in the State-Navy-War Building right next to the White House. Mudd's upward career track had just begun.[23]

It may be a coincidence, but at the same time Mudd was promoted, hundreds of pages of Vatican files disappeared. No trace of the original copies can be found in any U.S. intelligence agency. The only problem for Angleton was that Mudd had already written a summary report about the Croatian Nazis on the San Girolamo list, which was circulated throughout the CIC. Although Mudd's report named only twenty Croatian war criminals, it was enough to arouse Gowen's curiosity. He began to dig further into the secrets of San Girolamo.

Gowen developed another source, a Hungarian Fascist named Ferenc Vajta, who had recently defected from the Vatican's intelligence service after first working for the French secret service. Vajta confirmed that the Vatican and British and French intelligence services were recruiting ex-

Fascist "freedom fighters" behind the Americans' back. Gowen wrote a report that blew the lid off the Vatican's intelligence operations and passed the information on to "higher commands so that its full international importance can be evaluated."[24] Although several pages of this report are censored even today, Gowen recalls that he disclosed that Father Draganović's Croatian network was being funded by British intelligence, which had taken it over from the French.

Gowen had no idea just how important his discovery was. He was just following up leads to Nazi smuggling and had stumbled onto the crucial link between the Nazis, the British, and the Vatican intelligence network. On July 6, 1947, he submitted his report to the U.S. Army. The response was immediate. On July 7, 1947, the head of the army CIC in Rome obtained permission to break the Croatian smuggling ring and to take "Pavelic into custody on sight."[25]

From the State Department's point of view, the army's decision was a disaster. If Pavelić were put on trial, he might try to save himself by exposing the entire Argentine money-laundering scheme, not just the Nazi smuggling. If the investigation proceeded, a lot more people than Dulles and Menzies could go to jail.

Attempting to bribe Special Agent Gowen into silence was deemed too risky. He might tell his father, who was also in Rome as assistant to Myron Taylor, the president's personal representative to the pope. Gowen, Sr., was one of Taylor's favorites, and Taylor was one of Truman's favorites. In fact, both Gowens were later invited to the White House, when Taylor received a medal from President Truman for his work with the Vatican mission. Through Taylor, Gowen, Sr., reported directly to the president instead of through State Department channels.

That was why Taylor's discovery of the phony Vessel cable in 1945 was such a threat to Angleton and the British. Now, in 1947, young William Gowen became Angleton's worse nightmare. Here was an intelligence officer with a direct pipeline to the president through his father who was discovering the truth. The longer the Nazi smuggling continued, the greater the risk that President Truman would discover what really was going on in Rome.

When Gowen, Jr., began poking around the activities at San Girolamo, the damage control operation pulled out all stops. The State Department immediately recalled Gowen, Sr., to Washington. On July 7, 1947, the same day that the CIC gave the arrest order for Pavelić, Gowen, Sr., escorted his replacement, Graham Parsons, for presentation to the Vatican Secretariat of State. One week later the CIC received a sudden change of orders: "Hands off Pavelic." One of the worst mass murderers of World War II was allowed to remain unmolested in the Vatican and then be shipped off to Argentina to pick up his share of the Nazi gold that had been transferred there to safety.

Agent Gowen conceded in one of his reports that Pavelić's arrest might deal a "staggering blow" to the reputation of the Roman Catholic Church. Gowen's willingness to be a team player did not impress the State Department. The risk was too great that Gowen's father might mention the San Girolamo incident to Taylor and Truman. Although Gowen did not know it, his source Vajta was at the same time submitting detailed intelligence reports on geopolitical strategies involving the ex-Nazis to the State Department.[26] Years later copies of Vajta's reports, written in French, were inadvertently declassified and discovered by the authors in the U.S. National Archives. Gowen was not aware until 1991 of the extent to which Vajta's proposals had been approved by the State Department in the summer of 1947, behind Truman's back.

In 1947 Gowen was still under the impression that, unlike the British and French, the U.S. government was not yet a player in recruiting anti-Communist émigrés. His opinion, which he wrote at the time, was that "the lack of United States activity in this, the larger intelligence field" was hampering the recruitment of "worthy elements" among the émigrés.

In fact, the State Department was not just supporting the anti-Communist émigrés with lip service. It had just made a deal in 1947 to take over the funding of Draganović's Nazi-smuggling activities from the British. In order to keep Gowen and the Rome CIC in the dark, an American agent named Paul Lyons was brought from Austria to Rome to finalize the funding of the Nazi "refugee" scheme behind Gowen's back. Gowen's questioning of the U.S. embassy about what it was doing with Vajta, the Vatican defector, was the last straw for the Dulles clique.

When Americans took over sponsorship of the Nazi Ratline, Special Agent Gowen just knew too much for others' comfort. His stay in Rome could not continue much longer. Every day he was getting more information from Vajta and other sources. This time Graham Parsons ran the cover-up personally, and it blew up in his face. Contact between the Taylor mission to the Vatican and the regular staff of the U.S. embassy in Rome had been strictly prohibited by order of President Truman. Truman's orders had never bothered the State Department before, and Parsons lost no time in presenting himself at the next embassy staff meeting.

It was, he explained, a delicate matter. Parsons said that the Vatican had complained to him that an American intelligence officer had violated Vatican sovereignty and burglarized some of their files. Would the embassy please solve the problem by transferring Gowen somewhere else? Parsons did not know it, but word of his unauthorized embassy meeting quickly got back to Gowen, whom most British and American military leaders in Rome liked and respected. The military ignored the transfer request and tipped Gowen off that Parsons was stabbing him in the back.

Gowen did not have the slightest idea what Parsons was complaining about. He had never burglarized the Vatican; he had obtained the Draganović files from someone with legal access. As Gowen himself had never even set foot in San Girolamo, he thought that Parsons must have been referring to a routine inspection of a Hungarian facility he had visited previously. As mentioned earlier, because he spoke no Croatian, Gowen just had no idea of the bombshell he had uncovered.

When Gowen politely asked Parsons what it was all about, Parsons lied and denied even making such a complaint. Gowen got word back to Taylor, who was furious that Parsons had broken the diplomatic rule that Vatican representatives abstain from U.S. embassy contact. Parsons was removed, and in the White House plans were made to bring back Gowen's father to the Vatican post.

The upshot of Parsons's bungling was that, in the last half of 1947, much of the Nazi-smuggling operation had to be shifted temporarily to Trieste. One of the senior leaders of State Department intelligence, Robert Joyce, was quickly dispatched as political adviser. Unlike the Italian CIC, the Trieste CIC was directly under the command of a joint British-American intelligence team that ruled the territory like a private fiefdom. Shifting the Ratline to Trieste for a few months was only a temporary palliative. William Gowen had to go. He was still debriefing Vajta, and the more he learned, the more damage he might do.

According to a number of our sources in the intelligence community, it was the British who decided to kill two birds with one stone: force Vajta out of Italy and then frame Gowen for smuggling a Nazi.[27] Word was leaked to the Communists in the Italian government that they might be able to arrest Vajta. By this time Gowen had learned that Vajta had contacts everywhere, from the head of the Christian Democratic party in Italy, to Vatican, British, and French intelligence.

Because of the sensitivity of Vajta's contacts, Gowen asked his superiors what to do with him. He was told that arrangements had been made to hide Vajta in Fascist Spain. Another U.S. agency would handle the relocation. All Gowen was asked to do was write a letter of introduction to the Italian authorities praising Vajta's work for the CIC. Gowen, never suspecting that the U.S. State Department was setting him up as a fall guy, was told to escort Vajta to Genoa on the day he sailed. The army had nothing to do with it. As Gowen recalled, the State Department initiated the transfer, and it was the Spanish government who made the actual shipping arrangements. Of course, Gowen knew that Vajta was a wanted Nazi, but if the State Department wanted to smuggle him to Spain, that was their business. After all, what was one more Fascist in Franco's territory?

What Gowen did not know was that he had been tricked. Vajta wasn't going to stay in Spain. The State Department promptly waived the visa restriction barring the entry of Fascists and put him on a boat to the United States. The only document in Vajta's State Department dossier was Gowen's letter of introduction. Although Gowen did not find out about it for forty years, he had just been framed for the crime of smuggling a Nazi into the United States.

Someone immediately leaked word to the American press that a Hungarian Fascist named Ferenc Vajta was due to arrive on November 16, 1947. The press had a field day, and Vajta was arrested the minute he stepped ashore. The U.S. Congress demanded an investigation. The State Department coyly informed the military that it had issued Vajta a visa in Madrid because he presented "letters from William Gowen . . . indicating U.S. interest in trip."[28]

The implication was that Gowen was a dirty Nazi smuggler who had protected a man responsible for the murder of American airmen downed in Hungary and had conned the State Department into giving him a visa. Gowen did not know it, but like Daniel Harkins before him, his career had just been ruined by "derogatory information" in State Department files.

It was important to keep Gowen in the dark while the Vajta investigation took place. He was reassigned to routine courier duty in Germany and was hardly in any one place long enough to learn what was going on back in America. All that he recalls is that he was asked to drop by army intelligence headquarters in Germany. The intelligence officers who met with him briefly mentioned that one of his informants, named Vajta, had been identified as living in the United States. Gowen told them, truthfully, that he knew nothing about how Vajta got to the United States and supposed that the Communists had fed the press some false material to try to create a scandal. Gowen never knew that the State Department had told a different story to the U.S. congressional inquiry.

Gowen neither heard nor thought about Vajta for the next forty years. In the meantime, he became the target of yet another campaign of secret defamation. During the mid–1970s, Congress again asked whether any Nazis had ever emigrated to the United States and ordered the General Accounting Office (GAO) to investigate. While concealing evidence of their own employment of Nazis, the intelligence community handed the GAO the Vajta file with Gowen's letter. The GAO issued a formal report to Congress that there was only one case where a CIC agent smuggled a Nazi to America, but that he had been arrested on arrival.[29]

Gowen could have rebutted the fraud on Congress easily, but his name was not mentioned in the GAO report. During the investigation he was never consulted or even contacted. An American historian, Christopher Simpson, obtained some of Vajta's files under the U.S. Freedom of Information Act in the 1980s. Gowen's letter was virtually the only document that would explain how Vajta got a visa. Simpson made the same assumptions as the GAO and identified Gowen by name as the CIC agent who smuggled this Nazi to the United States. Gowen did not read Simpson's book, *Blowback,* and knew nothing of the allegations.

In 1990, when we were completing our previous book on the Vatican, we attempted to find William Gowen but were told that the Pentagon locator service had no trace of him. In 1991 Gowen was shown a copy of that book and contacted us on his own. He insisted that he "had absolutely nothing to do with [Vajta's] visa or his visit to New York. . . . What . . . outrages me still is that other parties, American authorities who cleared Vajta for a U.S. visa and then issued that visa (and possibly financed his trip), sought to conceal those activities of theirs by blaming me publicly for those developments. They are and were, among other things, liars." We revised the American edition of the book accordingly.[30]

Gowen was appalled to hear that he had been condemned in the congressional report as the only American Nazi smuggler and was determined to vindicate his reputation. Through contacts in American and Italian intelligence, he began to discover what had been so carefully hidden from him and his father forty years earlier. The Nazi smuggling, the Vessel scandal, the Vajta frame-up, all of it came back to one man—James Jesus Angleton.

Our sources independently confirmed that it was Angleton who arranged to feed the phony Vajta file to Congress.[31] From various contacts in the intelligence community, Gowen confirmed that it had been Angleton who perpetuated the Vatican cover-up. Even after Angleton was discharged from the CIA, he kept a careful watch on Gowen over the years and even visited with him on occasion. Angleton's job was to intervene whenever anyone threatened to dig up the long-buried Nazi scandals.

For example, in 1973, the Australian government released a large number of its intelligence files about the presence of Croatian Nazis down under. Angleton went into a tirade and demanded that the United States break off its intelligence liaison with Canberra. In 1977, in a rare statement to the press, he denounced the Australians for revealing some of the "crown jewels" of Western counterintelligence.

In 1976 one of the Vatican's historians, Father Robert Graham, filed a request for the Scattolini-Vessel files under the U.S. Freedom of Information Act, which had been amended in 1974 to include the CIA. It was an innocent request about an apparently minor incident in Vatican history. According to Gowen, someone in the CIA alerted Angleton that a request for one of his old files had been received. At about the same time, Father Graham showed up in Washington and telephoned Angleton for an appointment.

According to Gowen, Angleton immediately called his sister, Carmen, in Rome to confirm that Father Graham was indeed a Vatican historian. Angleton then ducked all of Father Graham's requests for an interview, while he tried to get back into CIA headquarters to sanitize the Scattolini files before they were released. According to our own sources in the intelligence community, once back inside the CIA vaults, Angleton took a black Magic Marker and blotted out several lines on many of the originals, so that no one, not even a member of the CIA, would be able to discover what words once had been there. Angleton was very particular about what he crossed out.

In his haste, Angleton missed one such reference in the hundreds of pages of Vatican files. It reads: "Cipher number of telegraphic letter: D.G/21983.M89541.b. Prot. RB.38629.G.57492.v." These numbered references fraudulently indicated to U.S. intelligence that the alleged source of the JVX documents was the Vatican's secret code room. Angleton had to obliterate each of the "cipher telegram" references before the Vatican realized that no such coded telegrams had ever been sent and tipped off the U.S. government. An investigation quickly would have determined that Angleton had continued to feed the president more Vessel forgeries even after Scattolini had been discredited.

If you hold the original CIA files up to a strong light, you can determine that many of Angleton's blacked-out sections were the same size and in the same place as the one phony "cipher" reference that slipped through.[32] However, in 1978, when Father Graham finally received his set of the CIA's Vessel file, it was a Xeroxed copy, which rendered Angleton's blacked-out lines completely opaque. Father Graham had no idea that Angleton had used the Vatican code citations and telegram references to corroborate his fictitious Vessel reports to Presidents Roosevelt and Truman.[33]

In 1992 Gowen and the authors compared notes and conclusively established the CIA records as Scattolini forgeries. Gowen was adamant that someone inside the CIA, perhaps the director himself, had to have let Angleton, by then a former employee, back into the CIA archives. We confirmed Gowen's suspicions from our own sources.[34] The man who gave Angleton permission to go back into the vaults in 1976 was the director of Central Intelligence himself, George Bush. There is no evidence that Bush was aware that Angleton was altering or destroying Vatican records in the CIA. Bush may simply have asked Angleton to work on a difficult problem, without realizing the sensitive nature of the Vatican files. In addition to the Vessel scandal, Angleton had worked on the Vatican's smuggling network run by Croatian Fascists in Rome.

As chairman of the Republican National Committee from 1972 to 1974, Bush may have been one of those who knew that there was something politically explosive about the Vatican-Nazi connection, especially as it applied to the Croatians. The Croatian connection to Republican electioneering was no minor scandal, no mere footnote to the 1940s. The Croatian Nazis reached to the very heart of the Republican party's 1972 campaign to reelect Richard Nixon as president of the United States.

Just about the time that Bush was taking over the job as party chief, the U.S. State Department gave the Australian government a briefing on the role of the Croatian Nazis in American politics. David Sadleir, who is now the director general of the Australian Security Intelligence Organization (equivalent to head of the FBI, or Britain's MI5), met with one of his American counterparts. Sadleir then wrote a long memo on the Nixon administration's sensitive handling of Nazis among the Republican party's Eastern European émigré supporters.

Sadleir had been told in strictest confidence that, in the United States, the Fascists had to be coddled because the "emigre vote was important to several municipal, state, and federal office-bearers. Accordingly, the [Nixon] Administration needed to exercise care in its handling of extremist groups."[35] As the memo makes explicit, there is no doubt that Nazis were the "extremist groups" that were so "important" to the success of the Republican party's election campaigns.

Although Bush is not mentioned, it is clear from Sadleir's memo that the Republican leadership had taken precautions to hide its campaign association with Fascist groups, particularly the Croatians. Sadleir was told by his State Department counterpart that "prominent" federal, state and municipal American politicians were discreetly advised by the Nixon administration to stay away from Croatian gatherings on April 10, because that was the day they celebrated Hitler's establishment of Ante Pavelić's "puppet State of Croatia," an artificial nation under the complete control of Nazi Germany.[36]

There are grounds to suspect that George Bush may have been among those who knew of Nixon's Nazi secret. In the first place, Bush was one of the few people whom Nixon trusted completely. In the second place, Bush's position as head of the Republican party made him the logical person to take control of the program to warn other Republicans that they must avoid attending Croatian functions on April 10. While there is no direct evidence that Bush had personal knowledge of Croatian Fascist activities (at least before he became CIA director), it seems unlikely that Bush as head of the Republican National Committee could have remained out of the loop entirely. The Croatian election connection almost became a scandal during his tenure as party leader. In 1973 a large number of Australian intelligence documents were tabled for parliamentary debate and thus became open to public access. Buried in this largely unread stack of counterintelligence, police, and immigration files was a copy of Sadleir's secret briefing memo. The Nixon administration was distraught. No wonder Angleton was publicly furious with the Australians. The Croatian "crown jewels" were a potential political bombshell. Unfortunately, the indolent American press missed the story completely.

The truth was quite sordid: With the help of the Dulles-Angleton clique, the Vatican had sent many of the Eastern European Nazis to Western countries, including the United States, Australia, and Canada, where the right wing recruited them to get out the rest of the Eastern European ethnic vote. The man who ran the political recruitment campaign in the United States was Richard Nixon. The cover-up had been going on for a long time before Angleton censored the Vatican files, but the Australians inadvertently had let a tiny corner of the story out of the bag.

Although we explore the Republican-Nazi connection in Chapters 10 and 13, it is important for the reader to understand the size of the scandal that Angleton was trying to bury. As a young congressman, Nixon had been Allen Dulles's confidant. They both blamed Governor Dewey's razor-thin loss to Truman in the 1948 presidential election on the Jewish vote. When he became Eisenhower's vice president in 1952, Nixon was determined to build his own ethnic base.

Vice President Nixon's secret political war of Nazis against Jews in American politics was never investigated at the time. The foreign language–speaking Croatians and other Fascist émigré groups had a ready-made network for contacting and mobilizing the Eastern European ethnic bloc. There is a very high correlation between CIA domestic subsidies to Fascist "freedom fighters" during the 1950s and the leadership of the Republican party's ethnic campaign groups.[37] The motive for the under-the-table financing was clear: Nixon used Nazis to offset the Jewish vote for the Democrats.

In 1952 Nixon had formed an Ethnic Division within the Republican National Committee. "Displaced Fascists, hoping to be returned to power by an Eisenhower-Nixon 'liberation' policy signed on" with the committee.[38] In 1953, when Republicans were in office, the immigration laws were changed to admit Nazis, even members of the SS. They flooded into the country. Nixon himself oversaw the new immigration program. As vice president, he even received Eastern European Fascists in the White

House. After a long, long journey, the Croatian Nazis had found a new home in the United States, where they reestablished their networks.

In 1968 Nixon promised that if he won the presidential election, he would create a permanent ethnic council within the Republican party. Previously the Ethnic Division was allowed to surface only during presidential campaigns. Nixon's promise was carried out after the 1972 election, during Bush's tenure as chairman of the Republican National Committee. The Croatian Ustashis became an integral part of the campaign structure of Republican politics, along with several other Fascist organizations. Shortly after Australia released its Croatian memo, Nixon was forced to resign as a result of the Watergate scandal. At the same time, Bush was transferred from his post as head of the Republican National Committee to the CIA.

According to the "old spies," George Bush, a very likable fellow, was appointed head of the CIA partly because his good reputation in Congress would help to fend off any more congressional inquiries, particularly Elizabeth Holtzmann's ongoing investigation of Nazis in the United States. The last thing Bush or the Republican party needed was an exposé of the very origins of Angleton's Croatian Nazi connection. There was a real risk in the 1970s that the congressional investigations of Nixon might collide with the congressional investigations of Nazis. Bush was sent to the CIA to ensure that Nixon's garbage remained buried.[39]

Keeping the lid on the Nazi scandal was no easy matter. As director of the CIA from December 1975 to January 1977, Bush was up to his ears in Croatian Fascists, including an attempt to stop one splinter group of fanatical young terrorists who hijacked an American airliner in 1976. Controlling that episode had taken quite a bit of effort. The congressional investigation of Nazis was another matter.

The timing, for one thing, was particularly awkward. In 1976 Congress was about to tell CIA director Bush to stop funding the right-wing Angolan guerrillas. A number of our sources claim that in advance of the ban, Bush decided to use one of Dulles's old tricks and utilize the British back-channel to hire agents.[40] They were the bagmen for continuing the Angolan arms conduit behind the back of Congress. One British agent, himself a Nazi war criminal, boasted that his organization had helped with the transfer of arms and money to Angola. George Bush may have inadvertently become the last American CIA director to put Nazis to work on an intelligence operation.

As we shall see, there is a great deal of evidence to support the contentions of the "old spies" that some of the same Croatian Fascists were recruited for George Bush's presidential campaigns.[41] But in 1976 Bush had no way of knowing that Angleton was hiding one last dirty secret even from the director of the CIA. During all those furtive postwar years in Italy, someone else had been watching James Angleton's every move with the Nazis. For almost thirty years, up to his enforced retirement in 1974, James Jesus Angleton had been under the control of a special section of the Zionist, later the Israeli, intelligence service. By blackmailing Angleton, the Jews had made a window of their own in Italy, a window to smuggle guns, Jews, and money to Palestine, and to ensure that they were unhindered, they cleverly used the same routes as the British, Americans and Vatican were using to smuggle Nazis and their war loot out of Europe.

Israel's first prime minister, David Ben-Gurion, was the one who knew all the secrets of the American money launderers, the British Fascists, and more, much more. Only Ben-Gurion and Joseph Stalin knew the secrets behind the true identity of Vessel.

PART II

THE AGE OF GREED

1948–1973

There is one chapter of the Age of Bigotry that we have said very little about in Part I of this book, although it was the major event of the period for world Jewry: the Holocaust. For one thing, there are many good books about the subject. For another, there is a widespread sentiment among Western Jews generally, and particularly those from the United States and Britain, that they talk too much about it. Perhaps they do, but if so, it is to each other.

For many years the Holocaust was virtually a taboo subject, even among American Jewry. Alan Dershowitz, the noted American lawyer, recalled how in Brooklyn Jewish mothers would put rouge on their children's concentration camp tattoo marks before letting them out to play. For the first twenty years after the war, the only Jew to discuss the Holocaust on American television was an opera singer on the television show *This Is Your Life*. For many survivors, recounting the past meant reliving it in painful detail. Most wanted to get on with their lives and look to their children's future, not their own nightmare past.

Because of this, almost an entire generation of gentiles has grown up knowing little about the greatest crime in human history, a crime committed by what had been considered the most civilized country of Europe. Fifty years after Allied soldiers liberated the death camps, only the veterans and historians remember the consequences of ignorance, apathy, and racism. Too many among the generations that grew up in the postwar period think of the genocide against the Jews only in the context of a movie plot, if they think of it at all.

Some may find solace that in recent decades, the Holocaust has become fashionable in Hollywood. Despite the excellence of such films as *Schindler's List,* fiction, even when it is based on fact, is not a substitute for education. In the United States, the average child reads only six sentences on the Holocaust in twelve years of school. There have been attempts to remedy this. During the Reagan administration, for example, one organization applied for a grant to develop Holocaust curriculum aids in an effort to teach ethics, by showing what happens when the rule of law is swept away and that genocide is the end result of societal breakdown. The "Facing History and Ourselves" grant application was denied because it did not present opposing points of view—those who support the Nazi version.

Although we do not like admitting it, the hard truth is that those who deny the Holocaust ever occurred have gained a certain fashionability in the last fifty years. Our ignorant children are easy prey for these bigots. The recent worldwide spread of overtly racist and Fascist ideas that accompanies such historical revisionism is enough to demonstrate the vulnerability of even liberal societies to resurgence of bigotry. In the past five years the most advanced Western countries have reported an alarming increase in attacks on Jews, their synagogues, cemeteries, and schools.

True, the worst resurgence of fascism has been in the post-Stalinist countries of Central and Eastern Europe, where decades of totalitarian rule stultified political and social development and froze the national outlook in the era of Nazism. The neo-Nazi movement in Germany, especially in the former East Germany, is a national tragedy. The Russian Parliament is deadlocked by the strength of Vladimir Zhirinovsky's openly racist political party. Adherents of old Fascist movements, such as the Ustashi in Croatia and the Hlinka Guard in Slovakia, also have gained substantial minority support as Yugoslavia and Czechoslovakia have disintegrated.

It is dangerous, however, to be complacent about Western societies. In France and Italy neo-Fascist movements have captured considerable popular support, even respectability, with their xenophobic, anti-immigrant policies. Even in the United States, Canada, and Australia, nations founded on multicultural immigration, there is an insidious growth of support for white supremacist, pan-Aryan movements just when apartheid has crumbled in South Africa.

In the Asian nations of South Korea and Taiwan, there are well-funded and fanatical Fascist movements, while in Japan extremists have begun to translate the old Russian anti-Semitic forgery *The Protocols of the Elders of Zion*. From France to the Far East, the forces of fascism are emerging from obscurity. They proclaim the old solutions and denounce the usual scapegoats. The Age of Bigotry is far from over.

In contrast to many Western Jews, used to decades of stability and relative liberality, the Israelis are not surprised by these developments, perhaps because they have never enjoyed the illusion of acceptance by non-Jewish neighbors. The younger Israeli intelligence officers are particularly critical of Western efforts to combat racism in the last half century. One explained the difference in the following terms. In the West, the Holocaust is portrayed as a historical event that happened only to Jews, whereas Israeli children are taught that in the course of human history, there were many holocausts involving many different races, and although the treatment of Jews under Hitler was unique, it wasn't only Jews who suffered.

The purpose of such Israeli education policies is more to understand the *why* than the *what*. Genocide is a recurring disease of the human spirit that is not easily understood but that must be explored if its cure is to be found. The Israeli officer's remarks had particular poignancy, as they were made while we were walking through Yad Vashem, the Israeli memorial to the Holocaust. He has a point, indeed several. Jews were not alone in Auschwitz, although they were the largest group. During the last days of the death camps, four Christians were killed for every Jew.

In countries such as Yugoslavia, which had a relatively small Jewish population, the Nazis used genocide principally as a weapon to divide the population ethnically, especially among the Serbs and the Croats. Although Yugoslav Jews were substantially decimated during the war, along with the local Gypsy population, the vast majority of victims were from among the Serbs and Croats. The vicious war between ethnically and culturally close peoples, based mainly on religious and bogus racial differences, continues to horrify the world in the 1990s.

According to a former Soviet intelligence officer, Stalin suppressed information about the Nazi Holocaust in order to blur the extent of Communist genocide, both before and after the war. Census documents were altered to conceal the extent of Stalin's mass murders from Ukraine to Siberia. Recent disclosures show that the number of Hitler's victims was considerably undercounted. The total number of Jews killed may approach 7 million, not 6. The number of Gypsies executed may be closer to a million than the half million previously estimated. According to Soviet sources, the total number of other nationalities murdered was even greater and may exceed 10 million when all the captured Nazi records are finally released from former Soviet archives. As the Israelis have been saying all along, the Holocaust is *not* just a Jewish issue.

Bigotry alone is too easy an answer. Anti-Semitism may have been the seed of the Holocaust, but the rapid spread of genocide, and the multinational character of the victims, suggests that too many history books have missed something: the root of all racism. This, says one American intelligence officer, is *money*. Greed is the secret connection beneath the soil of racial politics that permits patches of bigotry to spread across the landscape.

"Forget the ideology. Trace the money," said one of the "old spies." Instead of exploring the philosophical underpinnings of communism and fascism, our source suggested that we examine the issue of who profits from genocide. Although this analysis is itself too simplistic, it does lend a useful insight in tracing the evolution of the secret war against the Jews.

In the first part of this century, bigotry was certainly the primary motive for men such as Hitler, Jack Philby, and Ibn Saud. Their anti-Semitic ideology compelled them to measures that made little economic sense. The Dulles brothers, in contrast, would take on anyone as a client, Nazi or Jew, who could make them a profit. If Israel, not Saudi Arabia, had held the oil deposits, Allen Dulles would have been Ben-Gurion's best friend, but there is not a drop of oil under Israel. Ibn Saud had the good fortune to be born atop the greatest source of natural wealth in the twentieth century. Whoever wanted profits from Saudi oil had to play Ibn Saud's game against the Jews.

Before World War II Saudi oil was only a small, but significant, factor in the equation of world power. Ibn Saud had enough influence to slow prewar immigration to Palestine, but not stop it entirely. During the war the threat of Saudi oil going to the Nazis was enough for Ibn Saud to extract some kickbacks and price increases, but in the end it had little impact on the Allied victory. It does appear, however, that the Saudi king had one major triumph.

Each of the Allied leaders agreed to place Palestine off-limits to Jews for the duration.

Why would Roosevelt and Churchill succumb to Ibn Saud's demands? Even rich bigots, such as the Saudi king, have limits to their influence. Western acquiescence to the Holocaust cannot be explained away on grounds of racism alone, although it played a very large role in the policies of Western governments, as Martin Gilbert demonstrated in his book, *Auschwitz and the Allies*. The Holocaust, we submit, was that point in history where greed and bigotry combined with deadly effect.

At the height of the slaughter, the U.S. assistant secretary of war, John McCloy, argued in writing that it would be unwise to divert Allied aircraft from military targets to bomb the gas chambers. He wasn't a bigot; he was a banker, whose memo reads like a balance sheet. The bottom line was that rescuing concentration camp inmates was not cost-effective, and so the Allied planes flew over Auschwitz to bomb routine industrial targets farther north. Bombing the gas chambers at just three death camps—Sobibor, Treblinka, and Auschwitz—might have shut down the killing system for months, sparing hundreds of thousands of lives. For the price of a few American bombs, however, the death camps remained open.

The British used similar economic arguments to justify their stand: Even if Hitler released the Jews, there were no ships to transport them, no food to feed them, no houses to shelter them. Yet this argument can be countered easily. Even if Palestine was closed, the United States, Britain, and Canada were not. As for transport ships, empty convoys sailed back across the Atlantic every week during the war. Nor was there any shortage of food in the Western Hemisphere. But, as American historian Walter Laqueur makes clear, despite all the war rhetoric of sacrifices back home, consumer consumption actually increased in the United States during World War II.

Had the case been put before the average American, the Jews would probably have been given sanctuary. There is a reason why most of the Jews alive in the world today are in the United States. Between World War I and World War II, nearly 2 million Jews emigrated to America. Another few million during World War II would have had very little effect on the food supply and might have helped alleviate the industrial labor shortage. As their British officers discovered in North Africa, Jews also were among the most motivated troops in the war. By any objective standard, taking in Jewish refugees would have been an Allied gain and Hitler's loss.

Why was nothing done? Most people were unaware there even was a problem. While a handful of newspapers, such as *The Boston Globe,* provided detailed reporting on Hitler's atrocities, most of the Western press behaved like *The New York Times* and buried a few minor articles on the back pages, a precedent that has been repeated several times since, in places such as East Timor. When an eyewitness described Auschwitz in 1943 to Supreme Court Justice Felix Frankfurter, himself a Jew, he replied: "I know that you believe what you are telling me is the truth, but I cannot believe it." If prominent

Jews could not believe these reports, it is not surprising that the average American was uninformed.

But Western politicians knew the truth about what was being done to the Jews and kept the public in deliberate ignorance. The Allied leaders classified the intelligence reports on Hitler's war against the Jews. U.S. military attachés filed weekly body counts from September 1941. The British Foreign Office and the U.S. State Department sat on a small mountain of eyewitness evidence that was corroborated by both British intelligence and the Vatican. As we documented in our previous book, *Unholy Trinity,* both the British and American governments pressured the pope not to condemn the Holocaust publicly.

It is indisputable that the Western leaders conspired to conceal Hitler's massacre of Jews. President Roosevelt wanted to help the Jews but was deceived by his own intelligence advisers, opposed by the British and Soviet allies, and blackmailed by the Dulles brothers. Our sources in the intelligence community say that beginning in 1995, the fifty-year ban on Roosevelt's personal files will be lifted. The picture that will emerge is of a man under secret siege, trying to avoid a rift among the Allies over Jews in the middle of the war.

As we discussed in Part I, Roosevelt also was looking past the end of the war toward the future American role in the Middle East. Long before he met with Ibn Saud in February 1945, Roosevelt knew the king's price for the continued domination of American oil companies in Saudi Arabia. The president also knew that the nation that controlled Middle Eastern oil would emerge as the dominant economic force for the rest of the century. There were many factors behind the abandonment of the Jews, and greed for oil was one of them.

Greed was not the dominant factor in the Western calculus of what response to make to the Holocaust, only a small consideration for postwar national interests. Yet the steady drip of oil upon the scales may have been what tipped the balance against the Jews during World War II. Roosevelt was not the last president to weigh humanitarian concerns against the national economy and discover that the cost of helping Jews was too high. As Truman would discover after him, a coterie of bigots in Congress and Western corporations blocked any attempt to assist postwar Jewish emigration to the United States and nearly succeeded in blocking the UN vote to create a Jewish state in Palestine.

The abandonment of the Jews during the Holocaust was only the beginning of the Age of Greed. In Part II of this book we consider the allegation that greed, not racism, became the dominant force in shaping Western policy toward Israel during the Cold War. After the collapse of the Third Reich, professing anti-Semitism in public became less fashionable. Bigotry diminished as postwar disclosures of the full extent of the Holocaust evoked a sympathetic response from the Western public, a clear majority of whom favored the creation of a Jewish home in Palestine.

The Western leaders were forced to pay lip service to the wishes of the voters, but used covert means to usurp the democratic majority and assist those Arab bigots who continued the war against the Jews. The secret records of the State Department and the Foreign Office disclose the horrible truth: The Jews were still expendable to the cheap supply of oil, while Nazi mass murderers were useful warriors in the Cold War against communism and found it easier to emigrate to Western nations than their victims.

In the following chapters we examine in detail allegations from the intelligence community that corporate profits biased Western policy toward Israel during the Cold War. In public Western governments were Israel's ally, but in private they gave secret military and intelligence support to the Arab armies. During the Cold War the oil companies were the principal sources of American policy toward, and covert intelligence about, the Middle East.

In this period the Dulles brothers perfected the corrupt system they had built in prototype during the Age of Bigotry, in which the profits and private interests of their corporate clients were substituted for the national interest. In the Age of Greed, the Dulles brothers reached their zenith, and as secretary of state and director of the CIA, they built a revolving door between the oil companies and the intelligence community. Through this door their spies walked in and out, one minute in government service, the next as oil company executives, always putting their corporate loyalties first. We examine the impact of corporate intelligence on Western covert policy toward Israel in some detail in this second part of the book. It is a shocking story, one largely unknown to the public.

CHAPTER 6

THE TRAP IS SPRUNG

History books mention Jewish resistance during the Holocaust and note that Jews served with distinction in several Allied armies. Yet one topic is almost never mentioned: espionage by Jews during World War II. According to intelligence sources in Israel, the former Eastern Bloc, and the West, the Zionists had the only intelligence organization to penetrate every one of the Axis and Allied powers.[1] This untold story, our sources assert, will change the way we look at the history of the struggle against Hitler.

"A handful of Jews won World War II," boasted one aging Israeli. The small group of Western and Communist intelligence officers who spoke on this subject agreed with some reservations that the boast is true. They are speaking of the Jewish spy network, code named "Max," that arguably did more to destroy the Third Reich than all Western intelligence operations combined. It is one of the most embarrassing, and confusing, stories to emerge from World War II.

In summary, Zionist intelligence piggybacked on Stalin's most secret operation to deceive Hitler's generals. Inadvertently, the Max network uncovered Allen Dulles's wartime efforts to create a Western alliance with Germany against the Soviet Union. When Dulles used the same network to launder Nazi money, the Jewish agents revealed their hand and demanded that he ransom Jewish lives from Hitler.

Rather than publicly condemning the Western-sponsored flight of the Nazis and their treasure, the Zionists buried Dulles's crimes and used the information to their own advantage. The Max network was used to create an underground railroad for smuggling Jews and guns out of Europe, to blackmail Stalin into supporting the Zionist partition of Palestine, and to recruit a spy for Israel inside the CIA. Max was the most effective spy organization of modern times. It was the key part of Zionist intelligence that helped win the battle to create the nation of Israel.

In this chapter we examine the following allegations made by our intelligence sources in detail:

- During World War II Soviet intelligence used a network of supposedly "Fascist Jews," code named Max, to penetrate the inner circles of the Third Reich and to destroy the German army on the Eastern front. The Nazis believed that the Max network was their secret intelligence source inside the Kremlin, and it did in fact give "good" intelligence to the Germans but it was strictly controlled by the Communists.
- The Jews of the Max network were mostly Communist double agents, but they also were Jews who defected to the Zionist cause toward the end of the war and revealed Allen Dulles's secret deals with the Nazis.
- The Zionists blackmailed Dulles's protégé, James Angleton, into setting up a parallel smuggling system for Jews and fugitive Nazis.
- Stalin agreed to support the partition of Israel in return for Zionist silence about Soviet penetration of the CIA.

For the last half century, David Ben-Gurion's secrets have been hidden by successive Israeli governments. Through all those years, apparently the only ones who knew the whole truth about Allen and John Foster Dulles's various schemes on behalf of the Nazis were the Jews who spied for the Zionists and then for the State of Israel.

American Jews, such as Arthur Goldberg and Henry Morgenthau, knew only the tiniest part of the story. Some British Jews, including the Rothschilds, gleaned a bit more from British intelligence. Soviet Jews, mathematicians, and linguists who worked for Stalin's intelligence services, had learned a few of the secrets of the Max network. Each of them had a piece of the puzzle, but they all guarded their secrets jealously. For years they had been divided by ethnic rivalries and separated by political ideologies. Some were Communists, some were capitalists, all were welded together by the fires of the Holocaust into a single overriding cause: "Never again."

In each of the Allied armies, there were Jews who saw what was coming. They buried files where Allen Dulles's henchmen could not find and destroy them. Sometimes the preservation of files was purely a personal initiative, not connected with the Zionists at all. For example, Walter Rockler, one of the young prosecutors at the Nazi bankers' trial at Nuremberg, found a German document listing all the U.S. banks that had laundered money for the Nazis. He took the original back to the United States for safekeeping when his investigation was closed down.[2]

In many other cases Jews who worked for Allied intelligence took matters much further: They stole classified documents and gave them to the Zionists. One member of the U.S. Army's Counter Intelligence Corps was under close scrutiny because of his suspected work for the Zionists. It was believed that he copied a large number of dossiers before retiring to

Tel Aviv.[3] Bit by bit the Jewish members of the Allied intelligence services collected the very evidence that the Dulles crowd sought to destroy.

Stolen documents trickled to the various Zionist factions. It is a tribute to Ben-Gurion's leadership that he convinced all of them to keep their mouths shut. Exposing the Dulleses' web would do no good. After Roosevelt's death, the Jews' last hope for justice at Nuremberg disappeared. The Soviets executed several thousand Nazi war criminals; the Western Allies executed a few dozen and quickly released the rest from prison. Ben-Gurion thought that if the Jews could not have justice, they should have something else.

According to sources in both the American and Israeli intelligence community whom we interviewed on this episode, David Ben-Gurion decided to collect evidence of Allen Dulles's complicity with the Nazis during the war and then use blackmail to rescue the Jews who had not yet been processed by the machinery of the Holocaust.[4] In the course of this secret collection effort, the Jews discovered, to their amazement, that they had something that Dulles wanted very badly: a very productive section of the most valuable spy network behind the Iron Curtain.

Just before World War II began, an Austrian Jew named Richard Kauder created a secret intelligence network, code named Max, that made Ultra a minor achievement in comparison. Under the cover name of Klatt, during the early part of World War II Kauder worked exclusively for Admiral Wilhelm Canaris, the German spy chief who collaborated with the Vatican and the British to topple Hitler during the war. Although those efforts came to naught, Kauder did hand Canaris a major success in anti-Soviet espionage.

Only the top ranks of the German General Staff were let in on the Max secret. Kauder's Jews were the only communication link to a secret network of "White" Russian Fascists inside the Kremlin, who had supposedly infiltrated Stalin's military headquarters prior to World War II.[5] In order to pass on their intelligence, Kauder recruited a group of secret agents, mostly so-called Fascist Jews, who were willing to spy against the Soviet Union, not for the glory of the Third Reich but to save themselves and their families from the concentration camps. The Jews of the Max network were bilingual, expert in radio transmission, coding, and covert operations. Max was the most successful, and most closely guarded, intelligence operation of Nazi Germany.

On an almost daily basis, the Max reports provided Hitler's generals with the most secret battle plans of the Soviet Union. From Fascist Russian sources inside Stalin's war room, the little network of "Fascist Jews" received regular radio reports in code that enabled the German divisions to know the exact disposition and movement of many units in the Red army. The Max intelligence was so valuable that Admiral Canaris convinced the German generals to ignore Hitler's edict that Jews could not work for Nazi intelligence. With the approval of the German High Command, General Reinhard Gehlen, chief of anti-Soviet intelligence, protected the Jews in the Max network by transferring them, on paper, to the Hungarian secret service.

With the help of the Max network's almost daily intelligence, the German General Staff hoped to hold the Eastern front despite Hitler's constant meddling in military affairs. For years after World War II intelligence analysts marveled at the efficiency of the Max network, even as they wondered why a group of Jews would spy for the Germans. As we documented in our last book, the Max network was not made up of Fascist Jews. They were, in fact, *Communist* Jews who risked their lives inside the heart of the Third Reich's intelligence service.

In one of the greatest sting operations of all time, the secret mission of the Max network was to feed true information to the Germans to lull them into a false sense of security. Then the agents lured the Nazi divisions into a series of death traps on the Eastern front, using rare bits of false intelligence planted through the Max network. The first trap was Stalingrad; the next was the giant battle of Kursk where Hitler's tank divisions were slaughtered. The final sting was to mislead Germany into believing that the Red army was on the verge of collapse in 1944, when in fact the Soviets were preparing for the most massive onslaught of the war.

It would not be an exaggeration to say that the "Fascist Jews" of the Max network did more to defeat the German army than all of the Western intelligence services combined. Seventy percent of all Hitler's divisions were destroyed on the Eastern front, largely as a result of the misleading intelligence supplied by Max. The extraordinary thing was that the German generals continued to believe in the Max reports right up to nearly the last day of the war. They were not the only gullible fools.

The Max network was a prize that Allen Dulles wanted eagerly. Not only would it make him the king of anti-Soviet espionage after the war, but Max had secret communication facilities that were undetectable by the Allies during the war. Dulles was not aware that the Max network really worked for the Soviets, still less that the ultimate loyalty of the Jewish section was to the Zionists. Shortly after Schellenberg and the SS took over Admiral Canaris's operations in early 1944, they discovered that Max had been using a crude form of radio and courier nets to transmit information to the Vatican. Some of these had been intercepted by the British Ultra staff, and Churchill promptly warned his Soviet ally that it appeared that the Germans had broken some of its codes.

Schellenberg equipped the Max network with a new German invention: burst transmitters that compressed a radio transmission down to a few seconds of static. The technology was untraceable at the time. The Jews in the Max network were among the privileged few who had the new device. They were able to stay in nearly constant communication with their White Russian contact in Rome, "Prince" Anton Turkul, leader of the "Russian Fascists" who spied on Stalin. What Hitler and Canaris did not know was that Turkul was also a Communist double agent. Turkul's mission from Moscow was to pose as the leader of the Russian Fascist spy ring, using the Max network to entrap not only the Nazis but their sympathizers in the West.

According to several of the former intelligence officers we spoke to, in the early stages of the war a small portion of the secret information that Max obtained from the Germans was sent to the Allies as bait, to whet their appetites. Sir Stewart Menzies and Allen Dulles were the intended targets of this long-term Soviet disinformation strategy.[6]

In order to disguise the "Jewish Fascist" source, the Max material was passed through "Source Lucy" in Switzerland, one of the few survivors of the famous Red Orchestra spy ring that had infiltrated Nazi Germany on the eve of World War II. The agent behind "Source Lucy" allegedly was Anton Turkul, who used Jesuit couriers with diplomatic pouches to hand-carry selected bits of the Max information to Switzerland and then had it passed to Allen Dulles. When the Vatican vouched for the reliability of the Max information, Dulles salivated for more.[7]

In May 1943 Turkul had come out of the closet briefly and attempted to make direct contact with Dulles by traveling to Switzerland. He was unsuccessful, so he then used a Georgian nobleman, Prince Irakly Bagration, as a go-between. Bagration was the pretender to the nonexistent Georgian throne and one of Turkul's inner circle, who had lived in Rome before the war. In May 1942 he went to Berlin to negotiate with the Nazis, and in September the Germans made him chief of their puppet Georgian Committee. The evidence indicates that he was yet another of the many Soviet agents in Turkul's network, who was spying on both the Nazis, who intended to launch an offensive into Palestine and Egypt in 1942, and on the Zionists in Palestine. As usual, oil was the crux of the matter, both Soviet oil in the Caucasus and Arab oil.[8]

Soon after his appointment to the Nazi-sponsored committee, Bagration was mysteriously sent to Switzerland by the Jewish agent, Kauder, supposedly to keep him out of the hands of the Nazi secret police. Not all of the Germans were fools. Several factions of Nazi intelligence suspected that the Max network, with its curious mix of Jewish and Russian Fascists, was a clever fraud by the Kremlin. However, the German generals continued to be taken in and based much of their military strategy against the Soviet Union on the "priceless" Max reports.

Getting Bagration away from the clutches of the Gestapo was yet another of the Max network's maneuvers to boost its credibility with the West. Just before Rome fell to the Allies in June 1944, Kauder used Bagration to make contact with Dulles on Turkul's behalf. Supposedly Bagration was to volunteer the Russian Fascists to work for Western intelligence in any future war against the Communists. Unfortunately, the Third Reich learned of the betrayal. The faction around the Nazis' Eastern territories expert Alfred Rosenberg was extremely suspicious of Bagration and had the secret police wiretap his conversations. Toward the end of 1944, the intercepts allegedly picked up his discussions with the British embassy, or so Kauder told U.S. intelligence after the war.[9]

It seems much more likely that this was actually one of Schellenberg's schemes to improve his separate peace negotiations by dangling Max as the bait to hook the Allies on joining Germany in an anti-Bolshevik crusade. Dulles's assistant, Paul Blum, handled the negotiations for the takeover of the priceless Max network. Blum, it should be noted, had not only trained in X-2 (OSS counterintelligence) with James Angleton but was one of his closest friends.

Our sources say that Dulles, Blum, and Angleton did not realize in 1944 that the White Russian Fascists were connected to Berlin by the Jewish section of the Max network.[10] In fact, the Jews ran their own espionage cell within the cover of Turkul's "Fascist" organization. The most vital part of the Max network—its communication and intelligence service—was run almost entirely by Jews, but Dulles was not informed of this in 1944. He thought he was dealing with Russian Fascists, not Jewish Communists. This would explain why Dulles trusted the Max system to continue his negotiations with both the Nazis and the Japanese to secure a separate peace.

According to Schellenberg's account, Turkul had the *only* communication system that the Germans would trust to negotiate with Japan. U.S. intelligence files later confirmed that Turkul was also the head of the Russian Fascist Union in Japan and that his White Russian network had been subsidized by the Japanese General Staff.[11] Dulles swallowed the bait of the Max network, hook, line, and sinker. Here, he thought, was a secure way to negotiate his German-Japanese-British-American alliance against Stalin without Roosevelt finding out.

Of course, Stalin found out first. The Vatican peace negotiations had been an object of intense Soviet interest for some time. Dulles had been conned into using a Communist communication network to replace the

Vatican's slow-moving couriers. Through Max, Stalin could watch every move Dulles made.

One former East Bloc intelligence officer said that Max uncovered one of Dulles's dirtiest tricks.[12] It was Dulles himself who warned the Nazis that the Japanese ambassador had inadvertently compromised the Vatican negotiations. This Communist source alleges that Dulles himself tipped off the SS about the Magic decrypts of the Japanese ambassador in Berlin. Despite other allegations that Dulles leaked information to the Nazis, we have not been able to corroborate through any of our Western sources that Dulles betrayed the United States's most secret code-breaking success to the Germans.[13]

There is, however, some circumstantial evidence to suggest that such a leak occurred. It may only be a coincidence, but shortly after the Japanese-Vatican negotiations began, the SS suddenly told the German High Command to use tighter code security and stop using radio. Hitler's generals were desperate to buy time for the Max team to bring about a new alliance against the Soviet Union. They suddenly stopped using the Ultra code and switched to couriers. For once, not a word of the impending battle was leaked to the Japanese ambassador in Berlin.[14] This may explain why the Battle of the Bulge came as a complete surprise to U.S. Military Intelligence.

Perhaps it is only a coincidence, but while the Americans and the Germans slogged it out on the Western front, Soviet troops stole a march on Berlin. The Battle of the Bulge cost thousands of American lives and helped to delay the end of the war for another half year. During that time, the Soviet occupation of Central Europe was completed. There is some evidence that the Soviets used the Max network to foster the Vatican negotiations for their own purposes and to great advantage.

Shortly after Turkul's emissary, Prince Bagration, began his negotiations in Switzerland on behalf of the Max network, the Vatican and Angleton began publishing the phony Vessel cables under the guidance of another Soviet agent, Kim Philby. Vessel was used to sound out the Western Allies' position on the Vatican peace initiative, while the real Japanese responses were being handled through the Max network, immune from the ears of Ultra. Every aspect of the Max organization bears the hallmark of a classic Soviet intelligence operation.

Despite our best efforts, we have been unable to obtain a single page of contemporary Soviet records to shed light on these issues. To this day, the wartime archives of Soviet Military Intelligence (the GRU) remain closed.[15] There is a logical explanation for fifty years of Soviet silence about Max: The ever-gullible Dulles hired the Max network and later brought it into the CIA for anti-Soviet espionage. The CIA is just as reluctant as the West Germans to release its own records on its embarrassing employment of a Communist cell. Despite this, enough evidence has leaked out of the intelligence archives to show what a devastating effect the Max network had on Western intelligence during the Cold War.[16]

One aspect of the byzantine Max scandal has never been discussed before: Its contribution to the wartime and postwar success of Zionist intelligence. Two Israeli and three American sources agree that Allen Dulles's greed tempted him to use the secure Max communications to launder his clients' money out of Nazi Germany.[17] Several of our British sources also suspect that Dulles handled at least one Japanese gold transfer to the Vatican via the Max network, in order to evade detection from Operation Safehaven.[18] Both Israeli sources agree that Dulles did not realize, until too late, that it was the Jews inside Max who were laundering his Nazi money.[19]

While few details are available, Dulles must have had a bit of a shock when he was informed by the Zionists that Jews were handling his most sensitive, and illegal, correspondence with the Nazis. To his dismay, Dulles was told that if he wanted to continue using Max, the Jews wanted something in return. He could launder money in the other direction, to ransom Jewish lives from the Nazis.

It has long been known that the early Zionists tried to barter with the Nazis for Jewish lives, both before and during the war. Indeed, the Zionists have openly acknowledged that as far back as 1933, they were attempting to negotiate with Hitler to trade money, equipment, and food for the release of Jews. Adolf Eichmann's and later Otto von Bolschwing's prewar missions to Palestine were simply an extension of a widely known but basically futile policy. Only a handful of Jews were saved by such deals.

Neither the Nazis nor the Western Allies paid much attention to the suffering of the Jews during the war. As we discussed in our last book, Pope Pius XII probably rescued more Jews than all the Allies combined. Even so, the Vatican's activities were pitifully small, and by 1944 the Zionists had given up hope of Allied rescue. It should be recalled that only a few months before, at Easter 1943, the British delegate to the Bermuda Conference rejected any American initiative to rescue the Jews for fear that it might result in an exodus from Auschwitz to Palestine.[20] Even after 1943, when Allied aircraft in Italy were in bombing range of the gas chambers, John J. McCloy, the U.S. assistant secretary of war, had ordered in writing that no American planes be diverted to the concentration camps.[21]

The Jews had tried humanitarian appeals with no success. Next they tried ransom. In mid-1944 the Third Reich was clearly starting to collapse, and negotiations began between Zionist agents and the Nazi government. Eichmann's last full-scale extermination program—the 800,000 Jews of

Hungary—was getting under way, and a Hungarian Zionist, Joel Brand, was sent to Turkey to ransom as many of his people as possible in return for supplies and 10,000 trucks, allegedly "to be used only on the Russian front."[22]

The British refused to commit themselves to the deal, and the negotiations were transferred to Switzerland, which just happened to be Allen Dulles's home base. Eventually both Jewish and American money was provided to the Germans in return for a pitifully small number of Jews. In fact, the ransom negotiations were a cynical ploy by the Third Reich to keep the Zionists quiet while Hungary's Jews were sent to Auschwitz for gassing. When the trucks-for-Jews proposal failed, the Zionists switched from ransom to blackmail. Blackmail worked.

According to some of our sources, one of the Jewish agents inside the Max network suddenly surfaced with an ultimatum.[23] If Dulles wanted to use the Max network to move his Nazi money across Switzerland to the Vatican, he would have to deal with the Jews. If the Nazis wanted to smuggle both themselves and their money out, the Jews would arrange safe conduct, for a price. The price was Jewish lives.

Dulles had no choice but to accept. Besides, as he later confided to a friend, it might do him and his Nazi friends some good to be associated with a program to rescue Jews. In the second half of 1944, Allen Dulles began one of the most bizarre "humanitarian" programs in history. He communicated the bottom line to Schellenberg. If the SS wanted to get its money out before the Third Reich collapsed, its leaders had to permit a window of opportunity for the Jews to survive.[24]

By then most Hungarian Jews had already been dealt with at Auschwitz. Even so, Nazis were very resistant to allowing any escape. Only reluctantly did Himmler agree to spare the last remnants of the concentration camps. Instead of being shot or gassed, the Jews were herded aboard cramped trains or force-marched westward toward the Allies. Many died anyway, but some did survive.

According to the "old spies," Hitler knew only of Dulles's peace negotiations, not the plan to smuggle German flight capital to the Vatican.[25] In order to hide the evacuation of the Third Reich's treasury from Hitler, the SS replaced real money with counterfeit. Himmler called it "Operation Wendig" (Window).[26] Under the watchful eyes of Jewish agents in the Swiss banks, Dulles was allowed to send Himmler's money out through Italy. The smuggling route across the Brenner Pass later became the escape window for Jews on the exodus to Palestine.

The government of Israel has publicly admitted that, toward the end of the war, the Vatican and U.S. representatives in Switzerland were particularly helpful in ransoming Jews. Although the Vatican has published eleven volumes of documents pertaining to its wartime rescue efforts, the records of these particular financial transactions have never been opened to the public.[27]

One surviving U.S. intelligence report corroborates our sources' version of Operation Wendig and adds some key details about the underground railroad for both Jewish survivors and Nazi money. The American investigators in the army's CIC could not make head nor tail of the connection between Swiss banks and "Fascist Jews," but at least they recorded some of the basic facts. The top-secret report is entitled "Illegal Jewish Emigration In and Through Italy":

> On the Brenner Pass route from Austria the first stop on the underground railroad in Italy is a Castle in Merano where German is the language of the directors. This castle is believed to be "Schloss Rametz" belonging to CRASTAN, Albert, a Jew, who poses as a Swiss consul and as a member of the International Red Cross. During the war he was an agent of the SS task force "SCHLOSS LABERS" sometimes called "GROUP WENDIG" under the command of SCHWENDT, Col. Frederick, who was responsible only to Kaltenbrunner and Himmler.[28]

"Freddie" Schwendt, it should be noted, established a gun-running and "security" operation in Bolivia after the war, where he was joined by his old SS comrade-in-arms Klaus Barbie, the "Butcher of Lyons."[29] Barbie worked for State Department intelligence for a while, before he was smuggled to South America by Father Draganović's Vatican network.

Strangely enough, the Jews who worked with Schwendt on Operation Window seemed to have no fear of arrest or retaliation from Angleton's or Dulles's agents, despite their known association with the SS task force. As the bewildered army CIC reported:

> Four other Jewish agents of this group are known to be at large. One, VAN HARTEN, Jaac, is at present at 184 Hayarkonstr., Tel Aviv, Palestine, from where he claimed 5,000,000 dollars from the U.S. Government for property confiscated at Merano at war's end. All this property was the loot of the SS group which had been stored in Schloss Rametz, Schloss Labers, Schwendt's HQ, and other buildings in Merano. Included in this loot were large quantities of counterfeit British Pound Notes. . . .[30]

Jewish counterfeiters who worked for the Nazis? It was a strange mix indeed. The Allies could certainly have investigated some of Schwendt's "Fascist Jews" if they wanted to. They were prominent bankers who lived openly after the war:

> Another of Schwendt's agents, LOVIOZ, Carlo, another Jew and ex-head of the "Banca Commerciale" in London, is now director of the "Banca Commerciale" in Como. He has a brother who is director of the "Basle

> Bank" in Switzerland. The remaining two are the MANSER brothers, one of whom used to come to Rome to the German Embassy in an IRC-tagged vehicle during the Nazi occupation. One of the Mansers was in Milan in the summer of 1944; both were in Venice in the winter of 1944–45. It is interesting to note that CRASTAN, VAN HARTEN, and the MANSER's all used the IRC as a front. . . . The exact connection between the remains of "SCHLOSS LABERS" and the Jewish underground is unknown at the present time, but the link seems to exist.[31]

While the U.S. intelligence officer could not quite make out what these "Fascist Jews" were up to with their Swiss banks and IRC (International Red Cross) documents, this one obscure intelligence report came close to exposing how the Zionists had cut their deal with Allen Dulles. The castle, or *schloss,* at the Brenner Pass became the clearinghouse for Nazi money, real and counterfeit, being passed through Dulles's window to Italy.

The counterfeiters themselves were skilled Jewish engravers imprisoned at a special Austrian concentration camp at Alt Aussee, where they manufactured high-grade phony passports and documentation for the SS. The Nazis were to use these documents to escape from Germany. Later on, after rescuing as many Jews as possible, the Zionists used the Alt Aussee records to keep track of fugitive war criminals such as Adolf Eichmann.

As far as the Red Cross connection is concerned, the explanation is very simple. American intelligence had used the Red Cross as far back as World War I. When the SS-Wendig deal first came about, Dulles had asked his friend, Count Folke Bernadotte, head of the International Red Cross, to provide the Zionists with diplomatic cover. Bernadotte, it should be noted, was a closet Nazi sympathizer and anti-Semite, who permitted the Red Cross to be used as a vehicle for Nazi intelligence during the war and to hand out Red Cross passports to fugitive Nazis afterward. U.S. intelligence later found that the fugitive Nazis systematically used Red Cross mail couriers to evade Allied censorship and surveillance after the war.

The Zionists barely tolerated Bernadotte's role in the SS-Wendig smuggling. Bernadotte showed up in Palestine as a "neutral" arbiter of peace talks with the Arabs at the height of the 1948 war and proposed that the Jews give up the Negev desert. In effect, the Jews would not be allowed to run their own country. It was a bit too much hypocrisy for those Jews who knew the true story. This time Ben-Gurion could not control the extremists, and the Stern Gang assassinated Bernadotte. The head of the Red Cross had kept the "window" for Jewish survivors much too small. Dulles had already replaced Bernadotte with another collaborator inside the Red Cross, a Frenchman named André François-Poncet, who kept the supply of Red Cross passports flowing to Father Draganović.[32]

A number of Jews wanted to kill the Dulleses as well. This time Ben-Gurion was able to stop them from carrying out their plans. For the Zionist leaders, the hardest part was that they had to help the Dulles brothers continue the cover-up. The long journey to the birth of the nation of Israel had begun.

Of all the secrets of those who spied on Zion, this was the most important. The source of the West's post-1945 intelligence war against Israel can be traced back to Allen Dulles's operations in Switzerland. The spy war began long before there was an Israel, well before the end of World War II. It is a history largely unknown to the present generation of Western intelligence officers because the previous generation has vigorously suppressed the record of its transgressions. The records of the CIA have been systematically stripped. The registry at MI6 has been shredded.[33]

But the founders of Israel knew the truth and used it to their advantage. Everywhere the Nazi money went after the war, Zionist intelligence followed. After the Brenner Pass, the next stop on the money trail was Rome. The only ones who knew about Operation Wendig were the handful of Fascist Jews who ran the castle at the Brenner Pass. All traces of the Nazi money-laundering scheme were buried. The Jews had found a new reason for silence. They followed the money to Rome and found the name of Dulles's contact. For the next forty-five years, they kept the secret to themselves.

Years later only a handful of people knew that a young American lieutenant had been blackmailed and then recruited in Rome in 1944 as a double agent for Zionist intelligence. By the time of his forced retirement thirty years later in 1974, James Jesus Angleton had become one of the most senior officers of the Central Intelligence Agency. His primary job was head of the counterintelligence section. From his second-floor command post at the Langley, Virginia, headquarters building, Angleton's mission was to keep the CIA secure from penetration by foreign governments, particularly the Soviet Union.

To this day, career employees still shudder at the recollection of Angleton's witch hunts for Communist moles, which lasted long after the McCarthy era. He never caught any spies inside the CIA, but his investigations were so disruptive, his power so vindictive, his obstructions so crippling to CIA operations, that Angleton himself was accused of being a Soviet mole. It was not true. Angleton spied only for Israel, never the Soviet Union.[34] According to our sources, it was Angleton himself who recruited young Aldrich Ames for his first summer intern job as a file clerk. It is ironic that Angleton never caught a Communist mole in the CIA, but he did recruit one.

There are several versions of how Angleton came to control the CIA's liaison with Israeli intelligence. One former U.S. intelligence officer, Bill Eveland, claimed the relationship stemmed from Angleton's "wartime OSS liaison with Jewish resistance groups based in London."[35] One of Angleton's many biographers traced the connection to Italy after the war, where he allegedly established a close connection of mutual trust with the Zionist underground, which was funneling Jews to Palestine.[36]

According to our Israeli sources, what kept Angleton in line was blackmail, not trust.[37] Some within American intelligence suspected where Angleton's true loyalties lay. As will be seen, on the eve of the Suez Crisis in 1956, CIA section chiefs for the Arab countries received overwhelming evidence that Israel was preparing for war. The analysts at CIA concurred. Angleton's dismissal of the reports provoked a bitter shouting match in which he was flatly accused of being a "goddamn Israeli mole" by a number of his fellow CIA officers.[38] They were correct about what Angleton was; they just did not know how or why he had been recruited.

Over the years Angleton was promoted into the perfect position for an Israeli mole. On the one hand, he was the man responsible for detecting Israeli spies inside the CIA. On the other hand, he also was in charge of spying on Israel. As the case officer for the Israeli account, Angleton alone handled the CIA's collection of intelligence from and against the Jewish state, almost from its inception as a nation.

It was a sweet arrangement. Angleton was in charge of investigating himself. Normal intelligence practice is to compartmentalize counterintelligence from active operations, or what was known as "secret intelligence." The CIA organization and methods staff could never understand how Angleton got away with crossing all the lines. According to the CIA organization chart, the Israeli desk belonged in the Near East Division, but Angleton kept it to himself in the counterintelligence section from 1951 to December 1974.[39]

The CIA could never prove that he had spied for another country. The problem was that they were investigating the wrong Angleton. They should have investigated his father. The forerunners of Israeli intelligence used the sins of the father to blackmail the son. It began with the father smuggling Nazi money and then the son helping to obscure the tracks.

In order to keep the cover-up going, James Angleton had to keep the CIA away from two key areas. Apart from controlling access to Israeli liaison, Angleton needed to monopolize the flow of Vatican information in order to protect his role in the Vessel forgery. In addition, he had to protect the role of his father and the Dulles brothers in smuggling wanted Nazis, and their treasure, out of Europe with the help of the Vatican. Angleton managed to keep these two major CIA accounts to himself throughout his long career.

Years later Miles Copeland, one of the CIA's spies against the Jews, inadvertently revealed that Angleton had used almost exactly the same forgery scam that had been used with the Vatican to seize control of the Israeli account. Copeland revealed that Angleton had begun his campaign to control the Israeli section five years before he officially took it over. According to Copeland's account, one of his colleagues, code named "Mother," had used forged documents to con the Israeli account away from OSS Secret Intelligence.

Both American and Israeli sources confirm that Mother was most definitely James Jesus Angleton.[40] Copeland wrote that Mother fabricated a dossier on the situation in Palestine, based on "secret" information, which was nothing more than news clips straight out of *The New York Times*. Angleton convinced his colleagues that it was genuine material from agents within the Zionist and Arab undergrounds.

Angleton seemed to be rerunning his Vessel tactics, only in a slightly amended form. This time Angleton bragged about the forgery.[41] Copeland explained it away as purely a factional maneuver within U.S. intelligence and a harmless demonstration of the importance of mundane intelligence collection. If our sources are correct, it was, in fact, the beginning of Angleton's takeover of the Israeli connection.[42]

It was a matter of self-protection. Angleton had to keep everyone else in U.S. intelligence oblivious to the fact that he was being blackmailed by the Zionists. His Middle East forgery certainly occurred soon after his recruitment by the Zionists in late 1944. By the beginning of 1946, he was thoroughly in their pocket. He could only sit back and keep quiet as the Zionists simply piggybacked on Father Draganović's Nazi smuggling operation.

The bewildered U.S. Army Counter Intelligence Corps noted in 1947 that some Nazis were going out through what they thought was the Jewish underground.[43] The truth is, it was often the same Ratline. As one American source who worked on the Nazi smuggling admitted, they even used the same trucks. "The Zionists told us that for every one of them [the Nazis] that you take out, you take out one of ours."[44]

The CIC launched a major effort, code named "Operation Circle," to unravel the bewildering connections between the several escape routes that seemed to operate simultaneously yet cater to different clientele. With Angleton covering their tracks, the Zionists had little trouble evading the CIC sweeps. To their credit, the CIC did manage to piece together a remarkable picture of the enterprise. The Zionists had a network of safe houses, passport shops, and feeding stations all over Italy. They even started shipping the refugees in organized groups by train across the border.

The CIC's colleagues at State Department intelligence collated the army's information and detailed Vincent La Vista to conduct a major investigation. La Vista had previously worked on Operation Safehaven, investigating Fascist espionage cells operating in the United States and financial, commercial, and industrial dealings between Italy and Germany. By 1947 he was with the State Department's Division of Foreign Activity Correlation, a supersecret intelligence unit that had become very interested in the various underground railroads engaged in illegal immigration through Italy.

La Vista's report was forwarded to his superiors in May 1947. It uncovered all the branches of the Vatican railroad for the various Nazi and Fascist groups, including all the émigré war criminals from Central and Eastern Europe. La Vista even discovered that the Vatican was pressuring the governments of Catholic states in Latin America to accept the Nazis. He also uncovered the parallel Soviet railroad for Communist agents seeking entry into the Western Hemisphere, particularly the United States.

La Vista discovered hard evidence that Communists were using the Jewish railroad. One case he investigated concerned two Yugoslavs, who crossed the border into Italy and posed as fleeing Jews. La Vista's enormous network of agents and sources tracked the men's activities and found that the Zionists had aided them. On the basis of the available intelligence, however, La Vista reported that the only conclusion "must be that the two men . . . are either Yugoslav Agents or Russian Agents."[45]

While the Communists seemed to be piggybacking on the Jewish railroad, they were not controlling it by any means. The Zionists appeared to be operating as a completely separate organization. It was all very bewildering to La Vista, especially as American Jewish groups seemed to be behind the funding, staffing, and logistical planning. To confuse matters further, the CIC had told La Vista that even fugitive Nazis had used the Jewish railroad. On one occasion they established that a wanted Croatian war criminal, Colonel Modic, together with his entire family, had used the Jewish network in Rome to escape to South America.[46]

La Vista really wasn't sure what he had stumbled onto. Thousands of genuine Jewish refugees were coming into Italy illegally and being helped by the Zionists to escape to Palestine or to Egypt, where there was another efficient Jewish underground. Then there were Communist and Fascist networks using the Jews' railroad, and all three networks seemed somehow to overlap. Although it was confusing, La Vista did not hide his admiration for the Jews: "The Jewish underground now operating in Italy for the sole purpose of assisting emigration to Egypt and Palestine is one of the most efficient underground organizations with which this writer has ever come in contact. As a matter of fact, there is no force in Italy of the Italian Government, or otherwise, capable of stopping its activities or even seriously interfering with it."[47]

By the time La Vista had finished his report, he had traced the entire Jewish railroad. By foot, landing craft, or train, the Jews would make their way from Western, Central, and Eastern Europe, through the Balkans, and down into Italy, where false identities were available, manufactured by Jewish counterfeiters. In Italy, a network of Jewish camps for genuine displaced persons was allegedly under UN control, but in fact the Jews ran the camps themselves, just as the fugitive Nazis ran theirs. While the Nazis went out through Genoa mainly to Latin America, regular convoys shipped the Jews to the Middle East.

As we will learn in Chapter 21, from Sol Shnadow, one of the Jews who made the first part of the trip, the British army's Jewish Brigade, stationed in Austria, coördinated the shipments of Jews under the noses of its own British commanders. But no matter how efficient the Zionists were on land, the Royal Navy was prepared for the Jewish ships, and "the great majority were stopped and taken to Haifa and the passengers sent to Cyprus."[48]

To be sure, there were routes other than the Vatican Ratline. The militant Irgun organization of Menachem Begin had built up its European operations mainly through France, helped by the sympathy of successive postwar governments. Many French Jews had worked in the Resistance and after the war lobbied for the Zionist cause. The Zionists made firm and lasting friends in French intelligence, especially inside Military Intelligence. Still, Angleton's Ratline smuggling system through the Vatican was so efficient that in 1946 the main headquarters of the illegal immigration group Mossad Aliyah Beth was moved from Paris to Italy.

Even before World War II had ended, the Zionists had chosen Italy as one of the principal illegal immigration routes to Palestine, and agents were sent to organize the operations. By the end of the war, the escape routes already stretched from Romania and Yugoslavia down through Italy, and over the next few years numerous small and larger craft took more than 40,000 Jews from Europe to Palestine.[49] Many were young men of fighting age, the sort needed to conquer Palestine.

Yaacov Tavin was the Irgun's top man in Italy, before becoming head of its Intelligence Department in Palestine. Tavin was brilliant at espionage, but he also was a master terrorist. In October 1946 he organized the bombing of the British embassy in Rome, "which had become the symbol of opposition to Jewish immigration, much of which passed through Italy en route from northern and eastern Europe."[50]

Special CIC agent William Gowen recalled the embassy bombing and mentioned that his office received a polite telephone call from the Zionists that the building housing his headquarters was to be the next target. The caller apologized, explaining that his target was really the British intelligence office on the third floor and that he had nothing against the Americans. The CIC commanding officer took the threat seriously and moved out in December 1946, well before Angleton left the same building and returned to the United States.[51]

The British, who were unaware that Angleton had been blackmailed into working for the Zionists, were adamant that the smuggling of Jews from Italy had to stop. No matter how many buildings were destroyed, the Jews were to be prevented from reaching Palestine. After the Irgun blew up the British embassy, even Ben-Gurion's more moderate Haganah faction sent a veiled threat to the Italian premier, while the Irgun itself was none too shy about its intention to use terrorism against the Italian government.[52]

The Zionists' spies were causing havoc to the British on all fronts. The British hit back. They labeled the illegal Jewish immigration railroad as a "Red plot." Throughout World War II, the British had repeatedly warned their American allies of the dangers of illegal Zionist immigration into Palestine. After the war these warnings became obsessively connected to fears of Soviet intentions in the Middle East, as "it appeared to the British, concerned with security, thousands of illegal immigrants were streaming into Palestine from countries under Soviet influence, actively aided by the Soviet occupation authorities."[53]

British investigations in Eastern Europe concluded wrongly that the entire emigration scheme was a Communist plot and that the Soviets were sending out mainly young men who had received military training as well as a plentiful supply of arms and ammunition. Naturally, many of the illegal Jewish migrants were Communist agents.[54] At the time, there were numerous public claims that the Jews dominated the governments of many of the countries behind the Iron Curtain, including Hungary, Poland, Czechoslovakia, and even East Germany.

The CIC was more confused than ever. Operation Circle had started off with investigations of Nazi smuggling, then branched out to trace illegal Jewish immigration, only to come full circle and discover that the Communists were involved as well. No one had any idea what it was all about.

No one except perhaps David Ben-Gurion. When Dulles and Angleton became involved with the Max network, they did not realize that one of the key members of Admiral Canaris's network of "Fascist Jews" was a secret Zionist. After the war U.S. intelligence debriefers were puzzled at the large number of Max employees who were Jews and had participated in wartime ransom efforts for Jews. One of the Jewish leaders of the Max network demanded a new price for his continued cooperation. He wanted Jews to be smuggled to Palestine. According to British historian Richard Deacon: "The Palestinian Jews were helped by a former German Jew who had been one of a number of such Jews especially recruited by Admiral Canaris as agents for his *Abwehr* (German Secret Service)."[55] Deacon inadvertently uncovered one of the best-kept secrets in Israeli intelligence: One of the leading Jews inside the Max network had defected to Ben-Gurion but it was from the Communists, not from Admiral Canaris. Ben-Gurion's files for this period are closed and highly classified, but two of the "old spies" said that the man who made contact with Ben-Gurion was one of the top leaders of the Max network, probably Richard Kauder himself.[56]

By the end of the war, it had become clear to Kauder and his other Jewish agents that rescue operations for Jews were going nowhere. Dulles and the Nazis were more interested in saving themselves and in hiding their money than in helping more than a handful of Jews to escape from the gas chambers. Some evidence does support our sources' claim that it was Kauder himself who became the Zionist defector.

For one thing, he was one of an elite group of Jews who had worked for Admiral Canaris. For another, no other Nazi network was able to assemble so many Jewish agents and keep most of them safe from the Gestapo. The postwar U.S. intelligence files reveal that several dozen of the Max network agents were Jews, and it is possible that one of them could have been the Zionist defector.[57] However, Kauder was the real brains behind the Jewish section of the network, and his profile most closely resembles that given by Deacon. Strictly speaking, Kauder was an Austrian, not a German Jew, as alleged by Deacon, but at the time Austria had been incorporated into the Third Reich. Technically, Kauder had become a German citizen, although despite repeated efforts he was never "Aryanized."

Even more significant was the fact that Kauder was the only one of the Max organization to refuse the Communists' offer of new identity papers at the end of the war, papers that would show that he was fighting in Yugoslavia against Tito and under the command of the Americans. "Believing that the Americans would see through the fraud at once," Kauder "declared the whole set-up as a swindle" and refused to have anything to do with it.[58]

Kauder was starting to look for a new home for his espionage ring, and the logical place was within American intelligence, where his knowledge of the Turkul network would prove an invaluable asset in bargaining for help for his Zionist friends. Kauder's refusal of the Communists' papers certainly put distance between him and the Turkul section of the Max network, as all the Russian Fascists carried the papers. Further, Kauder immediately went his own way, was picked up by the U.S. Army in Austria, and initially said he was completely separate from the Turkul network.

Unfortunately, his American interrogators were appalled when they discovered that a Jew had been working for the Nazis, and they beat him to a pulp. By the time Dulles's friends located Kauder and got him released, he was so bitter at his treatment that he decided to protect Turkul and work exclusively for his Zionist friends. He obstinately resisted all threats and inducements by a string of frustrated British and American interrogators.

Kauder's defection to the Zionists was more than an embarrassment to Dulles. It was a body blow to Stalin. After the war Soviet Military Intelligence, the GRU, intended to use the Max network against the Western Allies, just as it had against the Germans. In fact, the Soviets were going to trick the same Germans who had fallen for the Max reports during the war and were now working for the Western Allies.

Allen Dulles had arranged for General Reinhard Gehlen, chief of Nazi intelligence on the Eastern front, to receive special treatment. Gehlen was flown to Washington in 1945, dressed as an American general, where he regaled the Pentagon with tales of his prowess in infiltrating the Soviet secret service. Dulles had Gehlen set up in a secret compound in Pullach, West Germany, with orders to revive the Max network. When one of Gehlen's aides, Colonel Hermann Baun, insisted that the whole Max operation had been a Soviet scam, Gehlen had him silenced.[59]

Baun belonged to a select group of Nazi intelligence officers who always had believed that the Turkul-Max networks were riddled with Soviet agents and that Germany was pouring massive amounts of money into a Red sting operation. The remnants of the Red Orchestra network, especially in the Luftwaffe, insisted that Baun and his supporters were wrong and had the German High Command override all their entreaties to arrest the Max agents.[60]

When Baun protested to his postwar boss, General Gehlen, that Max's White Russian handler, "Prince" Turkul, should not be used for intelligence operations under any circumstances, he was framed and eventually removed in April 1947. The reason was simple: Gehlen intended to make Turkul's Max network the centerpiece of his new West German intelligence agency. As soon as a Republican president was elected in the United

States, Dulles intended to take over the CIA and make Gehlen and Turkul the heart of his anti-Soviet network. The Soviets, of course, were delighted as they watched Dulles and Gehlen attempt to plant a Communist spy ring in the heart of Western intelligence.

British and American intelligence spent years after World War II trying to unravel the extraordinary maze of the Max network. It was one of the largest espionage cases of the early postwar period, and eventually, in 1956, the Allies decided that the whole thing had been a giant Soviet-controlled operation. Dozens of operations, hundreds of agents, thousands of innocent contacts had been betrayed. The Soviets had Dulles and Gehlen completely conned for the entire decade after the war.

In the early 1950s one CIA director, General Walter Bedell Smith, admitted to the military that the casualty rate for agents sent behind the Iron Curtain was in excess of 98 percent. He feared that many of the Dulles's agent networks had been penetrated.[61] Dulles should have listened to his predecessor's warnings.[62] As discussed in detail in Chapter 11, three years after Dulles became head of CIA in 1953, his pet "Fascist," Turkul, broadcast the CIA codes to start the Hungarian uprising prematurely. Thousands of innocent Hungarians rushed on to the streets of Budapest to start the revolution. Instead of American paratroopers dropping supplies, they found Soviet tanks waiting in the suburbs.[63]

Foisting the Max network on Allen Dulles and General Gehlen turned out to be the key to Soviet supremacy in the first half of the Cold War. By 1959 U.S. Military Intelligence admitted to the National Security Council that it did not have a single network of couriers or safe houses left in Communist territory, apart from East Germany. Dulles's Nazi "freedom fighters" had sold him out.

If Kauder, the Zionist defector, had gone public in 1945, the whole Max-Turkul operation would have blown up in Stalin's face. Assassinating Kauder would have done the GRU no good, because by 1944 he had already told Ben-Gurion's agents too much.

According to two former Israeli intelligence officers, the GRU told Ben-Gurion to name his price for his continued silence about the Soviet spy operation. Ben-Gurion told them what he wanted: a country.[64] For the first time in the history of the Zionist movement, the Jews had the whip hand over Stalin. By threatening to disclose that Max was run by the Kremlin, the Jews had a brief window of opportunity to play one superpower against another. Ben-Gurion was not a Communist. He was a realist.

He knew that the Allies had not lifted a finger while at least 6 million Jews were killed. He knew that the British government would go to extreme lengths to stop the State of Israel from being created. The American people were enthusiastic supporters of the Zionist state, but the United States alone was not enough to counteract the votes of the British and their supporters in the United Nations. Ben-Gurion needed the votes of the Soviet bloc if he were ever to have a nation. He was willing to make a devil's bargain with Stalin: Max's silence, in return for a reversal of the Soviet position on Palestine.[65]

There is evidence that Ben-Gurion's blackmail worked. Suddenly, in 1947, the Soviet Union became one of the leading proponents of partitioning Palestine into Arab and Jewish states. To understand what a major reversal of Soviet policy this was, it should be remembered that Zionism had been one of the main targets of Soviet propaganda for the previous half century and that this precedent had begun even before the Bolshevik revolution of 1917. While British and American right-wingers were trying to portray the Zionists as loyal Marxist slaves to Stalin, the left wing was vehemently denouncing the Zionists on the ground that they were not Marxists at all, but merely liberal capitalists in disguise.[66]

Helping create a Zionist state was not an easy thing for Stalin to accept. The Soviet dictator was one of the great anti-Semites of all time. Russian Jews tell a bitter joke that a thousand years from now, Hitler will be remembered as a petty tyrant who lived in the time of Stalin. The Soviet leader was anything but a Zionist supporter.[67] In fact, the blood purges of the 1930s were part of Stalin's method to drive all of the leading Jewish Communists out of power in the Comintern, the military, and the party. Jews became the only group in the Soviet Union to have their religion stamped on their passports.

During World War II the Soviet government consistently opposed all negotiations with Hitler to rescue Jews. Stalin allegedly commented that he did not care how many boxcars Hitler wasted in sending Jews to the concentration camps, as long as he wasn't sending ammunition to the Eastern front. As late as the Yalta Conference of the "Big Three" in 1945, Stalin had opposed any concessions to Jewish interests in Palestine that were not approved by the Arabs.

The traditional explanation of why Stalin suddenly became Ben-Gurion's champion is that he wanted to oust Britain from the Middle East and break the "imperialist encirclement" of the Soviet Union. The timing of Stalin's dramatic policy reversal suggests there was much more involved than has been suggested hitherto. To Britain's utter dismay, the entire Soviet bloc switched in favor of partition. For one thing, it was only in May 1947 that the Soviet representative at the UN, Andrei Gromyko, called for the division of Palestine into two states, one for the Jews and one for the Arabs. Stalin had not only agreed to a *volte face* in the UN, he was forced by Ben-Gurion to open up the Iron Curtain to permit the wholesale emigration of Jews to Palestine.

Ben-Gurion kept his part of the bargain, at least for a little while. Kauder was told to go back to work for the Americans and keep his mouth shut. That was a difficult maneuver for the Jewish master spy. How could he convince the suspicious Americans of his own usefulness, while not exposing the Communists who had controlled the network throughout the war? Some Americans did suspect Soviet penetration of the Max network, but they were systematically misled and frustrated by the Red moles in British intelligence, especially by Kim Philby.

Kauder was extremely lucky and also very clever. For several years he was under threat of execution by American intelligence as the man most likely to be head of the Soviet ring, but then he was suddenly released. With the secret help of Philby and the Soviet double agents in MI5, Kauder and "Prince" Turkul eventually convinced the Western interrogation officers that the real double agent was another White Russian colleague, Longin Ira. Turkul survived to wreak his damage on Western intelligence. What the British and Americans did not know was that after his release, Kauder rejoined his network of so-called Red Jews and helped to build Israel.

If Ben-Gurion's deal with Stalin seems harsh and cynical, it should be understood that these were harsh and cynical times. Although American public opinion was favorable toward Jews, few Zionists trusted Roosevelt entirely. Roosevelt's promise to Ibn Saud of neutrality in favor of the Arabs in Palestine came as no surprise to them. As several leading Zionists admitted, if Roosevelt had lived, it is unlikely that Israel would ever have been born.[68] They knew what they were talking about.

In 1944 the Zionists sent a secret mission to the United States to establish a propaganda operation and a "miniature Secret Service . . . to glean political secrets from both the White House and the State Department."[69] The Zionist movement soon discovered what it actually was up against in the Roosevelt administration. The network found out that the pirates of Wall Street controlled policy in Washington, especially those in the oil business. The Zionists quickly established that one of Dulles's chief allies, Navy Secretary James Forrestal, was their most formidable opponent. By 1946 Forrestal was replacing Stalin as Zionist Enemy Number One.

Within a few short years, Ben-Gurion would betray Stalin, drive Forrestal to suicide, and switch his allegiance to the United States. The next round in the secret war against the Jews was about to begin. It was the most crucial round of all, for it would determine whether the international community backed the partition of Palestine into Jewish and Arab states. With no oil to barter for support at the United Nations, Ben-Gurion turned once again to his best weapon: blackmail.

CHAPTER 7

"A JEWISH–COMMUNIST CONSPIRACY"

Most history books credit the government of the United States with securing the votes in the United Nations to create the State of Israel. The truth is that several key members of Truman's Democratic administration did everything in their power to prevent the vote going through, and they nearly succeeded. Truman, only twelve months before what seemed a sure election defeat by his Republican rival, had lost control of his own government at a crucial moment. In the end, the Zionists had to rely on their own resources to ensure a victory in the UN.

The previous histories of the UN vote record that there was a dramatic switch of voting intentions by the majority of the Latin American nations, most of which had intended either to vote against the partition of Palestine into Jewish and Arab states or at best to abstain. According to the published record, it was Truman's State Department that "twisted the arms" in Latin America and ensured that Israel would be voted into existence. According to our sources among the former intelligence officers, Zionist blackmail was what won the day.

In this chapter we discuss the following allegations by our sources in detail:

- The United States' first secretary of defense, James V. Forrestal, was the leader of a cabal of senior State Department and intelligence officials within the Truman administration that worked behind the president's back to block the creation of the State of Israel.
- Forrestal was, in fact, a corporate spy for Allen Dulles within the Truman administration, while Dulles was working to elect the president's opponent, Governor Thomas E. Dewey.
- When the Zionists realized right before the UN vote on partition of Palestine that they might not have enough votes, they blackmailed Nelson Rockefeller, who delivered the largely hostile votes of the Latin American bloc.

The secret history of the birth of Israel has never been told before. Let us begin with the principal villain, the man who nearly succeeded in preventing Israel's birth.

James Forrestal was a manic, ambitious, and very right-wing investment banker who had joined Dillon, Read during World War I and had risen spectacularly through the ranks, beginning as a bond salesman and becoming a partner only seven years later. By 1926 he was a vice president, and in 1938, at the relatively young age of forty-six, he replaced Clarence Dillon as the company's president. Along the way, Forrestal had earned himself the title of the "boy wonder" of Wall Street.

What few remember is that Forrestal's company was one of the banking firms that financed Hitler. American business dealings with the Nazis were hushed up by Forrestal's vice president, who was in charge of postwar investigations into Nazi finances.[1] Forrestal was not himself a Nazi, nor even a Nazi supporter. He was an extremely strange mixture who supported President Roosevelt's New Deal banking reforms but was not himself a New Dealer. In fact, as will be seen, like several other of Dulles's allies, he was a corporate spy within the president's own ranks. While he didn't respect, let alone like, FDR, nevertheless, in mid-1940 he became one of the president's special administrative assistants.[2]

Despite deep dissatisfaction with the president and his successor, Forrestal rose through the ranks to become undersecretary and then secretary of the navy, and finally the first secretary of defense in September 1947. Truman did not realize for another year that Forrestal was quietly going mad. Virtually the entire American defense policy, indeed much of its strategy toward the Zionists, was in the hands of an extremely bigoted lunatic who would soon take his own life.

Even before World War II ended, Forrestal became concerned, even obsessed, with the threat of Soviet expansionist aims in the Middle East and alarmed by reports "that communist agents were increasing their activities in a number of Middle East countries, including those upon whom the free world was dependent for oil." If the Arabs cut off their oil, "the military and industrial capabilities of the entire free world would be significantly and perhaps decisively reduced."[3]

In short, James Forrestal believed that controlling Middle Eastern oil was far too important to squander for the sake of the Jews, let alone their Zionist dreams. The Arabs controlled the oil, and the Jews were expendable. As he told Secretary of State James Byrne, Saudi Arabia in particular was "a matter of first importance."[4] On the other hand, when it came to Jews, Forrestal was at best indifferent, and his generally positive biographer, Arnold Rogow, has recorded that:

> Forrestal lived most of his life in an anti-Semitic world. The early family circle was anti-Semitic, and many of his friends positively disliked Jews. During his Wall Street career a large number of prominent investment

> banking houses and law firms refused to employ Jews, and some of the New York and Washington clubs to which he belonged did not admit persons of Jewish origin. The Navy Department itself was notorious for its anti-Semitic promotion policy.[5]

Forrestal himself admitted that he thought that Jews were "different," and he "could never really understand how a non-Jew and a Jew could be friends." While he emphasized the need to support the Arab position over Palestine, "his attitude towards the Jewish survivors of Hitler's concentration camps was essentially one of indifference." Like many of his fellow Wall Street club members, especially close friends such as Allen Dulles, he opposed more than token Jewish immigration to the United States. He proposed on more than one occasion that Jewish survivors be dumped in South America instead.[6]

Forrestal was not the only businessman-politician with strong oil connections, to say nothing of a barely disguised bigotry against the Jews. The upper ranks of the Washington establishment were studded with the stars of the oil business. Throughout the war they even controlled government oil policy and, as will be seen, later passed their secrets on to a new generation of oil men, men like George Bush, who had impeccable records as war heroes in the fight against fascism. As we shall see, the new generation continued Forrestal's policies.

Forrestal was very particular regarding U.S. oil companies. As he stated in 1945, when it came to Saudi Arabia, he did not "care which American company or companies developed the Arabian reserves," they just had to be U.S. companies.[7] Like the Dulles brothers, Forrestal wanted the British out of Middle Eastern oil. "The prestige and hence the influence of the United States is in part related to the wealth of the Government and its nationals in terms of oil resources," Forrestal wrote, adding that "the active expansion of such holdings is very much to be desired."[8] Further, America "should not be shipping a barrel of oil out of the United States to Europe."[9]

He had not been so opposed to shipping oil to Europe when the Nazis were in charge. As discussed in Chapter 3, it was Forrestal himself who negotiated the deal to bring Standard Oil of California together with Texaco to form Caltex, which later became the Arabian-American Oil Company. He even raised huge loans for the company and then joined the board of the I. G. Farben–controlled General Aniline and Film Corporation, one of Allen Dulles's key Nazi clients.

While still undersecretary of the navy in 1941, and just before the United States joined the war, Forrestal gave immunity to Standard Oil of New Jersey ships supplying the Nazis with much-needed oil. He was also the banker for Caltex when it bought up millions of dollars' worth of Saudi Arabian oil and the man who pulled the strings to procure King Ibn Saud's secret bribes from President Roosevelt.[10]

In fact, Forrestal's company, Dillon, Read, had helped finance Hitler in 1934. One of Forrestal's close business associates was an American Nazi collaborator named Alexander Kreuter, who obtained favorable treatment for Western financial interests from the Nazis. Kreuter later served as one of Dulles's contacts in the secret peace negotiations with Germany.[11] This connection was not the only time Forrestal assisted Dulles's corporate clients, who were making profits from the Nazis.

Apart from his apparent bias toward Fascist Europe and against democratic Europe, Forrestal was ambitious, greedy, and extremely clever. He was also badly unhinged, both emotionally and mentally. He was very much attracted to conflict and strange situations. He married a Protestant, although he was a Catholic. He was a Wall Street arch-conservative, yet he chose to join the Democrats. He was an extremist who advocated tough action as the best solution to almost every problem. It has been said that "genius is the ability to live between extremes without losing one's sanity." In this respect, Forrestal was no genius, although he was ahead of his times when it came to communism.

Well before most of his colleagues had even started thinking about the Soviet menace, Forrestal was planning for the inevitable confrontation. Like Jack Philby, Forrestal believed that oil was the crux of Western geopolitical strategy. It was *the* most important U.S. interest, and idealism came a poor second. Unfortunately, the Jews did not see it that way. They were determined to stir up trouble, in what Forrestal and his supporters came to see as their obsessive and unreasonable desire to have a homeland in Palestine.

Between 1945 and 1947 the Zionists, especially the Haganah, but also the smaller Irgun and Lechi factions, waged a total war against the British in Palestine. From Forrestal's point of view, Britain's diplomatic failure was another unfortunate development. In its imperialist greed, London had managed to push the Zionists and the French closer together.[12] The Italians were no better in Forrestal's eyes. They caved in far too easily to Jewish threats and terrorist actions. The foreigners were all soft on Jewish communism.

This was bad enough, but some of the most ardent American Zionist supporters, including Eleanor Roosevelt and her son James, seemed to be playing down the Soviet threat. Jews in high government positions were even more dangerous. They seemed to be the strongest advocates of the Communist cause within the United States.[13] So too did many other Jews who were active in the Zionist cause.

Forrestal's suspicions of a Jewish-Communist connection were not completely without foundation. Despite the defection of Richard Kauder, Ben-Gurion did not know at the time that some of his closest aides were working for the Soviets, including his friend Lieutenant Colonel Israel Beer. Before 1948 Beer was head of training and operations for the Haganah. Allegedly a former member of the Communist-led International Brigades in Spain, in 1961 Beer was arrested as a Communist spy, after Israeli intelligence uncovered him as a double agent.

Another Communist agent, Robert Soblen, operated under cover of the United Nations Relief and Rehabilitation Administration (UNRRA) and helped to divert food, clothing, and transport to the Zionists' underground railway to Palestine.[14] At this time, U.S. code breakers were starting to read the secret telegrams of the Soviet consulate in New York. From 1945 on there was considerable hysteria in Washington about Soviet espionage in the United States, as dozens of Communist spies were unmasked.

With Dulles temporarily out of the government, Secretary of Defense Forrestal led the inside charge against the Zionists. In his mind, the Jews and the Communists had become almost one and the same. On November 6, 1947, a few weeks before the UN General Assembly was due to vote on the Palestine question, Forrestal

> buttonholed J. Howard McGrath, senator from Rhode Island and Democratic National chairman. Forrestal repeated his arguments that "no group in this country should be permitted to influence our policy to the point where it could endanger our national security." McGrath was not encouraging; he "replied by saying that there were two or three pivotal states which could not be carried without the support of people who were deeply interested in the Palestine question. I [Forrestal] said I would rather lose those states in a national election than run the risks which I felt might develop in our handling of the Palestine question."[15]

Forrestal was playing Russian roulette with the Democratic party's electoral prospects. As already noted, Harry Truman was acutely aware of the point McGrath was making. As early as 1945 Truman had brashly told top State Department aides that he had "hundreds of thousands" of pro-Jewish voters and virtually no "Arabs among my constituents." In 1947, however, Truman seemed to be treading softly on his support for the Jews. Forrestal wanted to go much further and have the Democrats abandon them altogether.

Leading Republicans were already making capital over the Truman administration's apparently equivocal stance on the Jewish homeland. It is an irony that Allen Dulles, on the inside of Dewey's Republican campaign, pretended to support the Jews, while his friend Forrestal worked from within the government to convince the Truman administration to oppose a Jewish homeland. Like Jack Philby, Dulles's pro-Zionist stance was only a temporary political expedient. Any defection of the Jewish vote from the Democrats could prove an unexpected boon and might even make the difference in deciding the presidential election in favor of Dewey the following November.

Forrestal was not the only one inside the Truman administration with reservations about Palestine. He had several allies, including Undersecretaries of State Dean Acheson and Robert Lovett, as well as the Middle East section head, Loy Henderson.[16] This cabal worked with others outside the government, especially the oil companies. Among the strongest opponents of Israel was Aramco, the Saudi oil giant. Aramco was more than willing to throw its support behind Forrestal's anti-Zionist line. On one occasion Brewster Jennings of Socony Vacuum bluntly pointed out that Aramco had suspended much of its Saudi operations "because of the disturbed condition in Palestine and the indications of its continuance."[17]

Forrestal, Acheson, Lovett, and the oil companies also had a powerful ally in the new secretary of state, George Marshall, who was seriously concerned that a war between Arabs and Jews might disrupt his own scheme—known as the Marshall Plan—to rebuild the wartorn economies of Western Europe and turn back the Communist menace in France and Italy. Since 80 percent of Europe's oil came from the Middle East, anything that threatened oil was a threat to the success of Marshall's plan.

Marshall's strategic concerns for his European plan meshed perfectly with the oil companies' desire to make a huge profit out of cornering European markets. Forrestal was the link man in this, while the Zionists were the obstacle. Forrestal had previously been involved with Dulles's client, John D. Rockefeller, Jr., of Standard of New Jersey, to control Europe's oil. Just after the war Forrestal had been quietly tipped off that Rockefeller believed that "Europe in the next ten years may shift from a coal to an oil economy, and therefore whoever sits on the valve of Middle East oil may control the destiny of Europe."[18]

On November 7, 1947, the day after he met with Senator McGrath, Forrestal attended a cabinet meeting where Marshall said he believed that the Middle East was "a tinder box." Forrestal jumped in and helpfully repeated his suggestion that Palestine should be made a bipartisan political issue, as "no question was more charged with danger to our security than this particular one."[19]

In order to strangle Israel at birth, Forrestal had to unite the cabinet against Truman, who knew he needed the Jewish vote if he was to have any chance of reelection. As Senator McGrath had said, the Jewish vote was small but crucial in winning at least three key states: New York, Pennsylvania, and California. Without more bipartisan support, Forrestal feared that the Jews had the president where they wanted him.

The State Department had been telling Truman that any further efforts on behalf of partition might cause a diplomatic backlash. The U.S. had already exerted considerable pressure to influence those countries that were opposed to the creation of Israel or were at best neutral. Truman ordered the State Department to keep up the pressure, and Forrestal's allies found that the president was twisting their reluctant arms more savagely than on any other question. The two men who bore the brunt were the head of the State Department's Near and Middle Eastern Affairs section, Loy Henderson, and Undersecretary of State Robert Lovett.[20]

Forrestal offered his support to the embattled State Department. This clique of secret Dulles supporters within the administration believed from the polls that Truman was a lame-duck president and would not be around after one more year. In fact, Truman's own State Department paid more attention to British views than to his. On November 8, the day after the cabinet meeting, Forrestal lunched with Henderson and heard about the views of the notoriously anti-Semitic British foreign secretary Ernest Bevin.

Bevin had made it known that he wanted a cooperative arrangement with Washington that would maintain London's important role in the Middle East. In essence, the British were proposing to share their "colony" with the United States if partition could be defeated. According to Forrestal, the British did not want to stay in Palestine by themselves nor fight either the Jews or the Arabs.[21] Especially not the Arabs. Bevin was not one of Harry Truman's favorite people, particularly after he described the president's support for Jewish immigration to Palestine as "a crude desire for votes in New York."[22]

Forrestal could not have put it better himself. He contemptuously declared that U.S. Palestine policy had been made for "squalid political purposes."[23] Forrestal had become a handy ally for the British, the leading voice in Washington to squash the Zionist dream of their own state in Palestine. By then Forrestal also was "one of the driving forces behind the rapid emphasis on covert action" by U.S. intelligence to fight the Red menace.[24] The Arabs and their oil were vastly more important to this battle than the expendable Jews.

Forrestal could not make the president see this "truth." In fact, Forrestal never realized that there was more to Truman's position on Palestine than the votes of American Jews. According to David McCullough's Pulitzer Prize–winning biography of Truman, the Palestinian issue was "a basic human problem" for the president. "When his Secretary of Defense, Forrestal, reminded him of the critical need for Saudi Arabian oil, in the event of war, Truman said he would handle the situation in the light of justice, not oil."[25] Rebuffed by the president, Forrestal was even more determined to prevent justice, even if he had to leak classified files to do it.

The UN General Assembly debate on the issue of a Jewish homeland was scheduled to commence on November 26, 1947. In a series of reports U.S. intelligence declared that Palestine was "a hotbed of unrest where the Soviets would seize any opportunity to secure advantage." The CIA repeatedly set out the grim realities, particularly the hostility of the Arab world to Western support for the Jews, the threat to Western oil production, and the mounting evidence that the Soviets were penetrating Palestine as part of a plan to take over the Middle East.[26]

On the same day that the General Assembly debate began, Forrestal received a CIA report on Palestine, which predictably emphasized these themes.[27] Finally Forrestal had the ammunition to scare Truman's supporters away from Israel. He immediately arranged to lunch that day with Democratic National chairman, J. Howard McGrath. Having been rebuffed previously by McGrath, Forrestal had attempted to soften up the senator by making him read the CIA's assessment of the Palestine question. McGrath was shaken, and at lunch he said "that he realized how serious the situation was and said he would like to come back and read more carefully the C.I.A. documents."[28]

The Democratic politician was greatly disturbed at the implications of Forrestal's information. The CIA was saying that a vote for Israel meant shutting off the United States' oil supply. On the other hand, the Jews might desert the Democratic party if Truman changed his mind now and abandoned them on the eve of the UN vote. McGrath was concerned about losing more than votes. He reminded Forrestal that the Jews gave big campaign donations to the party and that they wanted more vigorous action by the government to procure the necessary votes for partition.[29] Forrestal countered by firmly stating that the State Department did not want to take further action along these lines, as it "would add to the already serious alienation of Arabian good will."[30]

Secretary of Defense Forrestal had been cooking up schemes with the State Department behind Truman's back. Now he was trying to cut the political legs out from under the president by convincing the chairman of the Democratic party to back off on his support for Israel. It would not be easy, but it might be possible, McGrath said, to use a poll to convince Truman that, even if partition passed, the American people were not ready to go to war for the Jews. Forrestal insisted that McGrath should give the matter a lot of thought, "because it involved not merely the Arabs of the Middle East, but also might involve the whole Moslem world with its four hundred millions of people—Egypt, North Africa, India and Afghanistan."[31]

Forrestal had not underestimated the power of the Moslem world. Their leaders were about to teach the Jews a lesson in power politics. The Zionists had to face a series of test votes before the UN Ad Hoc Committee. This body, which was composed of all member states, considered a number of ancillary resolutions just a few days before the final partition recommendation was referred to the General Assembly.[32] Two subcommittee resolutions were thinly disguised attempts to block the creation of a Jewish state in Palestine by referring the whole thing off to the International Court of Justice, where it would be stalled for years.[33]

The Zionists had to stop what were patently pro-Arab resolutions. Both were defeated, the first by a vote of twenty-five to eighteen, with eleven abstentions, the second by twenty-one to twenty, with thirteen abstentions.[34] The Zionists had just barely carried the second resolution with 51 percent of the vote. This was a disaster. They would need a two-thirds majority vote to win the final vote for Israel in the General Assembly.

When the Zionists looked at the results of the test votes, they knew they were in deep trouble with the Central and South American countries, six of which had voted in favor of the Arabs.[35] Only days before the final vote, the Zionists learned that Chile, which had previously been a supporter, was now going to abstain. Worse was to come, in what was the key test vote as far as the Jews were concerned.

The only way for the UN General Assembly to even consider the partition of Palestine was for the Ad Hoc Committee to endorse it and refer the matter to the Assembly. At this stage only a simple majority of 51 percent was required. As both sides would presumably maximize their support on the question, the vote would tell the Zionists whether they had a two-thirds majority. On November 25 the Ad Hoc Committee carried the resolution by twenty-five votes to thirteen, with seventeen abstentions. Partition was referred to the General Assembly, but the vote was short of the two-thirds majority required for final passage. The handwriting was on the wall.

Several Western nations that previously had indicated support actually abstained on the November 25 vote.[36] If they did so at the final General Assembly vote, the Jews would certainly be denied their homeland. The Zionists had only three days, from Wednesday, November 26, the day of the first General Assembly debate on the partition of Palestine, to Saturday, November 29, when the final vote was taken, to obtain new votes, reverse the Western abstentions, and secure the two-thirds majority. The Zionists were losing momentum. If the final test vote held up, there would be no partition. There would be no Israel, and all because of a handful of votes.

On Thursday Truman had his delegation engineer an adjournment to ensure that the Central and South American nations changed their votes, either to vote in favor or at least to abstain.[37] The Zionists made their list, while the Arabs intensified their lobbying campaign.[38]

The American delegation wanted to help the Arabs but were told not to by the President. On the other hand, the delegation was not doing a lot to support Truman's position on the Jews. One leading American Zionist charged that the U.S. delegation had been "compelled to act with considerable restraint upon orders from certain officials in the State Department, like Under-secretary of State Robert A. Lovett."[39] Drew Pearson reported on how Forrestal's secret ally, Lovett, was pulled into line: "Few knew it, but President Truman cracked down harder on his State Department than ever before to swing the United Nations vote for the partition of Palestine. Truman called Acting Secretary, Lovett, over to the White House on Wednesday and again on Friday, warning him he would demand a full explanation if nations which usually line up with the United States failed to do so on Palestine."[40]

At this point, the Jews had little faith in Truman's ability to control his own delegation in the UN, let alone anyone else's. The Zionists needed to pick up at least four votes in three days to ensure their two-thirds majority. Only one man had that kind of influence in Latin America. Ben-Gurion decided it was time someone paid a visit to Nelson Rockefeller and showed him the file the Zionists had compiled.

In his pursuit of allies against the Zionists in the fall of 1947, Defense Secretary James Forrestal failed to realize that one of his key supporters unwillingly had defected to the Jewish cause. He did not know that one of the wealthiest and most influential oil men had become subject to Zionist blackmail in November of that year, just as the United Nations was about to vote on the future of Palestine. Forrestal thought that Nelson Rockefeller was on his side. After all, he had gotten Nelson his first government job, allegedly to build bipartisan support for Roosevelt's policies. In July 1940 Forrestal had offered Nelson Rockefeller the position of Coordinator of Inter-American Affairs, an intelligence shop, which Nelson himself had proposed should be set up, with himself, naturally, in charge.[41]

Rockefeller had discussed the position of Latin American spy chief with Harry Hopkins, one of President Roosevelt's top aides. It was hardly the kind of sales pitch that should have endeared Rockefeller to the Roosevelt administration. Rockefeller proposed that while Hitler and Churchill fought each other to death, the United States should be ready to pick up the pieces by seizing the opportunity to increase the economic influence of American businessmen. In effect, Rockefeller had proposed to Hopkins that regardless of which side won the war, the Nazis or the Allies, the country's international position had to be safeguarded by the use of "economic measures that are competitively effective against totalitarian techniques."[42]

By "totalitarian" Rockefeller meant the Soviets, not the Germans. As outlined earlier, the Rockefellers just happened to own the largest stock in Standard of New Jersey and were then in partnership with the Nazi-controlled I. G. Farben, which held the second largest share of the Rockefeller-controlled oil company, to develop synthetic gas and rubber. The sources among the former intelligence officers whom we interviewed on the Rockefellers say that the family was in complete agreement with the Dulles brothers and Forrestal on the question of preserving U.S. profits, no matter who won the war.[43]

After he accepted the job as head of the Office of Inter-American Affairs, Rockefeller told his staff, in essence, that their job was to use the war to take over Latin American markets. While Britain and France fought a bloody struggle against the Third Reich, Rockefeller's primary concern was to monopolize Latin America's raw materials and exclude the Europeans.[44] Rockefeller's definition of Europe was very interesting: He meant the British, not the Nazis. As discussed earlier in this chapter, his friend Forrestal had authorized the Rockefeller oil company, Standard of New Jersey, to ship oil to the Nazis in 1941. That was before the United States entered the war, but Pearl Harbor made no difference to Rockefeller.

All through the war, at least while Rockefeller was in charge, everything the Germans wanted in South America they got, from refueling stations to espionage bases. The British, on the other hand, had to pay in cash. Behind Rockefeller's rhetoric of taking measures in Latin America for the national defense stood a naked grab for profits. Under the cloak of his official position, Rockefeller and his cronies would take over Britain's most valuable Latin American properties. If the British resisted, he would effectively block raw materials and food supplies desperately needed for Britain's fight against Hitler. It was Rockefeller's own variant of Allen Dulles's oil blackmail.[45]

Naturally, Rockefeller's cronies were members of the Dulles-Forrestal clique. To implement his economic program to drive the British out of the lucrative Latin American markets, in each country Rockefeller set up coordinating committees composed of reactionary executives from Standard Oil, General Electric, and United Fruit, which promptly bled South America dry.[46] It was just the sort of thing that endeared Rockefeller to the State Department. In November 1944 he was asked to serve as assistant secretary of state for Latin American affairs.

Rockefeller did not exactly make South America safe for democracy. He was too busy shoring up profits to be bothered with minor details, such as convincing the Latin American governments to declare war on the Axis, let alone send troops. By February 1945 one-third of the nations on the continent had not even entered the war, while Dulles's friend, President Juan Peron of Argentina, led a bloc of decidedly pro-Fascist countries that were eager to help the architects of the Third Reich escape with their assets intact. In the end, these countries had to be ordered to declare war on Germany and Japan, under threat of exclusion from the United Nations.[47]

It was all a farce, of course. Argentina did not declare war until late April, two weeks before the German surrender. Peron quickly assured Rockefeller, with a straight face, that he was no longer a Fascist in sympathy or fact. Most of the South American dictators had made a fortune from the Nazis during the war.[48] These were the nations that were later to decide the fate of Israel in the United Nations.

Rockefeller's political and corporate strategy was to use his bloc of Fascist nations to "buy" the majority vote at the UN to favor U.S.-sponsored resolutions. It was simple arithmetic. The Latin American bloc represented nineteen votes to Europe's nine. Rockefeller made no apologies for his strong-arm tactics, insisting that unless the United States "operated with a solid group in this hemisphere, we could not do what we wanted in the world front." In June 1945 Rockefeller was invited to attend the first UN conference in San Francisco, where his job was to control the Latin American delegations.[49]

He was particularly effective at this job. The only problem was that Rockefeller was too preoccupied with representing the interests of big business, not the United States. With FDR dead, he acted as if the UN was *his* organization, bought and paid for. He could do whatever he wanted, and did, at least until he pushed President Truman beyond his limit. Roosevelt had told Stalin that Rockefeller's favorite pro-Fascist state, Argentina, would not become a UN member, but Rockefeller successfully pushed it through anyway.[50]

For Harry Truman, Rockefeller's behavior over Argentina was the last straw. On August 23, 1945, a stunned Nelson Rockefeller left the White House, telling his friends "He fired me!"[51] For the next two years Rockefeller went back to making money, something he did extremely well. His partner in moneymaking just happened to be John Foster Dulles, a trustee of the Rockefeller Foundation and a fellow conspirator in smuggling Axis money to safety.

Two years later the Jews were facing their most difficult test. The Zionist leadership contemplated their dilemma. In November 1947, with the vote for Israel agonizingly but effectively short of a two-thirds majority in the UN on the test vote, David Ben-Gurion had three days to convince the wavering Western nations or some Latin American delegations to come on board. If he didn't, then Israel might never be born. As he saw it, Ben-Gurion knew he had to try for both. He had relatively easy access to the Western delegations, but the pro-Fascists of Latin America were another thing altogether.

Ben-Gurion knew that somehow he had to convince Nelson Rockefeller to obtain the necessary votes in Latin America, just in case the Western delegations chose oil over principle. It must have seemed such a terrible shame to the Zionists. At a time when they needed him in an official U.S. government job, all Rockefeller's incredible arm-twisting power was sitting idle, too busy making money to be useful just when the Zionists needed it most.

In the 1980s we interviewed a number of British and American intelligence officials who claimed knowledge of Rockefeller's secret role in the UN vote for Israel. Some alleged that Nelson was a closet Zionist, others that he was guilt-ridden and wanted to make amends for his family's early financial support for the Third Reich industrialists. The Rockefellers, they claim, were never pro-Nazi, just pro-money, and Germany in the 1930s was where the most money was being made.[52]

Those Israelis who were present for the foundation of the Jewish state present a somewhat harsher but perhaps more credible version. Nelson, they insist, had crossed several lines and had made a profit on both sides of the war. He had been under intense scrutiny by British intelligence in both South America and New York. Our British sources confirm that Rockefeller's name arose in several incriminating wiretaps and add that it is entirely possible that the Zionists were given transcripts by sympathetic British officials.[53]

One Israeli intelligence officer admits the British connection, but notes, with some cynicism, that the British passed the information on to the Zionists with the suggestion that it be leaked to the American press.[54] Several of our British sources felt that Rockefeller deserved more than a little payback for his anti-British stance in South America.[55]

According to the sources in the American intelligence community we interviewed for this chapter, the British wiretaps were incomplete and irrelevant. Ben-Gurion had already accumulated more than enough ammunition against Rockefeller and had decided that he could not take any chances with an indirect approach. There was no time for a British-style media campaign. The Latin American votes were needed in three days. Our American sources insist that the Jews simply laid their cards on the table for Nelson to read and "blackmailed the hell out of him."[56]

One of our American sources hinted that both Rockefeller's headquarters and the offices of the Zionist delegation to the United Nations may have been wiretapped.[57] As we shall see in Chapter 8, this was not an uncommon occurrence. Another possibility, which we have not been able to confirm, is that subsequent to the Zionists' visit, Rockefeller made a flurry of international telephone calls during which an alarmed Rockefeller related the threat to expose his complicity with Fascist businessmen, foolishly discussed the extent of his potential exposure, and unknowingly handed the Zionist wiretappers all the confirmation they needed. Most of our sources, however, insist that what really happened was that a group of pro-Zionist Jews in the U.S. Department of Treasury passed purloined copies of Roosevelt's secret Safehaven intercepts to Ben-Gurion's agents.[58]

It seems likely from its sheer quantity that the information the Zionists collected on Nelson Rockefeller had to have come from a variety of sources, including wiretaps. These allegations are credible for one reason: They are consistent with the known behavior of Nelson Rockefeller and some members of his family before, during, and after World War II.

In 1936 the Rockefellers entered into partnership with Dulles's Nazi front, the Schröder Bank of New York, which, as we have already seen, was the key institution in the Fascist economic "miracle." In 1939 the Rockefeller-controlled Chase National Bank secured $25 million for Nazi Germany and supplied Berlin with information on ten thousand Nazi sympathizers in the United States. Except for a few months' interruption, the Rockefeller-owned Standard of New Jersey company shipped oil to the Nazis through Spain all throughout the war. The roster of the Rockefellers' known pro-Nazi behavior is horrendous.[59] As previously outlined, in 1942 Senator Harry Truman described the behavior of the Rockefellers' company as treasonous.

Under the U.S. Constitution, giving aid and comfort to the enemy in time of war is treason. On September 22, 1947, Federal Judge Charles Clark issued the following opinion in a civil case: "Standard Oil can be considered an enemy national in view of its relationships with I. G. Farben after the United States and Germany had become active enemies."[60] The date is significant. Two months later, just as Nelson Rockefeller was hoping that the damage could be limited to a few corporate scapegoats, the Jews arrived in his office with proof that he personally had committed treason against the United States of America. It was the perfect moment for blackmail.

Today, Nelson Rockefeller is remembered as the Republican millionaire who became vice president of the United States. But in 1947 he was still under a cloud of suspicion for his activities in Latin America. While Rockefeller was supposed to keep Nazi influence out of the region, Nazi agents were flooding South America. In fact, he had knowingly allowed Standard Oil to continue leasing its Venezuela headquarters from a known Nazi. Despite the fact that Rockefeller sat on the Proclaimed List Committee and was in charge of Latin American intelligence, he turned a blind eye to Standard's shipments of South American oil to Hitler.[61]

Our sources among the "old spies" say that there was a lot more in the classified files that never reached the public.[62] After Roosevelt died, Rockefeller must have breathed a sigh of relief. The investigations were swept under the table. By 1947 the Rockefeller publicity machine had things under control, notwithstanding what Judge Clark might have said. Then the Jews arrived with their dossier. They had his Swiss bank records with the Nazis, his signature on correspondence setting up the German cartel in South America, transcripts of his conversations with Nazi agents during the war, and, finally, evidence of his complicity in helping Allen Dulles smuggle Nazi war criminals and money from the Vatican to Argentina.[63]

The account of what happened inside Rockefeller's office comes from a very aged Israeli source. During the mid-1980s he flew to the United States to meet one of the authors. After several hours' discussion about Nazi war criminals, the conversation was steered to the topic of Zionist blackmail of Nelson Rockefeller. The Israeli was surprised but eventually admitted that he had been personally acquainted with Reuven Shiloah, Ben-Gurion's intelligence chief, who had masterminded the operation. Here is his account of what happened when the Zionists confronted Nelson Rockefeller.[64]

Rockefeller skimmed through the dossier and coolly began to bargain. In return for the votes of the Latin American bloc, he wanted guarantees that the Jews would keep their mouths shut about the flow of Nazi money and fugitives to South America. There would be no Zionist Nazi-hunting unit, no testimony at Nuremberg about the bankers or anyone else, not a single leak to the press about where the Nazis were living in South America or which Nazis were working for Dulles. The subject of Nazis was closed. Period. Forever.

The choice was simple, Rockefeller explained. "You can have vengeance, or you can have a country, but you cannot have both." His choice of the word "vengeance," not justice, left the Jews in no doubt where he stood. But the General Assembly would vote in only a few days. It was the last, best chance the Jews would ever have. If the opportunity slipped by, they would never get another.

According to our Israeli informant, whose account was corroborated by several other sources in the intelligence community whom we interviewed subsequently, Ben-Gurion's representative was heartsick. Counterblackmail had not been in the game plan. He made a telephone call to try to obtain guidance. It took several hours before the reply came back: "Yes." There really was no choice but to give Rockefeller whatever he wanted. On behalf of the still-unborn state of Israel, the promise was formally given to let the Nazis go free. The men who murdered the Jews of Europe were effectively given amnesty, except for the unlucky few who had already been punished.[65]

But the promise was conditional on Rockefeller delivering the votes. "Don't worry," he assured them, "every country in Latin America will either vote in favor of Israel or abstain."[66] Rockefeller said he would deliver, and he did. In three days he called every dictator, *caudillo,* and businessman he had in his hip pocket and told them the facts of life. As Western intelligence officers confirmed, the results were immediate and dramatic.[67]

Brazil and Haiti completely switched from a "no" on Wednesday, November 26, to a "yes" in the final UN vote on Saturday, November 29. Nicaragua, Bolivia, and Ecuador switched from abstaining to suddenly voting in favor of Israel. Argentina, Colombia, and El Salvador had voted against Israel on Wednesday but abstained from voting on Saturday. It was a remarkable *volte face,* and not just because of those who changed to vote in favor. Those anti-Zionist nations that switched from a "no" vote to abstain significantly contributed to the final successful outcome. Under the UN rules, abstentions were not counted in the calculations for determining the two-thirds majority; thus the number of votes the Zionists needed to obtain the necessary majority was reduced by however many countries abstained from voting.

To the amazement of the Arab world, on November 29, 1947, the UN General Assembly adopted a resolution recommending the partition of Palestine by thirty-three votes to thirteen against, with ten abstentions, a majority of almost 72 percent. Clearly, there was a significant turnaround in the voting blocs. Between the Ad Hoc Committee's reference of partition to the General Assembly and the final vote—only three days—eight countries had been added to the count in favor, while the number of countries voting against remained at thirteen, and the abstentions fell by eight. Although France and New Zealand switched from abstention to support, it appears that most of the extra votes came from Latin America. Of the Central and South American countries, Bolivia, Brazil, Costa Rica, the Dominican Republic, Ecuador, Guatemala (which was consistently pro-Zionist), Haiti (which had hitherto been opposed), Nicaragua, Panama, Paraguay, Peru, Uruguay, and Venezuela all voted in favor. Argentina, Chile, Colombia, El Salvador, Honduras, and Mexico abstained. The Caribbean nation of Cuba was the only "no" vote in the Western Hemisphere. Every single member of Rockefeller's Latin American bloc voted for Israel or abstained. London was bitter at its ally's actions but realized that by delaying the vote until Saturday, "the United States [had gained] time to bring certain Latin-American republics into line with its own views."[68] Our sources agree that it could not have been accomplished without Nelson Rockefeller's help.[69]

Still, the price for the margin of safety was steep. In effect, the extra votes for passage in the UN were bought with the blood of 6 million Jewish victims of the Holocaust. Ben-Gurion kept his part of the bargain. Rosters of fugitive Nazis were quietly buried in the Israeli intelligence archives. Plans for presenting evidence at ongoing war crimes trials were shelved. For the next twelve years while Ben-Gurion was either prime minister or defense minister, Israel never published a wanted list, never extradited a Nazi, never held a war crimes trial.[70]

Not until 1960 did Israeli intelligence obtain permission to break the agreement for one very special case. Its agents kidnapped Adolf Eichmann in Argentina, where he had taken refuge along with Ante Pavelić, who had worked as Peron's "security adviser." The West German prosecutor for Nazi war crimes has speculated that out of at least 150,000 war criminals, only one-third were ever apprehended, and even fewer punished.[71] Ben-Gurion had his country, but at what a price? He kept his silence because it was the only leverage he had. It was a particularly bitter pill for the Zionists to swallow, as it turned out they may not have needed the extra South American votes after all, as the Western nations which had abstained in the earlier vote changed their stand to vote in favor.

The Zionists' success at the UN General Assembly did not end the danger to their cause. There was no guarantee that the Jews would not be double-crossed. They knew that Forrestal, the Dulleses, and their other enemies would not give up. And they could not blackmail them all.[72]

The oil men's counteroffensive began almost immediately. The vote for partition was a setback for the anti-Israel forces but not a complete defeat. There was still time to ensure that the Jewish state was stillborn. At a cabinet lunch on December 1, Undersecretary of State Robert Lovett complained that he had never had so much pressure applied to him in his public life to compare with the pro-Zionist lobby effort in the days just before the partition vote. His friend James Forrestal sympathized. The pair were not about to give up.

The Jews could hardly have failed to notice that a vigorous campaign to reverse the partition vote, only two days old, was already under way or that Forrestal was at the center of it. There was a leak from Forrestal's Defense Department the same day as the cabinet meeting in Washington. Someone told the Associated Press "that United States military observers were opposed to partition, on the grounds that it might put Russian troops in the Mediterranean within minutes of flying time from the Suez Canal and American Middle East oil concessions."[73]

The implication was that either the Jews would provide the Communists with a Middle Eastern base or that the Soviets would send troops to help implement partition. The leak was the start of a new offensive to try to divide the consensus that the Zionists had built on both sides of American politics about the need for a Jewish homeland. Forrestal thought that such tactics might create a different sort of consensus—a bipartisan effort to stop the Zionists. As Truman had resisted Forrestal's urgings to seek an understanding with the Republicans, the defense secretary unilaterally decided to try to remove U.S. Palestine policy from party politics. He took up the issue with Governor Thomas Dewey of New York in mid-December, but received no great encouragement.[74]

As the weeks progressed, however, the Dulles-Forrestal team began to realize that the deal was not yet secure for the Zionists. The debate had just moved from the UN General Assembly to the Security Council, where increasingly it appeared that Moscow was exploiting the situation to promote the spread of communism. The anti-Zionist lobby in the United States watched with growing apprehension as the Soviets were praised by the Zionist leadership for their crucial role in getting the vote through the General Assembly.[75]

To Forrestal and his supporters, ignorant of the blackmail the Zionists had used against Stalin, it appeared that the Jews and the Communists were working hand-in-glove against U.S. interests. The Communists were just then waging vigorous campaigns in Czechoslovakia, Italy, and France, and Moscow was supporting revolutions in China, Greece, Korea, and Iran. The Soviets' worldwide revolutionary campaign seemed to confirm that their Palestine policies were aimed at building a Red-Jewish state right next to the West's most important oil fields. Both the British and American secret services reported that this was, indeed, the Communists' aim.[76]

Now even the president was worried about the Soviet-Palestine link. When the State Department had warned Truman earlier that Israel would be a Communist puppet state within three years, he had rejected its advice as scaremongering, but now there seemed to be something in it, after all. Truman finally authorized Forrestal officially to sound out the Republicans about adopting a bipartisan policy on the Middle East, thus removing it as a potentially divisive domestic political issue in a presidential election year.[77]

Encouraged, Forrestal went to work on his opponents within the Democratic party, and by the third week of January 1948, he had put together a strategy with his friend Robert Lovett at the State Department.

If enough key Democrats could be convinced that the partition of Palestine was not going to work without a major U.S. military commitment, then the president might still be forced to accept a policy reversal and the partition plan could be overturned by the UN Security Council.[78]

Armed with the crucial support of Lovett, on January 29 Forrestal met with Dean Rusk, Loy Henderson, and other senior State Department officers. Rusk handled the administration's policy at the UN, while Henderson, it will be recalled, was in charge of Middle Eastern affairs, including Palestine policy. Lovett's staff had prepared a paper that concluded that the partition plan would not work, and after some discussion Forrestal had no trouble in obtaining Henderson's agreement to the proposition that the whole matter of U.S. policy should be reexamined yet again. The pendulum was swinging, slightly but significantly, in favor of the Forrestal forces.

A few days later the pro-Zionist forces in the Democratic party visited Forrestal. Franklin D. Roosevelt, Jr., cautioned that only the Republicans could gain political advantage out of a bipartisan policy on Palestine, as American Jews would feel betrayed by the Democrats if they reversed U.S. support for partition. Forrestal's blunt reply reflects the degree to which things seemed to be going his way: Although "our failure to go along with the Zionists might lose the states of New York, Pennsylvania and California . . . it was about time that somebody should pay some consideration to whether we might not lose the United States."[79] Once again Forrestal was playing Russian roulette with the Democratic party's electoral prospects.

With Lovett, Rusk, and Henderson on board, the secretary of defense believed he now had the most important voices within the State Department behind him, and he began to pressure Secretary of State George Marshall. At a National Security Council meeting on February 12, Marshall brought up the State Department's working paper on Palestine, which outlined three alternative policies. The first was complete abandonment of U.S. support for the partition plan. The second was vigorous support for the Security Council to implement it, and the third was to refer the matter back to the UN General Assembly in an effort to alter the details. Marshall said he favored none of these views, at least not yet.

On the other hand, "possibly he was coming round to the view of Robert Lovett, and others that partition was not workable and that the United States was not bound to support it." Forrestal's strategy was paying dividends. Now only the president remained as the major obstacle. Even he seemed to be wavering under the constant pressure. On February 17 Truman tentatively approved "a State Department proposal to invoke the conciliatory powers of the Security Council."[80] However, the president insisted that he be shown the final copy before any speeches were presented formally.

Suddenly it seemed that the Forrestal forces were everywhere in the ascendancy. On February 24 the Security Council met to consider the first report of the UN Palestine Commission. It was not promising for the Zionists. Prevailing conditions were said to be such that the partition plan could be implemented properly only if the country were pacified by non-Palestinian military forces.

The U.S. ambassador at the Security Council, Warren Austin, made it clear that Washington did not believe that such intervention was permissible under the UN charter. He proposed to form a committee of the council's "Big Five" (the United States, the Soviet Union, Britain, France, and China)—to reconsider the whole matter. The British observed that "security difficulties" had prevented them from carrying out the wishes of the Palestine Commission in several areas, notably the opening of Tel Aviv as a port for Jewish immigrants and the formation of a militia of the Jewish state.[81] In effect, the British said that it was the Jews' fault they were unable to defend themselves.

Meanwhile, as recognition of Forrestal's maneuvers spread, Zionist-organized opposition to the alarming direction of U.S. policy had gathered apace. Former Vice President Henry Wallace, then a "Progressive" candidate for president, attacked Truman's apparent policy switch on the partition question. Organized labor joined in, together with prominent Democrat leaders, such as FDR's former undersecretary of state, Sumner Welles. One leading American Jew, Rabbi Stephen Wise, even proposed the involvement of Soviet troops, while others suggested that Forrestal and his allies represented the oil companies and Wall Street, which were said to be the real forces behind the "Red scare" campaign.[82]

The Jewish state had become inextricably intertwined with the Cold War. A few weeks later, on March 11, the Communists obligingly provided three examples of Forrestal's Jewish-Communist conspiracy. The first was a Communist rally in New York. As militant young Communists finished singing "Solidarity Forever" the speeches began. A statement was read to the crowd on behalf of Henry Wallace, which declared that the "Truman Administration is selling out the Jewish people for oil." The same day the Soviet delegate to the UN said exactly the same thing, and in Prague the Communists launched their coup. U.S. General Lucius Clay immediately sent a telegram from Berlin to the U.S. Army's director of intelligence that "warned that tension was rising and that war might be imminent."[83]

The Cold War was threatening to turn hot, and the president had to view Palestine in the light of wider international events. On March 17

Truman went to Congress and "asked for broad powers, which just fell short of mobilization, and prompt enactment of the Marshall Plan programme for European economic aid. In these circumstances, joining with the U.S.S.R. to promote partition of Palestine became an even less acceptable policy."[84] The president was caught between his commitments to the Jews and the hypocrisy of his political opponents in an election year.

Dewey's Jewish front man for the Republican party, Rabbi Abba Silver, launched a particularly violent diatribe, denouncing Truman for going soft on support for the creation of Israel. At the same time the president was taking a lot of heat from the right wing for seeming to support the Jewish terrorists in Palestine. "Silver and terror," muttered Truman, had become the chief obstacles to a moderate policy on Palestine.[85]

Dewey's cynicism, to say nothing of his presidential ambitions, had reached a new height. Forrestal had been pursuing his quiet campaign to bring Dewey round to a bipartisan policy on Palestine through their mutual friend, Winthrop Aldrich, head of the Chase Manhattan Bank. Dewey had sent a message back to Forrestal, telling him that he now agreed with his campaign on Palestine and was "in entire sympathy and would cooperate in any way for the best interests of the country." Dewey suggested that future discussions be held with John Foster Dulles, whose brother, Allen, was then manipulating Rabbi Silver's assault on Truman.[86]

While Truman was contemplating weighing his commitment to the Jews, with its likely impact on his reelection prospects, against the dangers of the Red menace, Forrestal was dealing with the campaign advisers of his major Republican opponent. Forrestal's tactics were having some considerable effect on the president.

Even before Silver's diatribes, Truman had been "very, very bitter against Zionist leaders for unbecoming conduct and unusual discourtesies," and had refused all requests to meet with the elderly Zionist leader Chaim Weizmann. On March 18 the president relented and had a brief, "off the record" discussion with Weizmann.[87] It was an emotional meeting. Each man spoke what was in his heart. At the end of their talk, the president gave Weizmann his solemn promise that the Jews would have a nation. The pendulum had swung back toward the Jews and away from the Forrestal-led forces.

What Truman did not know was that Forrestal's allies at the State Department had already put in place what amounted to their own *fait accompli.* Despite the president's explicit orders that he see all speeches to the UN in advance, on March 19 Ambassador Warren Austin defied the president and announced to the world that partition was a dead letter. The very next day after Truman's interview with Weizmann, Austin told the Security Council that Washington had a new position: Partition could not be achieved by peaceful means; the General Assembly should be called into special session to establish a temporary trusteeship in Palestine; and efforts to implement partition should be suspended.[88]

It is an indication of the State Department's disdain for the "lame-duck" president that Truman did not find out that a major change in the American position had occurred until he glanced at the morning newspapers on Saturday, March 20. Furious, Truman wrote on his calendar:

> This morning I find that the State Dept. has reversed my Palestine policy. [Truman wrote in a fury on his calendar.] The first I know about it is what I see in the papers! Isn't that hell? I'm now in the position of a liar and double-crosser. I never felt so in my life.
>
> There are people on the 3rd and 4th levels of the State Dept. who have always wanted to cut my throat. They are succeeding in doing it.[89]

The Zionists immediately began a counterattack against the Austin policy, focusing their anger on Truman for his perceived betrayal. One indication came in the strongly pro-Jewish city of New York, where a revolt suddenly erupted in the Democratic party against Truman's nomination as presidential candidate. Pro-Truman labor leaders denounced the move for a trusteeship. So did Governor Dewey, whose commitment to Forrestal regarding a bipartisan, anti-Zionist position seemed forgotten as he saw the opportunity to attack his Democratic opponent and perhaps gain some previously solid Democratic votes among the Jewish electors.

A number of the "old spies" we talked to about the Dewey-Forrestal-Dulles alliance say that Dewey actually was coordinating his political strategy with Forrestal, through the Dulles brothers, to undermine the president.[90] There certainly is corroborating evidence that Forrestal secretly had gone over to the Republican side by early 1948. By then Forrestal had "little doubt . . . that Truman's political future could be measured in months," and as will be seen in following chapters, his secret deals with the president's Republican opponents had not escaped Truman's notice.[91] In fact, they cost Forrestal his job, when Dewey was unexpectedly defeated.

Nonetheless, on March 19, 1948, when Austin made his "trusteeship" speech to the Security Council, Forrestal seemed to have won his long campaign against the Zionists. The imminent Soviet threat, combined with Middle Eastern oil, ultimately had carried the day in Washington. Ben-Gurion was not about to let Forrestal's obsession with U.S. oil interests defeat his own determination to create a Jewish homeland in Palestine. He had a few more aces up his sleeve in his battle with the Forrestal faction.

The first step was to embarrass the president into countering the

Dewey-Dulles-Forrestal political alliance. After the Austin debacle Ben-Gurion no longer believed in Truman's moral commitment and feared that the president was vulnerable. Truman was susceptible to pressure only during the election year of 1948. After that the Jews would have no leverage for another four years, by which time it would be far too late. The fate of Israel would be decided in the next twelve months. Either the Jews would have a free nation of their own, or be ruled by a "trustee" amenable to the Arabs and the oil interests. The Zionists knew that the real purpose of the U.S. policy maneuver on the partition of Palestine was to delay the question until after the November ballot, when the American public's strongly pro-Zionist sentiment would no longer have such a potent political significance. Although the recent horrific slaughter of the Nazi Holocaust meant little to Forrestal and his supporters, it still had a considerable impact on many ordinary Americans.[92]

The Zionists' next step in the counterattack was to step up the pace of events in Palestine by beginning to forge the State of Israel. They declared a provisional Jewish government in Palestine and wound up the Jewish Agency, which handed over its powers and functions to the new administration. Naturally, this created an Arab backlash, and a new round of fighting was soon under way in Palestine.

The next phase of the Jews' counterattack was to pressure the Soviets to launch a diplomatic offensive. The Soviet reaction to Washington's new policy was certainly very strong. On the one hand, Stalin may have been determined to prove himself in the revolutionary forefront by striking "a great blow" against the "imperialist foe." On the other hand, it is not unreasonable to suspect that Ben-Gurion might have given the anti-Semites in the Kremlin a gentle reminder of his powerful blackmail concerning the Max network.[93]

Whatever the reason, at the end of March 1948 the Communists took a strong stand against the Forrestal-Lovett-Austin plan at the UN Security Council. The Soviet delegate forcefully insisted that the General Assembly partition plan was equitable to everyone except the oil interests:

> Full responsibility for wrecking the decision . . . lay with the United States, which, in the opinion of most people, was not so much interested in a just settlement of the question of the future of Palestine and the relations between Arabs and Jews, as in its own oil interests and strategic position in the Near East. The U.S.S.R. opposed the calling of a special session, and also considered it would be wrong for the Security Council to instruct the Palestine Commission to suspend its work, which was directed towards implementing the decision on partition.[94]

Truman now found himself squeezed on several sides. In Palestine, events were moving rapidly and threatening to get out of control. The escalating hostilities between Arabs and Jews were creating a political backlash against the Democrats. In the diplomatic arena, Washington was being outflanked by its archrival, the Soviet Union, which now was seen as the leading force on the side of the Jews. Some feared that if the Americans did nothing, the Communists would become the Jews' major ally and gain a foothold in the Middle East.

On April 4 a meeting of top U.S. advisers was held at which Forrestal's ally, Dean Rusk, director of the State Department's Office of Special Political Affairs, summed up the dilemma: "If we did nothing, it was likely that the Russian could and would take definite steps toward gaining control in Palestine through the infiltration of specially trained immigrants, or by otherwise capitalizing on the widespread, violent civil war that would be likely to break out."[95]

Forrestal had created a self-fulfilling prophecy of a Jewish-Soviet alliance, but suddenly the tables had shifted. The Zionists were using the Soviet threat to their own advantage. The greater the threat of a Soviet-backed war in Palestine, the closer to realization came Forrestal's Communist menace. But the unintended result was an increase in the demand for President Truman to find an American response.

President Truman was already so angry with the State Department that it did not take long for the various pressures to have an effect. In part, it was a matter of wounded pride. He would not put up with State's public sabotage of his foreign policy any more. The first strike was not long in coming. At the end of April 1948 he ordered that Forrestal's ally, Loy Henderson, be removed from his responsibilities for Palestinian affairs in the State Department and that the strongly pro-Zionist official, J. H. Hilldring, should replace him. The president was relentlessly winding back all the work that Forrestal had done at the State Department.

Next came the secretary of state, George Marshall. Truman waited until almost the last moment to spring the news. "The meeting in the President's office on the afternoon of May 12 began at four o'clock, just two days and two hours before the British mandate in Palestine was to expire."[96] Truman had his counsel Clark Clifford break the news. The president was considering the immediate recognition of the State of Israel: " 'As I talked,' remembered Clifford, 'I noticed the thunder clouds gathering—Marshall's face getting redder and redder' . . . Marshall, looking directly at Truman, [said] if the President were to follow Clifford's advice, and if in the elections in November, he Marshall were to vote, he would vote against the President."[97] It was as close to an attempted palace coup as Truman would ever face. He could remove the bureaucrats in the State Department and replace them with his own men, but Secretary Marshall was one of the most popular and respected figures in the United States, with an independent political base. Truman was down to 36 percent in the polls. If Marshall went against him publicly, he would likely lose the election in November. Truman said he would think it over and let Marshall know his decision.

On May 13, 1948, the day before the British mandate expired, the political potency of the issue was demonstrated at a mass rally at Madison Square Garden in New York. Three of New York's congressmen called for immediate recognition of the new Jewish state as soon as it was declared and denounced the influence of the oil companies and their political allies.[98]

That same day, May 13, Ben-Gurion proclaimed that Israel would come into being at midnight—6:00 P.M. Eastern time—on the following day. Truman had less than twenty-four hours to decide whether to recognize Israel or face Marshall's wrath. Would he go with James Forrestal's version of the Soviet threat? Or would he take the gamble that Israel would become an ally of the West against the Soviets?

Forrestal and his friends at the State Department did not know it, but Truman was about to show them that he was the "son of a bitch" in charge of the foreign policy of the United States. He was still smarting with embarrassment from being made to look like a liar after his promise to Weizmann, so this time the president waited until the last moment to pull a fait accompli of his own.

Marshall was quick to sense that Harry Truman was about to drop the diplomatic bombshell in a few hours.[99] He called the White House to recant his previous threat and now decided that he would not, after all, oppose the president in public. Not if he wanted to keep his job, he wouldn't. Truman waited until the very last minute to tell Austin at the UN about *his* change of policy. No matter what anybody else thought, the president had decided that the Jews were going to have their own country.

That evening, at midnight, the Zionists declared the State of Israel had come into existence, and a few minutes later, at 6:11 P.M. Washington time, the White House extended de facto recognition. The U.S. diplomats at the United Nations were virtually speechless, especially as they had received no warning of Truman's move. "Ambassador Austin, the only one of the delegation who had been notified in advance and only at the last moment, was so upset he went home without telling any of the others."[100]

At the State Department, meanwhile, Marshall had dispatched his head of UN affairs, Dean Rusk, by plane to New York to keep the whole delegation from resigning. There was also a serious eruption at the oil companies. Forrestal's friends at Aramco were furious and began a frenetic lobbying campaign. After "consultation with Arab leaders, James Terry

Duce of Aramco along with other oil leaders recommended to the departments of State and Defense that the United States repudiate its stand."[101]

To their chagrin, the oil men had played their cards too late. Truman was not about to change his mind and allow the Republicans to exploit the Jewish vote in November, especially after Dewey's sanctimonious and hypocritical lectures about his supposed failure to stand up for the Jews. Truman would not be known as the president who sold the Jews out for oil.

The Forrestal-led Dulles forces were routed again. The Zionists had won the second round in the diplomatic fight, but the war was not over. Ben-Gurion's victory against the pirates of Wall Street would be complete unless the Jews could be beaten on the battlefield. It was one thing to fight Forrestal, Dulles, and the oil companies in the UN; it was another to fight the well-funded Arab armies in the Middle East.

Here Forrestal thought that he could not possibly lose. Militarily it looked as if Ben-Gurion did not have more than a handful of soldiers, let alone modern weapons. With an effective fighting force of less than 20,000 lightly armed men to oppose the Arab armies ranged across five fronts and armed with modern British weapons, Forrestal and his friends were confidently predicting a rout. The Arabs, many of whom had sided openly with the Nazis during the war, declared that as soon as the British pulled out, they would drive the Jews into the sea.

The Jews knew they had problems and had been facing them for some time. There was a lot more to the Zionists' intelligence operations in Europe than illegal immigration. The Jews knew that their homeland could not come into existence by political means alone. They desperately needed guns. Over the last few years they had procured a great deal of weapons, ammunition, and equipment from the West, some illegally, some by subterfuge, and quite a lot from their sympathizers in Western military and intelligence services.

The Arabs had received far more, and in the wake of the UN vote in November, several Western nations, especially Britain, had stepped up their deliveries. Even some countries that had supported the partition plan were arming the Arabs. Ben-Gurion's colleagues, such as Golda Meir, the head of the Jewish Agency's Political Department, worked hard to redress the imbalance and procure weapons from Jewish networks in the United States. Contrary to conventional wisdom, however, the result of her American arms-for-Israel campaign was almost nil.

The surveillance of U.S. intelligence seemed so all-encompassing, the countermeasures so effective, that only a trickle of weapons actually reached the Jewish fighters in Palestine. Somehow the FBI seemed to be listening to every secret conversation of the Jews. Forrestal had one last ace up his sleeve that even Ben-Gurion did not know about. It was the ultimate dirty trick.

CHAPTER 8

SPYING ON ZION

President Clinton was surprised by Admiral Bobby Ray Inman's decision to withdraw his nomination for secretary of defense in January 1994. Inman blamed the Republican Senate leader, Robert Dole, for pursuing a partisan political campaign and the American press for instituting a McCarthy-like witch-hunt against him. Inman particularly accused *New York Times* columnist William Safire of collusion with Dole in this alleged campaign, a charge both men dismissed.

Safire speculated that there must have been another reason for Inman's withdrawal only a week before congressional hearings on his nomination. There may indeed have been a skeleton in Admiral Inman's closet, a very old skeleton that predated his tenure as director of the National Security Agency (NSA), the U.S. communications intelligence agency. According to our sources in the intelligence community, the skeleton is this: Inman's predecessors allowed the British to bug any American they wished, without warrants. Admiral Inman himself misled Congress in 1977 about this program.[1]

Several history books have recorded that American intelligence agencies have conducted wiretaps against U.S. citizens without warrants, but these allegations have concerned operations aimed mostly at the left, particularly Communists and radical black groups. Our sources say that the history books have missed the most important elements of this story of the violation of democratic rights: the systematic electronic eavesdropping employed against American Jews engaged in legitimate political activities. In this chapter we discuss the following allegations:

- During World War II the covert British wiretap program in the United States against Nazi sympathizers was extended to surveil American supporters of a Jewish state in Palestine.
- After the war this program was continued, and massively expanded, as the British gained the cooperation of FBI director J. Edgar Hoover and Secretary of Defense James Forrestal for the illegal collection of electronic intelligence on Zionist activities in the United States.
- The once highly secret Communications Intelligence arrangements between Britain and the United States have been deliberately twisted by

the intelligence agencies of both countries to allow illegal British wiretaps of American Jewish citizens using American facilities. A reciprocal arrangement exists in Britain.

- The illegal campaign against the Jews reached its height during the Reagan-Bush years in the White House, when even Jewish children in summer camp were monitored for "subversive" activities.
- Over the years this illegal arrangement has been extended past Jews, Communists, and black radicals, to reach virtually any citizen, including mainstream political candidates, no matter how harmless their activities may have been.

The "old spies" say that electronic surveillance of Jews started in 1944, when American Zionists were first wiretapped on a broad scale. The wiretaps were the product of secret wartime agreements between British and American intelligence calling for long-term cooperation to spy on each other's "subversive" citizens. Since that time the bugging of American and British Jews has never stopped. In fact, the wiretaps have been greatly expanded.

Our sources, who include a former special agent of the FBI, a former liaison to the NSA, several former NSA officials and employees, a number of former consultants to both American and British intelligence on communications security, and several former officers of the U.S. Army Security Agency, make one point very clearly: *For the last fifty years, virtually every Jewish citizen, organization, and charity in the world has been the victim of electronic surveillance by Great Britain, with the knowing and willing assistance of the intelligence services of the United States.*

This massive and systematic violation of both American and British law has continued, with only slight interruptions, for nearly half a century. As will be seen later in Chapter 12, dealing with the *Liberty* incident, electronic espionage has been the most deadly threat to Israel's existence from its very inception. It also has been the most continuous criminal violation of the Fourth Amendment to the U.S. Bill of Rights. Jews are not the only ethnic group to be wiretapped at their homes or jobs, although, as we shall see, they are the most frequent targets.

To put it bluntly, no citizen is safe anymore. Privacy is gone, search warrants are meaningless, the protections of the courts and constitutions have been overthrown entirely, without the knowledge or consent of our legislatures, presidents, or prime ministers. This ugly corner of Western history has never been fully explored before. It is, perhaps, the most shocking revelation of this book. Because of the sensitivity of this topic, we deal with it in some detail from the beginning.

Our sources' first thesis is simple. It is not American intelligence that mounted an intensive surveillance operation against Ben-Gurion's arms purchases in the United States, and cut off this promising source of weapons and equipment. It was *British* intelligence that wiretapped American Jewish citizens without warrants and leaked the information to the FBI. The truth is that the British had been eavesdropping on the United States for a very long time.[2]

The advent of British "electronic" espionage against American citizens goes back to the end of World War I. The British knew that money and guns sent by Irish-Americans were making the difference in the Republic of Ireland's war for independence against the British Empire. The British government compelled American telegraph companies to hand over all message traffic, in order that it could obtain intelligence on Irish nationalist and international Communist activities and take appropriate countermeasures.

As the heads of the Western Union and other telegraph corporations revealed to a shocked Senate in 1920, the British were reading *all* American telegrams. Apparently, even official U.S. government communications were included among the material handed over.[3] As a result of these revelations, Congress passed a law making it a crime to intercept telegraphic or diplomatic communications. There the matter rested, along with the false legend of Secretary of State Henry Stimson's edict that "gentlemen do not read each other's mail."[4]

Rested, that is, until the early years of World War II. As previously discussed, while the United States remained technically neutral, the British secret service obtained Roosevelt's permission for Sir William Stephenson to establish an illegal wiretap unit in New York to spy on Americans who were aiding the Nazis. As discussed in Chapter 3, several of our sources say that Roosevelt also was using the British wiretap team to dig up dirt on his political opponents.[5]

Without the knowledge of the State Department or the FBI, Roosevelt sent a two-man team of his top code breakers to Britain in January 1940. To the horror of the British, the Americans were Jews! One was Abe Sinkov, who had monitored South and Central American traffic. The other was Captain Leo Rosen of the Army Signal Corps.[6] The last thing British intelligence desired was to let two Jews know that British code breakers had targeted American Zionists as well as Nazi sympathizers. The empire had lost Ireland after World War I because of American supporters and were not about to lose Palestine after this one.

Just before the war broke out, the British "White Paper" had stopped Jewish immigration to Palestine, while British code breakers worked with the military to crush the Haganah's growing resistance. British intelligence was not about to let a few American Jews learn the secrets of Britain's war against the Zionists. The American mission was sent home empty-handed, except for a few nonessential bits of cryptographic intelligence.

According to one of our sources who served in England with U.S. code breakers, the situation changed dramatically in April 1943.[7] The British, then desperate for further assistance from their American ally, finally shared the Ultra secret with the Americans, after a three-year delay that "greatly hindered the work of the [American] Special Branch in both short-range and long-range planning in the European theater."[8]

Even then the British insisted that the dissemination of Ultra information be restricted to reliable Americans who received special training as liaison officers. By "reliable," they meant pro-British intelligence officers. As mentioned earlier, one of the few Americans posted to London for this training in 1943 was James Jesus Angleton, who would later head the domestic wiretap program for the CIA. In all fairness, the CIA's involvement with domestic bugging pales beside the FBI.

As mentioned in Chapter 3, J. Edgar Hoover started his own illegal wiretap shop in the 1920s and continued it until Roosevelt's assistant attorney general ordered him to stop in the late 1930s. Several sources suggested that Hoover had bugged too many congressmen and cabinet members for Roosevelt's comfort and that the president may have retaliated by permitting the British to wiretap Hoover's own office in the Justice Department.[9]

The first British bugging shop on U.S. soil actually was created by Sir William Stephenson before the U.S. entry into the war. Stephenson leaked wiretap information on pro-Nazi American businessmen to Hoover. In New York City, the wiretaps included several floors of the Rockefeller Building, selected clubs and law firms, and a score of shipping agencies. Hoover, unfortunately, refused to investigate the British leads. As he later admitted Stephenson resorted to murdering American Nazis. The FBI tried to keep Stephenson's hit team under surveillance but could never quite catch it in the act.

After the United States entered the war, J. Edgar Hoover dropped his surveillance on British agents in America, and the FBI joined in the effort to track down "subversives." The British had a newfound ally. The deeply anti-Semitic Hoover had always thought that Jews were subversives, even as early as the 1920s when he had ordered an investigation of the Irish nationalist politician Eamon de Valera on the grounds that he was a suspected Jew.[10] Through its own extensive spying on American Communists, the FBI had formed the view that far too many Jews were Red sympathizers.

The British played Hoover's paranoia like a violin. They established extensive electronic surveillance facilities in the United States during

World War II and did not want to dismantle them after the Nazis were defeated. As early as 1944, the British were wiretapping great numbers of American Jews and passing the information on to Hoover.[11]

British intelligence liaison reports are the most sacrosanct of all secret documents. However, through an incredible gaffe, one U.S. agency has released a stack of completely uncensored documents. In file after file, the FBI reported that it had received information from British intelligence on American Jews who favored an independent Jewish state in Palestine. The FBI put the Jews under surveillance and worked with the British to identify those Americans who were supporting Israel, either financially or otherwise. Here is an example from J. Edgar Hoover's secret archives:

> British Intelligence authorities have advised that the above captioned individual . . . left Palestine for the United States November 21, 1947, in contravention of the Supervision Order in force to prevent his departure. . . . [subject] has for several years been suspected of membership in Irgun Zvai Leumi, an underground Jewish terrorist group. It is believed that he is at present inactive in this organization due to ill health. British authorities reported that his address in the United States will probably be in care of Carmel Rabbinical College, 441 Garrison Boulevard, Baltimore, Maryland.[12]

Ben-Gurion did not know it, but the agents he sent to the United States were under surveillance before they even got off the boat. To her dismay, Golda Meir's arms-for-Israel campaign was a disaster. Everywhere she and her colleagues went in America, it seemed the FBI was listening.

From 1945 onward the FBI kept providing information from unnamed "confidential sources" to convince President Truman that American Jews were supporting the Zionist-Communist terrorists in Palestine and that the Soviets were behind the whole Jewish-Communist conspiracy. The FBI's liaison with British intelligence confirmed this outlook to the hilt. Hoover agreed with the British analysis. There was a worldwide Jewish-Communist conspiracy. In the last months of 1947 and throughout the next several years, the FBI uncovered a number of large stockpiles of ammunition and explosives destined for Palestine. The arms purchases had been organized by prominent American-Jewish businessmen.

At the time, buying surplus weapons was probably legal, or at least a gray area, so Hoover took his war against the Jews to the press. Shock waves resounded throughout Washington when the FBI exposed that one of Ben-Gurion's chief American agents, Haim Slavin, had procured millions of dollars' worth of U.S. arms and equipment for the paltry sum of $800,000.

The barrage of British-inspired propaganda finally convinced President Truman that he had to rethink his policy toward Israel. The information supplied by British intelligence to the FBI gave the anti-Semites in the State Department and the intelligence community the leverage they needed to use drastic means to stem the flow of weapons to the Jews.[13]

On December 5, 1947, a few days after the UN General Assembly had approved the partition plan for Palestine, the U.S. placed an "embargo on arms shipments to the Near East, and the State Department specifically forbade the issuing of passports to persons wishing to serve with armed forces not under the U.S. Government."[14] The British wiretap operations effectively stopped American Jews from providing more than token assistance to their embattled comrades in Palestine, but it was the FBI who claimed all the credit.

While the embargo covered the Arabs as well as the Jews, millions of dollars' worth of American arms had already been channeled to the Arabs before the new measures were announced. All of the Western allies followed suit in arming the Arabs. The British, who had sent the Arabs even more weapons than the Americans, now refused to join the embargo on the grounds that they had outstanding arm contracts with the Arabs that could not be terminated.[15] The British armed Iraq and Jordan to the teeth, while Hoover kept the Jews disarmed.

The Americans and British were not alone in this hypocrisy. The French also considered the Jews to be secret subversives and pumped huge stockpiles of arms into Syria and Lebanon to help the Arabs. At the same time the French, British, and Americans were sending each other the latest rumors of Jewish-Communist conspiracy to bolster their bigotry. Here is an excerpt from one of Hoover's informants inside the French embassy:

> A confidential informant, who in the past has furnished information of a reliable nature, reported that he had learned from one Andre Visson . . . that the Russians are now preparing two hundred thousand Jews sympathetic to the Russian [regime] in order to send them to Palestine. Our [FBI] informant said that Mr. Visson stated that this information had originated in the Balkans and that he believes it is attributable to English and American sources. Our informant further indicated that when an official of the French Embassy heard this information, he commented that it was very possible that the Russians were engaged in such activity and in his opinion, in view of the fact that Russia refuses even to permit children of mixed marriages to leave that country, it is evident that by letting two hundred thousand men out, Russia is branding its own acts.[16]

The diplomatic offensive hurt only one side—the Jews. But the arms embargo and visa restrictions were mild compared to J. Edgar Hoover's plans. At the FBI there was an even worse campaign under way. Along with the

Communists, American Jews were about to become the principal targets of FBI surveillance during what we now call the McCarthy era.

It did not matter to Hoover that loyal Jewish citizens had provided the FBI with considerable information throughout World War II. In fact, the Anti-Defamation League of the B'Nai Brith had been virtually the only source for rosters of Nazi sympathizers in the United States. Before Pearl Harbor, while Hoover was busy chasing "Irish Jews" and Jewish Communists, he had turned a blind eye toward American Nazi sympathizers. Having to ask the Jews for help rankled with him a bit.[17]

According to the intelligence officers we spoke to for this chapter, Hoover labeled his Jewish informants as "Premature AntiFascists" and placed them under surveillance as well.[18] According to our FBI and NSA sources, any American who voiced opposition to Hitler before December 1941 was considered suspect by J. Edgar Hoover. Such people were at least "pinko PAFs," and, at worst, "commie agents." Hoover adopted the British point of view completely. All Zionists were potential Communist terrorists. Anyone in the United States who supported Zionism or contributed money to Palestine was suspected as a Communist or a terrorist, or both. Anyone who even thought of emigrating to Palestine was most likely a Soviet agent in disguise.

It is no coincidence that this sounds like the kind of anti-Zionist propaganda that Defense Secretary James Forrestal was putting out at the time. Forrestal played a key role in continuing the wiretap link between the FBI and British intelligence, behind President Truman's back. It had to be done in secret because Truman had ordered the operation shut down on September 28, 1945, when he issued an executive order abolishing the Office of the Censor, which effectively stopped the interception of American telegraph cables.[19]

What Truman did not know was that the cables continued to be intercepted, only now they were sent to Forrestal's Army Security Agency, which continued the bugging under the code name "Operation Shamrock." Throughout 1945 and 1946 the cable companies wondered if cooperating in the interception program was legal, and their attitude threatened to expose Forrestal's operations. So Forrestal called in officials of the companies and asked them to continue their assistance because of the importance this electronic intelligence had to the wider national security.

One official apparently remembered the embarrassment caused after World War I by the congressional investigations of their operations with British intelligence and asked whether the president had authorized the intercepts. Forrestal replied in the affirmative.[20] What Forrestal neglected to say was that it was "President" Dewey he had in mind in 1947, not President Truman.

The history books record that the first approval for such electronic intercepts Harry Truman gave was not until July 1, 1948, when he signed a vague directive on Communications Intelligence, which, at any rate, required the unanimous agreement of all government agencies for decisions on targets and methods.[21] That made Truman's order useless as far as Hoover and the British were concerned. They had no intention of letting anyone know what they were doing, let alone of getting the unanimous approval of rival agencies, which were full of liberals or, worse, conservatives who believed in the Bill of Rights.

There is no record that President Truman was ever told of the manner in which Operation Shamrock was used for domestic espionage. Forrestal and Hoover found a "legal" way to subvert Truman's order to stop the intercepts. If they were found out, they would blame it on a dead president: It was Roosevelt who had requested the British to renew their domestic electronic surveillance business in 1939 and who then encouraged British and American code breakers to share facilities throughout the war.

In 1943 this resulted in the Britain-USA (Brusa) agreement to merge the Communications Intelligence (Comint) agencies of both governments. One of the little-known features of Brusa was that President Roosevelt agreed that the two governments could spy on each others' citizens, without search warrants, by establishing "listening posts" on each others' territory.[22]

After the war Hoover and Forrestal came up with a clever twist. They had the British bug American citizens on U.S. soil, and then the Americans, in turn, intercepted the conversations of British citizens on British soil. The foreign liaison shell game meant that Hoover could dispense with American court warrants as well as presidential approval. All he needed was the cooperation of the British secret service.[23]

Here was Hoover's secret: Truman had never repealed Roosevelt's decision to let the British wiretap American citizens. He had only ordered an end to American intercepts. Indeed, Truman had signed a document—probably without realizing the implications—agreeing that none of his presidential orders would change any Communications Intelligence agreement unless he made an explicit revocation.[24] Since Roosevelt had never told Truman that he had let the British set up listening posts on American soil, Truman never knew specifically to revoke the British eavesdropping agreement when the war was over.

This bit of lawyerly ledgerdemain was the work of Allen Dulles, according to our sources in the intelligence community.[25] Some evidence to support this assertion does exist. Years later, after he retired, Truman started complaining to the press that he had never meant to authorize the kind of intelligence empire that Dulles was running. Dulles visited the ex-president and explained to him the implications of the documents bearing his signature. Thereafter Truman quit talking to the press.[26]

The truth of the matter is that during the Truman administration, James Forrestal was running the Communication Intelligence operations, while he waited for Dewey, Dulles, and the Republicans to win in 1948. After the election, when the other U.S. agencies, particularly the CIA, voiced some criticism over his approach, Forrestal simply "locked the report in a safe and hoped the problem would go away." The problem did not go away, but in a few short years it did move to suburban Maryland. There, at the ultra-secure compound at Fort Meade, the National Security Agency was born on the very day Eisenhower was elected president in November 1952.[27]

According to several of the "old spies" who worked in Communications Intelligence, the NSA headquarters is also the chief British espionage base in the United States.[28] The presence of British wiretappers at the keyboards of American eavesdropping computers is a closely guarded secret, one that very few people in the intelligence community have been aware of, but it is true.

An American historian, David Kahn, first stumbled onto a corner of the British connection in 1966, while writing his book *The Codebreakers*.[29] One indication of just how sensitive this information is considered on both sides of the Atlantic is the fact that Kahn's publishers in New York and London were put under enormous pressure to censor a great deal of the book. In the main, Kahn simply revealed the existence of the liaison relationship, but when he wrote that the NSA and its British equivalent, the Government Communications Headquarters, "exchange personnel on a temporary basis," he had come too close to revealing the truth.

The U.S. government told Kahn to hide the existence of British electronic spies from the American public. Kahn eventually agreed to delete a few of the most sensitive paragraphs describing the exchange of codes, techniques, and personnel with the British government.[30] His innocuous few sentences threatened to disclose a larger truth. By the 1960s the "temporary" British personnel at Fort Meade had become a permanent fixture. The British enjoyed continued access to the greatest listening post in the world. The NSA is a giant vacuum cleaner. It sucks in every form of electronic information, from telephone calls to telegrams, across the United States. The presence of British personnel is essential for the American wiretappers to claim plausible deniability.

Here is how the game is played. The British liaison officer at Fort Meade types the target list of "suspects" into the American computer. The NSA computer sorts through its wiretaps and gives the British officer the recording of any American citizen he wants. Since it is technically a *British* target of surveillance, no *American* search warrant is necessary. The British officer then simply hands the results over to his American liaison officer.[31]

Of course, the Americans provide the same service to the British in return. All international and domestic telephone calls in Great Britain are run through the NSA's station in the British Government Communications Headquarters (GCHQ) at Menwith Hill, which allows the American liaison officer to spy on any British citizen without a warrant.[32] According to our sources, this duplicitous, reciprocal arrangement disguises the most massive, and illegal, domestic espionage apparatus in the world.[33] Not even the Soviets could touch the U.K.-U.S. intercept technology.

Through this charade, the intelligence services of each country can claim that they are not targeting their own citizens. The targeting is done by an authorized foreign agent, the intelligence liaison resident in Britain or the United States. Thus, in 1977, during an investigation by the House Government Operations Committee, Admiral Inman could claim, with a straight face, that "there are no U.S. Citizens now targeted by the NSA in the United States or abroad, none."[34] Since the targeting was done not by NSA but by employees of British GCHQ, he was telling the literal truth. Still, the congressional staff knew enough at the time to characterize Inman's statement in an unpublished report as "misleading."[35]

Whether Inman had personal knowledge of the British wiretapping may never be resolved. None of our sources claims to be present on any occasion when Admiral Inman met with the British liaison officers. It should be noted, however, that before Inman started his career with Naval Intelligence, he was assigned as an aide to London. The British connection may explain not only Inman's meteoric rise to become the youngest director of the NSA, but also why President Reagan later selected him to become William Casey's deputy at the CIA.[36]

The move surprised many who knew of Inman's reputation as a reformer and do-gooder. In fact, it was Admiral Inman who pulled the plug on the NSA's infamous "Task Force 157" while he was at CIA.[37] It is entirely possible that Inman may have been an innocent man, whose public reputation for integrity was used for window dressing. Inman's supporters in the NSA, of whom he has many, suggest that the blame for the British wiretap connection rests entirely with the FBI and that the NSA's job was only to carry out a targeting policy instituted by J. Edgar Hoover. That begs the question of whether Inman knew about the British targeting when he gave his misleading statement to Congress.

Whether Inman had personal knowledge of the origins or extent of British domestic espionage or not, the "old spies," several of whom served at Fort Meade, say that his denial of domestic targeting by the NSA is all "semantic bullshit." It is well known, even among low-ranking NSA employees, that the foreign liaison officers exchange all the targeting information anyway, including the names on the British target lists. Admiral Inman did not provide that information to Congress, although it was clearly relevant to its inquiries.[38]

According to a former special agent of the FBI, the you-spy-on-mine, I'll-spy-on-yours deal has been extended to the other Western partners, particularly Canada and Australia. The British, with the help of sophisticated NSA computers, can bug just about anyone anywhere. The electronic search for subversives continues, particularly in the United States.[39] The NSA conceded precisely that point when the U.S. Justice Department investigated its wiretapping of American protesters during the Vietnam War. The NSA assured the Justice Department that the information was acquired only *incidentally* as part of a British GCHQ collection program.[40] The "incidental" British exception has become the rule.

As discussed later in this chapter, illegal electronic surveillance, particularly against American Jews, continued past the McCarthy era, all through the Cold War, and past the collapse of the Soviet Union.[41] In modern times, commercial interests in the Middle East rather than security considerations have been the driving force behind the domestic bugging.

Where oil is concerned, the British and American wiretappers use their anti-Jewish intelligence as an under-the-table bargaining chip to appease the Arabs. Publicly, our nations are allied with Israel. Privately, we give secret intelligence to Israel's enemies in time of war. As we discuss in Chapter 12, on the *Liberty* incident, Congress does not have a clue how the British-American wiretap war works.

For that matter, U.S. supervision of American wiretapping has been minimal. During the 1975 Senate (Church Committee) investigations, the NSA was forced to concede that "there is not any statute that prohibits . . . interception of domestic communications." In short, the wiretappers were outside the reach of any existing law. Technology had outstripped the legal protections of privacy. While insisting that its efforts were mainly directed at overseas communications, the NSA also admitted that it was "technically possible" to monitor domestic conversations within the United States, "if some person with malintent desired to do so."[42] Some person like J. Edgar Hoover, for example.

Hoover was one of the biggest customers of wiretap information from its inception. In fact, the FBI made no bones about its right to listen in to domestic conversations without a warrant. It wasn't until a 1975 court case that the FBI was finally told that they had no legal right to wiretap individuals or organizations without a warrant, unless there was a proven "agency relationship" with a foreign power. In fact, until the stricter 1975 standards, the FBI could wiretap or place surveillance on any Jew who gave money to any Jewish organization that supported Israel. Here is an example of the type of innocuous information that was forwarded to the FBI as a result of their obsessive surveillance of American Jews:

> EMMA LAZARUS FOUNDATION OF JEWISH WOMENS CLUBS AMONG LARGER DONORS CONTRIBUTING $500 DURING A FUND RAISING DINNER HELD BY THE EMERGENCY CIVIL LIBERTIES COMMITTEE . . . [ON] DEC 15 1962 AT THE AMERICANA HOTEL NYC IN CELEBRATION OF THE 171ST ANNIVERSARY OF THE BILL OF RIGHTS.[43]

Apparently, Jews who celebrated the Bill of Rights were considered potential, if not actual, subversives. That remains FBI policy to this day. The FBI refused to accept the restrictions from an adverse 1975 court ruling and leaked its view to the media in a 1977 memo. The FBI still defended its right to spy on persons who "might" be supporters of a foreign power, or even anyone in the country who "might" be influenced by a foreign power.[44]

In light of the trivial intelligence haul from most of the surveillance, it was little wonder that over the years, Hoover had gone to great lengths to keep his surveillance of American Jews a secret, particularly from the Kennedy administration. Attorney General Bobby Kennedy made almost no effort to hide his desire to force Hoover out, and rumors spread that a Jew might actually step into his august shoes. Hoover and many in the upper echelons of the Bureau were absolutely outraged, and before long an ultimately successful campaign was under way to save the master wiretapper of U.S. intelligence.[45]

The electronic surveillance of Jews picked up during the Nixon administration but quieted down a bit after Watergate. In 1978 Congress finally passed the Foreign Intelligence Surveillance (FIS) Act, a feeble attempt to stamp out some of the worst excesses of domestic espionage. In another bit of lawyerly legerdemain, the FIS act was restricted *only to targeting by American agencies,* leaving the British liaison officer with a major loophole. The restrictive language added to the FIS act left unchanged the arrangement under which the British wiretapped American suspects and then passed on the information to the NSA. Inman, it should be noted, was not in the NSA during 1975–76 when the language of the British loophole was contrived, although he was its director in 1978 when the act finally became law.[46]

To this day Congress does not realize that the British liaison officers at the NSA are still free to use American equipment to spy on American citizens. And, in fact, they are doing just that. Congress has been kept in the dark deliberately. This is a fact, not a matter of conjecture or a conclusion based on anonymous sources.

In the early 1980s, during the Reagan administration, one of the authors of this book submitted to the intelligence community a draft of a manuscript that briefly described the wiretap shell game and mentioned that the secrecy provisions concerning British liaison relationships with the NSA have escaped congressional knowledge. The result was an uproar.

The intelligence community insisted that all passages explaining the British wiretap program had to be censored and provided a list of specific deletions. Even the simple mention of the existence of a secret agreement of which Congress was unaware was banned as classified information.[47] In 1985, when the author was called to testify about Nazis working for U.S. intelligence before a congressional subcommittee, he asked permission to discuss certain items pertaining to electronic surveillance in executive session. Permission was denied. So much for congressional oversight.[48]

Shortly after the Clinton administration took office, the intelligence community withdrew its previous objections to publication. In fact, many of the pieces of the jigsaw already had passed into the public domain. In 1982 James Bamford published his seminal history of the NSA, *The Puzzle Palace,* which disclosed some of the main points of the NSA-GCHQ liaison. The National Archives had been given dozens of declassified FBI documents citing British intelligence as the source of its information on Jews in the United States. And finally, in 1991, a pair of British authors confirmed a portion of the espionage on American Jews:

> Sometime in 1945 or 1946 a special unit, even more secret than the rest of the code-breaking agency, was set up to monitor the activities of Israeli agents and their sympathizers in the U.S. and elsewhere. The men who ran this organization held the view that because of the use made by the Israelis of sympathizers from the Jewish community, no Jew, however apparently loyal a U.S. citizen, should be permitted to work in the special unit or even be told of its existence. All reports from the unit carried the code name "Gold," signifying that they were not to be shown to anyone of Jewish origin.
>
> "We had them cold," recalls one former intelligence official who was cleared to see the Gold reports. "We knew who was shipping the arms, who was paying for them, who was being paid in this country, every illegal thing that was going on in this country. Because of politics, very little was ever done with [this intelligence]. But so far as I know the [National Security Agency] still has a group like that, buried somewhere deep.[49]

It does indeed. Its nickname is the "Jew room." Inside the National Security Agency is an intelligence center from which all American Jews are banned, regardless of their proven loyalty or devotion to country, just as the U.S. Navy banned Jews from electronic surveillance ships, such as the USS *Liberty*. The "Jew room" is where the United States and Britain spy on Israel and on anyone who supports Israel. Its name is a misnomer, as the intelligence center has more than one room in more than one agency.[50] As we shall see in the following chapters, it is, and has been, the heart of the secret war against the Jews.

Here are a few brief examples of the damage done to Israel. In 1956 the NSA provided the Egyptians with details of the abortive Israeli raid on the Suez Canal. In 1967 an NSA spy ship provided the British listening post in Cyprus with a detailed electronic map of the holes in the Israeli lines. In 1973 the NSA deliberately withheld information on the Arab surprise attack until the last moment. During the 1980s U.S. intelligence passed Israel's entire order of battle to various Arab governments and continues to do so as a secret compensation for the Camp David agreements negotiated by President Carter.

According to the "old spies" we interviewed, the back-channel relationship with British intelligence really came alive under Vice President, then President, George Bush.[51] From 1984 until 1991 the British-NSA communications channel was being used to direct the laundering of American money to the Palestine Liberation Organization. As we discuss in Part III, Congress still does not understand the foreign ramifications of the Iran-Contra affair. For that matter, neither does convicted spy Jonathan Pollard or the government of Israel.[52] Although Pollard does not know it, when he warned the Israelis that a PLO arms shipment was going through Greece in 1984, he inadvertently blew the whistle on the White House's first transaction of British arms to Iran.

Whatever the motive for his arrest, Pollard's blundering espionage had dramatic consequences for American citizens as well. According to one of our sources, in 1985 Bush authorized a widespread electronic surveillance program against American Jews to prevent any more Pollards. Other sources flatly disagree. They insist that the surveillance of American Jews had already reached staggering proportions long before Pollard.[53]

In 1982, shortly after President Reagan agreed to rescind the Carter-era restrictions on domestic Communications Intelligence operations, the FBI was asked to record all information on "potential" Jewish subversives. As one source wrote, the wiretapping had nothing to do with Pollard: "the arrest of Pollard [in 1985] was used as a pretext to expand a supposedly closed-down illegal covert operation by the FBI called 'SCOPE' whose purpose was to compile lists of Jews in government, research, and institutional leadership, et al. This operation was revealed publicly in the WALL STREET JOURNAL, January 17, 1992."[54] This source believed that *The Wall Street Journal* article was really an exercise in damage control, an attempt to shift the blame back to James Jesus Angleton and conceal the ongoing wiretapping. While there is some dispute about when and why the bugging resumed, the consensus of our sources is that the modern version of Operation Gold is horrendous. The FBI's collecting has gone beyond the pale of what could be considered legitimate intelligence gathering.

In addition to rosters of major contributors to Israeli funds, the Bureau has targeted the innocuous activities of children. "It's just gotten out of hand. . . . I saw FBI records where they collected lists of kids going to Jewish summer camp."[55] Other government officials who reviewed the FBI's "counterterrorist" program against American Jews said that while they did not catch any terrorists, they collected a lot of information on Jewish lobbyists.[56]

Another NSA source alleged that the FBI had custody of the Jewish surveillance files because a recent law made the FBI's "counterterrorism" files completely exempt from the Freedom of Information Act, under a special counterintelligence loophole.[57] Under the FBI's broad definition of an espionage suspect, anyone who communicates with a foreign government—for example, who calls a relative in Israel or donates to a charity that sends funds to Israel—gets swept up in the electronic vacuum cleaner. "Pollard paranoia" swept through the intelligence community, brushing aside the Bill of Rights.

Some of the "old spies," particularly those with FBI backgrounds, think this sort of activity is as harmless as it is stupid. The sad truth is that any of us can be the targets of electronic surveillance without a warrant. The Jews are not the only victims of the wiretapping, only the most frequent targets. Over the years the British back-channel inside the NSA was used for a variety of political dirty tricks. A large number of American candidates for public office have been placed under electronic surveillance by British intelligence officers sitting at their "temporary listening post" at Fort Meade.

Sometimes the surveillance has justification. The late congressman Adam Clayton Powell was wiretapped at his resort home in Bimini while he solicited campaign funds from a Communist agent. Sometimes the surveillance is naked political espionage, as with Hoover's request for telephone surveillance of a famous Washington brothel on 16th Street. Hoover used it to wiretap candidates for public office and then leaked word of their indiscretions, sexual and otherwise, to his incumbent friends on Capitol Hill.[58]

An admittedly secondhand source insists that British eavesdroppers were the source of the 1992 campaign stories alleging that presidential candidate Clinton had expressed pro-Soviet views while a student in London. Young Clinton's remarks were nothing more than an ambiguous comparison of Soviet and American efforts for peace in Vietnam, fairly innocent at the time. Because the wiretap itself could not be disclosed, it set off a scurry of searching through archives on both sides of the Atlantic for any incriminating documents. There was none, and in short order the British smear campaign died of its own weight.[59]

It is time that Congress and the public realize that in the age of computers, microwaves, and satellites, we are all Jews. Sometimes the British back-channel into the NSA has had a serious impact on American foreign policy. On several occasions it nearly destroyed the nation of Israel. To comprehend the origins of Hoover's illegal surveillance program, we should start at the beginning and examine the extraordinary circumstances that led up to Israel's 1948 war for independence.

In the next chapter we review David Ben-Gurion's frantic efforts to obtain arms despite Western surveillance. In that dark hour he was aided by an unlikely secret agent, an obscure Czech Jew who, more than anyone else, secured the weapons for Israel's survival. By the time he was given a state funeral in Israel, Lev Hoch had become the wealthiest publisher in Britain, at least on paper. Ben-Gurion's Czech spy had changed his name to Robert Maxwell.

CHAPTER 9

ROBERT MAXWELL'S CZECH GUNS

The history books say that the 1948 Israeli war for independence was fought with American guns and homemade weapons from underground factories in Palestine. It was a victory of brave Jews against much better equipped Arabs. Our sources in the intelligence community say there is a bit of truth in that, but not much.

In the first place, most of the guns came from the Czech Communists, not the Americans. The arms deals were negotiated behind the FBI's back by a rogue member of the British secret service. When Stalin discovered the Czech arms deal, he was furious and launched his own operation to take over Czechoslovakia and destroy Israel.

As soon as Israel had won its war for independence, Ben-Gurion secretly betrayed Stalin's double agents to American intelligence, but they ignored him for political reasons. Forrestal went mad trying to run the cover-up. If Ben-Gurion was right, the Nazi networks that Kim Philby and Dulles had smuggled to the United States were completely penetrated by Soviet intelligence.

In this chapter we examine the following allegations:

- A British intelligence agent by the name of Robert Maxwell provided the critical link to the supply of arms from Communist Czechoslovakia that saved Israel in 1948.
- Israeli prime minister David Ben-Gurion purged the Communists in Israel after the Jews defeated the Arabs and then warned James Jesus Angleton that Kim Philby was a secret Communist agent, but was rebuffed in his efforts to secure an intelligence liaison with the Americans.
- Defense Secretary James Forrestal went insane when his treacherous role inside the Truman administration was discovered after Dewey was defeated and after he was told that the Nazi "freedom fighters" he had helped Dulles bring to the United States were really "Red Nazis," i.e., Communists.

- Both Angleton and Allen Dulles buried the Israeli warnings about Kim Philby and Soviet penetration of the Nazi "freedom fighters" in order to conceal their own involvement with the recruitment of ex-Nazis as anti-Communist agents.

From the 1930s onward, guns were the key to the survival of the Jews in Palestine. The Zionists knew that some day they would have to fight the Arabs for the land. In the early days their best source of weapons was their British enemy. The Haganah had set up its own extraordinarily efficient intelligence service, the Shai, which infiltrated the British Palestine Police and spied on the British Special Branch as well as on hostile Arab agents.

During World War II Jewish agents serving with the British army in Palestine had begun to acquire large amounts of small arms, but they were not enough. After the war the Zionists made strenuous efforts to procure more from Europe via the fledgling Mossad intelligence service. A small but sophisticated arms-smuggling network was established in parallel with the illegal immigration network in Italy.[1]

The man who ran the Italian arms-smuggling operations was Yehuda Arazi, who had made his headquarters around Milan. He knew how the Eastern European émigré front game worked in Italy, for he disguised himself as part of the Polish Anders group in exile, one of the many émigré fronts for British secret service agents. Camouflaged behind this "respectable" anti-Communist émigré front, he successfully procured much of the arms, ammunition, equipment, and gas needed for the Jewish fighters in Palestine from the British army itself.[2]

In this way, the British unwittingly armed and equipped their Zionist enemies in Palestine. From modest beginnings, the Jews managed to smuggle in many of the arms they needed during 1947.[3] The Zionists needed a lot more, and they were not too particular where they picked them up. Obtaining the weapons, however, was far easier than trying to slip them into Palestine past the British navy.

In order to run the British naval blockade of the Mediterranean, the Zionists established a small navy of their own, run by an intelligence front in Tangier, opposite Gibraltar. The Zionists also were quite adept at laundering their financial transactions. Apparently they had learned some tricks from the Dulles brothers. Many of the ships were recently ex-Royal Navy, secretly bought for dollars in Tangier. The British author Richard Deacon, then a correspondent in the area for *The Times,* in mid-1947 reported that:

> British Intelligence sources now have adequate proof of how Admiralty agents have been deceived by the buyers. Arms, including machine-guns, ammunition and bombs, have been traced from Eire, Central America

> and Belgium, shipped by coastal cargo vessels through the Mediterranean. The arms are transferred at night to a ship in Tangier harbour.[4]

In his book on the Israeli secret service, Deacon reveals that this story had been part of a Zionist disinformation campaign in which he and the British were misled. The propaganda initiative effectively camouflaged the real arms smuggling by diverting the attention of the British to larger vessels, which were not running weapons, and away from the Jews' small ships, which could get through the blockade much more easily. It was a start, but the Zionist units in Palestine were still hopelessly outgunned by their Western-supplied Arab enemies.

To the Forrestal-led forces opposed to the creation of Israel, the Zionists' gun-running activities were extremely worrying. So much of the activities seemed to provide further evidence of the Jewish-Communist conspiracy. For example, one of the key organizers of the illegal smuggling routes from Soviet-dominated Central Europe via the Black Sea was Moshe Sneh, a Communist and former head of the Haganah who had broken with the mainstream Zionists because of their alleged pro-Western bias.

As the end of Britain's mandate approached, and the preparations for the war between the Arabs and the Jews intensified, the increasingly unstable and paranoid Forrestal believed that the Reds controlled the whole Zionist plot. At the same time that the Sneh scandal broke, Forrestal's friends in British intelligence made a series of claims about two ships sailing under Panamanian flags that had left from the Black Sea area en route to Palestine with 14,000 Jews on board. The British said the ships were part of Sneh's operations for the Soviets and that the passengers included many recruits for the Stern Gang, which then was carrying out a campaign of terror against the British, as well as "Red agents" specially trained and sent by the Soviets to further their aims in the Middle East.[5]

British intelligence was providing a stream of evidence that confirmed Forrestal's conviction that the Zionists' immigration and arms-smuggling traffic were part of a wider Soviet-inspired campaign. In fact, the Zionist leadership wanted to avoid any reliance on the Soviets as weapons suppliers, for fear that it would lead to just such allegations and alienate their cause from the West.

Indeed, it was Ben-Gurion himself who set about procuring the Western arms the Zionists needed for the looming war with the Arabs. He "persuaded various wealthy Jewish industrialists, mainly American, to raise not only capital, but to provide equipment for the establishment of an arms industry in Palestine."[6] Ben-Gurion naively believed that by turning so clearly to Western sources to arm his fighters, he could signal where he really stood.

His actions had the opposite effect. The British-FBI operations tracked the Zionists' every move. Although Golda Meir did raise a lot of money, as far as weapons were concerned, everywhere she went the FBI seemed to know in advance that her job was to break the American arms embargo on Israel. Apart from a handful of relatively small shipments, American intelligence closed the door almost completely on arms for the Jews.

While the British-FBI-Forrestal operations against American Jews prevented more than a trickle of U.S. weapons from getting through to the Israeli forces, the Arabs were allowed to build an arsenal of tanks, artillery, and aircraft. Israel had no air force, no tanks, and only a handful of antique artillery pieces. When the British pulled out, they would hand over their arms and forts to the Arab Legion, a unit established in the mid-1920s by Jack Philby, funded by his friend King Ibn Saud, commanded by a British officer, and specially trained to destroy the Jews.

To make the irony complete, Jack's Communist double-agent son, Kim Philby, had been smuggling Nazis to Damascus, Syria, since the immediate postwar years. The Nazi fugitives were training the Arabs for a new Final Solution. This time they would not let any Jews escape. They would drive the Jews of Palestine out and destroy all the survivors of Hitler's Holocaust. The Western world could easily see what was coming but did nothing except to make sure that the Jews' enemies were well supplied and armed.

The Haganah leader and first Israeli prime minister, David Ben-Gurion, faced a great dilemma. On the one hand, the West refused him the weapons he needed to fight the Arabs. On the other, his own intelligence confirmed some British and American charges that the Soviets were infiltrating Jewish Communist agents into Palestine.[7] If he turned now to the Soviets to provide the weapons his country desperately needed, then Forrestal's predictions might turn out to be self-fulfilling. If he did not turn to the Communists, then all his work might be in vain, and Israel would be destroyed before it had a chance to take its place among the nations of the world.

In those desperate times Prime Minister Ben-Gurion decided that his dilemma could be resolved in only one way. The weapons had to be found, even if they came from the Communists. Ben-Gurion knew that there was only one man who could help him solve his dilemma: An obscure Czech Jew who had changed his name to Robert Maxwell would become one of Israel's first, and most secret, national heroes.

Forty years later Robert Maxwell would be remembered as the brash British Labour member of Parliament who forged an international media and publishing empire, only to bring about its collapse through corruption on a grand scale, even stealing his employees' pension funds in a desperate effort to stave off financial ruin. His own corruption ended with his premature death, most likely by his own hand, and left his family to face the shame and legal consequences.

In 1948, however, he was the one man who could arm the nation of Israel. His remarkable success made him into an unlikely national hero, and whatever else historians may say about his legacy, this one act alone made Robert Maxwell a great man, one whose memory will be forever revered as one of Israel's founding heroes. Maxwell had many secrets hidden behind his façades of politician and publishing tycoon.

According to our sources among the intelligence community, his biggest secret was that he was a long-serving member of the British secret service.[8] But before he was a British agent and before he became an Israeli double agent, he was first a Czech Jew, driven from his homeland. His real name was Lev Hoch. Maxwell once wrote that "I have constructed during my years of exile a glittering surface as a kind of protection."[9]

Lev Hoch was born in the county of Maramures, in Carpatho-Ruthenia, a region conquered variously by the Habsburgs, Hungarians, Czechs, Poles, and Russians. There is an old Jewish proverb: "Ten measures of poverty were given to the world, nine of them were taken by Maramures."[10] The little town of Solotvino, with its salt mines, was an industrial wasteland in the old Austro-Hungarian Empire. Across the river, Maxwell had a distant relative named Elie Wiesel. Who would have thought that two such distinguished men, a prominent British publisher and a Nobel Prize winner, would come from such a desolate place?

In later years the British secret service thought he was a conservative member of the right-wing of the Labour party, a member of the club, a member of Parliament. Inside the protective shell, however, he had been someone else. At the age of twelve he was swept up in the exciting world of the Zionist movement, which had a not inconsequential presence in Solotvino. He became a member of a paramilitary unit that planned its escape to Palestine, but instead, World War II came to Solotvino, and Maxwell lost virtually his entire family in the Nazi Holocaust.[11]

British prime minister Neville Chamberlain had handed Czechoslovakia to Hitler in November 1938 as a bribe for "peace in our time." A Catholic priest, Monsignor Josef Tiso, was installed as Hitler's puppet. The slaughter was about to begin. Maxwell, then only sixteen years old, moved to Budapest and joined the French underground that was smuggling Czech volunteers to Western Europe. In December 1939 Maxwell was arrested as a spy, but the teenage Jew beat his Fascist guard to death and fled to Istanbul. He ended up in Syria, where he joined the French Foreign Legion. In March 1940 his unit was shipped back to France.[12]

At this time the French were collapsing, about to surrender to the

Nazis. Churchill promised to evacuate to Britain any Czech units that wanted to fight. It was a promise unfulfilled. Only 4,000 Czechs reached the port of Sète in time, and the rest were shot on sight, on Nazi orders. Any Jews among them were to be handed to the Gestapo for "special treatment." Lev Hoch decided it was time to become an Englishman, and he eventually adopted the name Robert Maxwell.[13]

The anti-Semitic commanders of the Czech division had ordered their men to leave behind any "political undesirables" to the Nazis. Only Jews and Communists fell into this category, although the commanders agreed with the Nazis that they were virtually one and the same. The scene on the docks was of unmitigated cruelty. People drowned trying to reach the ships, aged Jewish rabbis were left to die, soldiers were abandoned because of their religion. In fact, most of the Czech division was left behind.

By the time the remains of the unit arrived in England, the men were denouncing their own officers for cowardice and anti-Semitism. When the commander asked for all those who felt that way to step forward, Maxwell was among them. The 539 Czech soldiers who told the truth were discharged and sent under armed guard to a British prison camp. While the experience was dismal for Maxwell, it would turn out to be a stroke of good fortune for the nation of Israel.

In the British prison camp, Maxwell made a friend, an important friend. He was a Czech Communist, a former member of Parliament by the name of Vladimir Clementis.[14] According to our sources among the "old spies," the two were cellmates for a while and shared a common dislike of the Nazis, British politicians, and everyone who hated Jews. The two men never forgot their intimate friendship, forged under extreme circumstances.[15]

In order to get out of the prison camp, Maxwell volunteered for ditch-digging duty with an alien labor company called the Pioneers. He used a pick and shovel in England and Wales until 1943. During that time he took advantage of his relative freedom to have an affair with a widow from a British military family. Through this connection, strings were pulled, and Maxwell was transferred to the Somerset Light Infantry and then sent overseas.

He worked hard and by D-Day had become a sergeant in charge of a sniper section. He was recommended for a field commission but was turned down as unsuitable material for an officer. Maxwell convinced the British army it was wrong by knocking out a tank, capturing one hundred Germans, and leading an attack against the Twelfth SS Panzers. As a result, the British not only made him an officer, they made him an army spy.

Fortunately, for Maxwell, the British dropped their initial plans to parachute him behind enemy lines, a high-risk operation that had few survivors. According to several of the former intelligence officers we spoke to about Maxwell, he did very well at his next espionage job. Dressed in civilian clothes, he was sent to Paris, where he rounded up Nazis who had gone into hiding. Maxwell posed as a Czech black marketeer selling forged documents. It was this clever piece of impersonation and con artistry that first called him to the attention of the British secret service.[16]

Posted back to his unit, Lieutenant Maxwell won the Military Cross for bravery for rescuing a British platoon trapped by the Germans. As the war wound down, he extended his proficiency in foreign languages by studying Russian, and after the war, such skills became the key to his advancement in British intelligence. Intelligence interrogators skilled in foreign languages were in great demand, and Maxwell was sent to Spandau Prison in Germany.[17]

This was the prison where Rudolf Hess and many of the top Nazis were held. Maxwell's skill at interrogation got him a sensitive assignment. It is known that he interrogated several important Nazis, including the custodian of Hitler's will; the SS adjutant to Martin Bormann; Hjalmar Schacht, the financial wizard of the Third Reich; and Friedrich Flick, the Nazi steel tycoon who secretly had been one of Allen Dulles's clients.[18]

According to a number of our American intelligence sources, Maxwell may have picked up some incriminating intelligence information from these interrogations, but it is unlikely.[19] Maxwell's biographer, Joe Haines, says his most memorable interview was a German intelligence officer named Giskes. As a result, Maxwell correctly deduced that British intelligence had fed the Free French false information about D-Day and then deliberately parachuted French volunteers into German hands to be tortured. It was part of a greater deception strategy for the Normandy invasion.[20]

Several of our sources in British intelligence insist that it was Maxwell's perceptive insight into the British double-cross that convinced the secret service he was its kind of man.[21] Maxwell appeared to be a stereotypical ethnic Englishman: ambitious, even ruthless, clever, and eager to please his superiors. Maxwell was a war hero, spoke several languages, and worked like a fool. His army patron, who had just been promoted to director of staff at the War Office, tried to convince Maxwell to pursue a career as a soldier.[22]

Maxwell turned his friend down; he was already so attracted to the world of espionage that he was determined to be a spy. In March 1946 he was recruited by the British secret service and assigned to the British Control Commission for Germany.[23] Maxwell's Russian language studies served him in good stead, and in October he was appointed the British representative to supervise elections in the Soviet sector of Berlin.[24]

In Germany Maxwell stumbled across another Jew, Ferdinand Springer, a publisher who had survived in the Third Reich because German scientists had vouched for his expertise. According to Haines's "official" biography, Springer needed paper and Maxwell needed money. They started a publishing business on the sly.[25]

According to Alex Mitchell, a British journalist who investigated the matter extensively for *The Sunday Times* in the early 1970s, there was a lot more involved than that. Mitchell discovered Maxwell's role in interrogating Nazi dignitaries and scientists and concluded that he had used his official position to organize a strictly private trade in Nazi scientific papers, which he had taken to London and published in exclusive, and very profitable, editions.[26]

Twenty years later, when Maxwell died in November 1991, Mitchell wrote a retrospective. In the 1970s he thought that Maxwell had acted out of greed, but in hindsight he wondered whether someone had put him "up to this illegal plunder of scientific documents and where did this penniless former refugee get the money to pay for them? In all probability the secrets have gone to his grave in Israel."[27]

Not according to the "old spies" who supplied the information for this chapter, who say that Mitchell was closer to the truth than he imagined.[28] Someone was behind the enterprise, but it was not the Jews. Maxwell, under his cover of "press officer," had been ordered by the British secret service to set up a series of publishing firms as a means of identifying German scientists for possible recruitment. It was the British equivalent of the American Operation Paperclip, the code name for U.S. recruitment of German scientists. It is not a coincidence that Springer's firm received the first British license to begin publishing.[29]

In 1948 the recently formed Maxwell-Springer company merged with Butterworth Press, another front for MI6. The merger involved the German scientists, Maxwell, and a "shadowy and influential person," Count Frederick Vanden Heuvel.[30] Maxwell's new partner Vanden Heuvel was one of the most senior officers of the British secret service. In fact, he was Allen Dulles's counterpart as the MI6 station chief in Bern during the war.[31]

Vanden Heuvel knew all about Richard Kauder's Max network of "Fascist Jews," the window for Dulles's Nazi clients and their money, and the Vatican's role. Vanden Heuvel was one of the British mutineers.[32] Another of Maxwell's new partners was a German spy for the British, who revealed the first information to the West about the V-2 rockets.[33] After the merger, the new front company was called Pergamon. It was, according to several of the "old spies," a covert scientific intelligence collection service disguised as a publishing company.[34] Maxwell clearly was swimming with the sharks.

Maxwell, however, swam faster than they did. The impoverished British secret service could not afford to keep pumping money into a losing company for long, regardless of the inroads it gave them with the Nazi scientists. In 1951 Maxwell bought out 75 percent of Pergamon for the now-paltry sum of £13,000.[35] It was the beginning of a publishing empire.

At the time, the buy-out was a great relief to the British secret service, which favored Maxwell with the odd government publishing contract. Maxwell kept up his old contacts with Vanden Heuvel, and, in return for Maxwell's tips about the newest German scientists to surface from the postwar Nazi underground, the count supplied him with juicy pieces of information. Over the years the "odd couple" of Vanden Heuvel and Maxwell did quite well.[36]

It is true that Maxwell was a charlatan, a chameleon who overreached himself. He built publishing businesses on top of newspapers on top of a mountain of debt. Suddenly, many years later, the British secret service discovered through an informant that Maxwell's true loyalties were with Israel. His old intelligence friends punished him. All over the city of London, MI6 loyalists spread the word that Maxwell's credit was canceled. Hounded by MI6's contacts in the city, unable to continue refinancing his debts, he apparently committed suicide. To the surprise of many in the press, he was given a state funeral in Israel, buried on the most sacred ground next to the Temple Mount in Jerusalem. The "old spies" say that he deserved it.[37]

What no one in British intelligence realized until too late was that Maxwell was a committed Zionist. He had been since the age of twelve. MI6 thought that Maxwell was one of "our Jews." They were wrong. He was an Israeli double agent. Maxwell was a consummate con artist, picking at the rotten edges of the British Secret Intelligence Service. He had made a few inroads of his own, with tidbits gleaned from both the Nazis and their new British employers.

By 1946 Maxwell had learned that MI6 was moving against the postwar government of Czechoslovakia. This may seem strange, as it was the only democratic country in the Eastern bloc, with less than a 30 percent vote for the Communists. But then, it should be remembered that Kim Philby of MI6 was the golden boy of the Balkans at that time. His Soviet employers had told him that the Czech social democracy, with its free trade unions, political liberality, and stubborn independence, was an embarrassment to Stalin himself and must be destroyed. Philby told MI6 that Stalin was secretly controlling the Czechs and that the government had to be replaced by a coup of more "reliable" supporters.[38]

And who, Philby asked, was a more reliable anti-Communist than a Czech Nazi? MI6 pumped a fortune through the Vatican into Ferdinand Durčansky's Slovakian Liberation Movement. As we documented in our previous book, Durčansky was a Fascist and an opportunist, but he was a good Catholic. He also was one of the most senior Slovak war criminals at large. MI6 equipped him with a radio station in Spain, a propaganda outlet in Rome, and tons of money funneled through the Vatican.[39]

When Maxwell learned that the British were attempting to back the ex-Nazis in a Czech civil war, something snapped. He remembered how the British and upper-class Czechs had left the Czech Jews on the shores of France. He remembered the members of his family who had been shipped to Auschwitz by the Nazis. He remembered his old cellmate from the British prison camp. He remembered Vladimir Clementis.

Clementis was one of the leaders of the Czech Communists and, with Maxwell's help, about to become foreign minister of the Czechoslovak government. Maxwell gave him chapter and verse about MI6's plans for the Durčansky coup. The Communists passed the information to the non-Communist Czech Security Service, which confirmed the information and quietly put Durčansky's cronies under surveillance.[40]

Many members of the postwar Czech parliament were secretly involved with Durčansky's Fascist underground. The scandal, which was publicly exposed in late 1947, brought the Socialists and Communists into power as a new broom in early March 1948. The West reacted with horror. Cables poured into Washington from its embassies and agents that the Iron Curtain had just clanked over Czechoslovakia.

It was nothing of the sort. Stalin was furious. The last thing he wanted was an *independent* socialist country in Eastern Europe. The Czechs were even more Western-oriented than Tito became in Yugoslavia a few months later. Soviet intelligence worked overtime to mount a countercoup. Maxwell's former cellmate Clementis, who served as Czech foreign minister from 1948 to 1950, was hanged by the Stalinists in Prague in 1952 after supposedly confessing to being an agent of "Western imperialists."[41] So were many other Jewish Communist leaders.

Still, it took Stalin three more years to get control of Czechoslovakia. In the meantime, the damage had been done. In 1948 Foreign Minister Clementis had done the one thing that Stalin wanted to avoid: He armed the Jews in Palestine and helped them to win the war against the Arabs. This was what Maxwell had requested in return for betraying MI6's Durčansky net to the Czechs.[42]

Maxwell had watched the buildup of Arab arms from France, the United States, and Britain with secret horror. He knew that Truman's arms embargo tolled the death knell for the Jews of Palestine. In return for saving his native country from Durčansky's civil war, Maxwell begged the Czechs for weapons for his adopted country, Israel. He wanted Clementis to send guns to Ben-Gurion, when no one else in the world would supply them.

Maxwell's intervention infuriated Stalin and the hard-liners in the Czech Communist party, who were already plotting to overthrow Clementis and take power in Prague. Maxwell's arms deal ultimately killed Clementis, but he saved Israel. There is considerable evidence that Maxwell's Czech strategy was coordinated by Ben-Gurion's secret double agent inside Soviet intelligence. In fact, it is almost certain that in the aftermath of the Communist coup, Maxwell was supported by another secret Zionist agent, an Austrian Jew. It was, say our sources in the intelligence community, Richard Kauder, code-named Klatt, the head of the Max network.[43]

At the end of 1947 Kauder helped a team of Zionist intelligence agents to travel to Prague, where they quickly made contact with the Czech government through his local sources from the Max network. By early 1948 they had concluded the first of a series of crucial arms deals with the Czech authorities, thanks to Maxwell's warnings about the Durčansky plot. Even British historians have alluded to the Max network's role in the arms deals, deals that made the difference between victory and defeat for the Jews of Palestine.[44]

The official Israeli version is that the Czechs were keen on the deal because the Zionists paid for the arms in U.S. dollars. A whole genre of fiction was created to disguise the Maxwell-Clementis-Kauder connection. In an irony of history, many historians gave the credit for saving Israel to Clementis's archenemy, Stalin.[45] It must have been very galling for Clementis when he stood on the gallows a few years later. His tormentor, Stalin, had gotten the credit for his own brave actions.

At least the risk had been worth it. As soon as the deal had been struck, Ben-Gurion had designated Munya Mardor to direct an underground network to channel Czech arms to the embattled Zionists in Palestine.[46] The Czechs then shipped the arms by plane, in defiance of the Soviets, who never approved any part of the operation. In fact, as soon as Stalin learned that the Czechs were shipping fighter planes to Israel, the Soviet Union canceled its promised shipment of replacement aircraft to the Czechs.[47]

In an act of incredible bravery—some say stupidity—Clementis, as head of the Foreign Service, told the Soviets that the Czechs would send their fighters in defiance of Stalin's orders. Clementis may have been about to be murdered anyway, but this single action ensured his death. The Czechs shipped the aircraft to Israel by packing the fuselages inside American cargo planes, which had been smuggled out of the United States in violation of Truman's embargo.[48] Stalin was furious.

James Forrestal was furious too when he learned that American Jews had set up an entire airbase behind the Iron Curtain. Forrestal would never allow his countrymen to sell arms to the Jews because they were all Communists. Stalin would not sell the Jews guns, or tanks, or planes, because they were all working for the Western imperialists. The Western nations would not sell guns to the Jews because they had no oil, and the Arabs did.

In 1948 only one nation in all the world, Czechoslovakia, came to Israel's aid with everything it had. Within a few years, those involved paid for it with their lives. In 1952 Stalin's puppets executed virtually the entire Czech government. Eleven members were Jews. The charges were simple. According to Stalin's prosecutors, the Czech government was plotting with the West to break the country away from its alliance with Moscow. The accused were working with the Zionists to bring their plan to fruition.[49]

It is a pity that the United States did not stand by either Israel or Czechoslovakia in those days of indifference, lost opportunities, and friends abandoned. There would not be another "Prague Spring" until 1968, twenty years after Clementis's act of bravery. Even then, Alexander Dubček's nascent independence movement also would be crushed by Soviet generals with long memories. There was to be no "socialism with a human face."

But for a few brave hours in 1948, Maxwell's friends in the Czech government had done what no other nation on earth was courageous enough to do. They had, for the first time in two thousand years, given the Jews a fair fight. In addition to artillery and ammunition, they had given the Jews the cream of the Nazi air force, the Messerschmitt Bf-109, which had been built for Germany by the formidable, and expert, Czech arms industry.[50]

With Maxwell's help, Israel had an air force. On the afternoon of March 29, 1948, the first four Messerschmitts had been unpacked from the cargo planes and reassembled. The plane arrived just in time, for although the British mandate had not yet expired, the fledgling state of Israel already was besieged by its Arab enemies. Maxwell's air force turned the tide of the war for Israeli independence:

> That afternoon an Israeli observation post had reported that an Egyptian column consisting of five hundred vehicles, including artillery and tanks—the full rolling stock of an entire brigade—was moving along the coastal road. It was more than enough to make good the Egyptian boast that they would overrun Tel Aviv, only twenty-five miles away.[51]

Tel Aviv was the heartland of the Jewish defense of Palestine. If the city was lost, all was lost. The first four planes from Czechoslovakia were thrown hastily into battle. Only one returned. Ben-Gurion thought that he had lost the key battle of the war. There was nothing between Tel Aviv and the Egyptians to stop the tanks. Plans were made to evacuate the capital of the short-lived State of Israel. But thanks to Maxwell's Czech-supplied planes, the Egyptians hesitated and decided not to advance on Tel Aviv. They never recovered from this setback and did not come closer to the beleaguered city in the course of the 1948 war.[52]

At the first sight of the enemy's weakness at the end of March 1948, Ben-Gurion launched the Jews' great offensive. For a few critical weeks, the shuttle service from Czechoslovakia supplied 90 percent of the arms, equipment, and vital supplies, such as food and walkie-talkies. Golda Meir and David Ben-Gurion raised most of the money to buy the goods from the wealthy Jews of the United States and, to a lesser extent, Britain.[53]

The offensive opened on March 31, and the Czech arms were a significant factor in the ultimate Jewish victory. The World War II combat experience of Jewish fighters in the U.S. and British armies was another. The battle for Haifa, toward the end of April, proved a decisive military and psychological turning point. The Zionists reinforced their military superiority with ruthless psychological warfare. With rumors of military atrocities abounding, thousands of Arabs fled from their homes, although the mainstream Jewish civilian leaders begged them to remain and settle in the new state. By April 24, with Haifa captured and the Arabs in retreat, the Jews seemed near their ultimate goal, despite what the Dulles brothers and James Forrestal might be plotting in Washington.[54]

By the beginning of May, the position of the Palestinian Arabs was so desperate and their military setbacks so severe that the Arab League decided to intervene. When the British Mandate expired on May 15, 1948, and the Israeli state was declared, the war became even fiercer. The Jews needed more Czech guns urgently. As a semiofficial Jewish history recorded many years later, now the shipments included not only rifles, machine guns, and Messerschmitts, but also World War II vintage Spitfires.[55]

The formerly small-scale Zionist units were transformed into the skeleton of a modern army. The war was no longer basically low level; it had become fully mechanized. Haganah was using tanks, fighters, and "Flying Fortress" bombers. After May 20, 1948, less than a week after Israel officially came into existence, Clementis ensured that the Jews had a military airfield at their command in Czechoslovakia to keep the pipeline operating at full speed.[56]

Some American pilots who flew the desperate missions from Czechoslovakia (code-named "Jockstrap") to Israel (code-named "Oklahoma") later reminisced on those frantic times, flying arms to the Israelis. Their accounts of these desperate flights help to explain why the Jews won and the Arabs were defeated:

> You took on all the gas the plane would hold, filling the extra tank that had been installed in the fuselage as well as the regular wing tanks. From Jockstrap it was an 1,800 mile hop to Oklahoma. A C-46's normal range, with less of a load, was 1,500 miles; and you took off sure of only one thing—you weren't welcome anyplace else. If you landed in Greece, they would impound the airplane and its cargo. If you landed in any of the Arab countries, they would hang your manhood on a pole and parade it around.
>
> . . . But it was when you landed [in Israel] that you realized what it was all about . . . There were men standing in the trucks, new immigrants who would do the unloading, and the way they stood there, in their gray caps and shabby clothes, with their haggard unshaven faces, reminded you of the newsreels . . . of similar people riding in similar trucks to their deaths in Nazi concentration camps. The look of them came back to you in your hotel room in Tel Aviv that night. And the thought of making the whole trip back again in a couple of hours didn't seem like such a big deal.[57]

These American airmen were the heroes of the logistical war for Israel's survival, but behind them stood a greater hero. Almost half a century later Robert Maxwell allegedly committed suicide, hounded to his death, so the "old spies" say, by the British secret service. The orders to cancel Maxwell's credit came directly from Century House. His publishing empire rested on a fraud using other people's money, rolled over year after year as Maxwell tried to wait out the recession. When all the credit lines suddenly collapsed at once, there was only one way out, suicide.[58]

The truth is that Maxwell had embezzled millions from his own employees' pension funds, part of a total debt of more than $5 billion. He died penniless and despised by the British public, but there was a different reaction in Israeli intelligence and political circles. His naked body was wrapped in a prayer shawl and lowered into the soil of Israel. Dozens of old men who knew the other truth came out to pay their last respects to the man who had saved Israel from defeat.

It was an honorable burial. Whatever else can be said of the man, he saved a nation. Who of us will have, let alone deserve, such an epitaph, even in secret? The man he defeated, James Forrestal, had been buried long since, and with equal honors, in Arlington National Cemetery. As we will see in the second part of this chapter, in Forrestal's case, he was publicly honored by his president but privately despised by Truman's team.

Robert Maxwell and his friends among the Czech Communists had saved Israel in its first months from the Arab armies. By early 1949, the Jews had won a famous victory. The minute that the war for independence was won, however, Prime Minister Ben-Gurion moved quickly to dump the Communist connection. Contrary to Forrestal's dire predictions, there weren't that many Communists in Israel to begin with. In the 1949 elections for the Israeli parliament, the left was left behind.

The radical socialist party, Mapam (which Stalin supported, but secretly despised for its independent outlook), won only nineteen seats. The Communist party itself won only four seats out of 120, mostly with Arab support.[59] This 3 percent vote for the Communists was something of an embarrassment for the State Department, which in 1945 had predicted that Israel would be a Communist puppet state within three years.

The "hundreds of thousands of Jewish Communist agents" who supposedly had been infiltrated into Israel by the Soviets apparently defected as soon as they set foot in the Zionist homeland. While the Communist party in Israel was an outright joke, the radical socialists of Mapam had 15 percent of the vote, a small but irritating leftist minority. Prime Minister Ben-Gurion hated Mapam and tried to suggest that the Soviets had established a fifth column of their own inside the Jewish state through Mapam, although it turned out that Stalin's suspicions of its independent outlook were well-founded.[60]

A Communist-inspired civil war was just what Forrestal and his friends in the State Department had been predicting all along. To their astonishment, Ben-Gurion took strong action and abolished the Palmach, which had several pro-Mapam officers in its ranks.[61] As soon as the war against the Arabs was over, he asked for American military advisers to crush the remaining Mapam influence. Then Ben-Gurion reorganized the entire Israeli intelligence service under the control of pro-Western leaders. Reuven Shiloah, the man who allegedly orchestrated the blackmail campaign against both Stalin and Rockefeller, was placed in charge.[62] Shiloah made no bones about his personal political leanings: He was in favor of an alliance with the United States and for the closest possible relationship with U.S. intelligence.[63]

As soon as he had the votes for the State of Israel and the guns from the Czechs to defend it, Ben-Gurion blew the whistle on the Soviets. In 1949 Teddy Kollek went to James Angleton and exposed Kim Philby as a traitor. According to the former intelligence officers we interviewed on this point, Angleton was horrified.[64] Philby was a close friend, a closet Fascist, a supporter of the Vatican, and a fellow mutineer.

If Philby was a Communist, then all of Angleton's Nazi "freedom fighters" were penetrated by the Kremlin as well. This was not the way the scenario was supposed to play out. The Jews were supposed to be the Communist agents, not the British and the Nazis. Dewey was supposed to be the president, not Truman. Everything had gone wrong. Angleton kept his mouth shut about Kollek's warning and quietly began to lose his mental stability. He was not the only one to lose his mind over the alarming turn of events.

The notion of anti-Communist Jews as American allies, while Communists were posing as Nazis, was too much for James Forrestal. President Truman's reelection in November 1948 seemed to be the final straw, and the defense secretary's uneasy grasp on reality became increasingly shaky.

He had been sure that Truman would go down to a crushing defeat at the polls and "was shocked and disturbed by the reelection of Truman."[65] The Saturday after the election, Forrestal had his good friend and secret ally in the campaign against Truman, Allen Dulles, over to dinner, and they sadly discussed Dewey's stupidities in losing the unlosable election.[66] Dulles couldn't console his fellow conspirator. Everything was ruined for Wall Street's "boy wonder."

Worse was to follow. In the aftermath of Truman's stunning election victory, the president had discovered Forrestal's treacherous dealings with the Dewey-Dulles camp and worked out that he had been planning to jump ship when the election went as all the polls were predicting.[67] Many of Washington's best-informed insiders believed that Forrestal had been planning to keep his job under Dewey and that Dewey's defeat helped cause his nervous breakdown.

In January 1949 the president told Forrestal he had to go. Truman gave him a few months and allowed him to leave of his own "free" will, but his supporters knew what had happened. Poor James had been fired. On March 1 Truman suddenly demanded he "send in a resignation letter promptly."[68] Forrestal's public career came to the abrupt end of a traitor within a government that was not meant to be. As if to torment Forrestal, Truman gave the traitor a hero's farewell. A few weeks later, on March 28, his penultimate day in office, he paid a courtesy call on the president and was surprised to be received by a large group of dignitaries: "Truman read a citation honoring Forrestal for 'meritorious and distinguished service,' added his own personal congratulations, and pinned on Forrestal's coat lapel the Distinguished Service Medal. The retiring Secretary of Defense was visibly flustered, and he was totally unable to respond to the President's action."[69] Forrestal undoubtedly knew the truth of Truman's contempt for him, and although further honors were showered on him the next day at a special session of the House Armed Services Committee, it was the end of the road. The Jewish Communists were to blame. As the diplomatic victory of the Jews in the UN, then on the battlefield in Palestine, had sunk in, Forrestal's paranoia had reached unbearable levels. The Zionists, he believed, had him under surveillance twenty-four hours a day, and his firing from Truman's cabinet was the result of a lobbying campaign by American Jews.[70]

By late 1948 news of Forrestal's obsessive paranoia about the Jews had already reached Truman, and "he quietly ordered an investigation," which found that Forrestal was suffering "a total psychotic breakdown . . . characterized by suicidal features." It was enough to give the president the excuse he needed to fire the defense secretary. After all, how could the defense of the United States be left to a man who had gone mad?

The day of his appearance at the House Committee, Forrestal returned to his office for the last time, where shortly after one of his aides found him "sitting in an extremely rigid position . . . still wearing his hat . . . staring at the bare wall directly opposite. Forrestal appeared not to know that someone had entered the room."[71] He was taken to his home in Georgetown, but things would never be the same again. His whole world was collapsing.

Only a year before, when Dewey had a commanding lead in the polls, Forrestal had helped the Dulles brothers set up a separate spy organization called the Office of Policy Coordination (OPC), completely hidden away from the liberals in the CIA. The Cold Warriors of OPC took orders only from Forrestal and the Dulles faction in the State Department. In anticipation of a Dewey election victory, they had already begun smuggling Philby's Nazis into the United States.[72]

Now the Nazis they had hired to fight the Soviets were supposed to be Communists. Instead of admitting that he had been a fool, Forrestal's by-now delusional mind conjured up a conspiracy, involving Communists, Jews, and White House staff, who were out to "get" him. It was arranged to fly him on an air force plane to join his fellow anti-Zionist conspirator and State Department official Robert Lovett on vacation in Florida. His first words to Lovett were: "Bob, they're after me."[73]

Soon after arriving in Florida, he tried to commit suicide. Some of the "old spies" we asked about Forrestal suspect that part of the blame for his demise rested with Ben-Gurion, who also believed that Dewey would be elected instead of Truman.[74] The Zionists had tried unsuccessfully to blackmail Forrestal with tape recordings of his own deals with the Nazis, but they had much less evidence than they had against Rockefeller. Still, it was enough to tip Forrestal over the edge. His paranoia convinced him that his every word was bugged.[75]

To his many critics, it seemed that James Forrestal's anti-Jewish obsession had finally conquered him. He was admitted to the mental ward of

Bethesda Naval Hospital in April 1949. At the end, Forrestal allegedly could be heard "screaming that the Jews and the communists were crawling on the floor of his room seeking to destroy him."[76] His suicide came in the early hours of May 22, 1949.

Left unattended, Forrestal busied himself by writing verses from Sophocles' *Ajax*: "No quiet murmur like the tremulous wail of the lone bird, the querulous night—" Forrestal left the word "nightingale" half written, went to the nearby kitchen to which he had been allowed unsupervised access, tied his dressing gown sash to a radiator near the window, knotted the other end around his neck, and jumped out. The sash broke, and he fell to his death, sixteen floors below.[77]

A number of our sources among the old intelligence officers say they know exactly what prompted him to commit suicide. The word "nightingale," which Forrestal could not bear to write, was the code name for the Ukrainian Nazi unit, the Nachtigall Brigade, members of which Forrestal had recently helped smuggle to the United States as part of the planned OPC takeover of Philby's "Anti-Bolshevik Bloc of Nations" (ABN), an émigré umbrella group that had been recruited by MI6 to unite all the Fascist factions. Behind the back of Truman and the CIA, Forrestal had worked with the British to recruit the Fascist "freedom fighters" in time for President Dewey's inauguration.[78]

Intelligence reports had been trickling in to the CIA that the Nightingale and ABN were largely comprised of ex-Nazis that had been heavily penetrated by the Communists. Jaroslav Stetsko, one of the political commanders the Nightingale Brigade, had become head of the ABN just before Forrestal's death. Within a few weeks of his funeral, the anti-Dulles faction of the State Department quietly issued instructions that Stetsko was not to have a single piece of paper that he could use to claim U.S. support.[79] While the CIA did not know it, their investigations helped to kill Forrestal but did not affect Dulles's support for the Nazis of the Nightingale Brigade.

The CIA quietly informed the Immigration Service to bar entry to dozens of known Nazi war criminals, such as Stanislav Stankievich, Ferdinand Durčansky, and Yaroslav Stetsko, on the grounds that they were secretly working for the Communists. To Dulles's dismay, the CIA informed Kim Philby, who had just arrived in Washington in January 1949, that it wanted nothing to do with these extremist émigrés or any of the other ex-Fascist networks the British were trying to sell to Washington.

Philby hurriedly assured Angleton and Dulles that there was no truth to any of the CIA charges that the British networks were riddled with "Red Nazis." Angleton kept his mouth shut about the warning he had received from the Jews. The sad truth is that Dulles and his cronies had staked their careers on "anti-Communist émigrés." Too many Nazis had already been smuggled into the United States illegally by the Dulles clique in the State Department and Philby's allies in the British secret service. For political reasons, there could be no admitting the truth to the "liberals" in the CIA. President Truman and the Congress might want to know how Communist agents, posing as Nazis, had gotten into the country in the first place.

They were in too deep to pull back. Emanuel Jasiuk, a notorious war criminal who murdered tens of thousands of Jews in Belarus during the war, had already appeared on a stage with Alben Barkley, Truman's vice president. The occasion was, ironically, a convention of Ukrainian émigrés, some of whom, like Jasiuk, had fought against the Allies and helped obliterate the Jewish population of their homeland. Jasiuk and many of the other top leaders of the Nazis' killing units were already in the country. Angleton and Dulles could only watch silently as the first wave of Nazi recruits sponsored their followers for emigration to the United States. By the time Truman was sworn in for his second term in January 1949, the whole operation had gotten out of control.[80]

For the mutineers, 1949 was the year of no turning back. With Forrestal gone, they needed a new cover for the Nazi networks. It was time for a new "Vessel" scam to deceive the president and the CIA. In May 1949, within days of Forrestal's death, the ex-Nazi intelligence chief, Reinhard Gehlen, concluded a contract to supply the CIA with intelligence against the Soviet Union.[81] By some estimates, the CIA received over 90 percent of its intelligence from the Gehlen organization during the second Truman administration.

There was only one little problem. Gehlen was getting his information from the same Fascist émigrés the CIA had previously discarded as unreliable. Several of Gehlen's own agents and officers warned him that the Soviets were disseminating phony intelligence on a massive scale and that nearly all the material supplied to the Americans was most likely bogus, but he ignored all their pleadings to put a stop to it.[82]

This made Angleton's Vessel scam look like a minor fraud indeed. Yet Gehlen kept sending the phony intelligence, and Angleton kept vouching for Gehlen's bona fides to the CIA. In his own sick mind, he had no other choice. He simply could not believe the warning from Israeli intelligence that Gehlen was a fraud and Philby a Communist agent. As Philby himself recalled with a smirk, "the CIA lost no time in taking over the anti-Soviet section of the German Abwehr, under von Gehlen. . . . Angleton [defended] with chapter and verse, the past record and current activities of the von Gehlen organization."[83]

As we documented in our previous book, *Unholy Trinity,* the heart of

Gehlen's émigré operations was the Max network, now hidden within "Prince" Turkul's front group, the NTS (Narodny Trudovoi Soyuz, or People's Labor Alliance).[84] When Philby was finally confirmed as a Soviet spy by the code breakers in 1951, even Dulles and Gehlen had to purge themselves of Philby's pet Nazis. The only "trustworthy" group left was Turkul's NTS. Gehlen had already fired one of his best operators, Hermann Baun, for insisting that Max was a Communist network. Now his own staff told him that the NTS was a Communist vehicle. Again he ignored the warnings.[85]

Gehlen, like Dulles, was a con man. Max was his only meal ticket, his last source of Soviet intelligence reports to sell to the rich and gullible CIA. He did drop Turkul for a while, but then brought him back. Covering up the scandal cost him quite a bit. According to several of the "old spies" we asked about this question, Ben-Gurion not only blew the whistle in Washington, Israeli intelligence broke its deal with Stalin and revealed the Max secret to General Gehlen. Like Angleton and Dulles before him, however, Gehlen told the Jews to shut up about it. If Gehlen wanted to use a riddled network of spies, that was his business; but the Jews wanted something in return for their silence.[86]

One of our sources, the late John McIntyre, served with American intelligence inside the Gehlen organization from 1948 until 1951. To his amazement, Gehlen's Nazis were training the Mossad, Israel's infant foreign intelligence service. Another source confirmed the account and added that whatever the Jews had on Gehlen, it was so powerful that for the next four decades, even after Gehlen retired, they were allowed to operate freely inside West German intelligence, even piggybacking on its electronic espionage against France and Britain. As evidence of the Mossad's untouchability, this source pointed out that not a single Israeli agent had ever been arrested by the West German government.[87]

One of our sources, who is not a Jew, said that in fairness to the Israelis, they did try to warn Western intelligence, but no one would listen. Angleton sat on Teddy Kollek's warning about Philby for two years. By 1951 Dulles had joined the CIA. When the Israelis warned him about Max, he told them to take it up with Angleton and no one else. Angleton was working overtime on damage control, until Eisenhower was elected the following year. He told the Israelis to keep their suspicions to themselves.[88]

Ben-Gurion was appalled. He had bent over backward to show his good faith, even offering to send Israeli troops to Korea and voting with the United States in the UN. All it had earned him was Stalin's wrath. Not only did Stalin completely close down the Czech arms conduit in 1950, but he closed the door to Jewish emigration from behind the Iron Curtain.

By 1953 Stalin had gone mad as well and concocted the Jewish "doctors' plot," in which Jewish doctors to the top Communist leadership were accused of devious attempts at political assassination through medical manipulation. This new wave of anti-Jewish persecution would last for nearly the next forty years, long after Stalin died.

Ben-Gurion had betrayed his deal with the Soviets, only to have the West reject him. There would be no special intelligence relationship with the Americans; rather it was to be a one-way street. There would be no mutual defense treaty. The Americans were secretly arming the Arabs. The irony is that Israel had the only reliable network of agents behind the Iron Curtain, a network for which Angleton and Dulles took full credit, while they continued to fund the shambles of their Nazi networks with CIA money laundered through the Office of Policy Coordination.[89]

Going public would have done Ben-Gurion no good. Truman was a lame-duck president, and the Republicans would be elected in 1952, no matter what scandals Ben-Gurion exposed. None of them touched General Eisenhower, the American war hero. When President Eisenhower appointed John Foster Dulles as his secretary of state and Allen Dulles as head of the CIA, it was all over. Ben-Gurion quit as prime minister and retired to the desert for two years in disgust. He could not bring himself to deal with the men who financed Hitler. It was clear to him that the Dulles brothers would rather work with the worst Nazis than ever trust the hated Jews.[90]

Even after Eisenhower was elected, Allen Dulles was in too deep to pull back. Angleton simply sanitized the CIA files to keep the OPC-Nazi connection buried. Still, no one could hide the body counts. Franklin Lindsay, one of the OPC intelligence officers running the "freedom fighter" networks, went to Dulles's house in Georgetown with a written warning that these large and loosely controlled émigré nets were so insecure that they would inevitably be penetrated by the Communists. Dulles fought with Lindsay all day and finally browbeat him into watering down his report.[91]

The OPC's losses in Eastern Europe increased alarmingly. Yet, millions of CIA dollars continued to flow through the OPC to Turkul's Communist-dominated "freedom fighters." Why, we asked one of the CIA officers, did the CIA not drop the whole OPC operation when it became clear that the NTS was penetrated? She shrugged and said that all the OPC did was write checks. If the NTS turned out to be anti-Communist, fine. If it was Soviet-controlled, all the CIA had lost was money.[92]

That was not quite true. The OPC had lost the lives of hundreds of innocent people behind the Iron Curtain who hated both the Communists and the Nazis. The CIA had lost control of its own filing system to a forger and madman named James Jesus Angleton. The Americans had lost the support of Israel and driven the Mossad into the arms of British and French intelligence. They had sown the seeds of twin disasters that would haunt them in 1956: Budapest and Suez.

Many among our sources say that it is unfair to blame the CIA or even its rivals in the OPC. They were good troops with bad leaders. The Dulles brothers sold them all out. The whole "freedom fighter" program had nothing to do with intelligence. It was a political ploy to control the Eastern European ethnic vote in the United States. It was all about politics.[93]

CHAPTER 10

THE REVOLVING DOOR

Israeli disgust with American politics in the 1950s can be summarized in a single word: "Dulles." It was Allen and John Foster Dulles who led the American investors into Germany and then obstructed the hunt for Nazi war criminals after the war. It was Allen Dulles who pioneered the use of Fascist émigrés to offset the Jewish vote in the United States. The Dulles brothers were at the height of their power during the Eisenhower administration, and as secretary of state and CIA head, Foster and Allen pursued a number of policies that were hostile to Israel and favorable to its Arab enemies. The height of their achievements was the Suez Crisis, during which they were able to achieve twin goals: the humiliation of Britain and the isolation of Israel, which also shored up their clients' huge oil interests in the Middle East.

The Western response to this Israeli mind-set is incredulity. It is simply too hard to believe that Allen Dulles, a paragon of conservative virtue, would have obstructed the Nuremberg war crimes trials for profit or political advantage. Several elderly American intelligence officers admitted privately to the authors that the Israelis are right, but we would never get the public to believe it.[1] There are too many holes in the history books to fill. In this chapter we examine the following allegations:

- During the early 1950s Israel switched its allegiance to British and French intelligence in disgust with the Eisenhower administration's policies, which were established by the Dulles brothers, Allen and John Foster.
- During the Eisenhower administration the Dulles brothers recruited Nazi war criminals as intelligence agents and sponsored their immigration to the United States.
- A key figure in the Dulles brothers' program was Eisenhower's vice president, Richard Nixon, who utilized Eastern European Fascists for political purposes.
- Both before and during the 1956 Suez Crisis, the Dulles brothers

betrayed British, French, and Israeli military secrets to the Arabs in order to gain the dominant role in the Middle East.

- During Eisenhower's second term the primary goal of the Dulles brothers' policies was to further American oil interests in the Middle East, even at the expense of U.S. intelligence.

The secret scandals of the Eisenhower administration have their roots in the Holocaust. Immediately after World War II, Senator Harley Kilgore's committee attempted to probe the links between Allen Dulles's investor-clients and alleged obstruction of the American de-Nazification program in occupied Germany. Congress was deluged with denials, and in the absence of media interest, the investigations withered. There the matter rested for almost the next four decades.

In May 1982 one of the authors obtained CIA permission to expose a small corner of the U.S. intelligence-Nazi connection on CBS TV's *60 Minutes*.[2] Although the program won the Emmy award for outstanding investigative journalism, the revelations from classified files were met with some skepticism, particularly from *The New York Times*.[3] However, in 1985 the General Accounting Office confirmed to Congress that there were at least half a dozen classified instances where Nazi war criminals had been protected by Western intelligence agencies.[4] Although the hearings were ignored by the press, the initial disclosures had prompted further investigations.

In 1983 Charles Higham published *Trading with the Enemy*, which described the extent of the underlying corporate-Nazi connection of the Dulles brothers' clients. This too was ignored.[5] Moreover, when Burton Hersh published his book, *The Old Boys*, in 1992, endorsing and expanding on Higham's research, the author was viciously attacked in *The New York Times*.[6] Dulles was still a sacred cow.

Finally, in 1993 Christopher Simpson published *The Splendid Blond Beast: Money, Law and Genocide in the Twentieth Century*.[7] To the chagrin of many skeptics, including *The New York Times*, Simpson laboriously documented the extent to which Dulles's corporate clients had financed Nazi Germany and then blocked postwar investigations into their misdeeds.[8] Simpson's irrefutable evidence came directly from declassified government archives. Almost half a century after the Kilgore committee, the harsh record of Dulles's criminal conduct is beginning to emerge from the secret files of the State Department.

The truth is that politics *and* oil were intertwined in Dulles's secret war against the Jews. Not that Jews were his only target. As Simpson noted, the Armenian genocide was Allen's first experience at a cover-up. Dulles, then a young State Department employee, worked for an extreme bigot, Mark Bristol, who wished to advance American interests in the Mosul oil fields in Iraq, which were then controlled by Turkey. Bristol described the Armenians as "a race like the Jews—they have little or no national spirit and poor moral character."[9]

Dulles's State Department files show that he was the man assigned to cover up the Armenian massacre. In 1920 Dulles wrote to his boss that "Our task would be simple if the reports of the atrocities could be declared untrue or even exaggerated but the evidence, alas, is irrefutable. . . . I've been busy trying to ward off congressional resolutions of sympathy for these groups."[10] Where oil was concerned, Dulles was very good at heading off congressional inquiries.

Simpson's research fully documents the equally repugnant cover-up engineered by Dulles and his sources during the Jewish Holocaust of World War II. Dulles's wartime intelligence sources were the Nazi bankers themselves. Their bias was so evident that Dulles's intelligence reports to Washington were given a "lower rating than any other source by OSS headquarters."[11]

Dulles did not care about OSS ratings: He cared about protecting his clients and himself. Consider the case of Karl Blessing, former Reichsbank officer and then head of the Nazi oil cartel, Kontinentale Öl A. G. "Konti" was in partnership with Dulles's principal Nazi client, I. G. Farben. Both companies had despicable records regarding their treatment of Jews during the Holocaust. After the war Dulles not only "lost" Blessing's Nazi party records, but he helped peddle a false biography in the ever-gullible *New York Times*.[12]

Our sources in the intelligence community say that in one respect Simpson missed a major point. Dulles personally vouched for Blessing as an anti-Nazi in order to protect continued control of German oil interests in the Middle East. Blessing's Konti was the Nazi link to Ibn Saud and Aramco. If Blessing went down, he could have taken a lot of people with him, including Allen Dulles.[13] The cover-up worked, except that U.S. Naval Intelligence scrutinized a set of the captured Konti records.

According to several of our sources among the "old spies," Richard Nixon's political career began in 1945, when he was the navy officer temporarily assigned to review these captured Nazi documents.[14] Allen Dulles allegedly told him to keep quiet about what he had seen and, in return, arranged to finance the young man's first congressional campaign against Jerry Voorhis.[15]

In 1947 Nixon the freshman congressman saved John Foster Dulles considerable embarrassment by privately pointing out that confidential government files showed that one of Foster's foundation employees, Alger Hiss, was allegedly a Communist. The Dulles brothers took Nixon under their wing and escorted him on a tour of Fascist "freedom fighter" operations in Germany, apparently in anticipation that the young congressman would be useful after Dewey became president.[16]

When Truman was reelected in 1948, Nixon became Allen Dulles's mouthpiece in Congress. Both he and Senator Joseph McCarthy received volumes of classified information to support the charge that the Truman administration was filled with "pinkos." When McCarthy went too far in his Communist investigations, it was Nixon who worked with his next-door neighbor, CIA director Bedell Smith, to steer the investigations away from the intelligence community.[17]

The CIA was grateful for Nixon's assistance, but did not know the reason for it. Dulles had been recruiting Nazis under the cover of the State Department's Office of Policy Coordination, whose chief, Frank Wisner, had systematically recruited the Eastern European émigré networks that had worked first for the SS, then the British, and finally Dulles.[18]

The CIA did not know it, but Dulles was bringing them to the United States less for intelligence purposes than for political advantage. The Nazis' job quickly became to get out the vote for the Republicans. One Israeli intelligence officer joked that when Dulles used the phrase "Never Again," he was not talking about the Holocaust but about Dewey's narrow loss to Truman. In the eyes of the Israelis, Allen Dulles was the demon who infected Western intelligence with Nazi recruits.[19]

In preparation for the 1952 Eisenhower-Nixon campaign, the Republicans formed an Ethnic Division, which, to put it bluntly, recruited the "displaced Fascists" who arrived in the United States after World War II. Like similar migrant organizations in several Western countries, the Ethnic Division attracted a significant number of Central and Eastern European Nazis, who had been recruited by the SS as political and police leaders during the Holocaust. These Fascist émigrés supported the Eisenhower-Nixon "liberation" policy as the quickest means of getting back into power in their former homelands and made a significant contribution "in its first operation (1951/1952)."[20]

In 1976, after twenty-three years in the White House, the Republicans issued a secret memo that recognized the valuable contribution made by the Ethnic Division of the party over the years, especially in defeating the Democrats in 1952.[21] The irony is that the ethnic Fascists never played a credible role in winning any election and, in later years, caused the Republican party considerable embarrassment when pieces of the Nazi connection began to surface.[22]

To be sure, over the years the Democrats had acquired one or two Nazis of their own, such as Tscherim Soobzokov, a former member of the Caucasian SS who worked as a party boss in New Jersey.[23] But in 90 percent of the cases, the members of Hitler's political organizations went to the Republicans. In fact, from the very beginning, the word had been put around among Eastern European Nazis that Dulles and Nixon were the men to see, especially if you were a rich Fascist, such as Nicolae Malaxa of Romania.[24]

To illustrate the influence of the former Fascists, we have to go back and trace the complex web of interrelationships between such men as Malaxa and Richard Nixon. In 1946, soon after the war had ended, Malaxa had arrived in the United States. Two years later he asked for permanent admission under the Displaced Persons Act. For the next ten years he fought a lengthy, and very expensive, legal battle to stay. Luckily for Malaxa, he had the funds to pay his lawyers, having successfully claimed millions of dollars of Nazi money from the Chase National Bank that had been frozen as enemy assets during World War II. The Treasury Department official who had frozen this money was the same man whose legal firm won Malaxa's case to retrieve it.[25]

Such interrelationships were very common between émigré Fascists and the right-wing of the American establishment. When an Immigration and Naturalization Service official involved in the case against Malaxa resigned his government post, he too was hired to help Malaxa's legal battles. The Dulles brothers' old firm of Sullivan & Cromwell was brought in, as were the law firms of other senior cabinet officers and government bureaucrats, one of whom actually testified on Malaxa's behalf before a congressional subcommittee.[26]

Even such widespread and influential contacts and supporters were not enough for so senior a Nazi as Malaxa. He needed the personal help of Nixon, because the eyewitness evidence against him was so powerful. The problem for Malaxa was that he had, in fact, been the financier of the Fascist Iron Guard party and one of the plotters of an unbelievably bloody *pogrom* against Romania's Jews in January 1941. To protect his business interests, at the end of the war he even had collaborated closely with the Romanian Communists. The Displaced Persons Act expressly barred anyone who even had been a member of such a Fascist movement, let alone anyone who worked with the Reds. It would take an act of Congress to admit a VIP Nazi like Malaxa, and that is what Nixon tried to do in 1951, when he introduced a private bill to allow Malaxa to stay in the United States.[27]

When Nixon's bill failed, Malaxa was forced to leave, but he came up with an inventive scheme to get himself back in. In 1951, with the Korean War raging, Malaxa pretended to go into business making seamless tubes for the oil industry and argued that the enterprise was a vital defense industry. He set up his company in Nixon's hometown of Whittier,

California, and registered it in the same building as the law firm of Bewley, Kroop & Nixon. Nixon's former law partner, Thomas Bewley, was secretary of Malaxa's company, and the vice president was another Nixon crony.[28]

Even such sponsors were not enough, however, so at the height of the Korean War, Nixon intervened personally for his Fascist friend. In order to help Malaxa reenter the country, Nixon sponsored the company's application to give its personnel wartime priority and Malaxa's petition for a U.S. visa because he was allegedly indispensable to its operations. Although both applications were successful and in 1953 Malaxa was given permanent resident status, nothing was ever done to make seamless tubes.[29] The company was used to evade millions of dollars' worth of taxes and then dissolved.[30]

Such windfall profits were not enough for Malaxa, who continued to be active in the Nazi business network established in Argentina by Allen Dulles and his cronies at the end of World War II. In the mid-1950s he visited Juan Peron in Argentina to set up business links and also met with former SS man Otto Skorzeny who, as we shall see, was recruiting Nazi scientists for Egypt's war against Israel. When Malaxa tried to return to the United States, the Immigration and Naturalization Service again blocked him, and in 1958 he was ordered deported. Once again he won his legal battle, thanks to the attorney general, another of Richard Nixon's allies.[31]

To be fair, Nixon was not the only influential public figure in the United States to help the Nazis. Consider the case of Valerian Trifa, the Romanian Fascist who actually led the bloodthirsty mobs on Malaxa's Jew-hunt in 1941. After immigrating to the United States, Trifa forcibly seized control of the small but politically powerful Romanian Orthodox Church there. Trifa had himself declared an archbishop, then "moved in influential circles throughout Cold War America. He made broadcasts over Radio Free Europe to Romania, broadcasts he bragged were arranged by 'my good friend, J. Edgar Hoover.' He sat on daises with the Governor of Michigan and his picture appeared in newspapers shaking hands with a smiling Hubert Humphrey." On May 11, 1955, at Nixon's invitation, Trifa "had the honor of offering the opening prayer before the U.S. Senate."[32]

One of our sources in the intelligence community, a staunch Nixon supporter, insists that the vice president had no idea of the Fascists' background of atrocities and Nazi collaboration but was simply honoring a request from his mentors, the Dulles brothers.[33]

Yet there is reason to doubt the Dulleses-made-me-do-it rationale. As we shall see in Chapter 13, Nixon himself personally recruited ex-Nazis for his 1968 presidential campaign. Moreover, Vice President Nixon became the point man for the Eisenhower administration on covert operations and personally supervised Allen Dulles's projects while Ike was ill in 1956 and 1957.[34] Over the years Nixon maintained a studied silence when confronted with suggestions that he was the highest-ranking American official to have knowledge of the Nazi immigration.[35]

Several of our sources say that the Nixon-Dulles-Nazi connection goes much of the way toward explaining why Israel tried to switch its support to British and French intelligence in the early 1950s.[36] Repugnance for the Eisenhower administration was certainly one of the factors in Ben-Gurion's attempt at rapprochement with the despised British.

With no real allies among the superpowers, the Israelis were eager to cooperate with someone in the covert sphere, although they had no illusions about London's real objectives. They knew that the anti-Semite prime minister, Anthony Eden, was not out to help Israel but wanted to restore Britain's primary role in the Middle East and reverse the influence of the American oil companies.

The issue of British-Israeli cooperation started in 1954, with the victory of Gamal Abdel Nasser over his rivals. Nasser wanted more than an independent nation of Egypt. He wanted the British imperialists out of the entire area, which he would then dominate as the supreme Arab nationalist leader. Nasser also wanted the complete annihilation of Israel. His program called for the reversal of the UN decision to create Israel, an act he termed the "greatest international crime" in history.[37]

The Israelis knew that the British were not really interested in saving them so much as beating Nasser. But if Eden would assist Israel to destroy the one Arab leader who seemed able to unite the Arab world in a crusade to destroy the Jewish state, then Israel could live with Britain's peculiarly aristocratic brand of anti-Semitism. In any case, the April 1956 announcement of an overt anti-Israel military alliance among Egypt, Saudi Arabia, Syria, and Yemen demonstrated that Israel had few options. War loomed, and the Jews needed allies. Thus, on the basis of mutual enmity for Nasser, was built the Anglo-Israeli alliance around the Suez Crisis. In the words of the old proverb: The enemy of my enemy is my friend.

The other member of this alliance was the French government, the joint operators and owners (with Britain) of the Suez Canal, through which two-thirds of Europe's oil flowed from the Middle East's fields. The French were no particular friends of Nasser. The Egyptians were being considerably short-changed by the European shareholders in the canal, especially the British government, which took the largest share of the annual $100 million oil tolls. To the French, Nasser's desire for a larger share of the tolls was bad enough, but Nasser also was aiding the nationalists in France's North African colony, Algeria.

French intelligence had not had a warm relationship with the Zionists during World War II. Many French collaborators tried to outdo the Nazis in shipping French Jews to Auschwitz. As documented in our previous book, President Charles de Gaulle was the postwar originator of the Vatican's Nazi-smuggling activities and tried to employ Fascist fugitives to recreate a French corridor in Catholic Central Europe, before being forced to bow out of the émigré Nazi game by the aggressive British secret service.[38]

As will be discussed in detail in Chapter 13, after the war French intelligence began a massive effort to replicate illegal Nazi biological and chemical war experiments in a secret North African base near Beni Ounif in the French colony of Algeria. According to top-secret U.S. intelligence reports, the French had begun to manufacture an extremely toxic form of nerve gas, GA or Tabun, that had been tested on Jews at Auschwitz: "Starting from the stocks of German munitions charged with GA which they captured during the war, the French have advanced to the point where they are now making pilot-plant quantities of GA . . . so that performance trials can be carried out at the research station in Beni-Ounif, in North Africa."[39]

Another American intelligence report confirmed that the Nazi nerve gas was tested successfully on sheep and that the French were then using the North African range to test a "large amount of BW."[40] "BW" stands for biological warfare, and the intended target was the Soviet Union.

It was the last straw for the French Communists, who had heavily infiltrated the postwar Sûreté, France's secret service, known as the DST. Although there were anti-Semites among the French Communists, the pro-Jewish faction tipped off the Zionists, who promptly blackmailed several members of the French government.[41]

There were non-Communist Frenchmen who voluntarily supported the Jews as well, particularly François Mitterand, who had himself been interned in a Nazi concentration camp. A number of our sources in the intelligence community say that it was Mitterand who, as mayor in the immediate postwar period, allowed the Zionists to use Marseilles as a base for illegal immigration and gun-running.[42]

Gradually, a genuinely cooperative relationship developed between French and Israeli intelligence, although the Beni Ounif blackmail was always in the background. The Zionists proved to be helpful to their secret ally, providing France with information on dissident Arab activities in Algeria. The French connection bore fruit at the time of the Suez Crisis, with Israel using French Naval Intelligence to watch for a stab in the back from Britain. This link was particularly important, as the French access to British plans provided the Israelis with a window into the duplicitous schemes of their "ally."[43] The British needed close watching. Some of Eden's senior cabinet members were scarcely less hostile to Israel than Nasser.

The British and French had done a deal in 1954, which they hoped would resolve the Egyptian impasse peacefully. British troops stationed in the Suez Canal zone would be withdrawn by early 1956. However, the British became increasingly hostile when Egypt turned to the Soviet Union for arms. In September 1955 Nasser signed a $450 million arms deal with the Communists. Ironically, the Egyptian army was supplied by the post-Clementis Czech government, whose weapons had won the 1948 war for the Zionists. The Czechs were now firmly under Moscow's thumb. Despite the watchful eye of the KGB, the British had an Egyptian spy in Nasser's embassy in Prague, who kept them well informed of Communist arms deals to Israel's enemies.[44]

The French had their own problems with their former colonies. Israel's northern neighbor, Syria, signed a $100 million arms contract with the Communists. All the Soviet guns were pointed at the tiny nation of Israel. There were limits, however, to French support for Israel. France secretly had been selling tanks and advanced Mystère jet fighters to Israel, but refused to supply the weapons needed for an offensive war. Although retaining a close, secret liaison with Israel, the French government rebuffed Ben-Gurion's request to buy bomber planes for the looming conflict. Returned to office in February 1955 as defense minister, Ben-Gurion wanted the offensive bombers to destroy the Egyptian air force on the ground, but the French told him that he "should concentrate on a defensive strategy."[45]

Egyptian demands to gain more control over the canal's operations were rejected by the British at the end of 1955. At the same time, the British secret service advised that a war over the canal could benefit London "by accelerating the division appearing between Egypt and the United States, given the fundamental American commitment to Israel."[46] The American people may have been committed to Israel, but their leaders certainly were not. The Dulles clique was in control of U.S. Middle Eastern policy, and as a number of our sources said, the last thing Dulles wanted was a division between Egypt and the United States over Israel.[47]

The Dulles brothers' strategy was to side with the Arabs, even if they were temporarily in league with the Communists. Ideology was irrelevant when it came to commerce. The real enemy was the British oil industry, which was trying to usurp American corporations in the Middle East. In public, the Dulles brothers stated that the United States should oppose European colonialism in favor of Arab self-determination.

This was a bit of hypocrisy, coming from the very people who had quashed Muhammed Mossadeq's nationalist movement in Iran in 1953 and launched the Guatemalan coup in 1954. The real reason for supporting Nasser was not anticolonialism but commerce. The Dulles brothers had been assured that Nasser was bribeable and that, in any event, Egypt was expendable as long as the United States had oil-rich Saudi Arabia.[48] As long as he did not threaten the most important American interest—oil—the Dulleses had no reason to plot to get rid of Nasser.

Given the dreadful state of the British economy in the mid-1950s and its lack of gold and dollar reserves, the Dulleses knew they had London in a vulnerable position. Closing the canal might wreck Europe, but it would be good for American domestic oil prices. The Dulleses wanted to reduce Britain to a second-class player in the Middle Eastern oil business. They cared even less about Israel. Let the Europeans, Arabs, and Jews bleed themselves to death over Suez. A neutral, "anticolonial" foreign policy would ensure that the United States would emerge the winner in the oil game.

The Israelis no longer had friends in the American government. The Republicans were in, and they would stay in. Although 1956 was another election year, American Jews' money or votes could not sway the Republican party. The Dulles brothers knew that they could count on campaign money from the pro-Arab oil lobby. They could afford to ignore the 3 percent of American voters who were Jews. Most of their contributions and votes went to the Democrats, anyway. According to one British author with good connections in British intelligence circles, in 1956 Eisenhower refused to supply weapons to Israel because of the oil lobby.[49]

Through the judicious employment of the Dulles brothers' friends, the oil industry penetrated American policy and even its intelligence operations in the Middle East. The fact is that many U.S. spies either came from the oil companies or ended up working for them. The Dulles brothers' least-known, but longest-lasting, achievement was the creation of the "revolving door" for unemployed spies. Some intelligence officers like Miles Copland were double agents, and their activities too often were not part of their official duties for the U.S. government but extensions of their business interests. As their business interests often involved being anti-Jewish, and thereby hostile to Israel, they used their official positions to pursue pro-Arab and anti-Israeli operations. Sometimes their policy was anti-American as well.

One of the earliest examples of how this double-agent game worked concerned the Standard Oil Company. While busily shipping oil to the

Nazis during the war, Standard "provided officers in Spain and Switzerland to watch Axis oil shipments."[50] It just so happened that Spain was the very country through which Standard's oil was routed to the enemy, and Switzerland was the intelligence base of Allen Dulles, the mastermind of the whole dirty business. As previously discussed, the foxes were guarding the henhouse.

The rosters of Office of Strategic Services men contain numerous examples of the oil business–U.S. intelligence connection. Standard Oil also provided John Archbold, the OSS security officer in Calcutta. Colonel William Eddy was the OSS man in Tangier, who was posted in 1944 to Saudi Arabia as ambassador and arranged Roosevelt's historic meeting with Ibn Saud in 1945, when the president promised to be neutral in favor of the Arabs. After the war Eddy became head of State Department Intelligence in 1946 and 1947, just when the Dulles-Forrestal forces in the department were waging their war against the Zionists. Then he became the Middle East consultant for the Arabian-American Oil Company (Aramco) "and an official of the CIA-funded American Friends of the Middle East."[51]

Kermit "Kim" Roosevelt, the grandson of President Theodore Roosevelt, was another of the "oil spies" who used the revolving door. Kim was an OSS expert on the Arabs and later was the CIA's chief Middle East operator. Then he became vice president for government relations at Gulf Oil and, later still, set up his own consulting firm to make large profits from selling his "expertise" to oil companies and other related businesses. By the 1970s *Business Week* reported that "Roosevelt may charge up to $75,000 just to listen to a problem. The solution costs extra."[52]

There were many other examples of the syndrome, including Franklin Canfield, Howard Palmer, and Laurence Gordon. Canfield served with the OSS in London and "spent many of the postwar years on the legal staff of the Standard Oil Company in London." Palmer served with the OSS in Thailand and then became legal counsel for Aramco. Gordon had worked for Caltex (the merged Standard of California and Texaco company, which Forrestal had put together) and joined OSS in Indochina. After the war he went back to Caltex as director of the overseas division in Paris.[53]

These are only a few examples of how the revolving door was set up after World War II. At that time the oil-intelligence link expanded dramatically, especially under the Dulles brothers in the 1950s. In fact, the CIA seemed to be a prime recruiting ground for the large oil companies, and vice versa. Like several other companies in the oil-related business, including the Bechtel construction firm, the oil corporations provided good cover for CIA agents, many of whom after leaving the CIA provided their intelligence expertise to the oil companies for large salaries.

As Frank Jungers, the board chairman of Aramco, explained in 1978: "For years out there [in Saudi Arabia] we had a good relationship with the agency [CIA], partly because I thought it would make things easier."[54] It did, and not just for Aramco, but also for the CIA and the State Department.

During the 1950s it was really very hard to tell at any time where many U.S. spies owed their true loyalty: to the oil conglomerates or the CIA. Many of our sources in the intelligence community agreed that, with no oil, Israel was expendable to the Dulles brothers' foreign policy.[55]

In fact, with Foster and Allen directing policy under Eisenhower, the corporate influence in the intelligence community became so extensive that it became common American practice to endlessly mouth pro-Israeli slogans, while simultaneously betraying the Jews to their oil-rich Arab enemies. By the time of the Suez Crisis of 1956, the pirates of Wall Street held unparalleled sway over U.S. policies and the Dulleses had two major agenda items in the Middle East.

The first was to complete the historic drive to oust the British empire from this oil-rich and strategically important region where the Dulles brothers' corporate clients dominated economically, but London pretended it was still the major political force. The second was to shore up their clients' oil interests, which were threatened by Arab perceptions of Washington's pro-Jewish policy, even if this was at the expense of Israel, the only reliable, pro-Western democracy in the area. The men they chose for these tasks were those who constantly went in and out of the revolving door between the oil companies and the spy world.

The whole complex web of interrelations between the espionage world and the oil business is exemplified by one man who used the revolving door to further his own ends and those of the oil companies. If the Dulles brothers had a James Bond, it was Miles Copeland, or at least he thought so. "A legend in his own mind" was the caustic analysis from one of our sources.[56]

In 1941 Miles Copeland joined the OSS and soon after was sent to London as a counterintelligence expert. At the end of the war he was in the supersecret Strategic Services Unit and then ostensibly transferred to the State Department. In 1947 Copeland was sent under diplomatic cover to Damascus in Syria, but in reality he was an OPC operative.[57] He became one of Kim Roosevelt's key agents in the Middle Eastern team.

Copeland's experience in engineering the 1949 Syrian coup became the model for CIA operations in the area. U.S. companies such as Aramco and its close partner, Bechtel, worked hand in glove in this and many other covert operations and made huge profits as a result.[58] The revolving door was a symbiotic relationship between the spies and the corporate world.

In one of his own books, Copeland candidly outlined some of the tensions in U.S. policy on the Arab-Israeli conflict. For example, he recounted how, in 1952, he ran a series of disinformation propaganda operations against the Saudi Arabian representative at the United Nations, designed to demonstrate that he was too soft on the Israelis as a result of being under "Western influence." Copeland's boss, Kim Roosevelt, disapproved of this campaign, as he believed "there was nothing wrong with the Saudis' position on the Arab-Israeli conflict."[59] The Saudis, after all, were financing, arming, and training the Arab forces that wanted to wipe Israel off the face of the map. What was good for the oil companies was good for the United States.

One of Copeland's major tasks in the 1950s was to court Gamal Abdel Nasser, the president of Egypt and the man leading the Arab world in its fight against the Jews. Nasser was making strenuous efforts to dominate Lebanon at the time, and Copeland himself summed up the problem that Egyptian policy created for U.S. oil and other big business interests:

> Increasingly, during the 1950s, big oil companies were in evidence—and, naturally, they were followed by sellers of engineering equipment, by investors who foresaw the possibilities offered by the growing communities of American oil company families, and, finally, by representatives of companies selling a wide variety of consumer products. And when oil production finally got into full swing, newly rich Kuwaitis and Saudi Arabians began to spend vast sums of money in Lebanon, causing a boom-town prosperity which drew more and more investors and sales representatives into the area. . . . By the mid-1950s our commercial interest in the area, almost nonexistent ten years earlier, was tremendous. Beirut was the business world's "New York" in the Middle East.[60]

There were megaprofits at stake here. Nasser's pan-Arab movement seemed to hold the key to ensuring a stable environment in the Middle East so that the profits would continue to flow, along with the oil. Like Allen Dulles and Jack Philby before him, Copeland found he could make a lot more money if he joined the business club while retaining freelance status in the intelligence world. So in 1953 Copeland took up duties with the international management consulting firm, Booz-Allen & Hamilton, while agreeing to stay on as a "CIA alumnus."[61]

As Copeland admitted, "the CIA would be my cover for the BA&H job and BA&H would be cover for my CIA work as a loyal alumnus."[62] The man who got him the job was Frank Wisner, who as head of the State Department (later CIA) Office of Policy Coordination had run many of the covert operations using fugitive Nazi war criminals in the late 1940s and early 1950s. In March 1953 Copeland went to Cairo on a joint mission for his two employers. His most important job for the CIA was to offer the Egyptians technical assistance in their war against Israel, although he did not put it that way.

In Cairo, Copeland met with one of Nasser's most trusted advisers, the head of the Egyptian secret service, the Mukhabarat. Under his business cover, he offered to provide CIA intelligence and counterintelligence training to the Egyptians. It was a good offer and was promptly accepted.[63] The training would come in handy when it came time for Egypt to settle scores with the hated Jews. So would the generous assistance the British secret service extended to the Mukhabarat around the same time. As we shall see, both the United States and Britain, while ostensibly maintaining friendly intelligence liaisons with Israel, were simultaneously providing its Arab enemies with the technical knowledge and expertise to destroy the Jews.

It was, and still is, the custom that men like Miles Copeland treated the business world and the CIA as interchangeable jobs. In 1955 he rejoined the CIA and, "as head of a five-man political action unit, he helped to organise a 'games room' in Washington, where international problems could be imaginatively played out."[64] If our sources among the "old spies" are correct, Copeland did more than play games, much more.[65]

After he rejoined the CIA, Copeland became involved even more closely with Egypt and Nasser. He was later open about the conflicting interests of U.S. policy, to say nothing of his own personal interests: "Although we were irrevocably committed to the support of Israel, we had no illusions about what it would cost us in Arab hostilities and in risk to an important source of oil."[66]

It was, allegedly, an even-handed policy. Copeland's job, under Kim Roosevelt's and Allen Dulles's guidance, was to provide support for the Jews, tempered only slightly by American oil interests. Contrary to Copeland's claims, he was hardly "irrevocably committed" to Israel.[67] In fact, most of the intelligence officers we spoke to about Copeland agreed with *The Times* of London's January 1991 obituary: "Much of his function . . . was to explain Nasser's point of view to the State Department and the White House and to counterbalance the effect of the Jewish lobby. He always insisted that he was not specifically pro-Arab or anti-Israeli, simply pro-American: but, like many foreign service officers whose experience has been principally in Arab countries, he tended not to understand Israel. . . ."[68]

Copeland thought he understood Israel only too well. In his view, the Jewish state was causing untold trouble in the Middle East, and damaging American interests, by opening up the area to Soviet penetration. In fact,

Copeland had exactly the same view as that put forward by James Forrestal a decade earlier: The Jews of Israel were a threat to U.S. oil interests in the Arab world and a potential cause of Communist expansion into what had to be kept a purely Western domain.

Around the time Copeland rejoined the CIA in 1955, the buildup to the Suez Crisis was under way. For several years Nasser had been launching terrorist attacks on Israel from Egyptian bases in the Gaza Strip and calling for the destruction of the Jewish state. According to Copeland's version, the Israelis' February 1955 raid on Gaza was a deliberate provocation of Nasser, aimed at pushing Egypt into an increasingly hostile anti-Israeli stance. This, in turn, was calculated to ensure continued and growing support for Israel in Washington, and the success of this Israeli strategy ultimately led to Nasser's decision to ask for, and receive, Soviet weapons.[69]

Copeland's own strategy was to counteract the Jews, which meant doing everything possible to help their enemies. The two prongs to his approach were to buy Nasser's loyalty with Western arms and to woo him away from the Soviets with intelligence against Israel. Our sources say this was all part of a wider espionage war against the Jews that was planned and executed by the Dulles brothers and their supporters in the Eisenhower administration, largely behind the president's back.[70]

Both after rejoining the CIA and later when he was working for various oil companies and other U.S. business interests, Copeland and his boss, Kim Roosevelt, were frequently utilized by Allen and Foster Dulles for "a kind of crypto-diplomacy." Their job was reminiscent of that of the British agents who went before them: to get close to the shah of Iran, the president of Egypt, and the kings of Jordan and Saudi Arabia, so that when the Dulles brothers needed to exercise their influence, there were always well-placed agents ready to do their bidding.[71]

Thirty-five years earlier the British secret service had Jack Philby, Gertrude Bell, and Lawrence of Arabia to do this work. The Dulles brothers had Kim Roosevelt and Miles Copeland. It was a very cozy relationship. By the time of the Suez Crisis, American commercial interests in the Middle East were so important that, as Copeland recorded, the Dulles-dominated State Department organized the oil companies into a quasi-cartel:

> the United States Government sought the advice of business leaders through a number of committees which it sponsored, mainly committees of oil company executives. Oil company lobbies, which until that time had been largely on the defensive ("anti-tycoon" feeling in Washington had been strong throughout the administrations of Presidents Roosevelt and Truman), began to exert some influence on our foreign policy. Although the companies lost enthusiasm for the committee approach after

> the Justice Department threatened one committee with anti-trust proceedings (despite the fact that it had been formed at the request of the State Department) their new boldness on Middle East policy questions survived.[72]

Indeed it did, thanks in no small measure to Copeland himself, to say nothing of the influence of the Dulles brothers, who wanted their corporate clients included as key players in official policy formulations. The Suez Crisis presented both the Dulles brothers and their friends in the oil business with the long-awaited opportunity to expel the British completely from the Middle East and shore up the Arabs' oil for U.S. companies. British policy had been to promote the Arab League in an effort to ensure that the Arabs, particularly the imperial jewel, Egypt, effectively would remain clients. London also wanted to promote "an independent Arab Palestinian State" to "keep the Jews in their place."[73]

As discussed in Chapter 7, Labour's foreign secretary, Ernest Bevin, had tried to prevent Israel from coming into being because, like the U.S. State Department, he believed it would become a Soviet puppet state. However, after Israel was born in May 1948, Bevin told M16 head Stewart Menzies to open a station in Israel and "liaison was soon established" with the Mossad, which received considerable help from the British secret service. "From 1948 onwards the SIS Station in Tel Aviv, its incumbent usually one of the few women officers, ensured a two-way flow of intelligence during years when overt relations between the governments varied from cool to frigid."[74]

According to several of our sources among the "old spies," the key to this relationship was Maurice Oldfield, a bisexual British intelligence officer who established good ties with the Zionists in Egypt during World War II.[75] Anthony Cavendish, a former member of the British secret service, met Oldfield in Egypt soon after the war, and the two became close friends. From Cairo the two spied on Palestine, where Oldfield was mainly responsible for combating Jewish terrorism. After the bombing of the King David Hotel by the Irgun the British army banned all contact between Jewish civilians and its own soldiers, an order that was couched in almost vicious anti-Semitic language.[76]

Of course, those orders applied only to Palestine, not Cairo, where the ubiquitous Israeli agent, Teddy Kollek, had many friends among British intelligence. One of our sources suggested that Oldfield may have been working with, but not for, Kollek at the time.[77] Oldfield later became head of MI6 and was one of the very few pro-Israeli officers in the secret service. Cavendish was another.

According to his own account, Cavendish was particularly upset when he discovered in 1947 that ex-Nazis were moving from Egypt to Palestine to continue their war on the Jews. The Germans were prisoners of war and possessed precisely the military skills that the Arabs required if they were to drive the Jews into the sea before Israel could become an established fact. Cavendish's network discovered that the Arabs organized the "escape" of the Nazi prisoners and then spirited them away across the desert to the Sinai, where they became instructors for the Arab units.[78]

Although Cavendish's memoirs were heavily censored, the Nazi "escapes" in Egypt bear a striking similarity to the numerous escapes of Nazi war criminals from prisoner-of-war camps in Italy that had been engineered by MI6. As with the Egyptian Nazis, the Italian Ratline also sent German volunteers to the Middle East, especially to Syria and Egypt. As will be seen Chapters 11 and 13, these volunteers became important players in the secret war against the Jews. As Cavendish recalled, the climate of the times was markedly against the Zionists, and anti-Jewish feelings erupted among the British soldiers in Palestine in response to Zionist successes.[79]

Where Bevin had opposed the creation of Israel on strategic grounds, his Conservative party successor as foreign secretary, Anthony Eden, had "no sympathy for the Jews. His Middle East comprised Arab clients, not citizens, or victims of persecution."[80] To put it bluntly, Eden was an anti-Semite who during World War II had opposed any suggestion that the Allies should try to prevent the extermination of the Jews. In 1955 he became the prime minister of England. When he moved in to 10 Downing Street, Eden realized that, although he hated the Israeli government, he needed to maintain the covert relations the British secret service had made with its Israeli counterparts.

It was the old imperialist game, and could be applied equally to Arabs and Jews. According to several of our sources, the policy was to manipulate the Jews by publicly being cool toward Israel while simultaneously maintaining a profitable, secret relationship with the Jews' intelligence services.[81] As we shall see, the British were playing a most duplicitous game. While enjoying close relations with the Mossad, MI6 was simultaneously giving Israeli secrets to the Arabs. At the same time, Eden was refusing to sell weapons to Israel. So was Dulles.

In 1956 most Western leaders knew that another war was coming between the Arabs and the Jews. The Jews were to be left, once again, to fend for themselves. Not only did the United States and Britian refuse to supply Israel with the modern weapons it needed, nearly every Western government closed their arms warehouses as well. The Arabs, on the other hand, found willing sellers everywhere.

As Nasser collected weapons from both Communist and Western

sources, the power of his pan-Arab movement had become apparent. In April 1956 the British foreign secretary, Selwyn Lloyd, met Nasser in Egypt and warned him that the Suez Canal was a vital link in Britain's Middle Eastern oil interests. Nasser responded that he wanted 50 percent of the toll profits, but this was brushed aside. The British had no intention of giving some cheeky little "wog" an equal share in his own country. When Foster Dulles canceled U.S. support for the Aswan Dam project, Nasser moved and seized the canal.

The British and French tried everything, but diplomacy didn't work, nor did withdrawing the European pilots who guided the oil tankers through the dangerously shallow canal. The "natives" had been educated too well and could run it without the British and French. Eden was very stubborn. On October 24, 1956, senior British, French, and Israeli officials secretly met in France and finalized their very dirty deal. The British and French actually asked the Jews to be the scapegoats for a naked act of aggression: Israel had to invade Egypt to get things rolling. The Jewish "invasion" would create an excuse for the French and British to seize the canal by force.

The Israelis were tired of the terrorist raids from the Gaza Strip and were afraid that Nasser would eventually make good on his bellicose boasts to destroy the Jewish state. In this war, at least, they would have secret allies. Britian, France, and Israel would be the three musketeers. All for one, and one for all.

The next phase of Operation Musketeer would be the most devious. Britian and France would pretend to be horrified at the Israeli invasion and would demand that both sides stop fighting. When this did not happen, the British and French armies would invade and occupy the canal to protect an international waterway. The covert scheme even had a semblance of legality. The 1954 agreement with Nasser to remove British troops provided for their return in the event of war. Musketeer was a dirty little scheme, but according to the "old spies," the Israelis agreed because it would give them a permanent French-British buffer zone, dividing Egypt and Israel forever. The Arabs would never know what hit them.[82]

According to a number of our sources in the intelligence community, the Arabs were, in fact, provided with excellent intelligence on the Israeli plans. They knew the whole scheme in advance. Even before the secret British-French-Israeli pact, the Egyptians and Syrians were preparing for the war. Both nations had unified their military command structures under Nasser.[83]

Part of the story was told later by a veteran Israeli intelligence officer, Yaacov Caroz. He was in a particularly good position to know, as he was well connected with the French secret service. According to Caroz, in

August 1956, the deputy head of Egyptian Air Force Intelligence was approached by an agent acting on behalf of the British secret service, who proposed a plot to incite a revolt against Nasser within the Egyptian Army. Later the Egyptian intelligence officer was introduced to a British intelligence offier.[84]

Suddenly the British had an important agent inside the enemy's Military Intelligence. The Egyptian agent was paid a considerable sum of English pounds and agreed to carry out the coup. It was obvious that the plot would fail unless the Egyptian had some real intelligence to offer his superiors, so:

> it was agreed that in order to make it easier for him to travel to and from Egypt for consultations about the coup, he would receive secret information about Israel which would enable him to explain to his superiors that his journeys were to meet his "sources." *He was in fact given valuable items of intelligence about Israel,* the type that would convince those concerned of the importance of his missions. The source of the information was none other than the British Secret Service. [Emphasis added.][85]

The British were perfectly willing to betray their Israeli "ally" when the ally's back was turned. The British betrayal took place in the midst of the frenzied preparations for Operation Musketeer, when relations between Israel and MI6 were ostensibly very close. Discovery of the treachery came in December 1957, when Nasser announced that the Egyptian intelligence officer had reported the whole thing to his superiors from the beginning.[86]

Everything including the British-supplied intelligence, had been handed straight over to Nasser. No wonder he had the Syrians combine their forces with Egypt's, under his own command. The colonial "natives" had learned a thing or two about intelligence techniques, thanks largely to the Americans and the British themselves. As Caroz noted: "The British were the instructors and also among the first victims of the Egyptians."[87]

But if the Egyptians knew all about Israel's military preparations, the Americans, who were privately backing the Egyptians, were even better informed. Allen and John Foster Dulles had received very accurate intelligence from a number of reliable sources, especially from the United Nations Truce Supervisory Organization in the Middle East, which confirmed that another Arab-Israeli war was coming at the end of 1956.[88] Yet the Dulles brothers were not the only ones receiving the UN intelligence. Somebody on the UN team was handing it straight over to the Arab intelligence services.[89]

The Dulles boys were plotting to double-cross the British and French and, with them, Israel. U.S. intelligence was playing some dirty games of its own against the Jews. According to a number of our sources, American leaks to Israel's enemies were fairly common at this time. One extremely well informed source said that prior to the Suez Crisis, the NSA had broken several British and Israeli codes and was passing selected details to Nasser.[90]

The intelligence liaison relationship between the United States and Egypt was probably the closest of all the Arab nations at the time. Egyptian counterintelligence officers were, or at least pretended to be, on good terms with their U.S. counterparts, whom they met on the various American training courses.[91] The Americans even gave them sophisticated bugging and phone intercept equipment, and the CIA had a permanent representative in Cairo "who kept in constant touch with the Egyptian authorities."[92] This meant that the Dulles brothers knew what each of the players in the Suez Crisis was going to do.

Secretary of State John Foster Dulles kept the British government at arm's length while his brother, CIA director Allen Dulles, pretended to welcome the British with open arms. British cabinet secretary Norman Brook used the secret service's liaison with the CIA "as a means of telling the President [Eisenhower] what was really at stake."[93] Allen Dulles listened to the whole briefing, nodding his head and puffing on his pipe. The British thought they had an ally.[94]

The Americans had been given some idea of the scheme a few months earlier, in a series of joint meetings Wilbur (Bill) Eveland had with MI6. Eveland had been a U.S. intelligence officer in the Middle East during the early 1950s, and now the British wanted to explain their new policy. According to Eveland, Musketeer was a small operation compared to the original British program. MI6 deputy director George Young suggested that the governments of Egypt, Saudi Arabia, and Syria all had to be overthrown.[95]

Naturally, Eveland thought he had "entered a madhouse," but Young actually asked for American help to overthrow the Saudi king, whose vast oil wealth was making huge profits for the Dulles brothers' clients and whose political attitudes made him the safest pro-American ruler in the region. The British were so unbalanced during the buildup to Suez that they apparently had no idea that not only did the Americans not approve, but they were setting up their ally for betrayal.

According to nearly all the old intelligence officers we interviewed for this chapter, the CIA merely told MI6 that King Saud was an American puppet and not to be touched.[96] The British reluctantly agreed and backed off considerably by the time Operation Musketeer, Israel's military attack on the canal, was finally launched on October 29. The British secret service had toned down its list of demands. Saudi Arabia was off the coup list.

But in return for ignoring the American puppet, the British would replace Nasser with a puppet of their own. They wanted more than merely to restore the Suez Canal to normal operations. They wanted their colony back. The British thought they had cut a deal with Allen Dulles. This was the only time during the whole Suez Crisis that the Americans gave any help to their British ally. The CIA dropped a few crumbs by sending some aerial intelligence to the British, but it was only a ploy.[97]

In fact, there were wheels-within-wheels inside the CIA. The head of the agency, Allen Dulles, was pretending to help the British. The Middle Eastern desk was working to subvert the British and protect Nasser. At the same time James Jesus Angleton, whose own shop was a bitter rival of the Middle Eastern desk, was warning the Israelis not to trust the British under any circumstances. He was unofficially helping Israel, which was strictly against the president's policy.[98]

The Israelis thought that Angleton was out of the loop on Musketeer and promised that they would not get involved. On October 27, just two days before the Israelis attacked the Sinai, Allen Dulles held a top-level conference of senior CIA officers. Just back from a world tour, Dulles knew that the Isralis were about to attack. Apart from his British and French sources, which were impeccable, the U-2 photos of British convoys in Malta and Cyprus and of French preparations in Marseilles and Toulon made everyone certain of Israeli intentions. Perhaps not quite everyone; Angleton was certain of the opposite.

Deputy CIA director Robert Amory even predicted Israel's attack, on the basis of a fairly low-level Military Intelligence report filed from Israel, which could not have meant anything other than war was about to break out.[99] Amory quoted the intelligence report to the gathering, and Angleton:

> . . . listened to this with a smile of disbelief on his face. . . . He was considered by Allen [Dulles] to be the Agency's great expert on Israeli affairs because, over the years, he had increased and consolidated his close liaison with the Israeli intelligence apparatus, Mossad, which passed him useful information and sometimes participated in actions with his operatives. He now said:
>
> "Amory's remark may sound alarming, but I think I can discount it. I've spent last evening and most of the early hours with my Israeli friends in Washington, and I can assure you that it's all part of maneuvers and is certainly not meant for any serious attack. There is nothing in it. I do not believe there is going to be an attack by the Israelis."
>
> He spoke with such authority that Amory's information was dis-

> counted, for the moment, anyway. If [Angleton] said the Israelis were not going to attack, then he had to be believed.[100]

According to another account, Amory didn't take Angleton's smug put-down very well. It was well known that he "did not like Angleton and loathed his arrogant, self-confident air." He snarled back that Angleton was "this co-opted Israeli agent," although he later backed away from this and merely claimed that Angleton was "duped and not duplicitous."[101] According to several of the "old spies," Amory was not the only one who accused Angleton. There was a chorus of support for Amory's claim.[102]

Luckily for Angleton, his slip-up was buried as a piece of unwitting gullibility to Israeli deception operations. His uncharacteristic bungle threatened to focus attention on him just when Israel needed the CIA to be diverted elsewhere. The Zionist intelligence agents who had blackmailed him in Italy must have held their breath. Angleton had nearly gone too far.

The strange thing about the whole affair is that Allen Dulles knew that Angleton was wrong, that the Israelis were feeding him disinformation. Dulles had far better sources than any of them, Amory and Angleton included. He had been personally briefed by the British secret service. He knew exactly when the Israelis would move into the Sinai. Some of the "old spies" suspect that Dulles appeared to accede to Angleton's assessment precisely because he knew about the Jews' blackmail of Angleton in Italy ten years before Suez.[103]

With the precise details of Musketeer in their hands from British intelligence, the Dulles brothers played all sides against each other. Up until the end, the British believed that the Americans would pretend to be critical of Musketeer in public but in fact would be secretly on Britain's side. Foster Dulles let it be known that his decision to close down communications with the British Foreign Office was merely a ploy, to enable the United States to use the UN Security Council to condemn the British-Israeli-French military campaign, while actually siding with them.

At the same time, Allen Dulles kept up the stream of intelligence reports to the British, showing Nasser's troop locations, thereby proving the Americans' sympathy for the operation. What the British didn't know was that while they were leaking Israel's secrets, Dulles was simultaneously giving both Israel's and Britain's plans to Nasser.[104]

For the Americans, everything was going according to plan, but not for long. There was one nasty secret that the Dulles brothers did not know: The British had let Jack and Kim Philby reemerge to launch a joint Middle Eastern operation. Allen's unpredictable friend, Jack Philby, had teamed up with his now-disgraced son, Kim, to play a major part in the Suez Crisis. The Philbys did not trust the Americans to deliver the death blow to Israel. They had to make sure.

CHAPTER 11

THE REVENGE OF THE PHILBYS

The history books record the Suez Crisis as the last gasp of British colonialism in the Arab world. The "old spies" say that a few holes in history must be filled in. First, there was no Israeli surprise attack on the Suez Canal. Everybody leaked Israeli secrets to the Egyptians: the British, the Americans, and the Soviets. The Soviets had stage-managed their own invasion of Hungary to take advantage of the confusion and outrage over Suez.

The American public never realized that Soviet intelligence had penetrated most of Dulles's émigré networks and could manipulate them at will. In the 1950s the Communists were winning the Cold War, while a corrupt handful of American intelligence leaders were trying to bury their political scandals. Among the ugly stories was the fact that the United States sent Nazi scientists to help Egypt build missiles to destroy Israel. This action caused a major escalation in the Middle Eastern arms race.

In this chapter we examine the following allegations:

- The major thrust of the Dulles brothers' policy in the Middle East was to betray both Britain and Israel in order to increase the influence of American oil companies.
- The influence of oil company agents on American intelligence was so powerful that it could alter U.S. policy toward Nasser at will.
- The result of the revolving door between the oil companies and the intelligence agencies was an escalation in covert attempts to aid the Arab armies against Israel.
- Allen Dulles's radical policies had severe domestic political consequences for his protégé, Richard Nixon, in the 1960 elections.
- American oil companies subsidized Jack Philby's anti-British propaganda campaign, only to have it blow up in their faces.

The Suez Crisis was St. John Philby's last major act on the stage of world events. Jack had decided that if he was to see the end of Israel in his lifetime, this was perhaps the best chance he would ever have. Many of Philby's friends thought he was quite mad at this time, but he most definitely was not deranged, as was James Forrestal. Eccentric old Jack

Philby had made a few twists and turns in his political outlook. He had been a Nazi, a Moslem, a British spy, and a secret American agent. By the time of Suez, some even said that he had defected to the Reds, but he was never actually a committed Communist. He just wanted the gullible to think he was. The Jews' victory in 1948 only made him more determined than ever to destroy their state and even less scrupulous about the means he was prepared to use, if that was possible.

After World War II Jack continued his work for the Arabian-American Oil Company while adopting increasingly contradictory stances on developments in Palestine. It was all part of his game. Even his closest friends could make little sense of what he was doing. For example, Philby argued with Ibn Saud "furiously all the time" about what he saw as the king's failure to assert his leadership in the Arab world and deliver a crushing blow to the Zionists.[1]

It was just one more game, and Philby was building yet another persona for himself. The circle had swung round again, to where it had been in the late 1930s, when the king and Philby had their earlier "disagreement" about the future of Jewish immigration to Palestine, and Philby's enemies at court had accused him of being a British imperialist spy. This time Philby "provoked" a series of spectacular arguments with Ibn Saud. There was renewed talk in the king's circle that Philby was actually an agent of the British secret service and a Zionist-Communist spy.

Jack also was building some bridges with his son, Kim, who was now living in Beirut, after he had been forced out of England amid the barrage of American accusations that he was a Communist spy. Jack suddenly began to see the Soviet Union in a similar light to Kim. He denounced the British and trumpeted the Soviets as the leading anti-imperialists. Jack's newfound support for the communists seemed to be a case of like son, like father. It certainly gave his many enemies at court a free shot. "At Riyadh, where Communism and Zionism were accounted twin evils, few could understand why Ibn Saud tolerated, even enjoyed, his company."[2]

Philby said that his disagreements with the king were caused by the corruption and decadence oil money brought to Saudi Arabia. He claimed that it had made the Arabs inferior even to the Jews, who, he said, were at least honest in their business dealings.[3] This was the ultimate in Jack's deceit: Having advised and helped Ibn Saud to acquire massive oil wealth, he now condemned the consequences. In fact, he became quite pious about it all.[4]

As usual, Philby's sanctimonious pronouncements masked his real activities. While condemning the corrupting influences of oil money in Saudi Arabia, he himself was moving freely in Aramco's senior circles. While publicly rebuking the king about the state of his country, he was secretly introducing more and more of Aramco's senior executives to Ibn Saud.[5] In fact, the king and Philby were running their old game again. Philby had a good idea. According to our sources in the intelligence community, he would pretend to defect from the Saudis to the Americans.[6] The Jews may have won the first war for Israel, but in the second they would be driven out. To do it, Philby needed the oil companies, especially Aramco.

For years Philby's friends put his continuing relationship with Aramco down to his obsessive need to find publishers for his long-winded, old-fashioned books. It was partly true. Philby did have a great need to be published, to satisfy both his ego and his greed, and in the early 1950s top Aramco executives assisted him to continue his faltering literary career by finding publishers for him. Two influential American oil men in particular, Bill Mulligan and Tom Barger, were very helpful to Philby.[7]

The relationship went well beyond common literary and historical interests. Mulligan had a bird's-eye view of the revolving door among Aramco, the Bechtel Corporation, and various U.S. intelligence agencies, while Barger, an old friend from the 1930s, was the local president of Aramco in Saudi Arabia.[8] Philby's plan was long term. He had to have the ear of such important executives. With their help, the Jews might yet be driven out of the Arab world.

In fact, executives such as Barger treated Philby with considerable respect, even deference. There was much more to Aramco's generosity toward Jack than simple gratitude for his part in securing its lucrative oil concession twenty years earlier: Philby was chief ideologist and propagandist for Aramco's view of Saudi Arabia. He knew that the key to U.S. policy was the amount of pressure the oil companies could mount in Washington. If U.S. policy was based on the pro-Ibn Saud, anti-Semitic propaganda that he had perfected, the Jews might be beaten yet.

According to our intelligence sources, Philby's plan was very simple. He had to sell his version of the Middle East to the U.S. president and his top advisers.[9] Dwight Eisenhower's victory in 1952 made that possible. By the mid-1950s, as the Middle East stood on the edge of another war, the major U.S. companies operating in Saudi Arabia, particularly Aramco and the Bechtel Corporation, held complete sway in official U.S. circles. President Eisenhower and his secretary of state, John Foster Dulles, supported Aramco's line in every significant aspect.

In January 1956, for example, when Anthony Eden visited Washington to see Eisenhower, the president told him that he supported the idea "that the whole Arabian peninsula belonged, or ought to belong, to King Saud." So much for British influence in Kuwait, Iraq, and Oman. This was exactly the line that Jack had crafted for Aramco to push in Washington, and Ike's use of it demonstrated the success of Philby's propaganda efforts at the very top level of U.S. policymaking.[10]

In short, the man who provided Aramco with the intellectual content for this propaganda campaign was the same man who was "denouncing" the oil-corrupted Saudis. As discussed earlier, Philby was a master propagandist. He even assisted Aramco to adopt its own "style and imagery" to project its propaganda message to the United States: "Saudi Arabia as a mirror-image of the Old West, a wide, unfenced land where nature was unsubdued, where religion was simple and fundamentalist, and the law of the gun prevailed—the desert of Arabia, in short, as America's last frontier."[11]

By the time the Suez Crisis came around, Jack Philby was rightly very pleased with his propaganda work in Washington. Through Aramco, he could influence the most powerful men in the world. The Dulles brothers, of course, needed little persuading by Jack's propaganda on behalf of Aramco and the Saudis. Allen and Foster were pleased, though, that Philby had mended some bridges with another of their powerful allies, the Bechtel Corporation.

For some reason, Jack did not get off to a good start with Bechtel when it formed a partnership with Aramco in Saudi Arabian oil ventures. Instead of helping Bechtel, Philby tried to sabotage it and promote his contacts in the British construction business.[12] His friends in Aramco soon put Jack into the picture. Bechtel was a good business partner and part of the corporate-intelligence team fighting against the Zionists. Like Aramco and several other U.S. oil companies, Bechtel operated so closely with U.S. intelligence that it was hard to tell where private enterprise left off and official government business took up. The company was an ally, not to be undermined for a few British pounds on the side. Philby understood, gave up his secret commission, and ended his anti-Bechtel campaign.

The Dulles boys were relieved. Bechtel was one of their long-standing allies, which had stepped in to play its part in the secret war against the Jews. This giant multinational engineering and construction company was a powerful force on both the domestic and international chessboards. In fact, Bechtel was a major player in the war against Israel.

Through its rugged head, Steve Bechtel, Sr., the company had forged close business relations with the oil business in the 1930s, and like the oil companies, Bechtel was infused with hatred for the Jews. Mostly Bechtel's anti-Semitism sprang from the same corporate wellspring as that which infected the pirates of Wall Street, although Bechtel is a West Coast company. Its early experience in Palestine certainly confirmed its hatred for the Jews when, during the 1948 war, Bechtel had to abandon a major project because of the Zionists and lost millions of dollars in profits. The company was giving military assistance to Ibn Saud in his preparations to drive the Jews into the sea. When war broke out, Bechtel allegedly helped the Arabs to procure European weapons.[13] Despite Bechtel's denial, the arms did improve the company's relations with Ibn Saud.

Like the other anti-Jewish corporations, Bechtel soon learned that it was better to side with the Arabs, and banned the employment of Jews on its Saudi projects. It was hardly surprising that Bechtel soon established good connections with U.S. intelligence and became one of the leading corporations to use the revolving door between business and the espionage world. Bechtel's intelligence connections were not accidental. They came through John L. Simpson, a director of the J. Henry Schröder Bank and close friend of the Dulles brothers.[14]

By the time the Republicans won the White House for the first time in twenty years in 1952, Bechtel had contacts at the very highest political levels, including President Eisenhower, Vice President Nixon, and Secretary of State John Foster Dulles. Bechtel's intelligence connection went right to the very top, and Allen Dulles even disclosed top-secret government information to the company. It was a two-way trade.[15]

According to Jack Philby's Aramco executive friend, Bill Mulligan, Aramco's and Bechtel's Saudi teams were "loaded with CIA. . . . The agency didn't have to ask them [Bechtel and Aramco] to place its agents," Mulligan told Laton McCartney, author of the seminal history on Bechtel. The key Bechtel man in these joint operations was probably C. Stribling Snodgrass, who "functioned—both for the CIA and for Bechtel—as a Middle East intelligence agent."[16]

For a while Snodgrass worked for Bechtel, and then, after returning to government service, he frequently participated "in National Security Council meetings and CIA briefings." It was, again, a mutual relationship. While ostensibly working for the government, Snodgrass passed on to Bechtel "an ongoing stream of classified political intelligence" to which he was privy, while relaying to the intelligence community information Bechtel obtained on Saudi Arabia and other oil-producing countries. Before long it was rather difficult to tell what was legitimate business activity and what was covert action for the U.S. government. Bechtel had access to the top-secret reports of the CIA and the departments of State, Commerce, and Defense. The government had access to Bechtel's facilities to run its intelligence operations.[17]

As will emerge in Chapter 19, Bechtel went on to wage its anti-Jewish campaign for many decades. By the time that the Reagan-Bush team moved into the White House in the 1980s, Bechtel provided several key cabinet appointments who played crucial parts in the modern war against the Jews.

Three decades earlier it was Jack Philby who established the themes that came to dominate American policy, and by the early 1950s the Saudis were very satisfied at the success of his propaganda campaign in Washington. The oil companies were dictating foreign policy and, with Jack's skillful expertise, tilting the intelligence reports that Aramco and Bechtel sent back to the CIA. The White House, the State Department, the CIA, and several other key government departments were all under the control of people who had adopted Philby's view of the Middle East. Just at the peak of his success, however, Philby had a stroke of bad luck. In 1953 Ibn Saud, his partner and patron, died.

To Philby's dismay, the Western-educated heir to the throne, Crown Prince Saud, was far more interested in making money and living luxuriously than in waging a holy war against the Jews. Jack spurned the Saudi royal family with even greater spleen—and this time he was not faking it. In April 1955, eighteen months after Ibn Saud had died and been replaced by one of his sons, Philby was expelled from the country. According to several of the "old spies," Jack's anger at the king's stupidity was mostly genuine but partly a calculated maneuver on Philby's part.[18]

Philby proclaimed the end of the Wahhabi empire: Saudi Arabia was beset by "appalling corruption," and the royal family's morals were being picked up "in the gutters of the West." The new King Saud summoned Philby and joined the rest of his court in humiliating his father's old friend. They spat on Jack and demanded an apology. He was ordered to submit all his future writings for censorship. He refused and soon after was expelled.[19]

Philby was out of Saudi Arabia, at least for the time being, but he certainly was not down. He launched another propaganda campaign, this time explicitly against the Jews. Ever since the Zionists had won the 1948 war, Philby had been waiting for this moment. Now he had no need of restraint. He realized that there would be no more misleading negotiations with Weizmann, Ben-Gurion, and Sharett. The Jews had Israel and no longer needed to talk with such elderly Jew-haters and Fascists as Jack Philby.

Philby became almost fanatical in his own condemnation of the Jews, while simultaneously defending the reputation of his old anti-Jewish friend, the late King Ibn Saud. In public, Philby dismissed any suggestion that Ibn Saud had been a Jew-hater—which, of course, simply didn't stand up to the evidence. The Wahhabi culture was thoroughly racist when it came to Jews, and Ibn Saud wanted the State of Israel wiped off the face of the earth.[20] Philby could not help but reflect the underlying Saudi racial bias in his own tirades:

> the true basis of Arab hostility to Jewish immigration into Palestine today is xenophobia, and instinctive perception that the vast majority of the central and eastern European Jews, seeking admission into Palestine owing to persecution in their own countries, are not Semites at all. . . . Whatever political repercussions of their settlement into Palestine may be, their advent is regarded as a menace to the Semitic culture of Arabia. . . . the European Jew of today, with his secular outlook and his repulsive foreign ways, is regarded as a stranger and an unwelcome intruder within the gates of Arabia.[21]

As discussed at the beginning of this book, education, democracy, and human rights are anathema to a dictator, and the House of Saud contains arguably the most powerful dictators in the Middle East. According to Philby, the Moslem Arabs preferred Christianity to Judaism, which "has always been regarded in Islam with feelings akin to contempt as the faith of down-trodden minorities scattered around the world in Ghetto communities without political rights or importance."[22]

After decades of deception, Philby's own views on Israel had suddenly surfaced. Just a few years before he had pretended to negotiate deals with the Zionists to give them Palestine. Now he revealed his true loyalties: "I have always held, and still hold, that the Jews, in whose favour the Balfour Declaration and the mandate were drafted, have no shadow of legal or moral right to go to Palestine."[23]

Philby finally had revealed his true attitude after years of deceit. During World War II, when he thought he could subvert the Zionists through secret negotiations, Jack had proposed exactly the opposite. In return for £20 million, the Jews could have all of Palestine and the Arab inhabitants would have to move on.

By the mid-1950s, with Israel a reality, Philby had changed his tune. With the benefit of hindsight, he was convinced "that Britain and America have from the beginning been firmly minded to ride roughshod over all considerations of right and justice in favour of Zionism, and that they could at all times bring irresistible force to bear against the Arabs on that issue."[24]

Allen Dulles must have been stunned when he learned that Philby was condemning American imperialism as well as British. It was one thing for Philby to launch a propaganda attack on the Jew-lovers in the West, but it was quite another for him to adopt the Pan-Arabist, pro-Communist jargon of Egypt's President Nasser. Philby barely muted his blasts. In one of his many diatribes against the Jews, he said he was "convinced that any military argument which the Arabs might be able to bring to bear on the issue would be strongly, and irresistibly, countered in favour of Jewish aggression by the great 'freedom-loving' democracies of the world."[25] The

Jews must have been surprised at Philby's claim that the Western nations would send armies to defend Israel. None of them had even signed so much as an arms deal, let alone a mutual defense treaty. Jack's son, Kim, also must have been surprised to find himself in agreement with his father's propaganda. It sounded so familiar to Moscow's refrain of the twin evils of Zionism and imperialism.

Suddenly father and son were in genuine alliance for the first time in twenty-five years. As far as Jack was concerned, Britain's secret alliance with Israel against Egypt must be stopped. If the Soviet Union was the only country willing to stand up for the Arabs against the imperialists and the Jews, so be it.

One U.S. intelligence officer later bitterly regretted his association with the Philbys at this time. Bill Eveland later recounted how he came across the father-and-son team in Beirut through the help of the local correspondent of *The New York Times,* Sam Brewer, and his wife, Eleanor, who would soon become Kim's lover and then wife. Like everyone else in U.S. intelligence, Eveland wasn't aware that the British had let Kim back into the fold again.

After Kim's fellow double agents Guy Burgess and Donald Maclean defected to Moscow in 1951, many in both British and American intelligence suspected that Kim had tipped them off. The British secret service had promised the CIA that Kim had been dropped from all intelligence work, but it was a lie. In fact, the British secret service had obtained Kim's Beirut job with the editor of *The Observer,* David Astor. The new intelligence assignment was arranged by Kim's old friend and supporter within MI6, Nicholas Elliott. It was no simple reporter's job. In reality, Kim was back on the payroll for the British secret service, as a freelance "informant" on retainer.

While at the time even the British didn't know that father and son had teamed up together to back Nasser, the Philby connection led to Bill Eveland's disgrace and ultimately terminated his career. In September 1956, on the eve of the Suez War, Sam Brewer asked Eveland for a favor. Suddenly sent on assignment by *The New York Times,* Brewer was unable to keep an appointment with his old Spanish Civil War colleague, Kim Philby. Instead, Eveland went with Eleanor to meet with Philby, whom father Jack accompanied.[26] Eveland thought little about the meeting at the time, but according to several of our sources, the father and son had gotten together for more than just a social visit. The Philbys were about to add their own twist to the Suez Crisis.[27]

Kim had arrived in Beirut in August 1956 and taken up residence with Jack just outside Beirut. The two became very intimate—strangely intimate for two men, albeit father and son, who supposedly were on opposite political extremes. As the Suez Crisis developed, Jack and Kim were firmly on Nasser's side. It was almost exactly the same as their relationship in the early years of World War II, when Jack introduced Kim to his establishment friends and unwittingly helped him to penetrate MI6. Now he was introducing his son to his impressive list of contacts in the Middle East.[28]

Kim's major targets were to be the Arabs, especially Nasser's Egypt and Saudi Arabia, where his father's extensive contacts were thought to be useful in the buildup to Suez. Once again, just as in the days of Jack's Spanish oil deals in the late 1930s, Kim was assigned by MI6 to spy on his own father.[29] And just as Kim had let MI6 down earlier, once again things did not work out the way British intelligence hoped.

Most historians who have written about Kim Philby's Beirut interlude have concluded that at first he was inactive in the spy world. Phillip Knightley, the only Westerner to interview Philby before he died in Moscow in 1988, says there "is no evidence that during this period in Beirut—his first three years—Philby was very active in the intelligence world for either side." Patrick Seale, who knew Kim at this time, claimed that the "delicate nature of his covert duties for both the British and the Russians forced him to move cautiously."[30] Both Knightley and Seale insisted that Philby was not drawn back into the spy world until 1960, when the British secret service sent Kim's old friend, Nicholas Elliott, to Beirut as SIS station commander.

According to a number of the best-informed "old spies" among our sources on both sides of the Cold War, Knightley and Seale are both wrong. Our sources insist that Kim was extremely active in the intelligence world as soon as he arrived in Beirut. He was, in fact, the second-in-command to the SIS point man for Operation Musketeer, the British-French-Israeli plan to attack Egypt and destroy Nasser. Naturally, Kim was obeying orders from Moscow, which meant sabotaging British interests.[31]

Kim's betrayal of Musketeer was unwittingly aided by his father, who was doing much the same job for the Americans by helping to undermine the British-French-Israeli operation. What Allen Dulles did not know was that Kim and Jack were playing the Western superpowers off against each other. Both Philbys privately agreed that the Soviets were the only handy antidote to another victory for British colonialism and American exploitation. Between Kim's access to British intelligence and Jack's access to Aramco, there was little they did not know about Musketeer. The father-and-son team was in a perfect position to betray the operation to the Soviets, and they did.[32]

Although Jack actually did not share Kim's ideological fervor for communism, he was swayed by his son to help Nasser at the height of the

Suez Crisis. Now that Ibn Saud was dead, Nasser appeared to be the uncrowned king of Arab nationalism. Petty motives may have intruded as well. Some of those among our intelligence sources believe that Jack felt abandoned and betrayed by Ibn Saud's son. They say that Jack made one last effort with the king, briefing him about what was at stake and how playing the Soviet card would save Nasser. To Jack's disgust, the young king replied that he didn't care what happened to Egypt, just as long as more oil money flowed into the royal coffers.[33]

Rejected by the westernized Saudis, Jack became a propagandist for President Nasser and sent an endless stream of articles and letters to any newspaper that he thought might even consider publishing them. His rhetoric was anti-imperialist, especially anti-British imperialism.[34] Kim followed his father's propaganda lead on Nasser, a strange thing given British policy and what Kim must have assumed about his post in Lebanon being another test of his loyalty set by the British secret service. One study says that Kim's newspaper articles were balanced and impartial, except in one very important area: "The exceptions were his references to Nasser. He maintained close links with a group of Arab Nationalists, mostly Palestinian refugees, centering on Dr Wahid Khalidi of the American University of Beirut. This group regarded Philby as easily the most pro-Arab foreign journalist stationed in the Lebanon and by pro-Arab they meant pro-Nasser. . . ."[35] Of course, the Philby family was not the only source of Soviet information on Musketeer, only the earliest. Jack and Kim gave the Kremlin time to consider a variety of options. The Philbys wanted the Soviets to expose the Musketeer fraud in the UN and lead the Arab nations in the fight against imperialism and Israel. The Soviets did not want to risk World War III, so they settled on a compromise. They would denounce the West for trying to steal the canal and use the uproar to conceal their own theft of a nation. The Kremlin was having problems in its own empire in Eastern Europe, especially in Hungary, East Germany, and Poland. It was time to crack the whip.

On Tuesday, October 26, 1956, three days before the Israelis were scheduled to attack Egypt, the Soviets launched their secret weapon, the Max network, for the last time. The CIA had thoughtfully equipped "Prince" Turkul with his own transmitters in Germany, so that he could broadcast propaganda into the Soviet Union. This time Turkul aimed his broadcast at Hungary. Using genuine CIA codes, he triggered the premature uprising of the Hungarian underground. For the first three days it looked as if the resistance was winning. The Soviet garrison force pulled out of Budapest and an independent government was proclaimed. The Western nations watched with admiration and then, on October 29, turned their attention to the Middle East, where Operation Musketeer had begun.

At first the military campaign went well, especially for the Israelis. Bad planning cost the British and French a couple of days before they could implement their threat of intervention if Israel and the Arabs didn't stop fighting. Then all hell broke loose. The Soviet government exposed the entire scheme in the United Nations and gave the British and French an ultimatum: Withdraw from Egypt or face nuclear war. The ultimatum was "couched in the most brutal language . . . threatening the bombardment of Britain with long-range guided missiles equipped with atomic warheads."[36]

A forewarned Nasser had blockaded the Suez Canal immediately by sinking every ship he could as quickly as possible. Instead of securing Europe's oil supplies, the British-led operation had the opposite effect and had closed down the tanker route. When the British government asked for emergency oil supplies from the United States, Eisenhower told his aides with a smile that the British should be left "to boil in their own oil."[37] He was not about to fight World War III to save Britain's oil profits. The Dulles brothers could not have agreed more.

Neither could the Kremlin. On November 4, while the West was bickering over the Middle East, the massive tank divisions of the Soviet army sprung the trap. They raced across Hungary, crushing everyone in their path. The West was too split over Suez to react. Instead of fostering a Western alliance against the Soviets, Foster Dulles was screwing the British to the wall. On November 6 the British chancellor of the exchequer, Harold Macmillan, spoke by telephone to Foster. The British position seemed hopeless. The Arab world had unanimously supported Nasser and cut off oil supplies to Britain. Reserves would only hold for a few weeks, and gas would have to be rationed in the near future.

Huge amounts of Britain's currency reserves had already been lost because of the international finance community's reaction to the operation. "Dulles made his terms, as a corporation lawyer would: cease fire, and you get American help with sterling; no cease fire, and sterling can go down the drain and take Britain with it."[38] The Suez debacle was almost at an end. The Americans had won, especially the Dulles brothers' oil friends. A few days later Eisenhower indicated just how well he regarded the oil companies, when he gave them special presidential approval to avoid antitrust indictments so they could "cooperate" in supplying Europe with oil and make large profits from Britain's folly.[39]

The Dulles brothers' longtime oil clients were in the driver's seat. On the other hand, the British and French had to be punished. There would be no U.S. oil for them, or the rest of Europe, until they had pulled all their troops out of Egypt. By the end of November they had no choice, and the last trace of Britain's Middle East empire was extinguished when Operation Musketeer came to its conclusion.

A few weeks earlier, on November 12, the last sparks of the Hungarian uprising were being extinguished as well. While the West bickered over Middle Eastern oil, Turkul's network had broadcast false promises that American paratroops would join in the struggle. The last teletype line from Budapest carried the death rattle of the freedom fighters:

> The fighting is very close now and we haven't enough Tommy Guns in the building. . . . I don't know how long we can resist. . . . Heavy shells are exploding nearby. . . . What is the United Nations doing? Give us a little encouragement. . . . They've just brought a rumor that American troops will be here within one or two hours.[40]

But it was only a rumor. The Americans would do nothing. The UN would do nothing. Everyone was too busy fighting over oil and the Suez Canal. Allen Dulles's chief of covert operations, Frank Wisner, read the last words just before the line went dead: "Goodbye friends. Goodbye friends. God save our souls. The Russians are too near."[41] Wisner's heart was broken. His dreams of an underground army to roll back communism had crumbled in Hungary. No one in Eastern Europe would ever trust the Americans again. A few years later Frank Wisner went mad, just as his friend James Forrestal had before him. Like Forrestal, Wisner killed himself.

His daughter spoke to us of those bitter days and said: "Allen Dulles used my father."[42] Our sources say that Wendy Wisner is correct. Her father was one of many decent men, neither fools nor bigots, who devoted themselves to the cause of rolling back communism, only to be ensnared in the Dulles brothers' corporate agenda. As Paul Nitze later admitted, Dulles's hard-line anticommunism was largely for domestic consumption. Other sources from the Eisenhower era agree that the Dulles brothers were frauds and that their campaign to use American intelligence for private profit ruined the careers, even the lives, of many people.[43]

The Dulles brothers used the British as well and led them into a trap for the sake of their oil clients. The year 1956 was a complete disaster for London. Instead of strengthening the empire's hand in the Middle East, Operation Musketeer had left Britain more isolated and weaker than ever. Saudi Arabia, already firmly in the American camp because of its lucrative relationship with Aramco, took the opportunity provided by the Suez Crisis to break off diplomatic relations with Britain.

Anthony Eden's temporary alliance with the Jews against the Arabs had turned into a disaster. It was time for the British to switch policies again. Now the secret service's job was "to convince the Saudi ruling family and its advisers—several of the latter on close and confidential terms with SIS officers in the Middle East—that the era of counterrevolution was also one of renewed support for the Arab case on Palestine."[44] So much for the alliance with Israel. Instead of the three musketeers, it was every man for himself.

While the British secret service agents were courting the Saudis, Foster Dulles, on the advice of the oil companies, decided to drop his support for Nasser. Of course, that meant convincing the U.S. government to do an about-face. Allen Dulles put Kim Roosevelt and Miles Copeland on the reverse propaganda job. Now that Britain was out of the Middle East picture, Nasser was no longer a useful asset. Over the next two years, Copeland and the oil companies exerted enormous pressure on both the White House and Congress, and completely turned round the State Department's pro-Nasser policy. In its place, they put the plan that Jack Philby and his friend, Ibn Saud, had hatched so many years earlier: Saudi Arabia was to be the number-one country in U.S. Middle Eastern policy.[45]

In the aftermath of Suez, Copeland went back through the revolving door, left the CIA once again, and went to work for the oil business. At first he was engaged in finding solutions to the impasse over who should operate the Suez Canal and the oil pipelines. Together with an old intelligence colleague, Jim Eichelberger, Copeland floated the idea that there should be a "government-and-industry consortium" to "own and manage" the canal and pipelines. Allen Dulles agreed, and Copeland and Eichelberger took the proposal to the main U.S. companies—Standard Oil of New Jersey, Socony Mobil, Gulf Oil, Texaco, and Standard Oil of California.[46]

Predictably, none of the companies was interested in the proposal. They were private enterprise to the core and while eager to take large profits from government contracts, they did not want to go into business with the state. The companies all had counteroffers. Three wanted Copeland and Eichelberger on their payroll, and the other two offered them consultancies. A few weeks later both men accepted Gulf's consultancy offer. Their plan was to bring their boss, Kim Roosevelt, on board the gravy train soon after.

The firm of Copeland & Eichelberger opened for business in Beirut in July 1957. Within a week it also had as clients "one of the world's largest banks and one of the world's largest airlines." Over time it ended up working for most of the major oil companies, several of the leading independent oil companies, and "a major construction company" for which it "did a bit of industrial espionage."[47]

Copeland was up to his old trick: doing business for the oil companies while spying. The intelligence reports he and Eichelberger now compiled as part of the private sector were still forwarded to Roosevelt at the CIA, who resigned a year later, not to join Copeland & Eichelberger but to become a vice president of the Gulf Oil Corporation and, as Copeland observed, "once again, for all practical purposes, our 'boss'!"[48] It was yet another illustration of the way in which the Dulles brothers' revolving door operated. Roosevelt was Copeland's boss at the CIA, and then when Copeland switched to Gulf Oil, he turned up there too, once again as his boss in the espionage business.

It was all so convenient. Everyone made much more money than they did from the government, and they were doing the same job anyway. Copeland was working for Gulf, where Roosevelt was vice president for relations with the government. At the same time Roosevelt was still secretly reporting directly to the CIA. Copeland still sent his reports to Roosevelt, who passed them to the CIA, as coming from "an exceptionally well-informed source." Copeland was not at all embarrassed about the whole arrangement. He wrote it up in his autobiography: "With our enthusiastic agreement, he [Roosevelt] took over both our contact with Gulf and our contact with the Agency."[49]

Although Copeland does not name it, there are good reasons to suspect that Bechtel was the major construction company on his list of clients. As previously discussed, Steve Bechtel cultivated extremely close relations with Allen Dulles and others in U.S. intelligence, especially the Middle East experts. His friendship with Kim Roosevelt went back to October 1950, when they met in Tehran.[50]

Three decades later this intelligence connection would prove useful to Copeland in the modern espionage war against the Jews, when Bechtel executives such as George Shultz and Caspar Weinberger were in the Reagan-Bush administration and Copeland was active in plotting to implement viciously anti-Israel policies as part of the "retired spies" network.

Copeland's work in Beirut in the second half of the 1950s combined spy business with pleasure: "Thanks to our old CIA colleague, Jim Angleton, we began to entertain." In return for Copeland's reports, Angleton paid all expenses to entertain lavishly the local Western colony, especially Kim Philby, the suspected Communist agent.[51]

According to Phillip Knightley, Philby was keeping an eye on the CIA as well as on his friends in British intelligence. American Bill Eveland was suspected of being indiscrete, allegedly providing Kim with a great deal of top-secret intelligence about the CIA's covert operations. Although Eveland strenuously denied the allegations, his career in intelligence was ruined.[52] What Eveland and Philby did not know was that Copeland had bugged Kim's apartment. After Suez, Angleton was finally convinced that perhaps Teddy Kollek was right about Kim's true loyalties.[53]

For almost an entire decade, James Jesus Angleton, Reinhard Gehlen, and the other paragons of Western intelligence had completely ignored Israeli warnings that the Soviets had penetrated their friends on the far right. Philby's Fascist "freedom fighters" had a pipeline to Moscow, all right, but the intelligence flowed in the wrong direction.

From the Israeli point of view, if the Dulles brothers wanted to continue running penetrated agent networks, they had only themselves to blame for the Max debacle in Budapest, which occurred at the same time as Suez. Israeli intelligence knew that nearly every secret they shared with the West went straight into Arab hands. As the decade of the 1960s opened, the Israeli intelligence services began making quiet overtures to the Soviets. They would never trust the American government again. After Suez, their disgust with the Dulles brothers was complete.[54]

Suez was the crowning achievement of the Philby family. From Kim's point of view, he had tricked the West one last time and helped create the climate of chaos necessary for the Soviets to suppress the Hungarian uprising. Jack was not as satisfied as his son. Although he had tried his best to help the Arabs wipe Israel off the map, to Jack Philby's utter disgust, the hated Jews survived.

Jack, who reconciled with the Saudi Arabian royal family and returned to live in Riyadh, died a bitter man in September 1960, while on a visit to see his son in Beirut. Kim was at his father's bedside when suddenly he sat up and muttered "God, I'm bored," and then died. Forty years of ceaseless effort to defeat the Jews had come to naught for this extraordinary spy; the State of Israel showed no signs of disappearing. His son had his father's tombstone inscribed with this epitaph: "Greatest of Arabian explorers." It did not do Jack justice. Philby, Sr., was arguably the most effective of the earliest agents in the secret war against the Jews.

In the aftermath of both the Suez and Max debacles, Vice President Nixon came to realize that Allen Dulles's Nazi networks were dangerously close to exposure. Tough-minded CIA agents were digging into the dirt of the Hungarian uprising and had identified the "Fascist Prince" Anton Turkul as the culprit who had broadcast the CIA's codes for armed revolution on his own NTS radio transmitters in Germany, impersonating the CIA-funded Radio Free Europe. There were rumblings in the Pentagon and in the lower levels of CIA that old Bedell Smith was right: All the émigré networks probably were penetrated by the Communists.[55]

Angleton snuffed out further investigations into the "Red Nazi" scandal and tried to run his own émigré uprising in Czechoslovakia the following year. This time Operation Red Sox/Red Cap was shut down and Turkul's NTS network was rolled up. Because of the potential political fallout, there was no further inquiry into Communist penetration of the émigrés in the United States. The CIA filled four huge safes with NTS records, locked them up, and walked away. It tried to terminate, and eventually succeeded in terminating, all CIA funding for the various émigré groups that the State Department had sponsored. The CIA would not take the blame for Dulles's Nazi networks.[56]

J. Edgar Hoover had protected himself by removing the FBI from security checks on Dulles's émigré recruits. FBI files on Nazi émigré informants were transferred from headquarters archives to the New York and Washington field offices. By 1959 Nixon was left holding the bag. It was hardly the time to play the "ethnic card" and revive the Eastern European campaign strategy. The Nazis kept their heads down in the 1960 election, and the Eastern European ethnic vote stayed at home.[57]

In many ways, Nixon's 1960 campaign was the last victim of the Dulles strategy during the Suez Crisis. A few weeks after Philby's death, Vice President Richard Nixon's run for the presidency was narrowly defeated. He lost by one-tenth of 1 percent, the closest margin in American history. The old taunts of 1956 that a vote for Eisenhower was a vote "for Nasser, Nixon and Dulles" came back to haunt him.

Nixon's choice of running mate, Ambassador Henry Cabot Lodge, was particularly unfortunate, as he had been the main spokesman for the Eisenhower administration's condemnation of Israel during the Suez Crisis. Lodge was considered one of Nasser's main supporters, hardly the kind of vice presidential candidate to win support from Jewish voters.[58]

American Jews overwhelmingly supported Kennedy and claimed credit for his victory. To everyone's surprise, Israel's politicians endorsed his Republican opponent. To this day, many American Jews do not understand why the leaders of Israel openly backed Nixon and vehemently denounced John Kennedy for his father's well-known pro-Fascist, anti-Semitic views.[59] True, Joseph Kennedy was a despicable man who invested secretly with the Nazis and encouraged Britain to ally itself with Hitler against Stalin, but was that any reason to hate his son? According to a number of our sources in the intelligence community, Ben-Gurion had nothing against JFK personally, but he had a ton of dirt on Nixon.[60]

Some Israelis felt that Nixon's involvement with Dulles's Nazi networks left the candidate dangerously vulnerable to exposure. While there is no evidence of political blackmail, as will be seen in Chapter 14, when Nixon did gain the presidency in 1969, he turned out to be the most generous arms supplier that Israel ever had. Kennedy, on the other hand, was an unknown quantity to the Jews.

According to some of the former intelligence officers we interviewed for this chapter, one of the secrets that Ben-Gurion was keeping to use against Nixon involved a program run by Allen Dulles to help the Arabs get missiles to use against Israel.[61] The operation started in 1953, when Dulles asked his ex-Nazi friend General Gehlen to send a few Nazis to Egypt, as a sort of under-the-table training force for Nasser. Miles Copeland was the point man for laundering the American money. Former SS colonel Otto Skorzeny did the hiring, using CIA money, and a large number of Nazi war criminals were funneled to the Egyptian secret service.[62]

This was a bit too much for the Israelis to stomach, and they launched a clumsy retaliatory strike in 1954 that was quickly exposed as the "Lavon Affair." Emboldened by this setback to Israeli intelligence, Nasser asked for more Nazis, this time scientists who could build him a rocket with enough range to hit Israel. The Gehlen man who handled the hiring of German rocket scientists was none other than Alois Brunner, one of Eichmann's top assistants in carrying out the Final Solution, who had settled in Damascus, Syria, where he still lives.

In his account of the Nazis-for-Nasser operation, Miles Copeland was uncharacteristically coy about his own role. According to Copeland, his idea was to sabotage Nasser by having Gehlen send him incompetents who "could be counted upon to screw up the Egyptian army so thoroughly that it wouldn't be able to find its way from Cairo to Ismailia, let alone fight the British after arriving there." It was a lie. The ex-Nazis Gehlen recruited for Nasser were anything but incompetent, particularly some of the rocket scientists. By this time, the Israelis had well and truly burrowed their way into the "Org," as Gehlen's espionage networks were known.

Copeland passed off the Nazis-for-Nasser program as a little joke, one that he shared with his friends in the Mossad, who "admitted that they, too, were using ex-Nazis for a number of nefarious purposes, and for the same reasons that they were attractive to us."[63] In fact, the Israelis had begun to take notice of the program in the buildup to the Suez Crisis, through several of their agents in Western intelligence, as well as inside the Gehlen Org.[64] But because the Suez Crisis went so badly off the rails, it took the Israelis a little while longer to discover fully what was going on.

The actual construction of the rocket facilities had begun in 1959, but it was not until September 1961 that Israeli intelligence discovered that Egypt could have as many as one hundred ground-to-ground missiles ready by the end of 1962.[65] By that summer the Mossad had a full team established to study the progress of the German rocket scientists in Egypt. With the help of an agent in the German post office, they obtained some key proof, a letter "dated 24 March that year from a leading German scientist called Professor Wolfgang Pilz, to the Egyptian director of a rocket factory code named 333. According to the document, 900 missiles were to be constructed, and there was additional, although flimsier evidence of research work being carried out to fit the weapons with gas, chemical, or biological warheads."[66] The Israelis nearly went berserk. Dulles had used CIA money to fund a German "technical research" section that could mean the death of their nation. The Jews knew how deadly the Nazi nerve gas was. They did not even want to think about missiles armed with biological weapons. Kennedy's response was immediate, firm, and decisive. In September 1962 Kennedy decided to supply Israel with defensive ground-to-air missiles capable of stopping aircraft, but not the Egyptian offensive missiles.[67]

It was the first arms sale by the U.S. government to Israel. Not a word was said about the CIA-funded Nazis or the nature of the weapons payload. According to a number of the "old spies," Kennedy promised the Israelis that as soon as the 1964 election was over, he would break the CIA "into a thousand pieces and scatter it to the winds." Our sources say that Kennedy's ire would have been better directed at the State Department, as the CIA was making small but genuine efforts on its own to undo the Dulles legacy.[68]

Like Roosevelt's revenge against the bankers, it was not to be. Allen Dulles, in quiet retirement over the Bay of Pigs fiasco, was never prosecuted. With Kennedy's assassination in November 1963, the Israelis lost the best friend they had had in the White House since Truman departed. They would shortly discover that Lyndon Baines Johnson had a very different attitude toward the Jews.

When the next war with the Arabs came around in 1967, instead of backing Israel to the hilt, LBJ sanctioned a continuation of the Dulles brothers' policies of 1956. The Israeli government thought it had cleared the preemptive strike of the Six Day War with Washington, but they discovered that the U.S. president's sympathy for the oil corporations and their Arab friends was more powerful than the Democratic party's traditional support for the Jews. As they had done in 1956, the American intelligence agencies would betray Israel's military secrets to its Arab enemies.

CHAPTER 12

THE *LIBERTY* INCIDENT

The history books, particularly the Israeli ones, say that the 1967 war was the high point of Israeli military prowess. Abandoned by the UN, attacked by the Egyptian-led Arabs, the Jews fought alone and in six days defeated the entire forces of the united Arab armies. The prime minister's office later issued a moving video showing battle-hardened Israeli veterans weeping as they liberated the old city of Jerusalem and touched the Western wall of the Temple.[1]

For the first time in two thousand years, Jews around the world swelled their chests with pride. When an American ship, the USS *Liberty,* was accidentally damaged in the conflict, President Johnson graciously accepted the immediate apology of the government of Israel. Despite some American casualties, the United States and Israel remained firm friends.

Our sources say that there is more to the story than that, much more. The U.S. and British governments, while pretending to be on Israel's side, were giving all of Israel's secrets to the Arabs. In many ways, it was the Western spies who indirectly started the war. In this chapter we examine the following allegations:

- Western intelligence informed the Arabs that Israel would not have a nuclear defense shield finished in 1967, thus leaving a window of opportunity for attack.
- Realizing the danger of a massed Arab attack, the Israelis informed the United States of their intention to launch a preemptive strike, which the CIA promptly betrayed to the Arabs.
- U.S. intelligence attempted to curry favor with the Arab oil producers by giving the precise details of Israel's order of battle to the Arabs during the war.
- Israeli intelligence discovered the American betrayal and attacked the U.S. ship, the *Liberty,* which was gathering electronic information on Israeli troop movements and sending it to British intelligence, which in turn relayed it to the Arabs.
- Both the American and Israeli governments agreed to suppress the truth about the *Liberty* incident from the public.

Israel mourned the loss of President Kennedy deeply. Before he died, Kennedy had blunted Nasser's missile threat, made the first arms shipment from the U.S. government, and backed Israel repeatedly in the United Nations. The Israelis did not know what to make of his successor, Lyndon Baines Johnson. In public, Johnson had been an ardent supporter of Israel. In private, however, they feared that he was, and would always remain, an oil man. In fact, the Israelis did not trust Johnson at all. After the Suez debacle, they would never trust any American with the lives of their citizens. They launched a crash program to complete their first atomic warhead.

During the early 1960s the Kennedy administration watched the construction of the Israeli nuclear reactor at Dimona with some concern and increased the number of American spies in Israel. Kennedy offered Israel a deal. If it would stop its nuclear project, the United States would provide $600 million for a nuclear-powered water desalinization plant. The Israelis refused. They knew that sooner or later, one of the Arab states would start manufacturing poison gas and germ warfare weapons. The threat of a nuclear weapon would be the only thing that could deter the Arabs from starting another holocaust.

After Kennedy died, Johnson watched the reactor at Dimona go into full production with French assistance. The Jews had atomic energy, but they did not yet have an atomic bomb. Although Seymour Hersh's excellent book covers this subject in some detail, there are a few key details he missed.[2] As will be seen in the next chapter, the Israelis had used their window inside West German intelligence during the 1960s to obtain Argentine uranium and South African testing facilities. The Israelis were using both the German and the French A-bomb programs to further their own purposes.

What Hersh also did not know is that the CIA had several agents working in Israel under various cover assignments. One of them confirmed to us that in the spring of 1967, the Israelis had the potential to make a nuclear warhead but had not succeeded yet. They were at least a year away from making a working prototype.[3]

During that time the Jews still would be vulnerable to surprise attack. Somehow this information found its way from the CIA to the Arabs. Some of our sources among the "old spies" say that it was Miles Copeland's handiwork; others say that it was the long arm of British intelligence, aided by NSA technology.[4] As we shall see, the NSA routinely shared Israel's secrets with the British, who just as frequently passed them on to the Arabs.

Whoever was responsible, the leak of the Israeli atomic schedule set off a race against time. The Arabs had one last period of opportunity to smash the Jewish state with conventional weapons. The Israelis had less than a year to try to finish one weapon before the united Arab armies launched their attack. In fact, it would take Israeli scientists much longer than they had estimated to get the A-bomb.

The American intelligence reports that Israel could not prepare a nuclear defense shield in 1967 gave the Arabs some breathing room to plan their next battle against the Jews. In the spring of that year, Nasser was temporarily occupied fighting a war in Yemen, where he was testing chemical and biological weapons in preparation for his final solution of the Jewish problem.

According to Nasser's original timetable, he would launch the final attack on Israel in late 1967. The cooler fall weather would greatly facilitate an armored invasion. The Soviet tanks had no air conditioning and were ovens in the summer. A fall attack also would give him the time to pull his 50,000 men and their heavy armor out of Yemen and move them into the Sinai. Israel would be crushed long before its first warhead was completed.

As the summer of 1967 approached, it was clear that war was coming again to the Middle East. The tiny nation of Israel was not even twenty years old but appeared headed for extinction by its powerful neighbors, which surrounded it on nearly all fronts. President Gamal Abdel Nasser, the radical nationalist who ruled Egypt, had begun with a massive radio propaganda campaign calling on the Arab nations to unite in the destruction of the Jews.

The powerful Egyptian army, massively equipped by the Soviet Union, had begun its slow, ponderous movement over the Sinai Desert toward Israel. Israeli intelligence suspected that Syria and Jordan were preparing to launch simultaneous sneak attacks from the north and east, as soon as the Egyptians had everything in place in the south. Egyptian artillery moved to close the Red Sea to any vessel flying the Israeli flag and blockaded the Israeli port of Eilat. This was a clear violation of international law, but the UN did nothing, except accede to Nasser's request and order its Emergency Force out of harm's way in preparation for the assault.

The Americans agreed that Egyptian interference with Israeli shipping on international waters was an official act of war. Even Nasser had acknowledged as much back in 1956 as a condition for Israel's withdrawal after the Suez campaign; in 1967 the United States offered its sympathy but refused to provide any military assistance whatsoever. President Johnson turned his back. The Israelis told their American ally that if it would not help, it should keep its planes and ships away from the combat area, and Israel would fight by itself. One of the most widely reported, but least understood, battles in the secret war against the Jews was about to begin: one of the few espionage battles in the war to be fought entirely at sea.

By early June 1967, the Israelis knew that Nasser's invasion could come at any time. On June 5 Israel launched a preemptive attack before the Egyptian army could finish its buildup and reach its borders. The first three days of tank battles saw the tiny Israeli army pushing the Egyptians back across the Sinai, away from Israel, and the destruction of the Arab air forces. It was a heroic achievement that was marred by one unfortunate mistake, or so the Israeli government says. The "unfortunate mistake" was the attack on the USS *Liberty* stationed off the Sinai Coast. There are many contradictory accounts of this "error," but first, here is the official Israeli version.[5]

On June 8 Israeli reconnaissance spotted an unknown freighter steaming northward from the direction of Egypt approaching the Israeli coast. The photos showed what appeared to be an American vessel, but the U.S. embassy formally denied that claim. The Israelis concluded that the Arabs were trying to masquerade one of their warships as an American vessel. According to the Israeli version, one of their junior officers did recognize the photo of the USS *Liberty* in *Jane's Fighting Ships*. Through a breakdown in communications, however, the attack planes had already taken off before word passed up the chain of command.[6]

At 2:00 P.M. a pair of Israeli fighter planes strafed the vessel with machine guns and small rockets, but the ship kept coming. Another flight dropped napalm, while three Israeli motorboats fired torpedoes. During the smoke of battle, one of the motorboats hooked one of the enemy liferafts and pulled it on board. To their horror, the Israeli sailors saw the words "USS Liberty" stenciled on the rubber wreckage and called off the attack. They had been shooting at an American ship.

The Israeli cabinet responded quickly, and honestly. By 4:00 P.M. they reported the tragic mistake to the American government. Although the *Liberty* was not supposed to be near the combat zone in the first place, the government of Israel offered its apologies and promised to pay reparations for the damage. The U.S. government agreed that it was an honest mistake in time of war, but still made Israel pay compensation to the *Liberty*'s crew, thirty-four of whom had been killed in the attack.[7]

The official American version of the *Liberty* incident supported the Israeli story. The Americans accepted that it was a case of "mistaken identity" and that the Israelis had thought it was the Egyptian ship the *El Ksair*.[8] The United States and Israel were allies and would never deliberately attack each other. The United States accepted that the Israelis never would have knowingly fired on a ship flying the American flag. The *Liberty* attack was a horrible error.

There is, however, another American version—one that is somewhat different, to say the least. That story is told best by the surviving crew. Lieutenant James M. Ennes, Jr., an officer on board the *Liberty* that fateful summer day, has even written a book about it.[9]

According to Ennes, his ship had been ordered to patrol near the combat zone, but was still in international waters at the time of the attack. If anyone interfered with the *Liberty*'s right of free passage on the high seas, help was available from a U.S. aircraft carrier stationed farther offshore in the eastern Mediterranean. American fighter planes would be overhead the *Liberty* within minutes of a distress call. Not that there was much danger. The Israelis had knocked out the entire Egyptian and Syrian air forces in the first two days of the war. The Israeli air force was the only one left in the sky, and it had been following the *Liberty* from the moment it arrived off the Israeli coast at 6:00 A.M.

All morning there had been overflights by Israeli reconnaissance, nine passes in all. One of them flew less than two hundred feet from the ship, so close you could see the pilots and give them a friendly wave. No one could mistake the *Liberty* for an enemy ship with its American flag flying and its U.S. Navy identifiers gleaming in large white numbers on the hull. The number of fly-bys was unusual, but the crew thought that the Israelis were just keeping a constant eye on their position to make sure that a friendly ship did not sail into harm's way. There was a war on, after all, but the *Liberty* was minding its own business. It was really nothing more than a floating radio set, very lightly armed, and a threat to no one.

At 2:00 P.M. another flight of Israeli Mirage jets appeared on the radar screen. A few people on the bridge watched their approach with idle curiosity. Suddenly the Israeli aircraft opened fire and strafed the deck of the *Liberty* with machine-gun fire and rockets. People were screaming, running for cover. The Israelis left as quickly as they had come. They must have realized their mistake and broken off the attack. For a few seconds there was silence and then the sound of wounded men calling for help. The rockets and gun rounds had chewed up the deck and everyone on it. Some of the radio antennas had been badly damaged, but the *Liberty* still managed to get an emergency message to the Sixth Fleet that it was under attack and needed immediate air cover.

While they waited for the U.S. planes, another huge American flag was hung on the *Liberty* to prevent any further possibility of misidentification. Instead of the promised American fighter support, however, Israeli Mystère jets were spotted on the horizon. Everyone took cover. The Israeli planes fired rockets at the *Liberty* and dropped napalm, which is a kind of jellied gasoline that burns everything it touches. Some components of the *Liberty*'s radar dishes and antennas were made from aluminum. The only problem is that aluminum does not melt, it burns when it is hit with napalm.

Walls of flames rolled over the *Liberty*. As soon as the jets left, the crew rushed out to try to control the fires. Where was the American fighter support? They should have been over the *Liberty* minutes ago. What else could go wrong? That was when they saw the three speedboats approaching from the Israeli coast. They were not rescue craft, they were torpedo boats. One torpedo struck the starboard side of the *Liberty*, and the stricken vessel tilted ten degrees over, its steering gone, portions of the deck still burning. Luckily, the watertight compartments below decks had contained the torpedo damage. The ship would not sink, but that was the least of the problems.

The captain of the *Liberty* realized that something had gone terribly wrong, and the ship was alone. There was no American air cap to protect it, and it had become a floating target for the Israelis. Although the upper structures of the ship had been badly hit, almost 90 percent of the crew had been belowdecks and were still alive. After the Israeli torpedo boats picked up his crew and realized they were Americans, his ship finally would be safe.

The problem was that the Israeli boats were slowly circling the *Liberty*, firing at anyone who stuck his head out of a hatch. The three rubber rafts they did manage to toss over the side were ripped to shreds almost before they hit the water. Finally the Israelis left for good. Out of the 293 crewmen aboard the *Liberty*, only thirty-four had died. The crew thought it was a miracle that so many had survived.

Of course, few of the crew believed the Israeli government's apology that it was all a case of mistaken identification. Nor did they believe the American government was telling the whole story. When the crew of the *Liberty* were finally rescued, they found out that their fighter cover had been ordered out and then canceled by "higher authority."[10] Incredible as it may seem, the U.S. government had deliberately left one of its own ships defenseless while knowing it was under attack. Several of the officers and crew were interviewed by Navy admirals and then sworn to secrecy about the entire *Liberty* incident, in the interests of "national security."[11] The crew described the report of the navy's official Board of Inquiry as a farce.

Years later some members of the crew had their own theory about what had happened. The day the *Liberty* arrived off the coast of Israel was the very day the Israelis were planning to invade the Golan Heights, the Syrian chain of hilltops that loom over the valleys of northern Israel like a shadow of death. Ever since 1948 the Syrians had bombarded the Jewish settlements below, and now the Israelis wanted to end this, by stealing another country's mountain range before the Americans could find out and stop them in the UN. That is why they attacked the *Liberty*, or so several of the crew believe. The Israelis wanted the seizure of the Golan Heights to be a fait accompli before the Americans got wind of their plans.[12] What the crew members do not understand is why their own navy covered it up and let the Israelis get away with it by pretending the attack was a mistake.

One of the "old spies," Bill Eveland, put forward an interesting explanation of the official U.S. cover-up in his book on American Middle Eastern policies. As previously discussed, Eveland was one of the nation's spies against the Jews and was very hostile to Israel. He did not care too much, either, for Israel's co-opted double agent in the CIA, James Jesus Angleton. According to his account, there was "a pattern pointing to American connivance in Israel's 1967 attack on Egypt." Angleton was allegedly at the center of the plot, and partly as a result of his connections with Israeli intelligence, the *Liberty* suffered its fate.

Eveland believes that Angleton took advantage of President Johnson's known anger at Nasser's bellicose stance. Angleton wanted Nasser destroyed, so that the Arabs would be forced to negotiate peace with Israel. So did Angleton's liaison at the Israeli embassy in Washington. According to this version, Angleton went outside of official channels and used his liaison to encourage the Israelis to attack Nasser. Remembering American duplicity in 1956, the Israelis were reluctant unless they received approval from President Johnson himself.[13]

As the crisis deteriorated, Johnson "authorized Angleton" to tell his Israeli contact that "the U.S. would prefer Israeli efforts to lessen the tension but would not intervene to stop an attack on Egypt." Johnson was adamant that Israel must not attack Jordan, Syria, or Lebanon. The Pentagon, briefed on Angleton's discussions with the Israelis and concerned that the war might give the Soviets the pretext to intervene, sent the *Liberty* to monitor the fighting. According to Eveland, the generals were afraid that Israel would use the atomic weapons that the CIA had helped it procure, and the *Liberty* was sent to ensure that the United States could warn both the Israelis and the Soviets that it would retaliate if either country used nuclear warfare.[14]

According to Eveland's one-sided account, the *Liberty* discovered that Israel had broken its promise and had no intention of limiting the attack to Egypt. The Israelis were sending disinformation by radio to Jordan and Syria to encourage the belief that Nasser's forces were winning, and it was time for those nations to join the victorious side. Eveland insists that the Israelis *tricked* the Arabs into attacking but then discovered that the *Liberty* had uncovered their deception. According to Eveland, the reason the ship was attacked was to conceal the Israeli disinformation strategy. The U.S. government decided to bury the whole thing because the Jews threatened to expose all the details of Angleton's covert involvement in planning the war to the Soviets and the Arabs.[15]

A few historians support Bill Eveland's theory, at least to some extent. The highly respected British espionage writer Richard Deacon put forward a similar version of the *Liberty* incident in his book on the Israeli secret service, but made a more plausible case. This version comes a little closer to the truth, but Deacon was misled by his sources on several important matters. Deacon agrees with Eveland that Israeli and American intelligence had struck a secret deal for a limited war between Israel and Egypt, as long as Jordan and Syria were not attacked.[16]

Then, according to Deacon's explanation, the U.S. State Department got in the way. The Mossad discovered that the State Department had invited an Egyptian agent to Washington to negotiate some sort of deal and feared that its agreement with the CIA was about to be betrayed. For its part, the CIA feared that the Israelis would renege on their promise not to attack Jordan and Syria and thereby provoke the Soviets into entering the conflict, another point on which Deacon agrees with Eveland. In order to monitor the situation, the *Liberty* was sent to listen in to all the radio traffic.[17]

Deacon further agrees that it was the Israelis' clever use of radio deception that ultimately caused the ship's destruction. The Israelis had broken the Arabs' ciphers and codes, enabling them to feed false messages to the enemy. The phony messages led the Jordanians to believe that the war was going well for Nasser, when, in fact, the Egyptians already had been effectively knocked out of the battle. Such signals deception was bound to make King Hussein think about joining in on the victorious side. It was then, Deacon asserts, that things started to go badly wrong for the Israelis:

> on the night of 7 June the Mossad . . . knew that their deception plan had been spotted by the Americans. The Israeli Ambassador was called to the State Department and told that the Israeli attack must be halted forthwith as a cease-fire was to be ordered by the United Nations. . . . When the Ambassador protested, he was informed in diplomatic language, that the United States knew that Jordan had been lured into fighting by signal deception. It was obvious that, if *Liberty* continued with her transmissions, it could be disastrous for Israel as they would be able to reveal that the Israelis were in violation of a UN cease-fire order.[18]

According to Deacon, the Israelis ordered that the ship, which was a threat to the Jews' plans, must be put out of action, "whatever flag it was flying." The Israelis feared "there could be leakages from the State Department to the United Nations and, even worse, the latter, whose administrators were already biased against Israel, could pass on information to the Egyptians." The Israelis were not stupid. They knew that the State Department's Middle Eastern policies had a pronounced anti-Semitic tilt.[19]

Further, it was not idle speculation that Israel's secrets *might* end up in Egyptian hands. According to our sources in the American intelligence community who talked to us about the *Liberty* incident, passing Israeli secrets to the Egyptians was the whole idea of stationing the ship off the Sinai coast. They believe that all the published versions of the *Liberty* incident—the crew's, the Israelis', the U.S. government's, Eveland's and Deacon's—are wrong.[20]

When the authors described what we already knew from Western sources, several Israelis reluctantly provided corroboration of the best-kept secret of the Six Day War.[21] Contrary to the Israeli government's categorical denials, the assault on the *Liberty* had been deliberate, but it was an act of self-defense.

The "old spies" are adamant that the *Liberty* crew only knows the *what,* not the *why,* of what happened. Similarly, although Eveland and Deacon exposed the fact that the Israelis knew what they were doing when they attacked the ship, they did not know the real reason. Even U.S. Naval Intelligence did not piece together what had happened until years later, and they had to get most of the answers from the British, who got them from the NSA. This is the real version of the *Liberty* incident, as told by our sources among the former intelligence officers who were there on both sides of the battle.[22]

In the weeks preceding the 1967 war, the Israeli embassy in Washington fully briefed the CIA and the White House on its strategy to preempt the Arab invasion. Once before the Israelis had launched a preemptive strike in the Sinai without Washington's explicit approval. The 1956 Suez debacle still rankled in everyone's memory. This time the Israelis wanted to make sure that they had not crossed wires with their most important, perhaps only, ally in the world. Every major facet of the impending campaign was discussed in advance, *including* the strike against Syria.[23]

Our sources insist that the U.S. government knew that the Israelis were going to attack the Golan Heights weeks before it happened and gave them the green light. Syria was in the Soviet camp and no particular friend of the United States. Jordan was another matter. According to the "old spies" we interviewed on this point, a CIA agent in Amman, Jordan, leaked word to Jordan's King Hussein about the secret Israeli briefing. Everyone likes to tell good news: The Israelis would counterattack only in the north and south against Egypt and Syria.

Under American pressure, the Israelis had agreed not to send troops into the West Bank. As long as Jordan did not attack Israel from the east, King Hussein could stay out of the war and keep the provinces of Judea, Samaria, and the old city of Jerusalem, which the Jordanian army had stolen from Palestine back in 1948.[24]

It was a good deal for Jordan, but not good enough. King Hussein was under pressure from the Arab world to join in the attack against Israel. It would be a little embarrassing for him to sit back and do nothing while the Egyptian and Syrian armies came hundreds of miles to fight the Jews. From one point in Jordanian territory in the West Bank, it was less than a ten-mile drive across Israel to the ocean. A Jordanian armored column could cut the country in half.

The king had to do something to appease his Arab brothers, so he sent Jordanian troops to attack *from Syria,* while promising the CIA that not a single Jordanian soldier would attack Israel from the West Bank. Hussein slyly omitted his plan to place Jordanian troops under Nasser's control. The CIA passed the word on to Israel not to worry about an attack on its highly vulnerable eastern flank.

Through one of their spies, the Israelis quickly found out about the CIA deal with King Hussein, and they were furious. It may not have made a lot of difference to the CIA if Jordanian troops were fighting on the northern front, but it made a lot of difference to the Jews. But this was nothing compared to what the Jews found out next.[25]

When the Israelis discovered that the Americans also had made a deal with the Egyptians, they became even more furious at the CIA. To be fair, our sources in the intelligence community acknowledge that, by and large, the CIA was just a messenger boy. The real decisions were being made in the White House. Aramco and the other big players in the oil business were extremely concerned that American aid to Israel would alienate the Arab oil producers. It was not enough to withhold military assistance in the coming war. Everyone in the Moslem world knew that the United States was still neutral in favor of Israel. The oil men wanted some under-the-table help for the Arabs.[26]

President Lyndon Johnson had been in the "erl bidness" himself down in Texas and knew how the game was played. The oil producers got to LBJ or someone very close to him in the White House. Our sources were never able to find out who. The oil men asked if the president could throw the Arabs a bone, some sort of secret assistance that the public would never find out about but would make the Arab leadership grateful. The point was to keep the oil flowing no matter what happened in the 1967 war.[27]

The White House approved a contingency plan to send the Arabs a little intelligence about the Israeli Defense Forces, not too much, nothing that would tip the balance of war. Just a little something to let the Arab leaders think that the Americans were secretly on their side, no matter what was said about Israel in public. Unfortunately, the small-scale contingency plan escalated. No one planned it that way. Only a handful of staffers in the White House, the National Security Agency, and the CIA knew what had happened, and they all pointed the finger at each other.[28]

Even though the Dulles brothers had been in charge of policy in Washington for years, the real successes of American covert action had been very limited in the Middle East. Apart from the 1949 Syrian coup and installing the shah of Iran in 1953, the CIA had not had much luck in rolling back communism and keeping the Middle East safe for the oil companies. Egypt had been particularly disappointing, given the extraordinary amount of attention that Kermit "Kim" Roosevelt and Miles Copeland had put in. Instead of becoming a tame puppet, Nasser was drifting more and more into the Soviet camp.

A decade before the 1967 war, Roosevelt had sent CIA agents to bribe Nasser. As discussed in Chapter 10, Roosevelt used the "revolving door" and at one stage left the CIA to become vice president of Gulf Oil for government relations. Whether at the CIA or at Gulf, he worked closely with Copeland in anti-Israel operations. His CIA agents even built Nasser a sophisticated communications tower in downtown Cairo. Nasser laughed as he took the CIA's money, called the tower "Kermit's phallic symbol," and kept on bringing in more and more Soviet advisers. Something more was needed to impress him. Exit the CIA, enter the National Security Agency, the U.S. government's signals intelligence agency.

A few days before the war broke out, the USS *Liberty* was detached from navy control and placed under the authority of the National Security Agency. The ship was ordered to pick up two Hebrew translators (non-Jewish NSA employees) from Spain and head for the eastern Mediterranean.[29] The whole operation, to spy on Israel and betray its secrets, was clearly planned in advance.

When, on June 4, 1967, the CIA courier first passed on the news that the Americans were willing to provide secret intelligence about Israel, the Egyptian military was less than impressed. It had been passed "chickenfeed" before. Perhaps without authorization, the courier insisted that this time the offer was bona fide, approved by the president himself. Whatever the Egyptians wanted, they could have. But they just laughed. They had an entire air force that could fly over Israel and collect all the intelligence they wanted. Soon there would be no Israel anyway. That evening King Hussein called Nasser to say that the CIA had just alerted him that the Israelis would attack in the morning.[30] Again, Nasser laughed off the CIA's betrayal of Israel's plans.

The Egyptians stopped laughing on the morning of June 5. The Israelis wiped out virtually their entire air force in one strike. Then they destroyed the Syrian air force. Without air reconnaissance, Arab intelligence was blind. Within forty-eight hours the Israelis had captured the Gaza Strip, sent the Egyptian army in a rout back down the Sinai Peninsula, taken the West Bank from Jordan, and, for the first time in two thousand years, returned to their ancient capital of Jerusalem.

King Hussein screamed at the CIA that he had been betrayed. The CIA had promised that the Jews would not attack him. This was not the time to remind him about the Jordanian troops under Egyptian command in the north or about the shooting that they had started at Jerusalem before Israel had fired one shot at Jordan, to say nothing of the Jordanian air attack on Israel before the war even started. Kings can get very selective about the rules.[31]

The Egyptian generals were considerably easier to get along with. They desperately needed intelligence now and begged the CIA for its promised assistance. It was not long in coming. On June 8, the morning of the fourth day of the Six Day War, the USS *Liberty* arrived off the Sinai coast. Although its crew did not know it, it was the only hope the Egyptian army had of retrieving anything from one of the quickest and most decisive military victories in history.

The *Liberty* was more than a floating radio set. It was a giant magnet for electronic intelligence and could do much more than simply eavesdrop on radio communications. Anyone could do that. The nation of Israel is so tiny that the U.S. embassy in Beirut could monitor all the radio traffic in the entire country. The embassy even taped the Israeli pilots talking back and forth when they hit the *Liberty*. For that matter, the Egyptian embassy in Jordan could listen to radio traffic, and it was a good deal closer than the *Liberty*.

So what was the *Liberty* doing there? Our sources among the "old spies" have an interesting explanation.[32] They believe the *Liberty* was making a war map. Every time an Israeli soldier squawked on his walkie-talkie, the ship recorded his voice and indexed it with the direction and the strength of the signal. The same thing happened with tank radios, headquarters' telephones, even coded cable traffic. The ship swept up everything in the airwaves while noting the location of every speck of electronic dust in Israel. This is called a raw intelligence take.

The *Liberty* was one of the most sophisticated spy ships in the world at that time. Even so, it was not big enough to process all the electronic garbage it collected. Processing intelligence requires banks of computers and teams of analysts. All the ship did was record the garbage, compress it electronically, and transmit it to a land station. What happened next was none of its concern. The crew members did not know it, but the land station was located on the island of Cyprus. That was the clever part. The navy's paper trail would show that no American computer had even begun to process the *Liberty*'s troop movement data at the time of the attack. If asked under oath, the few officers involved in the scheme could swear that the ship never gave any Israeli secrets to the Arabs. They would be telling the truth, as far as it went.

The British secret service has one of the largest electronic listening posts in the world on the island of Cyprus. It had little difficulty in downloading the transmissions from the *Liberty*. All of Israel's electronic garbage was sifted by an enormous computer that began to make sense of the random noise. One section of the British computer began to decode Israel's cable traffic. Another went to work on plotting the military radio transmissions, while still another began to sort the telephone calls intercepted from microwave relay towers across Israel.[33]

First, the frequencies and locations of the major Israeli headquarters were identified, then the smaller regiments and battalions, then the individual units. A great deal of preparatory work had been done before the war began. Spectrographic analysis of known voiceprints enabled the computer to identify each Israeli commander as soon as he spoke on the radio or telephone. The voice was matched to a name and unit number and then the unit's location was placed on an electronic war map that was updated constantly in Cyprus from the *Liberty*'s input.[34]

The British were about to make good on the promise they had made to the Arabs after the Suez debacle in 1956, when they had abandoned their Israeli ally and told the Saudis that they would support the Arab case on Palestine. In 1967 the plan was for the British to hand the final product of the *Liberty*'s intelligence haul to the Egyptians. The finished war map was a detailed order of battle intelligence report, or OB. It is the most useful information generals can have in time of war. Using such a map, they can send their troops wherever the enemy is weakest and exploit an undefended region with an attack that penetrates the enemy's rear areas and cuts off its supply lifeline.

Our sources insist that, with the *Liberty*'s assistance, the Arabs might have been able to turn the war around to some extent or at least force an honorable stalemate.[35] For the first time they would know as much as or more than the Israeli generals did themselves about the movements of the Israeli army. The Arab generals would have details of every Israeli counterstrategy from the moment it began. They would have every Israeli battle order in close to real time.

Just as the Israelis were beginning to pull some of their mobile reserves out of the Sinai for the Golan assault in the north, the *Liberty* was letting the Egyptians know the location of each hole in the southern front. As soon as the Israeli army turned its attention to the north, the Egyptians could launch low-level, but irritating, attacks on Israeli settlements and military formations in the south.

"You have to understand what this means," said one of our sources. "The Government of Israel was already pissed off about the CIA leaks to the Jordanians. But that was nickel-and-dime stuff. This was as serious as lung cancer. As long as the *Liberty* was transmitting, every Israeli troop movement would be known to the Arabs within an hour, maybe within minutes. It meant that Israel could lose the war."[36]

Other sources do not put the threat this high, although they do agree that, at the very least, the Egyptians could drag the war out to a stalemate with the help of the ship's intelligence.[37] As best as can be determined, the purpose of playing the *Liberty* pawn was to help even the score on the chessboard. Despite Arab radio broadcasts announcing their triumphant victories, by the morning of June 8 nothing could stop the Israeli army from marching on Cairo, Egypt, Damascus, Syria, or Amman, Jordan. The united Arab armies were in ashes. But with the sly help of British-American intelligence, the tables could be turned to some extent giving the Arabs time to gain a diplomatic victory from the certainty of military defeat.

One of our American sources, after conferring with several others, described for us how the Israeli military planners saw the potential of the *Liberty*'s intelligence. Here is a brief paraphrase of what our source says the Israelis believed could have happened if they had not taken the ship out:

> After forcing the Egyptian army to retreat across the Sinai, the Israelis would have launched the Golan assault on the morning of June 8, as planned, and committed their southern mobile reserves to the northern campaign. Most of the Israel Defense Forces' units en route to the Golan would have been withdrawn past Gaza where the *Liberty* was listening.
>
> Once Israel was committed to a two-front war, everything would go wrong. On June 9 small elements of the surviving Egyptian brigades would thread their way through the holes in the southern front left by the withdrawal of the IDF. To the horror of the Israelis, the Egyptian reconnaissance forces would have been able to maneuver in the Sinai, eluding the few remaining Israeli forces. That would not have been surprising since the Egyptians would have had a map of all Israeli troop movements, courtesy of the *Liberty*.
>
> The cat-and-mouse game in the Sinai would have gone on for several more days, with Egyptian hit-and-run units inflicting damage on Israeli civilian settlements in the Negev Desert. Sooner or later the Israeli politi-

> cians would start screaming at the generals that they must withdraw their armored reserves from the Golan, to protect the civilians in the south. A week into the war, the Egyptian reconnaissance forces would have continued to sneak back and forth through Israeli lines at will.
>
> The *Liberty* could constantly monitor the arrival of Israeli forces from the northern front and map their deployment. It would have been as if the Egyptians were reading the minds of the Israeli generals, concentrating their forces where the Israelis were weakest. The new Egyptian hit-and-run tactics would have done a lot of damage to the spread out Israeli units by virtue of the *Liberty*'s superior intelligence. The more troops the Israelis pulled out of the Golan, the better the odds became for the Syrians. A two-front war is a no-win situation, especially when the enemy has a map of all your troops.[38]

One well-informed Jewish source disputes, in part, our CIA source's version, noting that, whatever the original plan, no ground units from the Sinai were in fact diverted to the Golan. This source asserts that the Egyptians intended to use the *Liberty*'s intelligence to exploit gaps between Israel's three Sinai divisions after the diversion of Israel's air force—not land forces—to the Golan campaign. All of our sources agree that, if the *Liberty* had continued to support the Arabs, there would have been a longer conflict involving greater Jewish casualties instead of a quick Israeli victory.

When both sides were bloody enough, the United States and Britain would step in as the peacemakers. The Israelis would be enormously grateful; so would the Arab leaders, but for different reasons. The *Liberty*'s intelligence could snatch a face-saving stalemate from the jaws of defeat. *Pax Americana,* the oil would flow. Of course, the impertinent Israelis would have to give back Jerusalem to King Hussein.

This was a worst-case scenario for the Israeli military leaders, and in light of the devastating losses taken by the Arabs in the first three days, it may never have come to pass. But the Jews could not take any risks. The history books contain certain intriguing references that tend to corroborate our CIA source's scenario. Israel's foreign minister, Abba Eban, recorded that Defense Minister Moshe Dayan initially opposed "any proposal to storm the [Golan] Heights" because he feared that Israel's forces "were becoming overextended."[39]

Eban was at the United Nations in New York the day the *Liberty* was attacked. Twenty-five years later he recalled that before the Israelis launched their attack against the ship at 2:00 P.M. Israeli time, the Egyptians resisted "any cease-fire resolution unless it was accompanied by Israeli withdrawal." A few hours later, after news of the attack had reached New York, the Egyptian ambassador, El-Kony, was in tears after he "was told by Cairo to get a cease-fire as soon as possible."[40]

Apparently Dayan, concerned that the Egyptians might make some sort of comeback in the Sinai, would not agree to move on the Golan until the *Liberty* was put out of action. On the other hand, the Egyptians, supported by the Soviets, resisted all suggestions of a cease-fire until after the *Liberty* had been attacked. A day earlier, on June 7, Israel had been prepared to accept the same terms and conditions finally forced on the Egyptians.

Finally, it is true that one Egyptian commander, General Saad Shazli, had evaded the Israeli encirclement in the Sinai, where he had been stationed right on the Israeli border with orders to cut off the port of Eilat from the rest of Israel. The Israeli military planners, realizing that the elusive Shazli may have been in a position to utilize the *Liberty*'s intelligence to force his way eastward through their lines, could have been concerned enough to believe that the worst-case scenario posed certain real dangers. As it happened, Shazli was retreating back to Egypt at the time of the attack on the *Liberty,* but the Israelis were neither sure of his whereabouts nor whether he intended to launch a counterattack.[41]

On balance, we think that the Egyptians were not in a position realistically to take full advantage of the ship's intelligence and that our source who called the situation "as serious as lung cancer" has exaggerated the actual military threat. But it is clear that the Israelis could not, and did not, know that at the time. They had to be sure that the potentially lethal betrayal of their battle strategy and deployment of forces by the United States would not undo all the gains they had made. Here is what the "old spies" say happened next.

According to our sources, Israeli intelligence had discovered the *Liberty*'s espionage mission before it even arrived off the coast, although there is some disagreement about how they did so. Later on the Egyptians executed someone whom they claimed was an Israeli mole inside their headquarters. On the other hand, there has been considerable speculation about an Israeli agent inside British intelligence.[42]

It does appear that, by whatever means, the Israelis were prewarned about the ship's real mission. By the time the *Liberty* arrived off the coast at 6:00 A.M., the Israelis were waiting. At first light on the morning of June 8, they sent a reconnaissance flight to map the ship's position. Shortly afterward a "flying boxcar" crammed with electronic information-gathering equipment flew over the *Liberty.* There was no doubt that the order of battle information being processed at the British base in Cyprus originated with this American ship.[43]

The Israeli forces were supposed to cross the forward battle line at the Golan Heights at 11:30 A.M. on June 8. An emergency session of the Israeli war cabinet was called for early morning, as soon as the flying boxcar returned with the tapes of the *Liberty*'s transmissions.[44] One source claimed that some other kind of tape was played, and suggested that Israeli intelligence had tapped a CIA phone or even the British computer in Cyprus.[45] Whatever the source of the information about the *Liberty,* the Israeli cabinet was absolutely convinced that the government of the United States was secretly betraying its ally, the only democracy in the Middle East, in order to curry favor with Arab dictators who were friends of the Soviets.

The Israeli army was asked to give the cabinet an estimate of what would happen if it went ahead with the Golan Heights operation as scheduled. The initial estimate was 25,000 Israeli dead, higher if the *Liberty* continued to help the Arabs.[46] The level playing field sought by the Americans was a minefield for the Israelis. There are 1 billion Moslems in the world. There were less than 3 million Jews in Israel. Any war of attrition always favored the Arabs.

The cabinet members postponed the Golan Heights operation for twenty-four hours while they considered their options. There were really very few. A diplomatic protest would do no good. The Americans would deny everything, the UN would stall, and meanwhile more Israeli soldiers would be killed. The Israelis would be challenged to come up with proof, and they could not do that without exposing their own intelligence agents, in both the Western and the Arab camps.

It came down to a choice between 25,000 of their own dead or attacking one American ship. One fighter-bomber loaded with high-explosive ordinance could blow the *Liberty* to splinters. Cabinet members asked if there was any option other than drowning nearly 300 American sailors, for no matter what the American politicians had done to them, Israel had always been friends with the American people. A plan to put the ship out of commission with a minimum loss of life was requested. Somehow, the Israelis had obtained a copy of the ship's building plans,[47] and the *Liberty*'s fireproof and waterproof compartments gave the IDF staff an idea.

The general staff reported their minimum-damage plan to the cabinet. During the first run, the aircraft would fire only light rockets at the antenna masts and strafe the deck. That would send the crew scurrying safely belowdecks to their battle stations. As soon as they were buttoned up, the second run would drop napalm to burn off the antennas and communications gear without breaching the structural integrity of the fireproof hull where the crew was hiding.[48]

The one problem was the electronic intelligence center belowdecks in hold number 3. One carefully aimed torpedo could take that out without sinking the ship, but whoever was in that compartment would die. The Israeli military staff estimated that American casualties could be kept to a few dozen. Most of the crew, maybe 80 to 90 percent, would survive. It was the best they could do.[49]

The cabinet members gave the order to disable the *Liberty* with minimum loss of American life. Because they could no longer trust their own telephones, they sent a courier to the nearest Israeli air squadron to ask for volunteers. Half the squadron refused to fly, because they had friends or relatives in the United States. "They just could not bring themselves to shoot at the American flag," said one of our Israeli sources. The ones who did fly were heartsick. Two of the pilots later had nervous breakdowns. The Americans on the ship were not the only victims of the *Liberty* incident. Two American-born Israelis volunteered to fly in the squadron.[50]

The air crews needed only a little while to unload the heavy-explosive ordinance and replace it with napalm canisters. It took longer to get the torpedo boats briefed and under way. Everything had to be coordinated for 2:00 P.M. so that the planes and torpedo boats arrived at exactly the right times, one after the other, like a ballet sequence. If the napalm was dropped too early, crew members might still be on deck. The Israeli torpedo could not be fired until the *Liberty*'s crew had sufficient time to close all the watertight doors.

In the meantime, a reconnaissance plane would make one last pass over the *Liberty* to confirm its identity and position. Only then would headquarters give the attack order to launch the fighter squadron. The reconnaissance pilots made their report in code, using a scrambling device. Tel Aviv used the same precautions when giving the attack order, as it knew U.S. intelligence was listening. The lead pilot on the strafing run would not break radio silence until he had made visual contact. He was to announce, *en clair,* when the ship was in sight.

As soon as the attack was under way, a senior official of Israeli intelligence paid a surprise call on his CIA counterpart. He told him what they were doing to the *Liberty* at that moment, and why. Before the second Israeli run even arrived over the ship, the CIA had told the navy to call off air support for the *Liberty.*[51] Although upon hearing news of the attack, the U.S. Joint Chiefs of Staff at first wanted to launch a "quick, retaliatory air strike on the Israeli naval base which launched the attack,"[52] this idea was quickly rejected. There would be no retaliation of any kind.

Why were the U.S. fighter planes, which had taken off while the debate was still under way, ordered back to the carrier and the retaliation strike abandoned? The Israelis had proof that the U.S. government had committed an act of war against Israel by betraying its military secrets to the enemy in the middle of a war in which Israel's very survival was at stake. The Israelis had sources in the Arab world that the CIA didn't even know about. The CIA's low-risk strategy had blown up in its face, along with any hope of plausible deniability.

The White House certainly was not happy, but it did not take long to work up a cover story. The American intelligence officers begged the Israelis to pretend that the attack on the *Liberty* was a mistake. To make it look good, Israel would be quietly reimbursed for whatever compensation it paid to the surviving crew members and the families of the dead. By 4:00 P.M. that afternoon, the deal was cut.[53]

According to our sources in the intelligence community, the governments of Israel and the United States have spent the next twenty-seven years lying about the *Liberty* incident.[54] There is a substantial amount of circumstantial evidence to show that this version of the affair is correct. There is, moreover, convincing and direct evidence to demonstrate that the official versions told by both governments are false.

In the last quarter of a century, more disinformation has been spread about the *Liberty* incident than any other episode in U.S.-Israeli relations. The cover-up continued with stories planted in the press during 1991 and 1992. The fact that both the United States and Israeli governments continued to lie about the incident a quarter of a century later is testimony to the sensitivity felt by them both about what really happened. Let us examine the lies, one by one.

The first lie had to do with the *Liberty*'s mission. What was it doing off the coast of Israel? Immediately after the attack, a U.S. diplomat in Egypt said that "we had better get our cover story out fast, and it had better be good."[55] Within hours the Pentagon had released a media statement claiming that the *Liberty* had been stationed there to facilitate communications in case American citizens had to be evacuated from Egypt or Israel. It was a pretty thin story and was attacked almost immediately by the American press. In order to deflect accusations that the *Liberty* was spying on Israel, the Pentagon quickly floated a rumor that the ship was observing newly installed Soviet radar systems, which implied that it was spying on Egypt.[56]

The problem with the spying-on-Egypt story was that the *Liberty* was so close to the Israeli coast that its crew literally could see buildings on the Gaza shore only twelve miles away. A few attempts were made to lie about the ship's position, such as the claim that it was "73 miles off the Sinai desert," but that lie was contradicted by an admission that it had been stationed "as much as 13.5 nautical miles" off the coast in international waters, and was never "closer than 12.5 miles" from Israel.[57] So much for the spying-on-Egypt theory.

The navy retreated to its original cover story. The *Liberty* was merely a relay station for evacuee messages, and it had to be stationed exactly where it was for "technical reasons." It was suggested that the radios in the U.S. embassies were weak, or that batteries were low, so the ship had to get in close to hear them.[58] The problem with this story is that Alexandria, Egypt, was the only place in the Middle East from where Americans might have had to be evacuated. There the U.S. consulate had been burned and Americans had been attacked by angry mobs. Yet as soon as this attack was reported, the *Liberty* steamed in the opposite direction, toward Israel. There were no angry Arab mobs in Tel Aviv, nor was there any immediate risk that Israel would have to be evacuated. The Israelis were clearly winning the war.

Anyway, the phone lines were still working at all the U.S. embassies throughout the Middle East, each of which had a radio transmitter powerful enough to reach Washington, D.C., not to mention an adjacent country. The State Department had years of experience in relaying messages from hostile countries without any help from the U.S. Navy. In fact, there was so little concern about evacuating American citizens during the Six-Day War that the U.S. Navy had pulled the entire Sixth Fleet away from Egypt and Israel. The closest carrier with evacuation helicopters was the *America,* stationed 400 miles away off the coast of Cyprus.

The navy had been ordered to forget about evacuees and keep all its ships far away from the Middle East to avoid antagonizing the Arabs. On June 6 President Nasser and King Hussein had sought to divert attention from their embarrassing losses on the first day of the war by blaming the British and American navies. The Arabs claimed that it was not the Israelis who smashed their air forces, but U.S. and British pilots flying off aircraft carriers in the Mediterranean.

Remembering that a similar conspiracy had occurred in 1956, the nonaligned countries believed Nasser's cynical lie and began to break diplomatic relations and impose an oil embargo against the United States and Great Britain. Both nations made vociferous denials in the UN of any assistance whatsoever to Israel. The closest British carrier was 1,000 miles away. In fact, only one U.S. reconnaissance plane had taken off on Monday, June 5, but it had been ordered to stay 100 miles away from the coast. Since then every plane and ship in the U.S. Navy had been ordered to stay as far away as possible from the Arab-Israeli war.

Of course, one ship never had been pulled back. The press wanted to know why the *Liberty* remained twelve miles off the coast on June 8. For the first several weeks after the attack, the navy stuck to the relay-evacuation-messages story, but then on June 29 it admitted that it did not know why the *Liberty* remained behind. Both the Joint Chiefs of Staff and the

Admiral of the Sixth Fleet had ordered the ship to pull out, but apparently it had never received the messages.[59]

The missing-message explanation immediately raised questions about the previous lie that the *Liberty* was to play a vital role as a radio relay station. If it could not even hear its own admirals broadcasting from a powerful aircraft carrier, how could it pick up a group of evacuees with weak radios and low batteries? The navy countered with the admission that somehow the messages were never sent to the *Liberty.* There had been an embarrassing foul-up in communications.

It was strikingly similar to the Navy's explanation of how it had misrouted the "low-priority" warning message to Pearl Harbor. The orders to pull the *Liberty* out of the combat zone had inadvertently been given a low priority. The routine messages were then bounced around from Washington to the Philippines and ended up "back on a desk at Fort Meade."[60] Deacon hints at an Israeli spy in the CIA, but concludes that this was improbable.[61] Of course, there was an Israeli mole in the CIA, but Angleton played no part in this charade of the misrouted messages.

We now know that the low-priority story was a half-truth wrapped in a double lie. The pull-back messages were not sent low priority, and they were in fact received by the *Liberty.* It is true that a desk at Fort Meade, home of the United States' ultra-secret service for electronic espionage, was involved, but the pull-back message was not lost there. In fact, Fort Meade told someone on the *Liberty* to ignore all orders from the Joint Chiefs. The ship was not under the command of the navy on June 8, 1967. It was assigned to the National Security Agency.[62]

First, the low-priority orders to pull out were actually sent on the highest priority, code-named "Pinnacle." We now know from the declassified files that both the Sixth Fleet and the Joint Chiefs of Staff were trying desperately to order the *Liberty* away from Israel. At least three high-priority messages were sent, the last only a short time before the attack.[63]

It is incredible that for two days none of the navy's messages got through to the *Liberty*'s communications center. The ship had radio receivers so powerful that it could pick up a transmission from a field radio inside a tank forty miles away. Even the navy admitted that the ship was perfectly equipped to monitor communications in the Arab-Israeli war. Of course the ship could hear orders from its own headquarters. It was designed as an electronic listening post. The *Liberty* could receive radio messages better than any ship in the world at that time.

There is no doubt that the ship's radio was working. Even after the Israeli attack blew away all of its masts and antennas, its communications gear was so powerful that Commander William McGonagle could still broadcast a request for assistance to the Sixth Fleet. Sending a radio message is much harder than receiving one. Even if the radio had been out of order, the *Liberty* also was equipped with multiple transmitters, teletypes, and satellite dishes. It had a Trsscom system for bouncing signals off the moon back to the other side of the planet. It had an early form of the ELF system for sending long-range messages to U.S. submarines. It had synchronized dishes to match the orbit of communications satellites in outer space. In fact, it was the one ship in the U.S. Navy that could stay in touch with anyone, anywhere, anytime.

The problem was that the *Liberty* was not taking orders from the navy at the time it was attacked. The navy was furious and leaked part of the story to *The New York Times,* which published an editorial denouncing the interference with the chain of command. The story did not blame a faulty radio, but pointed out that the ship was not under the command of either the Sixth Fleet or the Navy commander in chief for Europe. The blame was put on "the Pentagon" for leaving it in a danger area.[64]

This story does not work either. The Pentagon is under the command of the Joint Chiefs of Staff, and we know now, from their declassified messages, that they were sending pull-back orders independently of the Sixth Fleet.[65] The fact is that no one in either the Pentagon or the navy could send orders through the *Liberty*'s communications center. None of the ship's officers could even set foot in that area. Commander McGonagle did not know it at the time, but the real masters of his ship were the civilian spies of the NSA.

On June 2, 1967, three days before the Six Day War erupted, the *Liberty* had been taken over by a special three-man civilian crew from the NSA, picked up at Rota, Spain. The senior officer among them was known to the ship's crew simply as "the Major," and only he and his men had access to the supersensitive communications areas in the hull.[66] This confirms what our sources among the "old spies" told us: The ship was on a secret mission for the NSA, about which the navy neither had understanding nor control.[67]

We now know a little more about the civilians who came aboard the ship in Spain. They were experts in Hebrew.[68] The *Liberty* had nothing to do with evacuating civilians, observing Soviet radar systems in Egypt, or even monitoring Arab communications; it was there to spy on the Jews. That was its *only* mission. On-the-record confirmation comes from a former NSA officer who had been stationed in Turkey during the Six Day War. While the navy could not communicate with the *Liberty,* the NSA was receiving a great deal of intelligence from the ship and relaying summaries back and forth to other NSA stations in Crete and Turkey. It is clear, from this officer's firsthand account, that the NSA was using the ship to spy only on the Jews.[69]

It should be noted that this Turkish NSA report later was corroborated by *The New York Times*, using its own sources.[70] While confirming much of the version of the *Liberty* affair given by our intelligence sources, the young NSA officer in Turkey was simply too far out of the loop to know why the ship's mission was so sensitive to the White House. It had nothing to do with uncovering Israeli strategic planning. In the first place, both the CIA and the White House already had been briefed in full about Israeli strategy. They knew full well that the advance to Cairo was only a feint and that the Israelis were planning to move north to the Golan Heights.

In any event, the *Liberty* was in the wrong place for eavesdropping on an Israeli move into Syria. Although it could listen in on the entire theater of operations, the ship would have been much better positioned off the coast north of Tel Aviv, near the Lebanese border, if the attack on Syria was its target. Instead, it was over a hundred miles farther south, below Tel Aviv, off the Gaza Strip. What was it doing there, so far from the action on June 8?

The position was not accidental. The ship was given specific orders. It left its station off the Egyptian coast and sailed all through the night of June 7 in order to reach this position. Then it stopped and sailed in slow circles for the rest of the day, as close to the Gaza shore as possible without crossing the twelve-mile limit. But why? What was the *Liberty* listening for? Certainly not the Syrians, and there had been no major Egyptian forces there for several days. The only ones left to listen to were the Israelis. On June 8 the mobile reserves and support units of the Israeli army on the southern front were scheduled to pull out of the Sinai, travel northward past Gaza, and prepare for the assault on the Golan Heights.

The only reason the *Liberty* would have come in so close to shore by the Gaza Strip was to monitor the transmissions of Israeli squad and tank radios, which virtually were impossible to intercept without the powerful listening devices on board the ship. These were the only low-range, battery-powered units that it could have been listening to. This was the type of information the Egyptian army needed most: intelligence on the withdrawal of the Israeli forces from the Sinai. As each unit moved north past Gaza, the ship tracked it, identified it, and placed it on the war map. The only possible purpose for such close monitoring of the Israeli troop withdrawal was to tell Nasser where the holes were in the remaining Israeli forces.

It seems that the "old spies" were right. The *Liberty* was the Arabs' best hope. While the Israelis were stripping their forces in the Sinai, whether ground or air, or both, for an attack in the north, the Arabs were planning a counterattack in the south in an effort to retake Gaza. The American ship was there to keep track of the exhausted and undermanned units and show the Arabs where Israel's weak points were located on the southern front.

Military historians have wondered for years why Nasser kept fighting and refused the UN offer of a cease-fire. Actually, he was waiting for the overextended Israelis to open the northern front. He was waiting for the *Liberty*'s order of battle intelligence to reveal precisely the exact locations of the remaining Israeli forces in the Sinai. With the help of the ship's war map, Nasser might be able to bloody the Israelis where their forces were weakest and perhaps restore the status quo in the Sinai.

There is another piece of evidence, albeit circumstantial, to corroborate our sources' revelations about the *Liberty*'s real mission. For two days prior to the Israeli attack on the ship, Arab propaganda had been screaming that the U.S. Navy was secretly aiding the Israelis with planes from their aircraft carriers. Yet when an American spy ship was discovered just twelve miles off the Gaza coast, after the worst military defeat in Egyptian history, not a single Arab leader even alleged that Israel had been receiving American intelligence assistance against Arab forces in the south. It seems the Arabs knew whose side the *Liberty* was on.

So did the Israelis, who have now confirmed that one of the Egyptian majors in charge of signals intelligence in the Sinai during the 1967 war was a long-term Israeli spy.[71] Israel knew that orders had been given to prepare for a counterattack in the Sinai in the early hours of June 8. It has also acknowledged that it had broken the Egyptian, Jordanian, and Syrian codes as well.[72] That was not what worried the White House.

As the Israelis themselves revealed two days after the *Liberty* incident, they also had intercepted the telephone links between Cairo and Amman. Much to Nasser's chagrin, Israeli radio broadcasts presented the Arabs with an actual recording of Nasser and King Hussein conspiring to falsely accuse U.S. and British aircraft carriers of helping the Israelis destroy Arab air bases.[73]

The Israelis, however, never played the tapes of Nasser discussing the covert assistance he had been promised from the Americans. The White House was reeling from the threats of an oil embargo and diplomatic isolation in the Arab world that resulted from Nasser's propaganda. June 7 was when the secret offer of the war map was made and the *Liberty* diverted to the Gaza shoreline. That was what the Israelis heard when they tapped Nasser's phone line.[74]

Perhaps some people cannot believe that the United States would ever betray Israel by giving intelligence to the Arabs in time of war. Yet the *Liberty* was not the only example during the 1967 Six Day War. For example, two British historians reported a conversation that occurred on June 4, 1967, between King Hussein and a CIA agent in Jordan, who warned the king that Israel would attack Egypt the very next day. Hussein, of course, phoned Nasser immediately to tip him off.[75]

As we now know, Israeli intelligence had tapped the phone line between Hussein and Nasser. They had tape-recorded proof that the U.S. government had betrayed Israel's battle plans to the Arabs. It was a miracle that Nasser was so arrogant as to ignore the CIA's tip. Even before the first Israeli airplane took off the next morning, the Israeli government knew that all the war plans it had cleared with the CIA were being given to their Arab enemies.

The Israelis also knew in advance of the *Liberty*'s mission. On the day before the ship arrived at Gaza, the NSA "Major" informed Commander McGonagle that the *Liberty* had picked up Israeli transmissions that caused him "concern."[76] An Israeli air patrol was waiting at first light when the ship arrived off the Gaza coast. For the next four hours, the Israelis tried to jam the ship's frequencies, to no effect. The *Liberty*'s equipment was much too sophisticated to be stopped in that fashion.

There can be no doubt whatsoever that the *Liberty* was continuing to spy on Israeli battle communications. At 12:30 P.M. Israeli time the ship intercepted a discussion from an Israeli reconnaissance plane, positively identifying the ship as American. It took about half an hour to decode and translate Tel Aviv's response. The U.S. ambassador in Beirut, Dwight Porter, was later shown a transcript of the exchange. For twenty-five years Porter never mentioned this tape intercept until someone, presumably in the Bush administration, tipped off two columnists for *The Washington Post.* The Israelis regarded Rowland Evans and Robert Novak as front men for White House disinformation against Israel during the Reagan-Bush terms.[77]

Between 1988 and 1991 they had run at least seven stories that were later proven to be false, according to a count made by Abraham Foxman, national director of the Anti-Defamation League.[78] This was before the contretemps of 1992, when Evans and Novak falsely accused Israel of selling U.S. missile technology to the Chinese, a story that was completely discredited after a thorough investigation by the Department of Defense.

On November 6, 1991, Evans and Novak took on the *Liberty* incident. They were told that Ambassador Porter had seen a transcript of a conversation between the Israeli fighter pilots who attacked the *Liberty,* knowing it was an American ship. Two days later the Israeli government issued its rebuttal statement to columnist A. M. Rosenthal of *The New York Times,* saying that no such message had been sent or received. Hirsh Goodman, a respected Israeli journalist, reported a few weeks later that he had listened to the tape of the fighter pilots' conversation from fifteen minutes before the attack and for several hours afterward. Goodman insisted that

Evans and Novak were completely wrong. The fighter pilots never once mentioned that they had identified their target as an American ship.[79]

The truth is that both the U.S. and Israeli governments had planted false information in the press. The exchange that Ambassador Porter had read was not an intercept of the fighter pilots, who attacked at 2:00 P.M. It was a transcript of the coded broadcast made by the last reconnaissance flight at *1:30* P.M. The Israeli government, seizing on Evans and Novak's error, released only the fighter pilots' tape beginning at 1:43 P.M. They deceived their own friends in the press by concealing the earlier reconnaissance tape.[80]

That reconnaissance flight identified the *Liberty* as an American ship and received Tel Aviv's coded confirmation that the attack would proceed. It appears that this was the message decoded by the *Liberty* and later read by Ambassador Porter.[81] At approximately 1:59 P.M., a minute before the attack, the NSA communications center finished unscrambling Tel Aviv's reply and alerted the bridge that the next flight of incoming Israeli planes was not a reconnaissance mission. The planes were going to attack.[82]

Lieutenant Commander Philip M. Armstrong was the officer on the bridge. Although both he and the NSA crew died during the attack, it is clear from several eyewitnesses that Armstrong sounded the call to General Quarters *before* the first shot was fired. Shortly after the *Liberty* incident, three crewmen told *The New York Times* that they were running to their battle stations just before the Israeli planes appeared, having received the call to battle stations from the executive officer just before the attack began.[83]

Why, after nine peaceful overflights, did the *Liberty* realize that the next group of Israeli planes would attack? Why were crew members at their battle stations *before* the first attack plane even arrived? They had not been called to General Quarters on any of the other passes that morning. How did the *Liberty* know that the next plane to come over would be hostile, unless it had intercepted the conversation from the previous reconnaissance flight? The only possible answer is the one suggested by our sources in the intelligence community: The NSA "Major" decoded the earlier reconnaissance tape and warned the executive officer to expect an attack.[84]

It seems that someone in the United States played a trick on Evans and Novak and switched the source attribution: the coded reconnaissance tape for the fighter pilot tape. Someone in Israeli intelligence caught on to the deception and played a trick of his own. Hirsh Goodman was allowed to listen to the tapes beginning at 1:43 P.M. only, *after* the incriminating reconnaissance conversation was over. Neither side in the press war realized it had been used.

There was a purpose behind this American disinformation. The source of the tapes had to be switched to disguise the method of interception. The fighter planes did not have room for sophisticated scrambling and coding equipment. Their conversation was broadcast over open frequencies that the U.S. embassy in Beirut could plausibly have recorded, without admitting espionage.

As previously mentioned, the earlier reconnaissance flight was made by a flying boxcar jammed with top-secret Israeli coding equipment. The Americans could not admit they had intercepted that conversation without admitting that the *Liberty* was spying on Israel and had broken its most secure codes. That is why Evans and Novak were misled. Confirmation of the code breaking might have opened an inquiry that would have discovered that the ship's mission was to spy on the United States' ally and help Israel's enemies in the midst of a war that could bring about the Jewish state's destruction.

There has never been an independent inquiry to put the matter to rest. In order to head off a congressional probe, President Johnson asked Clark Clifford, a renowned Washington lawyer, to investigate the *Liberty* affair. However, he was told to limit his research to the information produced by the navy. Thanks to the Evans and Novak disinformation, few knew, until now, that the original tape of the Israeli order to attack an American ship came from the records of the NSA and not from the U.S. embassy in Beirut. To his credit, Clifford admitted in 1991 that he does not know what really happened to this very day, either who authorized the attack or why.[85] Buried in the files of the NSA are the records of transmissions to British intelligence during the *Liberty* incident, along with the data collected by the ship to assemble Nasser's war map on the southern front.[86]

It is no secret that the Israelis identified the *Liberty* as an American ship before the attack. The secret is that Israel attacked an American ship in self-defense. Almost a quarter of a century later, the White House still must lie about the incident. The reason is simple: If the Israelis told all they knew about American aid to the Arabs, Congress might start poking around the oil companies. There are far too many skeletons in that closet. The Israelis had Lyndon Johnson over the barrel, a barrel of oil.

As a result of the *Liberty* incident, the White House gave Wally Barbour, the U.S. ambassador to Israel, a new set of marching orders. No further intelligence was to be gathered on the Dimona nuclear reactor, nor were joint anti-Israeli operations to be run with the British and Canadian secret services. Israel was to be the main ally of the United States in the Middle East and was now more important than Arab oil.[87]

No one really believed it. But, in public at least, the United States and Israel were allies again, but only for a little while. As the Jews would find out during the next war, American intelligence continued to back the Arabs in defiance of the "new policy." Six years later, in 1973, the NSA got their payback for the *Liberty,* by waiting until the very last moment before telling Israel that the Arabs were planning a surprise attack on Yom Kippur. The warning came too late to avert a tragedy, and Israel barely survived the sneak attack. According to one NSA employee:

> I learned of the planned October 6, 1973, invasion of Israel by Syria and Egypt—30 hours before the US notified Israel. Upper echelon [National Security] Agency personnel knew of the planned attack hours, if not days, prior to that. Not passing the information along in time resulted in the unnecessary deaths and maiming of thousands of young Israelis. . . . Now I live haunted by the possibility that, somehow, I could have . . . saved some measure of the anguish that became known as the Yom Kippur war.[88]

Whatever intelligence "benefits" accrued to Israel from the *Liberty* incident, they were very short-lived. The Soviets were the only ones really to profit from the 1967 war. As soon as the Israeli victory seemed clear, the Saudis and Libya announced an oil embargo against the United States and Great Britain for the alleged help they provided during the war.[89] Nasser closed the Suez Canal. Oil prices began to skyrocket. Lyndon Johnson did not care, as the embargo caused the price of Texas oil to increase as well.

The British, however, had a problem. They would have to beg the Soviets for oil. Only a week after the war, *The New York Times* reported that British oil importers had asked their government for permission to buy Soviet oil and that London was considering lifting its embargo on such imports.[90] At the same time that the Soviets were defending their Arab allies in the UN, they were stabbing them in the back by undercutting the power of the oil embargo. Soviet salesmen scoured Europe opening new markets for their own oil exports.

As one editorial said in the immediate aftermath of the war: "When it comes to oil . . . the Russians are not customers, but competitors."[91] There was a new player in the Middle East, and the Soviets now were ready to compete with the United States. Within a few short years, some in Washington would view the Communist menace as so strong that the entire balance of power had shifted in Moscow's favor. Far from being more important than Arab oil, Israel was more expendable than ever, even as the threat of a chemical and biological holocaust loomed large over the Jews.

CHAPTER 13

THE FINAL SOLUTION REVISITED

The history books on nuclear proliferation have been quite harsh regarding Israel's decision to join the atomic club. The popular view is that Israel's nuclear program set off an arms race in the Middle East. Our sources say that the popular view is completely wrong: The Arab arms race had begun long before the Israeli atom bomb project. Indeed, Western covert aid to Arab nations to construct weapons of genocide was the very reason Israel began the program in the first place.

In this chapter we address the following allegations made by our sources in the intelligence community:

- Several Western nations, including France, Britain, West Germany, and the United States, recruited Nazi scientists for their expertise in biological and chemical warfare.
- Israeli intelligence penetrated Western intelligence and discovered that Nazi genocidal research was being shared with several Arab states.
- France and West Germany were blackmailed into supporting the development of the Israeli atom bomb.
- The Israeli decision actually to construct its first A-bomb was motivated in part by the resurgence of former Fascists in Western countries, particularly in the political campaign staffs of Richard Nixon.

One of the side effects of the *Liberty* incident was that President Johnson agreed to stop pressuring Israel to sign the Nuclear Non-Proliferation Treaty, much to the surprise of his aides.[1] Furthermore, he ordered that all intelligence operations with the British against Israeli nuclear programs be stopped. For a brief time Israel was regarded as the "main ally" of the United States, and Arab oil was not as important to American interests.[2]

For Israel, the paramount lesson of the *Liberty* incident was that the United States could not be trusted and that it must be responsible for, and able to, defend itself. The Israelis knew that it would be just a matter of time before Nasser regrouped his armies for the final solution of the "Jewish question." Next time the Jews would not have to depend on tanks, guns, and planes. They would have the atomic bomb.

Much of the history of the Israeli nuclear weapons program was ably documented in Seymour Hersh's book, *The Sampson Option.* Yet a number of our sources among the former intelligence officers say that Hersh's seminal account missed several important points.[3] It is true that Israel benefited substantially from French scientific advice; however, after 1967, the French terminated all weapons support for Israel in a fawning attempt to please the Arab oil kingdoms. Despite the ban, the Israelis were able to convince the French contractors to finish their work on the nuclear weapons project.

The Israelis had several threats to use against the French government. As previously discussed, the Zionists had penetrated the Vatican's Nazi-smuggling networks fairly thoroughly. As a result, they were aware of President Charles de Gaulle's scandalous role in recruiting Fascist fugitives as French agents to fight the Communists in the Balkans in the immediate post–World War II years. As fully documented in our previous books, these anti-Soviet groups were organized in various fronts, such as Intermarium and later the Christian Front, headed by Paul Reynaud. French intelligence ran them until the British secret service took them over in the second half of 1946.[4]

Equally scandalous was the cover-up of the Vichy government's role in Nazi atrocities. Some Frenchmen were themselves wanted Nazis and were smuggled down the Ratline under the watchful eyes of Jewish intelligence. Many more benefited from de Gaulle's cover-up and simply resumed their lives in postwar France. The scandal still endures; only recently have some of the French mass murderers, including Vichy officials, been exposed and a handful charged.

In fact, the Zionist intelligence service in France knew that several prominent members of de Gaulle's administration had been secret Nazi collaborators, among them André François-Poncet, the prewar French ambassador to Berlin. During the war François-Poncet had become an informant for SS intelligence, reporting to Klaus Barbie, the Butcher of Lyons. Another of Barbie's informants was Henri Lebrun, later an important member of the French judiciary.

After the war François-Poncet became the French high commissioner for Occupied Germany as well as head of the International Committee of the Red Cross. As discussed in Chapter 6, instead of hunting Nazis, François-Poncet was helping Allen Dulles smuggle them out of Europe. He had little difficulty in supplying Dulles with all the Red Cross passports he needed. In our previous book we detailed how the François-Poncet–Lebrun cover-up gave Dulles considerable leverage in French intelligence affairs. Dulles's mistake was allowing James Jesus Angleton to develop his own French liaison, a connection that some say was instrumental in the Zionists' acquisition of French secrets.[5]

According to a number of our sources, the Zionists discovered that the French were giving passports to a few Nazi scientists and relocating them in North Africa. Their curiosity aroused, the Zionists tagged along and discovered that the French were building a massive testing range for atomic, biological, and chemical weapons in its colony.[6] It was a hideous place. The brutal Nazi experiments on human beings at Auschwitz had produced a bewildering series of poisons. The French had captured German stocks of Tabun, Sarin, and even more toxic nerve gases, which could kill on skin contact. In addition the Germans had developed new and more virulent strains of anthrax, typhus, cholera, malaria and plague.[7]

The French were secretly testing the Nazi formulas and compounds on farm animals and then building a secret network of factories and research institutes to carry on the work that Hitler had started. This was, of course, a flagrant violation of France's public promise to shun chemical and biological warfare.[8] Seymour Hersh knew only that the French had conducted atomic experiments at a secret base in North Africa. He did not know that the base at Beni Ounif was also the heart of de Gaulle's effort to manufacture the same chemical and bacteriological substances that the Nazis had developed in their human experiments at Auschwitz and elsewhere. The Israelis knew. They had penetrated the base from the outset and were using the germ warfare scandal to blackmail their way into the heart of the French illegal weapons program.[9]

No matter how furious de Gaulle and other French leaders became at Israel, their military intelligence advisers cautioned them not to push the Jews too hard. Even after the French government publicly halted the sale of tactical weapons to Israel in 1967, the French contractors finished the plutonium factory at Dimona. The French-Israeli covert weapons program continued in secret despite the arms embargo. Apart from the blackmail of Beni Ounif, there was a second, and even more practical reason for the French to continue clandestine cooperation with the Israeli nuclear effort: It was the French scientific community that was piggybacking on Israel's research, not the other way around.[10]

In the field of chemical weapons, for example, the Israelis had perfected the use of Atabrine as an antidote to the Nazi nerve gases. In terms of atomic research, the Israelis had such a wealth of scientists that they had no need of French aid. Indeed, the head of the French nuclear weapons project was himself a Jew, with strong sympathies for Israel. In addition to scientific expertise, the Israelis had something else that the French lacked: an ample supply of enriched uranium and a place to test an atomic bomb in secret. Not in Israel, of course. In a manner of speaking, the Israeli nuclear weapons program was hidden inside West Germany.[11]

As previously discussed, John McIntyre was a U.S. intelligence agent assigned to General Reinhard Gehlen's headquarters in the late 1940s. The CIA had established a base at Pullach for Gehlen, where the remnants of Wehrmacht and SS intelligence were housed along with considerable numbers of German scientists.[12]

During the war the scientists, scholars, and physicians of the Third Reich had conducted very advanced research into biological and chemical warfare, including live testing on human beings. Allen Dulles's client, I. G. Farben, had equipped the Nazis with the largest pathological laboratory and pressurized gas chamber in the world. The Soviet gulags may have used more human beings as guinea pigs for military weapons, but Auschwitz was the most sophisticated research facility ever built for testing toxic compounds on people. In fact, the infamous Dr. Josef Mengele was only one of a team of German physicians at Auschwitz performing contract work for the prestigious Kaiser Wilhelm Medical Institute in Berlin. The "Brain Cancer" section was the Nazi cover for the biological and chemical warfare program.[13]

Only now are traces of this research, which had been buried by the German medical community, beginning to emerge in the declassified files of Western intelligence.[14] In fact, German doctors and scientists have popularized the view that Hitler forbade any research in biological and chemical weapons because he had been terribly scarred by chemical warfare in World War I. The newly declassified German documents reveal this to be a lie. During World War II scores of German universities, physicians, and scientists volunteered to participate in a massive research program to turn the tide of war against the Soviets.[15]

One of the reasons for continued silence is that prestigious Western institutions, such as the French Curie Clinic, the Rockefeller Foundation, and the Carnegie Fund, all played a part in German scientific research before the war began, and many German scientists resumed their lucrative Western connections when the war was over.[16]

To be fair, most of the German biological warfare scientists went to the French and British after the war; the Americans concentrated largely on nuclear physicists and rocket research. Such companies as Dow Chemicals, W. R. Grace, Imperial Chemical Industries, and Poudré were the new employers of choice for fugitive German scientists.[17] Some, like Josef Mengele, were too well known for their war crimes and eventually had to be smuggled down the Ratline.[18]

By the late 1950s a large pool of fugitive German scientists lived in Argentina and South Africa. By 1962 the West German government had grown anxious about the fact that President Kennedy might someday pull U.S. troops out of Germany, leaving the country defenseless against the Soviets. Not knowing that the base at Pullach was heavily infiltrated by

Communist agents, Bonn commissioned the head of the West German secret service General Gehlen to assist the military with a massive development program for atomic, biological, and chemical weapons.[19] It was all quite illegal, of course. Most of the dirty work was done in foreign countries, such as Argentina.[20]

To Israeli intelligence, it was far worse than illegal; it was horrifying. They knew exactly what General Gehlen was doing. Agent McIntyre recalled that there had been Jews inside Pullach since the late 1940s. When McIntyre first arrived at Gehlen's headquarters, he was amused to see a Jewish American air force sergeant walking down the streets of the secret compound, cursing at the "Nazi bastards" and making them get off the sidewalk when he passed. After Israel was born, sections of the Mossad arrived inside Gehlen's base to receive special training. McIntyre could never understand why the Jews kept quiet about what was going on.

While the naive Americans in the CIA took Gehlen's assurances that he was not employing war criminals at face value, the Israelis knew who the killers were and quietly blackmailed them. Gehlen could not expose the Israeli penetration program without revealing some of his darkest secrets to the Americans. Even he had no idea how many of his staff also were reporting to Tel Aviv. Gehlen hid the secret from his own superiors in Bonn, in order to preserve the fiction of the incomparable spy master.

Consequently, in the mid-1950s when Dulles's agent, Miles Copeland, asked Gehlen for scientists to help Nasser's military program, the Israelis were promptly informed that the Americans were using German war criminals to help the Arabs build a rocket. As previously discussed, Copeland tried to cover his tracks by claiming that he only recruited "incompetent" Nazis, but that was a lie. Through the Gehlen network of former Nazis, "Egypt was engaging Germans not by the dozen, but by the score." One former SS aeronautical construction specialist personally interviewed 220 men for work on the Egyptian rocket program.[21] And he was only one of many recruiters.

To his dismay, Copeland discovered that the Israelis had a few Nazis of their own on the payroll and had thoroughly penetrated Gehlen's operations. They knew that Copeland's "incompetent" Nazis were really skilled technicians and scientists. They were not about to sit back and let the Americans curry favor with Nasser by helping him build a missile capable of hitting Israel. The Israelis stopped the rocket program not by public exposure but by a series of assassinations and letter bombs.

Why didn't the Jews go public? The answer is that they could not expose the Dulles-Gehlen connection without revealing their sources inside Gehlen's Pullach compound. It was their only reliable window into the seamier side of Western intelligence. Gehlen spied on everyone: the French, the British, the Americans, even his own government.[22]

In 1962 one extremely well informed British journalist was tracking the activities of a Nazi cell in the Middle East. His friends in Israeli intelligence showed him a series of letters between one Nazi in Egypt and another in West Germany. This demonstrated that Israeli intelligence was able to intercept German mail, copy it, and then forward it to its intended recipient.[23] The reporter had discovered only one small part of a very much bigger Israeli operation.

According to several of the "old spies," by blackmailing General Gehlen the Israelis actually gained widespread access to letter opening, wiretapping, and coded communications inside Germany. Bonn did not know it, but Gehlen was spying on his own superiors, not to mention most of the West German population. Since Gehlen's organization was an integral part of NATO, the West German base gave the Jews unparalleled access to the nastier side of Western intelligence operations as well.[24] If the Israelis blew the whistle, the Germans would launch a massive house-cleaning operation at Pullach and the Jews' sources might be swept away along with the general.

Whatever Gehlen saw, the Israelis saw. According to some sources, it was Gehlen's copy of American intelligence reports on French experiments in chemical and biological warfare that tipped off the Israelis about the French North African testing range. The French were not alone in these types of experiments. The Americans filed quarterly reports on the progress of each country's efforts to expand on the Nazi germ and gas research. Nearly a dozen European nations had scientists working full time on perfecting the illegal weapons of the Third Reich. There were just too many scientists for another assassination or letter bomb program similar to that used against Copeland's Nazis in the 1950s.[25]

Even if the Jews had been able to kill all the French Nazi scientists, the British-controlled Germans alone would have been able to carry on with the program. The British had sent their Nazi scientists to play on a 1,000-square-mile testing range in Canada.[26] On the other side of the Cold War, the Soviets had built an entire city around the Nazi nerve gas factories that had been moved piece by piece to the Soviet Union.[27] In sum, all of the Allies had Nazis on the payroll.

By the early 1960s the Jews knew that some of Copeland's "incompetent" Nazis in Egypt were already working on gas and germ warfare and testing it in their war against the Yemeni royalists. As *The Sunday Telegraph* reported in mid-1963, the gas and bacteriological weapons could be delivered by conventional bombs or by missiles.[28] Over the next few years there were numerous reports of Egyptian use of mustard and other poison gases and suggestions of various bacteriological attacks as well.[29]

The Egyptians' rudimentary program was nothing compared to the sophisticated formulas developed by the various Western nations. Still, Nasser had more than enough tools to do horrible damage to the Jews, and it was only a matter of time before one of the Western nations shared its more advanced Nazi weapons expertise with the Arabs. As Jonathan Pollard later discovered to his horror, that is exactly what occurred in the 1970s and 1980s. The German nerve gas factories recently constructed in Libya and Iraq are using the identical formulas perfected on Jews at Auschwitz.[30]

Many people have criticized the nation of Israel for commencing a nuclear bomb program. As already discussed, President Kennedy begged the Jews not to introduce atomic weapons to the Middle East and offered them $600 million to build a nuclear-powered freshwater desalinization plant instead. Tel Aviv refused the offer and plowed 10 percent of its national budget into the Dimona facility, a move that some people believed irrational.

Many of the former intelligence officers we interviewed on this subject say that the Jews had no other choice. During the 1950s the proliferation of Nazi technology in chemical and biological warfare had spread like wildfire around the world. Nasser already had his Nazi scientists on the job, and soon the Arabs would perfect these weapons of mass destruction for use against the Jews. A few suitcases full of Rycin could effectively poison the entire national water system of Israel. A truckload of canisters filled with Soman nerve gas released downwind could wipe out the population of Tel Aviv in an afternoon. A barrier of anthrax spores in the soil would isolate Beersheba for decades.[31]

The Israelis were not paranoid. The threat of another "final solution" was, in fact, increasing every year. As American intelligence reports now confirm, the Soviet Union had taken the Nazi human experiments and developed new forms of toxic warfare. By the mid-1950s the Soviets had produced enough Nazi nerve gas to poison the population of the world several times over. Huge stockpiles of anthrax, plague, and "designer bacteria" were in place in each Soviet city. In the event of war, barriers of poison ground would isolate Soviet cities from invaders. More frightening, the Soviets had developed new offensive systems of germ warfare for genocide.[32]

There is little defense against this kind of attack, and what few antidotes exist are withheld from the public as military secrets. One of the best examples of this is Movidyn, a substance that the Soviets discovered in their satellite state of Czechoslovakia way back in the 1950s. Movidyn is a form of colloidal silver, odorless, tasteless, and cheaper to produce than chlorine disinfectants. One part per billion of powdered Movidyn in water has a germicidal effect. In a study of infected wells, it completely destroyed typhus, malaria, cholera, and amoebic dysentery. Drinking containers washed in Movidyn retained their germ-fighting abilities for several weeks.[33]

Movidyn seems to be a cost-effective prophylactic for most of the waterborne diseases that infect the Third World. To the astonishment of the Soviet military, Movidyn also disinfected every germ warfare bacteria in the Soviet arsenal, even their newest designer poisons. In other words, Movidyn was *too* good. The Czech factory was disassembled and carted back to the Soviet Union. To this day, the Movidyn formula seems to have been suppressed from the world, but then so have reports of germ warfare experiments that went wrong. Every country, including the United States, has a few skeletons in its closet when it comes to research on weapons of genocide.[34]

The fact that the Soviets went to such lengths to develop antidotes to chemical and biological warfare techniques is testimony to the devastating effects they can have on the defenses of any nation, let alone the tiny nation of Israel. It also would be naive to think that such weapons are too frightening to use in war. The Japanese army successfully used germ warfare, including plague, against the population of China during World War II. Recently declassified Japanese files indicate that they intended to conquer Australia with rats infected with bubonic plague, cholera, anthrax, typhoid, and hemorrhagic fever.[35] The U.S. Air Force dropped potato bugs on Nazi Germany to destroy crops. Saddam Hussein used both nerve gas and germ warfare against the Iraqi Kurds. There are too many precedents to ignore.[36]

The Israelis always have known that, sooner or later, someone would think about targeting them. The genie of germ warfare had been let out of the bottle by the Nazi laboratory at Auschwitz. During the 1950s and early 1960s they watched nation after nation perfect the technology. Even if the Jews went public, the Western governments would deny that they were using Nazi scientists to research illegal weapons of genocide. Probably all that would happen from such a pronouncement would be that Western nations would simply do a better job of concealing their toxic warfare programs. No one in the West would give up the Nazi scientists, not as long as the Communists were using them too.[37]

The Soviets were relying on germ and gas warfare as their primary defense, for their atomic program lagged several years behind that of the West. By 1948, the Soviets had the bomb, but no guidance system for missiles to transport it. The military depended on radio beacons inside each Soviet embassy to home the missiles in, an unreliable and extremely vulnerable system that remained in effect until the 1960s. Stalin and his successors would not give up their germ warfare programs—at least they knew they worked.

In the short run, only international agreement might have some effect on stopping the programs. The Israelis recognized that the Western governments had sat silent during one Holocaust and might well do so again for the sake of their Middle East oil supplies. The Jews knew from bitter experience that the West had shown more interest in recruiting Nazis than hunting them.

The Israelis' brief spurt of Nazi hunting in the 1960s met with little success. The Eichmann kidnapping in 1960 had aroused the ire of South American governments, which encouraged a wave of anti-Semitic attacks against Jews in Latin America. The West German minister of "refugee resettlement," Theodore Öberlander, was charged in the 1960s with war crimes while in command of the Nazi Nachtigall Brigade, but dozens of his grateful Ukrainian Fascist subordinates testified on his behalf and obtained an acquittal. Nobody believed the Jewish witnesses.

The Jewish press in the United States, Canada, and Australia identified a series of Nazi war criminals, but nothing was done. In fact, the Australian government simply blackmailed its tiny Jewish population of Holocaust survivors into silence. They were told to shut up about Nazi émigrés living "down under," or all the money they were sending to Israel would be frozen permanently. In frustration at the West's cynicism, the Israeli government told their Nazi hunters to close up shop.[38]

It was a case of "if you can't beat them, join them." The reluctance of the Western nations to pursue Nazi war criminals was a small but critical factor in Israel's decision to go nuclear. As long as the Nazi scientists roamed around free, their genocide research would continue. In the long run, the Jews would never find an antidote to every germ and gas weapon, but in the short run, they could build a deterrent. Ironically, the old Nazis in Pullach would help them build the atomic bomb.

The problem for Israel was not nuclear technology. The Israelis had enough skilled scientists to solve the design problem. The French contractors provided the machinery to build a plutonium reprocessor. The real obstacles were a constant supply of uranium and a remote test site. Israel has only trace amounts of uranium in its soil, which would be prohibitively expensive to retrieve. Even if enough was scraped together, the country is so small that an atomic detonation, even underground, would be detected easily. The Germans solved both problems.

Argentina had a large natural supply of uranium and an equally large contingent of Nazi scientists. During the early 1960s a senior West German diplomat in Buenos Aires, who had long been involved with the intelligence service, successfully negotiated a trade treaty with the Argentine government. A secret annex to the treaty was discovered years later by one of our sources, a member of the Argentine Foreign Ministry. The secret protocol called for the West German government to finance a massive Argentine effort to process enriched uranium. The West Germans secretly provided funding as well as reactor design technology they had obtained under a license from the American Westinghouse Corporation.[39]

A similar protocol was executed with South Africa, which had an equally large contingent of Nazi Germans. There the scientists would take the enriched Argentine plutonium, design a crude but effective tactical nuclear warhead, and test it. The West German government, despite its public allegiance to nuclear arms control, was, in fact, responsible for the single largest proliferation of nuclear arms technology in the world.[40]

Bonn was astounded when the Mossad revealed its knowledge of the entire scheme and demanded a continuous supply source of uranium as the price for continued silence. In March 1968, even before the Argentine facilities were fully on line, the West German intelligence service arranged for the first illegal diversion of enriched uranium to Israel.[41] Shortly afterward, the Dimona reactor began producing weapons-grade plutonium. Israel's decision to join the nuclear club in 1968 was prompted by several factors, not the least being the U.S. decision to join the arms embargo against Israel after the 1967 war. The Arab states, of course, continued to receive massive arms shipments from the Soviets, while the Western states continued their chemical and biological warfare programs.

In 1968 Henry Kissinger, a campaign adviser for Nelson Rockefeller's bid for the Republican nomination for that year's presidential election, told the Israeli leaders the facts of life. In essence, Kissinger's stated policy was that the West should stand by and do nothing if Israel was attacked by Soviet missiles. The Jews were on their own. The United States would not risk starting World War III over Arab territories occupied by the Jews, and Moscow knew it.[42]

A few months after Kissinger's bombastic lecture, the first Israeli nuclear bomb was assembled. The State of Israel quietly and efficiently had achieved the counterweapon to ensure its long-term survival. As long as the Jews could wipe out the Nazi scientists and their Arab sponsors with a nuclear strike, the threat of chemical and biological attack from the Arabs would remain on hold. The code name given to the first Israeli bomb: "NEVER AGAIN."[43]

It is an axiom among the Western press that the Jews make too much of the Holocaust and that Israel is paranoid about its security. The truth is that the Israeli policy has been to keep quiet about the subject, especially when it touched Western aid to Nazis. As will be seen here, the Israeli decision to go nuclear in 1968 also coincided with the emergence of ex-Nazis in Richard Nixon's campaign to become president of the United States.

Twenty years after the birth of Israel, the Nazis were coming out of the closet in the United States. One of the most prominent Eastern European Fascists was Laszlo Pasztor, the founding chair of Nixon's Republican Heritage Groups council. During World War II Pasztor was a diplomat in Berlin representing the Arrow Cross government of Nazi Hungary, which supervised the extermination of the Jewish population.[44]

As a member of a wartime "movement hostile to the United States," Pasztor would have been barred by the Displaced Persons' Act from entering the United States. However, in the first year of the Eisenhower administration, that act was replaced by the Refugee Relief Act of 1953. Former members of Fascist governments became eligible for visas, as long as they did not advocate forming a totalitarian government in the United States.[45]

Pasztor labored on the fringes of the Republican party's Ethnic Division during the Eisenhower administration, but the loyal Fascists were always dropped as soon as the election campaign was over. The Ethnic Division was allowed to be active only during presidential campaigns. In 1968 Nixon changed all that. According to Pasztor, Nixon personally promised to establish a permanent ethnic organization in the Republican party if he became president.[46]

Nixon kept his promise. As discussed in Chapter 5, the 1972 secret Australian memo revealed that the Nixon administration had discovered that Fascist groups were useful to get out the ethnic votes in several key states. Nixon needed the Nazi vote to avoid another Dewey debacle. Just a few more votes would have made all the difference in Nixon's race against Kennedy in 1960. In several key states, the Eastern European vote could provide the margin for victory in 1968.

The road to temptation was clear, and after Nixon won, he approved Pasztor's appointment as chief organizer of the ethnic council. Not surprisingly, Pasztor's "choices for filling émigré slots as the council was being formed included various Nazi collaborationist organizations."[47] The former Fascists were coming out of the closet in droves.

The policy of the Nixon White House was an "open door" for émigré Fascists, and through the door came such guests as Ivan Docheff, head of the Bulgarian National Front and chairman of the American Friends of the Anti-Bolshevik Bloc of Nations (ABN).[48] The ABN, as we documented in our previous book, had been condemned even during the Eisenhower administration as an organization dominated by war criminals and fugitive

Fascists.[49] Yet Nixon welcomed them with open arms and even had Docheff to breakfast for a prayer meeting to celebrate Captive Nations Week.[50]

In late 1971 a series of Nazi scandals hit the press in the United States and President Nixon was accused of being too close to notorious Fascist émigrés. On November 10, in a piece headlined "Nixon Appears a Little Soft on Nazis," Jack Anderson recapitulated a number of his charges in *The Washington Post.* Anderson had reported that the president had "invited an ex-Nazi to the White House for a prayer session and that he sent a letter of tribute to a notorious anti-Jewish editor."[51]

The Nixon White House had protested that the president "has never condoned and does not condone anti-Semitism in any form." Anderson agreed but pointed out that "men with histories of Nazi sympathies have managed to endear themselves to the Nixon administration." Five weeks earlier Anderson had cited the case of Dr. Joseph Pauco, "a prominent GOP adviser and White House guest" who was "a pro-Nazi propagandist in Slovakia during World War II." Pauco may have been a Fascist, but he was a good Christian. Like Pasztor, he too had prayed with the president during his White House visit and was one of the controllers of the Republican party's Heritage Groups Council.[52]

Anderson also had reported previously that both Nixon and Vice President Spiro Agnew had sent warm tributes to Geno Szebedinsky, editor of the Hungarian-American newspaper *Magyarsag,* "which foams with anti-Semitism." Nixon had written that "his distinguished career . . . is well known to me." In the five weeks since the charge was first made, Nixon had done nothing to repudiate his letter of greetings.[53]

It should be recalled that the State Department told its Australian counterpart that local officials in "several key states" depended on the Nazi vote. In fact, the émigré ethnic factions, such as the Croatian Ustashi, were important in federal elections as well. The "Nixon for President" campaigns appear to have been the primary beneficiary of their support. The president himself needed the Eastern European vote so desperately that he was not about to condemn the Fascist ethnic editors who could reach the voters, even if their hatred of the Jews was well documented.

During Nixon's "Four More Years" campaign in 1971–1972, Laszlo Pasztor again played a key role in marshaling the ethnic vote. No longer a marginal player on the fringes, now he held a key position as the Republican National Committee's nationalities director. At a two-day organizing convention in November 1971, Pasztor castigated the "ultra-liberal" and leftist Democratic party, which he felt had abandoned ethnic Americans, and boasted of the work he had done to funnel their votes to the Republicans. Several grateful Nixon cabinet members responded with promises of increased federal funding for their favored ethnic groups.[54]

The Republican leadership cannot claim ignorance as a defense. Anderson's famous exposé of Nixon's Nazis appeared in *The Washington Post* at the same time as the November 1971 convention. Among those mentioned was Laszlo Pasztor, "the industrious head of the GOP ethnic groups, [who] was never asked about his wartime activities in Hungary by the four GOP officials who interviewed him for his job." It was too embarrassing for Nixon to admit that Pasztor had been a ranking member of a Fascist government at war with the United States.

In his defense, Pasztor claimed that he was never a Jew-hater and that actually he was trying to rid the Republicans of extremist émigrés.[55] If so, he had a funny way of doing it. It is one thing to promote obscure Eastern European Fascist movements in the Republican party. It is quite another to let the German Nazis have a major influence. After 1953, the Republican administration changed the rules, and even members of the Waffen SS could immigrate to the United States as long as they claimed only to have fought the Communists on the Eastern Front.[56]

By the 1970s Pasztor wasn't afraid to associate publicly with former supporters of German fascism. Nor did Nixon seem to care, as long as the Germans voted for him. In October 1971 the second All German-American Heritage Group Conference "received a letter of 'warm greetings' from President Nixon and a note of welcome from Mrs. Nixon, who accepted the title of honorary chairman and noted her own German ancestry." It does not take a genius to realize that some of the conference members were not typical German-Americans. Among the Fascist propaganda offered at the conference were advertisements for books that denied that the Final Solution had taken place; one of the featured speakers had argued that the reports of 6 million Jews killed by the Nazis were "part of a Communist-Zionist propaganda effort."[57]

If these were the "moderates" Pasztor was promoting against the "extremists," then the far corners of the right must have been very extreme indeed. Another "moderate" leader was Romanian-born Paul Deac, a vociferous supporter of Nasser and a bigot about black Americans. On one occasion his front group ran a full-page advertisement "attacking federal plans to recruit more Negroes for defense jobs" under the headline "Is Your Job Next?" Deac himself said: "We spend millions and the Negroes get everything and we get nothing." Nothing except from Texaco, that is, which was one of the partners in Aramco's holdings in Saudi Arabia that funded Deac's group.[58]

In fact, the jockeying for power and competition over lucrative funding between so-called moderates and extremists in the Fascist ethnic groups caused more factional fights than did any fundamental political differences. When it suited them, representatives of all factions worked together under the leadership of the Republican party.[59]

The evidence is unequivocal that successive Republican leaderships knew exactly what they were doing and with whom they were working. Nixon could not have failed to notice the adverse press the Fascists' relationship with the Republican party was getting, but apparently the votes they could deliver outweighed any doubts he may have had about their credentials.

Pasztor was absolutely self-confident. He knew that even after the press scandals, the Fascists would remain as part of the Nixon team because of the importance of the ethnic Fascist vote as a counter to the Jews. "It was my job to bring [them] into the Republican Heritage Groups Council. . . . In 1972 we used the Council as the skeleton to build the Heritage Groups for the re-election of the President."[60]

According to several of our sources in the intelligence community who were in a position to know, the secret rosters of the Republican party's Nationalities Council read like a *Who's Who* of Fascist fugitives.[61] The Republican's Nazi connection is the darkest secret of the Republican leadership. The rosters will never be disclosed to the public. As will be seen in Chapter 16 dealing with George Bush, the Fascist connection is too widespread for damage control.

According to a 1988 study by Russ Bellant of Political Research Associates, virtually all of the Fascist organizations of World War II opened up a Republican party front group during the Nixon administration. The caliber of the Republican ethnic leaders can be gauged by one New Jersey man, Emanuel Jasiuk, a notorious mass murderer from what today is called the independent nation of Belarus, formerly part of the Soviet Union. But not all American ethnic communities are represented in the GOP's ethnic section; there are no black or Jewish heritage groups.[62]

According to a number of former intelligence officers, Nixon was funding the Nazis in the United States with the taxpayers' money. Each of the ethnic groups was the beneficiary of covert CIA support for "anti-Communist propaganda" that enabled them to publish right-wing newspapers, hold conventions, and generally establish dominance over the democratically inclined, anti-Nazi, ethnic immigrants. For years the money was taken from the CIA's covert accounts and laundered through legitimate organizations, such as Radio Free Europe and Radio Liberty.[63]

The CIA got wise to the illegal funding conduit in 1970 and asked a friendly member of the U.S. Senate to publicly expose the radio stations as covert cash conduits, hoping that the organizations would be abolished. Instead, Nixon issued a top-secret EXCOM, or Executive Committee order, to Henry Kissinger to find a way to save the stations. Kissinger did so, and they were promptly transferred to a quasi-public front under the State Department.[64]

The unwitting head of the new radio front, alarmed at the number of staff complaints about anti-Semitism and pro-Nazi leanings among the ethnic broadcasters, ordered an investigation. State Department Security ran complete background checks on employees and found that many were prominent Fascists. Stanislav Stankievich, for example, was a known war criminal—the Butcher of Borisov in Belarus. The scandal was swept under the rug, and the Nazis stayed on the payroll.[65]

Between the Six Day War in 1967 and the Yom Kippur War of 1973, the Israeli intelligence service watched in silent fury as the Nixon administration hired and gave honored places in public life to the men who had murdered their families. This is not to say that hiring Nixon's Nazis was a program of the American government or even the Republican party. If there is one thing that both Republicans and Democrats agree upon, it is that Nazis are bad.

The truth is that the Nazi immigrants were "tar babies" that no one knew how to get rid of. Dulles had brought in a handful of the top émigré politicians in the late 1940s. They in turn sponsored their friends in the 1950s. By the 1960s ex-Nazis who had originally fled to Argentina were moving to the United States. Everyone turned a blind eye.

FBI director Hoover, for example, knew that many of Dulles's "freedom fighters" had backgrounds that disqualified them for legal entry under the Displaced Persons' Act. According to the top-secret files of the International Rescue Committee, Hoover protected himself by removing the FBI from the process of background checks.[66] No one was checking the Nazis' background, except for a few "experts," such as Angleton, who was already in Dulles's pocket.

The Zionists' blackmail of Angleton had a devastating effect on him as well as the Israelis themselves. Angleton hated them, and at the same time that he built his reputation within the CIA as the Jews' best friend, he secretly was betraying them and helping to build Dulles's Fascist "freedom fighter" networks. His best work was an extension of the Vessel fraud, as Angleton covered the CIA's files on Central and Eastern European émigré groups with a cloud of disinformation.[67]

Only the initiated could tell which of the groups were legitimate anti-Communists and which were Dulles's Nazis. To this day, the CIA files for Eastern European Fascist groups are a hodgepodge of error and political fantasy constructed by the émigrés themselves. The U.S. intelligence community was crippled by political corruption in the 1950s and to this day has never fully recovered.[68]

The KGB, of course, exploited the confusion fully. Dulles did not know it, but his "refugee" chief, Carmel Offie, was a Communist mole.

With Kim Philby running the British end of the émigré operation and Offie an important part of the American side, virtually all of the Cold War projects launched by Richard Nixon, Allen Dulles, and Frank Wisner came to an explosive end. The Communists had penetrated the Fascist networks in the United States from top to bottom. The Soviets even were using Dulles's secret lists of relocated Nazis to blackmail potential recruits to work for them. When the Nazis warned the FBI, they were told to keep their mouths shut.[69] Even Hoover swept the scandal under the rug when told there was a Communist agent inside the New York FBI office.

To this day, the CIA still refuses to declassify its files for "Prince" Turkul's network. It is just too embarrassing to admit that the Eastern European Fascist groups, whom Dulles had hired, turned out to be working for the other side. The solution Dulles devised, and that Nixon adopted, was to pretend that the Soviets had never infiltrated the émigré groups.

Hoover, in fact, knew the whole story. The FBI's own sources inside the Nazi community kept him apprised of the latest developments, including the extent to which the Nixon campaign put the same agents on the campaign payroll in 1968 who had worked for Dulles from 1948 to 1958.[70] Without particularly referring to Nazis, as Nixon later admitted, Hoover had enough on him "to bring the Temple down."[71] By 1968 Nixon's Nazis had become a permanent fixture of American political life, and Hoover held Nixon in a political headlock.

To be fair, the resurgence of Fascist organizations between 1968 and 1988 was not merely an American phenomenon. The failure of the Allied leadership to pursue Nazi war criminals after World War II had disastrous consequences. In Australia, the Eastern European Fascists almost seized regional control of a mainstream, conservative political party. In Canada, the Ukrainian Fascist movement controlled the swing vote in several national elections. In Latin America, the Fascists' power reached its peak, with several dictators propped up by force of arms and with the help of ex-Nazi intelligence agents.

The young men who fought for Hitler in the 1940s had become "intelligence consultants" in the 1960s. By then they were in their late forties and early fifties, at the peak of their physical and political health. They in turn trained the "death squads" of South America in SS techniques. As amply documented by Scott Anderson and Jon Lee Anderson in their book on the World Anti-Communist League, *Inside the League,* the old right and the new right merged beneath the broad umbrella of anticommunism.[72]

The resurgence of the ultra-right around the world would have failed, however, without Japanese funding. Just as Nixon was toying with a few Fascists on the fringe of his 1968 campaign, all across the world Nazi and

Asian war criminals were coming out of the closet and forming a sort of Fascist International, called the World Anti-Communist League (WACL), which owed its early start to Allen Dulles's brother, John Foster.[73]

In 1948 Foster and General Douglas MacArthur released Japanese war criminals from prison and they immediately formed a thinly disguised neo-Fascist front in Japanese business and politics. One of their protégés, Kishi Nobosuke became prime minister in 1959. During the 1960s the former Japanese Fascists conducted extensive propaganda in the United States, under the umbrella of the WACL.[74]. Several sources have linked John Foster Dulles's network of Japanese Fascists into an ongoing covert disinformation campaign in the Western press.[75] While there is some dispute as to the origins of the WACL propaganda front, our sources have little doubt that Jews have been its most consistent target.[76]

But over the years greed, more than bigotry, has been the motive for Japanese anti-Semitism. Japan, which obtains 90 percent of its oil from the Arabs views American support for Israel as an irritant to the smooth supply of oil. The Japanese viewed favorably any right-wing organization that would lobby effectively against the Jews. Their anti-Israel strategy was subtle. An organization like WACL, dominated and supported by Japanese-Korean Fascists and old-time Nazis, was a perfect back door to American politicians.

The propaganda scheme was so good, in fact, that the Arabs moved into WACL in 1979 and successfully pushed their hatred of the Jews and Israel. Even pro-Communist Arab regimes, such as those of Syria, found a warm welcome in the Fascist circles of WACL. The reason was simple: Whether from racial hatred or political ideology, they all saw Jews as their sworn enemies and Israel as a state to be destroyed. "With membership in the League, the Arabs could now play both sides of the fence, subsidizing the far left for its pro-Palestinian sentiments and bankrolling the far right for its anti-Israel ones."[77]

WACL was the logical outcome of old schemes: Use the right against the center to isolate the Jews. As Jack Philby said, it was all about oil. The conventional view of the first Nixon presidency is that the White House armed Israel in 1970–71 in order to preserve U.S. Middle East oil interests from the Soviet threat. Perhaps Nixon was an anti-Semite, but at least he was pro-Israel, if only for strategic reasons. For Israeli prime minister Golda Meir, however, the old enemies had come back. For Israeli prime minister Golda Meir, the old enemies had come back. When Nazis were received as honored guests in the Nixon White House and Asian Fascists joined the Arabs in lobbying for the destruction of the Jewish state, the world had become a very frightening place. After the 1967 war, Israel was more isolated than ever before. The little bomb named NEVER AGAIN was the only security the nation possessed.

CHAPTER 14

THE REAL HERO OF YOM KIPPUR

The history books say that Israeli intelligence broke down in the 1970s and allowed the Arabs to launch a simultaneous sneak attack in 1973. The invasion on Yom Kippur, Israel's most holy day, caught the entire country unawares. Only the heroic intervention of an American Jew, Secretary of State Henry Kissinger, saved the tiny nation from destruction. Despite the threat of an Arab oil embargo, the Americans airlifted arms to save the Jews. When the Soviets threatened to intervene, Kissinger had President Nixon put the U.S. military on full alert for nuclear war. The Soviets backed down, the Arabs retreated, and Israel was saved.

Some of the "old spies" make gagging noises when presented with this version of history. Others pretend to be convulsed with laughter. More just shake their heads in quiet anger and insist that it wasn't that way at all, not at all. Rather than a hero, Kissinger was a military incompetent, whose petty intrigues and dabbling in covert operations nearly caused the destruction of Israel. This, say our sources, is what really happened:

- Kissinger failed to appreciate the danger of the Saudi-Egyptian alliance against Israel and created the climate for war by sabotaging the Sadat-Rogers peace negotiations.
- In order to curry favor with the Arabs, the White House ordered the National Security Agency to suppress information that a sneak attack against Israel would take place on October 6, 1973.
- Kissinger's strategy was to let Israel get "bloodied" a bit and then force both sides to the peace table.
- Kissinger underestimated the consequences to Israel of delays in intelligence, mobilization, and resupply, which nearly caused a military catastrophe.
- The man who saved Israel from Kissinger's blunders was the White House chief of staff, Alexander Haig.
- The man who became the scapegoat for Kissinger's blunders was the CIA counterintelligence chief, James Jesus Angleton.

Before the outbreak of the 1973 war, Israel knew that something was brewing in the Arab world but didn't know exactly what was involved.

Israel's old nemesis, Nasser, was dead, but his successor, Anwar Sadat, was not considered an improvement by Prime Minister Golda Meir, who recalled his pro-Nazi stance during World War II as evidence of his hatred for Jews.[1]

But Sadat was more than just another Nazi in Arab clothing. He was a brilliant politician who had tried, unsuccessfully, to obtain American mediation in the Middle East for a peaceful settlement with Israel. However, Kissinger was too busy sabotaging Secretary of State William Rogers's negotiations with Sadat for fear that Rogers, and not he himself, would get the credit.[2] In fact, Sadat's initiative was a missed opportunity, a tragic blunder. If Sadat could not persuade Israel to negotiate for the return of Egyptian land, he would force Israel to meet his terms.

Disgusted with White House in-fighting and the consequent lack of American response, Sadat had turned to the Soviets for military support. They were glad to receive him. According to several former members of Communist intelligence services, the Soviets had taken the Arab military commanders under their wing and explained that it was the lack of Egyptian intelligence security, not the failure of Soviet arms, which accounted for the 1967 debacle.[3]

In order to assist their Arab clients and recoup Soviet standing in the Middle East, hundreds of Soviet Military Intelligence (the GRU) agents poured into Israel. Between 1967 and 1973 the GRU had penetrated Israel's most secret communications channels, identified Israeli sources in Arab countries, and probed for weak points in Israeli electronic surveillance.[4]

After 1967 the Israelis had grown overconfident. In the meantime, forced deportations and Arab persecution had destroyed their massive human network of Jews living in Arab countries. The Mossad was blinded. The Soviets deafened it as well. Our sources say that Arab agents were equipped with the best communications gear available—ironically, American-made satellite communication sets developed by the NSA.[5] For the first time, the Israelis could not listen in to Arab war plans.

The Soviets were more than willing to give Sadat covert intelligence assistance, but their promise to give him offensive missile systems to threaten Israel fell through. Consequently, in 1972 Sadat threw the Soviets out and told both superpowers that they had squandered his peace initiatives. He would redeem Egyptian honor by force of arms.

No one took him seriously; everyone laughed at him—the Soviets, the Israelis, and the Americans. To the superpowers, he was just another insignificant Third World leader who could be pulled into line whenever they wanted to. The Israelis were too confident that they had Sadat's measure. They should have anticipated that Saudi Arabian oil was crucial to

American interests, and that President Sadat of Egypt was putting immense pressure on King Faisal, head of the Saudi royal family.

Not that there was any real political difference between the two leaders—both were Arab nationalists. In fact, King Faisal was even more emphatic than Sadat about the need to destroy the State of Israel. Faisal, who had inherited more than a little of his father's, Ibn Saud's bigotry, made no bones about hating Jews. For example, the king had once warned his French hosts that it was dangerous for their children to go out at night on a Jewish holiday. The Wahhabi tradition of ignorant racism was alive and well.

Still, there were practical limits to Saudi anti-Semitism. As late as 1972, Riyadh had resisted Sadat's pressure and insisted that oil should not be used as a political weapon. The wealthy Saudis were frightened of the potentially drastic consequences on the kingdom's revenues. But suddenly, in 1973, Faisal announced that he was changing his mind about an oil embargo. Several key factors were involved in the king's new position.

For a start, the oil marketplace had changed radically. The United States was already dependent on Saudi oil, twelve years before the previously predicted date of 1985, and the equation could only continue to favor the Saudis.[6] Another factor in King Faisal's mind was the death of Nasser. The strained relations between Egypt and Saudi Arabia that had existed during the years Nasser had been in power now had improved. Sadat's repudiation of Nasser's pro-Soviet stance also weighed heavily in the king's deliberations.

For the first time, the Egyptians were looking to Saudi Arabia for support. If Faisal didn't back Sadat, the Egyptian leader might turn to the Communists again. The Saudis geared up for economic war against the Jews' patrons in the West. In May 1973 Faisal fired the opening round of his propaganda offensive, telling senior Aramco executives that they had to change the pro-Israeli policies of the American government or face the consequences of the Arab oil weapon.[7]

A few weeks later Faisal met with oil executives in Geneva. His warning was again very blunt: Time was running out for U.S. interests in the Middle East, and the oil companies risked losing everything. The king was adamant that he would not let Saudi Arabia be isolated from its Arab brethren. It looked like the moment of truth had come. The oil men could see billions of dollars of profits going down the drain, and all because of Israel. It was unthinkable that a few million Jews should hold them, and the greatest power on earth, to ransom. The oil executives hurried home to Washington and promptly began to exert enormous pressure. To their chagrin, they found that the White House, State, and Defense departments refused to believe Faisal.[8]

The government bureaucrats had heard it all before, and now they seriously underestimated the strength of Faisal's determination. It was, however, one thing for the king of Saudi Arabia to threaten oil executives in private; it was quite another for the threats to be shown on prime-time television. This time the king meant business. He took the propaganda offensive in a series of media interviews that made it clear that by supporting Israel, the United States was placing its oil supplies at risk.[9]

Even the State Department must have known that Arab kings do not back down from their public statements. If that didn't make Washington sit up and take notice, then a new war would. On August 23, 1973, Sadat told Faisal that he intended to attack Israel. Faisal had no choice but to go along, but in fact, he wasn't reluctant. The Saudis were ready to fight the Jews to the last Egyptian soldier. The king promised his support, financially and by way of the "oil weapon."

A few days later the powerful Saudi oil minister, Sheik Ahmed Yamani, began dropping hints to the oil companies about a cutback in production that would affect the United States. Yamani emphasized that Henry Kissinger and others in the U.S. administration were misleading President Nixon about the seriousness of Faisal's intentions and that the United States must change its policy of supporting Israel or suffer the consequences.[10]

With such explicit public and private threats hanging over them, the oil companies became frantic. The king was uncompromising: If the oil companies wanted to avoid the oil weapon, then the United States must disavow its pro-Israeli policies. The companies recognized that the time had come to state these facts plainly to the Nixon administration. This time they got their message through: Bashing Jews was good for business.

Although the Arabs had done all the saber rattling, suddenly Nixon was blaming both the Arabs and the Israelis equally for the problems of the Middle East and urging the start of negotiations.[11] To make things worse for Israel, the whole world was suddenly seized by the new "energy crisis," and even the Nixon administration realized that a new policy was needed to avert a potential disaster. By the fall of 1973 U.S. consumers were on the brink of panic, and gas prices had begun their steep rise.

In mid-September 1973 the Arab oil producers turned the pressure up a few notches. The Organization of Petroleum Exporting Countries (OPEC) demanded a new deal from the oil companies, and a showdown was set for October 6, in Vienna. The U.S. oil giants wanted to form a bloc and then ally with the Europeans, but doing so required special approval from the Justice Department, because it breached antitrust laws designed to break the old cartel arrangements. The lawyers at Justice suspected that the oil men were just trying to force another price increase, under the guise of foreign policy.

The companies chose John J. McCloy as their lawyer to push their case for a counter-cartel against the Arabs. McCloy was not well disposed to Israeli interests. As previously discussed, McCloy was the U.S. official during World War II who ordered, in writing, that no American planes be diverted to bomb the gas chambers and then released Nazi war criminals imprisoned at Nuremberg. McCloy took up the cartel request on September 21. He finally overcame problems with both the Justice and State departments and obtained permission for the companies to conduct joint negotiations.[12]

However, the American response for a countercartel was too little too late. The Moslem world had been preparing secretly for battle. For most of 1973, the various U.S. intelligence agencies had noticed a slight increase in the threat of war in the Middle East. When the Egyptian army began its military buildup in the Sinai, the CIA passed a new estimate to the Israelis on September 26 that war was growing more likely.[13]

The Israelis told the Americans not to worry and explained that the Arabs would not attack for several more years at least. The Egyptians' autumn buildup was only a routine training exercise, code named "Tahir 41," that had long been scheduled. By the beginning of October, both the CIA and the Israeli intelligence services had found additional information to confirm that the training exercise was planned to end shortly, as Egyptian reserves were demobilized and officers went on a pilgrimage to Mecca.[14] By the end of the first week of October, everyone was relaxed. The Israelis were blissfully ignorant of the storm building around them.

On October 1 only ten people in Egypt knew that their training exercise was about to be converted into a genuine attack. On October 3 the date and hour of the attack was agreed upon with the Syrians: 2:00 P.M. October 6. The Syrians then briefed their Soviet advisers.[15] It was the best-kept secret in the Arab world.

The only outsider to know was the National Security Agency, which continued to monitor Soviet communications. Due to the CIA's September suspicions, it increased its electronic surveillance dramatically in early October. On October 3 and 4 the NSA decoded several messages from the Soviet embassy about the evacuation of personnel. By October 4 the NSA knew beyond a shadow of a doubt that an attack on Israel would take place on the afternoon of October 6.[16]

According to several of our sources among the former intelligence officers, the Nixon White House ordered the NSA to sit on the information.[17] "We knew it [the sneak attack] was coming. We knew when. We knew where. We were told to shut up and let it happen."[18] Once again

American intelligence was helping Israel's enemies in time of war. To cover the Nixon White House from political fallout, word of the NSA's warning would be leaked to Israel—but only on the morning of the attack, a few hours before the Arab onslaught.[19]

The politicians in the White House did not seem to realize that the Israeli generals could do little with only two or three hours' notice. As unconventional as it may seem, the Israeli mobilization plan requires sixteen hours to call up its reserves for war. During that time a few front-line units try to hold the borders at all costs, while the reservists grab their weapons and hitchhike to the front. In wartime, everyone in Israel uses their own cars to transport hitchhiking soldiers to their positions. This quaint mobilization plan works well, with sixteen hours' notice. Eight hours' warning causes chaos in Israel. Two hours' notice is a disaster.

In many respects, the White House caused the disaster of the Yom Kippur War by sitting on the NSA's intelligence until the last moment. As discussed in Chapter 12, one NSA official later confirmed publicly that he knew of the planned attack on Israel by Syria and Egypt thirty hours before the United States notified Israel, while other NSA officials "knew of the planned attack hours, if not days, prior to that."[20] The NSA's warning was not circulated to the Israelis or to other members the U.S. intelligence community.

As late as October 5, with the Soviets evacuating dependents of their officials in Egypt and Syria, both the CIA and the Watch Committee reported that there was little chance of war. On the same day Israeli intelligence continued to rate the risk of attack as a "very low probability."[21] In fact, only the NSA knew that the Arab version of Pearl Harbor was about to happen. Dozens of summaries based on electronic intercepts were sent on a restricted channel to the Nixon White House. As one source admitted, Nixon's staff had at least two days' advance warning that an attack was coming on October 6.[22]

But no one in the Nixon White House warned the Jews until the last few hours on the day of the attack. It was, the "old spies" say, Nixon's way of teaching them a lesson.[23] Although our sources think that incompetence, not malice, was the reason for delaying the warning, Nixon certainly had a motive for revenge. As previously discussed, Nixon was well aware that, apart from J. Edgar Hoover, only the Israelis knew enough about his past to cause him major political damage.

As the Watergate tape-recordings show, Nixon was terribly afraid of the Jews. He made lists of his enemies and kept track of Jewish Americans in his administration. Indeed, Nixon's paranoia about the Jews even caused a minor scandal for the Republicans, when a party official had to resign over his private census of Jews in a government agency on behalf of the president.[24] Anti-Semitism in high places in the United States was nothing new, and like previous Republican leaders, Nixon knew that Jews didn't vote for him anyway.[25]

Perhaps 1973 was time to show the "uppity Jews" that Nixon could not be pushed around. Perhaps the White House believed that its conspiracy of silence with the NSA would never be discovered. Perhaps the Nixon administration believed that American oil interests would suffer no harm if it quietly aided Arab intelligence by telling the NSA to keep their mouths shut. Whatever the motive, during September and October 1973 the Nixon White House turned a blind eye toward Sadat's plans for a consolidated sneak attack against the Jews. Not one word of the NSA's information leaked out until the morning of the attack.

For once in their lives, the Arab dictators kept their mouths shut as well, stayed off the telephone lines, and successfully planned an attack without Israel knowing about it. They played the game perfectly right up to the last minute, diverting the attention of Israeli intelligence elsewhere. Arab negotiations with the oil men were scheduled in Vienna for October 6. Everything seemed to be business as usual. But between the time the Saudi delegation took off from Riyadh that day and its arrival in Vienna, the world was shocked out of its complacency. Egypt and Syria had attacked Israel, and the Yom Kippur War had started.

A few hours before the invasion, the White House belatedly alerted Tel Aviv that the nation was in deep trouble. An attack was coming on both fronts, but the White House insisted that the Israelis do nothing: no preemptive strikes, no firing the first shot. If Israel wanted American support, Kissinger warned, it could not even begin to mobilize until the Arabs invaded.[26] Of course, there was little the Israelis could do on such short notice anyway, so they caved in to the American demands. No general mobilization was issued after the warning from the United States. The cabinet was still in emergency session when the attack came. Prime Minister Golda Meir was supposedly the person who overruled all entreaties from Defense Minister Moshe Dayan for immediate offensive action. She cited Kissinger's threats as the major reason.[27]

The 1973 sneak attack, was, to put it bluntly, a catastrophe for the Jews. The Israeli front-line units were crushed as the Egyptian army used high-powered water cannon to blast down Israeli sand forts and then cross the Suez. In the north, Syrian tank brigades obliterated significant sections of the Israeli battle line within hours. Kissinger was conveniently absent on the day the war broke out, sitting "incommunicado at the Waldorf Astoria in New York when the Department of State's Intelligence Bureau indicated the conflict was but a few hours away."[28]

A number of the intelligence sources we interviewed about the Yom

Kippur War, including several Israelis, insist that Kissinger had set up the Jews. He sat on the NSA's information, disappeared on the day of the invasion, and waited three days before convening the Security Council at the UN.[29] To be fair to Kissinger, the Soviets were stalling for time too, as both superpowers believed they could gain advantages from sabotaging an immediate cease-fire.[30]

Kissinger was eager that Israel should be forced to comply with UN Resolution 242, which would reverse all the territorial gains that Israel had made in 1967 and return the Jews to the days of maximum vulnerability. Stalling was clearly the policy of the Nixon administration. Instead of rushing arms to Israel, Defense Secretary James Schlesinger cautioned that the United States had to keep a "low profile in order not to create an Arab reaction" in the oil markets.[31]

The outbreak of hostilities gave the Arabs at the Vienna oil negotiations a great morale boost. The oil companies offered a 15 percent price increase, but the Arabs wanted to double their take. The Arab armies were winning for once, and the time was ripe to squeeze the West. Any country that helped Israel in the war faced an oil embargo. With Israel's very existence, to say nothing of Western economies, hanging in the balance, the oil men wanted their political masters to abandon the Jews.

On October 12 the oil companies sent a letter to Nixon via McCloy, suggesting that the Arab producers should receive some price increase. The companies were aghast at the prospect of increased U.S. military aid to Israel, which "will have a critical and adverse effect on our relations with the moderate Arab producing countries."[32] It could even produce a major gas crisis and open up the Middle East to Japanese, European, and Soviet penetration. The economy and national security of the United States were at stake.[33]

While the oil talks dragged on, the Israelis were being slaughtered and the White House dithered. When the Jews begged for the spare parts for their war equipment they had been promised, they were told that no American airline was willing to fly them to a war zone. The Israeli ambassador called Kissinger hourly to complain: "These delays are costing lives. Who's playing games?"[34]

By Monday, October 8, the third day of the war, the American games had cost Israel heavily. Several thousand soldiers had died, more in the first day than had died in the entire 1967 war. Over 500 tanks were destroyed. The Israeli air force had been crippled by Soviet SAM missiles. There were no spare parts for the planes, and the long-promised American replacement aircraft were stuck in the Washington bureaucracy. It was down to a tank war, in which the Arabs had an enormous numerical advantage. Moreover, at the start of the war, the Israelis had had only a seven-day supply of ammunition for some units.

On that same Monday, Israeli commanders reported that in another four days at most, the guns of the Israeli army would begin to fall silent. For once Moshe Dayan was despondent. He said sadly: "The situation is desperate. Everything is lost. We must withdraw."[35] Golda Meir told one of her closest friends that her defense minister had advised her to discuss terms of surrender with the Arabs. The end of Israel seemed imminent, and Meir's friend made plans for the two of them to commit suicide.[36]

Only when Israeli ammunition was almost exhausted did the Americans act. The war had been going for six days, and the Arabs continued to inflict huge casualties on the Jews. The White House had the Jews where they wanted them. The United States proposed a truce, followed immediately by negotiations. One senior official summed up U.S. policy as aimed at an Israeli victory, but one in which Israel "had its nose bloodied in the process" and was forced to the negotiating table.[37] The secret architect of this "let Israel come out ahead, but bleed" strategy was none other than Henry Kissinger.[38]

But six days into the Yom Kippur War, the White House was beginning to realize that it might be much worse than a small "nosebleed" for the Jews. The Israelis were on the verge of collapse. They were running out of nearly everything required to fight the war. On October 12 Nixon received Meir's desperate plea for assistance. The Soviets had started a massive resupply operation to Syria and Egypt; without a similar response from the United States for the Jews, Israel would surely be destroyed.

The man publicly credited with saving Israel at this desperate moment was Henry Kissinger. Allegedly he told Nixon, in no uncertain terms, that the country could not stand by and allow Israel to be defeated by Soviet arms. He himself may have stood by and not warned Israel about the imminent Arab attack, but when it seemed that the United States' Cold War enemy might triumph, Kissinger acted decisively. According to the version commonly accepted by most historians, when Prime Minister Meir secretly wrote to Nixon "warning that Israel was being overwhelmed and might soon be destroyed," Washington gave her some comfort. The Americans told the Israelis they could have supplies for the war, as long as it was done secretly.[39]

Kissinger and Defense Secretary Schlesinger decided on covert shipments in the hope that the Arabs might not learn of American military support. The arms were to be shipped by plane, and only at night. Nixon personally leaned on Portugal to supply a refueling base in the Azores, and the operations were timed to land in Israel under cover of darkness. This would enable the U.S. planes to be out of Israel before dawn and preserve Washington's supposed impartiality. The plan fell apart because prevailing winds in the Azores delayed the very first shipments, which meant that the American cargo planes landed in broad daylight on October 14.

To the Arab world, it seemed that the United States was publicly backing Israel and giving it the means to fight back. The very next day, October 15, the Israelis did exactly that, launching a successful counteroffensive that threw back the Egyptians just as they seemed likely to destroy Israel. Kissinger and Schlesinger had saved the day with their arms shipments, risking the wrath of the Arabs but preserving Israel. Or so the history books have recorded.

Our Israeli and American sources in the intelligence community state unequivocally that this version is simply not true. The man they blame for betraying Israel in 1973 is Henry Kissinger. This supposed savior of the Jews, they say, played chess with Israeli lives with an arrogance exceeded only by his incompetence. Many of the American comments about Kissinger are unprintable. All of our sources among the former intelligence officers agree that while Kissinger was not an anti-Semite, he was hardly an adherent of Zionism. The gist of the Israeli comments is that Kissinger's religious affiliation should be changed from "Jewish" to "self-promotion."[40]

The "old spies" say that to understand Henry Kissinger, you need to know where he came from. Like them, he was an intelligence professional for the Dulles brothers. In fact, Allen Dulles thought quite highly of him. Kissinger was not your typical spy.[41]

After World War II, Sergeant Kissinger's prestigious intellect got him promoted from army counterintelligence into the more prestigious Military Intelligence Service, which worked with Dulles in recruiting "anti-Communist" émigrés. In 1946–47, just as Dulles was putting together his OPC network to recruit ex-Nazi "freedom fighters," Captain Kissinger suddenly became a civilian instructor at the intelligence school in Germany, which coincidentally also became a cover for OPC agents.[42]

No one has ever accused Kissinger of personally recruiting Nazis, but several of our sources among the "old spies" say he must have been aware of what Dulles was doing.[43] Says one: "For chrissakes, Kissinger worked in the classified library vault over there. All he had to do was read what was in front of him."[44] For example, the 1947 version of the army's *Consolidated Orientation and Guidance Manual* listed the various war criminals living in the U.S. zone, indexed them by atrocity, and cross-referenced them to their various employers in Western intelligence.[45] This top-secret manual was considered a basic reference for intelligence officers at the time Kissinger was teaching intelligence courses.

If Kissinger knew about the OPC's Nazi recruiting, he kept his mouth shut. In the fall of 1947 he worked on covert operations at Harvard University as part of a foreign student recruitment team for OPC. After graduation, Kissinger was a consultant for Dulles's Operations Research Office, which, among other things, interviewed Nazis for intelligence against the Soviet Union.[46]

In 1952 Kissinger became a consultant for the National Security Council's Psychological Strategy Board, which supported Dulles's entire program of covert paramilitary operations.[47] Among other responsibilities, this office consulted on the employment of Nazis as "freedom fighters" behind the Iron Curtain for the rest of the Eisenhower-Nixon administration.[48]

In 1954 Nelson Rockefeller took over as Cold War coordinator for the White House. Shortly thereafter Kissinger was promoted to consultant to the NSC's "highest policy-making board for implementing clandestine operations against foreign governments."[49] Kissinger remained in this post briefly after Vice President Nixon took charge of clandestine operations in 1955.[50]

By the time Nixon ran for president in 1968, Kissinger was an old professional in spy work. A few days after the election, Nixon asked him to head his NSC, setting up a new organization "to exclude the CIA from the formulation of policy."[51] Kissinger, obsessed with being accepted by Nixon, went out of his way to prove his loyalty. He went so far as to keep his Jewish staffers, such as Morton Halperin, away from meetings about Israel.[52] The new president barely disguised his contempt for Jews and, as we have seen, openly brought Fascists into the Republican National Committee.

Kissinger has always denied involvement with Dulles's Nazis and insists that he was ignorant of the seamier side of the intelligence world.[53] But, by 1973, few Israelis were prepared to believe anything he said. From the Israeli point of view, Kissinger might as well have been an Arab. Israeli intelligence remembered that it was Kissinger who told them not to mobilize and wait for the Arabs to fire the first shot. It was Kissinger, they suspected, who sat on the attack warning in the first place. It was Kissinger who went into hiding on the first day of the war. The Israelis also saw Kissinger's hand in the three-day delay before the Arab invasion was brought up in the UN.[54]

It was Kissinger, they believed, who delayed the resupply operation at the height of the Yom Kippur War and then refused to send Israel arms except under the dark of night. Instead of standing by the only democracy in the Middle East, Kissinger had sold the Jews out for Arab oil. Then, as the new secretary of state, he wanted to take the credit for "peace" negotiations in which Israel would have to give back the territory it had won in 1967. The mere mention of Kissinger's name was enough to send the Israeli cabinet into a rage.[55]

To be fair, Kissinger never meant to do as much harm as he did. He may have been an "old spy," but he was no general. The problem was incompetence, not bigotry. He just did not understand the drastic consequences of delaying mobilization, nor did he appreciate the logistical implications of a seven-day ammunition stock. His aim was to let the Jews win the war, but to wound them a little in the process. However, his scheme nearly destroyed Israel.[56]

Neither Kissinger nor the Israelis knew that the Soviets now were encouraging the Arabs to press on for a knockout blow. The Soviets, who had completely penetrated Israeli communications, were relaying to the Arabs the despair within the inner circle of Golda Meir's advisers.[57] With Soviet prompting, other Arab nations had jumped into the war. Two Iraqi tank divisions, with 30,000 men and 1,200 armored vehicles, had suddenly appeared on the Golan Heights.[58] When Kissinger asked for cease-fire discussions in the UN on October 9, the Arabs laughed.

Our "old spy" informants say that Henry Kissinger was not the man who saved Israel. Just as President Nixon was considering Meir's desperate plea, which reached him on October 12, Israel had some help from the White House chief of staff, General Alexander Haig. Haig held up the oil companies' letter recommending a price increase for Arab oil producers for several crucial days.[59] If Nixon had known that the oil men were united, he would have backed away from the Jews, our sources say. Haig's action helped Israel, by allowing time for Meir's dramatic plea to have its effect on Nixon and for the cold hard facts of the Arab and Soviet threats to sink in at the White House.[60]

But Al Haig did much more for Israel. In fact, he was making policy behind Kissinger's back. By then Nixon already was enmeshed in the Watergate scandal. The unwitting Kissinger, intent on letting the Jews bleed a little, had opened an artery instead. Defense Secretary Schlesinger had dragged his feet too long on military supplies. He and Kissinger did not decide until Wednesday, October 10, that they would even supply Israel with arms. The U.S. airlift did not even commence until Sunday, October 14. Haig realized that there was a good chance that the Israeli Army would be crushed before the bulk of the supplies reached the front. The logistics loop was too long.

Behind Kissinger's back, General Haig took matters into his own hands within minutes of hearing about the attack on Israel. On Saturday, October 6, Alexander Haig told Israeli intelligence that there was a new weapon that could stop the Arab tank onslaught. If they could get a team to the United States, he would give it to them.[61]

On that Saturday evening, one of the authors, John Loftus, was assigned as the duty officer at the battalion headquarters of the Infantry Officer Candidate School in Fort Benning, Georgia. This is where the U.S. Army trains its own officers as well as those of allied nations. Some were more "allied" than others in those days. One week the Iraqis would be trained; the next class might be the Iranians. Sitting at the battalion night desk was standard duty for second lieutenants, but this time, on the first night of the Yom Kippur War, the orders were a little different. Loftus's commanding officer told him:

> A CIA plane is en route from Israel with about 40 Israeli field-grade commanders. They will arrive after midnight. You are to hide them in one of the empty barracks. You will give them an orientation on the TOW missile system and answer any questions they have. The Israelis will be here . . . for training, while we ship every TOW we have over there. If the press calls and asks if we are supplying Israel with a classified weapon, you are neither to confirm nor deny.[62]

These were sensitive orders, to put it mildly. The U.S. Army had just developed the tube-launched, optically tracked, wire-guided (TOW) missile and so far had shared it only with Britain and West Germany. The TOW could be fired from a foxhole and destroy a moving tank three kilometers away. As the missile was flying, it unreeled three kilometers of cable behind it, connected to a steering telescope. As the enemy tank moved, trying to get away from the missile, the missile followed, even up- and downhill. A teenager could steer the missile to the tank just by following it with the telescope. The "kill ratio" for the TOW was 97 percent.

The planeload of Israeli commanders who arrived that night did not look like soldiers, let alone crack infantry officers. The Israeli captains and majors had long hair, mustaches, and wore hippie-style civilian clothes. They were amazed when Loftus briefed them on the TOW's capabilities. The Israelis disappeared the next day for training. The Israelis were back in Israel by October 14, just in time to repulse a massive Egyptian armored attack in the Sinai. It was the turning point of the war.[63]

Thus, while Kissinger and Schlesinger were playing games with Israeli resupply, Al Haig was stripping every TOW missile off the eastern seaboard of the United States and from Germany and shipping them to Israel.[64] It was not hard to do. As Oliver North later discovered, you can pack a lot of TOW missiles into one aircraft.

A number of histories of the Yom Kippur War have made a great deal of the Israeli threat to use the atomic bomb. In point of fact, both the

United States and the Soviet Union believed that Israel had only three low-yield tactical warheads at the time, which would have had little effect against four thousand Arab tanks dispersed around Israel's borders.[65]

On the other hand, four thousand TOW missiles could make quite an impact. According to our intelligence sources, they did just that. Al Haig's missiles arrived in time to blunt the next Egyptian offensive.[66] Israeli intelligence learned that Egypt's armored divisions would attack the Mitla and Gidi passes in the Sinai—the last line of Israeli defense in the south—on October 14. The opening of the final Egyptian assault on Israel turned into a rout as the Arabs' tank force was cut to ribbons.

Haig had saved Kissinger's reputation by giving Israel the TOWs. If the vital Mitla Pass had fallen, Israel's fate would have been sealed. The American arms authorized by Kissinger had arrived too late to help with the defense of the pass. In fact, before the first official U.S. airlift had even started to unload weapons on Sunday, October 14, the crucial defensive battle in the Sinai was all but over.

It is no coincidence that the Israelis put their atomic bombs back in to storage on October 14, the day the TOWs were first tried out in Israel.[67] On October 15 the Israeli army counterattacked, crossed the Suez Canal, and began to drive toward Cairo. By October 16 the Soviet premier flew to Cairo and advised Sadat to call for a cease-fire.

The Soviets and Egyptians still had not figured out why their tanks were being blown up all over the desert. Knowing that Haig had stuck his neck out a long way, the Israelis kept quiet about the TOW missiles. Afterward, action reports revealed that the Egyptian tanks were not destroyed from the air, as has been popularly believed, but were hit on the side, consistent with TOW damage.[68]

Why did Haig authorize a covert TOW missile shipment, which could have cost him his career, as it was totally against U.S. policy at the time? The answer, according to several of the former intelligence officers we asked, is that as a young Army captain in the late 1940s, Haig had served briefly in General Gehlen's Nazi base and hated what he saw.[69] One of Haig's American colleagues inside the Pullach compound also witnessed Gehlen's recruitment of Nazis as Cold War "freedom fighters," the revival of anti-Semitism, and programs aimed directly at the new State of Israel, and was sickened by the hypocrisy and cynicism of his superiors. According to this source, young Captain Haig felt the same way.[70]

Perhaps in October 1973 Haig saw an opportunity to right some of these old-time wrongs and took it with both hands. Perhaps Haig thought that Nixon and Kissinger were dangerous. As cogently argued by Len Colodny and Robert Gettlin, it was Haig who became "Deep Throat" in the Watergate Affair.[71] Haig vehemently denies that he was the source of the leaks against Nixon.

Kissinger's supporters attribute his *volte face* on supplying Israel with the sudden appearance of nuclear weapons. The more likely reason, as Seymour Hersh points out, is that Kissinger mistakenly believed that the Soviets were sending paratroops to join the battle and nuclear arms to Egypt to protect their forces. Bad intelligence about Soviet actions and intentions probably caused Kissinger to hit the panic button and put American forces on full alert.[72]

Most of the "old spies" say cynically that the U.S. nuclear alert was just a lot of smoke designed to protect Kissinger's image as the man who saved Israel from the Soviets, and the Arabs from nuclear holocaust. Seymour Hersh documented that it was Kissinger himself who first leaked word to the Egyptians that Israel had three nuclear missiles.[73] The Arabs were not impressed. They had a more powerful weapon: oil.

On October 16 the Arab members of OPEC unilaterally announced a 70 percent oil price rise. By the next day President Nixon was already deeply worried about the consequences of U.S. policy for the supply of oil, to say nothing of the "national interest."[74] That same day the Arabs met to start planning for an oil embargo. The Saudis, in one last attempt at diplomacy on October 17, led a delegation to visit Nixon and Kissinger. They threatened the president with an oil embargo unless the American resupply of Israel was stopped, but Nixon, to his credit, refused to back down.[75]

Nixon and Kissinger argued that the supplies to Israel were anti-Soviet, not anti-Arab, and Nixon promised to work for a resolution of the Middle East conflict that would return land to Egypt, Syria, and Jordan. Kissinger agreed, and the president promised that his secretary of state would play the part of U.S. negotiator. Apparently to assure the Arabs of his sincerity, Nixon made some gratuitous comments about Kissinger's Jewish origins and pledged Kissinger's absolute neutrality. Little did the president know that the Israelis were even more alarmed than the Arabs at being offered Kissinger as a negotiator.

Although Nixon drew comfort from the fact that there had been no mention of an American oil embargo in the last round of talks with the Arab delegation, such action was still possible. In fact, Iraq wanted to nationalize all U.S. interests in the Middle East. The Arabs finally decided only to cut production by 5 percent every month until the West changed its policy on Israel. From October 17 the buyers were to be sold oil based on how much support they offered the Arabs, as opposed to Israel. This meant punishing the United States with the harshest measures, up to and including a complete halt in oil sales.[76]

On October 19 Nixon announced a $2.2 billion military aid package for Israel. Washington's policy supposedly was to preserve the military balance between the Jews and Arabs and to force negotiations. The Arab response was entirely predictable to everyone except Kissinger. Libya immediately announced a total embargo on the United States, and on his way to Moscow to broker a cease-fire on October 20, Kissinger learned that Saudi Arabia had done likewise. Further, the Saudi cutback in production was increased from 5 to 10 percent each month, and then to 20.[77] Once again the House of Saud was trying to blackmail an American president over Israel.

October 20 was the same day that Nixon fired special Watergate prosecutor Archibald Cox. The Watergate scandal had caught up with the president, and Middle East policy was effectively in Kissinger's hands. The Arabs were not about to give Kissinger an easy time, however. On October 21 Yamani told Aramco president Frank Jungers that the Saudis expected the American company to police the oil cutbacks and the embargo against its own country, and threatened drastic measures if Aramco broke the new rules. Jungers expected the worst: complete nationalization, and probably severance of diplomatic relations.[78]

Never before had the dual loyalties of Aramco been tested so rigorously. To implement the embargo, the company had to act against the interests of the U.S. government, including cutting off all oil supplies to the military. As usual, profit triumphed over principle and Aramco cut off oil supplies to the U.S. Navy. Washington actually had to turn to London to ask if it could supply the Sixth Fleet, much as Britain had been forced to turn to the United States in 1956.

The oil companies, fearful of a public backlash, made frantic efforts behind the scenes to turn the Nixon administration around. The oil men found an ally in the new U.S. ambassador to Saudi Arabia, Jim Akins, who, instead of advising the State Department about what policy to pursue, told the oil companies how to convince the government to adopt their viewpoint.[79] It showed just how powerful the "revolving door" had really become.

In the meantime, the Israeli army kept mopping up pockets of Arab resistance. Then the Soviets began to threaten unilateral intervention if a joint U.S.-Soviet force was not sent to implement the cease-fire thrashed out by Kissinger and the Soviets on October 20. For a few hours on October 25, it even seemed as if the two superpowers were squaring off for a nuclear confrontation, but then Kissinger pressured the Jews to allow the Arab armies to retreat unmolested. The cease-fire held. By October 26 the Yom Kippur War was over. Soon thereafter Israel and Egypt began their first direct talks in a quarter of a century.[80]

The first priority for the White House was to find a scapegoat for the failure to give Israel timely intelligence. Considering the extent of Israeli anger, the cover-up was remarkably successful in diverting the American press.[81] As luck would have it, just at that moment the nation's attention was turned to the previous quarter of a century of wiretapping and espionage scandals, which soon engulfed U.S. intelligence in congressional inquiries and bad publicity.

By throwing James Angleton to the wolves, the White House could kill two investigations with one stone. Angleton became the scapegoat for the illegal NSA interception programs as well as for the blunders of the 1973 war. Golda Meir could understand Kissinger's antics, but one of the things the Israelis wanted to know was why their trusted source, James Jesus Angleton, had not given them any warning of the Arab attack. The truth is that Angleton just did not know, as much of the NSA's late-breaking information was held back from the CIA until the last moment to prevent just such a leak.[82]

It was perhaps fitting that Angleton's failure helped end his long-standing liaison with Israel. But even before the intelligence disaster of the Yom Kippur War, his iron grip on the CIA's Israeli desk was being questioned. In the first half of 1973, new CIA head, James Schlesinger, had begun to clean up some of the more blatant Cold War operations that had begun to seep out into the public domain.

After discovering Operation Chaos, the CIA's program of domestic spying on the anti-Vietnam War movement, Schlesinger called Angleton into his office and ordered it closed down. He then started digging around in one of the two areas that Angleton had kept to himself for the past twenty-five years. Schlesinger later told Angleton's biographer, Tom Mangold, that "he was unhappy at the intimacy that had developed . . . between the Counterintelligence chief and the Israelis. He believed it was a mistake to allow Angleton to continue to control this power center so tightly."[83]

However, after only five months in the job, Schlesinger left the CIA and became defense secretary in July 1973. Angleton's control of the Israeli account was given a reprieve while William Colby, the new CIA head, took office, but not for long. Colby and Angleton were both OSS veterans, both had served in postwar Italy, and both had been close to former CIA director Richard Helms. There the similarities ended.

In fact, Colby was not a strong Angleton supporter, and six months after the Yom Kippur War, he took steps to loosen Angleton's secretive grip on the CIA's Israeli desk. Colby discovered the absurd restrictions Angleton had imposed that prevented the CIA station in Israel from communicating with any other Middle Eastern station. This only strengthened his resolve to remove Angleton.[84] The truth is that Angleton had become quite obsessive and paranoid and, although only 66, was long overdue for retirement.[85]

His departure could not have come at a more opportune moment for the White House. In addition to taking the rap for illegal surveillance programs such as Operation Chaos, Angleton became the major fall guy for all the failures of U.S. intelligence during the 1973 war. CIA director Colby announced that "Angleton's obsessively secret and uniquely cumbersome restriction unnecessarily slowed down vital communications, especially during the Yom Kippur War of 1973."[86] Angleton resisted all attempts at his removal in a most ferocious manner.

In deference, allegedly, to Angleton's long years of service, Colby didn't take the Israeli desk away from him immediately, although he was inclined to do so. In fact, Colby later claimed he "feared that Angleton's professional integrity and personal intensity might have led him to take dire measures if I forced the issue."[87] Perhaps Colby feared that Angleton, like James Forrestal, would have committed suicide. In his autobiography, Colby set out the official reasons for wanting to remove the Israeli account:

> Angleton had . . . traditionally handled [Israel] in the same totally compartmentalized fashion as counterintelligence. He had . . . played a valuable role in the exchange of intelligence between Israel and the United States during the years of his highly personal and special relationship with them. But however appropriate that may have been in past quieter years, the artificial segregation of CIA's contacts with Israel, which inevitably accompanied Angleton's secretive management style, from its officers working in the Middle East as a whole, and to a considerable extent the analysts, was impossible at a time when the Middle East had become one of the crucial foreign-policy problems of the United States.[88]

Colby has a rather peculiar version of modern Middle Eastern history. Apparently Angleton's secretive "management style" was acceptable for all those "past quieter years," such as during the 1956 and 1967 wars. Contrary to Colby's explanation, in fact, the region had occupied a critical role for U.S. strategic interests throughout Angleton's entire tenure.

Angleton's rule of the Israel desk was not Colby's only problem in 1974. As the media and Congress probed into the murkier corners of CIA operations, more exposés followed, especially the widespread ramifications of Operation Chaos, in which Angleton had been so intimately involved. In December 1974 Colby finally acted. After twenty-three years of officially holding the Israeli account, and nearly thirty since he first seized de facto control over it with his Zionist intelligence forgery, Angleton was removed as the Israeli liaison. Colby transferred responsibility for Israeli matters to the Near East Division, "where, according to the CIA's organizational chart, it should have been all along." A few days later Angleton lost his last remaining job as head of counterintelligence.[89]

It is significant that Colby never mentioned Angleton's equally "compartmentalized" and rigid control of the Vatican account, either in his autobiography or in his interview with Tom Mangold. Actually, neither Colby or Mangold even mentioned the Vatican or the Vessel forgery scandal in their books. In his biography of Angleton, Mangold says he deliberately culled out the material he had collected on Angleton's long hold over the Israeli desk, as it "would fill another book." He did record that the Israelis did not share Colby's concern at the way he handled the liaison and continued to hold him in the highest regard.[90] After his death in 1986, his friends in Israeli intelligence gathered to dedicate a memorial to his memory.[91]

According to Seymour Hersh, many inside the CIA shared this high regard for Angleton's handling of the Israeli account, even some of those who were his severest critics in other areas.[92] Whatever the official stance, several of our sources in Israeli intelligence have a much less charitable view of Angleton than public acknowledgments such as the memorial might suggest. According to several Israeli officers we interviewed, Angleton helped Israel, but only so far as he could be blackmailed into doing so. As soon as their back was turned, Angleton stabbed.[93]

After his forced retirement, it was discovered that Angleton also had been in charge of a major investigation into the influence of American Jews in government service, especially within the intelligence community. The program aimed to determine whether the views or Zionist contacts of such Jews might lead them to hand over classified information to Israel. It was enough for Angleton if they were active in Jewish affairs or had a Zionist relative. There was hardly a Jew in the American government whom Angleton had not bugged.[94]

Perhaps Angleton harbored lingering hopes that he might be able to exact some form of revenge against the Jews as payback for their blackmail of him in the mid-1940s. Whatever his motive, Angleton's secret files on the Jews were discovered during the investigation of Operation Chaos. Later it was revealed that Angleton also was instrumental in using Chaos to spy on both the Israeli embassy in Washington and domestic Jewish groups. This covert operation involved the CIA buying a trash collection company to collect the garbage of both the Israeli embassy and the B'Nai Brith for intelligence purposes.[95]

According to our intelligence sources, Henry Kissinger was heard around the corridors muttering about Israel's "blackmail" in its attempts to get President Nixon to resupply the embattled Israel Defense Forces in

1973.[96] There was enough scandal to go around, to be sure. The Nixon White House was a circle of snakes swallowing each other's tails.

When the dust had finally settled on the 1973 war, Nixon had resigned, Angleton had been fired, Kissinger was discredited, but Israel had received more arms in three months than from all previous U.S. presidents combined. Now was a time to make peace. However, even that process would be a time of betrayal for Israel, especially by the men and women of the intelligence community, whose job it was to wage the secret war against the Jews.

PART III

THE AGE OF STUPIDITY

1974–1992

Many readers will be surprised that there is a third section of this book. They might believe that the secret war against the Jews petered out with the Yom Kippur War in 1973 and ended with Angleton's retirement in 1974. Any reasonable person might expect that the peculiar combination of bigotry and greed that gave momentum to previous anti-Semitic operations could never be repeated in these modern times.

We understand the argument that Western civilization has progressed too far to tolerate another devious bigot like Jack Philby. The courts and legislatures would not permit another greedy manipulator like Allen Dulles to arise. The press and public scrutiny would never again permit Israel to be endangered for the sake of oil. Our nations have outgrown their fathers' secret sins. The "old spies" belong to another age.

After all, the old order has crumbled away. Jimmy Carter, Menachim Begin, and Anwar Sadat signed the Camp David Accords, the Berlin Wall came down, the Soviet Union has been overthrown from within, the United Nations smashed Saddam Hussein, and peacekeepers are trying for the first time to intervene in places such as Bosnia-Hercegovenia and Somalia. Even the Israelis and the Palestine Liberation Organization are shaking hands and slowly learning to live together. The wars are over everywhere. The world has changed. We have learned that what is past is not always prologue. We have learned to let the Jews live in peace.

Our sources in the intelligence community say that we have learned nothing and that nothing has changed except the levels of secrecy. Every evil thing that happened behind the scenes in the Holocaust and the Cold War happened again recently. The secret espionage war against the Jews continued. It was just better concealed, that's all. Like a great stage shrouded in darkness, the play went on with new characters playing the same parts, acting out the same scenes. Only the names on the playbill are different.

Thirty years later Jimmy Carter played the part of the naive but honest President Truman. Neither man knew that he was not in control of his own government, let alone the intelligence community. Just as the Vessel fraud deceived Truman in the 1940s, the "disappearing oil scam" completely conned the Carter White House in the 1970s. It was virtually the same trick, only the victims had changed.

Ronald Reagan recently revived the part of President Eisenhower. Both were affable grandfathers, beloved by the general public. Both were elderly men with serious health problems who took long naps and paid more attention to outdoor recreation than the affairs of state. Both relied on unscrupulous aides to make their policy for them. Both claimed "plausible deniability" and shifted the blame when caught in a lie. Both were gifted liars, who paid smiling lip service to Israel while aiding its Arab enemies.

James Baker played the part of Secretary of State John Foster Dulles. Both were anti-Israeli; both secretly sent arms and money to appease Jew-hating dictators; both were surprised when the dictators declared war on Israel. Saddam Hussein of Iraq and President Hafez Assad of Syria alternately played the part of Hitler.

The part of CIA chief Allen Dulles was played by his own protégé, Bill Casey, a genial crook with no sense of personal morality or national principles. Both used the intelligence services for personal profit and for the benefit of the oil companies. Both used the British secret service to hide illegal operations from Congress. Dulles put the Nazis on the payroll; Casey hired Arab terrorists. Both had "useful idiots" who did their bidding.

In Dulles's day, Frank Wisner played the part of loyal buffoon and private spy. In Casey's day, it was Oliver North. Both were narrow-minded patriots who hated bigotry but elevated stupidity to an art form. Both ran secret offices outside the normal channels of government, without any supervision or screening of their agents. Wisner hired Nazis who turned out to be Communist agents. North hired a PLO terrorist who turned out to be a Communist agent. Wisner killed himself when he realized what he had done. North may be too unaware ever to understand how much harm he has caused to the United States and Israel.

Caspar Weinberger re-created the role of Secretary of Defense James Forrestal. Both were anti-Israeli, pro-Arab, hard-nosed businessmen, determined to make the Middle East safe for American oil companies. The Bechtel Corporation starred as the Bechtel Corporation. The corrupt British secret service played itself. Some things never change.

Finally, George Bush played the part of Vice President Nixon, but with different motivation. Nixon's tragic flaw was excessive ambition, which caused him to do despicable things. Bush's flaw was excessive loyalty, which caused him to close his eyes to despicable people. Nixon craved the presidency; Bush inherited it. Both abused it.

Just as Jack Philby was our archetype for the Age of Bigotry, and Allen Dulles for the Age of Greed, George Bush is our archetype for the Age of Stupidity. Never did a person with such good intentions fail so thoroughly, and in so many different ways. As a young man, Bush was a war hero who secretly was ashamed of his grandfather's and father's work for Hitler. Bush voted to admit Jews and blacks to his college club, while his father was trying to keep them out. After graduation, George moved as far away from his Wall Street roots as possible: first to China, then to Texas.

Slowly, but surely, he began to be caught in the previous generations' web of oil and politics. At first it was a little work for the CIA, then a Mexican oil deal with corrupt influence-peddlers and political bagmen, then a foray into politics himself. George spent his time in the political stables, cleaning up after his mentor, Richard Nixon, who had institutionalized Dulles's Nazis in the Republican National Committee. He was learning the tools of the trade.

Bush had good teachers. The British secret service taught him how the Bank of Credit and Commerce International (BCCI) could be used for money-laundering and how not to trust or tell the CIA what was going on. He learned how to use British mercenaries to run a war in Angola in anticipation of an explicit congressional ban. Once again the "revolving door" established by the Dulles brothers was at work. Angola's rich oil reserves were the major motive of Bush's corporate friends. Then the oil industry and Bush's CIA fed a biased intelligence report to President-elect Carter that threw the United States into turmoil.

By the time he returned to Washington, Bush's confidence was exceeded only by his incompetence. In 1982 the Office of the Vice President became a secret spy cell for a host of ill-considered and illegal activities. He supported a secret war in Cambodia that lost millions and inadvertently helped the genocidal Khmer Rouge of Pol Pot. Then he copied the Angolan formula and used his British contacts to continue the Contra war in Nicaragua, despite another explicit congressional ban.

Finally the vice president's office sent a team of kidnappers to capture terrorists in Lebanon. When the leader of this hit team, Bill Buckley, was himself kidnapped, Bush's staff panicked and unwittingly hired a Syrian-born PLO terrorist to ransom Buckley back. The Syrian terrorist, Monzer Al-Kassar, had been trained by Soviet Military Intelligence and played Bush like a flute. By 1984 both the British secret service and the vice president's staff were hopelessly enmeshed in an arms-for-hostages trade that threatened to explode in the media at any moment.

A bizarre cabal of White House aides and British intelligence agents arranged in 1985 for Israel to establish a parallel channel to the Bush-British secret service operation for smuggling arms to Iran. The Jews could be blamed if something went wrong. It did, and they were. At the same time that the real British arms channel was threatened with exposure, the secret British spy bank, the BCCI, was also collapsing.

The cover-up was not that difficult. Then, as now, intelligence professionals easily can circumvent congressional investigations. The Iran-Contra inquiry was a classic American farce; the BCCI cover-up was scripted by the British secret service. When Congress went back to sleep, the Soviets were waiting for Bush. Through their Syrian surrogates, they tried to extract the highest possible price for continued silence about the White House's covert operations.

The Syrian terrorist who pretended to be Oliver North's hostage negotiator turned out to be one of the world's leading drug smugglers and gunrunners. Monzer Al-Kassar was taking millions from the White House at the same time that he was murdering Jews for Syrian intelligence.

By the time Bush became president, he reversed American policy toward the "pariah state" of Syria and welcome the men who tortured and murdered

American hostages to Washington as VIP guests. Bush had no one to blame but himself and his own stupidity. Still, he learned nothing from the Syrian scandal, nothing from his close calls with disaster.

As will be discussed in Chapter 16, in the 1930s Bush's grandfather had secretly armed and financed Hitler. In the 1980s George Bush was behind the arming of Saddam Hussein. George Bush secretly signed an intelligence order permitting the guns-for-oil trade. George Bush arranged for billions of American tax dollars to be loaned to Iraq, money that Saddam used to purchase chemical weapons factories and nuclear components.

Loyal to the end, Bush was convinced by his British friends and the American oil companies that Iraq could be appeased. Supposedly Saddam was someone you could do business with. They were all shocked when Saddam, like Hitler, broke his leash, invaded Kuwait, and declared war on his Western investors.

The Age of Stupidity had come full circle. Bush made every mistake of his parents' generation. Without meaning to, he had become his own grandfather and made life hell for the Jews. The play closes where it began: a willingness to tolerate Arab racism for the sake of oil, an indifference to oil men's deals with friendly dictators who inflict atrocities on the Jews.

The "old spies" say that we have learned nothing, taught our children nothing, and the curtain will inevitably rise again. When his troops invaded Kuwait, Saddam Hussein was only twelve months away from inflicting a nuclear holocaust on Israel in the Gulf War. Next time we may be too late. Those who fail to learn the mistakes of the past are condemned to repeat them.

CHAPTER 15

THE DISAPPEARING OIL MYSTERY

The history books say that the Camp David Accords were the only major achievement in Jimmy Carter's flawed presidency. But at least Carter did begin the process of reconciliation and peace in the Middle East, while maintaining the United States' historic commitment to Israel. He successfully balanced strategic and energy interests against principle and somehow managed to bring sworn enemies together. It was the only bright spot in an administration marked by a major oil crisis, gas shortages, Soviet threats in the Middle East, and hostage-taking in Iran.

Our sources in the intelligence community say that some of the most important events of the Carter administration took place without the president's knowledge and never made it into the history books. First, fraudulent intelligence reports tricked Carter into arms deals that marked the beginning of the end of Israel's military supremacy over its hostile Arab neighbors. Then an intelligence protocol to the Camp David Accords arranged for the systematic betrayal of Israel's secrets.

In his effort to be even-handed between American strategic interests and oil holdings on the one hand and his commitments to Israel on the other, Carter allowed the military and intelligence balance to be skewed in favor of the Arabs, especially the Saudis and the Egyptians. It was not the president's intention, say our sources, but he was induced to take foolish steps by groups within his own intelligence agencies that virtually were in revolt against his policies.[1]

In fact, Carter was even more susceptible to the oil men's plans against Israel than his Republican predecessors. It was not that Carter hated Jews, far from it. He has been a strong supporter of Israel most of his life. Yet he sincerely wanted to go down in history as the man who brought peace to the Middle East. No one really expected that this Baptist peanut farmer from Georgia could succeed where Kissinger the brilliant diplomat had failed. The Carter record is mixed: He negotiated the first peace treaty in the Middle East, but he also was tricked into a disastrous arms race that shifted the balance of military power away from Israel and in favor of the Arabs.

Arming the Egyptians and Saudi Arabians was a major *volte face* from the policies pursued by Richard Nixon a few years earlier, when American weapons had saved the Jewish homeland from destruction in October 1973. Nixon's arms package assured Israel that it would remain the foremost military power in the Middle East, at least for a few more years. But the disintegration of Nixon's presidency, with its loss of direction and focus both domestically and internationally, was an opportunity for the anti-Jewish spies and their friends in the oil companies to plot once more to betray Israel.

Ironically, it was the victory of Jimmy Carter over Gerald Ford in 1976 that gave the oil men their best opportunity for years. Traditionally, the Democratic party supported the Jews, while the Republicans undermined the Zionist movement and sided with the oil producers of the Arab world against Israel. The key objective of this new phase of the secret war against the Jews was to change President Carter's mind by supplying him with fraudulent intelligence reports.

The sources we interviewed for this chapter say that the oil industry had a well thought out scheme to deceive the president and control U.S. policy in the Middle East.[2] The first part involved intelligence falsification on a grand scale. This was no small-time Angleton Vessel forgery. This time, our sources insist, the president of the United States was to have his "pants scared right off him." The CIA was used to produce phony oil data to show that the world's two greatest oil producers, the Soviet Union and Saudi Arabia, were running out of oil. The Soviets would be forced to fight the United States for control of Middle Eastern oil. Carter was led to believe that war was coming to the region and that the United States had to arm the Arabs to defend Western oil. If that meant that Israel would be more vulnerable, so be it.

In this chapter we examine the following allegations from our sources in the intelligence community:

- At the end of the Ford administration, the CIA concocted a phony estimate that the Soviets would run out of oil by the mid-1980s.
- When that failed to sway President Carter sufficiently, the CIA concocted another phony estimate that the Saudis were running out of oil too.
- As a result of these false intelligence reports, the president of the United States was deceived into believing that a Soviet invasion of the Middle East was likely, if not imminent, and that the Arabs had to be armed to defend themselves.
- Behind the president's back, the U.S. intelligence community agreed to hand over to the Egyptians virtually all of Israel's military secrets as an inducement to sign the Camp David Peace Accords and subsequently entered into the same arrangement with Saudi Arabia.

Many of the "old spies" are fairly contemptuous of President Carter. Recently public opinion has been kinder to him. Like Harry Truman, his stature grows the longer he has been out of office. He has a deserved reputation as a peacemaker and an honest man. It is hard to recall why he was so despised when he was in office. Much of it has to do with the secret history of oil politics. Even during the 1976 election campaign, the oil companies viewed the Democratic candidate as Public Enemy Number One. Carter certainly had some radical ideas about energy policy, which made the oil companies fearful for the future and their profit levels.

Carter's first move after the election didn't please them. He nominated former CIA head and defense secretary James Schlesinger as his secretary of energy. Schlesinger had been the first CIA director to confront James Angleton in twenty-five years. He had been around during the "stable cleaning" at the CIA earlier in the 1970s and knew where many of the bodies were buried. Worse still, Schlesinger was now a convert to "environmentalism." Conservation and efficiency were the new buzz words. In their first few months in office in 1977, Schlesinger and Carter made energy their number-one policy issue.

The oil companies had noted that during his campaign, the incoming president "had promised a national energy policy within ninety days of inauguration day." The oil men also noticed that Carter "was dedicated to making good on his word."[3] For most of 1977, new energy and oil policies were practically all that was on the agenda. The energy crisis virtually became a moral crusade.

Even before Americans voted for Carter, the oil industry had launched a quiet crusade of its own, in anticipation of a Democratic victory. In the last months of the Ford administration, the CIA had developed a series of papers on energy and oil issues. Just after his victory in November 1976, Carter was shown a classified CIA analysis of global oil supplies. The "old spies" we asked about this point insist that the report had a powerful impact on Carter and helped to define his policies on the "energy crisis."[4]

When Carter launched his national energy plan in April 1977, he confirmed that the CIA had provided him with intelligence assessments which made dire predictions about future energy supplies in the Soviet Union. The CIA warning made front-page news: "Russia would be importing oil from the Middle East by 1985." The Soviets would need to buy three and a half million barrels per day, to be precise, whereas in 1977 they actually exported one and a half million barrels daily. "Previously, the assumption had been that the Soviets would continue to be self-sufficient in meeting their oil and gas needs."[5]

In order to bolster his "energy crusade," the president was using the CIA to whip up a public frenzy about a looming conflict in the Middle

East between the Soviet Union and the United States. The Associated Press ominously reported that "in a few years [the USSR] will face an energy crisis that is likely to sharpen U.S.-Soviet rivalries in the Middle East, CIA analysts predict."[6] In effect, the CIA was telling President Carter that the Soviet Union would face a domestic oil shortage in 1985, causing the worst energy crisis in American history. When the Soviets ran out of domestic oil supplies, they probably would look to the traditional oil suppliers of the United States, especially Saudi Arabia and Kuwait.

Our sources in the intelligence community say that the CIA's "oil shortfall" probably was the greatest intelligence fraud in American history. James Jesus Angleton would have been envious. His Vessel fraud had hidden one tiny corner of Allen Dulles's covert operations, but in the long run the forgeries he passed to Presidents Roosevelt and Truman only had limited foreign policy effects. The oil fraud of the 1970s succeeded in getting the U.S. president to change his policy toward Israel and the Arabs completely and directly promoted the massive defense expenditures of the 1980s, all based on the false premise that the Soviets needed oil and were planning to invade the Middle East.[7]

Some of the former intelligence officers we spoke to are adamant that the CIA was not to blame. They claim that CIA contacts in the oil industry cooked the books on the Soviet shortage by feeding misleading data to the CIA.[8] "The Agency had grown fat and lazy in the Middle East," explained one of our sources. "The oil companies were a big retirement area for ex-CIA staff. There were so many ex-CIA working for the oil companies, that it was easy to fake the data."[9]

Others in the intelligence community say that it was not the underlying data that were bad as much as the analysis that was skewed back at headquarters.[10] "You have to understand who was screwing the Jews," one "old spy" told us. "The whole phony scheme—the oil shortages, the predictions about Soviet troops in the Middle East, the Saudi arms buildup—all of that crap started coming out of the agency back in '76. The CIA told their boss what he wanted to hear, and in those days, the head of the CIA was an oil man."[11] Perhaps the truth was somewhere in between. The CIA field agents slanted the data a bit to suit the oil industry, and the analysts exaggerated a bit more.

According to several of our sources, the scheme to manufacture phony CIA estimates and push them on Carter began in the last days of Gerald Ford's term. They claim that a cabal within the CIA realized that Carter would be the new president, produced the first phony report, and then promptly gave it to Carter as soon as he won, knowing how it would affect his view of the energy crisis.[12]

It should be recalled that George Bush was the director of the CIA at the time the oil scam was put in place in 1976. There is some evidence to suggest that it was Bush himself who passed the fake oil estimates to Carter. In the immediate aftermath of Carter's win, Bush traveled to Plains, Georgia, to brief the incoming president. According to Bush's own autobiography, halfway through a five-hour session with Carter "one of my deputies, Dan Murphy, began outlining long-range national security problems facing the country. He mentioned a particular problem, due to come to a head around 1985. . . ."[13] Now, it may be just a coincidence, but the "CIA report, prepared in late 1976" that influenced Carter's energy policy also predicted that 1985 would be the crunch year for Soviet oil production. Perhaps Bush was referring to some other matter "due to come to a head around 1985." But it seems like a very improbable coincidence.

According to several of our sources, George Bush made a stupid mistake by mentioning his November 1976 briefing of Jimmy Carter. These sources believe that George Bush himself had wanted to emphasize the most pessimistic estimates of future oil production.[14] Although it is impossible to verify their claims, it seems highly probable that Bush was, at the very least, present at the moment when the first CIA oil estimate was passed to Carter. It is possible that his last major official act as CIA head was to approve the overly pessimistic estimates; but, on the other hand, it all just may be coincidental. As will be seen in the concluding chapters, such coincidences kept recurring throughout George Bush's career.

Whatever the truth of Bush's own knowledge of the false predictions planted on Carter, there can be no dispute that someone in the CIA gave the new president the bogus information while Bush was still CIA director. Whoever it was kept up the forgeries on a regular basis right through Carter's term, well after Bush had departed.

There were, of course, many who suspected right away that the CIA's predictions of a Soviet oil crisis by 1985 was just a con. *The Washington Post* was particularly critical, noting that even some of Carter's own cabinet members did not accept the "Red threat" thesis:

> That [oil shortfall] projection is widely disputed because one of its key premises is the Central Intelligence Agency's prophecy that the Soviet Union and its satellites—which now sell energy to other nations—will be importing 3.5 million barrels a day by 1985. This prediction, unveiled by the White House when President Carter announced his energy plan, is now regarded with considerable skepticism.[15]

In fact, the CIA's "revisionist analysis" came under immediate "serious challenge by West European intelligence agencies, by the Library of Congress, by the Soviets and, somewhat surprisingly, by [James] Schlesinger."[16] Although Energy Secretary Schlesinger was the loudest voice in support of Carter's plan for dramatic policy changes to deal with the gas "shortfall," he was less than impressed by the CIA predictions.

Perhaps, as a former CIA director, Schlesinger smelled the unpleasant odor of a set of "cooked figures." Although he was careful in his public comments to defend the Agency from any hint of such a charge, Schlesinger simply couldn't "believe the Soviets would let themselves be boxed into a position where they'd have to buy oil from anybody." He was supported by most reputable oil experts, one of whom claimed that far from facing oil imports, "the Russians are floating on a sea of oil."[17] On the other hand, Carter's new CIA head, Admiral Stansfield Turner, defended the analysts' predictions eloquently and forcefully. He had no idea someone at the CIA was forging the figures in favor of the oil companies.

The common view at the time was that the CIA figures had been produced to support President Carter's energy program. Our sources say the opposite. The sudden shortage of gasoline was a propaganda ploy by the oil industry, an opportunistic bid to frighten the American people into allowing it to increase their profits by removing domestic price caps.[18]

To the dismay of the industry, the president refused to lift the price ceilings. Instead, Carter and Schlesinger favored curbing domestic consumption through conservation and gathering higher taxes from the oil companies. In a dramatic declaration, they called the energy crisis the "moral equivalent of war." Of course, Carter's call for a strict conservation policy was not what the oil companies or the Saudis were hoping for. Conservation, which would lower oil prices by creating a glut, would diminish the importance of the Aramco-Saudi connection. Carter's conservation plan was a direct threat to the oil companies that didn't want to cut their profits by paying higher taxes.[19]

The flip-flop was astounding. In 1977, the oil companies, which had spent much of the previous few years bemoaning the depletion of worldwide oil reserves, had a sudden change of mind and declared there was no oil crisis. The CIA's phony prediction of a foreign oil shortage had backfired. The American people, Carter later wrote, "deeply resented that the greatest nation on earth was being jerked around by a few desert states."[20] Now that Carter was talking about using less oil, rationing, and government intervention to avoid windfall profits, the oil companies scrambled to reverse course.

Their new propaganda direction was that the United States did not need to depend on foreign oil, there was plenty left in the domestic oil reserves. Unfortunately, Carter's refusal to raise the price caps made domestic exploration uneconomical. According to the oil companies, the free market laws of supply and demand would solve all the problems—for a price. By July 1977, three months after the Carter-Schlesinger energy plan was announced, the oil companies were suddenly pursuing the line that "there's plenty of oil and other energy waiting to be developed, if only the government will get out of the way."[21]

It was not a convincing new catch phrase, not in light of the companies' very recent doom-and-gloom forecasts. The oil companies took out advertisements decrying President Carter's interference with the free market and pointing out that the long lines at gas stations were proof that the president was pursuing a "socialist" economic policy.

The Carter administration hit back, charging that the oil companies were using "a crass political tactic, designed to yield tax breaks and higher profits." It was once more a question of "profits" versus the "public interest."[22] Secretary Schlesinger certainly had no intention of swallowing the oil companies' argument that "the natural, inevitable consequence" of the oil shortage was "to jack up prices for us, so that we have higher prices and profits, as befits a period of national emergency." As he stated rather pointedly, the oil companies first had insisted there was a major oil crisis, but after Carter refused to allow any price increase, they then wanted Americans to believe that there was no crisis at all.[23]

When the oil companies could not sell the first theory that the Soviets were running out of oil, they tried a new tack. This time the companies' agents in the CIA said that the Saudis were running out of oil too. The fraud increased by several levels of magnitude and was directly connected to two interrelated aims of the oil companies and their agents in the intelligence community. The first was to convince Carter to tilt toward the Arabs in peace negotiations, especially about the territories captured by Israel in the 1967 Six Day War. The second was a scheme to force the president to arm the Saudis as a counterweight to the Jews, under the guise of the "Red threat."

The second phase of the forgery operation was put in place at Christmas 1977. Behind Admiral Turner's back, an "informant" at the CIA leaked a top-secret intelligence report to *The New York Times* that was even more alarming than the previous Soviet "shortfall" estimate. Soon, the CIA argued, the Saudis' oil wells would dry up. They would have little or no oil to export. This second "revisionist analysis" of the Saudi oil field capacity "claimed that the Saudi oil fields were, in effect, wearing out, partly because of mismanagement, and that their ability to produce oil was far less than previously believed." Everyone in the media suddenly was investigating the "case of the vanishing oil," as the CIA's estimates of Saudi oil capacity had dropped by 3 million barrels a day in just three months.[24]

Something about the whole affair was very strange. The CIA was adamant that both the Soviets and the Saudis were in danger of running out of oil and that by 1985 the Soviets would be confronting the West aggressively for the remaining share of Middle Eastern oil. The new bottom line was that the Saudis might not have enough oil to avert a major energy crisis in the West, even without Soviet competition for dwindling supplies.

The response to the new CIA report ranged "from ridicule to astonishment." This time the critics included "the State Department, the General Accounting Office, the Arabian American Oil Co. (Aramco), the Saudi government and, to a lesser extent, Schlesinger."[25] Schlesinger seemed to be a common factor in all the lists of critics.

Schlesinger, a former CIA director during the Nixon administration, flatly rejected the Saudi "revisionist analysis." His advisers just happened to include several former CIA energy experts, among them the former director of the CIA's energy analysis department.[26] There were plenty of ex-CIA critics outside Schlesinger's own department. For example, the international oil specialist for the General Accounting Office who savagely criticized the CIA's Saudi estimate, also was a veteran CIA oil analyst.[27]

Many other experienced hands shared the unanimous skepticism of these former CIA oil experts about the accuracy of the CIA's alarmist reports. For example, James Akins, the former U.S. ambassador to Saudi Arabia, had also been the director of the State Department's Office of Fuels and Energy and was widely acknowledged as an energy expert. He described the CIA's analysis of the Saudi oil fields as "absolutely pernicious" and warned that it gave "the Saudis the perfect excuse to cut production" when the United States actually wanted them to lift it because of the predicted oil shortage.[28] Akins, it should be noted, was the ambassador who secretly had advised the oil companies on tactics during the 1973 Yom Kippur War, as discussed in Chapter 14.

The oil companies and the Saudi government both had access to similar advice from old CIA hands. It almost seemed that Aramco had more of its ex-employees inside the CIA than the CIA had agents in the Middle East. In public, the Saudis dismissed the report as "ridiculous and obviously untrue."[29] In private, they went along with the CIA's "declining production" fraud. After some reflection, the House of Saud realized that here was an opportunity to sell less oil but make more money.

In public, the Saudis continued to insist that they had plenty of oil. In practice, they helped create an oil shortage. The CIA had created a self-fulfilling prophecy. The Saudis' reserves mysteriously fell by millions of barrels a day, and their pumping efficiency was said to be atrocious and sure to get worse. In a very short time, American consumers would find themselves running out of gas.

In light of the almost unanimous criticism of the CIA's forecasts, there was much speculation "about the agency's motives and integrity," and there was open talk of its "political motivation." Frank Church, the head of the Senate Committee that had investigated the CIA, claimed that the Agency "tended to accept a level of [oil] production that they'd hoped for without weighing other information."[30] The implication was that the Agency was supporting the president's new energy policies.

Our sources in the intelligence community state bluntly that someone in the CIA was manipulating the truth for political ends, but not to bolster the president. The idea was to undermine Carter and destroy his support for Israel. In fact, our sources say that the whole "oil scare" campaign was designed to justify supporting a pro-Arab peace initiative and then to make the Saudis the new superpower in the Middle East. In the long run, the revisionist CIA predictions on oil were nothing more than a ploy permanently to reverse U.S. policy toward Israel.[31]

In the short run, of course, the motive was more money for American oil companies. Our sources in the intelligence community say that the oil industry used its CIA contacts to fabricate both the Soviets-will-steal-our-oil hysteria as well as the dry-wells-in-Saudi Arabia predictions. The immediate goal of the phony predictions was to scare the White House into doing what the oil companies wanted: (1) lift the laws holding down the price on domestic American oil; (2) provide a panic to excuse raising world oil prices; and (3) appease the Arabs, by arming the Saudis instead of the Israelis.[32]

The oil men in the intelligence services promoted the fear that the Soviets would have no other option than to move down into the Middle East, invade Saudi Arabia, Kuwait, and Iran, and seize U.S. oil for themselves. If Carter didn't move soon, there would be no hope of withstanding a Soviet invasion of the Middle East. The most powerful army in the area was Israel's. But the Jews could hardly be expected to go to war to save the Arabs' oil for the West's often anti-Semitic oil companies. The time had come for the president to make a clear-cut decision: Either bow to the Jews' resolute opposition to U.S. arms sales to the Arabs and risk losing Middle Eastern oil to the Soviets, or arm the Arabs, thereby ending Israel's military supremacy—a sacrifice that would have to be made in the American national interest.[33]

Our sources say that the oil companies, and their friends in the CIA, had a very willing ally in the Saudis, who secretly cooperated with the CIA's fraud by artificially decreasing production and simultaneously increasing the price per barrel of oil. It was all meant to be a very profitable game, in which both the Saudis and the companies would get huge windfalls, while their Jewish enemies were finally put in their place. The Arabs soon would have the weapons they needed to see to that.[34]

From the oil lobby's point of view, the Saudis were practically the only nation in the region with the political clout, to say nothing of the money, to oppose the Soviet encirclement of the Middle East.[35] The only problem with this theory is that the Saudis lacked enough manpower to defend their own soil, let alone for them to act as a proxy army against the Soviets in the Middle East.[36]

Where oil and arms sales were concerned, the facts did not matter. Suddenly Saudi Arabia was being promoted in Washington as the Middle Eastern superpower, and Israel was seen as an irritant for opposing this new trend. A very definite change of policy took place in early 1978: President Carter tried to strike a compromise in the fine balance between U.S. commitment to Israel and U.S. interests in the Arab world, especially safeguarding Saudi oil from the Communists.

This policy change has to be seen in the context of the mid-1970s. At the beginning of the Carter administration, the nation of Israel was technically still at war with Egypt and Syria. Every month brought a new atrocity from Palestine Liberation Organization (PLO) terrorists. Every vote in the UN went in favor of the Arab bloc. But at least Nixon had provided a massive injection of arms to the Jews. Egypt's most influential ally was still Saudi Arabia, which, from its oil revenues, financed President Sadat to the tune of $3.5 billion a year. The Israelis looked for evidence that yet another American president would sell Israel short. They found it at the end of 1977, when Carter began to show a marked turn in favor of the Arabs.[37]

To the shock of many Jewish supporters of the Democratic party, to say nothing of the Israelis, Carter began to indicate that he was tilting toward the Arab position on several major issues. As the phony oil data fed him by the oil companies' friends in the CIA began to have its effect in late 1977, Carter appeared more and more eager to embrace the Arabs, especially Anwar Sadat. In fact, Carter became an enthusiastic supporter of the Egyptian president's "peace initiative."

In a dramatic speech on November 9, 1977, Sadat had said that he would go to Israel if it would save the life of even one Arab soldier. Israeli prime minister Menachem Begin, who thought it was just a public relations move, tried to embarrass Sadat by promptly issuing an invitation. The Israelis were more than a little embarrassed themselves when Sadat accepted just as promptly.

At the time, the Israelis didn't believe that Sadat was sincere about peace and didn't trust his initiative at all. A few days before he arrived in Jerusalem on November 19, Israeli intelligence's assessment was "that Sadat's move might be a new Egyptian deception to mask real aggressive designs." The Israeli government was advised that, in reality, Sadat was planning another war. Just five days before Sadat arrived in Jerusalem, Israeli defense minister Ezer Weizman was told by his intelligence advisers that the Egyptian move was a ploy to hide preparations for another sneak attack.[38]

In its way, the war-is-imminent concept was almost as disastrous an intelligence blunder as the no-one-will-attack-us prediction leading up to the 1973 war. There was even more consternation among the oil companies when Sadat actually showed up in Jerusalem and shook hands with the Jewish leaders. Even worse, he addressed the Knesset and, in a single speech, dramatically changed the chess board in the Middle East:

> . . . I come to you today on solid ground to shape a new life and to establish peace. We all love this land, the land of God, we all, Moslems, Christians and Jews, all worship God.
>
> Under God, God's teachings and commandments are: love, sincerity, security and peace.
>
> . . . If I said that I wanted to avert from all the Arab people the horrors of shocking and destructive wars I must sincerely declare before you that I have the same feelings and bear the same responsibility toward all and every man on earth, and certainly towards the Israeli people.
>
> Any life that is lost in war is a human life, be it that of an Arab or an Israeli. A wife who becomes a widow is a human being entitled to a happy family life, whether she be an Arab or an Israeli.
>
> Innocent children who are deprived of the care and compassion of their parents are ours. They are ours, be they living on Arab or Israeli land.
>
> . . . I have come to you so that together we should build a durable peace based on justice to avoid the shedding of one single drop of blood on both sides. It is for this reason that I have proclaimed my readiness to go to the farthest corner of the earth.[39]

Sadat's words sounded so sincere, so humane and rational. They certainly appealed to the large section of Israeli public opinion that desperately wanted peace with Egypt. Although there is some dispute over this point, many members of the Israeli cabinet didn't believe Sadat's promise of "peace in our time." They remembered Hitler's promises to Neville Chamberlain all too well. Even as Sadat addressed the Knesset, Defense Minister Weizman scribbled a note to his chief of staff: "Start preparing for war."[40] Some claim that Weizman was being jocular, to highlight the absurdity of the previous intelligence assessment; others state that he was deadly serious.

In Washington, Jimmy Carter certainly saw things differently. With just a little luck and some deft diplomacy, he could go down in history as the man who brokered a genuine peace between the Jews and their Arab neighbors. Better still, the United States could have both its friendship with the Jews and a stable oil market. Everyone would be united against the Soviets. It was a noble dream.

According to our sources, the Camp David Accords were not part of the agenda of the intelligence community.[41] That Carter, Begin, and Sadat managed to thrash out a deal was a fluke. No one ever expected Carter to convince an ex-Nazi Arab and a former Jewish terrorist to shake hands, let alone sign a peace treaty. But Carter had a certain way with these two men. Unfortunately, the Saudi royal family was not as susceptible to the president's charm.

Carter had hoped that Egypt's closest regional ally, Saudi Arabia, also would be drawn into the ongoing peace process even before Sadat's "epoch-making gesture." In June 1977 the Saudi ambassador in Washington had told Carter that there were "no disturbing differences at all" in their policies toward peace. Unfortunately, the Saudis were not the close ally that Carter wished for. They were quite disturbed in July when Carter announced that he would provide Israel with $100 million worth of tanks, helicopters, and some advanced American aircraft, the FS-16, none of which had been sold to the Saudis.[42]

To make matters worse, the new Israeli prime minister, Menachem Begin, announced within a week after visiting Washington that July that Israel would increase the number of Jewish settlements in the West Bank. In August Begin also declared that he was reversing the previous government's position on the land-for-peace formula. The PLO was a terrorist organization, "serving the interests of Soviet imperialism."[43]

Actually, the Communists were not the PLO's biggest backers at all. By 1977 Saudi Arabia had almost replaced the Soviets as the major financier of the PLO, which by then had built up a treasury of over $1 billion. The Saudi royal family broadcast flattering reports of Yasser Arafat on the kingdom's news service and extended a regular warm welcome to the PLO leader as grand as that offered to any prime minister or president of a sovereign nation. On every visit the Saudis handed the Palestinian leader "several million dollars" as bribe money to finance his cause.[44]

Little wonder that the Saudi royal family felt betrayed by Sadat's November 1977 reversal of the Arabs' longstanding policy to annihilate Israel. The Saudis, who gave their Egyptian ally $3.5 billion every year, were furious when Sadat did not even inform them of his imminent Jerusalem trip, let alone consult them about this momentous policy reversal. Now, moderate, pro-Western Saudi Arabia was caught between Washington and the fury of the Arab world.

To make matters even worse, Sadat had made the one symbolic gesture that was calculated to inflame the passions of the entire Moslem world: The Egyptian leader had prayed in the holy al Asqa Mosque in Jerusalem, something the Saudi royal family had promised not to do until the Jews were forced out of the city altogether. The reaction of the entire Arab world was completely predictable. The PLO quickly denounced Sadat's trip as treason; on December 5 the Arab League decided to frustrate the peace process.[45] The Saudis had to decide quickly which side to support—Presidents Carter and Sadat, or the PLO and the Arab leadership, of which they counted themselves an influential member.

The problem for the Saudis was that neither President Carter nor the Arab world understood that there were in fact "disturbing differences" between the Egyptian and Saudi positions. Already under attack for its pro-Western policies, Riyadh was denounced by many Moslems for appearing to agree to Sadat's betrayal or, at least, for not condemning the peace initiative more forcefully.[46] Under intense pressure from the Arab world, the Saudis decided against supporting any peace initiatives, and the talks began to break down.

Carter decided to use the carrot-and-stick approach to get things moving again. His first act was to travel to Egypt to shore up Sadat's perilous position in the Arab world. On January 4, 1978, he made a speech in which he praised Sadat's strength and courage. His main message, however, was to support the Palestinians. If peace were to work, the U.S. president said, then Israel must withdraw from the territories it occupied in 1967, and the Palestinian problem had to be resolved by recognizing their rights to self-determination. On the other hand, the Arabs had to recognize Israel.[47]

Carter's next move was in the military arena. Israel had requested a ten-year defense commitment of $12 billion. Carter offered only $4.8 billion, but the deal included seventy-five of the most advanced U.S. aircraft, the F-16 fighter. That was the carrot; then came the stick. In February 1978 Carter announced that, for the first time, the U.S. government also would sell aircraft to the Arabs, although nothing quite as advanced. Egypt would get fifty F-5E jet interceptors, and Saudi Arabia would get sixty F-15 fighter-bombers, which were still powerful offensive weapons.[48]

The whole package was linked. If the Israelis wanted the best aircraft, then the Saudis and Egyptians had to get something too. The Israelis complained long and hard, but Carter rammed the deal through Congress. The military balance was being subtly altered, and the Saudis got the F-15 shipment.[49] Then, in the spring of 1978, the president gave a further sign of his growing tilt toward the Saudis, when he welcomed Crown Prince Fahad to Washington and declared that the United States had received more friendship and cooperation from the Saudis than from any other nation.[50]

The Israeli leadership wondered where the president's true loyalties lay. Carter was playing hardball with the Jews in order to shore up his nation's dwindling oil supplies. For a brief period, the Saudis were mollified, but only for a little while. In September 1978 the old order of Arab anti-Semitism was turned upside down. The leader of the largest Arab state met with the leader of Israel at Camp David, the private retreat of the U.S. president, who did the impossible and cajoled Begin and Sadat into hammering out the framework for a peace treaty.

The draft peace agreement reached among Carter, Sadat, and Begin at Camp David in September 1978 only made things worse for the Saudis. From the point of view of the wider Arab world, Sadat's deal at Camp David was the ultimate betrayal. Egypt had regained only its own land in the Sinai; Gaza, the West Bank, and Jerusalem were left in Jewish hands, subject to very uncertain negotiations. Although the section dealing with the Palestinians would ultimately form the basis of the Israeli-PLO agreement of September 1993, fifteen years earlier the Arab leadership declared the Accords to be a betrayal, and accused Egypt of abandoning the PLO.[51]

After the Camp David framework was announced, the Arab world was even more outraged than it had been after Sadat's treacherous visit to Jerusalem. In November Iraq called a summit to formulate sanctions against Egypt. The moderate faction of the Saudi delegation tried to slow things down, at least a bit, by insisting that sanctions should not be implemented until Sadat actually signed the Camp David agreement.

These Saudi moderates still hoped that Sadat might pull off some sort of peace-with-honor deal for the PLO. But the feeling throughout the Arab world was outrage, and the Saudis increasingly were inclined toward opposing the deal. In an effort to shore up the agreement, Carter promised that Saudi support would be rewarded. Unfortunately, at that very moment, events took the worst possible turn for the president.

In January 1979 the shah of Iran fell to the radical and fundamentalist Moslem Ayatollahs in Iran. Carter's "dangerous" policies of criticizing the Shah's human rights abuses were seen, unfairly, as the main cause. The Saudis' record on human rights was scarcely better than the Shah's. The opponents of the Camp David Accords within the Saudi royal family suddenly had the upper hand, and the moderates could not dispute the argument that American power, which had not saved the shah in Iran, was unlikely to save the Saudi dictators either. As the Saudis saw things, if they supported Carter, then it would not be long before radical Palestinians, and their supporters in Iraq, Syria, and Libya, would begin to gather support inside their own country.

The Saudi royal family believed Carter was asking them to gamble its own existence, to say nothing of billions of petrodollars, against the unlikely odds that the Jews would eventually give the PLO what it wanted. The response was dramatic. Crown Prince Fahad, who had led the moderate faction which wanted to give Camp David a chance, suddenly canceled his scheduled trip to meet Carter in Washington in March 1979.

It was a calculated but very obvious snub. Fahad wanted Carter to know that he meant business. The crown prince was rapidly losing the room he needed to hold out against the pro-PLO radicals. He needed a sign from Washington, and fast. A few weeks later, just before Sadat signed the agreement on March 26, 1979, the Saudi government decided that it would have to join the general Arab response immediately, unless some deal could be worked out with Carter and Sadat. Carter, apparently adamant that he would not be "jerked" about by a desert state, did not heed the warning signs.[52] But Prince Fahad, in an effort to preserve the American relationship, floated one last proposal.

The Saudi strategy was subtle. Once the Egyptians and Israelis had signed the deal, the peace process could be widened to test whether the sections dealing with the Palestinians and Jerusalem could be made to work. A wider Moslem delegation would be sent to Washington to claw back Israel's gains on the West Bank and in Jerusalem. Carter had to be made to see that there was more to dealing with the Arabs than one man, representing one country. Secretly informed of the proposal, even Sadat was enthusiastic, but Carter rejected the initiative, as he wanted to finalize the deal with some "shuttle diplomacy" between Jerusalem and Cairo, not plunge the whole process into uncertainty with wider talks involving a group of stubborn Arab leaders.[53]

The president was tilting toward Egypt and Israel, away from the Saudis. He came to consider Sadat as his "special friend," whom he admired "more than any other leader," while Begin was "quite congenial, dedicated, sincere."[54] By the time the Saudis realized that Carter had pulled off the biggest coup in the Middle East, it was too late to sabotage the Camp David talks. In fact, they got the cold shoulder for trying. Carter made it known that he would not even receive Fahad's proposed Moslem delegation. The crown prince, who genuinely had thought that he had been trying to help the U.S. president, now would do nothing to oppose the radicals.

Predictably, on March 31, 1979, the Saudis severed diplomatic ties with Egypt, cut off their $10 million a day subsidy to Sadat, and joined the Arab boycott of Egypt without reservation. Carter was furious, and his administration began to characterize Saudi Arabia as an unstable regime, likely to fall to Soviet aggression at any moment.[55]

In an ironic twist, this time the Red menace was being used against the Arabs, not the Jews. The U.S. president rubbed in the insult with a vengeance. He declared that no Arab leader really wanted a genuinely independent Palestinian state, which directly contradicted Saudi king Khalid's stated position. Although Carter's statement was the truth, it was one of several public relations mistakes by the president, as in fact, Khalid was fearful of the close ties of the PLO with Moscow, although he passionately wanted the destruction of Israel.[56]

Only a few years earlier Sadat had assured the Jew-hating Khalid that this was his greatest wish too. Now Sadat was as furious with the Saudis as President Carter. After all, there was a lot of money at stake here for the Egyptian treasury—$3.5 billion a year, to be precise, almost exactly what Carter was offering if Sadat would sign on the dotted line.

Several of our sources among the former intelligence officers say that President Sadat had other reasons in addition to the $3 billion annual subsidy to accept the Camp David agreement. After the spring of 1979, there was no reason for Egypt to fear the Israelis. A secret addendum to the Camp David Accords provided Egypt with all the security it needed. After Camp David, the United States would supply Sadat with all of Israel's major military secrets, as part of a covert intelligence liaison between Washington and Cairo.[57]

One of our sources, a former officer of U.S. Army intelligence, put it very brutally: "We gave Sadat everything. Satellite photos, intercepts, the location of Israel's nuclear force, everything he needed for a successful first strike. As it turned out, the Israelis discovered that we had bribed Sadat, but Begin told everyone to keep their mouths shut. America was the only ally Israel had left. Still, betraying all of Israel's secrets was a pretty shitty thing for us to do."[58]

There is some evidence to support the old spies' claims. One former Israeli Military Intelligence officer went to Australia to write a book about his experiences, until the Australian government mysteriously threw him out. While there, he was interviewed by one of the authors. Although his knowledge of the Camp David affair was limited and his credibility on the "October Surprise" has been attacked harshly by numerous commentators, this Israeli source insisted that:

> There was a whole intelligence exchange between Egypt and the United States in the period after the Camp David agreement. There were actually two annual, scheduled intelligence exchange meetings between the CIA and the Defense Intelligence Agency with Egyptian Military Intelligence, one in Cairo and one in Washington. This was part of the Camp David agreement. It started in 1979, as a result of the agreement.
>
> [The United States] worked very hard with the Egyptians, trying

> basically to bring Egypt on to the same footing as Israel. Remember, they promised them the same amount of money. Sadat was promised $3 billion a year, just like Israel was, and they promised military aid and, very importantly, intelligence.
>
> . . . This was specifically about the Middle East, including Israel. I believe this is called "betrayal."
>
> Specifically, the Egyptians, through the Americans, got the disposition of all Israel's missiles and contingency plans for war. They got copies from the Americans of the Israel Defense Forces' Planning Department's various contingency plans and scenarios if war breaks out. The American interest was first of all to build up trust in Egypt, believing that in the long run Egypt is going to turn out to be the leader of the Arab world and the most powerful country in the area.[59]

Our other sources in the intelligence community have substantially corroborated these comments. They confirm that this treacherous intelligence relationship did come into being as part of Camp David and exists right up to 1994, and not just with Egypt, but with Saudi Arabia as well.[60] Our Israeli source conceded that the Saudis were being given American intelligence on Israel from at least 1979. "They were pouring intelligence about Israel into the Saudi's military headquarters," he insists, but "the Saudis were in no position to read it, or do anything about it."[61]

Our other sources, particularly in American intelligence, say that this is correct only up to a point. True, they say, the Saudis lacked some of the skills to interpret and analyze part of the intelligence the United States fed them and the military competence to act on it, but they didn't need to. The whole idea was for the United States to provide such expertise and later, military hardware. The Saudis were to share the U.S. supplied information about Israel's weak points with the other Arab states, not to mention the PLO, which is exactly what they did. No one in the Middle East had to spy on Israel anymore; the Americans were doing it on behalf of the Arabs.[62]

The former intelligence officers we spoke to about the Carter years agree that the president never knew the extent to which the intelligence community used the Camp David Accords to push its own agenda. The whole point of the intelligence exchange was to make up to the Saudis for the way Carter snubbed them during the peace negotiations. The Saudi reaction to Camp David was the opening bid in a claim for more American money and for sophisticated military equipment.[63] To demonstrate the seriousness of the threat, Crown Prince Fahad promptly bribed the Moslem Pakistanis to provide military forces as an alternative defense to American protection. The Saudis were demonstrating an alarming tendency toward independence from the United States.[64]

Carter may have felt that his commitment to supply the Egyptian and Israelis armies was a sufficient extension of American military power in the Middle East. But the State Department and CIA didn't want Egypt and Israel to be the dominant military powers in the region. They wanted oil-rich, pro-Western, and politically conservative Saudi Arabia to play that role. In fact, there was a quiet but vicious revolt going on in the foreign policy and intelligence establishments during Carter's term. Their favorite in the Middle East was the same as the oil companies' favorite—the Saudi royal family.

Carter did not know it, but he was being tricked at every turn. He had lost control of his own government, especially the intelligence community, which manipulated him at will. They had tricked him into being the first president to arm the Arabs. Once the F-15 sale went through to the Saudis, the trickle of advanced weapons would become a flood. The days of Israeli military supremacy were coming to a rapid close. The new age of arms for oil had begun.[65]

To the oil companies and their agents in the CIA, the defense of Saudi Arabia took on greater significance after the collapse of the shah in January 1979 and the Soviet invasion of Afghanistan in December. The new trend in Arab arms deals was just what the oil men wanted. There would be no more trouble from radical Arab states, or Jewish threats to stable oil production. Modern U.S. arms and technology in the Saudis' hands would see to that. There would be a genuine "balance of power" in the Middle East, but it would favor U.S. oil interests, not Israel. As soon as the peace treaty was signed, Israel was to be abandoned quietly.[66]

President Carter didn't mean it to turn out that way. He had begun the elevation of the Saudi military to regional superpower status, ending Israel's role as "America's largest aircraft carrier." That, according to several of our intelligence sources, was the long-term result of the phony CIA estimates about "Russians marching into the oil fields." The "Red scare" and the "Saudi oil shortage" had tricked the U.S. president into making the Saudis the best-armed military power in the region.[67]

The "Red scare" even had an impact on Carter's energy secretary, James Schlesinger. From the very start of the false CIA reports on Soviet and Saudi oil production, Schlesinger had disagreed strenuously with the revisionist predictions, as had his ex-CIA aides. But by the time he departed his post in August 1979, Schlesinger was beating a very familiar Cold War drum. In fact, he seemed to have changed his whole tune. Over the next few years, he became one of the loudest voices supporting the Reagan administration's push to make Saudi Arabia the main force in protecting Middle Eastern oil supplies.[68]

As he left office in 1979, Schlesinger, like Admiral Turner and the president, was obsessed with the Soviet menace to the Saudis, the very premise of the whole CIA forgery. Schlesinger declared that "the United States must protect its oil interests in the Mideast with a military presence capable of balancing the Soviet Union's nearby forces."[69] Although he tried to inject a sense of a brand-new Red threat, it sounded like the same rhetoric James Forrestal had used three decades earlier:

> Schlesinger, in a farewell speech Thursday at the National Press Club, warned that "Soviet control of the oil tap in the Middle East would mean the end of the world as we have known it since 1945 and of the association of free nations."
>
> The dependence of the United States and its industrial allies on Mideast oil has injected a dangerous new element in the long-standing power contest between the United States and the Soviet Union, said the departing energy secretary. And he added the United States cannot expect ever again to produce all of the oil and natural gas it needs.[70]

Unfortunately for Schlesinger, he had been too persuasive in his earlier arguments. The experts still agreed that the CIA figures were wrong. It was a little late to try to convert them to the imminent Soviet threat. Even the Soviets had more credibility in debunking the CIA's theories.

A few months after Schlesinger quit, the *Oil & Gas Journal*, a specialist energy magazine, published a lengthy article by a leading Soviet economist. It was unusual for a respectable magazine to publish Communist propaganda, but as the editor noted, "because of the controversy over future production capabilities of the Soviet Union, this article is presented in order to place the precise Soviet position on the record." The article was the sort of propaganda to be expected from an economist working at Moscow University during this neo-Stalinist time.

It completely dismissed the CIA's most recent forecast of a Soviet oil crisis, which "creates the impression that CIA people think mostly about the political effect of their forecasts and are not troubled by the fact that they have nothing to do with reality." The article set out the facts from the Kremlin, stressing that the Soviets would produce almost 600 million tons of oil in 1979 and would continue to outproduce both Saudi Arabia and the United States. Even when hampered by the very severe winter of 1978–79, Soviet oil production had remained unaffected, and "there are absolutely no grounds for the CIA to allege that in the 1980s the Soviet Union will become a major oil importer."[71] According to Moscow:

> Such "forecasts" can be explained only by the CIA's desire to back the assertion about the "Soviet menace" to U.S. oil interests in the Middle East and to make the public believe that the U.S.S.R. is threatened by the same energy crisis now ravaging the West.

> The Soviet Union develops its energy industry on a basis which has been and will be independent of foreign crude and products.
>
> . . . The Soviet Union also will continue fuel exports to the West, including crude oil.[72]

Nevertheless, the barrage of criticism had only a minor effect on those who were producing the phony intelligence estimates. By early 1980, at the beginning of another presidential election year, the CIA slightly downgraded the scope of the looming Soviet oil crisis. But it still predicted "that, by 1985, the USSR would be importing more than two million barrels of oil a day—equivalent to 6.6 per cent of current output by the Organization of Petroleum Exporting Countries (OPEC)." The problem for the electorate was simple: whose propaganda to believe: the Soviet Union's or the CIA's?

The debate became quite heated at times. There was certainly a great disparity in the argument, even over basic facts. One independent study estimated Soviet oil reserves at "150 billion barrels, just a little under Saudi Arabia's. The CIA puts the figure at between 30 and 35 billion barrels."[73]

Yet, as time went by, the facts seemed to count less and less. In April 1980 CIA head Turner went on a major offensive. A strong supporter of the CIA's analysis of Soviet oil problems from the very beginning, he claimed that any development toward Soviet dependency on oil imports "would cause a major disruption of the U.S. economy." Even worse, the Communists would upset the balance of power in the Middle East by offering to sell weapons to the Arabs in return for reduced oil prices.[74] The clear implication was that the United States had to preempt the Soviet threat by selling more arms to the Arabs while buying less oil.

Admiral Turner, who seems to have spent most of his years at the CIA thoroughly loyal to, if totally misled by, his own employees, was as certain as Forrestal and Schlesinger about the Red threat to U.S. Middle Eastern oil interests. His analysts' predictions about the imminent collapse of the Soviet oil industry completely convinced him.[75] According to our sources, Turner was what was called a "useful idiot."[76] Despised by the rank and file, he was only nominally in control of the CIA and was completely unwitting that many of the files he was fed by his staff were forgeries. Encouraged by some Chinese disinformation, Turner truly believed that the Soviets were getting ready to attack across the desert in 1980.[77]

The fact is that the CIA reports on the Soviet threat were as false as they were frightening. As one of our sources put it:

> Look, the Soviets couldn't even hang on to their puppet colonies in Afghanistan. They were bleeding themselves white. At one point during

> the Afghan war, the military was consuming nearly 28 percent of the gross productivity of the Soviet Union. The last thing the Kremlin wanted was all out war with the Moslem world. They couldn't finance their own PLO hit squads, let alone start a second front in the Middle East. The whole idea of the Russian army marching into the Saudi oil fields was a fraud.[78]

But the fraud worked. According to the Red scare scheme, there was only one thing to do: arm the Arabs so they could defend the oil fields themselves.

In September 1980, less than two months before Ronald Reagan defeated a lame-duck Jimmy Carter and was elected U.S. president, the CIA was still circulating its phony estimates of Soviet oil production. One CIA working paper reiterated the 1977 forecast "that Soviet oil production would decline to between eight and 10 million barrels of oil a day by 1985 from its current production levels of 12 million barrels daily."[79]

Coincidentally, in that same month things seemed to be getting even more serious in the Middle East. The Iraq-Iran war was in full swing, and it was feared that the Soviets could take advantage at any moment. The Saudis already had the promise of the Pakistani units, but now they were thinking seriously of compulsory military training. In 1979 fundamentalists had led a terrorist raid on the Grand Mosque in Mecca—fundamentalists who, like Jack Philby before them, were sick of the corruption oil money had brought to the kingdom. The bloody attack had rocked the royal family, and it feared both external subversion and internal dissent.

Carter was receiving a great deal of criticism for not expanding the defense budget to meet the imminent Soviet threat. Already engulfed by the Iran hostages drama, Carter fought his losing battle for a second term. No president can go soft on Communists in an election year.

With the Soviet threat to Middle Eastern oil supplies now firmly entrenched in the public mind, the time was ripe for the anti-Israeli forces in Washington to begin dramatically to boost the Saudis' arsenal. Carter had already bent over backward to give the Saudis the F-15 fighter-bomber, but in September 1980 they also got their first experience of AWACS—Airborne Warning and Control Systems. The AWACS were the most sophisticated aerial radar platform in the world, capable not only of defensive actions but also of directing offensive operations.

Because the AWACS net could neutralize the Israeli air force, the first four were only on loan from the United States, supposedly to keep an eye on developments in the Iran-Iraq war. Crown Prince Fahad apparently was impressed by these new toys. He wanted more, with no strings attached. As soon as Carter was out, he would get them. It was almost time to end the farce of the forged oil figures.

As soon as Reagan took office, the CIA began to admit that its estimates had been wrong, drastically wrong. In March 1981, less than two months into Reagan's term, the news was leaked to Marshall Goldman of Harvard University's Russian Research Center that the CIA had revised its forecasts of 1985 Soviet oil production to 11 million barrels a day, well above the panic figures of the 1970s. In effect, Goldman was announcing that under Carter the CIA had grossly overestimated the extent of a real Soviet threat to Western oil interests in the Middle East:

> [Goldman] said the 1977 CIA report made catastrophic predictions on Soviet oil needs and raised the prospects of some potentially dangerous scenarios.
>
> . . . "The original report implied that the Soviet Union needed to physically take possession of countries like Iran and Kuwait," Dr. Goldman said, adding that revised projections took an edge off the idea of a Soviet compulsion to enter the area.
>
> The September 1980 CIA report declared that the Soviet officials were "trapped in a rat race of their own making" in regard to oil production.
>
> Although it noted that the Soviet Union has the world's largest oil reserves, the CIA report said substantial growth in the 1980s was not achievable because the new oil was found in difficult to tap areas and required massive amounts of capital and manpower to develop.[80]

The Reagan team was horrified at the leak and rushed in to rebut any suggestion that the CIA figures had been cooked. Goldman was completely wrong, they said. If the Saudis were to get their AWACS, the public had to believe in the Soviet threat. "The Soviet Union will almost certainly become a net energy importer," Reagan's new defense secretary, Caspar Weinberger, said the same month, adding "this must be viewed along with the Soviets' 'economic necessity for eventual access to [Persian] Gulf oil.'"[81]

As will be seen in Chapter 19, although his father was a Jew, Weinberger had a similar corporate background to James Forrestal and his views on Israel sounded just like a 1980s version of his predecessor too. Like George Shultz, whom Reagan appointed secretary of state in 1982, Weinberger came to Washington direct from the powerful, Israel-hating Bechtel Corporation. They both were strong advocates of the AWACS sales, which just happened to coincide with Bechtel's profit-making enterprises in Saudi Arabia. To boost the case, Weinberger "cited Soviet oil needs to justify efforts to increase American military presence in the Persian Gulf region."[82]

No matter how much Weinberger and his supporters wished, the CIA's wildly erroneous oil estimates could not be maintained. In May 1981, just a couple of months after Weinberger had flatly contradicted Goldman, the CIA "grudgingly acknowledged" that the Soviets were producing more oil than it had predicted.[83]

Goldman thought some sanity had at last been restored to what had begun to look like an argument in a lunatic asylum. "This is a significant change," he said. "Our whole foreign policy debate has been disoriented because of the belief that their economy will collapse unless [the Soviets] march into the Middle East."[84] In fact, the CIA had done a complete *volte face* and now said that Soviet production was going to remain at about 12 million barrels a day through the mid-1980s.

According to our sources among the "old spies," Democratic Senator William Proxmire knew what the whole fraud had been about.[85] He claimed that "the CIA's pessimistic forecasts influenced U.S. policy in the Middle East, causing a tilt toward Arab nations and away from Israel and spurring efforts to establish a U.S. military presence there."[86] It was too late for the pro-Jewish Democrats to do anything but sit back and wonder how they had been taken in. It would be twelve long years before another Democrat would be in the White House.

For the Jews, the facts were even more horrible. When the dust had settled on Camp David, Israel had a piece of paper, and the Arabs had guns, money, and all of Israel's military secrets.[87] Carter had tried to be a force for good. He genuinely wanted to support Israel and bring about a lasting solution to its conflict with the Arabs, without harming U.S. economic and strategic interests in the Middle East. But unfortunately for Carter, he was never in control of his own government. The cardinal sin of statesmanship is naïveté. Carter and Turner never suspected that their own people would lie to them. The phony CIA oil reports completely fooled them.

"Don't you get it?" asked one of our sources. "The gas shortage during the Carter administration was as phony as the CIA's prediction about the Soviet oil shortage. The god damn Middle East was swimming in oil during the Carter administration, but less and less of it was shipped to America. For chrissakes, there was so much oil in South America that they had to shut down refineries in the Caribbean to keep it away from the U.S."[88]

This source has a point. One of the largest refineries in the Western Hemisphere is located on St. Croix, in the U.S. Virgin Islands. Most of its capacity went unused during the Carter administration's "oil shortage," yet it was greatly expanded during Reagan's term, despite the world glut of oil and falling prices.[89] Most of the "old spies" are adamant that the oil companies cut refinery production to cause as much damage to the Carter administration as possible.[90] On the other hand, Daniel Yergin asserts that it was the Arab exporters who were cutting supplies to the refineries.

By mid-1981 it was embarrassingly clear that all of the CIA's predictions, upon which Carter had relied, were completely false. Not only was there not an oil crisis, the whole industry had suddenly gone the other way. There was a worldwide surplus of oil, not a shortfall. The CIA figures on Saudi oil were just as false as their Soviet production estimates. By June that year, the Saudi Arabian government had created an oil glut and was under intense pressure in the Arab world to cut its production. The Middle East was drowning in oil.

In fact, the new Reagan administration was exerting considerable pressure on the Saudis to use their oil surplus in a price war against Libya. When Reagan asked, the Saudis were happy to open the spigots to oil fields that supposedly were dry. Radical Arab nations such as Libya were selling oil way above the Saudis' price, and the Saudis were "determined to stabilize prices largely because any new oil 'shock' would jeopardize their own huge investments in the West while spurring the West to a more rapid search for alternatives to Saudi oil."[91]

The last thing the Saudis wanted was a return to Carter's conservation and alternative energy policies. In return for cooperating with Reagan, the Saudis got to shop at the biggest arms bazaar in Middle Eastern history. Reagan and his advisers clearly decided that Saudi Arabia should become the most powerful nation in the Middle East. They used the same old excuse: The Communists might march on the oil fields. Even into the early 1980s, with the CIA's forecasts in shreds, the Reagan team was pursuing basically the same policies, based on the same false assumptions, as its predecessor.

There was a major difference between the Carter and Reagan teams, however. Carter's senior officials were deliberately misled by the CIA forecasts, while Reagan's advisers knew, by this time, that the CIA had retracted its previous estimates as false.[92]

Despite the collapse of the fundamental premise—that oil shortages would force the Soviets to invade Saudi Arabia—the defense buildup continued. The Reagan administration had a profound influence on the balance of forces in the Middle East, tilting military power decidedly against Israel. In arguing the case for selling the AWACS to Saudi Arabia, the Reagan team stressed the Saudis' key role in providing a stable oil market. The AWACS were crucial to Saudi Arabia, "to help it guard its oil fields." One senior U.S. official put the matter very bluntly: "There is no doubt that Saudi security is our security."[93] In the autumn of 1981, Prince Fahad got his AWACS.

By early 1983 the price of oil was falling and the United States was gloating, "because it signifies the effective end of OPEC power. Compared to the official OPEC benchmark price of $34 per barrel, the spot-market price for Persian Gulf oil last week appeared to be in the $28–$29 range. Meanwhile, the Russians lowered their price by $2.15 to $29.35."[94] The Soviets didn't mind. After all, they had never imagined such profits. Oil had been selling at $14 per barrel before the CIA pulled its fraud on Carter. The Soviets were laughing all the way to the bank.[95]

What the Reagan administration had done, according to most of our sources in the intelligence community, was change the tide of Middle Eastern affairs.[96] Where once Israel had been "America's largest aircraft carrier," Saudi Arabia was now the designated superpower in the Middle East. It was a policy of more arms and more oil for everybody.

The phony policy of selling guns to the Arabs to keep the Soviets out of Saudi Arabia and Kuwait was also good for American domestic politics, at least in the short run. Under the Republicans, lucrative arms factories sprouted in what had previously been rural Democratic states. The votes went where the jobs were. In the course of the Reagan-Bush administrations, the defense budget was increased to a point where more money was spent on arms than in all the wars in U.S. history combined. To accomplish this massive defense buildup, the Reagan-Bush administrations borrowed three times more money than all U.S. presidents combined. The largest debt in American history was based on the faulty premise that the Soviet Union was going to attack the Middle East.

Whoever initiated the 1976 oil fraud that influenced President Carter so dramatically, the effect was clear: The balance of military power in the Middle East had swung away from Israel and toward the Arabs in just four short years. In the following twelve years, it would get worse, and under the Reagan and Bush administrations the secret war against the Jews would become even more vicious.

The strange thing about these years is that neither Reagan nor Bush is anti-Semitic. The disasters that we now know as the Iran-Contra and Bank of Commerce and Credit International scandals did not spring from either bigotry or greed, but from stupidity. To understand how George Bush led his party into the mess, we must go right back and trace the roots of Bush's own folly.

CHAPTER 16

THE MEXICAN CONNECTION

The history books say that George Bush was a war hero, a Texas entrepreneur, then a senior figure in several Republican administrations. As president, he worked for a kinder, gentler nation. Our sources in the intelligence community said that the American public knows more about Kurt Waldheim's background than they do about President Bush's. George was himself one of the "old spies."[1]

The American voters who read Bush's 1987 autobiography, *Looking Forward,* certainly would have had no idea about many of the seamier sides to his family background, his business and espionage activities, and his political career. It was a thoroughly sanitized version of history. But does that make him a bad man?

According to a recent history, *Spider's Web,* by Alan Friedman, George Bush was certainly a devious man. The American arms sales to Egypt and Saudi Arabia begun by Carter were illegally diverted to Iraq soon after Reagan and Bush took office. Once American arms started going to the Arabs, only a few regimes, such as Gadhafi's Libya, could not obtain shipments. It was Bush himself who arranged the financing, established the policy, and created the covert arms network that backed Saddam Hussein.[2]

As discussed in the last chapter, when Bush was director of the CIA in the 1970s, the Agency published false oil data to justify the arming of the Arab nations. After Bush returned to office in the 1980s, his arms-for-oil agenda became clear. According to Friedman's analysis of CIA files, U.S. purchases of Iraqi oil increased twelvefold to over 1 million barrels a day, which helped finance Iraq's war machine.[3]

From the beginning, Bush's policy was clearly tilted toward the Arabs and away from Israel. In 1981, when the Israelis destroyed Saddam Hussein's nuclear reactor at Osirak, Bush was the first world leader to say that Israel needed to be punished.[4] Even after Iraq turned American weapons against Israel in the Gulf War in 1991, Bush refused to permit Israeli pilots to defend their country for fear it would irritate the other Arab nations. The Israeli intelligence officers we spoke to regard Bush as their most vicious American opponent since Allen Dulles.[5]

There is, however, no consensus among the Western intelligence community. Some of our sources agree with the Israelis that George Bush was the last, and the worst, of the Dulles clique that brought the CIA into discredit.[6] Others say that George Bush is a good man with bad friends. His only major character flaw was an excessive personal loyalty to friends and family. Bush himself was ignorant of the plotting that went on around him.[7]

Although it is true that your friends will do you more damage than your enemies, at some point Bush's defense of ignorance wears a bit thin. A joke going around during the Iran-Contra scandal said that "The two biggest lies in Washington are that Ronald Reagan was in the loop and George Bush was out of it." Because of the importance of Bush's role in the history of covert operations against Israel, we discuss his background in some detail. It is a history that has never been revealed fully before.

In this chapter we consider the following allegations:

- Bush's father and grandfather worked with Allen Dulles to finance the Third Reich and then, when war broke out, cloaked their activities under the cover of intelligence operations.
- George Bush established an oil leasing business in Texas, the biggest client of which was Edwin Pauley, Dulles's confidant, Nixon's bagman, and a front man for CIA money laundering. Bush himself played a minor role in CIA covert operations from the early 1960s.
- Through Pauley, Nixon recruited Bush to handle a variety of sensitive assignments. Bush later asked Nixon to resign for fear that the Watergate investigations might uncover further scandals.
- While not anti-Semitic, Bush was definitely anti-Israeli and pro-Arab, a bias that colored American oil and arms policy in the Middle East.

The real story of George Bush starts well before he launched his own career. It goes back to the 1920s, when the Dulles brothers and the other pirates of Wall Street were first making their deals with the Nazis. To understand Bush's role as a senior official of the Republican party, as head of the CIA, as U.S. vice president, and then, ultimately, in the White House, it is important to trace the Bush family roots right back to the beginning of the secret espionage war against the Jews.

Bush's family, say many of the former intelligence officers we interviewed for this chapter, was nothing to be proud of. The family, and especially his grandfather and father, dragged him into some dirty business, and he stayed with it too long, trying to make a bad thing good.[8]

George Bush's problems were inherited from his namesake and maternal grandfather, George Herbert "Bert" Walker, a native of St. Louis, who founded the banking and investment firm of G. H. Walker and Company in 1900. Later the company shifted from St. Louis to the prestigious address of 1 Wall Street. The obituary in *The New York Times,* which recorded Walker's death in 1953, mainly highlighted his sporting achievements, in both golf and horse racing, and his role in financing the "new" Madison Square Garden in the mid-1920s.[9]

Apart from disclosing that "Grandfather Walker" came from "a devout Catholic family," was named after the poet George Herbert, and formed his own investment firm, George Bush revealed practically nothing about his grandfather in his autobiography.[10] However, there was another, far seamier side to George Walker. Walker was one of Hitler's most powerful financial supporters in the United States. The relationship went all the way back to 1924, when Fritz Thyssen, the German industrialist, was financing Hitler's infant Nazi party. As mentioned in earlier chapters, there were American contributors as well.

Some Americans were just bigots and made their connections to Germany through Allen Dulles's firm of Sullivan & Cromwell because they supported fascism. The Dulles brothers, who were in it for profit more than ideology, arranged American investments in Nazi Germany in the 1930s to ensure that their clients did well out of the German economic recovery. "Dulles clearly emphasized projects for Germany . . . and for Mussolini's fascist state . . . All told, these and more than a dozen similar transactions had a combined value in excess of a billion dollars."[11]

Sullivan & Cromwell was not the only firm engaged in funding Germany. According to *The Splendid Blond Beast,* Christopher Simpson's seminal history of the politics of genocide and profit, Brown Brothers, Harriman was another bank that specialized in investments in Germany. The key figure in the firm was Averill Harriman, a dominating figure in the American establishment, who for almost half a century helped form many of Washington's major foreign policies. Some of his allies in this latter endeavor who also served on the firm's board included Robert Lovett, who as previously discussed worked closely with James Forrestal to lead the State Department's revolt against Truman's pro-Zionist policy during the UN debate on the partition of Palestine, and George Bush's father, Prescott, who later became a U.S. Senator.[12]

The firm originally was known as W. A. Harriman & Company. The link between Harriman & Company's American investors and Thyssen started in the 1920s, through the Union Banking Corporation, which began trading in 1924. In just one three-year period, the Harriman firm sold more than $50 million of German bonds to American investors.[13] "Bert" Walker was Union Banking's president, and the firm was located in the offices of Averill Harriman's company at 39 Broadway in New York.[14]

In 1926 Bert Walker did a favor for his new son-in-law, Prescott Bush. It was the sort of favor families do to help their children make a start in life, but Prescott came to regret it bitterly. Walker made Prescott vice president of W. A. Harriman. The problem was that Walker's specialty was companies that traded with Germany. As Thyssen and the other German industrialists consolidated Hitler's political power in the 1930s, an American financial connection was needed. According to our sources, Union Banking became an out-and-out Nazi money-laundering machine.[15] As we shall see, there is substantial evidence to support this charge.

While the United States languished in the Depression, Walker made millions for his clients by investing in Germany's economic revival. He decided to quit W. A. Harriman in 1931, to concentrate on his own firm, G. H. Walker, while his son-in-law stayed behind to run the show for Harriman. Some say that Walker left George Bush's father holding the bag. Others say that Bush specialized in British investors in Nazi Germany, while Walker handled the Americans.[16]

In that same year Harriman & Company merged with a British-American investment company to become Brown Brothers, Harriman. Prescott Bush became one of the senior partners of the new company, which relocated to 59 Broadway, while Union Banking remained at 39 Broadway. But in 1934 Walker arranged to put his son-in-law on the board of directors of Union Banking.

Walker also set up a deal to take over the North American operations of the Hamburg-Amerika Line, a cover for I. G. Farben's Nazi espionage unit in the United States.[17] The shipping line smuggled in German agents, propaganda, and money for bribing American politicians to see things Hitler's way. The holding company was Walker's American Shipping & Commerce, which shared the offices at 39 Broadway with Union Banking. In an elaborate corporate paper trail, Harriman's stock in American Shipping & Commerce was controlled by yet another holding company, the Harriman Fifteen Corporation, run out of Walker's office. The directors of this company were Averill Harriman, Bert Walker, and Prescott Bush.[18]

In order to understand the character of the firm, it should be recalled that Brown Brothers, Harriman had a bad reputation, even among international bankers, as hard-nosed capitalists who exploited every opportunity for profit in a harsh and ruthless manner. In a November 1935 article in *Common Sense,* retired marine general Smedley D. Butler blamed Brown Brothers, Harriman for having the U.S. marines act like "racketeers" and "gangsters" in order to exploit financially the peasants of Nicaragua.[19]

At some point, Prescott Bush must have realized that his father-in-law was, to put it mildly, a very shady character. A 1934 congressional investigation alleged that Walker's "Hamburg-Amerika Line subsidized a wide range of pro-Nazi propaganda efforts both in Germany and the United States."[20] Walker did not know it, but one of his American employees, Dan Harkins, had blown the whistle on the spy apparatus to Congress. Harkins, one of our best sources, became Roosevelt's first double agent. As previously mentioned, Harkins kept up the pretense of being an ardent Nazi sympathizer, while reporting to Naval Intelligence on the shipping company's deals with Nazi intelligence.[21]

To this day, we do not know if Prescott Bush stayed on board out of loyalty to his father-in-law or because the money was so good. Instead of divesting the Nazi money, Bush hired a lawyer to hide the assets. The lawyer he hired had considerable expertise in such underhanded schemes. It was Allen Dulles. According to Dulles's client list at Sullivan & Cromwell, his first relationship with Brown Brothers, Harriman was on June 18, 1936. In January 1937 Dulles listed his work for the firm as "Disposal of Stan [Standard Oil] Investing stock."[22]

As discussed in Chapter 3, Standard Oil of New Jersey had completed a major stock transaction with Dulles's Nazi client, I. G. Farben. By the end of January 1937 Dulles had merged all his cloaking activities into one client account: "Brown Brothers Harriman-Schroeder Rock." Schröder, of course, was the Nazi bank on whose board Dulles sat. The "Rock" were the Rockefellers of Standard Oil, who were already coming under scrutiny for their Nazi deals. By May 1939 Dulles handled another problem for Brown Brothers, Harriman, their "Securities Custodian Accounts."[23]

If Dulles was trying to conceal how many Nazi holding companies Brown Brothers, Harriman was connected with, he did not do a very good job. Shortly after Pearl Harbor, word leaked from Washington that affiliates of Prescott Bush's company were under investigation for aiding the Nazis in time of war. In February 1942 George Bush's father, who was by then the senior managing partner of Brown Brothers, Harriman, tried to wrap himself in the American flag. He became the national chairman of the United Service Organization's annual fund campaign, which raised $33 million that year to provide entertainment for Allied troops.[24]

The cover story did not work. The government investigation against Prescott Bush continued. Just before the storm broke, his son, George, abandoned his plans to enter Yale and enlisted in the U.S. Army. It was, say our sources among the former intelligence officers, a valiant attempt by an eighteen-year-old boy to save the family's honor.[25]

Young George was in flight school in October 1942, when the U.S. government charged his father with running Nazi front groups in the United States. Under the Trading with the Enemy Act, all the shares of the Union Banking Corporation were seized, including those held by Prescott Bush as being in effect held for enemy nationals. Union Banking, of course, was an affiliate of Brown Brothers, Harriman, and Bush handled the Harrimans' investments as well.[26]

Once the government had its hands on Bush's books, the whole story of the intricate web of Nazi front corporations began to unravel. A few days later two of Union Banking's subsidiaries—the Holland American Trading Corporation and the Seamless Steel Equipment Corporation—also were seized. Then the government went after the Harriman Fifteen Holding Company, which Bush shared with his father-in-law, Bert Walker, the Hamburg-Amerika Line, and the Silesian-American Corporation. The U.S. government found that huge sections of Prescott Bush's empire had been operated on behalf of Nazi Germany and had greatly assisted the German war effort.[27]

In the midst of the patriotic fervor over the war, it must have been a crushing experience for young George to know that his father and grandfather were among the men who helped finance Hitler's war machine. Little wonder that Bush made no mention of the whole affair in his autobiography. Still, his relatives were very lucky not to have gone to jail. Like Dulles, they volunteered to become spies for the war effort. George's grandfather, Bert Walker, went to Supreme Allied Headquarters in London to advise on covert "psychological operations." Prescott Bush's clients, including the Thyssens, fled to Switzerland, where they joined Dulles's anti-Hitler underground.[28]

Prescott himself had served in Military Intelligence during World War I, liaising with the British. According to our sources, he was trained by Stewart Menzies, later head of the British secret service during World War II.[29] Menzies knew that there were too many British investors in Brown Brothers, Harriman to make an issue out of their aid to Nazi Germany. It was better to bury the scandal.

By 1945 young George was a bona fide war hero, a fact that his father later used to good advantage in his successful run for the U.S. Senate. Like another naval hero, Jack Kennedy, who was also the son of an infamous Nazi supporter, George's war experience changed him, even as it redeemed the family's good name. The man who came back from the war was very different from the boy who had left.

George had grown up in Greenwich, Connecticut, an upper-class New York bedroom community. Greenwich was such a notorious hotbed of anti-Semitism that it became the site for the film *A Gentleman's Agreement*, which graphically exposed the prejudice against Jews held by many members of the nation's elite.

After the war, when George returned to Yale University, the school openly acknowledged that it had a policy to restrict the number of Jewish students in each class. Prescott Bush was a trustee at the time. The 1945 Annual Report of the Board of Admissions mentions a "Jewish problem" at Yale and publicly states that "the proportion of Jews . . . has somewhat increased and remains too large for comfort."[30] Apparently, Jews were good enough to fight for the United States, but Jewish veterans need not apply to Yale.

Such bigotry was appalling to young George. Our sources obtained access to George Bush's private files in Yale's most exclusive secret society, the Skull and Bones Club. George was in favor of admitting both blacks and Jews to this venerable institution.[31] The sources we interviewed on George's early life say it was a dig at his father, who was not the most racially progressive member in the history of the club.[32]

In 1949 the Skull and Bones class, which George Bush helped to select, finally succeeded in voting away all racial and religious barriers to membership. George's vote in 1948 for admitting Jews to the next Skull and Bones club was not his only act of rebellion against his father's generation. After graduation he shunned a seat with Brown Brothers, Harriman and asked for a job in China, as far away from Wall Street as he could get.

His father, who was also on the board of Dresser Industries, arranged it. There have been rumors that George's trip to China was somehow connected with espionage. True, Dresser has provided cover for CIA operatives over the years, but George's trip was strictly business.[33] It should be noted, however, that among George's classmates were a number of people who left college to work on intelligence operations with his father's friend, Allen Dulles.[34]

Try as he did, George Bush could not get away from Dulles's crooked corporate network, which his grandfather and father had joined in the 1920s. Wherever he turned, George found that the influence of the Dulles brothers was already there. Even when he fled to Texas to become a successful businessman on his own, he ran into the pirates of Wall Street.

One of Allen Dulles's secret spies inside the Democratic party later became George Bush's partner in the Mexican oil business. Edwin Pauley, a California oil man, was, like James Forrestal, one of Dulles's covert agents in the Roosevelt and Truman administrations. Like Forrestal, Pauley was a "big business" Democrat. The parallels didn't end there.[35]

During Roosevelt's presidency, Pauley was a major Democrat fundraiser and held a series of top posts, including treasurer of the Democratic party's National Committee.[36] He was also director of the Democratic convention in 1944 and had an unrivaled reputation as a man who could shake a great deal of money out of the oil companies, which were notoriously right-wing and pro-Republican. Pauley also had the loyalty of President Truman, especially for his role in getting him the delegate numbers to replace Henry Wallace as vice president in 1944, which ultimately took Truman to the White House when Roosevelt died in 1945.[37] Unfortunately, Truman's gratitude was not enough to sweep Pauley's dirt under the carpet.

The truth is that Pauley was committed to profit and, like the Dulles brothers, could not distinguish between his own interests and his public duties. During World War II he was in the perfect position to assist the Dulles clique in their Nazi oil deals. It was Pauley who recommended that Roosevelt appoint Interior Secretary Harold Ickes to the post of Petroleum Administrator for War, although Pauley later came to regret that action bitterly. Ickes, in turn, made Pauley his special adviser.[38]

Ickes's choice of Pauley, and several other top oil men, to hold key positions puzzled many liberals in the Roosevelt administration. Ickes believed that unless the oil companies were part of wartime policymaking, they "would take the bit in their teeth and run away with it given any chance."[39] Pauley and Ickes made a good team, at least while the war still hung in the balance. They worked to organize the Petroleum Administration for War, and more important for Allen Dulles, Pauley also held the key position of Petroleum Coordinator of Lend-Lease Supplies for the Soviet Union and Britain.[40]

There is some evidence that Ickes used Pauley, an independent oil man, as a counterbalance to the major oil corporations. For example, during the war Pauley had several run-ins with the foreign petroleum coordinator, Max Thornburg. He just happened to be a senior executive of Standard Oil of New Jersey, which, as previously discussed was owned by Rockefeller and I. G. Farben and was secretly sending oil to Hitler. While the war raged, Pauley and Thornburg fell to squabbling about Mexican oil, which had been nationalized in the 1930s, when the U.S. giants were thrown out.

In this particular fight, Pauley was supported by Ickes, who believed that the major companies were more interested in ensuring their profitable reentry into Mexico than they were in exploiting Mexican oil for the war effort. Pauley, then working for the Petroleum Administration while he pushed his own private interests in Mexico, could not have put it better himself.[41] Pauley's real concern, however, was not to help the war effort but to gain a share of Mexican oil profits. After the war he did so, in partnership with a young independent oil producer by the name of George Bush.

Despite the obvious conflict of interests, in April 1945 Truman appointed Pauley as the U.S. representative to the Allied Reparations Committee, with the rank of ambassador. Simultaneously, he was made industrial and commercial adviser to the Potsdam Conference, "where his chief task was to renegotiate the reparations agreements formulated at Yalta." As one historian noted, the "oil industry has always watched reparations activities carefully."[42] There was a lot of money involved, and much of it belonged to the Dulles brothers' clients.

As previously discussed, the Dulles brothers were still shifting Nazi assets out of Europe for their clients as well as for their own profit. They didn't want the Soviets to get their hands on these assets or even know they had existed. Pauley played a significant role in solving this problem for the Dulles brothers. The major part of Nazi Germany's industrial assets was located in the zones occupied by the West's forces. As Washington's man on the ground, Pauley managed to deceive the Soviets for long enough to allow Allen Dulles to spirit much of the remaining Nazi assets out to safety. Although Pauley knew that the Soviet zone contained less than one-third of Germany's industrial assets, as official U.S. representative he insisted to his colleagues on the Reparations Committee it controlled 50 percent.[43]

Pauley, a key player in the plan to hide the Dulles brothers' Nazi assets, then moved into another post where he could help them further. After successfully keeping German assets in Fascist hands, Pauley was given the job of "surveying Japan's assets and determining the amount of its war debt."[44] Again, it was another job that was crucial to the Dulles clique's secret financial and intelligence operations.[45]

In January 1946 Truman nominated Pauley as undersecretary of the navy. The move was "intended by . . . Truman as a steppingstone to his succeeding James Forrestal as [Navy] Secretary."[46] It also was designed to balance U.S. oil interests against the Zionists and their wealthy American-Jewish backers. Despite the strength of his support for the Jews, Truman was signaling that there was room for a strong oil voice in his administration. Pauley's nomination, however, ignited considerable political controversy, which eventually helped force him out of political life in 1947.[47]

Finally, the liberal Ickes had had enough of Pauley's machinations. Ickes decided that he would not lie to get Pauley's nomination endorsed by the Senate.[48] When his nomination came up before Senator Charles Tobey's Naval Affairs Committee for ratification, Pauley met his match, as evidence of his political bribes and "black bag" fund-raising operations for the Democrats began to seep out. Although the oil lobby, supported by President Truman, pulled out all stops to frustrate Tobey and make him abandon the hearings, Pauley finally had to retreat. But at least the cover-up was safe for a few more years yet, as the most damaging parts of Pauley's work for the oil companies did not emerge during the hearings.[49]

The most explosive allegations about Pauley's political bribes came from Ickes himself. It cost both men their jobs, prompting Ickes's resignation and, a short while later, Pauley's withdrawal from the navy job.[50] Despite pressure from Truman, Ickes was only too eager to tell Tobey's committee exactly the sort of scandal in which Pauley had been involved. When he testified, Ickes claimed that Pauley had promised to raise $300,000 for the Democratic party from among Californian oil men, if the federal government would drop a court case to establish that offshore oil title belonged to Washington and not to the state of California.[51]

At the time, Pauley was treasurer of the Democratic National Committee. Like Forrestal, he hated the fact that the Democrats were dependent on Jewish financial contributions. Large bribes from the oil companies, which happened also to suit their business interests, could tip the party away from the Zionists. Pauley also just happened to hold two key government oil posts at the time of his bribe offer. His arm-twisting tactics on the federal suit had been widely noted in the Washington bureaucracy. Evidence emerged at the Senate hearings that confirmed Ickes's claims and contradicted Pauley's own statement, made under oath, that he had never made such bribery attempts.[52]

If the hearings went on, the whole corrupt business eventually might seep out. When Pauley denied the bribery charge, it was like a red rag to the bull called Harold Ickes. No one was going to call him a liar and get away with it. Invited to reappear at the hearings, this time Ickes gave the committee chapter and verse. But if he had hoped for Truman's backing, he miscalculated.[53]

Indeed, despite Truman's support for the Zionists, the president was playing a careful balancing game with the oil companies. This time the oil companies won. Truman strongly and publicly supported Pauley and "questioned the accuracy and loyalty of Ickes's charges." The president had Ickes's resignation a few days later and promptly accepted it, "with alacrity and delight."[54] But the damage was done, and in "the face of further embarrassment to the Administration and certain rejection by the Senate Naval Affairs Committee, Pauley reluctantly requested that his nomination be withdrawn."[55]

It may have worked out for the best for Truman, who had enough trouble in 1948 convincing the American electorate that his administration wasn't toeing the oil companies' line about Israel, without having Edwin Pauley around his neck. Yet another scandal erupted around Pauley in 1947, which finally ended his political career and forced his retirement from public life. He now strictly worked behind the scenes, although, as we shall see, he continued as a secret Republican agent inside the Democratic party.[56]

Pauley went back to the oil business and, some years later, became an important factor in the secret war against the Jews. In fact, Pauley had a significant influence on George Bush's business career in Texas. In 1958 he founded Pauley Petroleum, which:

> . . . teamed up with Howard Hughes to expand oil production in the Gulf of Mexico.
>
> Pauley Petroleum discovered a highly productive offshore petroleum reserve and in 1959 became involved in a dispute with the Mexican Government, which considered the royalties from the wells to be too low.[57]

According to our sources in the intelligence community, the oil dispute was really a shakedown of the CIA by Mexican politicians. Hughes and Pauley were working for the CIA from time to time, while advancing their own financial interests in the lucrative Mexican oil fields. Pauley, say several of our sources, was the man who invented an intelligence money-laundering system in Mexico, which was refined in the 1970s as part of Nixon's Watergate scandal. At one point CIA agents used Pemex, the Mexican government's oil monopoly, as a business cover at the same time Pemex was being used as a money laundry for Pauley's campaign contributions.[58] As we shall see, the Mexican-CIA connection played an important part in the development of George Bush's political and intelligence career.

There was a substantial CIA presence in Mexico since at least the 1950s. Pemex was a perfect place to recruit agents of influence inside the Mexican government. Mexico became part of the "revolving door" between the oil industry and the intelligence community. One of the famous oil men–turned–agents was William F. Buckley, Jr., like Bush, a Skull and Bones alumnus, whose boss in Mexico was Howard Hunt, later of Watergate fame.[59]

According to *Regardie*'s magazine, the CIA-Mexican oil connection lasted for many years.[60] In the early 1980s, Pemex was listed as employer for another Bill Buckley, before he returned to the Middle East as CIA station chief. This Bill Buckley was to play a major role with George Bush in the Iran-Contra scandal and became a key figure in money laundering through the Bank of Commerce and Credit International, which played an important part in the anti-Israeli intelligence operations of the 1980s.

Pauley, say the "old spies," was the man who brought all the threads of the Mexican connection together. He was Bush's business associate, a front man for Dulles's CIA, and originator of the use of Mexican oil fronts to create a slush fund for Richard Nixon's various campaigns.[61]

There is clear evidence that Pauley, the conservative Democrat, played on both sides of the political fence. In 1972, after Nixon promised "a favorable climate for oil," the Campaign to Reelect the President (CREEP), together with Attorney General John Mitchell's secret "Finance Committee," collected at least $5 million in illegal cash donations from the oil companies. Some of Nixon's political bribe money came directly from Edwin Pauley himself.[62]

Although it is not widely known, Pauley, in fact, had been a committed, if "secret," Nixon supporter since 1960. It should be recalled that Nixon tried to conceal his Mexican slush fund during the Watergate affair by pressuring the CIA into a "national security" cover-up. The CIA, to its credit, declined to participate. Unfortunately, others were so enmeshed in Pauley's work for Nixon that they could never extricate themselves. According to a number of our intelligence sources, the deals Bush cut with Pauley in Mexico catapulted him into political life. In 1960 Bush became a protégé of Richard Nixon, who was then running for president of the United States.[63]

Bush's road to Mexico had begun innocently enough. After working in the oil equipment leasing business for Dresser Industries for several years, George Bush went out on his own. He "packed up his red 1947 Studebaker and set off for Texas," ending up in Midland, which soon became the "oil capital of west Texas." Bush began at the bottom, as a trainee painting pumping equipment, but didn't stay there for very long. He soon "caught the fever" and "formed an independent oil company in partnership with other ambitious young men no less eager to make money."[64]

In the mid-1950s, in partnership with such friends as Hugh Liedtke, Bush established Zapata Petroleum. Bush had energy and ambition, but he also had some family connections. One such contact led to a very lucrative deal with Eugene Meyer, the Jewish publisher of *The Washington Post,* whom he had met previously because Brown Brothers, Harriman "managed a lot of his accounts."[65] But Zapata had a much more powerful friend than Meyer.

George Bush's company leased oil rigs to Edwin Pauley and took a commission from all the oil Pauley pumped out of the Gulf of Mexico. Pauley was, according to a lengthy article in *Barron's,* George Bush's most important customer.[66] The "old spies" say Bush lost his virginity in the oil business to Edwin Pauley.[67]

In those days, Bush's business manager, Wayne H. Dean, owned a ranch extending across the international border into Mexico, thus qualifying Zapata as a "Mexican resident" corporation. In 1959 the Mexican government changed the rules and said that oil companies had to be run by Mexican nationals. It looked as if Bush's company would lose its most lucrative account, Pauley's Pan-American Petroleum Company. Instead, Bush, Pauley, and Dean met with their Mexican contact, Diaz Serrano, and worked out a deal.[68]

According to *Barron's,* Serrano was not above bending a few rules for his American friend George Bush, who apparently felt the same way about Serrano. Without telling his own shareholders in Zapata, Bush set up a new joint venture, Permargo, with Serrano at the helm, but with Bush associates holding secret control of a hidden 50 percent American share through a Mexican lawyer. Bush later sold Zapata's rig, the *Nola 1,* to Permargo, which took over the lucrative Pauley drilling contract.[69]

The only losers, said *Barron's,* appear to have been Bush's shareholders in Zapata. It is hard to know for sure, since the Securities Exchange Commission "inadvertently" destroyed all of the records for Permargo and Zapata for the period between 1960 and 1966. The destruction occurred shortly after Bush was sworn in as vice president in 1981.[70]

The Zapata-Permargo deal also caught the attention of Allen Dulles, who, the "old spies" allege, was the man who recruited Bush's company as a part-time purchasing front for the CIA. Zapata provided commercial supplies for one of Dulles's most notorious operations, the Bay of Pigs invasion. It was nothing terribly dramatic: Bush's company leased a few cargo vessels and shipped some CIA cargo as oil drilling equipment.[71] Coincidentally, all of Zapata's Securities Exchange Commission files for this period were "inadvertently destroyed" as well.[72]

Fletcher Prouty, a former U.S. intelligence official who worked on CIA support activities, says some circumstantial evidence implicates President George H. W. Bush as a contract agent supplying the CIA team for the Bay of Pigs invasion. According to Prouty, two of the CIA supply ships were named the *Houston* and the *Barbara J.*, in honor of Bush's home and wife. As further evidence, Prouty asserts that the Cuban resupply mission was code named "Operation Zapata," the name of Bush's oil company in Texas. Prouty's credibility, however, has been widely attacked because of his consultancy to Oliver Stone's film *JFK*.[73]

In 1988 *The Nation* magazine stumbled across an FBI memorandum dated November 29, 1963, reporting that "Mr. George Bush of the Central Intelligence Agency" had been briefed about the reaction of the Cuban exile community to the assassination of President Kennedy. *The Nation* added that a "source with close connections to the intelligence community confirms that Bush started working for the agency in 1960 or 1961, using his oil business as a cover for clandestine activities."[74]

The Nation's allegation that Bush's oil business worked for the CIA in 1960 matches *Barron's* description of the timeframe for Bush's creation of Permargo. When *The Nation* article appeared, Bush refused to be quoted directly on the Mexican-CIA connection, although his spokesman denied that he had anything to do with the CIA until he became its head in 1975. The CIA response to the article was both prompt and deceptive: It claimed the CIA agent working with the Cuban exiles in 1963 was in fact named George *William* Bush, clearly not the man running for president in 1988.[75]

The CIA had thrown a red herring to the press. When *The Nation* tracked down George *William* Bush, it discovered that in 1963, he was a social work trainee in Hawaii and had nothing whatsoever to do with J. Edgar Hoover's briefing of the other George Bush of the CIA on the Cuban exiles' reaction to the Kennedy assassination. Even after he joined the CIA George William didn't even know anyone involved with the Bay of Pigs.[76] On the other hand, President George Bush had a wide assortment of Bay of Pigs' veterans among his close friends and associates, among them Felix Rodriguez, who later worked for Bush and Oliver North on the Iran-Contra program.[77]

Another intelligence agent with ties to Bush was George de Mohrenschildt.[78] He had the names of all Zapata team members in his address book, including Pauley, Dean, and even the home address of "Bush, George H. W. (Poppy) 1412 W. Ohio also Zapata Petroleum, Midland 4-6355."[79] There is some reason to suspect that de Mohrenschildt was still working on both oil and intelligence matters at the time he was dealing with George Bush and Zapata.[80]

The most intriguing of Bush's early connections was to Richard Nixon, who as vice president had supervised Allen Dulles's covert planning for the Bay of Pigs. For years it has been rumored that Dulles's client, George Bush's father, was one of the Republican leaders who recruited Nixon to run for Congress and later convinced Eisenhower to take him on as vice president.[81] There is no doubt that the two families were close. George Bush described Nixon as his "mentor." Nixon was a Bush supporter in his very first tilt at politics, during his unsuccessful run for the Senate in 1964, and turned out again when he entered the House two years later.[82]

After Nixon's landslide victory in 1972, he ordered a general house cleaning on the basis of loyalty. "Eliminate everyone," he told John Ehrlichman about reappointments, "except George Bush. Bush will do anything for our cause."[83] Nixon knew what he was talking about. At the time, Bush had already been offered a senior post in the Treasury Department, under George Shultz, but Nixon wanted him elsewhere. According to Bush's account, the president told him that "the place I really need you is over at the National Committee running things."[84] So, in 1972, Nixon appointed George Bush as head of the Republican National Committee.

It was Bush who fulfilled Nixon's promise to make the "ethnic" émigrés a permanent part of Republican politics. In 1972 Nixon's State Department spokesman confirmed to his Australian counterpart that the ethnic groups were very useful to get out the vote in several key states. Bush's tenure as head of the Republican National Committee exactly coincided with Laszlo Pasztor's 1972 drive to transform the Heritage Groups Council into the party's official ethnic arm. The groups Pasztor chose as Bush's campaign allies were the émigré Fascists whom Dulles had brought to the United States.[85]

It seems clear that George Bush, as head of the Republican National Committee in 1972, must have known who these "ethnics" really were.[86] Columns by Jack Anderson and others had already made it clear, in 1971, that Nixon was a little too close to the Fascist groups. The Nazis for Nixon problem was one of those scandals that Bush inherited when he took over the Republican National Committee.

Although our intelligence sources are not unanimous on this point, several say that George Bush was included among the handful of people who knew about Nixon's deal to bring the Fascist groups into the Republican party in 1972.[87] Indeed, since Bush was the head of the National Committee, he was in the best position to supervise the transfer of the campaign staff's ethnic Fascists into the Republican party's own organization. A 1976 memo to Republican National Committee co-chairman Robert Carter contains an even more damning implication.

During Bush's time as Republican National Committee chairman, he appointed Colonel Jay Niemczyk as director of the party's ethnic Heritage Groups. Niemczyk's memo to Robert Carter praised Bush as having "added needed strength and impetus" to the Republicans' ethnic recruitment effort. Niemczyk reported that Bush "had *full knowledge of*" and, in the words of the memo, provided 'total support' for the party's ethnic Heritage Groups" (emphasis added).[88]

As head of the Republican National Committee, it seems likely that Bush did have "full knowledge," as did Richard Johnson of the State Department, that the ethnic Fascists were being coddled because the ethnic groups were useful to get out the vote in several key states. As previously outlined, in 1972 Johnson told the Australians that a selected group of American politicians had been briefed about the sensitivity of certain Fascist groups, such as the Croatian Ustashis.

If a lower-level State Department official like Johnson knew what was going on, it is likely that the head of the party—George Bush—would have been advised about the true background of the Croatians and the other émigrés in the party. As Johnson noted, the American government was advising Republican leaders not to attend Croatian gatherings on April 10—the memorial day for Hitler's creation of the Fascist Croatian state.[89]

When taken in conjunction with the earlier Australian report, and the *Washington Post* revelation that Nazis were being used for U.S. campaign purposes, the Republican memo confirming Bush's "full knowledge" of the ethnic campaign looks like a "smoking gun" as far as Bush's personal complicity is concerned. Nearly twenty years later, and after exposés in several respectable newspapers, Bush continued to recruit most of the same ethnic Fascists, including Pasztor, for his own 1988 ethnic outreach program when he first ran for president.

According to a number of our sources in the intelligence community, it was Bush who told Nixon that the Watergate investigations might start uncovering the Fascist skeletons in the Republican party's closet.[90] Bush himself acknowledges that he wrote Nixon a letter asking him to step down.[91] The day after Bush did so, Nixon resigned.

Bush had hoped to become Gerald Ford's vice president upon Nixon's resignation, but he was appointed U.S. ambassador to the UN. Nelson Rockefeller became vice president and chief damage controller. He formed a special commission in an attempt to preempt the Senate's investigation of the intelligence community. The Rockefeller Commission into CIA abuses was filled with old OPC hands like Ronald Reagan, who had been the front man back in the 1950s for the money-laundering organization, the Crusade for Freedom, which was part of Dulles's Fascist "freedom fighters" program.[92]

Although Governor Reagan may have been out of the loop in 1975, Rockefeller certainly knew all about the old Nazi connection, having counterblackmailed Ben-Gurion at the time of the UN debate about the partition of Palestine. In 1947 Rockefeller had been able to keep the Nazi scandal under control, and except for the occasional leak, it had stood up ever since. But by 1975 his damage control operation was floundering. In December Bush was brought back to become head of the CIA. After all, he had previous experience with protecting the Agency from the Watergate investigation.

According to our sources, it was Bush who, as head of the Republican National Committee from 1972 to 1974, told Nixon that he could not shift the blame for the Mexican slush fund to the CIA without wrecking the intelligence community. The "old spies" say that legitimate CIA operations in Mexico would have been hopelessly compromised if they were tarred with the brush of Nixon's money laundering.[93]

To Bush's credit, he did not allow Nixon to trash the CIA to save himself. On the other hand, Bush may have had his own reasons for blocking any investigation of the Mexican connection; after all, it involved his own business associate Ed Pauley.[94] In any event, Nixon resigned, and Bush became a hero for standing up for the CIA.

It was this action, and not his peripheral role in the Bay of Pigs or his company's minor role as a cover for CIA supply operations, that endeared George Bush to the Agency. His appointment as director of Central Intelligence was a big morale boost to an institution that had been severely tarnished by Senate and media exposés of some of its more bizarre practices during the Dulles-Angleton years. Though the practices had been concealed from the employees of the CIA, they were the ones who had taken the blame instead of their political superiors.

According to our sources, the rank and file viewed George Bush as the one man who would stand up to the White House if it ever again tried to politicize the CIA.[95] What these CIA staff did not know was that George Bush was appointed precisely to fend off any more congressional investigations. The nosy investigators had come perilously close to the heart of one of the many Dulles scandals: the recruitment of Nazi money and émigrés by the leading lights of the Republican party.[96]

Although many readers will not believe this, our sources insist the regular CIA staff were almost entirely ignorant of the true background of the ethnic Fascists and remain so to this day.[97] During the Eisenhower years, Allen Dulles merged the State Department's Office of Policy Coordination into the CIA, but kept the OPC's émigré operations separate from the CIA's geographical sections. The "freedom fighters" had their own files in the program branch that could be accessed only by a special set of cryptonyms. Before Allen Dulles was fired, he took the cryptonym cross-index with him. To this day, not even the director of Central Intelligence can retrieve an individual's record from the mass of files on Dulles's projects with the Fascist émigrés.[98]

After Dulles left, the CIA files on Fascist émigrés were a permanent shambles. Angleton remained to put out the occasional fire when someone requested a security check on a suspected Nazi. When Angleton was fired in December 1974, only a handful of people knew where the bodies were buried.[99] Then along came the new CIA director, George Bush, in December 1975, who inherited Dulles's dirty secrets.

Dulles's Nazis kept popping out of the woodwork, and it was getting harder and harder to keep the rest of the CIA in the dark. Ironically, the Vatican itself almost uncovered the story. As previously discussed, Father Robert Graham, the American-born Vatican historian, triggered Angleton's cover-up of the Vessel forgeries. In 1976 Graham had a conversation with Martin Quigley, an Irish-American Catholic from New York. Quigley had served with the Office of Strategic Services in Rome, before Angleton arrived on the scene and took over the Vatican connection. According to our intelligence source on this issue, Quigley told Father Graham an interesting but fairly minor piece of history.[100]

Monsignor Egidio Vagnozzi, from the Japanese desk of the Vatican Secretariat of State, had given the OSS some information about Japanese peace feelers. Quigley assigned the code name Vessel to Vagnozzi, who later became apostolic delegate to Washington and one of the most powerful cardinals in Rome.

This interesting and innocent bit of trivia intrigued Father Graham, who had written extensively on the Vatican's peace-making efforts during World War II. Graham promptly filed a request for Quigley's OSS reports under the new American Freedom of Information Act. What neither Quigley nor Graham knew was that Angleton had continued to use the "Vessel" code name after Quigley left. As previously discussed, Angleton had signed cover letters forwarding thousands of forged Vessel reports as part of Dulles's deception program against Roosevelt and Truman.

Father Graham had no idea that Vessel was only one of Angleton's covert operations in postwar Rome. During his takeover of the British-Vatican Ratline to smuggle fugitive Nazis, Angleton also had employed the very same Croatian and Eastern European Fascist organizations whose members Dulles and Nixon later brought into the Republican party in the 1950s and to which Bush had given a permanent home in the early 1970s. Vessel, the Vatican Ratlines, and the Republicans' Heritage Groups were all pieces of the same scandal. The Vatican request for documents threatened to open a very large can of worms.

When the CIA received Father Graham's request for all Vessel reports, the clerks retrieved not just Quigley's innocuous documents, but trunkfuls of highly sensitive intercepts of top-secret Vatican cables. The CIA, of course, did not know that the Vessel cables were forgeries, and Graham's request was brought to the attention of the highest levels of the Agency in 1976. According to our source the most sensitive material could not be released to Father Graham:

> By this time, George Bush had become CIA director, and because of the delicate nature of Graham's "semiofficial" request—which was viewed by the CIA, that is, as "a Vatican request"—that apparently would lead him, Graham, to conclude that the OSS had "spied successfully on the pope," it was decided by Bush and others that the Vessel files would have to be carefully reviewed and sanitized.[101]

None of our sources has personal knowledge of whether Bush was aware of the extent to which the Vessel files would reveal the old Nazi smuggling scandal in the Vatican, although they wondered whether Bush's previous campaign association gave him special knowledge of the ethnic Fascists' background. They do assert that a decision was made "at the highest levels" that the man who made the mess should clean it up.[102] "Angleton, though publicly disgraced and officially retired on pension, was asked to do the job. He was undoubtedly the most familiar with the material and the 'most responsible'—as he had long dealt directly 'with the Vatican' for the CIA. He was, apparently, paid a fee for reviewing the files, based on his recognized 'expertise.' "[103]

Thus Angleton, who had been fired in December 1974, was put back on the CIA payroll in 1976. He took one look at the huge pile of Vessel papers and realized it would take months to read and analyze them all. According to one source, Angleton went directly to Bush and explained just how sensitive the Vessel papers were.[104] According to another source, it is not certain that Angleton ever told Bush the whole story.[105] It seems, however, that someone in the CIA gave Angleton permission to violate the Freedom of Information Act and shred many of the Vatican files.[106] But not all the records could be destroyed:

> 'Eventually, some material would have to be released to Graham, but that material, [Angleton] was apparently informed, could be heavily censored. Moreover, he was given to understand that if other reports really could not be censored, they could be removed from the Vessel files and destroyed. Apparently, Angleton destroyed hundreds of such reports (as he himself reported to certain people). He seemed to have been given a completely free hand.'[107]

No matter how much censorship or shredding took place, Angleton knew that Father Graham would immediately, and correctly, identify some of the Vessel papers as Scattolini forgeries. Angleton contacted his sister Carmen in Rome and obtained Graham's phone number. Then Angleton asked Graham to drop his Freedom of Information request, but Graham refused.[108] He still thought that Vessel meant only the Quigley-Vagnozzi reports.

When, in 1978, Graham finally saw the little that had escaped the shredder, he was astounded to discover Scattolini forgeries. In 1979 Graham tried repeatedly to interview Angleton, who ducked every meeting. Angleton kept denying through intermediaries that he even knew Scattolini. While Father Graham did not know it, the lie could have been easily discredited by a number of people who served in Rome at the time.[109] Keeping the lid on the Angleton-Dulles scandals was becoming harder and harder.

Problems kept popping up for George Bush. In 1976 a militant splinter group of Croatian Fascists hijacked an American airliner, an act that sent all the other intelligence agencies scurrying for background files. As already mentioned, Croatian Ustashis operated the Vatican Ratline for Angleton and then went on to establish the Croatian Heritage Group for the Republican National Committee. The Australian report on Nixon's Nazis had mentioned this very group. Both the hijackers and the Croatian Republican group proclaimed loyalty to Ante Pavelić's Fascist government. Were there more Croatian Fascist terrorists running around in the United States? Somehow the link to the Croatian GOP had escaped the notice of the CIA.[110]

Some people in government, at least, were curious. In 1976, Congresswoman Elizabeth Holtzmann specifically asked if any Nazis had ever immigrated to the United States under the CIA's "100 Persons Act," which allows the Agency to bring in up to one hundred agents a year without going through normal immigration procedures.[111] The true answer was a bit of a problem. Back in the late 1940s and early 1950s, Dulles's cronies at the State Department had conned the CIA into sponsoring a handful of VIP émigrés for special entry, as a favor to Dulles's Office of Policy Coordination. The CIA did not know that the "émigrés" were, in fact, Nazi intelligence officers. But Bush's CIA told Holtzmann that "no war criminals, or terrorists, or persons of that ilk" had ever been admitted by the CIA.[112]

Some of our sources say that it is unfair to accuse Bush of personal knowledge of the Nazi cover-up, insisting that he was brought into the CIA precisely because he was ignorant and could plausibly deny any knowledge of some of the older, darker Dulles scandals.[113] But even if everybody in the U.S. government who knew about the Nazis conspired to keep Bush ignorant of past scandals, the "bumbling Bush" explanation does not explain why the CIA director was not aware of current ones. Somebody in the CIA had to know exactly what was going on in 1976, in order to keep the Nazi cover-up going:

> As late as 1976 the agency's practices in this regard were still so blatant that the CIA actually wrote an unclassified letter to a former CIA contract agent, Edgar Laipenieks, who was then facing deportation from the United States in connection with allegations that he had committed multiple murders, torture and other crimes against humanity at the Central Prison in Riga, Latvia, during the war. "We have been corresponding with the Immigration and Naturalization Service about your status," agency spokesman Charles Savage wrote to Laipenieks on official CIA letterhead. "It is our understanding that INS has advised their San Diego office to cease any action against you. If this does not prove [to be] the case, please let us know immediately. Thank you once again for . . . your past assistance to the Agency. Sincerely,"[114]

Laipenieks promptly released this CIA letter to the press. The whole war criminal cover-up was very much a current issue while Bush was CIA director. In fact, some of the Nazis were still working on covert operations in 1976. The Ukrainian groups openly fought with each other over who was receiving the most CIA money. Dimitri Kasmovich, the Nazi police chief in Belarus during World War II, boasted to his fellow collaborators that he was running guns to a new generation of anti-Communist "freedom fighters" in Angola.[115]

But, apart from a spot of gunrunning and occasional propaganda from

Kasmovich and other Fascists in the World Anti-Communist League, the old Nazis were just too elderly for covert operations. Now they were far more valuable to the Republican National Committee than they were to the CIA. Yet every time the CIA tried to get rid of the tainted émigré groups, someone kept bringing them back. Even when the CIA forced the transfer of Radio Liberty to the State Department, someone on Bush's staff agreed to bring the Dulles era files on Radio Liberty back to the CIA, where they remain to this day.[116]

As a practical matter, the CIA had no operational use for the elderly émigrés in Angola. Young agents were needed to fight in the jungle. There had to be another solution. Just before Congress ordered a halt to all CIA activities in Angola in 1977, the agency found the answer. Behind the back of Congress and of most of the CIA, U.S. intelligence turned to a little-known firm in London to recruit a private army for the Angolan civil war. Instead of hiring Nazi mercenaries, the CIA hired British mercenaries to evade the congressional ban.

Unfortunately, as we shall see in Chapter 17, the British mercenaries were also working with the Arabs. During Bush's twelve months as CIA director, the secret war against the Jews was entering a particularly nasty phase. British intelligence had replaced its Nazi agents with PLO terrorists. The Angolan operation would lead to a number of other scandals in the 1980s, especially Iran-Contra and the Bank of Credit and Commerce International. George Bush may not have realized it, but he was acting more like Allen Dulles all the time.

CHAPTER 17

REHEARSAL IN ANGOLA

Most of the Western histories of Israeli intelligence are quite negative. The book *Dangerous Liaison,* for example, portrays the Mossad as a group of gunrunning maniacs, shipping arms to Africa and Latin America for personal profit. Israeli arms deals have been widely exposed and just as widely criticized by the media.

Our sources in the Western intelligence community have a slightly different perspective.[1] In their opinion, the Mossad's arms transfers were quite small in scope, usually conducted at the behest of other Western nations, and often were submerged by much larger arms deals by Western intelligence services that have escaped public attention. Israel is a lightning rod for the media. Over the years it has become a convenient scapegoat for other countries' operations.

"The Jews get paid to take the blame for our screw-ups," one former Pentagon official admitted candidly. "The American Government cannot be seen in public as propping up violent dictators who torture their own citizens. The Mossad trains the security teams for America's clients. That is the price of doing business."[2] According to our sources, a small but significant portion of U.S. military assistance to Israel is diverted to fund operations of which Congress would never approve. It is a kickback that Israel must pay to the Pentagon, State Department, and CIA in return for their support on Capitol Hill.[3]

Our sources believe that Israel would not get a cent out of Congress were it not for the support of the military, the defense industry, and the intelligence community.[4] The myth of the powerful Jewish lobby is, unfortunately, just a myth, as is the claim that Jews dominate the American media. At less than 3 percent of the population, Jews are one of the tiniest minorities in the United States. Half of all American Jews live in the New York–New Jersey area and another group is concentrated on the southeast coast of Florida. All the rest of the states have less than 3 percent of Jewish voters. Jews account for less than 1 percent of the population in 80 percent of the U.S. congressional districts. They just lack the votes to get a foreign aid bill through on their own. They need help.[5]

Many Israelis privately fear that their country has become an economic colony of the American "military industrial complex." Annually that complex contributes $3.8 billion to Israel—almost ten times the amount raised by the United Jewish Appeal in the United States. "When 20 percent of our nation's budget depends on American largesse, we do as the Americans ask," said one retired Israeli officer. Whether it is training security forces for an African dictator or running guns to the Contras, the Jews do what they are told to do.[6]

In fairness, the Israeli involvement in under-the-table arms and covert operations is relatively small. Jews are small-time players in the world of international arms sales. When it comes to covert operations, the Mossad is almost insignificant compared to the American intelligence community. When compared to the British secret service, the Jews are Boy Scouts.

For the really dirty tricks, heavy-duty arms deals, and outrageously illegal covert operations, the Americans turn to Britain, not Israel. The British government has the most repressive combination of libel laws, press censorship, and criminal sanctions against disclosing intelligence operations of any country in the democratic world. It knows how to keep a secret from its own press, public, and Parliament. More important, it knows how to shift the blame to others when an operation is exposed.

While Israel has been roundly criticized for training Africans how to kill, smuggling guns to the Contras, and shipping arms to Iran, the British secret service was doing much worse, much earlier, and in complete secrecy. The Western public has no idea that the Jews were set up to take the blame for a series of British operations. To this day, the Israeli public believes that its intelligence service originated the Iran-Contra affair in 1985. They have never been told that the British secret service was running the arms pipeline several years earlier, at the request of Vice President George Bush.

To understand just how thoroughly the Jews were conned into taking the blame for recent covert intelligence scandals, we must examine how the British-Bush back-channel evolved. According to our sources, we must look back to Bush's largest covert operation as CIA director: the Angolan civil war.

In fact, the Angolan war was the beginning of a web of scandals that is known by a number of names: Irangate, the Iran-Contra Affair, and the BCCI. Compared to this, the CIA's phony oil estimates in 1976 were only a minor fraud and had a very minor impact on Israel. In this chapter we examine the following allegations:

- During the 1970s British mercenaries supplied PLO terrorists with weapons so the British secret service could infiltrate Middle Eastern intelligence organizations. MI6 did not warn either Israel or the United States of impending attacks by the Palestinian terrorists.

- When a British agent defected to the United States, the British secret service was compelled to supply mercenaries for the Angolan war after Congress banned CIA funding.
- The British secret service established the Bank of Credit and Commerce International (BCCI) as an intelligence collection center to track the movement of terrorist money. The bank was later used as a covert back-channel for arms deals and hostage ransom.
- The involvement of CIA director George Bush with the British back-channel in 1976 provided the model for his subsequent involvement in the Iran-Contra affair.
- The Carter administration was completely excluded from the BCCI-British connection. The CIA unwittingly purchased arms for the Afghan resistance from a PLO terrorist in the employ of the British secret service.
- Both the British and American participants agreed to exclude Israel from the back-channel intelligence and to use Israel as the scapegoat in the event of exposure.

Bush may not have realized it back in 1976, but the British secret service had replaced its Nazis with the Palestine Liberation Organization. The secret war against the Jews had entered a new phase. Where once British intelligence and its allies among the Dulles clique had relied on the Fascist émigrés, the modern espionage war would utilize the Arabs and their terrorist units. In 1976 the era of Palestinian and Syrian mercenaries had just begun.

The shroud of secrecy around George Bush's policy toward Israel can be unraveled by tracing the history of a British intelligence agent who defected to work for the CIA. His name was Leslie Aspin, not to be confused with the American politician of the same name, or with Michael Aspin, his brother, the convicted arms dealer. After Leslie's death in 1988, his family discovered the archives of his employment as a contract agent for the British secret service. Peggy Robohm, an American writer and researcher, passed them on to us.[7]

To put it mildly, Leslie Aspin left behind an intriguing record of financial deals, covert operations, and under-the-table deals. We have spent several years attempting to corroborate his information because it seems to contradict so much of the conventional history of the Iran-Contra affair.

Leslie Aspin's records indicate that he was the British intelligence agent who became the White House bagman to the Bank of Credit and Commerce International. It was Aspin who played a major role in Bush's plans to rescue the American hostages held in Lebanon by pro-Iranian fundamentalists in the mid-1980s. It was Aspin who helped Bush to circumvent the congressional ban on U.S. support for the Nicaraguan Contras. More important for the story of the secret espionage war against the Jews, it was Aspin who then helped the White House to set up the Israelis as scapegoats for the Iran-Contra affair, in which arms were sent to Iran and part of the proceeds used to fund secret, illegal assistance to the Nicaraguan Contras.

Because of the importance of the issue, and the widespread confusion and disinformation spread by a number of intelligence services, it may be useful to start at the beginning of Aspin's career. No one seriously can contend that he was a reliable source. In the absence of extensive independent corroboration, we would have dismissed his allegations out of hand. His own 1975 autobiography begins with some candid admissions: "Leslie Aspin is not a hero. He is a crook. He has never shot anyone, except from behind. He became a British Secret Service Agent, not out of patriotism, or even for money; but because he was blackmailed."[8] Even this confession is not entirely true. There was more to Aspin than he let on. He was not really as bad as he pretended to be. In fact, he was extraordinarily loyal to causes he believed in, as well as to friends and family. He was a tough kid who grew up in Britain, bold, brash, and very, very bright. In a way, he was quite modest. Throughout the Iran-Contra affair, he preferred to let everyone think that he was just a bit player.

Aspin was, by all accounts, a charming rogue with an exceptional skill for espionage, a sort of working man's version of James Bond. Before dropping out of the British military, he became a qualified paratrooper and a member of the elite British commando force, the Special Air Service. The SAS, as we shall see, does the British government's dirty work. It is not unusual for former SAS men to enroll with one or more of the numerous firms specializing in security operations, including providing mercenaries for secret and proxy wars. There is more to such operations than adventure and moneymaking. British intelligence carefully promotes these activities, especially when they are consistent with London's foreign policy objectives.[9]

Aspin did not wish to become dependent on the British government for his livelihood, so he became a smuggler. He was, by everyone's account, very good at what he did. By 1968 Aspin had a reputation in the Middle East as the kind of man who could move anything, anywhere, anytime, and without getting caught. Whether it was black market cigarettes smuggled out of Yugoslavia, or guns through Malta, Leslie Aspin was the man to see.[10]

He would have stayed happily on the fringes of the law for many years, had he not taken on the wrong client, in the wrong country, at the wrong moment in history. Aspin began to smuggle weapons for a PLO terrorist group known as Black September, which was sponsored by both Libya and Syria.

In 1970 the original Palestinian population of Jordan, swelled by refugees from Israel, were an unwelcome majority in their own country. The Hashemite Bedouin kingdom, established by Lawrence of Arabia, Jack Philby, and the British secret service many years before, ruled the native Palestinians with an iron fist. The Syrian government, against the wishes of the Kremlin, fomented a revolution to topple the pro-Western Jordanian government. When the Palestinians took to the streets, a small Syrian tank column invaded Jordan to aid the rebellion.

The CIA, Mossad, and the British secret service worked hard to keep King Hussein on the throne. The rebellion was crushed ruthlessly and thousands of Palestinians were killed. The Syrian tanks pulled out under international pressure, to say nothing of Israeli threats to intervene in a most brutal way, and the entire leadership of the PLO was expelled from the country. To the Palestinian radicals, the events of that month became known as Black September.

The Kremlin was appalled at the Palestinian debacle. The Soviets had warned the Syrians against premature uprisings. It was Soviet policy to engage the West not by direct military confrontation but by drawn-out guerrilla wars that would bleed the Western allies and provoke the democracies into harsh, reactionary policies. The protracted war in Vietnam had given Moscow the whole idea, but in the Middle East the Syrians had cost the PLO its best base on the very borders of Israel.

The Soviets engineered a coup and installed a new puppet in Syria, young Colonel Hafez Assad, who would follow the Kremlin's wishes more closely. As president, Assad established a series of low-profile training camps for Palestinian terrorists inside Syria. The new group called itself Black September, in memory of the events in Jordan. Over the next two decades, this militant terrorist organization would seize an influence in the Middle East in inverse proportion to its size.

Assad directed his chief of Military Intelligence, Ali Douab, to supply the Palestinian terrorists with all the arms and equipment they needed. In order for the Syrian government to be able to deny its role, most of the arms would have to be smuggled carefully to the Black September cells in Syria and around the Middle East. President Assad also directed his own brother, Rifaat Assad, the head of Syria's secret service, to work with Douab's Military Intelligence in handling the sensitive smuggling assignment. The two Syrian spy chiefs knew just the people to hire as agents: the Al-Kassars, a local family specializing in drug-smuggling.

Monzer Al-Kassar was one of three brothers who handled clandestine movement of money, drugs, and guns for the Syrians. His best friend was "the Prince of the Coast," Rifaat Assad, the president's brother, a decorated war hero from the Yom Kippur War and secret service chief.[11] When Monzer's brother married Ali Douab's sister, the Syrians kept the intelligence business all in the Al-Kassar family.

At the time it was Soviet policy to have their terrorist proxies become financially self-sufficient through the sale of drugs. Syria had a small but lucrative opium-heroin trade, which would, after the takeover of the Bekaa Valley in Lebanon, become a multibillion-dollar industry supplying 20 percent of the heroin sold in the United States. Monzer Al-Kassar had offices in Spain, Poland, and East Germany, but his financial transactions were laundered through a series of bank fronts in Switzerland.[12]

After being briefed by Rifaat Assad, Al-Kassar in turn recruited Leslie Aspin. Aspin would not handle drugs under any circumstances, but he loved the lucrative arms trade and helped recruit British advisers for the Libyan intelligence service. Aspin freely admits in his autobiography that he recruited a team of ex-SAS mercenaries, some of whom had already been training members of Black September.[13]

In his published writings, Aspin never referred to Al-Kassar by name, but simply called him the head of "the Bank," which directed the smuggling network. Aspin did good work and soon rose to the top of the motley crew of former French Legionnaires, British mercenaries, and American ex-military who worked on the smuggling ships. These high-speed boats ran cargoes past blockades all across the Mediterranean. In 1969 Aspin graduated from smuggler to shipper. Al-Kassar sent him to Libya.[14]

At the time, Libya's colonel Mu'ammar al-Gadhafi, was working with the Soviets and the Syrians to arm terrorist groups in Spain, Ireland, and Germany. Aspin was escorted to the secret school for terrorists in the desert, which one colonel in Libyan intelligence boasted trained "people who will strike fear into the very heart of Israel and anyone who helps them," and asked Aspin to supply some of his "many friends to fight for money—mercenaries," who were needed to assist in this fight against the Jews.[15]

So, Aspin's smuggling shop branched out from arms to human cargo. He escorted Irish Marxists to Libya for training and recruited several of his old British comrades to teach the terrorists how to kill, bomb, and attack more effectively. Both the Syrians and Libyans were delighted. Al-Kassar was pleased, and Aspin was getting rich. What none of them knew was that British intelligence had its own source inside Black September and was watching Aspin with growing interest. In February 1970 he had made a big mistake.

Life had been hectic for Aspin, channeling men to the secret training camp and smuggling weapons from Libya to the Basque terrorists in

Spain, so he decided to take a long holiday in England.[16] The British secret service was waiting for him at Heathrow Airport. It wanted Aspin to be an informant. For three days Aspin played dumb and resisted all requests that he turn into a double agent for MI6.

Finally the British agent played his trump card: He threatened to tell the Libyans and Syrians that Aspin was working for MI6 anyway. "We and our friends abroad have just sufficient knowledge to act against a few of the people you have worked with and that will convince your old pals that we are telling the truth," the British officer told him. "They will be convinced that you have betrayed them. That will put you in the same situation that you would be in if you actually did give us the help we require." Offered money as a final inducement, Aspin eventually agreed.[17]

When Aspin started to talk to the British secret service in 1970, the revelations first came as a trickle, then became a waterfall of information about the secret world of terrorism in the Middle East. He told the agent about the Al-Kassar family and provided all the other names of his key contacts in the Arab world, including the Libyan colonel and the names, addresses, and phone numbers of the colonel's European associates. He even provided the details of the Swiss bank through which the drug and gun money was laundered, the identities of the Irish terrorists who had been to the Libyan school, and the names of the men, and their boats, who shipped the Arabs' arms around the world.[18]

In the space of one conversation, Leslie Aspin became the most important source for the British secret service in the Middle East. He was given the code name Kovaks, then briefed on clandestine communication by his controller, "Homer," and put on the payroll of the secret service. The British had only one kind of intelligence operation in mind for him.

MI6 did not care about the Jews, so it did not want Aspin to warn the Israelis about arms to the PLO. Nor did the British care about its ally's drug problems, so they did not want him to help the Americans stop Syrian drug-running. All they wanted him to do was stop the shipments of guns from Libya to Northern Ireland.[19] Aspin did this extremely well. In fact, his ability to forewarn British intelligence of IRA weapons shipments earned him a place in Irish history books.[20]

According to Aspin's version of these counterterrorist operations, they were debacles, and his secret service controllers thoroughly botched nearly all of them. In fact, Aspin suspected that the British secret service was incredibly incompetent, although he made a lot of money on both sides, from MI6 and the Libyan arms dealers.[21]

Unfortunately for Aspin, the IRA had penetrated the Irish police counterintelligence force, the Special Branch, and quickly discovered Aspin's true role for the British.[22] He soon realized that he was becoming expendable. From the British point of view, Monzer Al-Kassar was a much more valuable source than Aspin. Al-Kassar was not only a friend to the president's brother and an in-law of Syria's intelligence chief, but also, his bank network handled the bulk of financing for the PLO, including the drug sales and arms purchases.

The British had been looking for a way to penetrate the Al-Kassar family for a long time. The father, Mohammed Al-Kassar, was one of the first major drug smugglers in the Middle East. He had four sons, the second of whom, Monzer Al-Kassar, was born on July 1, 1947.[23] Mohammed was a member of the powerful Alawite minority and an early supporter of the socialist Baath party favored by Moscow. One of their Alawite protégés, Hafez Al Assad, became president of Syria and the lifelong protector of the Al-Kassar family. Mohammed Al-Kassar rose quickly from a small-time drug runner to Syrian special ambassador.[24]

It should be recalled that British intelligence had its own spies inside Syria and discovered that the Kremlin intended to finance international terrorist groups with drug sales. Syria and Bulgaria were to front the networks, exchanging drugs for cash under diplomatic cover. It did not take the British long to suspect which Syrian diplomats were involved in such smuggling activities. Mohammed's eldest son, Ghassan, was arrested in Milan in 1969 in connection with a stolen car ring operating out of Bulgaria.[25]

Ghassan was released, but kept under surveillance to see where the trail would lead. On January 12, 1970, Ghassan and his younger brother, Monzer, were arrested in Vienna for the same crime. On February 3 the brothers were arrested again, this time in Trieste. The stolen car investigation had taken on international significance as a possible new method for Eastern Bloc drug smuggling, with its ramifications for the financing of international terror.[26] The British had the Irish end of the drug ring safely under control, but American kids were taking Monzer's drugs, and Israel's very existence was threatened by the Arab terror squads.

Aspin, although he knew only a little of the Al-Kassars' drug business, confirmed that the family also was running guns through Libya. He was told to keep working for the Swiss bank network, while the British waited for their chance to get one of the Al-Kassars on their own turf.[27]

In 1972 the Danish authorities were informed that Monzer Al-Kassar was smuggling hashish from Lebanon to Copenhagen in stolen cars. The charges were dropped, despite the fact that the Danes found a bag of hashish with Monzer's fingerprints on it. In 1973, however, a warrant was issued for Al-Kassar's arrest for trying to smuggle even more carloads of drugs into Denmark.[28] According to the former intelligence officers we spoke to for this chapter, the British MI6 liaison was tipping off the Danes about his every move, trying to keep the pressure on Al-Kassar.[29]

Soon after the Danish courts issued an arrest warrant on March 16, 1973, charging Al-Kassar with international drug smuggling, the British secret service made its move. According to our sources, MI6 made the same approach to Al-Kassar as it had to Aspin. If he cooperated, the British would reward him handsomely. If he did not cooperate, the British would spread the word that Monzer Al-Kassar was the informant who betrayed all the recent gun shipments by Libya and Syria.[30]

There is some circumstantial evidence that Al-Kassar was recruited in Denmark. Soon after the arrest warrant was issued, he was allowed to flee to England, where he set up an import-export firm called Espargo, with a subsidiary in Beirut. The smuggling continued, but this time under British auspices. According to the "old spies," Al-Kassar was the "supersource." Through him, the British could track money moving to every terrorist organization in the world.[31] To protect him, the British were perfectly willing to have the Arabs blame Aspin for all the botched shipments to the IRA. By 1973 Aspin believed that the secret service was about to make him a public scapegoat.[32]

Despite the fact that the IRA knew about Aspin, the British wanted him to go back to Northern Ireland to carry out an assassination.[33] He deliberately flubbed the job and escaped back to England, to the great annoyance of "Homer." Aspin realized that his short career with the secret service was coming to an end. In September 1974, just before the British leaked word of his double agent role to the Irish press, he made his own plans to betray the British and flee to the United States.[34]

As a safety measure, he had previously tipped off the Americans that the British were not telling them everything they knew about Monzer Al-Kassar's drug shipments to the United States. Aspin contacted Larry Katz, a narcotics agent in the U.S. embassy in London, whom he had known in Turkey, and warned that a trunkload of drugs was about to arrive in New York. "Homer" was not amused when the Americans intercepted the drugs and suspected Aspin as the source of the leak.[35] In order to continue Al-Kassar's bona fides as an Arab terrorist, the secret service was quite willing to let his drug business continue and keep the facts from its American liaison officers.

But that was nothing compared to what else the British were concealing.[36] According to Aspin, at the end of 1973 he bumped into one of his old friends from the Black September terrorist movement and got him drunk. The source:

> . . . gleefully told me that his colleagues intended to blow up a Pan American or El Al aircraft at Rome airport before the end of the month.

> This was in December, 1973. . . . At the next meeting with Homer, I passed on the information about the Arabs and made a particular point of the Rome threat.
>
> He promised to pass on this information to the three governments concerned.
>
> I'm almost positive that he never did this and the thought that I trusted him to do so and did not make sure myself that they knew leaves me sick every time I think of it.
>
> Before the end of the month a Pan Am plane was blown up on the Rome tarmac. I'll never forgive the bastard for that.[37]

The problem with Leslie Aspin was that he had developed a conscience. The British secret service had a good thing going with Monzer Al-Kassar, and Aspin was going to wreck it by telling the truth. Al-Kassar was the British government's best window into the Middle East, and MI6 did not want to share him with the Americans.

The British intended to promote Al-Kassar's bank network as a cheap and easy way to keep track of the terrorists, who trusted Monzer to mind their money and launder it for them so they could buy weapons and explosives. The Arabs believed in him because he kept the drug profits rolling in, but they were curious why none of his arms shipments was reaching Northern Ireland. In order to protect Al-Kassar, the British decided to publicly expose Aspin as their informant.

On September 6, 1974, the secret service planted an exposé on Leslie Aspin in the Irish press. The British blew the whistle on their own agent, leaking his true name, passport number, details of his role in one of the arms intercepts, and his relations with the MI6 provocateur, the Libyans, and the IRA.[38] Aspin knew he was a dead man if he did not run. He evaded British security, PLO hit men, and Libyan intelligence. In October 1974 Leslie Aspin arrived in the United States.

As soon as Aspin's defection was known, the secret service placed Al-Kassar in "administrative detention" in Britain. Officially he was charged with smuggling cannabis oil to Britain. Unofficially, the British wanted to keep him under wraps until they knew what Aspin planned to do.

After hiding out for a year, Aspin made his move. In 1975 he published his autobiography, *I, Kovaks,* candidly admitting his criminal activities, his work for the British secret service, and the manner in which he was betrayed. However, he never used Al-Kassar's name. At the end of the book, he coyly noted that "I have had two offers of work . . . from a government who knows all about me but for whom I haven't yet worked."[39]

Our intelligence sources say that the first offer was probably from the U.S. Drug Enforcement Administration (DEA). Only a handful of top people in DEA, including Larry Katz, knew that the British had recruited Al-Kassar, who was rapidly becoming one of the best drug informants in the world. The problem was that the British could not expose the PLO drug network without exposing their informant.[40]

As long as Al-Kassar worked for the British secret service, Aspin had a life insurance policy. That was why Aspin never mentioned him in his tell-all autobiography. Al-Kassar was his trump card over the British government. Aspin made it clear that if he was killed, he would take Al-Kassar with him. By the end of 1975, the British decided to leave well enough alone.[41]

So did his new employer, George Bush. In order to provide a steady stream of income, Aspin decided to work for the new director of the CIA. Our sources in the intelligence community say that Aspin's hiring was a closely held secret. None of the CIA section chiefs were briefed. His information about the British secret service's double-dealing gave George Bush the leverage he needed to form a new, and private, relationship with the British government.[42]

According to a number of the "old spies," it was a simple trade. The British wanted Bush to keep Aspin quiet, and Bush wanted the British to provide something he desperately needed: a secret army of mercenaries to fight in Angola.[43]

The Portuguese colonial rulers finally had pulled out of their African colonies in 1975 after decades of fighting guerrilla insurgencies. In Angola, the pro-Marxist Popular Movement for the Liberation of Angola (MPLA) had won the battle for power over its pro-Western rivals, Holden Roberto's National Front for the Liberation of Angola (FLNA) and Jonas Savimbi's Union for the Total Independence of Angola (UNITA). Before long, the civil war between the groups became complicated by international intervention, first by Western-backed South African forces, then by Cuban forces sent from thousands of miles away. Just as Vietnam had been lost to the communists earlier in 1975, now it seemed that Angola would join the Red Empire. It was an especially bitter pill for U.S. oil companies to swallow, as Angola contained a fabulously rich oil deposit.

The Angolan war was Bush's first major covert operation as director of Central Intelligence, and it was going badly. According to John Stockwell, the chief of the CIA's Angolan Task Force, it was an impossible assignment. On November 14, 1975, the White House top-secret advisory board, the Forty Committee, "had asked the CIA to outline a program which could win the Angolan war."[44]

On December 2 the CIA recommended that the only way to win was to put American advisors on the ground to direct the untrained anti-

Communist soldiers. Henry Kissinger just grunted and left without making any decision. No one was willing to authorize another Vietnam.[45]

When Bush arrived at the CIA in December 1975, the Angolan problem was the first mess dumped in his lap. He did not want his first operation to be a loser, but the war was going downhill at a rapid rate. Worse, the U.S. Senate was particularly opposed to sending American soldiers to fight in Africa and was on the verge of ordering the CIA to terminate all of its covert operations in Angola. There had to be some way to win the war behind Congress's back. Eventually the White House Forty Committee approved mercenaries as the solution, as long as they weren't Americans.[46]

Our intelligence sources insist that the only thing Bush wanted was victory. His political future could be crippled if it were known that the first thing he did as CIA head was to retreat and hand over Angola to the Communists without a fight.[47] If it took foreign mercenaries to win, so be it. So the CIA made formal approaches to the British for mercenaries and missiles. The British government said no to the missile request, as missiles were too easily traceable. However, it had no objections to supplying mercenaries to the CIA behind Congress's back.[48]

To avoid embarrassment to the British government, several "private security firms" of ex-SAS men in London are ready to carry out any sensitive operation requested by the British government. One of the "less impressively connected firms," run by John Banks, was assigned to help with Bush's problem in Angola. It was Banks who provided CIA director Bush with "the British mercenary corps for the Angolan civil war."[49]

Banks's partner, Leslie Aspin, kept his part of the CIA bargain: No mention of Al-Kassar's name in his book. Soon after the Aspin deal was cut with the Americans, it was safe for the British "supersource" to go back to work. Al-Kassar was let out of administrative detention in October 1975, at the same time the drug charges against him mysteriously vanished because of legal technicalities. By January 1976 the first shipment of arms and mercenaries from Britain were sent to Angola. Two of the Angola recruits, Leslie Aspin, and John Berry later joined Al-Kassar's arms smuggling apparatus.[50]

Without informing John Stockwell, head of the CIA Task Force in Angola, British mercenaries suddenly appeared.[51] CIA director George Bush was keeping more than one secret from Stockwell. According to our sources, not only were the British mercenaries being paid for by the CIA, they were being recruited by a CIA agent named Leslie Aspin. Without Stockwell's knowledge, Bush had sent Aspin back to London to help coordinate the mercenary program.[52] In 1976 Leslie Aspin "turned up as an assistant to John Banks in the mercenary recruitment scheme for Angola."[53]

The British secret service had no choice other than to accept this situation. Aspin and Banks had connections at the highest levels of American intelligence. More established and "well connected" British security firms were shouldered aside. Apparently, Aspin had told Bush too much. Aspin and Banks had the CIA contract for Angola, and there was nothing the British government could do about it.[54]

Banks enlisted the help of a friend in Special Branch, and at least four members of the Aspin-Banks private army were members of the British secret service.[55] But all in all, Aspin's mercenaries were a motley crew. The first group of mercenaries were pulled out shortly after President Ford terminated all CIA operations in Angola except for intelligence gathering. Nothing, however, precluded a British citizen like Aspin from recruiting replacements. By summertime, Aspin's forces would be the only Western army left in Angola. The anti-Communist Angolans were getting nervous.

Despite the Congressional ban, there were continued promises of American support. George Bush still had a few million dollars left in the CIA slush fund for contingencies, some of which was promised to the Angolans. Henry Kissinger told them to keep fighting no matter what Congress said and, within days of the ban, gave promises of aid to Jonas Savimbi's UNITA.[56] It was Leslie Aspin who stayed on the ground in Zaire, coordinating the war across the border. Before the Americans pulled out, he made at least one close friend from the American contingent, a young officer named Bill Buckley, who had been detached to the CIA from Special Forces, the U.S. army's elite Green Beret units, which specialize in psychological warfare and counterinsurgency. The two men forged a link that led them to work together on other under-the-table operations.[57]

As will be seen in Chapter 18, it was to be a fateful connection for the secret espionage war against Israel. Aspin and Buckley were two of a kind: ex-commandos, full of fun and energy, and willing to cut a few corners for the sake of the mission. According to our sources, what endeared the pair to the CIA was their disdain for bureaucratic niceties and their willingness to bend the law a little to get the job done.[58]

Officially, George Bush was telling the regular staff of the CIA that they had to obey the congressional ban and pull out of Angola. Unofficially, of course, the CIA and Kissinger were telling the Angolans to keep on fighting. Over the next year the mercenaries of the British secret service kept the Angolan guerrillas afloat. By 1977, when Carter was sworn in as U.S. president, Aspin's back-channel was well established. He had made the under-the-table link between Bush and the British and South African governments. Aspin's South African mercenary friends continued the major part of the program, with the covert support of at least one oil company.[59]

It does not take a genius to figure out why an oil company was paying for mercenaries after the CIA pulled out. Several U.S. oil companies had multimillion-dollar investments in the oil-rich Cabinda region of Angola, which they did not want to see in Communist hands. The irony is that the Communist Angolan Government quickly pledged that the American oil companies would be safe from nationalization and would continue to make healthy profits in Angola. Obviously, no one believed this pledge.

That, say our intelligence sources, was what the war was really about: As in the Middle East, the key was American oil rights.[60] Aspin's army eventually achieved its victory at the negotiating table, and the British mercenary troops eventually were called home, leaving the South Africans to launch token resistance raids. Everybody at the CIA, including Buckley, got medals. Aspin got a new job, as the unofficial British bagman for American covert operations hidden from Congress.[61]

As we shall see, Aspin was one of the first arms traders to open an account in the Bank of Credit and Commerce International, which played such an important part in the secret espionage war against the Jews in the twelve years when George Bush was vice president and then president.[62] It is no coincidence that Aspin went back to work on joint British-American money laundering just as U.S. intelligence was closing down one of the wildest, and most illegal, money-laundering schemes in American history: the Ed Wilson Affair.

The following version of events was told to us by an extremely reliable CIA official with in-depth knowledge of the Wilson case and then confirmed by other sources.[63] In 1971 Ed Wilson had been fired from the CIA and promptly hired by a Naval Intelligence–National Security Agency joint operation known as Task Force 157. The NSA was involved in this operation because as the U.S. Communications intelligence agency it was using the Task Force's rented fishing vessels to carry electronic surveillance and detection equipment to monitor the Soviet fleet in the Mediterranean.[64]

As bizarre as it seems today, officials of Naval Intelligence decided in 1971 that Gadhafi's loyalty could be bought with an under-the-table sale of American arms, which the Libyan dictator preferred to poorly made Soviet weapons. Using the NSA as an unwitting cover, the navy actually funded and approved Wilson's arms shipments to Libya during the early 1970s. This incredibly stupid initiative was flatly contrary to U.S. policy, and wholly illegal.[65]

The Department of the Navy was not alone in the scheme to cozy up to Gadhafi. The oil companies, in particular, continued to do business with the new madman of the Middle East, strictly in the interests of profits, and were supported by the Nixon administration.[66]

The British secret service had no intention of getting along with Gadhafi and sent the ex-SAS mercenaries of the Stirling Company to plan a coup. Colonel David Stirling had founded the SAS in World War II, and later formed a company which specialized in using mercenaries as cover for official British intelligence operations. However, the Libyan coup was blocked at the last minute. The British "Foreign Office obliged Stirling to drop out because the Americans felt that Qathafi *(sic)* would be fairly easy to control."[67] Shortly afterward Wilson's Task Force 157 began its feeble attempt to bribe Gadhafi with guns.

When bribery did not work, the United States tried to curry favor with Gadhafi by leaking information about the British coup plotters as well as his Libyan opponents.[68] Nothing seemed to work. The navy's Libyan initiative merely convinced Gadhafi that the West was weak. Subsequently, Admiral Bobby Ray Inman investigated the Task Force 157 fiasco and eventually had Ed Wilson fired.

What Admiral Inman did not know was that Wilson had a business associate, an Iranian Jew named Albert Hakim. The Washington address for Wilson's firm, Consultant's International, was 1618 K Street Northwest, Washington, D.C., the same suite as Hakim's "Stanford Technology."[69] Hakim, who became Oliver North's banker in the 1980s, later testified that Wilson had "penetrated" his Swiss banking operation and was acting without his knowledge in selling Hakim's high-tech surveillance and communications gear to Libya.[70]

There is reason to suspect that Hakim was Leslie Aspin's business associate, too. Wilson's gunrunning to Libya for Task Force 157 took place from 1971 to 1974. This was, of course, the same time that Aspin was infiltrating Libyan arms networks for the British secret service with the help of a banking source. Without ever mentioning Hakim's name, Aspin confirmed that the banker was headquartered in Geneva, was affiliated with Jewish financiers, owned several ships and traded in gold and other commodities.

With apologies to Albert Hakim if we have identified him unfairly, he does seem to be the only Jewish banker with an organization headquartered in Geneva who fits this description. Moreover, he certainly is the only one with an admitted connection (albeit an innocent one) to Ed Wilson's Libyan arms deals in the early 1970s.

Although Hakim never mentioned Aspin's name, he did tell the Iran-Contra investigators in Congress of his relationship with the Azima brothers in the United States. This is coincidental since the Azimas, Iranian expatriates who operated an air cargo business from their base in Kansas

City, worked directly with Aspin. The name of the company was Global International Airways, or GIA.[71] Congress censored Hakim's identification, believing that the Azima family was the crucial "first contact" in opening a secret channel to Iran for Oliver North.[72]

Because of the censorship, the press failed to realize that Hakim's friends the Azimas had prior experience with gun running. The local Kansas City press, however, has quite a file on the Azimas and their mysterious air cargo company. In 1979 a GIA aircraft that was supposedly hauling vegetables to Central America was found to contain rockets, mortars, and guns. GIA's pilots used to joke at their "vegetable" manifest and say that they were carrying "cabbages and cabbage launchers." The local press referred to GIA as the "little CIA."[73]

Hakim strenuously denied any knowledge of Wilson's shady activities. He insisted to Congress that his Swiss operation had been penetrated by unscrupulous individuals, such as Ed Wilson and Frank Terpil, the former CIA officer who worked with Wilson to supply Gadhafi with weapons. Hakim said that when he discovered that some of his employees had been involved in shady deals behind his back, he fired everyone responsible.[74]

On the one hand, it is possible that Hakim did not know that Wilson was using his company to smuggle guns to Libya. On the other hand, Hakim may not be at liberty to tell the whole story.

The former intelligence officers we spoke to on this point say that Hakim is actually not a bad man, but that he is afraid to tell anyone what really happened. Our sources say that Hakim was cooperating with the British secret service. After Aspin revealed how money for Libyan arms was channeled through Switzerland, the British secret service used Hakim's legitimate business network to monitor the financial transactions of the one family that controlled and directed the gun-running operations in the Middle East: the Al-Kassars of Syria.[75]

According to these sources, Hakim was an innocent pawn used first by the British secret service and then by U.S. intelligence.

There is a certain irony here. At the same time that the U.S. Navy and Ed Wilson were trying to run guns to Libya behind the backs of the British, Wilson was using Hakim's company while Hakim was working with the British secret service. According to our sources, the British let the navy make fools of themselves for a little while. Then, after Inman finally fired Wilson, the British had a chat with the new CIA director, George Bush.[76]

To put it bluntly, the Americans had been "caught with their pants down." Arming Gadhafi through Task Force 157 was just the kind of scandal that would tear the intelligence community apart. Bush realized that the Republican administration was in deep trouble over the Wilson affair. Instead of a thorough, searching investigation by the CIA, George Bush allegedly ordered a cover-up in 1976.[77] When Admiral Inman became deputy CIA director in 1981, he roundly criticized the so-called investigation of the Wilson affair and apparently concluded there had been a cover-up during Bush's tenure as CIA head.[78]

The "old spies" say that there is a lot more to the Wilson case than has ever been made public. Much of the money generated by Wilson in Task Force 157 went to bribe Republican politicians during the Nixon administration.[79] According to a top-secret Justice Department surveillance report, Wilson was also observed passing envelopes to several members of a congressional appropriations committee.[80] Because of the sensitive political scandal, the Justice Department investigation never went forward. Neither, as Inman later discovered, did the investigation at the CIA. The whole Task Force 157 scandal was quietly swept under a rug. Also in 1976, Hakim entered into a new business relationship with the Bechtel Corporation after being screened by Bechtel General Counsel Cap Weinberger, later secretary of defense in the Reagan-Bush Administration.[81]

Apparently in 1976 George Bush had become the Republican party's garbage man. He was the man in charge of the CIA when Hakim's connection to Wilson was first investigated, and when Wilson's Task Force 157 affair was first covered up. Bush was also the man in charge of the CIA during the coverup of the Angleton's Vatican-Vessel scandal, when he covered up when the CIA protected one of Nixon's Nazis, when the Wilson affair was exposed and during the Angolan mercenary operation.

Our intelligence sources insist that Bush did not create these scandals. He inherited them in 1976. One "old spy" was unequivocal: "Bush was a virgin in covert ops. He spent most of his one year as DCI testifying before Congress. There was one guy in the Republican party who knew where the bodies were buried. Bush trusted Bill Casey for advice. That was his big mistake."[82]

In 1976 Casey was running Reagan's presidential campaign. Casey had known Reagan since the early 1950s, when they had both worked on the Fascist "freedom fighter" program under Vice President Nixon.[83] Later on, as president, Nixon had appointed Casey to run the Securities and Exchange Commission. Casey was one of the Republican party's leading fund-raisers. As Oliver North later would discover, Casey also had considerable knowledge of international money laundering.

A number of past and present intelligence officers say that it was Casey who opened a new private channel to the British in 1976. It did not take a political genius to realize that the Democrats would take over the White House, the CIA, and the Securities Exchange Commission in 1977. Time was running out to hide a dirty chain of money laundering that stretched back to Dulles. Casey had worked with British intelligence before, and together they had no problem in devising a new and more reliable banking system that would permanently avoid congressional scrutiny. Casey, not Bush, forged the British banking-intelligence connection. George Bush just did as he was told. His only contribution was to chip in CIA funds to set up the new listening post in the Gulf states. The British took care of the rest.[84]

Through a series of coups, the British secret service had placed their own puppets on the thrones of the tiny bedouin kingdoms that comprised Oman and the United Arab Emirates. These tiny countries ("tribes with flags") were totally dependent on the SAS and MI6 for their survival. Virtually every aspect of their banking, intelligence, and foreign policy was handled by British advisers on the scene.[85]

The capital of the United Arab Emirates, Abu Dhabi, was a small town of less than 100,000 people, but it controlled 10 percent of the oil deposits in the world. The UAE was the perfect place to hide a bank, a bank to handle covert operations behind the back of the British Parliament and the U.S. Congress. The new bank would be called the Bank of Credit and Commerce International, or BCCI. Although it is now better known as the "Bank of Crooks and Criminals," the "old spies" say that BCCI really stands for the "British Cover for Collecting Intelligence."[86]

There had been a previous American attempt to use a financial facility for covert operations, but the Nugan-Hand bank operation was exposed by the Australian media and was on its way to bankruptcy by the late 1970s. The Nugan-Hand bank unraveled along with Wilson and Task Force 157, but not before it had established close working relations in Saudi Arabia with both Aramco and the Bechtel Corporation.[87]

As the old bank in Australia collapsed, the new one in Abu Dhabi was coming into being with the help of the British secret service, which used the same front men in another British colony, the Cayman Islands. In this "tax haven," Nugan-Hand's legal firm of Bruce Campbell & Company set up the International Credit & Investment Company (ICIC) as a front for the BCCI.[88]

According to our sources in the intelligence community, what no one knows is that this little British island played an integral role in international money laundering for several of the Arab intelligence services.[89] The British used their MI6 base on the Cayman Islands as headquarters for an "International Consortium for Intelligence Collection (ICIC)," a joint venture of several spy agencies that would secretly own the stock of an international bank. Later on several witnesses tried to tell Congress about the "consortium" entity for "Intelligence Cooperation," or IC, that had been established in the Cayman Islands. What no one realized was that the ICIC spy consortium was the same ICIC that secretly controlled all the stock of the BCCI.[90]

Here, according to the "old spies," is how the BCCI-ICIC fraud worked. In 1976 British and American representatives offered stock in ICIC to the intelligence services of the UAE, Pakistan, and Saudi Arabia. In effect, the British secret service "borrowed" the money to start the BCCI from various friendly intelligence services. The original investors, the Arab spy agencies, were then repaid under-the-table by the ICIC after the bank started to turn a profit. The BCCI had no capital of its own, but the public believed it was funded by wealthy Arabs.[91]

To Sheik Zayed of the United Arab Emirates, the scheme had appeal because the BCCI was also a perfect conduit for bribes. The sheik, whose country lived under a constant terrorist threat, was paying more than $10 million a year to the PLO. As discussed in Chapter 15, the Saudis were paying much more as bribes to Yasser Arafat. By laundering their bribes through the BCCI, the Arabs were able to let the British secret service trace the money to various terrorist cells, which would be identified quietly and then destroyed. The Saudis, in particular, were getting tired of paying ransom to every obscure terrorist group that popped up. It was cheaper, and better public relations, to let the British secretly eliminate the Arab extremists for them.[92]

Monzer Al-Kassar played a key role in this, as the "Banker for the PLO." He convinced all the terrorist groups, from Abu Nidal to the Marxists, to transfer their accounts to the new BCCI branch in London. There the secret service could easily wiretap and decipher every coded transfer of the Arab bribe money to each terrorist faction in the world. There was only one problem. According to a number of our sources, to make the scheme convincing and to protect Al-Kassar's role as an informant, the terrorists would have to be allowed some successes. There would be no intelligence sharing with Israel. No Jews would be invited to the ICIC. The BCCI would become the most anti-Semitic bank in its time.[93]

It took the Mossad a long time to figure out that the BCCI was an intelligence consortium among the British, the Americans, and the Arabs. It took them even longer to find out who was behind the setup back in 1976. Finding out the truth did not do them any good. Many years later, in 1992, when Israeli intelligence planted items similar to the following in the American Jewish press, no one would listen: "The CIA had a covert relationship with BCCI in 1976. At the very same time, George Bush was director of the CIA. We are told the late William Casey . . . met secretly and regularly with the BCCI bank's founder, Aga Hassan Abedi. Unfortunately there are so many coincidences."[94]

Israeli operatives were not the only ones to figure out that the BCCI had been founded as an intelligence front. Before he was deposed, the dictator of Pakistan, Zulfikar Bhutto also accused the BCCI's founder of having ties to American intelligence. "On several occasions, Bhutto said publicly that Abedi was in league with the CIA."[95] To be fair, the British secret service had told only a handful of people in the CIA about the bank. Abedi was only a hired hand, although he and his Pakistani friends later stole the bank blind. While the powers behind the scenes of the BCCI were the bedouin sheiks who set up the bank, behind them were their masters in British intelligence.[96]

The leaders of Oman and the United Arab Emirates owe their existence to Julian Amery, a former member of the British secret service and the brother of John Amery, the British traitor who, as discussed in Chapter 5, was hanged after World War II as a pro-Nazi propagandist. Forty years later brother Julian became a paid consultant to the BCCI and its biggest defender in the British Parliament.[97] In the late 1950s Amery was the undersecretary of war who was sent to reorganize the armed forces in the area. In 1967 British mercenaries replaced the sheik of Abu Dhabi of the UAE with his brother, Sheik Zayed.

In 1970 Timothy Landon of British intelligence launched another SAS mercenary coup in Oman, blasting the old ruler aside and putting Sultan Qabous on the throne. Oman and Abu Dhabi became loyal friends of Julian Amery, a staging ground for the SAS and headquarters for the BCCI.[98] The biggest British coup was in establishing liaison with Kamal Adham, the head of Saudi Arabian intelligence from 1963 to 1977. As discussed in Chapter 11, following the Suez debacle in 1956, British intelligence had wound back the Mossad connection and actively courted Saudi Arabia. One of the men who established close relations with Adham was Julian Amery.[99]

It is unlikely that Bush remained entirely ignorant of the new British-Arab intelligence alliance in 1976. After all, he was director of Central Intelligence. Moreover, in June 1976 the U.S. ambassador in Lebanon was killed by a terrorist bomb. It was Bush who instituted a new and "questionable policy": Instead of asking the Israelis for intelligence, Bush moved closer to the Arabs, especially Adham and his cabal of BCCI agents.[100] Bush's personal interest in the Gulf States went back to the mid-1960s, when his oil company, Zapata, had gained the contract to build Kuwait's first offshore oil rig.[101]

In support of the British initiative to create the BCCI as an intelligence collection source, in 1976 Bush authorized the expenditure of CIA clandestine funds to establish an NSA signals post in the Gulf States.[102] Through these signal posts, communications from both ends of the bank's headquarters, in London and Abu Dhabi, were systematically intercepted.

Because of the extreme sensitivity of British-American wiretap cooperation, the BCCI records remained with the British secret service, with access given to only a handful of CIA people.[103]

Our sources insist that none of the BCCI-British intercept results were shared with the CIA after Bush left office. After Jimmy Carter became president in 1977, a number of people suddenly resigned from the CIA, went through the "revolving door," and acquired connections to the BCCI. Others, including William Casey's close friends, Robert Gray and John M. Shaheen, appear to have played innocent roles in the Iran-Contra scandal. Gray's company also represented the BCCI. The original Arab investors, Abedi, Adham, and friends, secretly bought an American front for the BCCI, from Casey's friend J. William Middendorf.[104]

To be fair, Casey, his friends, and the CIA did not realize what a mess they were getting into. They did not know that the British secret service had relinquished day-to-day control of the BCCI to a group of Moslem bankers whose incompetence was exceeded only by their crookedness.[105]

All that Carter's CIA inherited was Leslie Aspin. For additional training in special operations, Aspin was sent to the JFK School for Special Warfare at Fort Bragg, North Carolina, where he earned his "Green Beret."[106] Since he had already gone through British paratroop school and earned his SAS commando beret, the course wasn't particularly difficult for him. Not many people in the world wore both berets, had experience as an intelligence agent in hostile territories, and possessed a vast knowledge of mercenary operations, smuggling, and the Middle East. Leslie Aspin was quite a find.

While assigned to Company E, 7th Special Forces Group (Airborne), of the First Special Forces unit, he was offered his first formal contract with the CIA in 1978. The Angola operation did not count—it was off the official books. Indeed, very few in the CIA even knew how the British mercenary link came about. But on April 25, 1978, the CIA director of personnel wrote to Aspin to start his official CIA career.[107]

Aspin was offered a job just as a "contract" agent, someone hired for a specific job, who then goes back to his own career. Aspin's family told us that he would go on the CIA books for a day, be briefed on a mission, and then quickly taken off the books again. In that way the CIA could state truthfully that "we have no employees named Leslie Aspin."[108] Aspin went home to England for a brief rest before his next assignment.

Most of the CIA's Angola staff, including Bill Buckley, headed off to the Middle East. Aspin was not far behind. In 1979 a group of radical Moslems seized the Holy Mosque in Mecca, Saudi Arabia. The Saudi National Guard was not quite trained for antiterrorist warfare, so the Saudis asked for help. As Mecca was off-limits to non-Moslems, the presence of

Western agents had to be a closely kept secret. The odd couple, Aspin and Buckley, went in on the British-American strike team, disguised in Saudi uniforms.[109]

They blasted the terrorists out of the mosque and stood the survivors up against a wall. Aspin photographed his firing squad as it executed the radicals. Then one of the strike team members took a photo of a grinning Aspin and Buckley, with their arms around each other. Aspin kept the photos as souvenirs of their secret mission.[110] Not surprisingly, the contract to clean up the mosque went to another early BCCI insider.[111]

Over the years, Aspin handled a number of covert assignments for both the British and Americans. Although Parliament had prohibited sending arms to South Africa, that was no hindrance to people like Aspin with connections in the Cayman Islands. By the late 1970s it seems that he was already involved with TransWorld arms, a Canadian firm that was later involved with Iran-Contra. Through his London contacts, Aspin was paying for his arms shipments through a "Geneva Bank," almost certainly the BCCI, which he used almost exclusively to service his varied clientele.[112] By 1980 Aspin's arm deals were going quite nicely. He bought a very expensive home in England.[113]

Unfortunately, he may have been selling arms to terrorists. But, as we shall see, this may have been part of another British intelligence operation to ransom hostages.[114] We have confirmed that, starting in the early 1980s, Aspin's BCCI bank account at the London branch shows several large deposits from Ghassan Al-Kassar, Monzer's brother and business partner.[115]

Our intelligence sources say the British tricked President Carter well and truly by foisting Monzer Al-Kassar's arms network on the unwitting CIA. The British secret service offered to supply Soviet-made arms to the Afghan resistance, which would disguise CIA participation as well as enable the mujahideen rebels to resupply themselves with captured Soviet ammunition. Carter gratefully accepted London's offer. As the naive president later conceded: "In a highly secret move, we also assessed the possibility of arranging for Soviet-made weapons (which would appear to have come from the Afghan military forces) to be delivered to freedom fighters in Afghanistan and of giving them what encouragement we could to resist subjugation by the Soviet invaders."[116] Our sources insist that Carter did not know that the British were buying the arms from Monzer Al-Kassar, who had become the main sales representative for the Communist-controlled Polish and Bulgarian arms industries. To this day, the CIA does not have an inkling that it bought Eastern Bloc weapons from one of the PLO's leading terrorists.[117]

Although the former intelligence officers we interviewed said that the

Carter administration was totally excluded from British intelligence information collected from the BCCI, there was accidental contact. After the 1979 Soviet invasion of Afghanistan, the CIA was searching for a way to launder guns and money to the mujahideen freedom fighters. It was, they say, purely coincidental that Abedi's Pakistani branch of the BCCI was chosen as the repository for CIA funds for the Afghan rebels.[118]

During the Carter administration, the "old spies" say, the only one who might have had an idea that there was more to the BCCI connection was Aspin's old comrade-in-arms, Bill Buckley. It was Buckley who oversaw the paramilitary side of things in Afghanistan for the CIA. The CIA money went from Buckley through BCCI, Pakistan, to the British secret service, and then to Al-Kassar.[119] If Buckley knew more about the British-BCCI connection, he took it to his grave.

Buckley may not have been able to connect the chain because his British friend Aspin was away working on a different operation with Al-Kassar. In 1980 Aspin's BCCI account in London shows that the Al-Kassars were buying guns from him, not the other way around. Aspin was selling arms through the Al-Kassars for delivery to Iran. It may have been the first of Monzer's and Aspin's hostage ransom operations. It would not be the last.[120]

In fact, Aspin's 1980 ransom deal was the beginning of what would turn into the American arms-for-hostages scandal, as it provided the prototype that later was used in the Iran-Contra affair. The Iranian Hezbollah had kidnapped two British citizens. Monzer Al-Kassar, playing the intermediary, told the British they could be released for a price, a small one. The Iranians just wanted to buy some machine guns for their war against Iraq. Leslie and his brother, Michael, opened a company called Delta Investments, which acquired American-made Browning machine guns.[121]

After one of the Al-Kassar brothers deposited the Iranian money in Aspin's London BCCI account, the American weapons were shipped to the United Arab Emirates, where they were transshipped to the Iranians, who promptly released the British kidnap victims. Michael Aspin, unfortunately, boasted about the ransom deal to the British press, which quickly confirmed the story.[122]

The media, which suspected that the British secret service was behind the ransom arrangements, made a big deal about the successful guns-for-hostages operation.[123] Leslie should have known then never to trust his brother to keep his mouth shut. Al-Kassar was too valuable to MI6 to risk any more press leaks.

By January 1981, when Reagan was inaugurated and Casey became head of the CIA, all the ingredients for the coming disasters were in place: Leslie's relationship with Monzer, Michael's big mouth, and, of course, the bedouin bank of BCCI that handled the under-the-table guns-for-hostages deal.

Casey and the British had created a bank for spies that no one supervised, where it was impossible to trace money, and which was immune from either congressional or parliamentary scrutiny. The BCCI was a perfect vehicle for Casey's contacts in the oil industry to make their own bribes to the PLO. The Jews of Israel would never know what hit them. Neither would the innocent victims of the Third World, who invested $20 billion in a con game. While Casey was playing spy chief, his old friend Aga Hassan Abedi was stripping the bank's assets.

The real villain was Monzer Al-Kassar. If he had been honest with the British, the secret service would have been able to strike a double blow against terrorism and drugs, not to mention keeping the BCCI under control. Al-Kassar could have been the best informant in the world. The problem was that he was not working for the British at all. He was working for the Communists. His only loyalty was to Soviet Military Intelligence, the GRU. Al-Kassar's antiterrorist work for MI6 was probably the best sting operation in recent Soviet history.[124] As we shall see in the next chapters, the one who got stung the worst was George Bush.

Within a decade Al-Kassar used his protected position within MI6 to become the world's leading drug dealer. By 1989 the drug enforcement agencies of West Germany, Italy, Spain, and the United States had pooled their information at a special Interpol conference concerned solely with Monzer Al-Kassar. There was no doubt about it. Al-Kassar had used political blackmail to build an arms, drugs, and terrorist empire from South America to the Middle East.[125]

And, of course, Al-Kassar was killing Jews.

CHAPTER 18

THE IRAN–CONTRA DEBACLE

The history books say that in 1985, the U.S. government discovered that an American intelligence officer and committed Zionist, Jonathan Pollard, was spying for Israel. Pollard was accused of leaking top-secret satellite photos that aided Israel in its attack on Iraq's Osirak nuclear reactor. He also was denounced for leaking hundreds of boxes of U.S. secret codes, plans, and operations. Pollard became a synonym for wholesale leaks of every kind that severely damaged U.S. intelligence. Secretary of Defense Caspar "Cap" Weinberger furiously demanded that Pollard be given the maximum sentence for espionage.

Pollard's forty-five-year jail sentence outraged the American Jewish community, which continues to advocate his release. Pollard, they argue, had simply passed on intelligence data that should have been shared with Israel in the first place. The "old spies" say there is a little truth in that, but not much. CIA director Bill Casey had indeed refused to give to Israel satellite photos that they desperately needed of Lebanon to counter Palestinian and Moslem terrorists who launched attacks across the border.[1] The United States also had withheld data on German sales of chemical warfare equipment to Libya and Iraq.[2]

But, our sources insist, the Mossad had more and better sources of their own. They simply did not need Pollard.[3] For example, the deadly Israeli raid on the Osirak reactor was not accomplished with the aid of satellite photos stolen by Pollard. "For chrissakes, photos show only the outside of the reactor shell: The Israelis had the goddamn blueprints and knew exactly where the construction was most vulnerable to air attack."[4]

As for the German chemical warfare sales, the Mossad had its own agents inside West German intelligence who provided far more details than Pollard obtained from NSA wiretaps.[5] Our sources believe that Pollard is still sitting in jail because the Mossad does not want him released and that he will stay there until the Mossad changes its mind. "Pollard screwed up their relationships with American intelligence and they hate him. The last thing the Mossad wants is for Pollard to be paroled, immigrate to Israel, and write a book exposing even more American secrets."[6]

The former intelligence officers we interviewed for this chapter agree that Pollard never worked for the Mossad, which would have fired him in a minute. Pollard was a loose cannon, an adrenaline addict, who stole whatever documents he could get his hands on, blabbed to everyone that he was an Israeli spy, and then whined that Israel would not protect him when he got caught. The truth is that Pollard was an amateur spy operation run by a group of right-wing Israeli politicians. They kept Pollard far way from the professionals of the Mossad. The whole operation was politically self-serving and poorly supervised. Rather than obtaining ongoing benefits from Pollard's hundreds of pages of documents, Israel got nothing but grief from the Pollard affair.[7]

Far from being the superspy that "Cap" Weinberger portrayed him to be, Pollard was a low-level incompetent with an exaggerated opinion of his own worth. CIA officer Ricky Ames may have exaggerated Pollard's leaks in order to conceal his own work for the Russians. As a practical matter, Pollard had little access either to communications intercept or satellite data, let alone secret NSA codes. According to the security officers familiar with the Pollard case, his primary access was to U.S. Navy data banks on ocean shipping. His private focus was on arms shipments to terrorists, which was fairly routine material.[8]

That, say the "old spies," is where the ugly truth lies. To this day, Pollard does not know how sensitive his "routine" shipping surveillance really was. In the spring and summer of 1984, Pollard noticed a pattern of vessels going back and forth from Greece to Yemen, where the PLO had a major base. Pollard passed the tip to the Israelis, who checked it out with their Interpol and West German sources. In the summer of 1984 the Israelis tipped off the Greek authorities to seize an entire shipload of arms destined for the PLO.

Neither Pollard nor the government of Israel was aware that they had smashed George Bush's first shipment of arms to Iran. The British secret service had arranged the Greek shipment to ransom American hostages in Lebanon. Pollard never realized that he had busted the most secret White House operation of modern times. The summer 1984 Greek shipment was a dagger over George Bush's head.

To this day, Congress believes that the Israelis started the Iranian arms-for-hostage deals in 1985. The problem with that is that Bush's shipment through Greece took place an entire year earlier. The Greek shipment in 1984 exposes the entire White House cover-up. Just recently have the Israelis begun to work out that they were dragged into Iran-Contra as scapegoats for a bungled Bush-British smuggling operation.

Our intelligence sources say that none of the parties to the deal—the Americans, the British, or the Israelis—could have had any idea at the time that the hostage deals were destined for unmitigated disaster. There was no great conspiracy, only a series of stupid mistakes. When it came to hostages, everything that could go wrong went wrong, and in the most spectacular way. The only thing that worked halfway well was the cover-up to shift all the blame to the Jews.

In this chapter we examine the following allegations in detail.

- The failure of President Carter's hostage rescue in 1980 was due to military ineptitude and not to some political cabal's "October Surprise" to prevent Carter from releasing the hostages in an election year.
- The Israelis encouraged Vice President George Bush to develop an aggressive counterterrorist program. He did so, but with the British as his ally, not the Jews. From 1982 onward, the Office of the Vice President ran a secret counterterrorist center without the knowledge of the CIA or Congress.
- In 1983 Bush and Casey assigned Bill Buckley and Leslie Aspin to a stupid and utterly illegal program to kidnap terrorists in Lebanon. Instead, Buckley himself was kidnapped by the terrorists in March 1984 and held as a hostage.
- The British, Bush, and Casey believed that Buckley's ransom could be obtained with the help of Buckley's associates who turned out to be Aspin and Monzer Al-Kassar. These two put together the Greek shipment of arms in the summer of 1984.
- From 1984 onward, Vice President Bush's staff worked desperately with the British to ransom Buckley and then brought in the Israelis in 1985 as unwitting "fall guys" for the Iran-Contra debacle.
- None of the parties realized at the time that their secret hostage mediator, Monzer Al-Kassar, was really working for the kidnappers, Syrian intelligence and the Soviets. Al-Kassar used his Western intelligence connections to build a drug and arms empire that was untouchable, while he continued his own war against the Jews.

There is an old saying that most of the evil in the world is done by good men, with the best of intentions. A case in point is George Bush. Most of the former intelligence officers we interviewed voted for Bush, only to discover that he did not have a clue about what he was doing.[9]

Not that everything Bush did was bad. In fact, he got blamed for a lot of things for which he was not responsible. One of the best examples was the first hostage negotiation effort during the last months of the Carter administration in the fall of 1980, the so-called October Surprise. Conspiracy buffs, and con men such as Richard Brenneke, have played a game of connect-the-dots to implicate vice presidential candidate, George Bush, in a plot to betray the hostages for political gain.

The truth, according to our sources in the intelligence community, is that there was no conspiracy, just a lot of stupidity in both the hostage negotiations and the rescue effort. The Joint Chiefs of Staff squabbled over pieces of the hostage rescue, so they could bask in the glory. Unfortunately, they did not have the slightest idea how to proceed, so they called in a consultant.[10] They picked Miles Copeland, the wrong man.

As already seen in previous chapters, Copeland had years of experience in the Middle East as he shuttled between his two masters, the oil companies and Allen Dulles's CIA. He was more of an expert on bribing Arabs than on hostage rescue. Therefore Copeland consulted the disgraced James Jesus Angleton, who introduced him to "a Mossad chap who confided that his service had identified at least half the 'students,' even to the extent of having their home addresses in Teheran . . . It was convincingly implicit in his remarks that, among those who managed to get out of the compound every now and then, Mossad had at least one agent and probably a lot more."[11]

Copeland thought he had the right answer. His plan was simple: Bribe a few of the Iranian students who were holding the Americans and smuggle the hostages out of the U.S. embassy. According to our sources, many of the "students" actually were KGB-trained Palestinians, so the bribe plan would not have worked, even in the unlikely event that Angleton's Israeli friend had numerous agents among them. The Joint Chiefs rejected Copeland's bribe plan out of hand. Their policy: "Millions for the defense budget, but not one cent for ransom."[12]

Somewhat miffed that the Pentagon had rejected his advice, Copeland convinced himself that no one in his right mind would authorize the kind of military rescue operation that the Joint Chiefs had talked to him about. Not realizing the damage he was doing, Copeland published many of the top-secret details of President Carter's hostage rescue plan in a Washington newspaper, several days before the actual assault.[13] The Iranians redoubled security. Not that Copeland's spiteful leak mattered. The Joint Chiefs had so thoroughly bungled the planning that not a single helicopter even reached the embassy. In the scramble for each service to get a piece of the glory, they used navy helicopters, which lacked sand screens. The desert crash of two American helicopters into a transport plane in April 1980 was as spectacular as it was avoidable.[14]

The "old spies" insist that it was the Iranians' own idea to release the hostages during the inauguration ceremony in January 1981, so that neither the old president nor the new one could claim credit. Far from being in league with the Iranians against the hostages, George Bush was trying to learn from the Israelis how to fight terrorism and put an end to the kidnapping.[15]

In 1979 Bush had attended the Jonathan Institute, an Israeli think tank on counterterrorism sponsored by the right-wing Likud politician Benjamin Netanyahu. Benjamin's brother, Jonathan, had died during the Israeli rescue raid at Entebbe in 1976. Bush, who had been CIA director at the time, was intrigued at the success of the Israeli commando raid. A large number of hostages were rescued at the cost of very few lives.[16]

Hostage rescues were one thing, but some Israelis favored preemptive strikes. The program of the Jonathan Institute was simple: Don't fight fire with fire, put the fire out while it's still small; hit the terrorists, hit them hard, and hit them first if possible. Massive retaliation against terrorist organizations has long been a major policy of the Israeli government. Some of the more right-wing Israelis thought that retaliation was not enough. They favored the Soviet model for dealing with hostage situations. When a few Soviet "diplomats" were kidnapped in the Middle East, the KGB kidnapped the family members of the kidnappers and mailed pieces of their bodies back to the terrorists until the Soviet hostages were released.[17]

Counterkidnapping worked. An even more extreme minority favored hitting the terrorists before they could kidnap anyone. The euphemism was "preventive action." However, most of the panelists at the Jonathan Institute favored the more moderate approach. Israel, the United States, and Britain should pool their intelligence resources and wage a common fight against a common foe. What the Israelis did not know was that Bush already had such an arrangement with British intelligence, but Jews were not allowed to participate.[18] They might not go along with the British plan to preserve Monzer Al-Kassar's cover by continuing terrorist acts against Jewish targets, while sparing British subjects. As the Interpol records show, Al-Kassar was behind a wide variety of terrorist operations, from assassinations in Spain to the hijacking of the *Achille Lauro* cruise ship.[19]

In the latter instance, a wheelchair-bound American Jew was murdered and thrown overboard. It was Al-Kassar who smuggled the murderers to safety. Killing Jews was a good cover for his work as an informant for British intelligence. After all, he was a vital cog in the bank interception program, the man who convinced the terrorists to keep their money in the BCCI.[20] Every time an Arab sheik deposited bribe money to the PLO, the British traced the distribution of funds through Al-Kassar to every terrorist sect in the Middle East. As long as Al-Kassar was useful, there was no question of allowing the Israelis to join the "Intel Cooperation" group behind the BCCI.

The Arabs who were the Middle Eastern principals of the BCCI would never allow Israel in either. They may have been sick of paying bribes to the PLO, but they didn't want to be involved with the Jews. For example, Sheik Zayed of the United Arab Emirates was violently anti-Israel. In fact, he was the first to declare an oil embargo against the United States for helping Israel in the 1973 war. It was a principal policy of the BCCI that whenever its banking practices were questioned, such inquiries were rebutted as Zionist racism against Arabs.

Bush himself, while sympathetic to the Israelis, had no intention of admitting them to the BCCI-intelligence club. Not even President Carter was allowed to join.[21]

Our sources say that the oil men wanted to ensure that Carter would be a one-term president.[22] As discussed in Chapter 15, the oil companies had a great deal of help in their anti-Carter campaign from their agents inside the U.S. intelligence community.

There were other games as well. As Carter prepared for his debate with Ronald Reagan, a copy of his briefing book ended up in Republican Campaign Headquarters. Although Carter did not explicitly mention the briefing book, in a 1991 interview he accused Don Gregg, one of the former CIA officers assigned to Carter's National Security Council, of betraying him by leaking information to the Republicans. Immediately after the election, Vice President Bush appointed Gregg as his National Security Adviser, making Gregg the only member of the Carter White House to stay on under Reagan.[23]

The leaking of Carter's information was not the only time that Bush received election help from disgruntled ex-CIA types. During Bush's 1988 presidential campaign, Miles Copeland wrote a letter to selected friends to organize an informal spooks-for-Bush team. Many Dulles-era members of the intelligence community who found their niche in the Reagan-Bush administrations continued their vehemently anti-Israeli stance. Copeland's campaign letter is, unfortunately, illustrative of their bias:

> The difficulty, however, is that we have "Israel around our necks," as one of our own senior diplomats said in a recent speech . . . in London . . .
>
> In the Middle East . . . our association with Israel so diminishes our "power to insist" that we must consider ourselves lucky [to achieve the minimum from the Arab states]. . . .
>
> George Bush has acknowledged an awareness that those who have given President Reagan his ideas on the Soviets are persons on the right who simply *assume* a "scenario" in which Israel can remain "our most valuable ally in the Middle East" . . . and who cry "anti-semite" at anyone who dares suggest that Israel may be more of a liability than an asset. . . .[24]

What Copeland was proposing was a Middle Eastern network of businessmen to conduct covert operations outside the CIA. It was to be a 1980s version of the "revolving door." To put it bluntly, Copeland was promising that Bush would do exactly what Dulles had done in the Middle East during his decade as CIA director: publicly praise Israel, while secretly working with the Arabs against the Jews:

> George Bush knows very well . . . that if he's going to get elected he'd better not do battle with pro-Israel forces in the U.S., and that his job, as President, will require some means of walking the line between ostensible sympathy for Israel and realistic understanding of what difficulties such sympathy makes for the few friends we've got left in the Arab world. I've been assured by old CIA types who have been close to him that unique among Presidential aspirants, he not only appreciates the problem but realizes that we can circumvent it only by the kind of covert operations that we propose.[25]

As we shall see, Copeland's manifesto was a virtual blueprint for the secret intelligence organization that Vice President Bush and CIA director Bill Casey had begun to construct in the earliest days of the Reagan administration. It all came home to roost in the scandal surrounding the secret initiative to trade arms to Iran for the hostages held by the Ayatolloh's friends, the Lebanese Hezbollah.

One of the first things President Reagan did in 1981 was to dismantle Carter's National Security Council structure and install his own highly compartmentalized staff organization. The NSC was relegated to a harmless study group, while policy was made in a bewildering maze of separate and secret cells. One top-secret National Security Decision Directive, NSDD #3, established a new intelligence organization for Vice President George Bush. The former CIA director now had become the head of his own separate spy agency in the White House:

> . . . the Special Situation Group (SSG) chaired by the Vice President . . . is charged, inter alia, with formulating plans in anticipation of crises. . . . In order to facilitate this crisis pre-planning responsibility, a Standing Crisis Pre-Planning Group (CPPG) is hereby established . . . and will: . . . For each potential crisis, insure that an interagency group is established and developing contingency plans. Provide guidance to the group and task it with the preparation of *preemptive* policy options to prevent a crisis if possible as well as the preparation of politico-military options for dealing with the eventual crisis. [Emphasis added.][26]

It is clear from this top-secret document that Bush asked for, and received, authorization to prepare "preemptive policy options." If this sounds strikingly familiar to the "preventive action" program of the Jonathan Institute, it is no coincidence. Bush intended to strike the first blow in the war on terrorism, having learned such strategies from the Israelis. In short, George Bush's job was to coordinate the State Department, CIA, military, and any other government agency in preparation for another terrorist attack or hostage crisis. No one but Bush was responsible for the disasters to come.[27]

Of course, as plans for dealing with the terrorists grew more ambitious, Bush's Special Situation Group needed a bigger staff. Bush's aide Don Gregg just could not do it all on his own. On May 14, 1982, the White House made another top-secret reorganization. A memo was sent to the secretaries of state, treasury, defense, the director of the CIA, and the chairman of the Joint Chiefs of Staff. They were told that under Vice President Bush's SSG, there would be created a "Crisis Pre-Planning Group" to handle the staff functions. The memo also announced that: "The first meeting of the CPPG is scheduled for Thursday, May 20, 1982, in the White House Situation Room from 1000–1200. Agencies are requested to provide the name of their CPPG representative to Oliver North, NSC staff (Telephone: 395-3345)."[28]

During a television interview, Oliver North insisted that he had always worked for the NSC and denied having kept Vice President Bush briefed on his work.[29] This was a lie. As the memo just cited shows, at least as early as May 14, 1982, North was already detailed from the NSC to work for Bush's CPPG. As a practical matter, the CPPG's staff work was done by an informal subgroup called the 208 Committee.[30]

Reagan had created a secret cell inside the White House, separate from the normal command structure. Reagan was a nice old guy who read his scripts well. When it came to intelligence operations, he trusted Casey and Bush to tell him what to do. They were, after all, both heads of the CIA. If Bush wanted a new spy service, he got it.

That did not go over well with the secretary of state, George Shultz, who wrote a memo in protest on May 25, 1983, complaining that the structure of the vice president's private intelligence organization was hampering the coordination of U.S. efforts in Central America. Reagan wrote a polite memo back to Shultz informing him that Bush's SSG/CPPG structure would stay the way it was and that Shultz should help make it work. An attached chart showed that Shultz's State Department was below the NSC, which was below the president. To the left of the NSC and above Shultz was Bush's SSG/CPPG apparatus. When it came to terrorism or the Contras, Bush's Special Situations Group had the final say.[31]

To put it bluntly, Bush was running a White House within the White House. Its members could co-opt, or circumvent, any government agency they wished. There would be no leaks, but, unfortunately, no independent criticism of their plans either. The vice president's SSG was the perfect hiding place for some of the bizarre operations dreamed up by Bush, Casey, Robert "Bud" McFarlane, Dewey Clarridge, and North. Our intelligence sources say that these five men are the "morons" who bungled their way into the Iran-Contra affair and then tried to shift the blame to the National Security Council, or to Israel, even to "Ollie" North—anywhere but back to the Office of the Vice President.[32]

It began in 1982, when Don Gregg drafted a proposed directive that was a virtual model of planning for the Contra scandal. Congress never saw this draft during the hearings, but in it Gregg laid out his scheme for third-country coordination and fund-raising.[33]

Bush knew from his Angolan experience that you do not circulate that kind of memo for approval. Not if you wanted to keep the operation secret. Gregg's draft was never circulated. Not even North knew that in 1982 Bush, McFarlane, and Gregg were already planning to use the British to go behind Congress's back. The vice president's private back-channel to MI6 was the best-kept secret in government.[34]

On June 15, 1982, two British businessmen incorporated a company called CSF Investments Limited in Bermuda. It was a very interesting company, with global ties. Its funds were deposited in the Republic Bank in New York, which had very close ties to Saudi Arabia. All the stock of CSF Bermuda was owned by CSF S.A., based in Geneva.[35] CSF Geneva later established the front companies for Albert Hakim, the banker for Oliver North. To show how this intricate web worked, it should be recalled that CSF Bermuda also was used to buy aircraft for the Contras.[36]

Leslie Aspin had been working as an "adviser" (read arms supplier) to the Lebanese Christian militia, while smuggling South African arms to Iran on the side. In 1983 he received a transatlantic telephone call from Bill Casey, the head of the CIA. Casey had gotten Aspin's name from Bill Buckley, who had just returned with bad news from Lebanon.[37]

Despite all the power given to Bush's SSG, planning for counterterrorism in Lebanon had not stopped the terrorists. An American ambassador had been kidnapped and hundreds of U.S. Marines had been killed. Everything was going wrong. The SSG had sent in a special military unit to carry out plans for "retaliative action," but the Pentagon had gotten cold feet and pulled the unit out. Our sources say Buckley told Casey that what was needed for the crisis was a private mercenary unit, like the one he and Aspin had worked on in Angola and Saudi Arabia. Casey agreed, and Bush approved.[38]

The time had come for a little of Bush's "preemptive" action. Aspin and Buckley had several meetings in 1983. They discussed their options against the terrorists, "some of them legal, some of them illegal," as Aspin dryly recalled. What Buckley wanted was a special mercenary unit to "take hostages and rescue them."[39] To put it bluntly, Aspin and Buckley were supposed to recruit an indigenous Lebanese force to kidnap terrorists, or their relatives, and hold them hostage until the Hezbollah gave up. On the side, they would blow up the terrorists' homes and headquarters in Lebanon.[40]

According to Aspin's account, he was a little taken aback, and asked who had approved the scheme. Buckley explained that it was to be run outside the CIA, but claimed that it had the approval of Casey and Vice President Bush himself. Money for the counterterrorist operation would go through the usual British channels to Aspin's account at the BCCI. Everything was set at the White House.[41]

Well, not quite everything. There was a slight problem with the law. Carter's executive order prohibiting assassinations was still on the books, and so were a host of laws regulating covert operations. North had talked about the proposed kidnap strategy to Vince Cannistraro, a CIA liaison to the oft-ignored National Security Council. He thought North was crazy or kidding. So did everyone else North explained the scheme to. Americans just don't run around killing or kidnapping people. People were starting to express opposition to the idea.[42]

It became clear to the White House staff that the CPPG's proposed kidnap operation required written presidential approval. At the end of 1983 Bush's planning group decided to draft National Security Decision Directive #138 for Reagan's signature. North was put to work on it, but soon ran into a blizzard of objections from the CIA and the Pentagon. It looked like a long, drawn-out bureaucratic war had begun.[43]

Casey threw his hands up in the air and told Buckley to head back to Lebanon as the new CIA station chief. He and Aspin could start recruiting on the ground, while the paperwork was plodding through the "nervous nellies" at the White House. In fact, it would take until April 1984 before even a watered-down version of NSDD #138 was signed.[44]

In the meantime, Aspin and Buckley began to plan the kidnap strikes, while they waited for what Aspin called "Defensive Directive #138" to give them the green light.[45] It would be a long wait. At the beginning of 1984 CIA deputy director John McMahon read North's kidnap proposal and hit the ceiling. He called North in the middle of the night, reprimanding him for proposing that the president should permit the "neutralization" of terrorists or, in plain language, assassinations. Apparently Reagan never explicitly approved such a strategy.[46]

What the president did not know was that "neutralization" planning was already under way. Casey had sent Buckley to Lebanon at the end of 1983, and he was already recruiting kidnappers without the president's authorization in early 1984, even while the assassination debate was dragging on.

Let us be perfectly clear on this point. Our sources insist that Bush personally approved both the sending of Buckley to recruit a Lebanese kidnap team to "take hostages as well as rescue them" and the NSDD #138 draft containing the proposal to neutralize terrorists by forcibly taking them back to the United States. However, the documents prove only that the kidnap draft was to be sent to Vice President Bush's aide Don Gregg for Bush's review. There is no document that confirms that Bush in fact did see or approve it; there is no document that indicates that Bush ever objected. Our sources' contention that Bush in fact approved it is lent credence by the fact that it would be unusual for a document of this magnitude to have gotten as far as it did without Bush's approval.

After CIA Deputy McMahon's furious rejection, the Vice President's CPPG staff repeatedly circulated revised drafts of NSDD #138, but received continuing criticism from other agencies of the executive branch. Things weren't going well with the CPPG's other major operation either, the effort to support the Nicaraguan Contras in spite of congressional opposition. Most of the blame lies with the vice president's penchant for relying on the old-boy network. In 1983 Felix Rodriguez (a.k.a. Max Gomez), one of Don Gregg's old friends from the CIA, was hired for the Contra operations.[47] Gomez, who liked to talk, later boasted that he was in charge of Contra supply operations. He also happened to mention that his friend Vice President Bush was "the real Darth Vader" behind the operation.[48]

By the end of 1983 the seeds of the twin operations that later became known as Iran-Contra had been planted. Eventually it would result in the decision to make the Jews of Israel the "fall guys" for the whole mess. The real planners were the close-knit members of Bush's planning staff, the CPPG. For example, in 1983 another CPPG staffer, Dewey Clarridge of the CIA, traveled secretly to South Africa to solicit foreign aid for the Contras. It was later reported that Clarridge's trip was part of a "vest pocket" operation run by CIA director William Casey outside of all normal channels.[49] In fact, Clarridge also had been Bush's personal deputy when he was CIA director. The vice president's office became the perfect place for Casey to hide operations from his own subordinates in the CIA.

In fact, Bush's group had now become the only White House channel to plan for the Contras. After Clarridge's 1983 trip, three South African planes were leased to the Contras.[50] Because no one in Congress knew of Bush's secret shop for contingency planning, no one realized just how early the Iran-Contra affair began. Aspin recalled that he first heard about Rob Owen as the paymaster in 1983.[51] Virtually all of the early planning for both the Iran and Contra disasters came from Bush's CPPG and its subgroups.

Because of Gregg's workload, Bush asked if someone in the White

House could work on the Senior Interagency Group (SIG) for Contra planning. Casey preferred North, who had shown enthusiastic support for the kidnap team proposal. In December 1983 North started to keep an office diary for his new assignment, significant parts of which were later released under the Freedom of Information Act.

One of his first entries was a reminder to "Thank Casey for SIG pref [erence]." North quickly busied himself writing memos for the vice president. By the end of January 1984 North presented his revised National Security Decision Directive on terrorism to the staff. North personally called the CPPG members, including Gregg, to pick up the vice president's copy. The next week North wrote another paper for Bush on the Central American death squads.[52]

During 1983 and 1984 North was often Bush's escort officer in Central America. Whatever else they may have done, these two men deserve a great deal of credit for pressuring the governments of El Salvador and Guatemala to end the slaughter of civilians. The irony is that at the same time, North was working with the vice president's CPPG staff to set up their own secret unit in the Middle East to "neutralize" anti-American, pro-Iranian terrorists.

North's diary for early 1984 shows that Bush's CPPG was planning a "London Summit" for cooperation on world terrorism. The next week North had to rewrite his NSDD on terrorism again, and again, and again. By February 23 he was preparing a briefing book for Vice President Bush to review. The diary does not specify the topic of the briefing book.[53]

Even before the British came on board with the antiterrorist hit squads, there were problems at home. Judge Webster of the FBI was upset about the kidnap directive and wanted to see the president. Then North had to explain the terrorism strategy to Attorney General Edwin Meese III, then respond to more queries from the Justice Department. Finally North was getting questions from Bob Brown of the Pentagon's Special Operations Force. It looked as if skeptics in Washington would slowly bleed the terrorism project to death.[54]

Meanwhile, back in Lebanon, word of Buckley's recruiting for a kidnap team was getting around. Unfortunately, it reached the wrong ears. Before Buckley could kidnap anybody, he was himself kidnapped in Beirut on March 16, 1984. North was told that the "CPPG principals" (Casey, Bush, and McFarlane) wanted an immediate meeting.[55] North was not allowed to attend. Far from being the central player in the reaction to the kidnapping of the CIA station chief, he just did not know what was going on. At this point, "Ollie" was still a low-level errand boy for the vice president's staff.

For Bush, the Buckley kidnapping was a disaster. If Buckley talked, he could reveal the entire kidnap scheme that Casey (and allegedly Bush) had authorized without even telling Ronald Reagan. He may have been sleepy, but he was still the president. At this time, NSDD #138 was not even ready for Reagan's signature, and it would not be for several more weeks. The CIA and the rest of the White House had to be kept in the dark. North was told to borrow $1 million from the businessman Ross Perot to ransom Buckley. Perot came up with the money, but the ransom offer eventually was rejected.[56]

While Casey, Bush, and the British were pondering their next move on the Buckley kidnapping, North went back to organizing support for the Contras and passing memos to Don Gregg. The topics of the memos are not revealed in the diary. North also noted that on the Contra front, the vice president was going to talk to Congressman Edward Boland, the author of the first of several pieces of legislation that had cut off funding for the Nicaraguan rebels. But calls started coming wanting to know what the plan was to rescue the hostages held by the Hezbollah in Lebanon.[57]

The problem was that without Buckley, there wasn't a plan. The next meeting of the Terrorist Incident Working Group was still bogged down in arguments about the paperwork. It seems that before a rescue group could be sent to Lebanon, it was necessary for the president to delegate his authority to Ambassador Bartholomew, Washington's man in Beirut.[58] But Bartholomew didn't have a clue what to do with a rescue team. After all, his CIA chief of station had been kidnapped and wasn't around to advise him.

So Bartholomew delegated his authority back to Oliver North. To cover Bartholomew, the State Department reported that "North was handling an operation that would lead to the rescue of all seven hostages" and that an American team had been sent to Beirut for the task.[59] In fact, North's diary shows that he wasn't doing much about the hostage team at all. That appears to have been delegated back to the CPPG, where Bush and Casey were wringing their hands and calling the British for help.[60] North's next diary entry for the Buckley rescue operation is censored to protect a foreign government, almost certainly Britain, because of a sensitive intelligence liaison relationship.[61]

While his superiors busied themselves with the British, North plowed along trying to get approval for some sort of National Security Decision Directive on terrorism. At the next meeting of the Terrorist Incident Working Group on March 29, there was a discussion about a newspaper report linking Buckley with the CIA. While the "group agreed that there is no utility in pressing French" and while apparently the British had not come up with anything, they were the only hope. There really was nothing to report to the president, so the staff agreed to "remove Buckley issue from [the National Security Planning Group] agenda." North went back to trying to convince the CIA to support new and more powerful antiterrorist legislation.[62]

North did not know that Casey had gone to London to make arrangements with the British for joint operations against terrorists, while the Saudi, Omani, and Kuwaiti intelligence services were sounded out separately. On April 19, 1984, the White House briefed the local British intelligence liaison, Derek Thomas, on the Arab reaction to a new antiterrorist strike team to take strong action in the Middle East, especially in Lebanon. North was called in to take notes while "J" briefed the British intelligence officer.[63] "J" may have been either John Poindexter or another White House aide, John Negroponte.

"J" explained to Thomas, the British representative, that the Kuwaitis were a little skeptical when shown the pro forma of the antiterrorist plan, which apparently called for direct strikes, similar to the original concept of NSDD #138. While the Kuwaitis were cool, the Saudis and Omanis agreed "that we had to." The British officer asked specifically what their feeling was about taking a tough stand against the Lebanese-based terrorist groups and was told that the Omanis were most supportive.[64]

Then the conversation switched to Libya. Thomas explained that someone inside Libya's embassy in London had just shot a policewoman, but the British government was trying to avoid provoking Gadhafi by arresting his diplomats for murder. The American pointed out that most of the occupants of the embassy did not even have diplomatic status.[65] It was an embarrassing moment for Thomas. The British government had decided to cave into the terrorists once again.

The British, who already had ransomed hostages in Iran, now were sending arms to Libya to bribe Gadhafi, despite the American call for a worldwide trade embargo. The British officer said: "We have sometimes not been helpful to your sanctions." The American said: "We know."[66] The British agent defended the arms shipments by pointing out that threatening Gadhafi would do no good. He was irrational and had threatened to take fifteen U.S. and British hostages in Libya for every Libyan arrested in London.[67] In the end, all the Libyan terrorists were allowed to go free, even the ones without diplomatic immunity.

It was an uncomfortable topic, and Derek Thomas suggested they move on to a general discussion of strategy to deal with terrorism. Following briefings about the NSDD #138 proposal, now there was "less nervousness in London" about the American program to neutralize terrorists. Thomas was instructed to say that, while the British government shared the objective of better methods, it was concerned about the "preemption options." These "could be counterproductive."[68]

Without mentioning kidnapping or assassination directly, Thomas pointed out that the White House's "preemptive options" violated several international conventions. Moreover, there was a "risk of contagion of terrorism," an "escalating spiral" of counterkidnapping that would "exonerate" the Iranians. If the Americans went ahead on their own, there was a danger of "strains developing" in the alliance with British intelligence. Apparently, this was a pointed reference to Buckley working with British mercenaries like Aspin without first clearing it with British intelligence.[69]

"We do want to work with you," Thomas assured the Americans, "but we want to discuss options with you before you act . . . to consult *before* a final decision is made."[70] Bud McFarlane had already agreed to consultations, and in any event, the Americans had not made the final plans on what to do in Lebanon. Now that Buckley was kidnapped, they had no plans at all.

The British agent pointed out that Geoffrey Howe, one of Prime Minister Margaret Thatcher's senior ministers, would be in Washington on May 29, for a meeting with Secretary of State George Shultz. Perhaps it would be a good time for the stepped-up intelligence exchange called for in NSDD #138. Thomas said that "We would like to have a team come (three or four people) and talk about a week before" Howe's visit.[71]

It is surprising that North took such copious notes on this early meeting with a senior British intelligence official. Even more surprising is that they passed the censors when North's diary was declassified. The truth is that no one outside the members of Bush's special group knew that British intelligence had agreed to work with the CPPG on hostage issues. While the CIA and the Pentagon each accused the other of doing nothing to rescue Buckley, arrangements were being made in the vice president's office to have the British secret service run the Buckley rescue show.

After Thomas's intelligence team came to Washington, North was briefed by Dewey Clarridge on April 27 and told that a decision had been made about the hostages. North was the last to know. Actually, the British made their decision in mid-March, soon after Buckley was kidnapped. The British, as was their wont, decided to try to ransom the hostages by offering arms to Iran.

Aspin was the perfect choice to coordinate the ransom deal. As mentioned earlier, in 1981 his company, Delta, had brokered the release of British hostages by selling American arms to the Iranians. In 1984 he would be glad to do the same for the Americans, especially as it might get his old friend Buckley released. Aspin had experience with American intelligence, so he was not an unknown quantity, especially to Casey and Bush.[72]

Several of our sources in the intelligence community say that Aspin had a special British connection as well. He had at one point hired Mark Thatcher, the prime minister's son, as one of his agents for his arms deals.[73] There have been rumors about Mark Thatcher for years. As a British resident of Texas, his name came up in several supposed arms transfers. Texas is also the site of the CIA warehouse for foreign firearms, and both Britain and the United States had been supplying foreign-made arms to the Afghan resistance since 1979.

According to our sources, Aspin paid Thatcher through an American cement company, which was a front for the CIA.[74] Although Leslie's brother, Michael, is not considered a reliable source because of his fraud conviction, he insists that he saw one such check from something called "Cementation" made out to Mark Thatcher.[75] By way of corroboration, Leslie Aspin's private files contain correspondence with a company called Cement International, including advances of several thousand dollars to himself against his 20 percent commission on sales.[76]

Since Aspin was an arms dealer, there may be a grain of truth to the story, especially since he had Mark Thatcher's business number in his private phone book.[77] The son of a prime minister would be just the sort of helpful person to expedite the red tape that surrounds every legitimate arms transaction. There was, after all, nothing illegal in helping the freedom fighters in Afghanistan.

The Mark Thatcher connection also may explain how Aspin, a small-time arms dealer, obtained access to 10 Downing Street. Before he died, Aspin said that Ian Gow, Margaret Thatcher's personal secretary, was his point of contact for the Iranian ransom negotiations. Although the Thatcher administration vehemently denied all these accusations, the unlisted telephone numbers for Gow, who is now dead, and several other prominent members of the British hostage negotiators, such as Terry Waite, were later discovered in Aspin's phone book.[78]

Moreover, as shall be seen, Margaret Thatcher and her senior officials were in constant contact, by cable and in person, with the secret White House hostage team.[79] The evidence is overwhelming that they facilitated Aspin's attempts to ransom Buckley, beginning in March 1984, only a week after the CIA man's capture. Long before the London Summit, scheduled for June, Aspin put together the first British effort to trade American weapons for the hostages held by Iran's agents in Lebanon.[80]

Here is how it began. Aspin knew that his old friend Monzer Al-Kassar had extensive ties with Syrian intelligence, which as a practical matter exercised de facto control over all the terrorist groups in Lebanon, including the *Hezbollah*. Al-Kassar was glad to hear from Aspin again, as the Al-Kassar family was about to move from small-time drug smugglers to big-time gunrunners.[81]

Aspin knew that the Iranians were desperate for American ammunition. Their war with Iraq was dragging on, and while the Iranian army was entirely equipped with U.S. weapons supplied to the shah, Iran was under a strict American trade embargo. They had U.S. Army howitzers but could not buy any more U.S. shells, while the Iraqis were being deluged with supplies from the Soviets.

Aspin proposed a trial run. He would ship American cannon ammunition in return for Al-Kassar contacting the kidnappers and obtaining proof that Buckley was still alive. In the spring of 1984 Al-Kassar called a conference in Hungary attended by the leaders of every Arab terrorist faction in the Middle East. In no time at all, he identified one particular faction of the Lebanese Hezbollah as the ones who held Buckley. It took a few more months, but his relatives in the Syrian secret services convinced the Lebanese to give Al-Kassar a videotape of Buckley in captivity.[82]

The Hezbollah might be loyal to Iran, but as a practical matter, Syria was an ally and, more important, controlled the lucrative Bekaa Valley drug trade necessary for the Hezbollah's financial survival. Besides, Al-Kassar was going to help the Hezbollah's friends in Iran to obtain badly needed ammunition.

The Kuwaitis were the reason the hostages were taken in the first place. They had recently arrested and imprisoned a group of Lebanese terrorists known as the "Dawa." This gang included several members of the clan that had kidnapped Buckley and the other Western hostages held in Lebanon. The clan hoped that the Americans would force the Kuwaitis to trade prisoners. The Hezbollah were glad to have Al-Kassar act as a mediator. After all, the Syrians were only asking them to make a videotape, not give up the hostages.

In the meantime, Aspin kept his end of the bargain. According to an invoice in his secret files, he placed a $40 million order in March 1984 with Hirtenberger, an Austrian arms firm, for American cannon shells. The size of the order was staggering: "140,000 rounds, Howitzer Ammunition M 107, filled with TNT, complete with Fuze PDM 557, percussion primer M 82 and charge MMA2," at $285 per shell.[83]

Still, the Iranians would be happy to pay the $40 million. They were awash in oil, which they were selling covertly to Israel and South Africa, their only remaining sources of supply for Western goods. It should be noted, however, that the Israeli shipments were quite small, consisting of nonessential military supplies such as truck tires and spare parts. Moreover, from 1979 to 1982 each Israeli shipment to Iran had been cleared with both the Carter and Reagan administrations. When the Reagan administration asked the Israelis to close down the channel in 1983, they quickly complied.[84]

As a result of the tightening of the American embargo, the Iranians had millions of dollars piled up in an Israeli bank and nowhere to spend them. Aspin's howitzer deal was a godsend, and they readily opened a letter of credit for his arms deal in Switzerland. Unfortunately, the Iranians were a bit lazy and used an Israeli bank to confirm payment for the order.[85] At this point in 1984, the Israelis received their tip from Jonathan Pollard about PLO arms shipments to Yemen. No one had told the Israelis that the Americans were smuggling arms to Iran. The Mossad thought it was helping the U.S. trade embargo by tracking the shipment. The West Germans and Interpol were doing the same thing, for the same reason.

Al-Kassar, oblivious to the surveillance net around him, was happy that he and Aspin were working for the Americans again. It was just like the old times in Angola. Two days after Aspin placed the order with Hirtenberger, Al-Kassar and his brothers, Ghassan and Haitham, applied for American visas to the U.S. embassy in Vienna. The Vienna office of the U.S. Drug Enforcement Administration (DEA) promptly telexed the State Department in Washington warning that the brothers were notorious arms smugglers and major drug traffickers.[86]

Like the Israelis, the DEA didn't know about Monzer Al-Kassar's role in the Buckley ransom, but the CIA knew why he was coming to the United States. According to Interpol records, the CIA had discovered in March 1984 that he had ordered a jet from Gates Learjet Corporation at a cost of $1.8 million.[87] Despite explicit warnings from the DEA in Vienna to the State Department that the aircraft would be used for drug smuggling, Al-Kassar got his jet. Someone in the White House must have pulled a lot of strings. And that was only the beginning.[88]

There were a few problems getting Al-Kassar a visa to the London Summit on terrorism—he had some outstanding drug warrants and had been banned from England. But the Syrian connection was necessary to the Buckley deal. On May 21, 1984, a few weeks before the June conference, the U.S. embassy in Damascus, Syria, sent a cryptic telegram to its European counterparts. The cable was a broad hint to leave the Al-Kassars alone: The Americans were vouching for them as accredited diplomats. People in the European intelligence community began to "talk of the USA connection of the Al-Kassars."[89] For a family of narco-terrorists, it had a lot of political clout. This made many European police very angry, and they decided to increase the watch on Monzer Al-Kassar.

When Al-Kassar traveled from Vienna to Germany in April, the West German Domestic Intelligence Service, the BKA, had already bugged his hotel room, and learned that a major arms deal was in the works.[90] What Aspin did not know was that Al-Kassar was going to "piggyback" a major PLO arms deal on top of Aspin's shipment to Iran. Aspin had made arrangements to truck the cannon shells to Greece, where he had obtained a phony "end user certificate" from the Greek government.[91]

Aspin later admitted that his partner in crime was a Greek national who had worked with him back in the Libyan smuggling network in the 1970s and who went on to assist him in many of the Iranian deals in the 1980s.[92] Unfortunately, Leslie's friend did not have quite as much pull in the Greek government as he thought he did.

The whole thing might have gone off except for the German wiretaps on Al-Kassar, which had been shared with the Israelis. At the same time, Pollard passed his tip about the unusual shipping patterns. Although they did not know Pollard was the source, the Mossad confirmed that the weapons were not staying in Greece after all, but were being loaded aboard a ship bound for South Yemen, where PLO terrorists were attempting to rearm themselves after being driven out of Lebanon.[93] The Mossad tipped off the Greek customs officials that there was a shipment of illegal weapons being loaded aboard a freighter. On the night of May 2, 1984, the Greek customs officers raided Al-Kassar's ship and found not just the few CZ pistols that Aspin admitted later, but twenty-seven tons of weapons.[94]

Instead of the 140,000 cannon shells that Aspin had ordered, the Greeks found "1.99 million rounds of ammunition produced in Austria by the firm of Hirtenberger. . . . Only much later was it learned that a close, very personal relationship existed between this firm and Monzer Al-Kassar."[95] Al-Kassar had added a few things to the shipment, hoping to slip his PLO arms out of Greece along with Aspin's arms to Iran. There was enough weaponry to equip a small army. As it happened, no one went to jail for the shipment through Greece, and our sources say that most of the arms eventually got to Iran.[96]

In order to get the arms-for-hostage deal moving again, Aspin contacted a licensed British arms dealer, Ben Bannerjee, a Pakistani resident who also handled most of Al-Kassar's arms transactions through the BCCI. In order to test Bannerjee's abilities, Aspin ordered a "trial run" and had the arms dealer deliver forty Czech pistols from Vienna to Iran.[97] These pistols were a "hot" item, as they were copies of a Western model made in Czechoslovakia without serial numbers. A quantity of the same type of Czech pistols had been seized in the Greek fiasco.[98]

Al-Kassar's friends behind the Iron Curtain could copy any Western small arm, produce it cheaply, and eliminate bothersome serial numbers needed to trace weapons. Al-Kassar was a useful man to have around. So was Bannerjee. He had enough friends at the BCCI and enough knowledge of export laws to make any shipment look like a legal transaction. Even the experienced Aspin learned some new loopholes in international gunrunning.[99]

Apparently, the bottom line was that it was illegal for the British government to bribe the Iranians with British weapons, but not with American arms. While Aspin was learning how to play in the big league, Oliver North was working with Ed Meese of the Justice Department to straighten out the legal end of the hostage rescue project.[100] The British Parliament may have been lenient about arms exports, but the U.S. Congress was not.

North had his own tutor. On May 10, 1984, North met with Andrew Green, another British intelligence officer whose specialty was arms transfers and antiterrorist operations. Later Green surfaced as an "antiterrorist expert" on Northern Ireland. We do not know what he proposed to North on May 10, but the next day Green had some second thoughts about the new British-American partnership and called him back. North's secretary, Fawn Hall, took the message:

> Ollie,
> Andrew Green (Brit you met with yesterday) called 745-4239. He said, "Of course, we certainly intend that the meeting be confidential, but just in case it should leak, the kind of defensive line we should take is as follows:
> " 'We have said in Parliament that we intend to consult our partners on measures to combat terrorism. We have already discussed this in the European community. We keep in regular touch with the U.S. as well.' "[101]

They certainly did. North's diary for May 15 is completely censored on the grounds that it concerns another meeting for hostage rescue and counterterrorist planning with a foreign intelligence service.[102]

Everybody in Washington except the State Department was getting ready for tough action against terrorists. North prepared a paper for Bush on the problems he was having. It appears from the intermittent diary entries that, contrary to popular belief, Gregg handled most of the terrorist strategy for Bush, while North only got the overflow. His office diary has occasional notes about "Air Commandos ready to move equipment" and the hijacking of an Air France Jet in Sudan. There are also entries about suppressing terrorists in the United States.[103]

It was the beginning of a warrantless surveillance program. As discussed in Chapter 8, the White House was about to launch a massive and widespread wiretapping operation against American citizens. It may only have been a coincidence that in 1982 President Reagan rescinded Carter's policies restricting electronic eavesdropping, at exactly the same time that Vice President Bush was establishing his secret espionage organization within the White House. The Americans who were subjected to the new campaign were not terrorists but members of the Jewish community, and the scope of the wiretaps would have made Forrestal and Angleton blush.

North had very little to do with that. His main preoccupation in early 1984 was with the Contras. In order to hide the fact that the U.S. government was buying Communist weapons, the Contras had been told by their CIA handlers to blame the Jews as their weapons suppliers.[104] On April 23 one Contra leader told reporters that "we received some weapons . . . the Israeli government took from Lebanon."[105] The Israelis vehemently denied the charges and sent a senior official to complain to Washington.

The Israelis were desperately afraid that Congress would blame them for circumventing the Boland Amendment, which had prohibited U.S. assistance to the Contras, and would retaliate by cutting Israel's foreign aid.[106] While in fact Israel had transferred some captured arms to the CIA, it stopped doing it as soon as the first Boland Amendment passed.[107]

According to published Israeli accounts, the head of Israel's Foreign Ministry, David Kimche, visited Robert McFarlane in Washington on April 17, 1984, a month after the Boland cutoff, and "rejected McFarlane's request that Israel, too, aid the Contras." McFarlane has confirmed the Israeli version and later testified before Congress that Israel was asked to supply both weapons and training to the Contras, but that Kimche turned him down.[108]

The Israeli cutoff of guns annoyed Casey greatly, and in April 1984 he tried to pressure Israel by leaking the story that the United States was trying to get Israel to take over the covert program of aid to the Nicaraguan Contras, in return for which Washington would increase defense and intelligence assistance to the Jews.[109] The Israelis did not take the bait. They knew that Congress determined Israeli aid, not Casey. Congress had said not to help the Contras. As long as Congress kept renewing the Boland Amendment, there would be no further transfers of Israeli weapons.[110]

Israel knew how the Washington game was played and leaked word of McFarlane's request to Secretary of State Shultz, who hit the roof on discovering that some low-level official on the White House staff was dealing with the Israeli government behind his back. Of course, McFarlane was not just any official. He was the National Security Council's sole representative on Bush's staff, serving as chairman of the vice president's Crisis Pre-Planning Group.

McFarlane was still smarting over Shultz's reprimand when Casey told him to forget the State Department and get the Israelis to obey by saying that when the Contras came to power, they would reverse the Sandinista's policy of support for the PLO. Further, Kimche was to be told in no uncertain terms that President Reagan would be greatly disappointed if Israel didn't cooperate. The Israeli answer was still "no."[111]

Israel's determination to reject all inducements and threats by the Bush team in the Reagan White House signaled a new phase in the secret espionage war against the Jews. According to our intelligence sources, the first step came when Casey told the Contras to blame the Israelis anyway.[112] And so, for the next several years, the Contras proudly admitted, even boasted, that the Israelis had captured the AK-47 rifles they were using from PLO terrorists.

The Israelis cringed every time they heard this and swore truthfully that they had not shipped a single rifle to the Nicaraguans. But according to the "old spies," Casey kept up the phony leaks to the media.[113] While the Israelis didn't have anywhere near enough "captured PLO weapons" to supply the entire Contra army, the blame-Israel fraud was a good cover to disguise the fact that the White House was actually buying weapons from Communist armaments manufacturers via Monzer Al-Kassar.

Our sources insist that the Contras needed "Communist" or "captured PLO" weapons mostly to conceal the fact that the White House was paying the bill. No one would ever suspect Ronald Reagan's staff of buying guns from the "Evil Empire." Yet that is exactly what was going on behind Congress's back.

On May 12, 1984, Oliver North met with General John Singlaub, the World Anti-Communist League (WACL) chief. Despite the fact that WACL was comprised partly of old World War II Fascists from Europe and Asia, Singlaub was then developing his own contacts through Taiwan and Korea with Chinese Communist arms dealers.[114] For a short time, Singlaub ran an Asian conduit to purchase Communist guns for the Contras.

At the same time, North also had an "arrangement" to buy Communist weapons from General Singlaub's rival, General Richard Secord, who dealt with the Soviet bloc arms dealers through his partner, Albert Hakim.[115] Hakim, as the congressional records confirm, was buying the Communist weapons from Monzer Al-Kassar.[116]

In other words, three separate U.S. networks were purchasing Communist weapons for Iran and the Nicaraguan rebels. All of them were run by Vice President Bush's planning staff inside the White House, and the Israelis plausibly could be blamed as the source for all these weapons. On the other side of the Cold War, Soviet Military Intelligence, the GRU, which coordinated all arms sales from the Eastern Bloc, must have thought that the White House was trying to solve the Soviet Union's foreign exchange problems by paying good American dollars to bolster an economy that was barely functioning.

Apparently, neither North nor the two dimwitted generals realized that the Communists were enjoying this bizarre game, which involved taking Contra dollars to pay for even better weapons for the Sandinistas.[117] When Al-Kassar told his Soviet controllers that the British secret service was paying him to smuggle weapons to the Iranians as well in an effort to save Buckley and the other American hostages, the Kremlin must have been very pleased. The Iranians did not control Buckley's fate; the Soviet GRU held a mortgage on him through its Syrian surrogates. The Syrians had a foreign arms debt of $13.5 billion, of which $8 billion was owed to the GRU's network of weapons factories.[118]

According to our intelligence community sources, the Syrians were working off their Soviet debt with drug sales to finance the GRU's support for "spontaneous" uprisings in Northern Island, the Basque region of Spain, the Japanese Red Army, and a bewildering "alphabet soup" of German, Bulgarian, and Middle Eastern terrorist organizations. In 1984 funding terrorists was Soviet state policy, and arms deals were the bread and butter of the GRU.[119]

The Communist sales to the Contras may have been a joke to the Soviets at first. But when Al-Kassar told them about the frantic British and American efforts to ransom Buckley, they stopped laughing. At the very least, here was a new and lucrative ransom racket. At the most, it was an opportunity to blackmail gullible American politicians into working for the GRU. What happened was somewhere in between, but it was not a positive development for Israel.

In the spring of 1984 the GRU told Al-Kassar to continue his support for the Western arms-for-the-Contras' initiative as well as the Iranian arms-for-hostages ransom. It was a strategy built on patient surveillance. The Soviet expression translates to something like "Let the mouse go down the hole and see where he comes out."[120]

A normal American intelligence officer would, in the usual course of events, have noticed that Al-Kassar was: (1) a well-known Communist narco-terrorist, who was suddenly, (2) selling arms to the Americans for a secret and illegal Contra operation, and (3) selling arms to the British for a secret and illegal operation to ransom Iranian hostages. It should not have taken above-average intelligence to realize that Al-Kassar was working on a different agenda from that of the Republican National Committee.

But these were not normal times. By the spring of 1984, Bush's SSG/CPPG structure had isolated the Iran-Contra initiative from the dreaded liberals in the U.S. intelligence community, not to mention the State Department and the Israelis. The dynamic duo, Casey and Bush, had concocted a structure outside the law where, unfortunately, it became impossible to submit Al-Kassar's name to the intelligence community for a routine security check. Because the SSG's operation violated U.S. law, Casey and Bush could not risk that some honest CIA officer might put two and two together and blow the whistle to Congress.[121]

Neither Casey nor Bush trusted his own people enough to ask for advice about Al-Kassar. Casey thought that the CIA was filled with liberal obstructionists who had repeatedly disobeyed his orders. Neither man ever ran Al-Kassar's name through a routine file check. If they had, a series of terrible tragedies might have been avoided. The British secret service had a vested interest in Monzer, and were not about to criticize their best, and only, agent inside the PLO. After all, it was Al-Kassar who had convinced the other terrorists to put their money in the BCCI so that their activities could be tracked by MI6. Still, the British had more than enough information about Monzer's drug sales, gunrunning and communist connections to raise the question of who was penetrating whom and for what purpose. MI6 closed its eyes and hoped for the best.

The intelligence services of the United Kingdom and the United States maintain close liaison and their cooperation will continue in the future. But if the CIA had learned anything from the Kim Philby scandal, it was that the incestuous clubhouse atmosphere of MI6 does not lend itself well to in-house scrutiny. In 1984 the British secret service presented Al-Kassar to Casey as the new supermole in the PLO; as the years went by and the disasters multiplied, the British were not about to admit that they had made another blunder and recruited yet another Communist double agent. Politics counseled perversion. Better a silent lie than an admission of an honest mistake.[122]

Once committed to a losing cause, British intelligence even kept Prime Minister Margaret Thatcher in the dark. No matter how much derogatory information they received about Al-Kassar, the British spymasters kept their mouths shut.[123]

There is an old, useless, and probably apocryphal British legend that one day the King of England told his secret service chief to reveal the name of a key foreign agent. The spymaster refused. Amused by the insubordination, the king threatened to cut off his subordinate's head. The master spy replied, "Then my head will roll with my lips sealed." Just this sort of juvenile romanticism caused British intelligence to suffer a series of public scandals and encounter secret penetrations unprecedented in the history of professional intelligence organizations. MI6 would rather have a good legend than a sound legacy.

It is, sadly, a legacy of distrust of even MI6's fellow spies, and continues even to this day. In 1984 the secret service (MI6) did not tell even the security service (MI5) that Monzer Al-Kassar was on the payroll. No vetting was done. No one even asked the retired British intelligence officer who was then head of Interpol to check on Al-Kassar's bona fides. The SIS mandarins of Century House kept their growing suspicions about him to themselves, just as they had forty years earlier in Kim Philby's case.[124]

Not all British agencies are as corrupted with hide-bound tradition as the secret service. According to the "old spies," a brilliant young woman in MI5 suspected Al-Kassar of foul play and recruited her own agent inside the BCCI in 1987. As a result of her efforts, Monzer was exposed and the BCCI closed down before it could swindle any more money out of MI6 and the British taxpayers.[125] The woman, Stella Rimington, is now the head of the British security service. The head of MI6 has been fired.

Other good cops also believed that open democracy should triumph over political secrecy. An ex-CIA agent culled U.S. intelligence files on Al-Kassar and leaked a story to *Reader's Digest* in 1986.[126] As bizarre as it may seem, any dentist's office in the United States that subscribed to the magazine had more information on Al-Kassar than the White House, which still had him on the payroll *after* the article came out. MI6 was not the only organization that carried compartmentalization to absurd lengths. To be fair, perhaps the British deluded themselves that being a terrorist was all part of Al-Kassar's cover.

It is ironic that the West Germans, who have the worst record on illegal arms sales next to North Korea, had the best arms investigator in the world. Manfred Morstein of the West German counterintelligence agency, the BKA, tracked Al-Kassar for almost a decade before quitting in disgust over the extent to which several nations protected the terrorist from arrest. A few years after the *Reader's Digest* article, he published a book, *The Godfather of Terror,* setting out Al-Kassar's arms and drug deals in great detail. Although Morstein never understood why Al-Kassar was untouchable in so many countries, the book was an authoritative exposé that quoted intelligence files from around the world.[127]

Unfortunately, Morstein's fact-filled book was never translated from German, at least publicly. One of our sources obtained an English-language translation made in 1991 by a subsidiary of the U.S. government with CIA funding. In keeping with our "Keystone Cops" theory of Western intelligence, the CIA did not discover Morstein's book until 1992, when a congressional committee published its own research on Al-Kassar. Then the CIA sent a messenger over to borrow a copy of the Morstein translation from Congress.[128]

As much as it rankles the "old spies" we interviewed about this tragicomedy, the first published American government analysis of Al-Kassar's White House connection came not from the intelligence community but from a staff report to Congress.[129] Although Republican members blocked it from being issued as an official committee report, this obscure staff study is well worth quoting:

> The al-Kassar brothers—Monser, Ghassen, Haitham and Mazin—control one of the world's largest arms and narcotics networks. . . . The al-Kassar's ability to provide governments with access to arms and equipment through irregular channels allows them to do business with high-level government officials who wish to deal "off the record" with terrorists or other politically sensitive groups. Although the risks of providing such services can be high, the dividends are at least equally high because governments who receive such services apparently "look the other way" with respect to the brothers' [drug] trafficking activities.[130]

Maybe the founding fathers were right in dividing the American government into three parts, so that each could spy on the others. What neither Bush nor Thatcher realized was that, in the long run, the system works. Neither leader trusted democracy enough to give it a chance, at least when it came to espionage. MI6 kept its secrets and North's superiors kept theirs, even from "Ollie."[131]

North still does not realize that the "big boys" in the vice president's office did not trust him fully in the early days. For several years he had no idea that Al-Kassar the hostage mediator was the same Al-Kassar the Contra supplier. In June 1984, North was not allowed to go to the London Summit on terrorism, so he did not meet Al-Kassar or even hear about his role in the Buckley ransom. North had to stay home and mind the store—and watch out for terrorists.[132]

On June 1, 1984, North received information from a "reliable source" that Ambassador Pickering was going to be attacked by terrorists in El Salvador. The CIA wanted to send in agents, but North wanted to send the Joint Chief of Staff's Special Operations Committee (JSOC), Admiral Moreau's version of a SWAT team.[133] North's problem: All his bosses were en route to the London Summit. Thinking that the threat was of international importance, he called "Bud" McFarlane aboard Air Force One to "ask Pres to tell Thatcher." A week later North's diary records lamely: "Threats to Pickering—subsource uncertainty."[134]

North was having a lot of problems with sources, none more so than Manucher Ghorbanifar, a Middle Eastern con man who went on to play a prominent role in the arms to Iran deal. Even before the June summit began, North should have realized that the CIA had dropped Ghorbanifar for fabricating intelligence. What North did not know was that now Ghorbanifar was working for the British secret service arranging arms sales to Iran. Al-Kassar had vouched for Ghorbanifar, and that alone should have set off alarm bells.[135]

Ghorbanifar's highly placed contact in Iran was none other than Mohsen Kengarlou, chief of Iranian Intelligence Operations, leader of the extremist faction that favored terrorist operations against the United States. Several years later the Iranians discovered that someone was leaking intelligence to the Soviets and admitted that "one of Kengarlou's associates was suspected of working for the KGB."[136]

Our sources say that the Iranians were right about the traitor in Kengarlou's intelligence headquarters. Except that he wasn't KGB. He worked for Soviet Military Intelligence, the GRU. Everything Ghorbanifar learned about the secret British-American operations during his negotiations with North, he passed on to Kengarlou and his Soviet mole. The more the GRU learned about the plans being made in London, the happier it was with Al-Kassar for foisting Ghorbanifar and his penetrated network onto the Americans. Even before the June 1984 summit began, the Soviets had their inside agent, reporting all of North's plans back to Moscow. Al-Kassar, of course, was already briefing the Soviets on the British end of the deal.[137]

The Iran-Contra debacle was to become the GRU's second major coup against the CIA in forty years. First there was the GRU-controlled Turkul-Max network in the 1940s and 1950s, and now it was Monzer Al-Kassar's Arab terror network in the 1980s and 1990s. Despite the involvement of the Soviets, it is our opinion that the entire "ABC" scandal (Al-Kassar, BCCI, and Contragate) was 90 percent stupidity and 10 percent conspiracy on the part of George Bush and his coterie of advisers. One should never underestimate the gullibility of the Western intelligence services, especially when politicians try to run their own spy service outside of normal channels.

Vice President Bush was leading the intelligence community into disaster. No one knew where the arms-to-Iran deal was headed because no one knew that Bush, Casey, and North had chosen most unreliable guides, who were taking them deeper and deeper into the swamp. Very soon Bush would realize that he was in up to his neck. Then it would be time for the White House to publicly blame the Jews for both ends of the Iran-Contra scandal.

CHAPTER 19

BUSH'S INNER SANCTUM

The conventional wisdom is that George Bush was the most qualified man ever to hold the post of vice president. He had been director of the CIA, U. S. ambassador to the United Nations, and a Republican party loyalist for many years. Despite his extensive background and expertise, Bush has always claimed that he was "out of the loop" on Iran-Contra and did not learn of Israel's 1985 arms-for-hostages initiative until a year after the Jews' first shipment to Iran. Bush claimed that when he first found out about the deal, he loyally supported the president. The impression was created that if only President Reagan, his national security adviser, John Poindexter, and National Security Council staffer Oliver North had consulted Bush earlier, the entire debacle may have been avoided.

Some of our sources in the Western intelligence community say that Iran-Contra was Bush's debacle to begin with. He played amateur spymaster until the operations began falling apart and then shifted the blame to the other end of the Reagan White House to save his own political career. Far from being a competent professional, Bush was a bungler when it came to espionage. He was willing to sacrifice Israel, Reagan's reputation, anything, and anyone to save his own neck.[1]

That assessment is a bit harsh, according to other sources. Bush was a good man with bad friends, they say. The vice president was misled, and even betrayed, by CIA head Bill Casey and his coterie of friends in the intelligence and foreign policy bureaucracy. They were the ones who caved in to the Arab dictators and once again made the Jews expendable for oil. Bush, like Reagan, was an unwitting accomplice. When it came to covert operations, Bush was an innocent pawn, who kept his silence to protect the guilty members of President Reagan's administration.[2]

By way of direct rebuttal, several former members of the Reagan administration have written books assailing George Bush as a man who was anything but "out of the loop." Reagan's secretary of state, George Shultz, said that Bush was an ardent supporter of the Iran-Contra initiative and pushed it over the objections of others. Secretary of Defense Caspar Weinberger's diaries for the period later were published by the special prosecutor for Iran-Contra, and confirm that Bush had been lying about when he first heard of these programs.[3]

As long as Bush was president, the "old spies" kept their silence, and their distance, from the cabinet in-fighting. Then, after Bill Clinton was elected, in 1992 and 1993 a spate of intelligence histories appeared that cast new light on Bush's protestations of ignorance. It turns out that Iran-Contra was not Bush's first experience with gunrunning. As far back as 1982, Bush and Casey had teamed up to convince Reagan to support covert operations in Cambodia. As a portent of things to come, some of the weapons ended up in the hands of the genocidal Khmer Rouge faction, while more than $3.5 million simply disappeared.[4]

According to Mark Perry's book, *Eclipse: The Last Days of the CIA*, the 1982 Cambodian gunrunning was one of the first covert operations to be advanced by Bush as vice president. It was not the only time Bush teamed up with Casey that year. In 1982, Casey flew to Baghdad to open a highly secret link to Saddam Hussein.[5]

According to Alan Friedman's book, *Spider's Web*, Vice President Bush played a covert role in Casey's Iraq initiative. Like Perry's discussion of Cambodia, Friedman makes a powerful case that Bush was inextricably intertwined with Casey's bizarre initiative to buy Iraqi oil, and Hussein's allegiance, with guns. There is no doubt that transferring American weapons to Iraq was highly illegal but was approved by both Bush and Casey. It also was hidden from both the secretary of state and Congress.[6]

Both times Casey and Bush teamed up, the operation involved gunrunning. It is no coincidence that both secret operations began in 1982, the same year that Vice President Bush established his Special Situations Group for counterterrorism. What neither Perry nor Friedman realized was that Bush and Casey worked together on a third covert operation, the arms-for-hostages deal with Iran. According to our sources, the story of Bush's role as the secret architect of Irangate has never been told before. It was run just as poorly as the Cambodian gunrunning and just as illegal as the arming of Iraq, but it was much better hidden from Congress.[7]

The special prosecutor's investigation missed this area entirely, because it was focused on the National Security Council, at the wrong end of the White House. The 1982 Cambodian and Iraq operations had given Bush and Casey a great deal of background in back-channel deals and how to hide them from Congress.[8]

Members of the Israeli government during the mid-1980s probably will be horrified to read the next two chapters. For several years they have been pilloried in the press as the instigators of Irangate, the ones who were to blame for the stain on the Reagan presidency. The truth, according to our sources, is that Israel was deliberately kept in the dark. The British secret service was running guns for Vice President Bush in 1984, one whole year before the Israelis were drawn into the Iranian scandal.[9]

In this chapter we consider the following allegations in detail:

- Former employees of the Bechtel Corporation, not Congress, dictated U.S. foreign policy in the Middle East for most of the 1980s, a covert policy that was anti-Israel and favored the Arab oil producers.
- The office of the vice president supervised covert policy in order to conceal illegal operations from the CIA as well as from the pro-Israeli secretary of state, Alexander Haig, who quickly was driven from office.
- The Iran gunrunning operations were carried out for Bush by the British secret service using Aspin, Al-Kassar and the Azima brothers as contract agents. These families established the original Contra conduits as well as the secret arms channel to Iran in 1984, a full year before Israel became involved.
- In 1982 the vice president's office recruited Oliver North, who served as a courier in 1984 to propose British and French arms deals to Iran, using the Bank of Credit and Commerce International as a conduit.
- Michael Aspin, one of the British participants, inadvertently exposed the Bush-British-BCCI connection.
- As the British arms channel collapsed, Israel was recruited in 1985 as the unwitting scapegoat for Irangate while Oliver North diverted the congressional investigation to protect Vice President Bush from further exposure.

According to some of the "old spies," Oliver North is almost as big a phony as Bush, and twice as stupid as the Israelis. At the time, neither North nor the Israelis realized that they were being set up as "fall guys." According to our sources in the intelligence community, there were some very good reasons why Oliver North was not included in George Bush's inner sanctum on the Middle East and not allowed to go to the 1984 London Summit on terrorism.[10] In the first place, North was thought to be pro-Israel, a suspicion that was confirmed after he left government service.

In his 1992 autobiography North noted the "corporate culture" prevalent in Washington policymaking circles during the Reagan-Bush years, which was strongly influenced by the many former Bechtel employees at the CIA and the Defense Department, who seemed to "relish any antagonism that could be fostered between us and the Israelis." North also blasted the "long-standing and barely hidden pro-Arab" bias at the State Department, "which I'm hardly the first to notice." North believed that the anti-Israel bias came from a deep strain of anti-Semitism that had been passed on from generation to generation of government officials.[11]

During the Reagan years, however, some senior cabinet members seemed to take this pro-Arab prejudice farther than others. As North recorded, neither Reagan nor Bush was anti-Israel, but Secretary of Defense Caspar Weinberger:

> . . . seemed to go out of his way to oppose Israel on any issue and to blame the Israelis for every problem in the Middle East. In our planning for counterterrorist operations, he apparently feared that if we went after Palestinian terrorists, we would offend and alienate Arab governments—particularly if we acted in cooperation with the Israelis.
>
> Weinberger's anti-Israel tilt was an underlying current in almost every Mideast issue. Some people explained it by pointing to his years with the Bechtel Corporation. . . . Others believed it was more complicated, and had to do with his sensitivity about his own Jewish ancestry.[12]

As North noted, "Cap" Weinberger has a Jewish background and was a former general counsel of the Bechtel Corporation, one of the most notorious anti-Semitic companies in the United States. During the 1980s Bechtel's executives, more than those of any other corporation, had a revolving door to the White House. In mid-1982 Weinberger was joined in the Reagan administration by George Shultz, previously Bechtel's president, who replaced the pro-Israeli Alexander Haig as secretary of state.[13]

Weinberger's appointment in the mid-1970s as a senior executive of Bechtel was most unusual, in that his father was Jewish, "not a plus at a company with extensive dealings with the Arabs and more than a little anti-Semitism in its own executive suite." Indeed, many within Bechtel "worried over how a man named 'Weinberger' would go down with the Arabs."[14] There were good reasons for such alarm, but Weinberger went out of his way to go to the other extreme, perhaps in an effort to demonstrate his credentials as a good Bechtel company man.

When Weinberger joined Bechtel, the company's profits were being threatened by an attack on its long-standing adherence to the Arab boycott, which had been imposed by the Arabs after the Jews won the 1948 war, and banned all trade between Arabs and Israel, or any company that did business with Israel. Bechtel absolutely carried out the provisions of the boycott to the letter; even when offered extremely lucrative contracts to do business in Israel, the company declined to deal with Jews.[15]

During Weinberger's tenure at Bechtel in the mid-1970s, a Justice Department investigation discovered that the company's contracts with Arab countries were completely in line with the boycott. Although the U.S. government had turned a blind eye to the boycott for the previous quarter of a century, and even had participated in it on occasion, a new policy was in force at the Justice Department. On the strength of the evidence, Attorney General Edward Levi decided to proceed with a suit against Bechtel, only to be vehemently opposed by Secretary of State, Henry Kissinger who was a great admirer of Bechtel's president, George Shultz.[16]

Eventually the case was settled by a consent decree, partly because the company wanted to settle quietly to protect "its publicity-shy Arab clients." The consent decree was highly favorable to Bechtel and American oil companies operating in the Middle East, effectively leaving the boycott's provisions in place. When the Carter administration later construed the settlement agreement in a more stringent manner, Bechtel appealed right up to the Supreme Court. Although the company eventually lost the case in 1981, as of 1989 it still did no business with Israel.[17]

During the 1980 presidential primaries, Bechtel at first strongly supported its favorite anti-Jewish candidate, John Connally. When his campaign failed, Bechtel had no trouble finding another candidate. The company had been close to Ronald Reagan for many years and had financed his political campaigns before. The most direct connection was between Shultz of Bechtel and William Casey, Reagan's campaign manager and later the CIA director at the center of the Iran-Contra scandal.[18] In light of such connections, it was hardly surprising that Shultz and Weinberger were elevated to their senior cabinet posts in the Reagan-Bush team.

However, many viewed Reagan's choice of Shultz to replace Alexander Haig as secretary of state as another signal of his hostility to Jews. In fact, neither Reagan nor Shultz were anti-Semitic; rather, both actually tempered the anti-Israeli bias noted by North. It was the other Bechtel appointee, Defense Secretary Weinberger, who conducted the administration's bitter campaign against Haig's pronounced pro-Israeli stance. Shultz helped oust Haig, but the evidence indicates that it was more to get the job for himself than anything else.[19]

Weinberger's opportunity to get Haig came when the White House called on Israel to refrain from attacking Beirut and resume talks on Palestinian autonomy on the West Bank. Haig, who had seen enough of the Republicans' anti-Semitic tendencies during Nixon's time, launched a strong public attack on this policy. It cost him his job. Weinberger and Shultz could hardly stand each other, and their brawls were legendary both in Bechtel's headquarters and in Washington. But both Bechtel alumni did seem to agree that the leader of the pro-Israel faction, Alexander Haig, must go. Shultz helped Weinberger to force Haig from office. President Reagan then promptly recruited Shultz as his replacement.[20]

To almost everyone's surprise, Shultz was much kinder to Israel than had been expected. Our sources attribute his *volte face* to his disgust at the many broken promises made by the Arabs during Middle East negotiations. This change of heart was one of the reasons that Shultz was shut out of the Iran-Contra deals and preserved a far better reputation than many others in the administration. Some of the "old spies" say that from the very beginning of his term Secretary of State Shultz had become too soft on the Jews for the hard-liners in the Reagan-Bush team.[21]

Shultz's confirmation hearings, however, did not go without controversy. He was pressed "for details of Bechtel's lobbying efforts to sell AWACS aircraft to Saudi Arabia, where the company had a total of $40 billion in contracts." While pushed aggressively by Shultz and Bechtel, as previously discussed, the AWACS sale "was bitterly opposed by Israel and its supporters in Congress." Despite Haig's vehement opposition, the Senate passed the deal.[22]

Shultz stood to gain a lot from the AWACS sales. As Bechtel president, Shultz oversaw "construction projects of extraordinary scale and geographical scope," including one Saudi Arabian project with an estimated budget of $30 billion, larger "than the entire U.S. space program."[23] The AWACS sale went through before Shultz headed for Washington in mid-1982, but it was Weinberger, not Shultz, whom North singled out as Israel's major foe inside the Reagan team.

Apart from being considered too favorable to Israel, North had another strike against his admission to Bush's inner circle. He was seen as an "Iraq-hater" as well. From 1981–82, Weinberger at Defense and Bill Casey at the CIA wanted to tilt U.S. policy heavily toward Iraq, but were blocked. In the first two years of the Reagan administration, Secretary of State Alexander Haig strongly advocated an anti-Iraq, pro-Israel line, including sending weapons to Iran to help in the war against Iraq.[24]

When Haig left, only a handful of "Israel-loving, Iraq-hating" staffers remained behind. North was one of them, because he believed that the Iraqis were anti-American terrorists, while Israel was a powerful antiterrorist force with which he worked closely. But as Iraq began to fare badly in the war with Iran, North's pro-Israeli influence within the Reagan team became almost nonexistent.[25]

North was temporarily isolated from the inner sanctum in the early 1980s because the insiders' policy had become decidedly anti-Israel and pro-Iraq. According to several of our sources, North was not told of this shift. The new policy had been decided secretly by Bush's Special Situation Group, and not even the president had been told all the details. The group was committed to a covert program to save Iraq from military defeat.[26]

In February 1982 CIA director Casey flew to Paris to meet the head of the Iraqi secret service. By late spring 1982 Casey was sending Saddam Hussein AWACS intelligence, obtained by the planes recently sold to the Saudis over Israel's strenuous objections. By 1983 Casey had a secret CIA station in Baghdad and was giving Saddam Hussein everything from satellite photos to the Iranian order of battle.[27]

U.S. policy—or at least Vice President Bush's policy—had changed sides, and North did not know it. From 1982 on Bush and Casey conspired to tilt U.S. policy toward Saddam Hussein.[28] Bush was good friends with Saddam's deputy foreign minister, contrived anti-Israeli votes in the UN, and made personal phone calls to one of his former Yale classmates to obtain American funding for Bechtel's oil pipeline in Iraq and later to finance Iraq's weapons purchases. The Iraqis received everything the Israelis were denied, from satellite down-links to advanced cluster bomb technology. The Bechtel Corporation was even building Saddam Hussein a chemical factory which he could use for poison gas production.[29]

In view of North's disgust at anti-Semitism and hatred of Saddam Hussein, it is not surprising that he initially was excluded from Bush's inner sanctum. That he stayed on the fringes of Bush's inner circle at all is remarkable. The fact that he retained his post as liaison on terrorism to the vice president's office had nothing to do with North's work on the AWACS sale, or that he was Bush's escort officer in 1983, or that his boss on Bush's Crisis Pre-Planning Group (CPPG) was "Bud" McFarlane, a fellow marine who also was detailed over from the National Security Council staff at the White House. It had to do with the fact that he would make a good "fall guy," if things went wrong.

When the Iran-Contra scandal was under investigation, McFarlane testified under oath that North had done it all on his own. At this point, even North finally realized that his "friend" had been stabbing him in the back all along. In his autobiography, North wrote that "Naturally, I felt betrayed by Bud's version of events."[30] Our sources say that it took some time before North realized that McFarlane had implicated him in an attempt to divert attention from the vice president, although "Ollie" still may not know the whole story of Bush's early involvement with the British.[31]

Since 1982 McFarlane had chaired the CPPG directly reporting to Vice President Bush. Only much later, in November 1984, did North take over Bud's job as Bush's covert liaison. McFarlane knew who was behind the 1984 London Summit; North did not. From 1982 until late 1984 North and the rest of the National Security Council were as far out of the loop on intelligence matters as Ronald Reagan.

The president was a nice old guy who read his speeches well. But his speechwriters were something else again. Reagan had trusted Bush to tell him what to say when it came to intelligence. Bush trusted Casey. That was Bush's most grievous mistake. Casey shafted him as badly as McFarlane shafted North. Years later, after Reagan found out a part of the truth, he allegedly told Bill Clinton that he had voted for him instead of Bush.[32]

The major scapegoat, however, was neither North nor Reagan but Israel. No matter how cooperative the Jews were, nor how many dirty operations they were prepared to ghost for Washington, they were entirely expendable compared to George Bush's political career.

The only reason North was even allowed near the vice president's office in 1984 was that McFarlane was "losing his grip" and had to be replaced. Casey vouched for North enthusiastically as Bud's de facto successor. To Casey, North had one redeeming quality: He was a "shooter," a no-nonsense guy who favored aggressive action against terrorists. Truth be known, North's support for the plan to kidnap terrorists was mild compared to Casey's, who became almost apoplectic at the refusal of CIA officers to involve themselves in such illegal and extreme actions.[33]

When Casey ordered the CIA to come up with a plan for an operation to kidnap a notorious terrorist, Agency staff pointed out, to his disgust, that Congress had not yet passed a statute giving them "long-arm" jurisdiction.[34] The U.S. courts would simply release any terrorist who was kidnapped without a shred of legal authority.

To Casey, the word "illegal" meant a sick bird. One former CIA officer told us how Casey even ignored the financial conflict-of-interest laws, until he was forced to put his assets into a blind trust so that he could not use his intelligence information to enrich himself. According to our source, Casey then used a CIA courier to fetch daily reports from the trust so that he could continue to handle his own investments. As CIA director, he had access to a great deal of inside information, particularly concerning the oil industry, which he allegedly used for his own profit.[35]

That Casey was a crook was disturbing enough for his subordinates. The CIA was afraid that he might try to resolve the jurisdiction problem by assassinating terrorists instead of just kidnapping them. "What really worried Agency officers was that Casey could count on support from an emerging group of pro-Casey activists ('my shooters,' he called them), who were only too happy to comply with his wishes."[36] Bill Buckley, the ex–Green Beret, was one of those "shooters" whom Casey most admired. For this reason Casey sent him to Lebanon. If the "liberal wimps" in the CIA did not have the guts to kill a few terrorists, Casey would set up his own force, using British and Lebanese mercenaries. Poor Buckley, however, was a marked man. It may have been Monzer Al-Kassar himself who leaked word of his antiterrorist mission.[37]

Just one month after Buckley was kidnapped in March 1984, British intelligence developed a severe case of cold feet about any more preemptive action. North took copious notes during the April meeting with the British, while not quite understanding what the fuss was all about.[38]

"The fuss" was that the British were a little frightened by Casey's fanatic desire to kill "Commie terrorists." By May Casey asked for and received a meeting in London with senior British intelligence officers, to put some "fire in their bellies" in the war against terrorism.[39] It should come as no surprise that Casey was asking British intelligence to do something that the CIA had refused. It had happened before.

At the end of World War II, Bill Casey was Allen Dulles's man in London. As discussed in Chapter 17, he was part of the team that put the Fascist "freedom fighters" program into action. After leaving the Office of Strategic Services, Casey served on the International Rescue Committee in New York. His job was to resettle ex-Nazis who had been recruited by British intelligence as anti-Communist agents. Casey had broken more than a few laws in helping the British then.[40] Now he wanted the favor returned. What was the big deal about killing a few terrorists anyway?

Many readers will find it inconceivable that Bill Casey would have gone to a foreign government, behind the back of his own CIA and in violation of American law, to ask the British to build him a private version of Murder, Incorporated. In fact, when the British turned him down again at the London Summit, Casey did not abandon his plans for a kidnap/hit team. Within a year the CIA director had taken up the kidnapping option with the French secret service. Casey's counterterrorism experts were even more appalled at this than they were at the approach to the British. The French were known to be "trigger-happy" and might cause even more problems for the CIA.[41]

Predictably, the CIA staffers dragged their feet while they tried to bring Casey to his senses. Eventually the French called off the hit squad.[42] Our sources in the intelligence community say that Casey's French initiative was merely a ploy to make the British think that he was abandoning their special relationship. Within a year of the London summit, the British secret service reversed its position and, with the help of Buckley's indigenous Lebanese mercenaries, tried to plant a car bomb in Beirut. Unfortunately, the target of the assassination, Hezbollah chief Sheikh Muhammed Fadlallah, had been delayed en route to his home. He escaped, but dozens of innocent citizens were killed by the blast. Although U.S. intelligence was blamed for the massacre, it was, according to our sources, a British operation.[43]

As we shall see, the British "on-again, off-again" hit squad policy started off slowly but came into high gear toward the end. If the British were reluctant at first to avenge Buckley's kidnapping by killing a few terrorists, they were more than enthusiastic about using a terrorist like Al-Kassar to negotiate Buckley's ransom. During the London Summit in June 1984, they told Casey they had the perfect team to deal with the kidnappers: Al-Kassar, Aspin, and the Azimas.

Casey, of course, knew of Aspin because of his recent work in Lebanon with Buckley's aborted strike team. Aspin was one of Casey's original "shooters," with a long track record from 1976, when Aspin hired mercenaries for the CIA in Angola, and, from 1979, when Aspin and Buckley fought the terrorist takeover of the Grand Mosque in Mecca. It also helped that Aspin was also a close friend of Buckley, who was one of Casey's favorites. More important to Casey's plans to ransom Buckley, Aspin had contacts with arms transporters everywhere. Aspin's business contacts were the Azima brothers of Kansas City. He had known them since the time their company, Global International Aviation, flew "cabbages and cabbage launchers" to Central America back in the 1970s.

The Azimas' GIA "often transported arms to Egypt from 1981–1983 under contract with Egyptian American Transport and Services Corp. (EATSCO), the company operated by Thomas Clines, Richard Secord, Edwin Wilson, and others."[44] Nothing the Azimas were connected with seemed to go well. Clines was convicted for overcharging the U.S. government during the EATSCO scandal, while Wilson went to jail for shipping plastic explosives to Gadhafi. General Richard Secord, who was simply a naive victim of the con, was eventually cleared but his career was tarnished, causing him to resign.

For some reason, the Azima brothers emerged from each scandal stronger than before. Despite its association with criminals and gunrunners, GIA received yet another U.S. government contract to send "humanitarian aid" to the Contras in Nicaragua. Long before the congressional ban went into effect, Aspin and the Azimas had already worked on the Contra supply operation. In fact, Aspin admitted that "my first contact with Rob Owen and North was in 1983."[45] Owen, it should be recalled, was the "paymaster" for the Contras.

While it does not appear that the Azimas were shipping anything more than humanitarian aid to North's freedom fighters, Monzer Al-Kassar certainly was. He turned out to be one of General Secord's primary sources for Communist weapons for the Contra army. Al-Kassar's early participation in the Contra game is not surprising since General Secord's partner was Albert Hakim, the contact for Aspin, the Azimas, and, of course, Al-Kassar. It appears that Aspin was the middleman for Al-Kassar's purchases in 1983 and 1984. Aspin even had Secord's home phone numbers. He knew all the players in the Contra game, years before Congress did.[46]

But in June 1984 Casey had not invited Aspin to talk about smuggling guns to Nicaragua. He wanted him to smuggle guns to Iran to ransom their mutual friend, Bill Buckley. Aspin, who attended Casey's secret conferences that took place at the same time as the London Summit, described what happened:

> In June of 1984, I was contacted by a Mr. Casey who was then head of the CIA in the United States of America. . . . He requested me to assist in the sale of [arms] to Iran in exchange for hostages held.
>
> These hostages were being held in Lebanon, so in June of 1984, I started [attending] a series of meetings in London. I suppose there were probably 6 to 8 meetings all told in that month, one of them being at the U.S. Embassy Grosvenor Square. . . . During these series of meetings, it was discussed as to how one could get the hostages released, ways of doing it, some of them improper, some of them proper.[47]

Aspin later amplified that the "improper" options included Casey's insistence to "take hostages" from the terrorists' families, just as the Soviets had done. Aspin said that the kidnapping had now been authorized by "Defense Directive 138."[48] The British, however, knew that the "neutralization" language of National Security Decision Directive #138 had been so watered down by the time it was signed that it authorized little more than a stepped-up intelligence exchange. The British told Casey to forget about revenge for a while and concentrate on getting Buckley back.

Here was how Aspin could help. His friend Monzer Al-Kassar knew all about ransom deals. Al-Kassar had learned all about kidnapping from his closest boyhood friend, Abul Abbas, who became one of Yasser Arafat's trusted aides in the PLO before Abbas moved over to the extremist wing. Al-Kassar was a long-time supporter of Abbas's Palestinian Liberation Front and an enthusiastic advocate of the PLO's kidnap-for-ransom schemes. In fact, most of the Al-Kassar family had connections to one PLO terrorist group or another.[49]

A little background is in order to understand Al-Kassar's role as a rising star in the terrorist constellation. In 1982 the Soviet's game plan was to split the PLO and weaken Arafat's control. The Palestinians had begun a dangerous tilt toward diplomacy and away from terrorist attacks on Israel. Al-Kassar's friends in Syria played a critical role in the Soviet divide-and-conquer strategy.

In 1983 a Palestinian colonel named Abu Musa broke with the PLO and, with Syrian backing, chased Arafat's Al-Fatah fighters out of the Bekaa Valley opium fields. Now Al-Kassar's family did not have to share. The Bekaa drug trade is so lucrative that even the Mafia ended up buying heroin from the Al-Kassars. French intelligence, always willing to bend a few rules to ensure France's Middle Eastern oil supply, used Al-Kassar's network to ship arms to the Middle East, while turning a blind eye toward the family's drug business. In August 1983 the French obtained the early release of Monzer's brother Ghassan, who was being held in jail on a narcotics charge.[50]

That same month in 1983, Ghassan and Monzer flew into Vienna, where Austrian intelligence wiretapped their meeting with European arms dealers. The West Germans still think that Monzer's Vienna negotiations were just a sting operation to trap a Jewish agent trying to infiltrate his networks, posing as an arms dealer. The Jewish agent had stumbled in and had to be killed by Monzer's old school friend-turned-terrorist, Abul Abbas.[51] In fact, Monzer's primary purpose was to meet one of his British arms contacts.

Monzer and his brothers were fast becoming the central switchboard for all the world's terrorist, arms, and drug networks. In fact, just before Casey arrived for the London Summit, the Al-Kassar family had hosted a summit of its own in Budapest, in Communist Hungary, for the major Palestinian terrorist leaders.[52] The result of the conference was a major increase in terrorist activities against Israel and against Jews residing in Europe. To keep up his cover, Monzer leaked some of the details to the British. According to our sources, MI6 told Casey but not the Mossad. Al-Kassar's information was much too valuable to risk exposure by sharing it. Yet again, the Jews and their state were expendable.[53]

The British secret service cannot deny knowledge that its top informant was killing Jews to protect his cover. Again, a bit of background is in order. MI6 had known all about Al-Kassar's role in terror bombing since 1981. That had become public knowledge, thanks to Leslie Aspin. Aspin had set up a British front called BAB Security Assurance Services. BAB stood for Banks, Aspin, and Berry, the company which had put together the Angolan mercenary team for Bush back in 1976. Banks soon quit, as Al-Kassar had quite an unsavory reputation, even in gun-running circles. Aspin and John Berry stayed on, but then Aspin started to get nervous.[54]

Aspin discovered that his partner, Berry, was making bombs for Al-Kassar. In 1981 Aspin "blew the whistle." Scotland Yard wiretapped Berry and then arrested him as he tried to export fuses for terrorist bombs. During his interrogation, Berry blurted out that the "fuzes were for the Syrian government . . . Monzer was the middle man."[55]

The Syrian government blandly denied any involvement, of course. In fact, Monzer Al-Kassar was a key agent in the Soviet-Syrian joint operation to split the PLO and undermine Arafat and Gadhafi, both of whom were much too independent for the Soviets. Al-Kassar's reinvigorated terrorist campaign helped persuade many of the Palestinian extremists to transfer their terrorist operations and headquarters to Damascus, where Syria's president Assad was handling things for Moscow. The only terrorist groups Al-Kassar would betray to MI6 were those who refused to obey orders from the Kremlin. Al-Kassar, of course, continued to fool MI6 by claiming that Berry's public arrest had jeopardized his status as a trusted confidant of the PLO's most radical factions.[56]

It was embarrassing for MI6 to have its rivals over in Scotland Yard and MI5 learn that Al-Kassar was the man behind the PLO's mad bombers, so MI6 arranged for Berry to "escape" to Al-Kassar's palace in Marbella, Spain, where British extradition did not apply.[57] Al-Kassar stayed on the MI6 payroll and the terrorist attacks continued. By 1985 Al-Kassar was accused of supplying a suitcase bomb for an attack in the Jewish Quarter in Paris. British police traced the explosives to Aspin's partner, Berry, living with Al-Kassar in Spain.[58]

In 1986 police wiretaps confirmed that Al-Kassar had called England to order six tons of TNT as well as machine guns for his terrorist friends. West German investigators were not allowed to question the British arms dealer. Then Interpol discovered that the British arms brokerage, Creative Resources Associated, in Shropshire, England, was shipping weapons to Cenzin, a Communist firm run by the Polish secret service. The weapons were "stolen" en route by terrorists in Vienna and later linked to Monzer Al-Kassar.[59]

This linkage is not surprising, as CIA files show that in Al-Kassar's Vienna company two secret service agents from Cenzin were partners.[60] Al-Kassar was the leading sales representative for virtually all Communist arms manufacturers. British arms dealers made a fortune dealing with him and were "shocked, *shocked*" when they later learned that he was dealing with terrorists. Among the intelligence and law enforcement agencies, his reputation was so well known that it almost looked as if he would not be allowed to obtain an entry visa for the London Summit. "In February, 1984 England had finally imposed upon him a life-time ban on entering the country because of arms and drug dealing."[61]

It was a ban observed more in the breach than in the observance over the next four years, as Al-Kassar continued to travel in and out of England with impunity to report to MI6.[62] He was still angry that the British had allowed the Mossad to stop his May 1984 arms shipment through Greece to the PLO. Didn't the British want information about Buckley's kidnappers? In short order, the May 21 cable from the U.S. embassy in Damascus greased the way for Al-Kassar to attend the London conference with Casey.[63]

By the time Casey arrived in London in June, the first arms shipment had already been captured in Greece. As Aspin recalled, the upshot of the conference was that Al-Kassar would help him send another arms shipment to Iran through one of his "Licensed British Arms Dealers" to make the Buckley ransom negotiations look legal. The Iranians, desperate for

American-type tank ammunition, were willing to provide information about Buckley in return for the privilege of buying arms from the West.[64]

Once there was proof that Buckley was still alive, Al-Kassar and Aspin would deal directly with his captors to negotiate the ransom price. The kidnappers would provide a newspaper with a recent date and Buckley's signature on it, as proof that they were the real thing. A signature was not good enough. As previously discussed, Casey asked for a videotape of Buckley to make sure that it was not a con, and Aspin agreed. Within a few weeks Casey had his videotape and the Iranians had their tank ammo.[65]

Here is how the first successful arms-for-hostages deal was planned in the summer of 1984. The Iranians would pay for the arms with oil credits deposited through the Bank Melli, the BCCI's correspondent bank in Iran since the time of the shah. No more Israeli banks for them. The Iranians had learned their lesson from the Greek fiasco. Moreover, the BCCI had no compunction about helping the Iranians evade the international arms embargo by selling oil on the black market.[66]

As soon as the Iranian money was transferred to the BCCI, the weapons would be shipped from Lisbon, Portugal, the only country in Western Europe that continued to trade with Iran. To disguise the transaction, the paperwork would show that the former British colony of Mauritius was the recipient of the weapons. The cover was a bit thin, as people might wonder what a tiny island nation in the Indian Ocean wanted with millions of dollars' worth of tank and artillery shells.[67]

As soon as they got the green light from Casey, Al-Kassar and his British arms dealer friend, Ben Bannerjee, contacted the Iranians on June 12, 1984. But the Iranians wanted to increase the size of the deal. In addition to the artillery shells and High Explosive Anti-Tank ammunition rounds, they wanted to buy five thousand TOW missiles. On June 29 Al-Kassar's front men in Portugal sent a cryptic message to Aspin that the "seller of black oil" [Iran] was also the "TOW buyer." It would mean another transaction on top of the tank rounds, but that only increased the profit potential.[68]

Al-Kassar could buy American-type tank ammunition from Communist arms factories, which would make anything for a price. There were also rumors that some of the tank shells came directly from the Soviets, who had warehouses of the stuff abandoned by the Americans in Vietnam. Bannerjee assured Aspin that Al-Kassar's price was good, the best in the world. "Only Israel" could sell old U.S. tank ammunition at a lower price, and Israel was obviously excluded from this particular deal.[69]

By the end of June, the parties were in agreement: Ship the tank ammunition to Iran first and the TOWs second. Bannerjee placed the order for six thousand tank rounds, fifty thousand high-explosive artillery shells, and fifty Soviet antiaircraft cannons. On July 7 Leslie and Michael Aspin wrote a pro-forma contract agreeing to pay $US 22,270,000 to Al-Kassar for the list of weapons, "Country of Origin: Poland & U.S.S.R." When the goods were received by Al-Kassar's front company, Exportex Mauritius Limited, Leslie and Michael's front company, Delta Investments of Great Britain and the United Arab Emirates, would take custody and authorize payment from the BCCI's letter of credit.[70]

On July 28, 1984, Bannerjee and the Aspins agreed to divide the profits left over "after deduction of thirty per cent net profit for buyer's agent."[71] Al-Kassar's cut came first. This time the arms shipment to Iran went off without a hitch. The Buckley videotape was promptly handed over to MI6. According to the Iranians, after Leslie Aspin delivered the second shipment, the five thousand TOW missiles, they would get Buckley released. Both parties failed to realize that this was easier said than done.[72]

Neither the Iranians nor the British secret service realized that, while the kidnappers were the pro-Iranian Hezbollah, the Syrian government paid the terrorists' bills and had effective control of the hostages. Soviet Military Intelligence (the GRU) knew, because it had the final say over its Syrian surrogates. Monzer Al-Kassar's Syrian relatives were making too much money from their share of the drugs-for-guns racket to let the British secret service slow them down.

The British thought they had Al-Kassar's activities covered because of the wiretaps on his BCCI transactions. MI6 kept the London BCCI bank headquarters under tight surveillance,[73] and the British thought that they could trace his BCCI accounts to identify, infiltrate, and destroy terrorist groups. Al-Kassar, however, took his money out of the BCCI's foreign affiliate, the Swiss Bank Corporation. From Switzerland, where the British could not get a trace of his activities because of secrecy laws, the money went to Spain, where Al-Kassar owned a 51 percent interest in the Bank of Bilbao. Owning your own bank is indeed convenient. Having broken the chain of BCCI surveillance, Al-Kassar was able to send the British on a wild goose chase after the dissident terrorists, while the GRU and Syria were building a secret empire.[74]

Al-Kassar had to tell the British something, so they would not start looking for terrorist money in the right places. It was the Libyans who were the bad guys, he claimed. They were working with the KGB to sell drugs for gun money. The truth is that Gadhafi paid for his arms shipments with oil and then gave guns to the Irish Republican Army (IRA) and other groups for free, as a gesture of "solidarity."[75] This charitable gesture by the Libyans had long annoyed the GRU, as it undermined Soviet influence with terrorist groups, not to mention their lucrative drugs-for-guns business. Soviet cooperation with Gadhafi began to wind down in the early 1980s.[76]

It was a stroke of genius by the GRU to denounce its KGB rival as Gadhafi's drug connection. There was a small grain of truth in the deception. Al-Kassar reported through Syrian intelligence to the GRU, which shared his information with the KGB until 1971, when a KGB officer in Kuwait defected to the CIA and told about terrorist training in Syria.[77] The KGB was taken off the terrorist project, and the GRU was given full control of the Syrian narco-terrorist network. By 1983, the KGB had lost control of Arafat's PLO as well.[78] By 1984 Al-Kassar had convinced most of the radical Palestinians to relocate to Damascus under the protection of Syrian intelligence and the GRU.[79]

From the GRU's perspective, the KGB and Libya made useful, although somewhat dated, scapegoats for its ongoing Syrian enterprise. Al-Kassar was primed with juicy anecdotes to misdirect British intelligence. He would betray only those narco-terrorists whom the GRU had already written off.[80] The British believed Al-Kassar's linkage of the IRA-KGB and Gadhafi, partly because MI6 really wanted to believe that groups like the IRA were Communist drug dealers, as that would make discrediting them easier in the British press. In a 1981 book called *The Terror Network*, a British author, Claire Sterling, had denounced the KGB while barely mentioning the GRU and implicated Gadhafi as "the Daddy Warbucks of Terrorism." The book was one of Bill Casey's favorites.

When Casey came back from the June 1984 London conference, he told the CIA that the KGB was supporting terrorist groups with drug sales. His staff laughed at him and insisted there was no evidence of a Communist narco-terrorist plot, but Casey insisted that Sterling was right.[81] In some ways, both Sterling and Casey were right, except that they were off on a few minor points: The terrorism was GRU-, not KGB-sponsored, and the drugs were coming from Syria, not Libya. Still, the CIA was wrong in saying that Soviet support for terrorists had ended long ago. As the CIA would find out, to its deep chagrin, worldwide terrorist operations were in fact coordinated from the Kremlin.

The key details began to emerge after 1989, when communism collapsed in Central and Eastern Europe. First, the Stasi secret service files from East Germany were released, and then Boris Yeltsin's Russian government confirmed that the Soviet regime had funded various terrorist groups. Casey might have been a bit of a zealot when it came to the "commies," but in 1984 he was right and his staff were wrong. Of course, Casey had received some recent evidence from the British, but he could not reveal Al-Kassar as the source. The British also had an East Bloc defector who confirmed many of the dribs and drabs Al-Kassar had provided to MI6 to build up his importance as an inside source.[82]

Even without knowing about Monzer, the CIA should have been paying more attention to the Al-Kassar family. According to the CIA's own files, Ghassan Al-Kassar's wife is Nabila Al-Kassar, a courier for the extremist People's Front for the Liberation of Palestine/Special Command as well as for Monzer's friend Abul Abbas.[83] West German intelligence files given to the CIA also show that Nabila's brother was the first secretary in the Lebanese embassy in Sofia at the same time her husband had his arms export business. CIA files also show that the Al-Kassar brothers were in frequent contact with the Yemeni intelligence service, which provided them with another set of diplomatic passports.[84]

But in those days, the CIA just was not watching Monzer Al-Kassar, and Casey was not about to blow the whistle on the British "superspy" inside the terrorist groups. Not while Monzer and Aspin stood a chance of getting his favorite "shooter," Buckley, back alive. Unfortunately, Aspin was having a devil of a time finding the five thousand TOW missiles the Iranians wanted. His brother Michael was ill, so Aspin turned to his old friend Paddy Matson in Dubai. Aspin's Delta Investment Company had long had a branch office in the capital of the United Arab Emirates.[85] Not only did Dubai have a BCCI branch and a major British intelligence outpost, it was a very convenient place to stage Middle East arms deals.

As previously mentioned, in 1976 the British had convinced CIA head George Bush to fund a joint British-American eavesdropping station in Oman. The huge complex could easily overhear telephone conversations at Sheik Zayed's BCCI operation in Abu Dhabi, just a few miles away in the United Arab Emirates. The helpful Omanis had a few contacts in their former colony of Baluchistan, in Pakistan, near the Iranian border. In short order, the British had the Pakistan end of the BCCI wired as well.[86]

Aspin told his friend Matson to go to the United States to find five thousand TOW missiles. Matson went to the Emerson and Hughes companies, and discovered the bad news. The TOW missile was a highly restricted item that could be shipped only to certain countries. The improved version of the TOW missile was completely out of bounds, except for foreign government sales under congressional oversight.[87]

However, a few nations still had older versions of the original TOWs in their stockpiles. The explosives in the warhead were good for only five years before they started to decay, so it might be possible to pick up some old "basic" TOWs under the table. According to Pentagon records, Oman and South Korea were among the five countries that were shipped the basic TOW from 1983 to 1986. The Omanis did not have enough, so that left the Koreans.[88] Aspin had good connections with a former Korean dictator through one of his friends in the smuggling business. Aspin also had contact with Horace Hsu, a Hong Kong resident, who was desperately trying to obtain U.S. citizenship. According to the Aspins, the Koreans and Omanis would provide the TOWS, while Hong Kong handled the financing. Hsu had previous experience with the British, as he had handled several large deals for the sultan of Oman. Hsu states that he refused to fill Michael's order.[89]

In August 1984 Aspin was temporarily sidetracked filling an arms order for the Contras.[90] By the end of September he was back on top of the Iran deal. Al-Kassar had lined up some good contacts in Lisbon. The Portuguese Ministry of Defense would purchase the Korean TOWs through a series of front companies and then sell them to one of Bannerjee's front companies. Aspin recalled that:

> I took Bannerjee to Lisbon in October, 1984 and November, 1984. Each time we booked into the Ritz Hotel. I then contacted [name deleted] of INDEP which is a member of the [Portuguese Government's] National Industries of Defense and [name deleted] whose address I received from my brother along with his phone number. . . . I also took Bannerjee at this time to the Director of National Armaments.[91]

Interpol discovered later that most of the organizations Aspin dealt with in Portugal had a long history of connections to Monzer Al-Kassar. With Al-Kassar's blessing, the Portuguese deal went smoothly:

> After meetings with them and various phone calls, it was decided that they would help me put the mechanics of all this together, [including] the arrival in Lisbon of the TOW missiles, and transfer from military aircraft to Tehran. . . . I had an agreement drawn up between National Industries of Defense, and Ben Bannerjee's Company, BR&W Industries, Ltd. . . . This was on the 6th of October, 1984, the reference number was P442. . . . the certificate [was] signed by General Alivares [*sic*] which has a serial number 333118-84SAQ and again, this is for TOW missiles.[92]

The Portuguese government would even sell twenty armored personnel carriers on which the Korean TOWs could be mounted. All Aspin had to do was provide an end-user certificate and freight insurance, and the deal was set. On October 23, 1984, he obtained a Nigerian end-user certificate for the purchase of "5,000 71A" Basic TOW missiles and twenty armored personnel carriers from the government of Portugal.[93]

Suddenly, at the end of October, just as Aspin was getting ready to ship the TOWs, the smiles faded. Casey had cold feet. The TOW missiles were too well known as an American weapon and too easily traced by their serial numbers. The Iraqis would start screaming that the United

States had changed sides in the Iran-Iraq war. Couldn't Aspin fix the Iranians up with some French antitank missiles?[94]

Aspin shrugged in disgust and went off to find a French arms dealer. Equipped with a letter of introduction from French intelligence, he and Bannerjee found one who was more than willing to sell them five thousand STRIM antitank missiles.[95] The only problem was that the French required $5 million in cash up front. No problem, said Casey. He would send a courier to arrange for a deposit to the Paris branch of the BCCI. Casey's courier was a young lieutenant colonel named Oliver North. Aspin would meet him in Paris on November 14, 1984.[96]

Contrary to Casey's directions, North stupidly recorded his instructions for the French missile deal in his notebook. To this day, Congress does not know why these thirty pages of North's diary are still classified. Two of our sources, who have independently read the entries, have verified, years after Aspin's death, that Aspin was right: The diaries confirm that North was the secret courier who left a meeting with British intelligence to arrange a French arms-for-hostages deal in 1984.[97]

These thirty pages of censored notes are the smoking gun that show that Oliver North was working with the British and French on an arms-to-Iran deal almost a year before the Israelis, who supposedly "invented" the ransom proposal, and shipped the "first" arms to Iran in the fall of 1985. The November 14, 1984, entries blow the entire Irangate chronology right out of the water. It seems that North never did tell the whole truth, even when given immunity by Congress. Whether by intention or stupidity, North withheld material facts that saved George Bush's neck.[98]

Since the London Summit in June 1984, North gradually had been insinuating himself into Bush's inner circle. McFarlane had already been criticized for not being aggressive enough and was about to be eased out of the White House. Oliver North was waiting in the wings to replace him.[99]

Despite his reputation as an Israeli supporter, North was known as a man who got things done. More and more, Bush's inner circle began to rely on "Ollie" when problems popped up that had to be hidden from both Congress and the CIA. From the recently declassified sections of North's diary, we can trace his gradual involvement, step by step, during the summer of 1984. While Casey and the big boys were off in London at the secret terrorism conference, North was left back at the White House to mind the store. On June 14 North had to deal with a problem in Angola. Bush's favorite anti-Communist faction, UNITA, had just picked up eleven foreigners for "protective custody" in connection with Angolan missionaries.[100]

North got his first glimpse of the secret Bush-British back-channel in dealing with the aborted Angolan missionary rescue. According to Sam Hall, a private British-American mercenary force had been dispatched to rescue the missionaries but had itself to be rescued by friendly UNITA forces. North liked Hall and soon put him on the Contra payroll. Apparently North learned too much and talked too freely to Hall about the man who really was in charge of the covert Contra operations. Hall was arrested a few years later by the Sandinistas in Nicaragua, and from prison revealed to the CBS television program *60 Minutes* that he was working for Oliver North and Vice President Bush.[101]

In addition to the Contra front, North was handling a part of the British liaison. While still just an errand boy, North slowly was becoming one of those "in the know." His diary for June 14 shows that he was one of the privileged few to receive intelligence about antiterrorist operations from the British secret service.[102]

There is no doubt that North had direct contact with British agents. Andrew Green of British intelligence called North directly to report that the next "terrorism summit" was set for July 11–12. In view of the previous problems with the State Department, Green asked if the American embassy in London would be involved. It appears from subsequent events that the answer was no. Bush definitely wanted the State Department kept in the dark.[103]

On June 17 North was informed that Congress would not rescind the Boland Amendment and that Speaker of the House Tip O'Neill had refused to make any deal continuing aid to the Contras. North noted in his diary: "O'Neill—no deal . . . call Brits."[104] As we shall see, Casey had arranged for British intelligence to help the White House evade the congressional ban and continue the Contra war. Contingency plans had been under way for a long time. As far back as February 1984, Casey had approached the "BCCI sheiks" to float the Contras, in the event that Congress cut off funds.[105]

As the Arab money started to pile up in June, Aspin was told to get ready to start shipping arms to the Contras. North noted on June 25, 1984, that he needed a Panama, or offshore, bank account number. The following day Contra leaders Carlos Morales, Estelle Morales, and Adolfo Calero were instructed to open an account in the Banco de America Central-Cayman Islands, under the name of the Human Development Council.[106]

Although Aspin had used the Cayman Islands before, doing so was a bit risky for British intelligence because of the BCCI connection. Aspin was told to use Barclays Bank instead. It made no difference to him; both Barclay's and BCCI were right nearby his office. North was instructed that the arms would move in twenty-four hours, but noted that strict conditions had been imposed by the British for money laundering. North foolishly wrote down all the secret British instructions in his diary:

> Never let Agency [CIA] know of amount, source, or even availability—No one in our government can be aware—Your organization must not be fully aware—[Take] care in communications [with] STEEL HQ—Accounting arrangement—No more meeting here in [British embassy] complex.[107]

Steel was the British liaison office for the Contras. Several former CIA agents were stunned when we showed them this passage from North's diary, which included several other references to London phone numbers for "Headquarters." North's diary confirmed that the vice president's staff had completely usurped normal intelligence liaison channels. Even the CIA had no idea that it had been replaced in Nicaragua by British agents. Outside of the vice president's office, the American intelligence community had been kept completely in the dark.[108]

So had the Jews. On the same day that the clandestine British conduit was established, North made a note about attending the next meeting of the Jonathan Institute. The records of the Israeli foundation for the 1984 meeting show that the Jews were still publicly appealing for a joint effort with American intelligence to combat terrorism. In 1984 the Israelis were still excluded from the game.[109]

Only a handful of people in the CIA knew what was going on. One of them was Dewey Clarridge, Casey's liaison to Bush's group and North's most frequent briefer.[110] Apparently word had already spread that foreign governments were being asked to fund the Contras. North noted some concern that the CIA thought that this might be "an impeachable offense." The CIA's general counsel was going to ask Attorney General William French Smith for a "ruling on U.S. seeking alternative funding."[111] No wonder the British wanted North to keep the Cayman Islands deal hidden from the CIA.

Clarridge, of course, was one of those who had already solicited third-country donors for arms. In fact, he provided North with a list of the ammunition that had just been shipped. In addition to the standard NATO 7.62 mm ammunition (which can also be fired from an AK-47), Clarridge's list included Communist weapons such as RPG-7 grenade launchers.[112] Since Al-Kassar was the leading arms salesman for the Soviet Bloc, he was able to buy direct from the factories in Poland, Bulgaria, and Czechoslovakia.

The shipment came just in time. North got a call from the Iran-Contra paymaster Rob Owen, saying that the RPG-7s were needed for a "private army of 75–100." Apparently Owen was trying to put together his own group of "shooters" to deal with terrorists in Central America. Casey just would not give up. While North was smuggling Communist arms through the British, things were heating up in the Middle East. Andrew Green of British intelligence called back within a week to move the counterterrorism summit to July 23.[113]

In a secure conference call, North was informed that the Hezbollah terrorists had just contacted the Algerians and asked them to serve as intermediaries for the hostage release. The terrorists discussed releasing the hostages in return for arms shipped from Portugal to Kuwait. Buckley's name had come up. The Algerians offered to pass the arms through their country, as it was a shorter route. The rest of the hostage ransom discussion recorded in North's diary was censored.[114]

Apparently the Iranians had learned about the Portuguese front companies from Al-Kassar. It should be recalled that these front companies were used in Aspin's July 25, 1984, shipment from Portugal. Word was starting to spread that the United States was in the market for Communist weapons. Rob Owen got a call from a man who offered to broker a South African RPG-7 deal, but wanted U.S. government verification that it was okay. Owen passed the information on to North.[115]

Favors also were given to those countries, such as Egypt, that were trying to help. McFarlane was asked to call the Export Import Bank to urge approval of a nuclear power plant for Egypt. Hostage and prisoner releases had become widespread. Even private citizens, such as Jesse Jackson, were trying to help release political prisoners from Cuba. North noted that the vice president's staff "has talked to Jackson party."[116] Bush's office had become the hostage clearinghouse.

On June 28, 1984, word already had reached the Associated Press that the United States was trying to build up its role in Lebanon by dispatching a thirty-man team. Whatever the British had to say to North regarding this premature disclosure also was censored.[117] The British were having their own problems. Their "#2 man in Rome" had just returned from Iran, where "he was representing our proposal." He had discovered that "one of [the] bankers of Hugh's organization [MI6] now at large as fugitive. Has jeopardized operation—Interpol looking for him."[118]

There were certainly enough leaks to go around. According to one of Clarridge's sources, "DEA thinks CIA leaked info to Gorman" of the Pentagon. Everybody was spying on everybody else, while Bush's inner circle spun its webs in secret, trying to run the Contra war and ransom Buckley at the same time.[119]

By mid-July 1984, Buckley's friends in the CIA were asking North "what's happening? Why aren't we doing something?" North was, in fact, doing something about Buckley. He was raiding the Contra accounts for ransom money. According to North's diary, one of the Contra leaders discussed with him that "part of $ will be turned into enterprise—forwarding checks for rest in $—Bank president supervising personally."[120] This is the first hint in North's diary of an early diversion of Contra funds to the ransom enterprise. The existence of the British banking channel was still a closely held secret.

On the next diary page North listed McFarlane, Poindexter, himself, and another as "those who know," while he listed Casey and Clarridge as "those who suspect."[121] The diary does not reveal what they "know" or "suspect." But in the context it appears to indicate which people were aware of the British government's role in helping the Contras. Apparently North took literally the British warning about not telling the CIA about the funding. North had yet to discover that Casey and Clarridge were in the inner circle long before he was.

By this time the U.S. embassy in London was beginning to suspect that something was going on outside the normal government-to-government channels. North noted that "Brits think we have to weigh in with [Ambassador] Price. Brits themselves have not done any serious arm twisting."[122]

As it turned out, Ambassador Price in London did not need much pressure when he learned that the British were trying to rescue an American CIA agent. On July 17 Price was allegedly shown the videotape of Buckley in captivity. Aspin and Al-Kassar had come through. North immediately went to brief Bush about the Buckley tape. One of the inner circle, perhaps Bush himself, asked North for rescue options: "Do we think there is anything that we can do?" North talked to Andrew Green and set up an early-morning meeting with British intelligence.[123]

In the meantime, there were more arms to smuggle. North met with a Contra leader, who said they needed an end-user certificate. Then there were the money men. A vice president of the Bank of America, which had been the BCCI's correspondent bank, was landing in Miami on Friday and had to get the VIP treatment. Finally, on July 24 the next "terrorism summit" with British intelligence took place. The next nine pages of North's diary regarding the summit were censored, except for one word: "Preemption."[124] Apparently Casey was still pressing the British for "shooters."

In its scramble to assemble the British back-channel, Bush's inner circle did not manage to keep its various operations compartmentalized. For example, North asked General Secord to take on one of Bush's old CIA acquaintances, Chi Chi Quintero, as his logistics man. Chi Chi had a lot of experience with "Canadian Arms dealers—Century Arms Ltd." Century Arms was much too close to the British, and Quintero was much too close to Bush.[125]

North knew next to nothing about the origins of the BCCI. He was too busy running the Contra operation long distance. Congress was hearing rumors about North's involvement and was starting to ask questions. Casey told North to "go ahead" and brief Congress along the lines of the agenda McFarlane had established. Later North admitted that his briefing of Congress was a deliberate lie, but it worked at the time to keep them off his back. Meanwhile, North kept writing memos to keep Bush informed.

In August North got another call from the British embassy to follow up on plans for a conference on September 19. Word of the British connection was still closely held inside the vice president's staff. The Pentagon's hostage rescue team, the Joint Chiefs Special Operations Committee (JSOC), was falsely told that the prime minister "was not dealing with us" but that Casey would be taking a trip on August 28 to start the ball rolling.[126]

In fact, Aspin had already been reporting to Ian Gow, Prime Minister Thatcher's personal assistant, for several months.[127] North's diary shows that the British already had begun to take over the Contra war. By the end of August, North was receiving résumés from former SAS officers who wanted mercenary work. One British citizen who had just gotten out of prison still wanted to charge North $50,000 for his services. Another, who was eventually fired, was described as a British expert on counterterrorism.[128]

North was learning more and more about the secret British channel. He noted in his diary that the next terrorism conference would be on October 4–5. On the agenda were such items as the use of force on the "secret level." The British embassy called and asked North if it should schedule still another terrorism "summit" in London. North replied that his side would prefer sometime between November 7 and 21.[129]

Despite all the secret meetings, the news was not good. The British had lost track of the hostages in Lebanon. On September 21 North reported "no precise info on Buckley et al. w/in last 2 weeks." Apparently as a result of Al-Kassar's tip, the White House decided to ask the Syrian government to help with the hostages. North noted that the U.S. ambassador to Syria was pursuing intelligence ties with the Syrians and questioned whether Vernon Walters, a senior intelligence official, should go back to the country.[130]

The next diary reference to British intelligence was censored but it was apparent that the British were under a great deal of pressure. North recorded Poindexter's announcement that there were efforts under way to learn more about Buckley, including "pressuring our allies to combine efforts and concentrate assets." Poindexter added that it was "time to take extraordinary measures" against the Iranian Hezbollah in Lebanon.[131] The rescue teams were ready and waiting, but were postponed while the diplomatic games went on in Syria.

Just as Aspin was getting the TOW missile deal lined up, there was bad news from the British embassy. Andrew Green was transferred from Washington to become head of assessment for the United Kingdom intelligence group in Belfast.[132] Green was a big loss, for he had been most helpful in the past. Still, North went ahead with planning for the next British meeting. Among the notes he made to himself were "special purpose forces," which apparently was a reference to the mercenaries, and "Spanish arms sales to Iran," which may have referred to the transfer that year of two hundred tanks from Spain to Iran that Interpol suspected Al-Kassar and the British were involved in.[133]

The rest of the notes about the British meeting are blacked out. However, on the following day, October 12, 1984, North drafted a cable to Margaret Thatcher.[134] It would be hard for her to deny any knowledge of North's activities, for his diary mentions "Thatcher cables" dozens of times. While their content is blacked out in the declassified diary, their frequency suggests that Thatcher had more than a little familiarity with the "black" end of the White House.

North also was doing more of McFarlane's work for Bush on domestic problems. On October 5 the terrorism bill seemed stalled in Congress. North made a list of topics for the vice president to discuss with key senators. While he had started out in 1982 as the messenger boy for the inner circle, by the fall of 1984, North had gradually learned most of its secrets. He was in frequent contact with General Secord at Hakim's Stanford Technology offices and also kept in touch with General Singlaub on "Iranian terror/alternatives."[135]

Just as things seemed to be progressing on Casey's plot to "neutralize" terrorists in Beirut, someone on the vice president's terrorism task force inside the White House leaked a copy of a Contra manual talking about "neutralizing" Communist officials in Nicaragua.[136] That leak was followed by another about British secret service help in Grenada.[137] Still, the British did not break off their cooperation. They needed something.

North's diary makes it clear that Margaret Thatcher's government wanted a quid pro quo for its help: more American cooperation in the war against the IRA. The "Thatcher Response" was a request for the U.S. government to prevent the transfer of funds from Irish American groups. North made a note to discuss the problem with Ambassador Price from London, who would be back in Washington during the week of October 22.[138]

Another "Thatcher cable" was discussed at the morning staff meeting on October 25. The "Brits issues" were the subject of a lunch meeting with the attorney general. Although most of the page of North's diary is censored, there are clear references to a "new legislative initiative" and a "White Paper on the IRA."[139] The Reagan administration later introduced and passed legislation to expedite the extradition of IRA agents to Britain. According to several U.S. intelligence sources, the White House also handed over the names of American sources inside the IRA. In at least one case, doing so resulted in the assassination of an American citizen by MI6.[140]

Such things were not part of the White House plan, of course. Still, British cooperation with American plans in the Middle East to "neutralize" terrorists was vital, so the quid pro quo was necessary. While the sideshow of shutting down the IRA in the United States was going on, the cables were flying between Syria, Saudi Arabia, and the members of the "London Summit."

It seemed that an earlier planning meeting between the State Department and McFarlane was, according to Admiral Moreau, "a disaster" and "a major tactical error" that "hardened all negative" attitudes at the State Department. Moreau said that "McFarlane losing grip on process—very, very bad."[141] McFarlane, the head of Bush's secret crisis staff, was beginning to crack up under the pressure and was on his way to resignation and attempted suicide.

Alan Fiers, who had just come on to the Contra program in the fall of 1984, seems to agree with Moreau's harsh assessment and said that only North was really in control of the covert Nicaraguan operation.[142] As a result of his success with the Contras, North was assigned the Iranian hostages as well. By the end of October it was clear that North would be brought in to replace McFarlane as the inner circle's representative to London. Oliver North was on his way to fame, glory, and Leslie Aspin.[143]

In the second week of November 1984, Oliver North flew to England on a secret mission. Contrary to Casey's instructions, North took his notebook with him. The next thirty pages of North's notes are completely blacked out—the longest section of censorship in the entire diary. It is, our sources say, the smoking gun, which has never been disclosed before.

The censorship codes reveal that the references to North's whereabouts and activities for the period November 12–19, 1984, have been classified on the grounds of intelligence liaison with a foreign government.[144] However, North himself stupidly wrote on his unclassified travel voucher that he was attending a counterterrorism conference in London. So much for secrecy.[145]

Since none of these documents was even discovered, let alone released, until well after Aspin's death, Aspin could not have known about North's secret November trip unless he was there. Although Aspin later got the exact sequence of events confused in his rambling, dictated statement, there can be no doubt that he was North's contact in November 1984. Aspin was one of the few in the world who knew what North was doing in London and later in Paris. North was Bush's bagman to deposit the Buckley ransom in the BCCI.

Before North turned over $5 million for the arms-for-hostage ransom, Aspin was told to make sure that the Iranians would agree to substitute the French STRIM missiles for the American TOWs. After a series of meetings in London and elsewhere, Aspin says he went to Zurich with Bannerjee in mid-November 1984 to meet with Ghorbanifar, who was acting for the Iranians.[146] Aspin specifically recalled that he and Bannerjee then left Zurich on November 14 for an evening meeting with Oliver North in Paris: "That night Ben and I had a meeting with Col. North [on] Bill Buckley, who was head of CIA Lebanon. Ben at this stage was 100% sure of official backing on the project as he had now met with North again, this seemed to give him more confidence."[147]

That evening Aspin briefed North on their meeting with Ghorbanifar. Bannerjee presented the purchase order invoices for TOW missiles but indicated that there might be long delays in getting them into Iranian hands. However, the immediate availability of the French STRIM missiles seemed to be acceptable to Ghorbanifar, who would clear it with his superiors. North had some banking business to transact alone with Aspin, so Bannerjee excused himself. According to Aspin: "After Ben had left, I was given details of bank accounts and the names of companies I could use, plus I was told . . . to open more accounts with Bannerjee in the name of 'Devon Island' . . . Devon Island was to open its account in Paris at the Bank of Credit and Commerce [BCCI] . . ."[148]

This is an astounding accusation. In it Aspin alleges that the Americans themselves chose the BCCI as the bank to handle the purchase of missiles from the French government in exchange for the hostages in Iran. Apart from Aspin, no one has ever mentioned North's secret trip to London and Paris in either the BCCI or the Iran-Contra investigations.

There is, however, evidence that Aspin was correct in describing North's secret mission. In 1993 we obtained copies of North's travel vouchers for November 14–15, 1984. In a reimbursement statement signed by North, he records that he flew to England for a counterterrorism conference and then departed London, arriving in Paris late on the night of November 13. He spent the entire next day in meetings in Paris and was reimbursed for a lunch and dinner in Paris on November 14. On the morning of November 15, he departed for a conference in Brussels, after buying some items at the duty-free shop at Orly Airport.[149]

We also asked two different sources to review North's classified diary entries for November 14–15. Although there is no mention of the BCCI, both sources confirmed that the entries concerned French assistance in an arms-for-hostage program, just as Aspin alleged.[150]

In its rush to conclude the Iran-Contra inquiry in just three months, Congress ignored several leads to the 1984 French connection and started its investigation with the Israeli involvement in 1985.[151] As a result, Congress missed the beginning of the Iran-Contra affair by a full year. No one even asked North, or Bush, or Gregg, or McFarlane what he was doing in 1984 and before. Congress fell for the cover story and assumed that the Israelis began the first arms-for-hostage deal in the summer of 1985. By that time all the operations had been shifted out of Bush's office. Blaming the Jews was their only chance for a successful cover-up. If the starting date of 1985 did not stick, the whole chronology would collapse.

Not only was the Iran-Contra Committee defrauded, no one ever realized that the BCCI was the early conduit for arms purchases for Iran for the vice president's intelligence operations. Albert Hakim testified that the BCCI was the bank used early on for arms deals, but no one picked up on the significance of his offhand remark.[152] Aspin was one of the few who knew that North was behind the BCCI transactions. Aspin had anticipated that he would be called as a Congressional witness to explain the purpose of North's secret trip to Paris. In May 1987, well before the Iran-Contra hearings even began, Aspin gave his lawyer in London a sworn summary of the 1984 arms-for-hostages deal with the White House. Aspin's hastily dictated statement is most unclear as to the subsequent chronology, although he is exact when it comes to the money.

Aspin told his lawyer that in November 1984, North and Ghorbanifar filled out signature cards for a BCCI bank account and, at a "later date"—apparently November 28 from his passport—Aspin and Bannerjee returned to Paris to actually open the BCCI bank account for the exchange of the STRIM missiles. Aspin recalled these details vividly, perhaps because the BCCI treated him like a VIP: "We were met [at the Paris airport] by the representative from the bank and driven in a black limousine to the Hilton Hotel where the bank has rooms at its permanent disposal. I remember very clearly on the way to the hotel that Ben used the phone in the car (in the bank's car, that is) to phone his wife in England."[153] The BCCI had good reason to be impressed with Aspin and Bannerjee. They seemed to be unusually wealthy customers with White House connections. Aspin detailed the numbers of the three accounts that were opened, including one that had $5 million deposited in it and another that could be operated by the signatures of North and Bannerjee.[154]

It is a pity that the Iran-Contra staff investigator dismissed Aspin's allegations out of hand. Several years later, the authors asked Senator

Kerry's staff, which was investigating the BCCI, also to check the bank records for the accounts described by Aspin. We were told that these were in fact genuine account numbers that once existed at the Paris branch of the BCCI, but that the signature cards had been removed from the BCCI files. The branch manager at the time of North's visit had returned to Pakistan. However, Senator Kerry took our allegations seriously enough to subpoena the replacement manager at BCCI Paris. He testified that he recalled being briefed about North's accounts and even remembered Bannerjee. But to his memory, the accounts were never used after they were established.[155]

What happened to the $5 million Aspin said North had deposited in the Paris BCCI branch? Albert Hakim's records show that exactly $5 million was later transferred from BCCI Paris to North's Swiss bank accounts. However, our sources confirmed that it was a different $5 million, belonging to one of the corporations owned by Saudi Arabian businessman Adnan Kashoggi, who also worked on Hakim's arms deals for North.[156] The truth is that the BCCI manager was right; the accounts were established but never used. As we later discovered, North never had a chance to deposit the $5 million ransom payment in the Paris account because the French operation was scrapped almost immediately. The Iranians had rejected the offer of STRIM missiles and demanded the American-made TOWS.[157]

According to Aspin, Ghorbanifar and Bannerjee helped sabotage the original STRIM deal, just as they later increased the price for the TOWs. There was just more profit for them in selling American missiles. The Iranians had upped their order from five thousand TOWs to twenty thousand. In early December 1984 Aspin was told to go to Germany to deal with the Iranians directly. He met with the Iranian ambassador in Bonn, who gave him an official letter outlining his government's requirements.[158]

Aspin was the first and, for a long time, the only person who realized that Ghorbanifar could not be trusted and that the Iranian government was perfectly willing to put its official commitments in writing. On the letterhead of the Iranian embassy, the ambassador confirmed "With Responsibility" on December 6, 1984, that his government was ready to deal in a big way:

> We hereby confirm that the amount for the purchase of 20'000 units of:
> TOW Missiles BGM 71A
> (First generation)
> is available in our account.
> The amount of 16'500'000.00 US Dollars (In words: Sixteen million five hundred thousand United States Dollars) for each shipment of 1250

units will be irrevocably released maximum 48 hours after the goods arrive in TEHRAN and the following documents are presented:

1) Satisfactory Inspection Certificate signed and sealed by the duly authorized representative of the buyer in TEHRAN. 2) Bill of landing for the transport and certificate of arrival and departure of the aircraft from TEHRAN Airport.[159]

The ambassador's certificate and two others for small arms and ammunition were signed and sealed with the stamp of the Islamic Republic of Iran. Aspin had the biggest deal of his life. Ghorbanifar had defrauded his own government and boosted the price to $13,200 per missile. The Iranians had committed to sixteen shipments of TOWs, with each shipment worth $16.5 million. It was a $264 million order, of which roughly $130 million was pure profit. Here was enough money to fund any secret war Casey wanted.

Aspin told his brother Michael, while British intelligence told North the good news. According to North's diary, on December 6, 1984, he had a late-night meeting, followed by a long conference call. All references to British intelligence liaison were again censored from his diary. On December 7, however, Admiral Moreau called to say that there was a problem with "Operational Security." There had been a serious leak.[160] Leslie's own brother Michael had blown the whistle on the entire TOW missile deal.

Michael had just gotten out of his sickbed in December when Leslie asked him to obtain insurance for the TOWs-for-hostages deal that was suddenly back on again. Michael thought that the whole "Buckley ransom" deal was phony and that Leslie was being set up by some sort of American sting operation. In order to protect his brother, Michael called his American source, Calvin White, director of Special Operations for the U.S. Customs Service.

The FBI does not know this, but Michael was the secret British witness who first informed on Ed Wilson's Libyan arms deals back in 1981. The federal prosecutor in the case promised Michael immunity from prosecution.[161] It was Customs Agent Calvin White who personally escorted Michael from London to Washington for a secret briefing about Wilson on December 9, 1981.[162]

Three years later Michael called White in Washington to ask if the U.S. government had authorized the sale of TOW missiles to Iran. When Michael learned that such a deal still was illegal, he offered again to become a government informant. Here is Calvin White's sworn statement:

At some time during December, 1984, I am unable to remember the exact date, I received a telephone call in my office from Michael Aspin. I recognized the voice as his and I assumed that he was calling from the U.K. Aspin stated that he had information about a deal that was being

> discussed to sell 200 TOW missiles to Iran. He stated that if the U.S. wanted to do something about this we should know about the deal and he also stated that a man named Garnick AZANIA [*sic,* actually Azima] of New York was involved in selling the missiles.[163]

When White relayed Michael's offer back to U.S. Customs headquarters, a message was sent to various Pentagon agencies to alert them of a possible diversion of TOW missiles. Apparently, Admiral Moreau's warning call to North on December 7 to say that security had been breached was based on this message. It must have caused quite an uproar in Vice President Bush's office.

There was an even worse uproar in London. Leslie Aspin had confided all of the details of the ransom deal to his brother, including the Iranian documents, the Portuguese connection, and the transfer of missiles through the Gulf states. Michael's well-intentioned efforts to protect his brother had inadvertently blown the whistle on every clandestine arms network used by the British secret service. The worst part of the debacle was that Michael himself had been asked to handle the insurance and letter-of-credit arrangements with the BCCI.[164]

Leslie was told to keep his brother quiet. In January 1985 he told Michael that Calvin White was nothing more than a "jumped up Customs Wally" and that Vice President George Bush personally had authorized the TOW missile sale. Michael told Leslie that he was a fool and that no one in the White House would back such a deal. When Michael insisted on calling U.S. Customs again, the White House decided to send a personal messenger to tell Michael the facts of life.[165]

Our sources have confirmed that in February 1985, Oliver North flew to London again. Michael admits that he met with North and that North told him that the TOW missile sale was for real. It was a follow-on to the tank ammunition deal that he and his brother put together in the summer of 1984. Michael thought that North was an even bigger fool than his brother, but he pretended to be convinced. While North and Leslie went on with their planning, falsely believing that Michael was now part of the team, Michael continued his efforts to inform on the TOW missile deal. Michael, however, believed that he could save his foolish brother from prison and make a great deal of money at the same time.[166]

Informing on illegal international arms deals can be very profitable, if you know how to do it. The trick is to blow the whistle *after* the advance payment or performance bond on a letter of credit is issued and *before* the arms are actually shipped. In return for stopping the first $64 million arms shipment to Iran, Michael wanted to keep the $1.4 million advance payment for the TOW missiles as his reward.[167]

Michael denies that he continued to try to stop the arms shipment for a reward and maintains that, after his February visit with North, he was sincerely trying to aid his brother's TOW missile deal. The American wiretaps and affidavits tell a different story. In March 1985 Michael recruited an American, Howard. He, in turn, presented Michael's $1.4 million reward scheme to various federal and state authorities.[168]

The local U.S. Customs officer in Alabama pretended to be Howard's banker and, on April 25, 1985, wiretapped Michael as part of a sting operation. When the Alabama customs agent reported his sting to Washington, all hell broke loose. The unwitting agent had just stung Bush's back-channel to the British secret service.[169]

By May the damage assessment was complete.[170] The BCCI could no longer be used for American arms deals. Michael also had exposed the Azima brothers, Bannerjee, the Oman connection, Paddy Matson, and the entire network of innocent businessmen recruited from Lloyds of London to help with his brother's hostage rescue. Leslie had told all of them that Vice President Bush had personally authorized the exchange of TOW missiles for Buckley. John Taylor, one of the innocent businessmen who had never been involved in an arms deal, decided to protect himself. Taylor learned from his own friends in MI6 that in fact Britain was secretly aiding Aspin's American hostage deal.[171] Even without Michael's disclosures, too many people knew about Bush's secret channel to Britain.

In the late spring of 1985 Leslie sent a message to North that the whole British channel had to be closed down. If the hostage deal was to continue, someone else would have to be the middleman. The problem was that the Vice President's Office did not have a trustworthy replacement for Aspin. There were not that many arms dealers around who had worked both for CIA and MI6, knew Monzer Al-Kassar, the BCCI and Bill Buckley, and had experience in smuggling guns to the Middle East.

The White House asked the British not to back out entirely. Leslie Aspin was ordered to continue working with Bannerjee and Al-Kassar on one channel, while allowing Michael, who now swore that he was a loyal member of the team, to see what he could come up with on his own. Neither brother realized that Michael was being set up. MI6 planned to frame Michael for a phony arms deal in order to discredit his previous disclosures about the real one. In the spring of 1985, while MI6 cynically told the Aspin brothers to keep both channels running, the vice president's staff had come up with a dirty little scheme of their own: the creation of a parallel arms channel that could be sacrificed if anything went wrong.

But where would they find an innocent government stupid enough to take the blame for the White House as well as provide cover for the British secret service's continuing arms deals? At that time someone in the inner sanctum had a good idea: The Jews could provide the perfect camouflage. They could be conned into opening a small arms channel that could be sacrificed, if necessary, to protect the British connection. While our sources could not establish who first thought of the scheme, they insist that Vice President George Bush's staff and CIA director Bill Casey ultimately decided that it was time to bring in the Israelis. If anything went wrong, the Jews would be the scapegoat. The only part of the entire Iran-Contra plan that worked well was the cover-up.[172]

CHAPTER 20

BLACKMAILING THE PRESIDENT?

The history books for the Reagan-Bush administration are still being written. But we can judge their likely content from the contemporaneous press coverage, which can be summarized in a single word: inadequate. Little of the truth has emerged, or is likely to emerge, from the usual channels. The American media itself has been critical of its own efforts. For example, a survey of American journalists "found that only twenty-four per cent felt coverage on Iran-Contra was good. Seventy per cent called it fair to poor."[1]

Part of the failure is that the American media has little institutional memory: Five years ago is ancient history. Part of the problem is economic. The impoverished newspapers cannot afford large research staffs. The wealthy TV networks would rather pay millions to anchorpersons who have no clue that they are being lied to. And so the lies are passed into the public domain while the media celebrities nod sagely to conceal their bafflement.

The intelligence community professionals do not put the blame entirely on the media. The truth, they assert, is that the Iran-Contra story was impossible to cover because the Reagan-Bush administration itself did not know what was happening. These politicians were entirely overtaken by clever adversaries who manipulated the White House's confusion to conceal their own covert operations. The "old spies" admit they themselves did not recognize who was doing what to whom at the time, although they have since laboriously plumbed the depths of the Iran-Contra quagmire. Here, for the first time, is what they say really happened:

- The abortive British arms to Iran deals of 1984 were buried beneath a massive cover-up, a transatlantic sting operation to protect George Bush's reputation and smear those who knew the truth. In addition to presenting false evidence to British counts, incriminating files were erased from White House computers and physically removed from the BCCI archives.
- The Israelis were recruited in 1985 as a cover story for continuing the highly illegal Bush-British partnership, which involved buying

Communist weapons for the Contras from a PLO agent and Syrian terrorist, Monzer Al-Kassar.

- The Syrian terrorist and drug king Monzer Al-Kassar also became the principal mediator for the release of the American hostages in Iran.
- What neither Bush nor the British knew was that their secret agent, Al-Kassar, really was working for the Soviets, who had penetrated the Iran-Contra operation at several levels.
- The American CIA agent William Buckley, who was told that Bush, Casey, and the British secret service had approved Middle East kidnappings, was tortured to death by Al-Kassar's accomplices in Syrian intelligence at the same time that Al-Kassar was "negotiating" for Buckley's release.
- After Bush became president, Syrian intelligence traded its silence about Iran-Contra, the BCCI, and Buckley in return for a complete reversal of U.S. policy toward Syria. The same Syrian agent and drug lord who tortured Buckley to death was given VIP passage to Washington. So was the Syrian general in charge of negotiating with the Hezbollah terrorists and of approving all drug shipments out of Lebanon.
- The British and American taxpayers lost billions of dollars from the collapse of the BCCI and the unpaid loans to finance Saddam Hussein's army.
- The government of Israel became the public scapegoat for the Iran-Contra affair. As a result of the Reagan-Bush administration's covert tilt toward the Arabs, the Israeli government lost its military superiority, most of its secret networks, and much of its reputation. At the same time, Israel was compelled to stand by helplessly as Iraq bombed their cities during the Gulf War. In the end, neither bigotry nor greed did the most harm to the Jews; it was George Bush's stupidity.

In addition to the information provided to us by our sources in American, Israeli, and British intelligence, we discovered the "smoking guns" of the Bush-British-Syrian debacle in the recently declassified office records of Oliver North, which were never shown to Congress, Colonel North's own records confirm that he has been lying all along. To this day, neither Congress nor Parliament knows how it was deceived.

The British did not realize it at Christmas 1984, but Michael Aspin had done them a big favor. His leak forced MI6 to close its BCCI connection and transfer the American operations to another British bank in 1985. One year later rivals in MI5 recruited an informant inside the BCCI and started passing word to the CIA about the amazing bank for terrorists in London. By then MI6 had covered its tracks. It had pulled all of the embarrassing signature cards from the BCCI.[2]

George Bush did not realize it, but Michael Aspin had done him a big favor as well. The near brush with exposure finally convinced the inner circle that it had to pay more attention to security. There just had been too many leaks. First, there had been Buckley's kidnapping in March 1984. Then, in May, Aspin's Greek shipment of arms to Iran had been exposed by the Mossad. The July 1984 shipment had gone through successfully, but word had leaked to the Algerians, who fortunately had kept their mouths shut.

Even the Iranians knew that the vice president was the man to see. Congress found notes in the White House from the Iranians demanding a meeting with Bush.[3] Apparently they were tired of dealing with his underlings. Bush's friends on the Contra side were no help either. North noted in his diary on January 9, 1985, "Felix [Rodriguez] talking too much about VP connection."[4]

By the beginning of 1985 people were starting to whisper in Washington that some kind of crazy spy operation was being run out of the White House. Even the CIA staff did not know about Bush's Special Situation Group. Agency insiders thought it was all "Ollie" North's fault that there was a "mini-CIA" operating over at the White House running such operations.[5] Actually, it was a mini-branch of MI6, and North certainly was not in charge. His diary shows that he repeatedly briefed Don Gregg, Bush's National Security Adviser, and, occasionally, Bush himself. There are literally dozens of diary entries covering North's dealings with the vice president's office.

According to our sources in the intelligence community, North was just a junior clerk to whom Gregg passed on orders from the vice president.[6] The special prosecutor for the Iran-Contra affair, Lawrence Walsh, now has confirmed that Gregg was one of his early targets, but he was unable to collect enough evidence against him. Without Gregg, the prosecutors knew there was no case against Gregg's boss, Vice President Bush, whom they suspected was the true architect of the enterprise.

The special prosecutor had come close, but not close enough. The cover-up was too sophisticated. George Bush did not even start to keep his office diary until well after his own involvement had ceased and the British channel had been covered up. Special Prosecutor Walsh was sent on a wild goose chase for post-1984 evidence of Bush's complicity. By then the trail had been thoroughly obscured.[7]

There was no paper trail for the investigators to track. Walsh did not know it, but the vice president's office used a separate, and totally secure, communications channel when dealing with the British. Casey had equipped both ends of the channel with an ultra-secret portable satellite system used by the U.S. Navy's SEAL teams for commando operations.

The SEAL's undetectable satellite communications were linked into the White House FLASHBOARD crisis alert network, which coincidentally was under Oliver North's supervision. That is how Bush's crisis unit originally communicated with the British back-channel in London. Key pieces of evidence were in North's diary all along, but the prosecutor did not realize it. According to a December 11, 1984, entry, Casey called to tell North that their "SEAL communicator" had been sent home.[8]

Leslie Aspin knew who the replacement was, but no one listened to him. Gregg had recruited a navy officer named Robert Earl to continue the secure SEAL phone links to England. Earl had been a classmate of Oliver North's at Annapolis, then a Rhodes Scholar at Oxford, and had worked with Gregg in the CIA. They were all in Vietnam at the same time working on hostage rescue plans.[9] Later on, when Gregg became Bush's National Security Adviser and North began taking over more of the Iran-Contra operations, Earl had joined his old friends in Washington. Earl testified that after spending a year in Newport, Rhode Island, he came to the vice president's Task Force on Terrorism in the summer of 1985.[10]

Incredible as it may seem, no one in Congress asked Earl if he had any *previous* contacts with North. No one appreciated the SEAL's role in setting up secure, untraceable telephone links for the Iran-Contra affair. No one in Congress even suspected that an earlier British channel existed before the Israelis came on the scene in the summer of 1985. According to our sources, Earl was not a major player, but he could have told Congress that a secure communications link with British counterterrorism existed in 1984. Earl also could have confirmed that he had inherited this communications responsibility when he traveled to England with North in February 1985, and that he repeatedly had met with North while attending the Naval War College months before arriving in Washington.[11]

Earl may not even have remembered his occasional dealings with North while he was stationed at Newport, but North remembered—he mentions the meetings throughout his diaries. He also mentions his phone calls to Earl before the February 1985 conference with Aspin in London. As brother Michael's leaks were discovered, Leslie claimed that he relayed several messages through Earl to North in the spring and summer of 1985. North's diary shows a half a dozen calls from Earl during this period, before Earl officially started to work for George Bush.[12]

Earl did not realize the significance of what he knew in 1984, and Congress did not know enough to ask him. Earl was not allowed to go to sensitive meetings in 1985 and did not even know about the Iranian initiative until 1986. He was just an answering service. Earl cheerfully volunteered much information about his secure phone-drop system during his official deposition. He was involved primarily with counterterrorist operations and never paid much attention to the messages he was giving North. Neither did Congress.[13]

Aspin remembered Earl very well, saying that in 1984 Earl gave him a special phone number to reach North. When we checked the phone number, we discovered that while it had a Washington, D.C., area code, the 355 exchange prefix actually rang across the river in Virginia in a secure intelligence facility. Albert Hakim testified that he also was given the same (202) 355 exchange, but the numbers for the phone drops changed constantly. The clever phone drops were only part of the vice president's enhanced security program.

The only problem with the security plan is that everyone in the inner circle forgot about North's notebooks. Casey had told North repeatedly not to make a written record, but he did anyway. Whether from self-preservation or poor memory, North kept jotting down every little snippet of incriminating information. In the short run, North's fastidious record-keeping did not matter to the success of the cover-up. North's diary was not declassified until long after the Iran-Contra hearings were over.

Here are Colonel North's contemporaneous records of how the arms deal evolved. If either Congress or the Mossad had seen his verbatim record of the original deals with the British in 1984, then the Israel-made-me-do-it-in-1985 story might have collapsed of its own weight. On December 20, 1984, North noted British plans for a meeting in Germany with the "Bonn Group" on December 24 and 25.[14] This, of course, is exactly the time that Aspin's telexes show that the Iranian embassy in Bonn was haggling over the BCCI letter of credit for the TOW missiles.[15]

North's diary shows that the British channel was truly international in scope. For example, his fumbling efforts to charter a supply ship of Al-Kassar's (who used it mostly for drug smuggling) almost exposed a major British covert operation in Africa.[16] On another front, a Canadian firm with MI6 connections, Century Arms Limited, reported on the progress of its negotiations with the People's Republic of China.[17] The White House believed that the Soviets were going to send the fearsome Hind helicopter to Nicaragua and wanted Chinese surface-to-air missiles to shoot them down. The Contras also wanted hand-held missiles as well, but those were harder to come by.[18]

The British were clearly involved with running the Contra war.[19] While they would not sell their hand-held "Blowpipe" missile directly to the Contras, they would allow Chile to do so through the back door. The Chileans needed credit and had "met with the Lady," apparently a reference to direct intervention by Margaret Thatcher. Some of these back-door deals with the British seem to have been explained to a few of Bush's friends in the Senate.[20]

Later North denied briefing Bush in 1984–1985, and claimed that he was not even in the Vice President's chain of command, but his own diary shows that he was still reporting to the Vice President for signature authority.

In other words, North was not making these decisions on his own. It is abundantly clear that someone had authorized him to conduct a series of sensitive international initiatives in the spring of 1985.[21] The scope of the international arms deals in which the Bush team was involved stepped up at this time, and North kept track of the players as they came and went.[22] But Bush had his mind on other matters.

The vice president was "pissed" about being named as the "drug czar," when no assets or resources were devoted to the drug trade, no direction was given to the ambassadors, and the Drug Enforcement Administration was still holding its information closely to its breast.[23] This complaint is a bit ironic, since the White House, through its own ignorance, was not telling the DEA that the biggest European drug dealer, Monzer Al-Kassar, was on its payroll.[24]

We must emphasize that Bush had absolutely no knowledge of Al-Kassar's drug connections. Both Bush and North actively screened out any member of the Contra forces who was even suspected of dealing in drugs. They were totally unaware that they were purchasing arms for the Contras from the biggest drug dealer in the world, Monzer Al-Kassar.

The tragic irony is that there was someone at the other end of the White House who could have told them all about Al-Kassar, but Vince Cannistraro was not admitted to Bush's inner circle. At that time, Cannistraro was President Reagan's National Security Adviser on Terrorism; later he would head the CIA's counterterrorist task force. Our sources say that it was Cannistraro who finally worked with Interpol to have Monzer Al-Kassar blacklisted around the world as an international terrorist and drug dealer.[25]

In 1992 we asked Cannistraro if he had known back in 1985 that Al-Kassar was being paid by the White House. Cannistraro refused to believe it, until we cited the million-dollar payments made from North's Swiss bank account in Al-Kassar's own name. When we told Cannistraro that the congressional investigators had confirmed North's payments to Al-Kassar, Cannistraro was stunned, especially when he learned that the investigators believed that Al-Kassar was just a minor figure connected with some Portuguese arms dealers. Cannistraro knew who Al-Kassar was, but no one asked him.[26]

Cannistraro was genuinely shocked to discover that, at the very time Interpol and DEA were hunting Al-Kassar, Oliver North and Richard Secord were recruiting him. One of the "old spies" compared Bush's war on drugs to a firing squad, in which everyone stands blindfolded in a circle and shoots each other in the foot.[27]

There is no doubt about it: The White House had hidden its operations even from the regular CIA staff. Bush's staff trusted no one beyond the inner circle, not even Vince Cannistraro, Reagan's own adviser on terrorism. The entire system of intelligence exchange and analysis had been turned upside down, with disastrous long-term consequences. In the short run, however, these excessive precautions helped make protecting the vice president from political exposure possible. Bush, after all, was Reagan's designated successor in the next presidential election. If the truth came out about Al-Kassar and the British arms network to the Contras and Iran, Bush might be impeached.[28]

Our intelligence sources say that the creation of the cover story to protect the vice president in 1985 was Casey's idea. There had to be a way to discredit Michael Aspin and everyone else in London who had heard about Bush's arms-for-hostages initiative. Bush's name already was being whispered in London, so why not plant false Bush stories to discredit the real ones? After all, the best place to hide a leaf was in the forest. In January 1985 Casey confided to one of his old OSS friends that the United States had secretly permitted the shipment of arms to Iran. His friend then went to London to start his own arms deals. As Michael said, "The word was out in the zoo."[29]

As rumors started to spread among British arms dealers that the U.S. embargo to Iran had been lifted unofficially, Casey arranged for U.S. Customs to plant an informant, Cyrus Hashemi, in London. Hashemi pushed the Bush-says-its-okay line even further. Casey's idea was to use Hashemi to arrest everyone in London, and later New York, who claimed to be helping George Bush ship arms to Iran.[30] It was Casey's last dirty trick, and a lot of innocent people on both sides of the Atlantic were caught in the fraud, including dozens of British arms dealers as well as a retired Israeli general. Hashemi eventually died in London in mid-1986, amid numerous rumors that he had been murdered by either Iranian or British intelligence.[31]

When the arms dealers in New York and London were arrested for shipping arms to Iran, they all claimed that they were working for George Bush, only to discover that the Bush arms-for-hostages deal was a fraud circulated by U.S. Customs agents. When Michael Aspin was arrested, he screamed loudly that he really *was* working for Bush, but by that time no one believed him.[32]

One document survived the White House shredder to show that Casey was behind the London sting operation. In the rush to discredit the arms-dealers-for-Bush group, one of Casey's accomplices got caught in the sting. Casey wrote to National Security Adviser John Poindexter that, at first, he was concerned that "some of the [real] principals were involved in the sting operation." Casey's friend later assured him that "none of the principals were involved, however, one of the players, Lawyer Samuel Evans, was the major indictee and is free on $4.5 million bond."[33] The American prisoners, including Evans, were quietly released and charges dropped. Michael Aspin remained in jail. He was not one of Casey's players, let alone a principal.

Several of the "old spies" say that his predicament was Michael's own fault.[34] His brother Leslie had warned him repeatedly to drop his Iranian arms deal. Michael was being set up, and fell into MI6's trap. There is no doubt that the British secret service was setting Michael up for a false conviction.

As mentioned in Chapter 19, John Taylor, one of Michael's codefendants, had secretly been in contact with British intelligence throughout the arms deal and had confirmed that the British government had endorsed the American arms-for-hostages trade. After he was arrested, Taylor protested to his lawyer that he had official permission to work on the ransom attempt. In short order, Taylor was told to keep his mouth shut about the MI6 connection in return for acquittal. He did, and he was acquitted.[35] Thus the evidence that would have acquitted Michael Aspin never came up in court.

Some people will never believe that the British judiciary would permit the suppression of testimony that would exculpate the defense. Perhaps they should see the recent film *In the Name of the Father,* which exposes a similar incident during the trial of the "Guilford Four."[36] Several of the lawyers from that case worked on Michael Aspin's trial.[37]

The prosecutor not only remained silent about Taylor's evidence of MI6 authorization,[38] but also about the fact that one confession was obtained from a witness who was being treated with psychotropic drugs for mental illness.[39] In the end, it was too much for Leslie. He came forward to confess that he was running the arms channel for the White House, but by then no one believed him. Michael, the only one on either side of the Atlantic who actually tried to expose the Bush-British gunrunning operation, was convicted, not as an arms smuggler, but as a fraud.[40]

Michael freely admits to previous criminal arms smuggling but continues to insist that he was framed on this one. It appears that, technically at least, Michael was innocent of this offense, but he was a lot better off in jail. The number of strange deaths of the principals multiplied greatly over the following years. In addition to Hashemi, Leslie Aspin and Ben Bannerjee later both died of mysterious heart attacks in their mid-forties. Their Israeli arms contact, Amiram Nir, who sat in the court watching

Michael's trial, died after his plane slammed into a mountain in November 1988.[41] Maybe Michael was lucky to have been framed. Being one of Casey's players could be very dangerous.

Apart from "neutralizing" the leaks concerning the Bush-British connection, Casey's most important contribution was to set up the Israeli government as the "fall guy" for the arms-for-hostages deals that were still continuing. As early as January 1985 a few Israelis began to suspect that someone was secretly organizing arms deals with Iran. They had tracked both of Leslie Aspin's shipments the year before and guessed that they were connected to the American hostages. They had no proof, of course, but the rumor alone was enough to throw the White House into a flap.

On January 14, 1985, North got a call from White House aide John Negroponte. Apparently, Negroponte was trying to determine how many people in Israel had heard about the 1984 British shipments to Iran. The results were grim: The "number one man" and the military were aware. It was "most unfortunate—serious adverse consequences." The "adverse consequences" were that the Israelis might realize that the White House was setting them up as the fall guys to protect the British arms channel. There was also a danger that the rest of the White House might discover what the vice president's staff was up to. Casey called North to warn him that "3 or 4 staffers [were] too aware" of what was happening.[42]

Apparently the British bugs on American phones were continuing. The fear that Israel might find out the truth later led to increased scrutiny of Jewish members on the White House staff.[43]

At the end of January North briefed Bush about the growing concerns. Casey insisted that there be no outside assistants at the Bush meeting. Apparently some of the staff members at the National Security Council had heard rumors about the back-channel operations. Shortly after this meeting, North called Poindexter to emphasize that there had been no CIA involvement in the requests for third-country assistance.[44]

This was a clear lie and suggests that Poindexter, who had previously criticized working with the British, was not admitted to the vice president's inner circle. It should be noted that most of the NSC reports during this period were harshly critical of any new initiative toward Iran. If Poindexter was out of the loop, North was getting more and more information from British intelligence.[45]

North noted that the "highest levels" of the British government were increasingly involved in the efforts to free the hostages. So were the highest levels of the U.S. government. Reagan, Bush, Casey, McFarlane, and White House chief of staff Donald Regan were all meeting to decide strategy. The next day McFarlane briefed North on their talks with the British liaison about hostages.[46]

There is clear evidence from North's diary that the vice president's office remained the center of the web. Bush met with his Contra friend Felix Rodriguez on January 28 to get some feedback on the war in Central America prior to Bush's own visit. Apparently Rodriguez was miffed now that the British were supplying pilots and flight engineers for the Contra shipments.[47]

On February 19 North was briefed about an Israeli firm, Ageo Economics Consulting, that also wanted to work with the Contras. The idea was quickly shot down. Apparently it would not do to let the Israelis find out they still were being credited as the source of Contra arms. To this day, most Contra leaders still believe their weapons came from Israel, which had captured them from the PLO.

While the Jewish arms dealers were shut out on the Contra front, the plans to make them the scapegoats for the Iranian arms were proceeding smoothly. On February 20 North met with the gullible Mike Ledeen, who was told he was being sent to Israel to do a survey on counterterrorism.[48] The White House later cited Ledeen as the man with whom the Israelis first discussed an arms-for-hostages deal. In fact, hostage negotiations were under way before Ledeen ever set foot in Israel.

On the same day that Ledeen had his first briefing, North was told that McFarlane would have "a complete English translation" of the negotiations with the Iranians.[49] This is exactly the time that Leslie Aspin and his associates were meeting with the Iranian arms brokers in London. The result of the negotiations was that the Iranians wanted Aspin to buy insurance for the TOW missile shipment. Aspin needed cash in advance to buy insurance, as his brother had blown their friendly connection to the BCCI.

At the same time, North noted that he needed an account number for the deposit. He soon got a call that the new correspondent bank was the British financial giant, Barclays International.[50] On February 25 North was notified that money had been wired from the Contra account in Miami to the new account at Barclays. Shortly afterward Aspin paid several hundred thousand dollars in insurance premiums for the shipment to Iran.[51]

North's notes of a March 21, 1985, meeting between himself and Poindexter reflect a classic example of excessive secrecy. The Iranian kidnappers did not want money; all they wanted was the release of the Dawa prisoners in Kuwait. Reference to the discussion of the British initiative was censored, but it was followed by the telling comment: "Nobody at State knows."[52]

At the last meeting of the Terrorist Incident Working Group in March, North reviewed their five options for rescuing the hostages:

1. Make a deal with the Kuwaiti Government to let the Dawa terrorists go free.
2. Make a private financial deal with the kidnappers.
3. Send the Joint Chiefs Special Operations Committee (JSOC) rescue team in.
4. Send aid to the Shia [the Shiite Islamic Republic of Iran].
5. Either a British or French deal with the Kuwaitis or the Shia.[53]

It is noteworthy that as late as March 1985, the Israelis were not even an option for an arms-for-hostages deal. The White House considered only the British and French reliable partners. North's Terrorist Incident Working Group (TIWG, pronounced "tee-wig") still thought it could bribe somebody, but was afraid that the ransom would only spur more kidnappings, which is exactly what happened. Still, naïveté reigned supreme in the White House. The task force was confident that the "ultimate outcome should be stability so that more hostages are not taken once this group is free."[54]

Portions of the next page of North's diary were censored on the grounds of "hostage release/foreign intelligence liaison." However, the censor released other portions containing a discussion of how to improve long-term stability with the Shia. Clearly North's fifth option, a British deal with the Iranian Shiites, was chosen. North thought that everything was under control. On the same day, March 26, that the British arms deal to Iran was approved, North met with General Secord, confirming the Contra supply arrangements with DEFEX, a Portuguese company run by Al-Kassar's friend. Secord thought he was in control of the Lisbon channel, reporting happily that the "Canadians are out of it."[55]

The Canadian firm was too publicly associated with British intelligence. Al-Kassar's Portuguese contact in DEFEX was a perfect front. Even Generals Secord and Singlaub did not know of the link to MI6. They thought DEFEX had been set up by the Portuguese government to help the Contras.[56]

The rush to bring the Israelis in for the Iran deal seems to have been prompted by British reluctance to stick their necks out any further in Nicaragua. Apparently MI6 had become nervous that its sister agency, MI5, would learn of its support for the Contras.[57]

Shortly after Aspin advised that the British channel should be closed down, at least temporarily, the White House plan to entrap the Israelis went into high gear. Apparently retired General Singlaub, who had worked on earlier arms deals with Israel, but did not know about the British channel, was asked to provide introductions for Mike Ledeen. Ledeen would present the "new and exclusive offer" to Israel.[58] In April 1985 Ledeen was just an innocent courier, sent to plant the seed of an Israeli hostage ransom. A meeting in Zurich, Switzerland, between Ledeen and Israeli representatives was set for the following month. Ledeen, a part-time NSC consultant whose primary qualification was that he knew nothing about the previous British channel, was, like the Jews, being set up as a scapegoat.[59]

However, on April 13, 1985, General Singlaub reported to North that the Israelis knew something about the previous Greek arms shipments to Iran. The head of Israel's defense ministry "Maundy" Maron, who was a close adviser to the Labor party's Yitzhak Rabin, "said that they had a positive I.D. on two shipments in 1984. Assumed that it [was hostage related]." News that the Israelis had seen both British shipments to Iran caused some tremors in the White House. On April 22, North met with General Singlaub again for the latest developments. The Israeli defense attaché had talked to Rabin. Maron was approached, as was Rafi Eitan of the Ariel Sharon faction.[60] The Israelis were still in the dark about the source of the weapons. The scapegoat plan went ahead.

Casey asked one of his old friends in the oil business, John Shaheen, to contact Cyrus Hashemi's business partner, Adnan Kashoggi. Kashoggi had his own investors who could privately finance the arms deals as well as extensive contacts in BCCI Monaco to ensure discretion. About the same time, in the spring of 1985, Manucher Ghorbanifar was told to keep his mouth shut about the previous arms deals with Aspin in London and to see if he could lure Kashoggi and the Israelis into taking over the arms-for-hostages game.[61]

While Kashoggi was willing to cooperate, the Israelis repeatedly ignored Ghorbanifar's suggestion that they trade arms to Iran for hostages. The soft sell by a private party did not work. The Israelis remembered that only two years before, the State Department had requested them to stop clandestine shipments to Iran. Officially, the American arms embargo was still in effect.

To overcome Israeli reluctance to break the law, Bush's staff sent their American emissary, Mike Ledeen, directly to Israel. No more subtle suggestions in Switzerland. Ledeen was told to ignore the normal State Department channels and coordinate his visit through the hard-line anti-terrorist leader Benjamin Netanyahu of the Jonathan Institute. Ledeen told the Israelis that "the White House" was asking for assistance in negotiating a hostage deal. Unfortunately, the skeptical Israelis reported Ledeen's initiative to the secretary of state, who hit the roof. McFarlane calmed George Shultz's ruffled feathers by telling him that Ledeen had gone off to Israel "on his own hook."[62]

Casey came up with a better angle. This time the Israelis were asked to help with an official CIA "research" initiative that had been approved by the State Department.[63] It wasn't quite true, but to the Israelis it finally sounded like a formal American request to see if the hostages could be ransomed. By July 1985 the Israelis agreed to "*start*" an arms-for-hostages deal with Iran.[64] Congress thinks this is the beginning of the "First Channel" to Iran.

The key to the scapegoat plan was to make the Israelis believe that they were the first as well. For the White House, the fear that Israel would discover the truth about the 1984 British channel was about to become an even bigger nightmare. Just as the Israelis were getting the arms shipment under way in the summer of 1985, the Pollard case erupted. As discussed in Chapter 18, Jonathan Pollard was a committed Zionist who went to work for the navy's Anti-Terrorist Alert Center in 1984 and later became an intelligence research specialist. That same year, a group of right-wing Israeli politicians had recruited Pollard, whose section coincidentally tracked all arms shipments to the Middle East. When Pollard was arrested in November 1985, Bush's inner circle was thrown into turmoil.

They need not have worried, as the politicians had never told the Mossad exactly what they were doing with Pollard in 1984. The Americans are not the only ones to shoot themselves in the foot with excessive secrecy.[65] Pollard was a hopeless amateur, who was stealing files by the thousands of pages and inviting his own arrest. Because the cabal of shortsighted politicians did not trust the Mossad enough to tell them what was going on, Pollard was left unsupervised. From the Mossad's point of view, Pollard was a loose cannon, an adrenaline addict, a proven *shmuck,* who went off to play spy and ended up embarrassing Israel. It was someone else's mess. Let them clean it up. The Mossad washed its hands and walked away. In a frantic effort to silence Pollard, the White House pushed for the heaviest sentence possible.[66]

As a result of the right-wing politicians' secrecy and Pollard's confinement in prison under maximum security, nobody in the Mossad recognized Pollard as the source of the report on the two unidentified arms shipments to Iran in 1984. If they had, the Israelis might have wondered if Pollard had stumbled across an early, and unknown, American connection to Al-Kassar's arms-for-hostages deals. The Mossad could have dug into the transcripts of the Iran-Contra hearings, found proof that he was on North's arms payroll in Switzerland, and could have blown the Bush-Casey cover-up out of the water. As it was, the Mossad completely overlooked Hakim's obscure deposition testimony about North's $1.2 million paychecks to Al-Kassar.[67] It was a huge intelligence blunder and a close call for the White House damage control squad.[68]

The crux of the cover-up was to deceive Congress into believing that the Israelis came up with the ransom idea on their own in 1985 and to conceal the role of Vice President Bush as the original architect of the Iran-Contra affair. In order to do that, it was necessary to conceal all the work done in earlier years by the members of Bush's Special Situation Group and pretend that nothing happened before the start of the Israeli initiative in July 1985.[69]

By the time the Israelis came on board in mid-1985, Bush had already begun to transfer the hostage operations out of the Office of the Vice President back to the unwitting staffers of the National Security Council. Even the vice president's Task Force on Terrorism was run "under the rubric of NSC." As soon as the report was completed, both Earl and North were quickly reassigned from the task force to the new White House Crisis Management Center. If anyone came looking for Iran-Contra evidence, he would be sent to the wrong end of the White House. The State Department, of course, was completely in the dark.[70] If the hostages were released, Bush would get the credit.[71] If the operation was exposed, someone else would get the blame. It was a proven method: Blame the Jews.

The Israelis did not know it, but Al-Kassar's British channel was operating parallel to theirs. On June 3 Ledeen reported that there were so many people approaching the Iranians that they were confused as to who were the real intermediaries. The mullahs at the head of the Iranian government wanted to meet with someone they could deal with.[72] Ledeen foolishly thought he was the only authorized mediator.

The Israeli files list a "Mundhir El-Qassar" as some minor informant from the Abul Abbas faction who got a lot of money selling hostage information to American intelligence.[73] Because Israeli politicians can be just as stupid as American politicians, the Mossad never got a chance to correct their bosses' mistake. The correct spelling of the name was Monzer Al-Kassar, and he was anything but a minor informant. Al-Kassar, as we shall see, was the true White House mediator for the hostages.

Everybody kept his secrets to himself. And so the farce went on as the Israelis were slowly sucked into the arms-for-hostages deal in the spring and summer of 1985. Only a handful of Israeli politicians knew the barest details of Al-Kassar's identity. To keep the Mossad out of the picture, they employed Amiram Nir as their exclusive channel to Al-Kassar and the White House. Nir was the Oliver North of Israel: an amateur spy with political ambitions. Nir actually met with Al-Kassar without knowing who he was.

The Mossad had lost several of its best agents trying to infiltrate Al-Kassar's operation and would have been outraged to learn that he was being paid by the Americans and meeting with Nir, the former TV journalist who had been appointed Israel's counterterrorism adviser by Labor prime minister Shimon Peres. But the Mossad, like the CIA, was kept out of the loop as the left-wing Israeli politicians tried to run an arms-for-hostages trade with Iran on their own, just as the right-wing politicians had tried to run Pollard on their own. Ironically, Israeli political secrecy helped to prolong Monzer Al-Kassar's career as a double agent.

Al-Kassar, of course, was not just sitting on his hands while the Israelis took over his profitable arms business with Iran. Not only did he keep his own channels open with the White House, he was busy keeping up his bona fides with his terrorist friends by planning to murder more Jews. According to Belgian intelligence files, Al-Kassar had been quite active during 1984 and 1985, planning assassinations and bombing attacks against Israelis in Europe under orders from Abul Abbas's Palestinian terrorist faction. One plan involved two Mossad agents who were trying to infiltrate Abbas's organization to prevent arms deals.[74] The Mossad was just trying to stop what it thought was a terrorist arms deal. It did not know that some of the arms were planned for Buckley's ransom.

At the same time, Al-Kassar also was building his bona fides with both the British and the PLO by betraying the Abu Nidal Organization, the extremist Palestinian group that had been causing trouble for both the West and the Palestinian "moderates." Abu Nidal had been thrown out of Iraq and was looking for new sponsors. In the eyes of Soviet Military Intelligence, the GRU, Abu Nidal was expendable because he would not follow Soviet orders. The GRU told Al-Kassar to get as close to Nidal's organization as possible in order to betray him to the West.[75]

Abu Nidal fell for Al-Kassar's pitch completely. Al-Kassar helped the Nidal group establish a Polish arms business, ironically called SAS, which were also the initials for Britain's antiterrorist commando unit; he also helpfully arranged for Abu Nidal's bank accounts in the London branch of the BCCI, where MI6 could monitor every deposit and withdrawal. In 1985 the British told Casey that Al-Kassar's sting was ready. The BCCI had tracked all the members of Abu Nidal's network.[76]

It was time for the "shooters." Casey knocked heads together at the CIA to create a new Counter-Terrorist Center that would cut across bureaucratic lines. While its staffers still did not know that Al-Kassar was Casey's secret source, they did what they were told. Abu Nidal thought that Al-Kassar was setting him up as an international arms dealer. In fact, he was being set up for the CIA.[77]

Of course, the CIA did not know that British intelligence was monitoring its transactions with Abu Nidal through the BCCI. MI6 had to make sure that none of the American "do-gooders" at Langley would stumble onto Al-Kassar's arms networks, while they chased after the red herring of the Abu Nidal organization. The CIA did not learn about Al-Kassar's

BCCI accounts for several more years, and then only because MI5 blew the whistle on MI6's bank for terrorists.[78]

To be fair, the CIA had a few skeletons of its own when it came to dealing with PLO terrorists. As the Agency busied itself with infiltrating the Nidal group, it sought allies. The best one turned out to be Nidal's enemies inside the Palestinian movement, especially among the "moderates" of Yasser Arafat's mainstream PLO, who provided a stream of intelligence to the CIA about Nidal's networks. The most senior contact between the PLO and the CIA was Arafat's intelligence chief Abu Iyad, who later was murdered on Nidal's orders.[79]

Some readers may be shocked that the CIA would deal with a thug like Abu Iyad, who had been involved in much of the Palestinian terror campaign against Israel over many years, especially after the explicit American promises that no one in the U.S. government would deal with the PLO behind Israel's back. After all, during the Carter administration, Andrew Young had lost his job as the American representative at the UN merely for having a conversation with the PLO delegate. The Israelis were particularly sensitive on this subject, as Abu Iyad continued to launch his own terrorist attacks on Israel, while he betrayed rival factions to the CIA.

According to our sources, the CIA secretly brought several moderate Palestinians to the United States for intensive briefing. This group, code named "Baker's Dozen," included most of the "official" Palestinian negotiating team with Israel: "Hanan Ashrawi, Hanna Seniora, Saeb Erakat, Sari Nusseibeh and other lower ranking Palestinians were summoned to Langley for a three day conference on integrating their politics with the U.S. . . . Ashrawi was singled out as a good Palestinian image spokeswoman dubbed by the Company—the Palestinian Golda Meir."[80]

The Israelis did not know that part of the PLO was being funded and trained by the CIA at the same time that the Agency was pretending to work with Israel against the PLO. Arafat himself wasn't crazy about the situation. He was getting squeezed on the right by the CIA's assets and on the left by the Syrian-controlled radicals. Of course, the CIA's agents among the Palestinians had to look like radicals too:

> [One of the PLO leaders] argued that unless his fighters . . . were allowed to commit some actions against Israel, they would not be taken seriously. The . . . CIA encouraged attacks on non-civilian targets. Military targets—Sha'ar Victor—Army Camps and Immigration Centers—the sole exception to the non-civilian target. At this point the head of the [Deputy Director of Operations] thought the operations were going too far and threatened to resign.[81]

How could the U.S. government arm some terrorists and hunt others? One of our sources explained the contradiction: "Y'see, Abu Nidal was a *terrorist* because he killed Americans. Arafat was a *freedom fighter* 'cause he only killed Jews."[82] This was something of a semantic fine point, as Arafat was responsible for the deaths of quite a few non-Jews too. Still, apparently this terrorist distinction salved some consciences down at CIA headquarters.

In fact, the CIA was doing everything possible to destroy the Mossad's antiterrorist networks. Instead of joining with the Israelis to hunt Abu Nidal, the CIA compromised Mossad's agents wherever possible. The anti-Israeli operations began when the CIA learned that several American companies had been dealing with Abu Nidal. Actually, several of these companies were fronts for the Mossad, which also was trying to penetrate the terrorist groups. Instead of cooperating with the Israelis, the CIA smashed a number of these companies and had their executives charged and jailed.[83]

The truth is that the CIA was far more interested in fighting the Mossad than in stopping the terrorists. Why? Because by the 1980s, oil company policy was CIA policy. The oil companies could bribe the PLO; they could not bribe the Mossad. The Mossad, in turn, had a long memory of CIA support for Arabs against Israel. Its members did not trust Bill Casey as far as they could throw him.

Instead of sharing information about Abu Nidal, Al-Kassar, and the more radical factions of the PLO actively engaged in anti-Western and anti-Israeli terrorist campaigns, the Mossad and the CIA treated each other like the enemy. Just as the White House was trying to get Israeli cooperation on the arms-for-hostages deal, the CIA was blowing up the Mossad's networks. One of the "old spies" explained American intelligence in terms of the "African centipede theory." The African centipede has fifty sets of opposing male and female sex organs, "and it sits around all day screwing itself."[84]

A classic example of the way in which one section of U.S. intelligence works against another is how Monzer Al-Kassar took over the arms channel to Iran established by Bush and his British secret service allies behind everyone else's back. In mid-October the FBI told the CIA that it had just received a report that could prove to be "embarrassing to the United States."[85] The FBI's Iranian agent had just returned from an inspection tour of Iran's military installations, during which he had witnessed an unmarked American plane unloading modern weaponry. The CIA curtly told the FBI that its agent was completely wrong.[86]

There was no mistake. The FBI's student-spy had just witnessed a shipment of top-secret Phoenix missiles that Monzer Al-Kassar had supplied to the Iranians. The CIA should have realized what was going on. Back in the fall of 1984, the Agency was told that Al-Kassar had been wiretapped at a Geneva conference with European arms dealers, where the sale of Phoenix missiles was discussed. Nine months later the Iranians were using his Phoenix F-14 missiles, then a closely guarded American "state secret," to blow Iraqi fighter-bombers out of the sky. Even then Al-Kassar could not be prosecuted, despite being classified among the most wanted international traffickers in illegal weapons.[87]

Perhaps Al-Kassar's remarkable immunity had something to do with the fact that he was working for the British secret service. In October 1985 North received a report that the Israelis were curious about rumors of the Phoenix missile deal.[88] The Israelis were getting ready for their first shipment of low-level Hawk missiles in November. They did not know that a secret British-American channel was operating one step ahead of them and selling a better grade of weapon: the newest Phoenix and Harpoon missiles, taken directly from British supply stocks.

Some clues in North's diary identify the "unmarked American aircraft" that flew the Phoenix missiles to Iran. On February 11, 1985, North listed "Race" under his problems report. Race was the new name for Global International Aviation, owned by the Azima brothers. To them, Phoenix missiles were just another cargo of "cabbage launchers."[89] Our sources say that in early 1985, the Azimas had been told to pick up some of the State Department's humanitarian aid and medical supplies from the Contras and fly it to Iran.[90] We have no idea when the first Azima airlift occurred, but there is a clue. On February 15 North received a report that the Iranians were suddenly pressuring the Hezbollah to let the hostages go.[91]

Apparently plans for the secret sale of sophisticated weapons to Iran had been in the works for some time. Our sources among the "old spies" say that the Azimas' airplane was also the one to ferry Al-Kassar's Phoenix missiles to Iran later that year. The October 1985 shipment represented the first direct transfer of American arms to Iran. That was why the Iranian parliament later identified the Azimas, not the Israelis, as the ones who first brought the Americans to Iran. The Azima connection was exposed in a November 1986 radio address from Tehran: "Iranian Speaker of the Parliament, Rafsanjani, named Azima as the man responsible for sending the Americans to Iran. Rafsanjani explained that Azima was an anti-revolutionary escapee who, nevertheless, sometimes worked for the Khomeini regime in purchasing arms for Iran."[92]

The American public does not have a clue about the Azima connection, because the White House conned the Iran-Contra investigators into censoring the name of the man whom Albert Hakim used as the secret arms contact. Azima's name is deleted from both the Tower Commission report and the Iran-Contra report. He is described only as "the first contact" who opened the "Second Channel" to Iran after the Israeli "First Channel" had difficulties.

The Israelis certainly fouled up their first attempt to ship arms to Iran. On February 25, 1986, North made notes of his discussions with the Iranian leaders: "Things were made very difficult with the hawk op." It seems that the Israelis had stupidly left Hebrew markings on the missiles and shipped the wrong parts in November 1985. Neither North nor the Iranians doubted that the Azimas' shipment of high-tech Phoenix and Harpoon missiles in October came *before* the Israelis November 1985 shipment of the almost-obsolete Hawks. "Re the relationship—we first started w/phoenix/harpoon and then there was hawk."[93] The Iranians, of course, knew that Azima was the unnamed first contact and also knew that the Azimas' "Second Channel" was really the first to deliver arms, not the Israelis.

In 1988, just before Bush was elected president, the Israelis finally figured out that the unnamed "first contact" was Ferhad Azima and that the mysterious unmarked aircraft that was seen in Tehran was "a Boeing 707 belonging to Ferhad Azimi [*sic*], an Iranian-American living in Kansas City, Missouri. The plane was chartered from a company managed by Farzin Azimi, Ferhad's brother."[94] There is no doubt that the "cabbage launchers" were frequent flyers. In July and September 1986 the Azimas' aircraft was identified ferrying still more arms to Iran. According to Elizabeth Colton, a reporter for National Public Radio:

> Witnesses at Tehran airport reported that the plane's tail carried American registry markings N345FA. According to the FAA, a Boeing 707, serial number, 20069, with those markings has been registered since August 1985 under the name of Ferhad Azima and his wife, Lynda of Kansas City, Missouri. . . .
>
> Some analysts, who have been following the unraveling of the secret White House dealing with Iran for hostages, believe the disclosure that Azima's plane was in Tehran . . . provides the missing link in trying to sort out how the National Security Council was making its deals with Tehran.[95]

When we interviewed the Azima brothers, each blamed the other brother, who was conveniently absent. Our sources knew exactly what the Azimas were trying to hide. They were not just working for Albert Hakim, they were hired by Hakim's boss, Leslie Aspin, formerly of the British secret service. Aspin was the missing link between Al-Kassar's missiles and the Azimas' aircraft.[96] The Aspin–Azima–Al-Kassar network had sent arms to Iran before the Israelis arrived and were still shipping them long after the Israelis had left.

In May 1987 Aspin dictated a sworn statement to his lawyer admitting his role in supplying the various missiles and radars to Iran. In fact, he admitted that the British arms-for-hostages deal had never been closed down:

> I'm still working towards the release of the hostages by arranging transactions in other types of equipment, mainly radar and missile systems. I categorically state that unless a High Court judge personally directs me to speak to any British officials including the police, I will not be available to anybody and this is the only statement that I am going to make. . . .
>
> There is no way I could entrust myself or the knowledge that I have [information] into the hands of the British police, in particular not to help certain persons further their career or for this information to be used for political scandal, in particular against the President of the United States.
>
> I would like to prefer that the British police continue to think of me as an idiot and a bit player in this whole affair. Also bear in mind that during the course of these transactions one of the parties involved was taken hostage himself in Lebanon and eventually tortured to death and he was head of the CIA in Beirut at that time.
>
> Once again, I say my name is Leslie Allen Aspin, I reside at 47 Desmond Drive . . . and this is the end of my statement.
>
> Would you be good enough, Mr. Powell [Aspin's lawyer], to destroy this tape so that there's no recording of my voice.[97]

Before Aspin died, he told his family to destroy all his business files as well. Fortunately they did not. Instead, they gave a copy to American researcher Peggy Robohm, who sent them on to us. There is absolutely no doubt that Leslie Aspin was the British bagman between the White House and the Azima brothers. We have all of his Swiss bank records for the British front companies. He used two silly cover names, "Willy Bringold" and "Jobri Frengold," one of which appears in a partially scratched out entry in North's diary. Aspin's front company, Multiplan Investments, had rented offices in Pall Mall and corresponded with the lawyer for the Azimas' bank in Kansas City. The lawyer's description of Mr. "Frengold" matched Aspin perfectly. In addition, Aspin's files contain dozens of Frengold signatures in his own handwriting.[98]

There is not a shadow of a doubt: What Congress thought was a new "Second Channel" to Iran was the original British network of Aspin, the Azimas, and Al-Kassar. If Congress was deceived, so were the Israelis. It appears that all the Israeli shipments of obsolete TOWs and antique Hawk parts was merely a cover to conceal the ongoing British channel for delivering sophisticated weapons to Iran.

Our sources among the retired intelligence officers were right. The Jews were nothing more than the "fall guys" for the whole arms-for-hostages scandal. Casey must have thought he was pretty clever. After letting North play with Ghorbanifar and the Israelis for one year, he ordered him to close down the Israeli channel in 1986. As Ghorbanifar, the contact for the Israeli "First Channel," was being eased out, Aspin, the Azimas, and Al-Kassar—the "Second Channel"—increased the volume of their shipments. The game went on long after the Israelis quit playing. From 1986 to 1988 Aspin laundered some $42 million through a series of British and European banks in payment for the Aspin–Azima–Al-Kassar network. Aspin's records show the last arms deal was on January 1, 1988, a $10 million ammunition order from Al-Kassar's contacts in Yugoslavia.[99]

Al-Kassar, however, was playing his own games with the White House while it was trying to close down the Ghorbanifar-Israeli channel. To the dismay of North and Amiram Nir, his Israeli counterpart, Al-Kassar invited Ghorbanifar to his home in Marbella and revealed that his "First Channel" was being dropped. Ghorbanifar then confronted Nir, angrily, who had to break the news to North.[100] The following references from North's notebook show that Al-Kassar had deliberately leaked word of the British connection.

On September 25, 1986, North made extensive notes about the discussion between Monzer (code name M, the Mediator) and Ghorbanifar (code name the Merchant): "Mediator ('M') spent some time in Syria, then came back—still has house in Marbella—has entertained merchant here last week—merchant saw local police guarding it." On September 30 Nir reported the worst to North: " 'Merchant' [knows] very much—Brit connections—talked to [Monzer]." Now Ghorbanifar was in a position to blackmail Casey and he did. He wanted money. Casey agreed to pay.[101]

Why would Al-Kassar help his competitor, Ghorbanifar, stay in the White House hostages game? Why did he expose the British connections to Ghorbanifar and the Israelis? Our intelligence sources say the answer is brutally simple. Al-Kassar was a senior Soviet intelligence agent. He was not in the business of hostage ransom. He was in the business of blackmail.[102] The Soviets and Syrians were plotting to set up George Bush for a big fall.

Here, for the first time, is what really happened to the hostages held by the pro-Iranian *Hezbollah* in Lebanon. As soon as Al-Kassar first heard about Casey's frantic efforts to ransom Buckley in 1984, he relayed word to Syrian intelligence. Within weeks Syrian intelligence had Buckley's kidnappers under its control. The Buckley case was immediately referred to the highest levels of Soviet military intelligence in Moscow.[103]

Youssef Haidar, the son of a senior Syrian intelligence officer, was suddenly rushed to the Soviet Union in 1984 for "special training" in interrogation. When he returned in 1985, his assignment was to torture

Buckley in such a way as to leave no visible marks. A long flexible tube with inflatable balloons was forced down the CIA man's throat. As the air pressure was increased, the pain became unbearable.[104]

One of the eyewitnesses to this torture was Lilly Boustanny, a Lebanese citizen who worked for British intelligence and later became an agent for U.S. Army Intelligence. We have a sworn statement from Kris Kolesnik, one of the Americans who debriefed Boustanny concerning the manner of Buckley's death:

> And she's in that room I guess where Haidar orders the air pressure turned up in the tube that's down his stomach. I'm assuming the reason why he's got that in there so they wouldn't leave any traces, but he's got a tube down his stomach and they torture him by increasing the air pressure. And she kind of throws up or gets sick or whatever, and she's begging [her Washington contact] to do something about it because this guy's going to die. And I have all this recorded on a daily basis.[105]

By the end of spring 1985, Haidar's torture sessions had gone too far for too long. He had increased the air pressure so much that Buckley's lung tissue was traumatized. Buckley developed pneumonia and strangled to death on June 3, although his death didn't become public until much later. Bush had been bargaining for a dead man.

Even after Buckley's death was revealed, the vice president's nightmare continued. Before he died, Buckley had signed a 400-page confession in which he revealed the whole plot, every detail of the White House's illegal plan for a private mercenary force to kidnap or assassinate terrorists. From the Hezbollah kidnappers the confession went to Iran and Syria, and the Syrian secret service sent it straight on to Moscow.[106]

Our sources say that the Soviets and Syrians played Casey and Bush like a flute. Al-Kassar knew they were desperate to get Buckley back and even more desperate to suppress his confession. The revelations about the American kidnap and assassination team would have ended Bush's political career and might have landed Casey in jail. But the Soviets did not want merely to blackmail Casey. They wanted Bush. Al-Kassar was just a straw man at the auction, pushing up the ransom price to see how high Bush and Casey would go. TOWs, Hawks, Phoenix missiles, F-14 radars, whatever the Syrians demanded as ransom for the "Iranian captors," they got. Then they wanted more. They wanted a visit from Vice President Bush.[107]

The "old spies" we interviewed for this chapter say that Bush was slowly sucked in by the Syrian government and that he should have known better.[108] North's contemporaneous records show an increasing awareness that it was the Syrians, not the Iranians, who were calling the shots with the kidnappers. The first clue was apparent in the spring of 1985, when North received a report that in Lebanon pictures of Khomeini were being replaced by pictures of Assad. By that time Iran had "little or no influence" among the Lebanese kidnappers.[109]

On May 22 North had yet another hostage release conference. U.S. intelligence advised that the Syrian officer in the area of the hostages controlled all exits and entries and even collected a "tax" at Lebanese checkpoints. North was warned: "If Syrians become aware, Syrians will grab hostages." French intelligence said that it already viewed the hostages held in Lebanon as a Syrian operation and was applying its own pressure. North passed the problem over to Bush's staffers. On June 24 the National Security Planning Group endorsed making a call to Assad. The plan was to keep "continual pressure on Syria re other 7" hostages.[110]

That, North discovered, was easier said than done. On July 9 he attended a briefing for McFarlane, who was being sent to cut a deal with the Syrians. The briefer characterized Assad as a "Pan-Arab bigot" looking for a "personal victory." McFarlane was cautioned on how to approach the Syrian hostage negotiations:

- Don't beg on a "deal"
- Don't imply he's a murderer . . .
- No gratuitous comments about Israel . . .
- Take a leak before going in . . .
- Will talk about endless time to get things done . . . Patience!
- Very likely to be a long meeting
- Sees himself as a statesman
- Personal description of distaste for Americans.[111]

Casey was more to the point. Not only would the Syrian president refuse to help with the hostages, "Assad will do everything possible to obstruct peace process." Fears that the Syrians would interfere with the ransom efforts continued to plague the White House.[112]

On August 8, 1985, there was an uproar about an article in *The Washington Post* identifying North as the administration's point of contact to the Contras and the author of the secret proposal to " 'neutralize,' meaning kill" terrorists. North received a call "to VP thru Don Gregg." The *Post* article was "not good for process, not good for country, national interest." Dan Murphy was told to call the publisher, Katherine Graham, and warn her that the article could "endanger TWA solution."[113]

Hoping that the storm would blow over, North went back to negotiating with the Syrians. On November 6 North was advised that the State Department was considering giving "Syria credits" to help its economy.[114] The descent down the slippery slope to bribery and counterblackmail had begun.

By now it was becoming clear, even to the Iranians, that the Hezbollah kidnappers were working for someone else. By December 6 North reported: "Iranians are having great trouble controlling situation—great urgency."[115] The Syrians were in no rush. All the hostages were safely in their pocket.

Apparently Assad wanted a more important negotiator. On March 31, 1986, Dewey Clarridge asked North "is VP going to meet w/[them]?"[116] On May 15 it was decided to arrange a meeting between Ambassador Murphy and "Shiabi (person close to Assad). Chief of staff of armed forces . . . this weekend—Europe—must be very private." It was just another stall. The Americans were told that the man who actually held the hostages was "out of country, probably in Iran. Syrians trying to find him."[117]

On May 28 Bush and Reagan decided "no further meetings till hostages come out."[118] That policy did not last very long. In July the State Department sent some diplomats who:

> . . . presented message to Assad . . . said statements made after TWA 847 [criticizing Syria's support of terrorists] were injurious . . . Assad promised that he would get mail to/from hostages . . . Assad said to tell Pres that "there would be good news soon" . . . Israeli embassy asked Dornan to ask abt Jewish [hostages] . . . Assad offended at unfair treatment by US . . . Assad said [Iranian Hezbollah group] does not hold [the hostages].[119]

The vice president sat in on the diplomats' briefing and discovered that the Syrians were not just go-betweens, but the people who controlled the hostages' fate. Now there was no choice but to deal with Assad face to face.

Lilly Boustanny relayed the message from Haidar of Syrian intelligence: "She was saying that all the Syrians were saying that they wanted to give the hostages to us, and the principal guy doing this was the then-vice president Bush."[120] Boustanny says that Vice President Bush made four secret trips to Damascus to negotiate personally for Buckley's release. We have confirmed one of these trips. The Israelis have admitted that on July 29, 1986, George Bush flew to Israel and met with Prime Minister Peres and senior cabinet members before flying to an Israeli air force base to watch maneuvers.[121]

Purely by coincidence, one of the authors visited the same base a few years later and had lunch with the pilots. The entire base was still talking about Bush's "secret" flight to Damascus. Several people remembered it because during that same week in July 1986 the Syrians released Father Lawrence Jenco, an American hostage held captive in Lebanon, as a goodwill gesture.[122]

According to another report given to us independently by a former intelligence officer who worked on counterterrorist issues, a reliable source in Lebanese intelligence told him:

> On the 17th of July [1986], an American official arrived in Syria and met the Syrian President Hafez Al-Assad and Abdul-Halim Khaddam. They discussed the hostages issue. President Assad promised the American official to release the hostages held in the Southern Suburb and those held at "Sheikh Abdulla" Barrack in Beqaa.
>
> - The hostages are in fact held by Syria and not by "Hezbollah" as the media portrays it.
> - The deployment of the Syrian Army in West Beirut and the southern suburb is as a result of an agreement between Syria and U.S.A. provided that Syria does two things:
>
> 1. Release the hostages.
> 2. Exterminate the elements of "the Iranian Revolutionary Guards" [which] specialized in executing terrorist and kidnapping acts and operations.[123]

Our sources in the intelligence community say that the Syrians were just playing with Bush, teasing him with promises to release more hostages and trying to find out how much the vice president would pay to keep Buckley's confession from hitting the American press.[124]

North noted: "vp trip to Israel—the longer this goes on—the worse it will be." That was an understatement. Bush was so aggravated by his July trip from Israel to Damascus that North noted the recommendation "that Israelis be taken off the short tether in the Bekaa."[125]

It was an idle threat to use the Israelis to up the pressure in Lebanon with some military action. Instead of launching a raid against the terrorists, North called to set up the date of the next Syrian meeting. Bush would meet with Kanifani, a senior Syrian official, on August 23. On the day before Bush's meeting, North was told the White House party line: We do not have an official deal with the Syrians. It is just a private discussion with Kanifani.[126]

After the meeting was over, North reported that "many strange things [were] going on in Syria—people taking pictures of hostages—U.S." The bad news was the Syrians were the only ones who had access to the hostages. The good news was that many of the hostages were still alive. The bad news was that "Buckley gave them much sensitive info, but protected."[127] The "sensitive info" was presumably Buckley's confession of the details of the private mercenary force. The Syrians had the vice president of the United States in a very compromising position. They were willing to sit on Buckley's information and even release the rest of the hostages, but only if Bush cooperated with the Syrian agenda.

One group almost blew the whistle on Bush: the members of the Intelligence Support Activity (ISA). This top-secret American commando group had been sent to Lebanon to rescue the hostages by force. The ISA got lucky and developed a network of Lebanese informants that uncovered the hostages' whereabouts. By November 1986 the commandos had gathered all the intelligence: maps of the various Iranian compounds and even the names of the Syrian officers who shuttled the captives back and forth. One Pentagon source showed us the documents, with details down to the license plate numbers. The commandos had a positive identification of all six surviving hostages. They were ready to rescue them when, suddenly, they were told to stop collecting intelligence and come home. In the end, the truth was too embarrassing.[128]

The problem with the ISA team was that it was too good. It was flooding U.S. intelligence channels with highly accurate reports on Monzer Al-Kassar, General Kanaan, and the Syrian drug-runners who controlled the kidnappers. The army had no idea that Al-Kassar was working for the White House on hostage ransom. The ISA's sin was success. It had dug up too much of the truth.[129]

Bush should have realized that the Syrians were playing good cop/bad cop. Al-Kassar and President Assad were the good cops. Haidar was the bad cop. They strung Bush along from 1985 to 1988, releasing a few hostages, kidnapping others. Just before Bush's election in 1988, Haidar made his move.[130]

According to Lilly Boustanny, Haidar was still using her as a courier to relay messages to the White House. Haidar discovered that Bush was planning another trip to Damascus in May 1988, trying to get the rest of the hostages out before the election. Haidar sent Boustanny to Paris with a message for Bush: "The answer you will get on Thursday is NO. You're not going to get them." If Bush wanted the hostages, he would have to deal with Haidar and no one else in Damascus.[131] Haidar later boasted that he had taken pictures of Bush in Damascus that "would be worth a fortune."

It is clear that Haidar believed he could blackmail Bush. We have found no smoking gun to show that Bush was blackmailed. However, the sudden reversal in American policy toward Syria did strike many across the political spectrum as inexplicable. We regret to confirm that Youseff Haidar, the man who tortured Buckley to death, was subsequently observed in Washington, D.C., with a VIP escort by Agent John Lipka of the FBI.[132] Shortly after Haidar's visit, Bush announced to the press that the Syrians had gotten a "bad rap" for terrorism. Soon thereafter, several more hostages were released. Shortly after that, the CIA was told to stop investigating a Syrian connection to the 1988 bombing of Pan Am Flight 103 over Lockerbie, Scotland, and focus attention on Libya. By this time conservative members of the Republican party began to mutter that Bush had gone soft on Syrian terrorism.[133]

If Bush thought that the Syrians would "protect" him from the release of Buckley's confession, he should have realized that Assad would demand a heavy price for continued silence. During the next four years, U.S. intelligence observed a bewildering number of Syrian terrorists, drug-runners, and intelligence officers arriving in Washington as "special emissaries" of President Assad.[134]

The Christian Lebanese accused Bush of making a deal to permit the Syrian takeover of Lebanon. The Arab press added to the suspicions by leaking copies of Bush's correspondence to Assad.[135] Even Congress berated the Bush administration for going soft on Syrian drug salesmen. Everyone from conservative Republican think tanks to the major media criticized President Bush's reversal of policy toward Syria, but almost no one knew what was behind it.

One of the "old spies" put it very succinctly: "Look, George Bush was a nice guy who got in over his head. The Syrians kept leading him deeper and deeper until there was no way out but to continue paying the blackmail."[136] Several other sources say that Bush was not the only politician to be caught in the Soviet-Syrian web.[137] Interpol records and classified files show that several prominent Latin American, Austrian, Spanish, and Lebanese politicians took a little piece of the illegal arms and drug deals and then were blackmailed by Al-Kassar and his friends.[138]

The Syrians kept the game going even after the collapse of the Soviet Union. They had been taught too well. Other Soviet clients followed suit. The next one to make a secret deal with George Bush was Saddam Hussein. This time it was not blackmail, but a trade of oil for guns. The secret war against the Jews was about to explode into flames.

CHAPTER 21

THE VICTORS AND THE VICTIMS

The "old spies" have a very interesting explanation for Saddam Hussein's invasion of Kuwait: American oil companies told him it was all right to invade, so he did.[1] The oil companies were the only ones who agreed that Iraq had a legitimate gripe against Kuwait.

The tip of a banana-shape oil field in southern Iraq extends three miles across the Kuwaiti border. Under the unwritten rules established, and enforced, by the international oil companies, profits from cross-border fields are allocated according to the percentage of the oil field that lies in each nation. But for years the Kuwaitis had been pumping the field madly without paying a cent of royalties to Saddam Hussein. The oil men agreed that Kuwait was stealing Iraq's oil.[2]

As the Iran-Iraq war wound down, Saddam needed money badly. The old Soviet economy was in shambles, the Syrians were broke, and the Kuwaitis were thumbing their nose at him. To add insult to injury, the Kuwaiti royal family was demanding that Saddam pay them $10 billion. They had loaned Iraq a lot of money over the years to fight Iran, and now they wanted it back, all of it.

According to the "old spies," here is how the 1991 Gulf War really began. For several years American oil companies in the region had been supplying clandestine aid to Casey's secret war in Iraq. Alan Friedman wrote about some of this in his exposé of the Iran-Iraq war.[3] But there is more that has never made it into the history books.

According to our sources, the oil men in Iraq had gotten quite close to the small army of CIA and British mercenaries who directed Saddam's war machine. Naturally they were all sympathetic to Iraq's point of view. One of the oil men suggested that Saddam had every right to seize control of the Kuwaiti portion of his oil field. It was, after all, only a three-mile strip of sand. The oil men in the White House would probably make some public protests, but in private President Bush almost certainly would continue to support Iraq. Some of the British and American intelligence officials nodded in agreement at the suggestion that Iraq could invade the oil field without meaningful American protest.[4]

The conversation apparently was reported to Saddam Hussein, whose ambassador sounded out the Americans further. Would the White House really be willing to turn a blind eye toward Iraqi seizure of the offending oil field? The answer, he was assured, would probably be in the affirmative. After all, George Bush was a fellow oil man, and he would understand that the Kuwaiti oil poachers had to have their knuckles rapped.[5]

Given an inch, Saddam would take a mile. Given three miles, he would take the whole country. The Kuwaiti banks would singlehandedly solve his balance of payments problem. He honestly believed that the Americans would not make a big deal about the invasion of Kuwait, which was under British influence anyway. Saddam was going to sell all the oil to the Americans anyway, as they were his best customers. With all sides getting bad advice from the oil companies, misunderstandings were inevitable.[6]

By 1991 Saddam's "misunderstandings" were raining down on Israel. At least the Bechtel Corporation, under Shultz's prodding, had not finished its chemical factory for Iraq. During the Gulf War, George Bush refused to let the Israelis defend themselves on the grounds that it might offend the other Arab states.

Because Bush did not trust the Jews, the Israeli air force was denied the American black box identification code. Without the IFF (Identification: Friend or Foe?) setting, Israeli planes would be mistaken for Iraqi forces and shot down. While the United States paid billions in bribes for token Syrian and Egyptian forces, the entire Israeli Army was grounded with Iraqi missiles falling all around the country. The Israelis found it hard to accept the American explanation that defending Jews was distracting from their liberation of Kuwaiti oil wells.[7]

In the last dozen years, Israel had lost its military superiority, seen most of its secrets handed over to the Arabs, and watched as foreign missiles, tanks, poison gas factories, and warheads poured into their enemies' hands. Now the U.S. president was standing by while Israel was bombed. What had happened to their American ally? the Jews wondered.

Saddam wondered the same thing. He thought his friends in Bechtel could sway the entire American government. Perhaps dealing with Bechtel was one of the reasons he thought the Americans were weak. For years the company had been bending over backward to please his every whim. Unfortunately for Saddam, Bechtel was having a spot of trouble right then.

In early 1988, just two years before Iraq invaded Kuwait, Bechtel found itself embroiled in a scandal that focused very directly on Israel and the company's Iraqi business interests. The origins of the affair went back to 1984, to "a tangled scheme to persuade the Iraqi government to build a $1 billion oil pipeline."[8]

By the time federal investigators were probing the Bechtel-Iraq scandal in 1988, it had become a major bribery inquiry, centered on whether a Bechtel representative had recommended trying to buy influence with the Israeli government. The scandal showed just how pervasive was the influence Bechtel had with Vice President Bush, and just how long-lasting Dulles's "revolving door" has been.

Bechtel's influence had seeped over from the CIA and the Defense Department into the Justice Department. As one business magazine commented on the scandal, "Attorney General Edwin Meese III's job may be on the line. So may Bechtel's reputation." It turned out that, like George Shultz and Caspar Weinberger, Meese had a close Bechtel connection: He had acted as an attorney for the company. He also was a close friend of the Saudi ambassador to the United States.[9]

The Iraqi pipeline idea was hatched in 1984, just when the Al-Kassar–Iran–Contra–BCCI scandals that haunted Reagan and Bush for the next decade also were on the drawing board. It was a time of plummeting oil prices, which had put an abrupt brake on the highly profitable "superprojects" several Middle Eastern countries had contracted Bechtel to construct. "The pipeline, which was to run from Iraq's northern oil fields through Jordan to the Red Sea, sounded like a surefire way to shore up Bechtel's business."[10]

The scheme is a good example of how the Jews were expendable at every turn. While one end of the Reagan White House was busily concocting a scheme to make Israel the scapegoat for the arms-for-the-Iranians-and-Contras operation, which had been inspired by one of Israel's greatest enemies, Syria, the other end was planning how to enrich another of Israel's deadly enemies, the Iraqi government of Saddam Hussein.

The problem was that in 1985, Bechtel's pipeline deal for Saddam Hussein seemed to have turned sour, because Hussein feared that Israel would allow him to spend billions on constructing it and then wipe it out, just as it had his nuclear reactor in 1981. Bechtel could see its profits going down the tube. And it had such a bad reputation in Israel, it needed someone "who had strong ties to the Israeli government."[11]

The man who Bechtel hired to try to influence the Israelis was Bruce Rappaport, who also was innocently involved in the 1985 arms sales to Iran. Rappaport just happened also to be one of Oliver North's bankers in the so-called "First Channel" through Amiram Nir.[12]

Rappaport then "sought out attorney E. Robert Wallach, a close associate of Meese, to line up Reagan Administration support." Subsequently, Meese referred Wallach to Reagan's National Security Adviser, Robert "Bud" McFarlane. In mid-1985 Bechtel and Rappaport entered into "a partnership," which entailed Rappaport securing Israeli agreement "not to damage the pipeline. In return, Rappaport would get a percentage of the oil, possibly for sale to Israel."[13] CIA director Bill Casey approved the plan, as it seemed to promote American interests in the Middle East, to say nothing of Bechtel's corporate profits.[14]

Apparently, Rappaport was successful in obtaining Prime Minister Peres's promise not to impede Bechtel's deal with Saddam Hussein.[15] At the same time, Vice President George Bush personally intervened to arrange ExImport Bank funding for Iraq's war machine.

The bottom line for the Bush-Baker initiative was that in three short years, Iraq went from supplying only a tiny portion of U.S. oil to an amount almost comparable to the 2 million barrels a day supplied by the Saudis. By 1987 the United States imported only 80,000 barrels of oil a day from Iraq. In 1989 President George Bush signed a top-secret order, National Security Directive #26, permitting the secret transfer of sensitive weapons technology to Iraq. Oil imports from Iraq climbed to 1,100,000 barrels a day in 1990. Billions of dollars' worth of loans guaranteed by American taxpayers went to Saddam Hussein, *after* U.S. intelligence reported that he was using the money to build atomic and chemical weapons of genocide.[16]

The British were brazen about sending arms to Iraq. One Whitehall aide wrote that "I doubt if there is any future market on such a scale anywhere where the UK is potentially so well placed." Iraq was "the big prize." More than six weeks *after* Saddam invaded Kuwait, the British government was still shipping large quantities of artillery shells to Jordan, with full knowledge that they would be diverted to Iraq.[17] None of this secret history was made public at the time of the Gulf War.

It is a matter of public record that many former members of the Reagan-Bush administrations had such heavy investments in oil companies that they had a clear conflict of interest in determining U.S. policy in the Middle East. As previously mentioned, George Bush secretly waived the Federal conflict of interest policy. Many members of his administration have enriched themselves in the Gulf states after leaving government service. Even Bush's son George Jr. was awarded a lucrative oil contract in the Gulf. No matter which side triumphed in the Gulf War, the oil men had won. To the victors go the spoils.

In the end, the pipeline deal fell apart, despite the support of Meese, McFarlane, Rappaport, and others.[18] But the whole episode illustrated the corrupt influence, and enormous power, of the multinational corporations that have spearheaded the secret war against the Jews. Whatever minor and temporary setbacks Bechtel and its friends may have suffered, the system goes on. In the end, Jack Philby was right. It was all about oil.

Now let us look at one of the victims. Just one. In many ways, though, this man fought back for all the Jews in the world.

Sol Shnadow was not a corporate giant. No one offered him an insider deal in Kuwait. He was not an imposing figure, just a stocky, round-faced barber with a great sense of humor. Few could see the deep pain he carried within—the despair of a man who has seen too much. Yet Sol Shnadow was a modern Jewish hero, one of the very few who honestly could say he had had some form of justice against the Nazis who murdered his family. But in the end, it was a small drop in an ocean of amorality.

Several years ago the Mossad found Sol Shnadow in the United States, where he had settled many years earlier, and flew him to Israel for the dedication of Yad Vashem, the Holocaust museum and institute. Golda Meir met him at the airport. He was one of the last living Jewish war heroes.

With him Shnadow brought a photograph of the partisan unit he had fought with in the forests of White Russia, what we know today as the independent state of Belarus, a nation of Slavs sandwiched between Poland and Russia just to the north of Ukraine. Sol's photograph is now one of the famous picture posters distributed around the world as part of the B'Nai Brith Holocaust education series. The poster is entitled "The Jewish Resistance." The men and women look so young and so grim. They posed in two rows, rifles at the ready, with crossed armbands full of ammunition. Sol Shnadow is in the front row, second from the right.

The Jewish partisans of White Russia were almost sacred to Israeli politicians, for reasons that are particularly poignant. Many of the prime ministers, cabinet members, and intelligence chiefs of Israel were born in or near White Russia. For the first forty-five years of Israel's existence, numerous government leaders came from that particular corridor of White Russia, Lithuania, Russia, and Ukraine. This was the region that lay within the extended boundaries of VorKommando Moskau, the Nazi unit that organized and carried out the mass exterminations of Eastern Europe's Jews in 1941 and 1942, before the machinery of the gas chambers even had been assembled and set to work.

The man who murdered Sol Shnadow's family was Emanuel Jasiuk. He also settled in the United States after the war, just half an hour's drive from where Sol made his new home. Unlike Sol, Jasiuk and his colleagues, such as Stanislav Stankievich, had high-level assistance to enter the United States and then inside help to obtain well-paid government work. Jasiuk and Stankievich, who ran the concentration camp where Shnadow had been imprisoned, were two of Allen Dulles's Fascist "freedom fighters" and then members of Nixon's ethnic Fascists, getting out the vote for the Republican party. Jasiuk, Stankievich, and their friends had murdered not only Shnadow's family, but the families of many of the leaders of the State of Israel.

Shnadow and the Jewish partisans had fought back for all of them. That was what made him a hero to Golda Meir and her colleagues. It was the only retribution, or justice, many Israeli leaders would ever have. Letting these Nazis go free after the November 1947 deal with Nelson Rockefeller was the hardest thing this generation of Jewish leaders ever had to do. It was a price they chose to pay. If they hadn't, there may never have been an Israel. They traded silence for security, keeping silent about the Nazis' escape in return for votes in the United Nations to guarantee that the Palestine partition resolution would be carried.

The truth is horrifyingly simple. The originators of the first, crude killing systems of the Nazi Holocaust were never punished for their crimes. The governors, mayors, and police chiefs who carried out these crimes against humanity under the direction of VorKommando Moskau deliberately were allowed to go free.

The reason was simple. At the end of World War II, every Western intelligence service competed to hire the members of VorKommando Moskau as anti-Communist intelligence experts. VorKommando Moskau knew the names of all the secret agents and collaborators behind the Iron Curtain. After the war, MI6 and Allen Dulles whitewashed as loyal anti-Communists, those whom the SS had screened as loyal Nazis. Their war crimes were ignored in the rush to rebuild the Nazi spy networks behind the Iron Curtain.

To the Western intelligence services, it made a cynical sort of sense. The Nazis were defeated, and the new enemy was the Soviet Union. Hitler's war was over, but the Cold War had only just begun. Why waste valuable intelligence assets just because of a few dead Jews? No one would ever learn that Nazi intelligence agents were still on the payroll, only with new masters. Even if the Jews did learn about the files of VorKommando Moskau, what could they do about it?

As was seen in earlier chapters, the Jews did a good deal. The founders of Israel used their knowledge of this unit to blackmail the Nazis' new employers in the West. For the founders of Israel, the cover-up was the cornerstone of continued Western support. It was the secret price they paid to have and to hold a Jewish state amid a sea of enemies. But what a terrible price: to let the men who murdered their own families go free.

The first two generations of Israeli leaders included men and women like Chaim Weizmann, David Ben-Gurion, Golda Meir, Moshe Arens, Levi Eshkol, Menachem Begin, Shimon Peres, and Yitzhak Shamir, all of whom were born within the operating radius of VorKommando Maskau. To understand how they must have felt about letting the mass murderers of their people go free under the deal with Nelson Rockefeller, you must see the events through the eyes of someone who went through it and survived.

Although he did not understand the *why,* Sol Shnadow saw the *what* and wrote it down for posterity. In his memoirs, he left behind a bewildered anger at the horror he had known during his lifetime. He described himself as both a victim and a witness. He was, in fact, a hero who had been betrayed.

For Shnadow, who was born and raised in Poland near the German border, the nightmare began in September 1939, one week after Hitler and Stalin signed the Non-Aggression Pact. It was the month that Hitler attacked Poland, with Stalin's connivance. On the first day of the war, September 1, Shnadow was called up for reserve duty with the Polish cavalry. He was an unlikely hero, just a twenty-seven-year-old barber, with a wife and two small children.

Three days after Germany attacked Poland with tanks and airplanes, Shnadow's unit counterattacked on horseback. The unit actually fought its way across the frontier and penetrated the Third Reich. Shnadow was probably the first Jewish soldier to invade Nazi Germany. The incident did not make it into the history books, however, because he was the only survivor. The German army caught the little band of Polish cavalrymen in an artillery ambush, followed by a machine gun attack. Shnadow's horse was blown to the ground, pinning him beneath it. In seconds the battle was over. The brave Polish cavalry surrendered. Then the German infantry moved in to take its revenge.

First, the Germans shot the prisoners of war and then the Polish wounded. Shnadow could hear the footsteps as the executioners approached. He could only lie there helplessly and close his eyes as the shots came closer. A German soldier looked down at him, covered from head to toe with the blood of his horse. "This one's dead," the soldier muttered, and moved on. For seven hours Shnadow lay still amid the corpses, waiting for the Germans to finish their killing and leave. When darkness came, he struggled from beneath the horse and threw off his helmet. To his amazement, all the hair on the top of his head was stuck to the dried blood in the helmet. He was alive, but partially bald.

Shnadow changed his uniform for some clothes he had stolen and snuck back across the border into Poland, the only survivor of the first raid on the Third Reich. He went back to being a Polish barber and waited for the victors to arrive. On September 15 the Germans finally arrived in Sol's little village of Ostrolenka, and the humiliations began. A Luftwaffe officer drew a line down the faces of two very religious Jews and ordered Sol to shave off half their beards, not realizing that the barber was himself a Jew. After making the Jews pay Sol, the officer forced them to crawl on their bellies for several blocks.

> I knew a new reality had come. Half a block from me there was a one-story building belonging to the Jewish community council. I saw the Germans bring about ten Jews there in a truck. They locked them in the truck and one German, in a white uniform, with a huge knife, called the first Jew inside.
>
> I was standing, watching. In five minutes, the German emerged alone. His entire uniform was soaked in blood, and the knife was bloody. One after another he marched a single Jew into the building, and emerged more covered with blood. It appeared obvious that he was killing the Jews, one by one. The fourth victim died before he entered the building. He fell on the ground, and had a heart attack.[19]

It was, in fact, a macabre German joke. They were merely slaughtering geese and wanted to see how frightened they could make the Jews. Their intimidation had a purpose: Terror made the Jews easier to deport. It had worked very well in Germany. In the early days, the Nazis did not murder Jews wholesale; they simply drove them out to someone else's country. When the order came that the Jews of Shnadow's village had twenty-four hours to evacuate, no one disobeyed.

The Hitler-Stalin pact of August 1939 had divided Poland, and the Nazis were driving the Jews en masse across the border into the Soviet zone of occupation. It is an irony that in 1939, the only national leader willing to admit Jews was that great anti-Semite Joseph Stalin. The deeply religious Jews of Poland dreaded the atheistic Bolsheviks.

Shnadow had already lost one brother fighting the Communists in 1920. He did not know it, but soon he would lose two more. First, his younger brother died of disease, then his older brother, a former officer in the Polish army, was arrested by the Soviets and sent to "Siberia."[20] In 1991 the Soviet government finally admitted that the NKVD had murdered thousands of captured Polish officers and buried them in mass graves in the Katyn Forest. Shnadow's brother was among them.

On October 5, Shnadow, his family and neighbors arrived in the city of Lomjew (Llodja) in the Soviet zone of Poland, where he opened a "Refugee Barber Shop." His easy manner and facility with languages (Russian, German, Polish, Hebrew, and Yiddish) made him a popular figure. In April 1940 the Soviet authorities decided to deal with the mass of Jews crowding into the Soviet zone of Poland. Legal Soviet passports were offered to those who agreed to relocate farther east. Getting as far away from the Nazis as possible seemed a good idea at the time, so Shnadow became a citizen of the Soviet Union. He and his family were relocated to the small town of Molchad in Belarus, or White Russia.

What Shnadow did not know was that the Nazis were preparing to follow him fourteen months later. Back in the Nazi zone of occupied Poland, the feared SD, the intelligence service of Hitler's SS, had recruited a group of White Russian Fascists who had fled west just as Shnadow was heading east. The White Russian collaborators were recruited as guides for Operation Barbarossa. Hitler was planning to betray Stalin and invade the Soviet Union. The region of Belarus, where Shnadow had relocated, lay in the path of what was to become the main invasion route of the German army.

The White Russian collaborators were assigned to the special intelligence unit within the SD, known optimistically as VorKommando Moskau. Their job was to serve the German conquerors as local officials for every town between Poland and Moscow itself. There were only a few dozen members of VorKommando Moskau at first, then a few hundred. Anyone who wanted to be on the winning side flocked to join up.

VorKommando Moskau was an elite forward unit of SS intelligence on the Soviet front. Its primary mission was anti-Communist intelligence collection, but it also was responsible for security screening of the occupied populations in a broad sector of the Eastern Front, which held nearly 6 million Jews. Precisely this security and intelligence experience made the men of the unit so attractive to Western intelligence after the war and led them to their journey to the United States and membership in Nixon's Republican "ethnic groups."

VorKommando Moskau did not kill the Jews. It hired the collaborators, who recruited the executioners, who killed the Jews. From 1940 to 1942 this one small unit acted as an employment agency for the architects of Nazi genocide in Eastern Europe. Contrary to popular belief, while the Germans masterminded and controlled the machinery of the Holocaust, the footsoldiers who carried it out were not primarily Germans, but local volunteers from Poland, the Baltic states, Ukraine, and White Russia. Those non-Germans who wished to serve Hitler's New Order first had to pass a security check by VorKommando Moskau.

The first loyalty test in the newly conquered areas was to organize the early experiments with mass executions of Jews in 1941 and 1942. As a reward, VorKommando Moskau appointed its collaborators as the police chiefs and mayors of the Nazi occupation on the Eastern front. The political collaborators recruited and screened the local police force. The policemen, in turn, screened other volunteers for service as auxiliaries with the SS mobile killing units. Later on in the war the police auxiliaries supplied the staffs of the concentration camps. Before there was Auschwitz, Treblinka, or Sobibor, there was VorKommando Moskau.

This one small intelligence unit was the nucleus of the secret cancer of genocide. Although the center of the cell was located in the Polish-Soviet border country of Belarus, its recruits carried the virus into several adjoining nations. Members of the VorKommando governed Nazi-occupied Soviet Union as far as the regions of Smolensk, Gomel, and Vitebsk. They ruled the cities of Brest Litovsk and Bialystok in Poland, extending their control southward to Pinsk in Ukraine and north to sections of the Baltics. The civic leaders recruited by VorKommando Moskau invented the first crude formulas for mass execution, tested various methods of organized liquidation, and then spread the Holocaust across the borders of war.

Despite ample warning from his spies, Stalin was completely surprised on June 22, 1941, when the German army roared across the Polish border. The attack was so swift and so overwhelming, and the German army conquered so many cities so quickly, that the SS had trouble finding enough Russian-speaking collaborators to run local security operations.

One Byelorussian, a doctor, became the chief agent recruiter for VorKommando Moskau and later for the Nazi mobile killing units, the Einsatzgruppen. After the war he was settled in the United States. Now retired in New York, the doctor is mentioned in many of the contemporaneous SS records. Leaving Warsaw, he took up his new job as mayor of Bialystok. Leaving there he supplied a steady stream of White Russian émigrés flocking to return home to Belarus on the heels of the conquering Nazis. The first assignment of agents of VorKommando Moskau in each newly conquered city was to open a recruiting office. The Germans were amazed, and grateful, for the speed with which the agents identified those local fanatics who would serve their cause.

Shnadow saw it with his own eyes.

> When the Nazis reached Molchad in July 1941, the collaborationist White Russians armed their youth and dressed them in black uniforms. Suddenly, they were police, just like that. . . . A German officer I shaved gave me a cigarette and in passing said "You are lucky you are not a Jew. It will be very bad for the Jews." Yes, this was already in 1941.
>
> In the first weeks of the war, the White Russian police did anything they wanted, took anything they wanted. Jewish girls were all raped. There was one young girl, a young Elizabeth Taylor, better looking. My landlady's son took her out into the fields and raped her. We lived from week to week.

With brutal efficiency, the collaborators of VorKommando Moskau organized a local police auxiliary in each county for the SD. With this added manpower, the Jews were herded into ghettos in the smaller towns. By the fall of 1941 everything was in readiness for the first experiment.

Stanislav Stankievich was one of the original members of VorKommando Moskau. Like the doctor, he had joined the SS intelligence service back in Warsaw and followed on the heels of the German invasion. Stankievich's first assignment for the Nazis was to organize the town of Borisov, not far from where Shnadow lived. According to German reports, at first Stankievich was regarded as something of a buffoon, but he was determined to prove his loyalty to the Third Reich.

On the night of October 19, Stankievich called his police force together. He told them that the SS was growing concerned about the huge Jewish population in Belarus, just behind the Nazi front lines. The SS had asked whether Stankievich could massacre every one of the eight thousand Jews in Borisov in a single day, without any German help. Stankievich thought it over and said that it could be done. He threw a wild party for his police force, to get them properly drunk for the work that was to come.

The raid began at 3:00 A.M. on October 20. It was all very systematic. The Jews were shuttled out one hundred at a time to a road near the airport where long ditches had been dug. There they were forced to undress and made to lie on top of each other, head to toe. Stankievich's idea was to shoot through a double row of bodies to save ammunition. It was his own unique contribution to the horrors of the Holocaust.

Of course, if the Jew on top was shot through the heart, the one on the bottom was only wounded. The police were told to cover the wounded with a thin layer of dirt and then suffocate them beneath another double layer of bodies. It went on all day: a layer of dirt, a double layer of bodies, another layer of dirt, and so on. Stankievich was very proud of his system. He called it the "sardine method."

After the war the worst part of the atrocities was discovered: The bodies of the smallest children had no wounds. Apparently, to save the price of a bullet, Stankievich buried the babies alive. Of course, he was not there to hear their muffled screams. After giving the orders, he went for a ride in the country to escape the noise of the massacre. He was a civilized man, after all. He even held a doctorate in humanities from a prominent Belgian university.

The SS was suitably impressed and promoted Stankievich. He was appointed mayor of Baranowitz, the second largest city in Belarus. When Stankievich arrived there in the early spring of 1942, about fifty thousand Jews lived in the region surrounding Baranowitz and about fifteen thousand in the central city itself. It took Stankievich only a few weeks to organize the Jewish ghetto. Then he was ready to repeat the success of the Borisov massacre.

The Jews in Shnadow's village heard the news of the first large-scale executions in Baranowitz in March 1942. Shnadow and the other Jews of

Molchad debated what was happening in the big city. "For us, the nagging question was: why did they kill these Jews? Did they not fulfil the contribution quota? Were they killed because they were Communists? We tried all kinds of excuses. Of course, there was no reason. They were just Jews."

As soon as the killings were under way in Baranowitz, Stankievich turned his attention to the outlying villages. No Jews were executed in Molchad for the first six months of the Nazi occupation. Then suddenly everything changed.

> Every week, every ten days, the German murderers gave . . . orders for more Jews to be assembled and killed. If people were not on the list, they were happy with relief. We lived from one week to the next. People were happy to live one more week.
>
> I began to think of where to flee. What could I do? I had responsibilities for my wife, my brother's wife and three kids. One daughter had already died. Where could one flee? There was the army of the Germans and the police were everywhere. There were rewards for catching a Jew—five kilograms of sugar for every Jew caught. I knew that if I tried to escape, they would catch me.

In September 1942 time ran out. At 10:00 P.M. the White Russian police took Shnadow and five hundred other young Jews out of the Molchad ghetto for slave labor. It was the last time he would see his wife, children, relatives, and neighbors alive. Everyone Shnadow loved was killed shortly thereafter.

Shnadow was transferred to the Baranowitz ghetto, directly under Stankievich's eye. "I was picked to work for the SD. Others were to work for the SS. At six in the morning we lined up at the ghetto exit, identity cards in hand. . . . We had to build a foundation for a brick building. Downstairs a jail, upstairs a headquarters. In the morning we got a square piece of bread—maybe a half pound for the entire day's ration. It was fall, going on winter, hell for heavy construction."

Shnadow knew that others had it worse. The Germans had suggested a more efficient method of murder to Stankievich. "We were working near SD Headquarters. We saw everything, how they bring the prisoners—women in the gas trucks—a black van. They were killed by exhaust gas. We saw the killing vans every day." Still, it was not enough. Stankievich gave a new order to his thugs. "In November 1942, the Nazis cleaned out the ghetto. . . . There were 2,500 Jews left all told in Baranowitz. Fifteen thousand Jews were killed between March and November 1942."

Shnadow did not know that the 2,500 Jews of the Baranowitz ghetto were all that was left of the 50,000 in the district. All the Jews in the surrounding towns and villages had been murdered already. All 4,000 Jews from his village of Molchad were dead. He had survived only because he listed his occupation as bricklayer, although he knew nothing about the trade. The SS needed bricklayers, so Shnadow lived to see the next chapter in Stankievich's crimes.

The White Russian Fascists of VorKommando Moskau had made an impression on a young SS officer named Adolf Eichmann. He designated the cities of Minsk and Baranowitz as the final destination for the condemned Jews deported from the rest of Europe. They arrived in Belarus by the tens of thousands. Because the gas vans and the liquidation squad simply could not keep up with the huge numbers of Jews to be killed, Eichmann conceived of poison gas as an alternative. Partly in revulsion against the cruel methods of Stankievich and his colleagues, and partly as an efficiency measure, he brought the gas chamber into use. Now VorKommando Moskau was obsolete. The remaining Jews of the Soviet Union began their final train journey westward, toward Poland.

"From Slonim, 2,000 Jews were sent to Auschwitz. A sister of mine with her two kids lived in Slonim. One girl, 16 years old, had won a prize for beauty in 1940. She was killed in the streets fleeing." Of the fifty thousand Jews under Stankievich, by December 1942 only five hundred were still alive. They were sent as skilled laborers to Stankievich's concentration camp, Koldychevo. It was a school for murder, the place where the White Russian police were trained.

Shnadow arrived at night in a convoy of trucks carrying two to three hundred Jewish prisoners. The camp guards began killing them for practice. "I was recognized by some of the inmates—'the barber Shnadow is here!' Perversely, they [the guards] beat the others to death. They exempted me. They needed a barber! They fixed me up with a chair. It was my own barber's chair from Molchad. Amazing!"

His barber's skills kept Shnadow alive. He was given a little room for a barbershop, adjacent to the camp headquarters building. He could see everything that was happening. When he arrived in Koldychevo in December 1942, there were about 500 Jews and 600 Gentile prisoners in the camp, mostly Polish but some French, including some priests and nuns. By the end of 1943 only 125 were left alive, 115 men and 10 women.

The horrors of Koldychevo are hard to describe. Shnadow remembered the macabre experiments vividly, as the young White Russian trainees tried to outdo each other in cruelty. A baby was thrown in the air and caught with a pitchfork. A young man was tied to a horse, drenched with kerosene, and then he and the animal were burned alive. One guard took a butcher knife and carved out human organs while the victim was still alive. "There are things," Shnadow said, "that I do not want to remember." He was a gentle man, thrust into a citadel of hell.

The day when the camp would be rid of Jews was fast approaching. It was the day when Stankievich came to visit Koldychevo. Shnadow said, "I would remember him in fire!" Stankievich had called a conference of the senior White Russian collaborators in his district. Shortly afterward one of the White Russian guards, who liked Shnadow, came into the barbershop. He whispered that the final decision had been made. All of White Russia must be "Judenrein," free of Jews, by a certain date. The young guard looked sadly at Shnadow, said, "Escape, save yourself," and thrust a pistol into his hand as he confessed that his brother was in the underground. Then he turned quickly and left.

Shnadow stood there trembling, not knowing if it was a trap. He had nothing to risk but his life, so he ran to the stable where the Jews slept at night. Inside was a young girl who worked at the camp laundry. "Take this and hide it," he said, thrusting the pistol at her. "If you say anything, I'll kill you." That is how Shnadow met Helen, the young girl who became his second wife.

Helen remembers little of the war years. Her memory has been erased by tragedy. She was only fifteen when the war broke out, beautiful and spoiled, the only child of one of the wealthiest men in Baranowitz. She remembers her father as a very religious man who was killed because he had stopped to pray. "This is when I stopped believing in God." Helen worked for the SS, sorting the clothes of the murdered Jews. One day she found her mother's coat and knew that she was an orphan. That was the day she stopped remembering. In Koldychevo, she worked as a slave in the laundry.

Shnadow and four others decided to plan a breakout. It was madness, but there was no other choice. Shnadow said that if even one of them lived to be a witness, to tell what the Nazis had done, it would be worth it. The last 125 Jews were marked for death anyway. Under the noses of the SS, they dug a tunnel out of the stable leading to the fence. The blacksmith's shop made a pair of wire cutters. Time was running out. Soon the fence would be electrified.

That night Shnadow led the breakout. His job was to kill the closest guard and cut the wires. But the guard already was dead drunk, and the heavy snowfall muffled their escape. In one of the worst blizzards of the season, the last Jews in the camp made their escape into the night. It was dawn before the guards realized what had happened. The Germans thought it a poor reflection on White Russian efficiency that Jews could escape from a school for camp guards. Stankievich ordered a massive manhunt and captured one of the inmates. Before he was tortured to death, he revealed who had planned the breakout. Stankievich put a price of 10,000 marks on Shnadow's head.

Six police battalions were after him, but Shnadow was nowhere to be found. No matter what happened, he kept moving. The first night he fell through thin ice, but he kept his frozen body moving. Then Helen's feet froze solid, and she begged to be left behind. Shnadow carried her on his shoulders. They hid in holes where the peasants stored potatoes. Once the camp guards were so close to their hiding place that Shnadow could have reached out and touched their boots.

He stole a horse and sleigh and raced for the woods where the partisans were active. They called the place Jerusalem. When they reached the edge of the forest, Shnadow slapped the horse to make it run away. Then he made his companions walk backward into the woods to confuse their trackers. Only a few dozen inmates found their way to the partisan camp—all the others died. The partisans could not believe that they had escaped from one of the most heavily guarded concentration camps, but Shnadow had done it.

Hundreds of miles behind Nazi lines, this tiny band of men and women, most of them barely out of their teens, had formed a Jewish resistance unit, Bielski's brigade. They lived in the swamps and forests of White Russia, hiding during the day in holes cut from the earth, attacking the Nazis at night. With arms and intelligence sent by the Soviets, the little band of Jewish partisans fought back. They took revenge against the men who had murdered their families. German military units had to be reassigned to antipartisan warfare, and Belarus became a linchpin of the Nazi collapse. The SS VorKommando never reached Moscow.

The partisans were so adept at blowing up bridges, railroads, and ammunition dumps that the main German supply routes to the Eastern Front were threatened. At the end of World War II, only a few dozen of the 1,400 Jewish partisans were left alive. Sol Shnadow was one of them. "There must have been a reason I survived all of this," he said. "I was to live and bear witness." Sol and Helen were heroes to the Soviet liberators, who allowed them to keep their arms.

Shnadow went back to the town of Molchad and found the man who had been in charge of the White Russian police. Shnadow forced the man at gun point to show him the mass grave under the bridge where his wife and children were buried. Then Shnadow blew his head off, walked back to town, and turned himself in to the Soviet commander for murder. The grizzled Soviet captain shook his head at Shnadow's confession. He said, "Just don't do that anymore, all right?" He then gave Shnadow back his rifle.

Shnadow rejoined Helen in Baranowitz, in what was once her parents' house. "It was all right for Jews for a little while. There were many Jews in the Soviet army, even junior officers." But then came the NKVD, the Soviet secret service. Apparently, Jewish partisan heroes who stayed and fought were an embarrassment to Stalin's minions, who had fled the German advance. At night, Shnadow would be dragged down for interrogation and asked to inform on the other Jews from Koldychevo. The new wave of persecution had begun. He decided to escape again.

Shnadow had a special reason. He had married Helen in 1944, while they were in the partisan underground. Now she was pregnant. Shnadow obtained a pass to search for any surviving relatives in Poland. He knew there would be none, but Poland was porous for refugees. Helen and Sol escaped on liberation day, May 8, 1945. They had no escape route planned. "We changed our names and went to Czechoslovakia."

In June 1945 they crossed the border from Czechoslovakia into Hungary. Sol and Helen were among thousands of refugees being sheltered by the Red Cross. Sol left the refugee center and went for a walk. Along the way a Soviet jeep carrying four soldiers and two officers passed. Shnadow saluted automatically and then froze. He had just alerted the Soviets that he was a deserter.

The jeep screeched to a halt, and the soldiers started chasing him. Shnadow ran like the wind and pulled himself over the brick wall that surrounded the Red Cross shelter. He took off his hat and crouched in the courtyard amid the hundreds of other refugees. The soldiers ran right past. The Soviets were looking for a young soldier with hair, not a balding refugee. Making him lose his hair was the only favor the Nazis had done for him.

It was a close call. Sol and Helen moved on. From Hungary they went to Romania and then to Austria. Their luck still held. "In Austria, we met the Israeli brigade—the Palestinian brigade—30,000 Jewish soldiers who were serving in the British Army. One of the soldiers came from Baranowitz, and knew Helen. They prepared white bread and English tea. We had not seen this kind of food for so long. They provided the women with dresses. We were there in Austria for a few days."

As a sideline, the Jewish brigade ran a very efficient smuggling system. Jewish refugees were bundled into army trucks and snuck over the Italian border. "Such mountains. We were in the Alps and saw the sun for only two hours a day. It was at the old Austro-Hungarian border, where it joined with Italy." Shnadow did not know it, but he was traveling down the Jewish-controlled section of the Ratline.

When Sol and Helen arrived in Florence, she was in her eighth month of pregnancy and so malnourished that she had to go right to the hospital. Sol was in worse shape. He had abdominal pain, bloody stools, and yellowish discharge. The diagnosis was possible intestinal gangrene, but no tests were done. When the doctors saw his circumcision, they realized he was a Jew. Instead of medical treatment, he was transferred immediately to a ward for the terminally ill.

"I distinctly remember the fan moving slowly. One patient died in front of me, and I knew that this was the room for the dead. They had decided to leave me isolated, and unattended. They were planning on letting me die." All around the world, from Australia to the United States, Jewish families were raising money to rescue the survivors of the Holocaust. Boatloads of food and rare antibiotics were sent to Europe. They arrived just in time for Sol Shnadow.

One of the nurses heard him muttering in Polish and called a young doctor who had come to Italy from Poland to study. He made a correct diagnosis and prescribed new medication. It was probably paid for by some anonymous Jewish family in the West who never knew how much good they had done.

"The pain went away, and eight days later I walked away—an eighty- to ninety-pound skeleton. Before the War I weighed 155 pounds. I could not walk until they gave me a cane. The Polish doctor came twice a day. 'You can go home,' he said. 'I have no home,' I answered." Sol did, however, discover that Helen was still alive and they had a baby daughter. It was a miracle that any child could be born alive after all that the mother had endured. Helen was too weak to produce breast milk, so Sol found some Italian mothers who were nursing. Slowly the three began to heal.

The Zionist underground offered to smuggle them on a ship to Palestine, but the newspapers said that the British were intercepting most of the Jewish refugees and interning them in Cyprus. Sol knew that he and his new family would not survive another concentration camp, even a British one. He had one relative left, a sister who lived in the United States. He had to reach her. All the other twenty-seven members of his immediate family were dead. Helen had no living relatives on the face of the earth.

> There was no mail, so I walked in the street until I saw an American soldier who looked like a Jew. I asked him for a favor—to contact my sister in America. I remembered her address by heart. I wrote that I was alive, and enclosed a small passport picture . . . what did I have to lose? Two weeks later a telegram arrived from my sister. This soldier had written his sister in Brooklyn, his sister called my sister in New Jersey. She explained that her brother had located her brother.

It took some time, but the immigration paperwork finally came through. When Shnadow arrived in the United States, he did not put the past behind him. Rather he sat down and finished writing the memoirs he had started in Italy. He wrote of the fifty thousand Jews from his little corner of the world who would never be able to speak for themselves. Sol Shnadow did not know it, but he was writing a bill of indictment before the bar of history.

Years passed, and then one day the FBI visited Shnadow and showed him a photograph of an alleged White Russian war criminal. Shnadow gave the FBI agents a copy of his memoirs, but told them he was quite sure that the man in the photo had never been in Koldychevo. It was all rather puzzling. Shnadow went back to work at his barbershop and thought no more about the visit.

Shnadow's story was hidden for many years, until one of the authors found a copy of his memoirs in a classified FBI file. In 1979, John Loftus was one the first attorneys assigned to the Justice Department's Nazi hunting unit, the Office of Special Investigations. By luck of the draw, he had been assigned to review the White Russian cases, the crimes of men from Belarus. But something was terribly wrong with the files. It almost looked as if the FBI had deliberately shown photos to witnesses from the wrong areas, refused to follow up leads, and ignored damaging testimony. Sol Shnadow could have been a key witness in at least a dozen cases, but he was never asked.

Each of the government agencies was asked to locate Shnadow, but they all replied that there were no traces of him. In view of his age he was missing and presumed dead. In fact, the FBI had misspelled his last name in their files. This was a common practice to avoid potentially embarrassing file checks.

Through unofficial channels, Loftus asked the Defense Investigative Service to run a computer check on a list of all the White Russians whom the military ever had investigated or interviewed, in particular how many had previously been issued security clearances by the U.S. government. To the Pentagon, it was an innocuous-enough request. No mention was made of a possible link between the Nazis and the FBI.

The computer printed out page after page, listing each of the intelligence files held on each of the White Russians by each of the government agencies. Yet when an official request was made for the same names through Justice Department channels, the official response was that no such files existed. They did exist, as Loftus discovered when he began searching the vaults on his own, without anyone upstairs knowing about it. In fact, the dossiers revealed that everyone was lying. Over the years, every major White Russian war criminal had been on one NATO payroll or another. Even the few German administrators from the SS had been hired. They were, so it seemed, good anti-Communists. VorKommando Moskau was alive and well in the United States.

Many of the White Russian Nazis had been resettled en masse in the town of South River, New Jersey. It was ironic. Shnadow had been living less than half an hour away from the men who murdered his family. This heroic Jew, who fought against the Nazis and the Communists, came to the United States to find freedom, only to end up living in the shadow of his family's killers. The truth was recorded in the classified vaults, in the files of Stanislav Stankievich.

Stankievich was part of the elite leadership group settled around the New York–New Jersey area by Allen Dulles and Bill Casey. Stankievich was certainly not alone. The immigration records showed that almost the entire Nazi puppet government of White Russia, which included large portions of Ukraine and Russia, had been smuggled in and given American citizenship.

Stankievich, in particular, had done very well for himself. He fled to Britain after the war and was financed by British intelligence. He returned to Germany just as evidence was given at the Nuremberg trials about his atrocities. Stankievich then transferred to the U.S. zone, where the State Department put him in charge of a refugee camp funded by the United Nations.

This was rather bold, as the Soviets just had denounced him by name in the UN as a war criminal and claimed that he was working for Western intelligence. The U.S. Army arrested Stankievich, who promptly confessed to all the posts he had held under the Nazis. He had nothing to fear. Dulles's friends in the State Department ordered him released, as he was a key anti-Communist agent of the British secret service.

Stankievich even got a promotion. He was placed on the board of the U.S.-funded Institute for Russian Research in Munich. Ronald Reagan did not know it, but the money he raised for the Crusade for Freedom went here. At the same time that Stankievich went on the U.S. government payroll, an American congressman read an intelligence report about his atrocities into the Congressional Record, citing him by name as an example of the sort of non-German war criminal who should be hunted down.

Instead, State Department agents smuggled Stankievich to New York City, gave him a job as a broadcaster with Radio Liberty, and arranged for him to become a citizen of the United States. During the Eisenhower administration, Stankievich added to his résumé by leaving State Department intelligence and joining the CIA as a contract employee for Radio Liberty. When he was located in 1980, Stankievich was alive and well, living on his government pension.

Loftus asked the deputy assistant attorney general for permission to prosecute an American intelligence agent as a Nazi war criminal. Permission was granted. It was an enormous research job. Every Nazi document ever written by or about Stankievich had to be located. When it was done,

Stankievich was lucky enough to drop dead two weeks before charges could be filed. He died in 1980, peacefully in his bed, a citizen of the United States.

There was a considerable sigh of relief at the British embassy, which suggested to the new Reagan administration that cases of this sort should be banned in the future to avoid potential embarrassment all round. The vaults were placed out of bounds. The whole thing was to be officially forgotten. The memoirs of the Jew would remain unknown in the classified files. Loftus quit in disgust and asked the CIA for permission to reveal the scandal to the public.

In 1982 Loftus exposed Stankievich's crimes, and the cover-up, on CBS television's *60 Minutes* show.[21] The segment won the Emmy Award for outstanding investigative journalism. After the program aired, Loftus received a telephone call. The FBI had concealed another secret. Sol Shnadow was still alive, in New Jersey.

During his last years Shnadow mustered all his waning strength to tell people about the Holocaust and to raise funds for Israel. He was so proud of the Jewish nation. He loved it as he loved the United States, with all his heart. It would have broken his heart if he knew how he had been betrayed.

Israeli intelligence had known about the White Russian Nazis for years and kept silent. The Nazi mayor of Minsk, Vitaut Tumash, ran the Slavic desk at the New York Public Library. Franz Kushel, the commander of the Belarus police execution squads, had a White Russian club in Brooklyn. Stankievich lived in Richmond Hills and worked at Radio Liberty's offices in New York. The doctor who was VorKommando Moskau's chief recruiter became the head of a county medical society. The list goes on and on.

In 1979 the internationally renowned Austrian Nazi-hunter Simon Wiesenthal visited the Justice Department in Washington and stepped into Loftus's office for a brief chat about VorKommando Moskau's activities in White Russia. Wiesenthal had an encyclopedic memory, rattling off details about the various SS subunits, the number of Jews killed, the sites of the worst atrocities in Belarus. He knew it all. Loftus asked if Wiesenthal had ever heard anything about Nazis working for Western intelligence. The old Nazi hunter looked at the classified file folders that buried the desktop, nodded, and started to speak.

After World War II, Wiesenthal himself worked for U.S. intelligence. "One day I arrested a Ukrainian Nazi and brought him in. The next week I saw him out on the street. What could I do?" Wiesenthal shrugged. To understand the enormity of what Wiesenthal had admitted, it should be known that his own mother had been killed by Ukrainian Nazis, yet he did nothing to pursue this man further. In over thirty years he had never criticized American intelligence for hiring Nazis. During the same thirty years, Soviet propaganda had frequently denounced Wiesenthal as an agent of Western intelligence, accusing him of hunting only those Nazis who were not on NATO's payroll.

Most people would agree that Simon Wiesenthal is a decent, dedicated man. For many years he was one of the few people in the world who kept the search for Nazis going. He single-handedly brought many of the most infamous German war criminals to justice. But did he have a blind spot for the members of VorKommando Moskau who worked for Allen Dulles?

Was it simple ignorance on Wiesenthal's part, or did he actively assist the cover-up? Shortly before the *60 Minutes* program went to air, Ira Rosen, the producer, asked Wiesenthal to appear. CBS had already interviewed some of the White Russian Nazis who had admitted contact with Western intelligence, including the FBI.[22] Wiesenthal asked CBS not to do the show, saying that it would do great harm. Rosen was bewildered but adamant. CBS's own sources had confirmed the FBI-Nazi connection.

There was a reason why Wiesenthal was afraid of Mike Wallace's *60 Minutes* investigation. It was Simon Wiesenthal's information that led the FBI to drop the investigation of its Nazis. After Loftus mentioned this, he received a heated telephone call from Marty Mendelsohn, Wiesenthal's lawyer, threatening to sue for libel. The threat was quickly dropped when Loftus mentioned that if he was sued, he would have to testify that he had read Simon Wiesenthal's FBI file. Wiesenthal's dossier had emerged from the top-secret vaults almost by accident. It had been cross-referenced among the White Russian Nazi files in the FBI dossier for Charles Allen, a New York journalist and Nazi hunter.

During the 1960s Allen had bombarded the Justice Department, and Congress, with accusations that Nazis were living in the United States. Allen specifically identified several of the White Russian Nazis, including one of Stankievich's underlings, a man named Emanuel Jasiuk. The attorney general asked FBI director J. Edgar Hoover to investigate.

The problem was that the FBI already knew Jasiuk. In 1950 the head of the U.S. Army's Counter Intelligence Corps wrote to Hoover, warning him that Jasiuk was a Nazi war criminal who had worked for U.S. Air Force Intelligence in Germany and had illegally immigrated to the United States, along with several others. Instead of arresting them, the FBI promptly recruited every White Russian Nazi it could find in the New York–New Jersey area. Even Stankievich's brother helped them with information. So did SS general Franz Kushel, who described the funding links to British and American intelligence.

The FBI quickly identified a White Russian Nazi front group, the Byelorussian National Center, formerly the Byelorussian Central Council under Hitler. The FBI report stated that the "new organization was so-named, so the members could avoid being called war criminals during the time of crisis in Germany." Jasiuk was one of the prominent Nazis mentioned in FBI File Number 105-40098. This sixty-three-page dossier provided only a summary of their history with the SS, but it was cross-referenced to every White Russian Nazi whom the FBI had interviewed.

Jasiuk's arrest could expose the whole cover-up, including Hoover's role in recruiting the White Russian Nazis. For help in dealing with Charles Allen's allegations, the FBI turned to their confidential informant Simon Wiesenthal. According to the FBI dossier, Wiesenthal told the FBI that the source of Allen's information came from Communist reports of their own war crimes trials. It was Simon Wiesenthal's information that gave the FBI the idea for its cover story. The FBI could depict Allen's charges as a Communist Cold War tactic to intimidate the émigré community with false charges of war crimes.

The FBI dropped the Nazi investigation and began a security check into Charles Allen instead. They discovered that Wiesenthal was correct. Many of his charges had originally appeared in Communist propaganda, following a trial of White Russian camp guards. Wiesenthal's information gave the FBI the excuse it needed to close the investigation. Although most of Hoover's personal files were destroyed at his death, the army kept a copy of its letter to the FBI director in CIC File Number X847230A2. Army intelligence confirmed that Jasiuk was in fact: "well known for his cruelty and persecution of the Polish populace in the area and was responsible for sending many persons to forced labor. . . . In 1942 . . . Subject submitted a list of certain residents of Nieswicz and other cities to the Sicherheits Dienst (German Secret Service) in Baranowitz, and as a result, a number of these persons were shot."

Charles Allen may have been a left-winger, but he was right about the Nazis. Army intelligence had confirmed that Emanuel Jasiuk was Stankievich's deputy in the Baranowitz region of VorKommando Moskau. Among the "other cities" liquidated by Jasiuk was the little town of Molchad. Jasiuk was the man who directed and supervised the murder of Sol Shnadow's family.

For almost forty years, the leaders of Israel knew what Shnadow and so many other survivors did not: The murderers of their families and friends had been living peaceful and prosperous lives in the West, having worked for one or more intelligence service as anti-Communist "experts." Wherever the survivors of the Holocaust went—Britain, the United States, Canada, Argentina, or Australia—the murderers went with them. Except to

Israel. The Jewish homeland was the only place where Jews could live and know that Nazis did not share the same sidewalks.

Over the last half century the government of Israel repeatedly kept its silence when informed of the West's hostile covert operations and used its knowledge for secret leverage against the West. As we have documented in chapter after chapter, the Israeli intelligence services and their Zionist predecessors uncovered many of these duplicitous operations but said nothing in public.

The Israeli leaders did, however, do a great deal in private. Beginning with James Jesus Angleton, through Nelson Rockefeller, James Forrestal, Reinhard Gehlen, and many more, the Jews chose silent but effective means first to create and then to defend their homeland in the Middle East.

If this was blackmail, was there a defense of necessity? What were the alternatives for Israel? Or for Wiesenthal? Instead of trading silence for secret advantage, should the Jewish leaders have exposed the bigotry, greed, and stupidity of foreign politicians? In hindsight, exposure might have meant punishment of their own leaders by the Western electorate and an end to the secret war against the Jews. On the other hand, why should the Jews trust in those Western voters who had not previously spoken out about the Holocaust?

The fact remains that the people's voice was never heard, either during the Holocaust or since, because no one either in Israel or the West trusted their judgment enough to give them a chance. To this day Israelis have little sense of the secret wars that shaped their history. Equally, Western citizens have no conception of what their governments have done to the Jews in the name of "national security."

It was a bit bizarre to watch George Bush on television as one of the honored guests at Bill Clinton's White House as the PLO and Israel exchanged their letters of recognition in September 1993. Former Secretary of State James Baker actually took credit for helping the peace process along.

"You shouldn't be surprised," said one of our sources in the intelligence community. "It's pure hypocrisy. In public, Israel is our ally. What the public doesn't know is that all Western nations have covert policies to side with the Arabs. It keeps the intelligence community busy. Screwing Jews is what I did for a living."[23]

The sad truth is that the men and women who spied on the Jews were aware that their own governments pursued a hypocritical policy. In public, they were Israel's allies. In private, they were enemies. Perhaps the most remarkable thing about this two-track policy is how first the Zionists, then Israel's leaders, blunted the clandestine offensive and quietly turned Western secrets into Western blackmail.

But what was the price of silence to the Jews of the world? What was the price to democracy, both in Israel and the West? How can free citizens judge the conduct of their elected leaders when one-third of modern history is classified? And, finally, what price have non-Jews paid in the secret war against the Jews? We live in an age where our lives are changed by the secret will of politicians who serve their own agenda, rather than the public mandate. As we have seen all too clearly, in the age of electronic surveillance, we are all Jews.

The first hopeful signs began to emerge in September 1993. For the first time in seventy-five years, the Jews and Palestinians had been left to themselves. Suddenly the superpowers had left them alone. No more interference, no more outside agendas, no more oil men disguised as diplomats. Eight months after George Bush left office, the PLO and Israel worked out the first hard step toward peace. The road has been rocky, as it was bound to be, but Yasser Arafat and Israeli prime minister Yitzhak Rabin represented the best hope of the moderates on both sides. Arab and Jewish extremists, though, continue to pose a major threat.

The worst extremists are not the individual mass murderers, such as Baruch Goldstein or the fanatical Hamas bomb-throwers, but the politicians of the Middle East who pretend to want peace but prepare for state-sponsored murder. Syria's president Assad was quietly furious at the peace pact, but publicly pledged not to intervene. It must have been hard for him to bite his lip.

Syrian schoolchildren are taught that not only is Lebanon part of Greater Syria, so are the West Bank, Gaza, and Israel itself. Peace between the moderate Palestinians and the moderate Jews is a major threat to such irredentist aspirations. Assad's world is like Slobodan Milosevic's idea of Greater Serbia in the Balkans, and like Milosevic, Assad prefers the extremes to fight one another. Little wonder that after Arafat signed his deal with Rabin the radical PLO factions in Damascus announced that they would kill Arafat. Or that Syria's ally, Iran, is pumping millions of dollars into fundamentalist opposition groups.

The Israelis and the Arafat faction are trying to ban all the extremists: American and Jewish, Syrian and Iranian. It will be interesting to see how long the foreign-funded terrorists hold out in the face of PLO-Israeli cooperation. This time waging another secret war against the Jews will be difficult. From September 1993 the cards have been on the table for all to see. It is, the "old spies" say, a hopeful time.[24]

As this book goes to press, there are more hopeful signs. King Hussein and Prime Minister Rabin met in Washington in July 1994 to sign an agreement ending half a century of war between Jordan and Israel, and committing them to a lasting solution of all the issues which previously divided their peoples. On the negative side, a wave of international terror has been launched against Jews—from London to Argentina—allegedly orchestrated by Iran using the zealots of the Lebanese-based Hezbollah. We wonder whether President Assad of Syria may, in fact, be the real controller of the Hezbollah assassins, and the terror campaign is one final desperate bid to derail the peace process and preserve Assad's own autocratic rule, and those of the feudal Arab states which have waged their war against the Jews in secret alliance with the Western intelligence services. In the end, only the dismantling of the feudal Arab dictatorships and their replacement by democracies will assure lasting peace in the Middle East. Assad and the other autocrats will only give up their power unwillingly.

Still, if the PLO and Mossad do decide to start working together, they could neutralize outside agitators within a decade. The process will be difficult for a while, but Israel will not become as dangerous as Northern Ireland, just New York. And then, if the "good cops" do their job, there will be peace, real peace in the Holy Land for the next generation.

Perhaps the most valuable commodity in Israel will be the little stamp marked "made in Jericho." If Israeli financiers and Palestinian businessmen team up, the Arab embargo will crumble and new markets, new ideas, will sweep aside the old dictators who have dominated the region for so long. As democracy, literacy, and commerce spread across the Arab states, the long, secret war against the Jews will be over.

Some of our sources among the former intelligence officers are optimistic on this point. The more cynical of the "old spies" claim that Arafat is preparing his own civil war with his exile loyalists pitted against the native Palestinians. The ruling council of the PLO is decidedly undemocratic. Its members may not be pleased with the concept of being voted out of office and losing their stipends. The first internal struggle may come over control of the Palestinian police force in the Gaza Strip. In the longer run, the fact that as this book goes to press the Palestinian Covenant still has not been altered to renounce the goal of destroying Israel leaves the door open for the extremists in the Palestinian movement to seize control of the PLO in the future and once again pursue wars of annihilation against the Jews. That such pressure exists is undoubted, and helps to explain embarrassing slips such as Arafat's speech in South Africa when he called for a holy war to liberate Jerusalem.

From the Israeli point of view, at least their own policemen will be out of harm's way while the Palestinians fight each other. Arafat's war of Arab against Arab may go on for a little while, but the desire to kill is losing momentum. In the end, Arafat's own survival may depend on the willingness of Israeli intelligence to warn him of attacks from his own countrymen. He needs the Israelis as much as they need him. Still, it will take time for the wounds to heal. Arafat remembers that his home was bulldozed so that Jewish visitors would have a bigger plaza to view the Wailing Wall. Israelis will visit the graves of their relatives killed by the PLO. Forgetting will take another generation.

In the meantime, there are still more concessions to be made. The "old spies" say that some sort of reciprocal dual citizenship is inevitable, as total separation of Jews and Moslems is as impractical as it is undesirable. In the end, Arafat will get his capital in Jerusalem. After all, how much square footage does an office building take? In return, Jews will get the right to purchase homes in the West Bank. After all, where the Jews go, so goes the Israeli water supply system.

In thirty years water, not oil, will be the most valuable commodity in the Middle East. As Turkey completes its vast Anatolian dam project, the waters of the Tigris and Euphrates rivers will be under the control of humanity for the first time in history. The downstream countries—Iran, Iraq, and Syria—are poorly prepared for the consequences. Someone with arms but not water will want to make war. In the course of the next generation, a new Arab dictator will look on the green fields of Israel and Palestine with envy.

When the next war comes, which side will the West be on? As oil supplies eventually dwindle, the cost of extraction will increase while prices will skyrocket. As long as the world is dependent on Middle Eastern petroleum, the West remains vulnerable to blackmail. In an oil economy, Israel always will be expendable. The truth is, we have turned our backs on the Jews before and may very well do so again.

And yet all things are possible. In the last year two sworn enemies, Yasser Arafat and Yitzhak Rabin, shook hands on the White House lawn. While it would have seemed impossible only a year earlier, since September 1993 Arafat and Rabin have sat across the table and worked on the practical, hard-edged problems of creating a new way, a new life, for both Jews and Palestinians in what has been a bloodbath for the last seventy years. The dialogue is not exciting, more the mundane task of creating economic, political, and law enforcement infrastructures that move the Palestinians toward their own homeland, while ensuring the security of the Jews.

The secret war against the Jews may not be over. There are still many among the West's political, espionage, and business elites who are bigoted against the Jews, hungry for Arab profits, and stupidly devoted to anti-Israeli intrigue. But left alone for a short while, moderate Palestinians and

Jews seem capable of making progress. Perhaps we have witnessed at least the beginning of the end of the secret war against the Jews. There is room for optimism.

The hesitant, painful steps taken toward a lasting peace between the Jews and the Arabs in 1993 and 1994 marked a departure from the West's silent siege of the Jews over the previous three-quarters of a century. We have traced those long decades through the Ages of Bigotry, Greed, and Stupidity, but it would be wrong to believe that any of these major impulses in the secret war have passed into history.

Too many of the players are still around. Monzer Al-Kassar has moved back to Spain from his hiding place in Poland and is reportedly back working on new arms and drug deals, although whether for the GRU or MI6 is uncertain. One thing seems certain, however: that Monzer's Syrian allies will ask him to carry out further anti-Jewish operations designed to frustrate the peace process. It seems hard to believe that the Russian GRU would not approve of such schemes, and perhaps even orchestrate them. Boris Yeltsin simply does not control this powerful section of Russian intelligence. The Tikriti mafia around Saddam Hussein is more entrenched than ever. The GRU is slowly reemerging as the focus of Russian chauvinism. The British secret service escaped paying for the BCCI downfall. Another generation of CIA men and women is retiring to work for the oil companies. The old Nazis have trained the skinheads to replace them. The Ustashi is still at work in Croatia and Bosnia. In one form or another, they all will be back.

It is not the individuals who are frightening. We have always been able to survive bigots, greedy businessmen, and stupid politicians. Sooner or later the truth will emerge. There will always be historians who dig up the ugly past buried in the intelligence vaults. What is frightening is that we have learned so little.

We have left our children vulnerable. So many know so little about the Holocaust, or the Armenian massacre, or the Cambodian Killing Fields, or East Timor, or Bosnia. Perhaps Eli Wiesel, who said that this century will be known as the most violent period of mankind, with 50 million murdered, is right. We began in World War I in Sarajevo and are still fighting there at the turn of the century.

If we are to keep future generations safe, we must first teach them the perils of ignorance. Then we must show them how to fight evil by exposing it. They must not continue the awful silence of previous generations. We must teach what Sol Shnadow told his children before he died. It was his most important lesson, his most enduring legacy: "You should never be afraid to speak the truth."

NOTES

LIST OF ABBREVIATIONS

The following abbreviations are used throughout the notes:
PRO—Public Record Office, London
CO—Colonial Office Records, United Kingdom
FO—Foreign Office records, United Kingdom
MIS—U.S. Army Military Intelligence Service
CIC—U.S. Army Counter Intelligence Corps
CIA—Central Intelligence Agency
CIG—Central Intelligence Group
DIA—Defense Intelligence Agency
NSA—National Security Agency
NSC—National Security Council
OPC—Office of Political Coordination
SSU—Strategic Services Unit
FBI—Federal Bureau of Investigation
IRR—U.S. Army Investigative Records Repository
USNA—U.S. National Archives

INTRODUCTION
THE SECRET WAR AGAINST THE JEWS

1. Originally published as *Ratlines: How the Vatican's Nazi Networks Betrayed Western Intelligence to the Soviets* (London: Heinemann, 1991) and as *Unholy Trinity* (New York: St. Martin's Press, 1992).
2. One version has it that a White House aide asked Baker "What about the Jews?" and his response was "Fuck'em, they won't vote for us anyway." The original story was confirmed by columnist William Safire in *The New York Times*, citing his own source.
3. Remarks attributed to Secretary Baker by reporter Seymour Hersh.
4. Memorandum, "Holdings of James A. Baker, III, and his immediate family," January 25, 1989, disclosing holdings in Amoco, Exxon, Texaco and a half-dozen petroleum trusts and partnerships.
5. Memorandum for the Attorney General, from the President, Subject: "Conflict of Interest Waiver, August 8, 1990." The waiver document was so sensitive that even Baker was not given a copy. Alan Friedman, *Spider's Web: The Secret History of How the White House Armed Iraq* (New York: Bantam, 1993), pp. 170–71.
6. As we go to press, the Clinton administration has taken the first steps to rectify the shameful record of the Carter, Reagan, and Bush administrations over East Timor. In a meeting with Indonesia's President Suharto in 1993, President Clinton raised the issue in a reportedly strong manner. Washington has suspended weapons sales, and there are tentative signs of some trends in Indonesia toward democracy.

CHAPTER 1
PHILBY OF ARABIA

1. For Philby's own account of his conversion from imperialism to the cause of the colonial people, see Harry St. John Bridger Philby, *Arabian Days: An Autobiography* (London: Robert Hale, 1948), esp. pp. 15, 40, and 268–269.

2. See, for example, Edward Said, *Orientalism* (London: Peregrine, 1985), pp. 196–197, 224, 235, 237, and 245–246; and Glyn Roberts, *The Most Powerful Man in the World: The Life of Sir Henri Deterding* (New York: Covici Friede, 1938), p. 344.
3. Confidential interviews, former British diplomat, former officer of Foreign and Commonwealth Office, 1988–1993.
4. Ibid.
5. "Young Philby was born in Ambala, India, in 1911." Anthony Cave Brown, *C: The Secret Life of Sir Stewart Menzies* (New York: Macmillan, 1987), p. 166.
6. Phillip Knightley, *Philby: The Life and Views of the KGB Masterspy* (London: Pan Books, 1989), pp. 19–20.
7. Philby, *Arabian Days,* p. 94; and Bruce Page, David Leitch, and Phillip Knightley, *Philby: The Spy Who Betrayed a Generation* (London: André Deutsch, 1968), p. 37.
8. Confidential interviews, former British diplomat; former officer, Foreign and Commonwealth Office, 1988–1993.
9. Cave Brown, *C: The Secret Life of Sir Stewart Menzies,* p. 169.
10. Confidential interview, 1989.
11. Confidential interviews, 1992–1993.
12. Our source from the British diplomatic service asserts that M16 deliberately assigned openly gay agents, such as Guy Burgess, to Washington as sexual bait for Hoover. The FBI director felt safe in sleeping with another member of the security club. The famous picture of Hoover dressed in women's clothing was, our source insists, taken surreptitiously by one of Hoover's British lovers and passed to the CIA to keep the FBI in check. Confidential interview, 1992. We have not been able to corroborate this allegation, but it would explain why the British secret service assigned a flamboyant homosexual like Burgess to work with the gay-bashing director of the FBI. Our source in the Foreign and Commonwealth Office vigorously denies that his government set up a "honey trap" for Hoover and denies any complicity in the photograph. Both sources agree that Burgess's defection to Moscow focused a great detail of attention on the sex life of the Philbys, father and son. Confidential interview, 1993.
13. Page, Leitch, and Knightley, *Philby,* p. 37.
14. Here is a brief example: "Twice St. John Philby disappeared from base, each time wandering the by-ways of Baghdad disguised as an Arab beggar. Two clever Germans were causing concern to the British forces at this time. One was the famous Wassmuss, who ranged with a band of guerilla fighters throughout Persia, swooping down on oilfields and generally upsetting the British lines of communication between India and Mesopotamia. The other German was Preusser, who claimed to be the master of the Persian Gulf. St. John Philby had to pit his brains against these two clever men. The sequel was inevitable. Preusser was knifed by an Arab one night and died. Wassmuss found a cordon closing around him in Persia and only escaped by a sensational ride through the night towards the rooftop of the world, where he took refuge in a Central Asian state. When this work was finished St. John Philby again disappeared." William J. Makin, quoted in Page, Leitch, and Knightley, *Philby,* p. 37.
15. Confidential interview, former officer of Foreign and Commonwealth Office, 1992.
16. The trio were among the most important members of the "band" later immortalized by T. E. Lawrence, whose "imaginative perspectives were provided principally by their illustrious contemporary Rudyard Kipling, who had sung so memorably of holding 'dominion over palm and pine.' " Said, *Orientalism,* p. 224. See also Philby, *Arabian Days,* pp. 99, 100, 191, 197–201, and 204.
17. Confidential interviews, former officer of the British Foreign and Commonwealth Office, 1988–1992.
18. A former president of the Zionist Organization of America admitted that: "Britain, hard pressed in the struggle with Germany, was anxious to gain the whole-hearted support of the Jewish people: in Russia on the one hand, and in America on the other. The non-Jewish world regarded the Jews as a power to reckon with and even

exaggerated Jewish influence and unity." Quoted in Alfred M. Lilienthal, *The Zionist Connection* (New York: Dodd, Mead, 1978), p. 21.

19. The Jewish establishment in the United States cared very little for Zionists, Palestine, or, for that matter, other Jews. There were less than a quarter of a million Jews in the country before the 1890s, and they were largely of Germanic stock. The leaders were upper-middle-class mercantilists, well educated and attempting to be fully assimilated. After the Russian *pogroms,* the old-line upscale American Jews were buried in a wave of 5 million Jewish immigrants inside a decade. The "native" Jews despised the new immigrants with a passion and treated them most severely, just as German Jews treated Russian and Polish Jews who had resettled in Germany. The new Jews barely spoke English. Far from controlling American elections, few of them could even vote. As far as public opinion went, the newspapers they read were written in Yiddish.
20. "It is a delusion to suppose this was a mere act of crusading enthusiasm or quixotic philanthropy. On the contrary, it was a measure taken . . . in due need of the war with the object of promoting the general victory of the Allies, for which we expected and received valued and important assistance." Churchill's speech to the House of Commons, July 1937, quoted in Lilienthal, *The Zionist Connection,* pp. 21–22.
21. The most pertinent of these documents are reprinted in Jeremy Wilson, *Lawrence of Arabia: The Authorized Biography of T. E. Lawrence* (New York: Athenaeum, 1990).
22. As First Lord of the Admiralty, in early 1915, Churchill had conceived a plan to force a passage through the Dardanelles and knock Turkey out of the war. Instead fifty thousand Allied soldiers, mainly British, Australian, and New Zealanders, were killed for no appreciable military gain. The British commanders tried to switch the blame to the colonial soldiers from down under, but there was even less regard in London for the value of Arab guerrillas against the Turks. The Australians redeemed themselves at the end of October 1917, in the cavalry charge at Beersheba in Palestine, which helped knock Turkey out of the war. It ended Philby's fantasy that the Turks threatened Egypt. There was no need for Britain to rely further on untrained, low-caliber Arab guerrillas.
23. Richard Deacon, *The Israeli Secret Service* (London: Sphere, 1979), p. 9.
24. As in everything else, Philby's views were reliably contradictory. Around the same time, he also said he wanted Britain to reaffirm the Balfour Declaration because Jews had every right to settle in Palestine at will, "on a basis of equality with the existing population." Elizabeth Monroe, *Philby of Arabia* (London: Faber and Faber, 1973), pp. 103–104 and 138–139.
25. Page, Leitch, and Knightley, *Philby,* pp. 37–38.
26. As the chief of the district containing the holy cities of Mecca and Medina, Hussein wanted to establish a united Moslem government with himself in charge. Lawrence advised that the union would be a purely religious one, not amounting to the kind of Arab republic feared by the British authorities in India. See T. E. Lawrence, "The Politics of Mecca," January 2, 1916, FO 141/461, folio 146, PRO.
27. The situation was a bit more complicated than that. The India Office, which feared that Lawrence and Hussein might actually establish an Arab republic, wanted to back Ibn Saud as a counterweight.
28. Our British diplomatic source asserts that Lawrence was the man who briefed Philby extensively on the British double game.
29. Confidential interviews, former British diplomat; former officer of Foreign and Commonwealth Office, 1988–1993.
30. As one historian has recorded, Jack Philby's interest in the genealogy of Arab tribes and potentates "developed into a lifelong fascination with perhaps the most powerful of all the potentates at that time, Ibn Saud, whom he first met while on a mission to Riyadh in 1917. That meeting . . . set the course of the rest of Philby's life." Daniel Yergin, *The Prize: The Epic Quest for Oil, Money & Power* (New York: Touchstone, 1992), p. 287.

31. Taking its name from a famous eighteenth-century fundamentalist reformer, the sect advocated *jihad,* or holy war, against all infidels and non-Moslems, which extended even to fellow Moslems who would not submit to their brand of fundamentalism. The Wahhabis were dedicated to constant aggression and expansion at the expense of those who did not share their "ideals." Ibn Saud—and indeed the whole modern kingdom of Saudi Arabia owed their existence to the Wahhabi spirit. Their methods against their "enemies" were merciless, too often involving not only the slaughter of men but also women and children. J. B. Kelly, *Arabia, the Gulf and the West* (New York: Basic Books, 1980), pp. 225, 231.
32. "The purpose of the Congress was, as the head of the Comintern told the Congress, to strike at Imperial London through Delhi and the other great capitals of the raj." Cave Brown, *C: The Secret Life of Sir Stewart Menzies,* p. 169.
33. Victor Rothschild's appeal to the prime minister was widely reported in the British press. The source of the suspicion was that Rothschild had attended parties with several members of the Cambridge net and had visited their homes.
34. Confidential interviews, former British diplomat; former officer of Foreign and Commonwealth Office, 1988–1993.
35. Monroe, *Philby of Arabia,* p. 103.
36. Telegram from P. Z. Cox to Winston Churchill, July 6, 1921, CO 537/822, PRO.
37. ". . . these Arabs found allies among the colonial officials and the military officers whom England sent to govern the country. . . . They deplored the prospect of the Jews taking over the country because it complicated the situation. . . . Some of the English officials had always been anti-Semitic; others now became anti-Jewish because they found it hard to get along with the Jews. The Jews could not be treated like backward colonials upon whom these officers were accustomed to look down." Solomon Grayzel, *A History of the Jews* (New York: Mentor, 1968), p. 619.
38. ". . . the upper class Arabs were encouraged to hope that, if they objected strongly enough, the idea of a Jewish homeland would be given up. . . . Not meeting with success, they sought to improve their argument by stirring the peasant Arabs to violence. Riots broke out in Jerusalem in April 1920 and, on a larger scale, in Jaffa in May 1921." Ibid.
39. According to a former CIA officer previously stationed in Jordan, the British secret service used Transjordan as a staging area for stirring up the Christian and Moslem populations against the Jews. Our British sources confirm that organized terrorism did take place in the early 1920s, but state that it was the work of French agents from Syria and Lebanon seeking to revive the Sykes-Picot terms and establish French control over Palestine. Our Israeli sources are of the opinion that all of these countries were involved, but that the policy was instituted by the British under Lawrence and then continued by his successor, Philby.
40. "Every expression of violent opposition by the Arab nationalists was the occasion for a reduction by England of Jewish rights in their homeland. . . . In 1922, the British Colonial Office issued . . . a government declaration, by which the promised homeland was deprived of any independent political foundation. It asserted 'that the terms of the [Balfour] Declaration do not contemplate that Palestine as a whole should be converted into a Jewish national home, but that such a home shall be founded in Palestine' . . . It was already clear, however, that the British government both in England and in Palestine was ready to do everything possible to win the Arabs over, if necessary at the expense of the Jews." Grayzel, *A History of the Jews,* pp. 654–655.
41. Monroe, *Philby of Arabia,* pp. 126–127. Interestingly enough, in his autobiography Philby failed to mention his meeting with Weizmann, although he made great play of taking "tea with Mr. and Mrs. Churchill in Sussex Square" and meeting with King George and the Prince of Wales. "Baron Rothschild and Wickham Steed were perhaps the outstanding personalities among many that I collected to lunch informally with the Amir," Philby wrote proudly. His new "friend," Chaim Weizmann, was to prove

a much more important contact than the king, the prince, and the future prime minister combined. See Philby, *Arabian Days,* p. 223.

42. Monroe, *Philby of Arabia,* pp. 126 and 129.
43. Philby went on: "Besides this, Abdullah has rather let me down by his personal extravagance, which is on such a scale that he is simply inviting interference, and getting it in full measure from H.M.G., which means the Zionist element. So I am off." Ibid., p. 132.
44. Both CIA and British intelligence sources agree that Philby had access to a great deal of secret intelligence that somehow found its way into Ibn Saud's hands. The military campaign against Hussein was a "cakewalk" as the Wahhabis were forewarned of the exact disposition of the forces opposing them.
45. In August 1924 the military campaign was launched and, by October, the holy city of Mecca fell to Ibn Saud's warriors. By the end of 1925 Ibn Saud's victory was complete. The holy city of Medina fell in early December, and a few weeks later he entered Jidda.
46. As his biographer put it, "Britain had betrayed its word to the Arabs; he must struggle to put right a wrong that could not be righted without sacrifice." Monroe, *Philby of Arabia,* p. 137.
47. Yergin, *The Prize,* p. 287.
48. Monroe, *Philby of Arabia,* p. 160. Unexpectedly, Philby's meeting with the Grand Mufti of Jerusalem gave him the chance to further his intrigues against the Zionists. Philby was approached by Dr. Judah Magnes, a moderate Zionist leader who believed in promoting cooperation between Jews and Arabs. (Mainstream Zionists have questioned whether Magnes really believed in the necessity of a Jewish state in Palestine at all.) For a whole day after their meeting, Philby shuttled to and fro between Magnes and the office of the Mufti's Supreme Moslem Council. The result was a draft constitution for a democratic republic of Palestine, in which electoral representation would be proportional under a continuing British mandate. Philby immediately sent the plan to the colonial secretary, Lord Passfield. Magnes showed it to the Zionist leadership, including Weizmann and David Ben-Gurion and to the high commissioner, Sir John Chancellor, but they were all hostile. With the Jewish population in a minority, proportional representation would have been tantamount to the Zionists' committing suicide. The Zionist Executive and Jewish Agency condemned it immediately. Passfield told the chancellor that Philby had no authority to enter into negotiations and did not reply to his letter. Ibid., pp. 160–162.
49. "On August 7, 1930, Philby set out for Mecca . . . With that last rite he abandoned Christianity and became a muslim. The King bestowed upon him the name of Abdullah, slave of God; he was given the right to visit the royal concubines, which he did frequently, and in due course his *bhint,* Muriel, arrived at his house, ready to bear his children, which she did." Cave Brown, *C: The Secret Life of Sir Stewart Menzies,* p. 171.
50. Ibn Saud later gave Philby beautiful slave girls, one of whom bore him children when he was in his mid-sixties.
51. Page, Leitch, and Knightley, *Philby,* p. 40.
52. Yergin, *The Prize,* p. 287, and Robert Lacey, *The Kingdom: Arabia and the House of Sa'ud* (New York: Avon Books, 1983), p. 233.
53. Lacy, *The Kingdom,* p. 234.
54. Philby, *Arabian Days,* p. 269. Jack's self-serving propaganda was aided from time to time by some "useful idiots," who were only too happy to reinforce this view in Western circles. One pro-Communist author called Philby "the bearded Mohammedan explorer," who was "Britain's agent at Ibn Saud's court." Roberts, *The Most Powerful Man in the World,* p. 344.
55. The official Soviet version of Kim Philby's recruitment was revealed in 1993, after Random House paid the KGB to open its archives. The result was *Deadly Illusions*—

The First Book from the KGB Archives, by John Costello and former KGB officer Oleg Tsarev, (London: Century, 1993).

56. Costello and Tsarev, *Deadly Illusions,* pp. 146, 152. The Soviets were so interested in Jack's Saudi Arabian operations that as early as mid-1935, they tried, unsuccessfully, to engineer Kim's appointment as an English-language teacher for Ibn Saud's son. Ibid., pp. 155–156.
57. As we shall see in subsequent chapters, the list was fairly extensive.

CHAPTER 2

THE SORCERER OF OIL

1. One example is an interview recounted by Robert Kaplan: "You simply cannot realize how powerful and unconscious a force anti-Semitism was in America at the middle of this century when Bill and I were in school. At Princeton and Wellesley, at the prep schools we went to, you almost never encountered Jews. It was a different America then." Robert Kaplan, *The Arabists: The Romance of an American Elite* (New York: Free Press, 1993), p. 4.
2. See, for example, Leonard Mosley, *Dulles: A Biography of Eleanor, Allen, and John Foster Dulles and Their Family Network* (New York: Dial Press, 1979), pp. 3–84.
3. The remarkable thing is the near unanimity of opinion on this point from sources on both sides of the Atlantic. Hatred for all things Dulles extends from American CIA officials to agents of MI6, the West German BND, and especially the Mossad.
4. Burton Hersh, *The Old Boys: The American Elite and the Origins of the CIA* (New York: Scribners, 1992), p. 49.
5. Confidential interviews, former member of British Diplomatic Corps; former officer of Foreign and Commonwealth Office, 1988–1992.
6. According to this version, the woman was a "pretty, good-natured Czech girl who helped out in the Legation's code room until British counterintelligence satisfied itself that she was blackmailed by the Austrians. Allen had been taking her out; by prearrangement one evening he bought her dinner. The two of them then ambled together in the direction of the Old Town, where Allen fed her to a couple of operatives from the Secret Intelligence Service lying low just outside the historic Nydegg Church." Hersh, *The Old Boys,* pp. 21–22.
7. Confidential interviews, former member of British Diplomatic Corps; former officer of Foreign and Commonwealth Office, 1988–1992.
8. For example, he favored the British line of establishing a Catholic "Pan-Danubian Confederation" in Central Europe, as a buffer between the Soviet Union and Germany. Dulles even continued to pursue that British-Vatican initiative during and after World War II, when it was flatly against U.S. policy.
9. Hersh, *The Old Boys,* p. 274.
10. Elizabeth Monroe, *Philby of Arabia* (London: Faber and Faber, 1973), p. 138.
11. The Bahrain concession started with Major Frank Holmes, an eccentric New Zealand adventurer and mining engineer, who had foreseen the oil potential of Saudi Arabia and neighboring Bahrain in the early 1920s. It was Holmes who introduced Gulf Oil to the region and apparently taught Philby how the game was played. The British saw Holmes as a "troublemaker with a 'capacity for mischief,' who was trying . . . to undermine British influence in the area." Just the sort of man Jack Philby could exploit for his own ends. Daniel Yergin, *The Prize: The Epic Quest for Oil, Money & Power* (New York: Touchstone, 1992), p. 281.
12. Ibid., pp. 282–283.
13. Ibid., p. 283.
14. Ibid., pp. 286, 341.
15. Robert Lacey, *The Kingdom: Arabia and the House of Sa'ud* (New York: Avon Books, 1983), p. 233.
16. Philby's version of the conversation goes this way: " 'You are like a man sleeping over

a buried treasure and complaining of poverty, while unwilling to do anything about it.' 'What do you mean?' [the King] asked sharply. 'I mean,' I replied, 'that your country is full of buried riches—oil and gold for instance—which you cannot exploit yourselves and won't allow anyone else to exploit for you.' 'I tell you, Philby,' he answered rather wearily, 'that if anyone were to offer me a million pounds right now he would be welcome to all the concessions he wants in my country.' 'They are worth a good deal more than that,' I said, 'and, if you really mean what you have just said, I know a man who can help you.'" Harry St. John Bridger Philby, *Arabian Days: An Autobiography* (London: Robert Hale, 1948), p. 291.

17. Ibid.; and Yergin, *The Prize,* p. 288.
18. Yergin, *The Prize,* p. 289. " 'Since he retired from Govt. service . . . Mr. Philby has lost no opportunity of attacking & misrepresenting the Govt. & its policy in the Middle East,' commented one British official. 'His methods have been as unscrupulous as they have been violent. He is a public nuisance, & it is largely due to him & his intrigues that Ibn Saud—over whom he unfortunately exercises some influence—has given us so much trouble during the last few years.' " Ibid., p. 287.
19. Lacey, *The Kingdom,* p. 234. According to Philby's own account, he had met with Loomis "on several occasions during the summer [of 1932] to discuss the prospects of an oil concession in Sa'udi Arabia. . . . His company had struck oil in Bahrain, and Twitchell's reports had encouraged it to desire exploration rights on the Arabian mainland." Philby, *Arabian Days,* p. 295.
20. Yergin, *The Prize,* p. 290; and Philby, *Arabian Days,* p. 295.
21. Lacey, *The Kingdom,* p. 234; Yergin, *The Prize,* p. 290; and Monroe, *Philby of Arabia,* p. 203. (He "was a free man, ready to work on behalf of any serious bidder.")
22. Lacey, *The Kingdom,* p. 235.
23. Monroe, *Philby of Arabia,* p. 204. Philby "kept that arrangement secret. At the same time, he kept up his contacts with the I[raq] P[etroleum] C[ompany]—so successfully that its representative, Longrigg, regarded him as a confidant. In fact, Philby's primary loyalty was, and would remain, to the King." Yergin, *The Prize,* p. 290.
24. Ibid., p. 291. As is clear, Philby actually became adviser to all sides. Longrigg "unwisely confided to Philby" that, as there was a world glut, "they did not need any more oil, as they already had more in prospect than they knew what to do with." The British offer was pitifully small compared to Socal's, and eventually Philby advised Longrigg that "You might just as well pack up," which the Englishman did soon after. Ibid., and Anthony Sampson, *The Seven Sisters* (London: Coronet, 1988), p. 106.
25. Lacey, *The Kingdom,* p. 235. When the bottom line was finally reached, Philby advised Ibn Saud to demand £50,000 and £5,000 per annum in gold in exchange for a concession covering the whole of the Eastern Province and a royalty of 4 shillings per ton once production commenced. On the other hand, he advised Socal to accept these conditions. It was a neat arrangement. Philby was acting for both sides. See also Monroe, *Philby of Arabia,* p. 205.
26. Yergin, *The Prize,* p. 291.
27. Sampson, *The Seven Sisters,* p. 106. "The gaining of the concession by an American company would inevitably begin to change the web of political interests in the region. When Philby told Sir Andrew Ryan, the British minister, that Socal had won the concession, he was 'thunderstruck, and his face darkened with anger and disappointment,' which delighted Philby no end." Yergin, *The Prize,* p. 292.
28. Monroe, *Philby of Arabia,* p. 205. Socal was the original company from which the Arabian American Oil Company (Aramco) grew, first through the merger with Texaco from which Caltex was formed, then after World War II, when the Rockefeller-controlled Standard Oil of New Jersey and Socony Vacuum (Mobil) were brought on board to form Aramco. On the Caltex development, see discussion in Chapter 3, including the role of Socal's partner, Texaco, in shipping oil to the Axis.

29. Ibid., p. 214, and J. B. Kelly, *Arabia, the Gulf and the West* (New York: Basic Books, 1980), p. 238.
30. Yergin, *The Prize,* p. 298. This was a period of boom for Philby. Before 1933 his trading company had been dabbling in a wide range of business enterprises. It was all rather small time: selling Sunlight soap for Lever Brothers, marketing kerosene and petroleum for Standard Oil, supplying British-manufactured silver and nickel coins to the Saudi government as well as British coal and Ford cars and trucks on commission. The Jidda merchants who had claimed that Philby's conversion to Islam was a mercenary step seem to have gotten it right. They called him "Slave of Sixpence." Hot on the heels of his success with the Socal deal, in the summer of 1934 Philby won the Ford Motor Company monopoly for Saudi Arabia. It was a case of turning a fast buck out of the holiest of the pilgrimages. The king had recently given permission for "pilgrims of all ranks to use motor transport" on their way to Mecca, revolutionizing the compulsory Moslem rite by replacing the traditional transport of camels and donkeys. Now Philby had the exclusive contract to deliver the new means. Little wonder that the locals changed his nickname from "Slave of Sixpence" to "the commercial pilgrim." Philby was a very greedy man, with some very greedy friends.

    In light of the abominations visited on him by his father, Kim was very loyal to Jack when it came to his capitalist ventures. Although Kim remained true to his Communist ideals right to the very end, he excused his father's capitalist greed, and was surprisingly defensive about him when speaking to Phillip Knightley in Moscow in 1988, shortly before his death. Kim Philby "was quick to defend his father against accusations that he made a fortune negotiating these oil deals for the Saudis. 'Let's get this clear,' he said. 'My father did not sell off oil concessions to the Americans. He played a part in negotiating one Arabian oil concession on behalf of the Standard Oil Company of California, the acorn from which Aramco grew. For his services, he was paid one hundred dollars a month for the period of negotiation, five thousand dollars on signature of the contract, and five thousand dollars on discovery of oil in commercial quantities. Less than twelve thousand dollars for one of the richest concessions in the world. . . . The picture of my father as a shifty businessman selling useless stuff to the Arabs is completely wrong.' " To his dying day, Kim defended his father. Perhaps he was confused or senile. The younger Philby must have forgotten that Jack's biographer had published the real figures for his father's income from the Socal deal, not including the commission he received from Ibn Saud. Most likely Kim was covering up yet another long forgotten secret from his father's past—to say nothing of his own. See Monroe, *Philby of Arabia,* pp. 154–155 and 210; Patrick Seale and Maureen McConville, *Philby: The Long Road to Moscow* (London: Hamish Hamilton, 1973), p. 14; and Phillip Knightley, *Philby: The Life and Views of the KGB Masterspy* (London: Pan Books, 1989), pp. 142–143.
31. "Virtually from the day in 1933 when the first of Aramco's four parent companies, Standard Oil of California, obtained a sixty-year concession for the Eastern Province, the company has served the house of Saud as guide, confidant, tutor, counsellor, emissary, advocate, steward and factotum." Kelly, *Arabia, the Gulf and the West,* p. 252. It was Philby who showed them how to do it. As discussed in Chapter 7, Aramco and its constituent companies were among the most vocal and persistent campaigners against the partition of Palestine and the formation of Israel, and after the Jews won the 1948 war, continued an unremitting anti-Jewish campaign in favor of their Arab partners: "Aramco and allied oil groups advised and fought against the United Nations decision to partition Palestine and create Israel. They warned against recognition by the United States, and then, after consultation with Arab leaders, James Terry Duce of Aramco along with other oil leaders recommended to the departments of State and Defense that the United States repudiate its stand . . . Aramco has accepted the Saudi Arabian stricture that it is not to sell any oil bound for 'Jewish

destinations' . . . Also, since the establishment of the Jewish homeland, major oil companies and tanker fleets have economically quarantined Israeli harbors in response to an Arab League black list that refuses trade with those who deal with Israel. Socony ceased supplying Israel in October 1956, explaining that 'we got out of Israel because of the continued and increasing difficulties of doing business simultaneously there and in the Arab countries.' " Further, at the request of the Saudi Arabian Government, Aramco screened its employees to ensure that no Jews visit the country as Aramco representatives. See Robert Engler, *The Politics of Oil. A Study of Private Power and Democratic Directions* (Chicago: University of Chicago Press, 1967), pp. 256–258.

32. For a full discussion of Standard of New Jersey's relationship with I. G. Farben, see Chapter 3, and also Yergin, *The Prize,* p. 331, Joseph Borkin, *The Crime and Punishment of I. G. Farben* (New York: The Free Press, 1978), pp. 89 and 92, and Peter Collier and David Horowitz, *The Rockefellers: An American Dynasty* (New York: Holt, Rinehart and Winston, 1976), pp. 225–226.
33. This story was reported independently by an officer from the U.S. Military Intelligence Service (MIS) and a CIA officer who previously had been stationed in Jordan.
34. Ibid.
35. During the 1970s von Bolschwing was interrogated by U.S. Air Force intelligence concerning his Nazi past. A copy of the report is in the authors' possession.
36. Ibn Saud went on: "How . . . would the people of Scotland like it if the English suddenly gave their country to the Jews? . . . It is beyond our understanding how your Government, representing the first Christian power in the world today, can wish to assist and reward those very same Jews who mistreated your 'Isa [Christ] . . . an accursed and stiff-necked race that, since the world began, has persecuted and rejected its prophets and has always bitten the hand of everyone who helped it." Lacey, *The Kingdom,* p. 259.
37. Confidential interviews, MIS officer, 1982; former officer, British Foreign and Commonwealth Office, 1989.
38. Monroe, *Philby of Arabia,* p. 218.
39. Some of the king's other advisers privately gloated that Philby had finally been exposed as a British intelligence agent. Ibid., p. 214.
40. Philby wrote of the plan: "We are to have another meeting . . . to continue the talk, the idea being roughly to get Faisal in as King of Palestine with some *quid pro quo* in the way of Jewish immigration—say 50,000 in the next five years." Ibid., p. 219.
41. H. StJ. B. Philby, *Arabian Jubilee* (London: Robert Hale, 1952), pp. 212–213. Philby's biographer puts the scheme slightly differently: "Philby suggested that in return for a subsidy of £20 million, paid to Ibn Saud, the Jews should take over western Palestine apart from a 'Vatican City' in the old city of Jerusalem; at the same time they should help with securing Arab unity and independence, which was attainable only under Ibn Saud. According to Weizmann's account of the talk, Philby's scheme included "considerable transfers of Arab population." Monroe, *Philby of Arabia,* pp. 221–222.
42. Weizmann told Philby that the Zionists were free to promise economic advantages which could be guaranteed by the Jews alone. He stressed, however, that "we could not give any promises in the political sphere where we had not the power to 'deliver the goods'; moreover, that we could not do anything that might conflict with our loyalties towards Great Britain and France." Jack must have gritted his teeth at this, but kept quiet in the interests of advancing the scheme. Ibid., p. 213.
43. Ibid., p. 222.
44. Ibid. In April 1940 Philby instructed his wife in Britain to copy one of his letters about the deal to Weizmann: "Ibn Saud . . . still won't say yes and won't say no. The truth is that he himself is quite favourably inclined towards the proposal and is just thinking out how it can be worked without producing a howl of anger among certain

Arab elements. . . ." It is revealing that Philby deliberately encouraged the impression in Weizmann that both he and the king favored the deal. Naturally he said nothing of his own duplicitous role in stirring up opposition. Little wonder that Philby could occupy so much of the Zionists' time on his fraudulent scheme. Ibid., pp. 222–223.

45. Ibid., p. 223.
46. David Wyman, *The Abandonment of the Jews* (New York: Pantheon, 1984), p. 342.
47. For accounts of the official policies of the various Allied governments, see Walter Laqueur, *The Terrible Secret* (London: Weidenfeld & Nicolson, 1981); and Martin Gilbert, *Auschwitz and the Allies* (London: Michael Joseph/Rainbird, 1981).
48. Richard Deacon, *The Israeli Secret Service* (London: Sphere, 1979), p. 29.
49. Monroe, *Philby of Arabia,* pp. 223–224. The king recounted how Philby had played the intermediary: "Furthermore, the promise of payment, the King was advised [by Jack], would be guaranteed by President Roosevelt. His Majesty said he had been so incensed at the offer and equally at the inclusion of the President in such a shameful manner that he had never mentioned it again." The king's anger was very strange, to say the least. By then he himself had already tried to extract a bribe from the U.S. president. In November Hoskins was sent to London to tell the British Foreign Office that the scheme had one or two minor problems. While there, he also filled in Weizmann and Namier. They promptly told Philby, who feigned astonishment. He refused to believe it and personally met with Hoskins to argue the facts. Philby tried to convince the American that the scheme had been botched because it had not been put to Ibn Saud firmly enough. Most important, Philby insisted, he definitely was not out of favor with the Saudis. He also may have dropped some hints to Hoskins that the king was being embarrassed in the Arab world by all the Jewish leaks and misrepresentations. If he did, Weizmann apparently was not told. The Zionist leader could not leave uncorrected the charge that he had used President Roosevelt's name as guarantor for the ransom money. Weizmann wrote and denied it to Sumner Welles at the State Department. Ibid., p. 224.
50. Neither our American nor British sources have any direct evidence on this point, but it seems logical in view of subsequent events.
51. Weizmann also wrote of the scheme: "It is conceived on big lines, large enough to satisfy the legitimate aspirations of both Arabs and Jews, and the strategic and economic interests of the United States and Britain." Monroe, *Philby of Arabia,* pp. 224–225.
52. On the eve of World War II, Philby had declared that Hitler had "no earthly intention" of attacking Britain and that the Italians were the "New Romans" who were going to sweep through a decadent Europe. Around the same time, Jack stood as a candidate for the pro-Fascist British People's party. Philby "was drawn into this dubious company by his anti-Zionism, fed by what he conceived to be the follies of British Middle East policy and by his conviction that the British government was as guilty as Hitler for leading the world to war." Bruce Page, David Leitch, and Phillip Knightley, *Philby: The Spy Who Betrayed a Generation* (London: André Deutsch, 1968), p. 36; and Seale and McConville, *Philby,* p. 136.
53. These embarrassing statements were quoted by the journalist and MI6 agent of influence, Robert Bruce Lockhart, who noted them in his diary. See Anthony Cave Brown, *C: The Secret Life of Sir Stewart Menzies* (New York: Macmillan, 1987), p. 180.
54. One retired colonel from the U.S. Army has made a second career tracing the intricate corporate links among the Nazis, the Dulleses, and Philby. We are indebted for his help and for his introduction to other amateur sleuths in the NATO countries.
55. Ibid.
56. Confidential interviews, former member British diplomatic corps; former officer, British Foreign and Commonwealth Office, 1988–1992.
57. Ibid.
58. Ibid.

59. Page, Leitch, and Knightley, *Philby,* p. 40. In fact, Philby had been "gleefully predicting the imminent collapse of his homeland" in Saudi Arabian court circles. Lacey, *The Kingdom,* p. 257.
60. Although considered a bit of a crank, Philby "was at this time a distinguished and well-known figure, and the British mandarin class to which he belonged was tolerant of his crankiness. Indignant at his detention, his friends such as Maynard Keynes, E. M. Forster, Dennis Robertson, campaigned for his release . . ." Seale and McConville, *Philby,* p. 137.
61. Philby and "Vee Vee" had been friends since their days together in India, when Vivian was in the Indian police and Jack in the Indian civil service. In 1925 Vivian transferred to the secret service, became head of Section V (counterespionage), and by World War II was deputy chief. It was Vivian who "was responsible for [Kim] Philby's transfer from SOE to SIS." Kim Philby, *My Silent War* (London: Grafton, 1989), p. 88*n*; and Page, Leitch, and Knightley, *Philby,* pp. 125–126.
62. An expert on both the Soviet Union and the Middle East, Footman "had known St. John since the twenties, when they met at a seminar on Middle Eastern affairs." Page, Leitch, and Knightley, *Philby,* pp. 144–145.
63. These were "the people who, St John said, 'had their fingers on the pulse' . . . Seeing London society partly through his father's eyes, Philby probably saw his life-work as an attempt to penetrate the intelligence services of a capitulated and pro-Fascist Britain." Ibid., p. 108.
64. Knightley, *Philby,* pp. 84–85. As "Vee Vee" told his colleagues, "I've got a bright young man for us—Philby, the *Times* war correspondent. Used to know his father in the old days." Page, Leitch, and Knightley, *Philby,* p. 144.
65. Lacey, *The Kingdom,* p. 258.
66. Monroe, *Philby of Arabia,* p. 231.

CHAPTER 3
THE PIRATES OF WALL STREET

1. Burton Hersh, *The Old Boys: The American Elite and the Origins of the CIA* (New York: Scribners, 1992), p. 69.
2. Ibid. In 1929 Standard of New Jersey had struck its first deal with Farben to get the non-German patent rights to the synthetics programs for oil and rubber, in return for 2 percent of Standard's stock valued at $35 million. In 1930 a joint company was formed "to share developments in the 'oil-chemical' field. Overall, a good deal of technical knowledge was flowing to Standard." Daniel Yergin, *The Prize: The Epic Quest for Oil, Money & Power* (New York: Touchstone, 1992), pp. 329, 331. As it turned out, the deal actually benefited the Nazis, as they kept most of their knowledge and had a decided advantage in the buildup to World War II.
3. Leonard Mosley, *Dulles: A Biography of Eleanor, Allen, and John Foster Dulles and Their Family Network* (New York: Dial Press, 1979), p. 75.
4. Various versions of these meetings exist, the best of which is contained in *The Men Who Financed Hitler.* To be fair, much of these contributions were "in the nature of insurance money, and was often intended to bolster the position of the so-called 'moderates' in the Nazi party. Like many on the right at this time, the business elite thought that the Nazis could be controlled and used against political adversaries on the left." "Who Paid the Piper? German Big Business and the Rise of Hitler," Book Section, *The Financial Times,* September 7, 1985.
5. Yergin, *The Prize,* p. 328.
6. They particularly wanted to stop the Nazis' criticism of Farben's synthetic oil and fuel program, which depended heavily on tariff protection and government support. The officials convinced Hitler that synthetic fuels would cut German dependence on foreign oil and reduce pressure on its foreign exchange.
7. Yergin, *The Prize,* p. 333.

8. The Bank of England was widely criticized in the British Parliament after the war for its lending policies toward the Third Reich. See generally *The New Republic,* January 9, 1984, p. 38.
9. Peter Padfield, *Himmler: Reichsführer SS* (New York: Macmillan, 1972), p. 106.
10. Ibid., p. 112.
11. ". . . [Allen] Dulles had no sympathy for the Nazis. Several of his law partners were Jewish; so were many of his German clients. By 1934, the law firm had already found it impossible to work within the framework of Nazi 'legality.' The Berlin office of Sullivan and Cromwell was shut down." R. Harris Smith, *OSS. The Secret History of America's First Central Intelligence Agency* (Berkeley: University of California Press, 1972), p. 206.
12. "It followed that those governments which encouraged Hitler, not merely with irresolution and dithering but also with sympathy as some kind of bulwark against communism, must also bear the blame . . . [including] the support that 'the Bank of England and English Capitalism generally' gave to Nazi Germany." *The New Republic,* January 9, 1984, p. 38.
13. *The New York Times,* Late City Final Edition, November 9, 1983, Section A, p. 2, Col. 3, Foreign Desk.
14. Ibid.
15. "Their book says Marcus Wallenberg told a British diplomat in 1946 that his bank bought confiscated property from the Nazis, and the diplomat reported that information in a confidential cable to Washington. Some of the stolen items were found after the war in Spain, Austria, Switzerland, Latin America and other countries. . . . The authors said one such company was the American Bosch Corp., which they said conducted research for the U.S. Defense Department and sent information back to Berlin. 'Swedish neutrality made all this possible,' Aalders wrote. Peder Bonde, a nephew of the brothers, told Swedish radio the family had no reason to be ashamed of the Wallenberg's [*sic*] wartime business dealings. 'They did business with businessmen who wanted to protect their own property. They were not Nazis,' said Bonde." Associated Press International News Wire, November 6, 1989.
16. Confidential interview, former officer, British Foreign and Commonwealth Office.
17. The generals had the backing of the businessmen, and their conspiracy against Hitler is discussed in Mark Aarons and John Loftus, *Unholy Trinity* (New York: St. Martin's Press, 1992).
18. "While never Franco's attorney, Dulles represented the Bank of Spain toward the end of 1938 when it was undeniably Franco's creature." Hersh, *The Old Boys,* p. 70.
19. Forrestal convinced the companies to marry "Socal's low-cost potential Middle East crude to Texaco's Eastern Hemisphere distribution system." Yergin, *The Prize,* p. 299.
20. Ibid., pp. 299–300, and confidential interviews, retired colonel, U.S. Army; former officer, the NSA; and former special agent, CIC. See also Charles Higham, *Trading with the Enemy* (New York: Delacorte Press, 1983), chap. 5.
21. Confidential interviews, retired colonel U.S. Army; former officer, the NSA, and former special agent, CIC.
22. ". . . in 1938, IG Farben director Hermann Schmitz . . . hired Sullivan & Cromwell to deal with the World War II version of U.S. Alien property regulations." Christopher Simpson, *The Splendid Blond Beast: Money, Law and Genocide in the Twentieth Century* (New York: Grove Press, 1993), p. 56*n*. See also Higham, *Trading with the Enemy,* chap. 8 passim.
23. A U.S. Senate Committee exposed the fact "that the use of buna rubber was delayed in this country 'because the Hitler government did not wish to have this rubber exploited here for military reasons.'" Joseph Borkin, *The Crime and Punishment of I. G. Farben* (New York: The Free Press, 1978), pp. 89, 92.
24. "In 1941, on the eve of Pearl Harbor, during hearings of the U.S. Senate Committee to Investigate the National Defense, Assistant Attorney General Thurman Arnold

read a letter from Standard Vice-President Frank A. Howard noting that the company had renewed the cartel agreement with the Nazis in Holland in 1939. The terms seemed so distinctly lacking in patriotic concern ('We did our best to work out plans for a complete modus vivendi,' the letter stated, 'whether or not the U.S. enters the war') that committee Chairman Harry S. Truman had left the hearings snorting, 'I think this approaches treason.'

"Ivy Lee had already been tarred with a similar brush. In 1934 the Jersey Company had sent him to Germany to consult with Farben on ways to improve its image, as well as that of the Third Reich, to which it had deep political and economic ties. He came home to face a severe inquisition by a Special House Committee on Un-American Activities. The committee testimony was released in early July, a week and a half after the 'night of the long knives.' The close coincidence between Lee's appearance before investigators and Hitler's blood purge of the SA resulted in headline news: 'Lee Exposed as Hitler's Press Agent' . . .

"With memories of the Lee scandal in mind, [John D. Rockefeller] Junior grew greatly concerned as the Truman Committee probed the intricacies of the Standard-Farben cartel. (By 1942, Farben was known to be operating with slave labor from the Nazi concentration camps.) He privately requested a memorandum from Standard executives explaining their dealings with the Axis powers which he could use in his defense if it should come to that. But it never did; he had become a citizen above suspicion." Peter Collier and David Horowitz, *The Rockefellers: An American Dynasty* (New York: Holt, Rinehart and Winston, 1976), pp. 225–226.

25. Confidential interviews, retired colonel, U.S. Army; former officer, the NSA; former special agent, CIC. The interview with Justice Goldberg arose over the authors' revelations that the U.S. government had used former Nazis as intelligence agents.

26. "In the boardroom Arnold sharply laid down his charges while the others looked hard at him. He spelled it out that he had the goods on Standard: that by continuing to favor Hitler in rubber deals and patent arrangements, the Rockefellers, Teagle and Farish had acted against the interest of the American government. Chewing his cigar to a pulp as he turned over the documents, Arnold coolly suggested a fine of $1.5 million and a consent decree whereby Standard would turn over for the duration all the [Nazi] patents. . . .

"Farish rejected the proposal on the spot. He pointed out that Standard, which was fueling a high percentage of the Army, Navy and Air Force, was making it possible for America to win the war. Where would America be without it? This was blackmail, and Arnold was on the defensive." Higham, *Trading with the Enemy*, pp. 45–46. Much of Higham's nonfiction work has been dismissed unfairly because of his previous books on Hollywood. We have taken a lot of trouble to verify his sources or obtain another source to corroborate his version. A careful review of Higham's source material by Burton Hersh has confirmed the accuracy of Higham's reporting on international finance. Interview with Hersh, 1992.

27. "By 1944 the United States was seriously short of oil. It cost Aramco ten cents a barrel to bring up oil in Bahrein and twenty cents in [Saudi] Arabia, plus a royalty of fifteen cents to the Sheik of Bahrein and twenty-one cents to Ibn Saud in addition to the existing bribe. Suddenly . . . Standard [of California] informed [U.S. Secretary of the Interior] Ickes that the price to America would be $1.05 a barrel, take it or leave it. With his back against the wall, Ickes had to accept." Higham, *Trading with the Enemy*, p. 84.

28. Hersh, *The Old Boys*, p. 70.

29. *The Washington Post*, September 17, 1989, p. C1.

30. Ladislas Farago, *The Game of the Foxes* (London: Pan, 1974), pp. 441–442.

31. Higham, *Trading with the Enemy*, p. 78.

32. Robert Engler, *The Politics of Oil. A Study of Private Power and Democratic Directions* (Chicago: University of Chicago Press, 1967), p. 431.

33. Ibid., p. 200.
34. *The Washington Post,* September 17, 1989, p. C1.
35. U.S. National Archives, Civil Reference Branch, Secret State Department Telegram, January 12, 1945, from U.S. Embassy, Paris. Memo of interview with Joseph J. Larkin.
36. Documents quoted in Paul Manning, *Martin Bormann,* (Secaucus, NJ: Lyle Stuart, 1981), pp. 72 and 268.
37. Interview with Walter Rockler, 1990.
38. See Tom Bower, *The Pledge Betrayed* (New York: Doubleday, 1982). Bower blamed the British military for the lack of effort in prosecuting Nazis.
39. *The Washington Post,* June 6, 1990, p. A20, "British Lords Kill War Crimes Bill in Rare Display of Parliamentary Power." Lord Shawcross stated that Jewish attacks on British troops in Palestine created an atmosphere in which it would have been impossible to continue war crimes trials and criticized the younger generation for their "more simplistic ideas of right and wrong."
40. Confidential interviews, retired colonel U.S. Army; former officer, British Foreign and Commonwealth Office, 1988–1990. See also Robert Kaplan, *The Arabists: The Romance of an American Elite* (New York: Free Press, 1993), p. 58: "As the power of Nazism increased in Europe, Philby despaired of a coming war against Adolf Hitler and began whispering in the King's ear that it would not be such a bad thing if England were to conclude a peace, more or less, on Hitler's terms."
41. CIA study, "German Intelligence in the Near East," part 1, p. 4, Modern Military Branch, U.S. National Archives.
42. Robert Lacey, *The Kingdom: Arabia and the House of Sa'ud* (New York: Avon Books, 1983), p. 257.
43. CIA study, "German Intelligence in the Near East," part 1, p. 6.
44. One version puts the relationship this way: "Saudi Arabia had intricate economic and political links with Hitler. On June 8, 1939, Khalid Al-Hud Al-Qarqani, royal counselor of Ibn Saud, was received by Ribbentrop in Berlin. Ribbentrop expounded to Khalid his general sympathy toward the Arab world and pointed out that Germany and the Arabs were linked by a common foe in the shape of the Jews. Khalid answered that Ibn Saud attached the greatest importance to entering into relations with Germany. . . . He stressed that the King hated the British, who hemmed him in." Jack Philby could not have expressed it better. Soon after Hitler received the king's representative in person, and gave Ibn Saud a token of his esteem: ". . . one and a half million Reichmarks from Hitler's personal treasury for the purchase of 8,000 rifles, 8 million rounds of ammunition, light anti-aircraft guns, armored cars, a special Mercedes for the King, and the building for a munitions factory. Soon afterwards, Emil Puhl arranged for a further loan of 6 million marks that was paid in installments for the rest of the war." Higham, *Trading with the Enemy,* p. 80. Others say that the Nazi arms were never actually delivered.
45. Lacey, *The Kingdom,* p. 258.
46. Confidential interviews, retired colonel U.S. Army; former officer, British Foreign and Commonwealth Office, 1988–1990.
47. "Moffett stated that in order to ensure that Ibn Saud remained loyal to American interests (in other words did not hand Caltex over to Germany or supply General Erwin Rommel with oil), the Treasury must advance $6 million a year to Ibn Saud. Moffett said that the $6 million per annum would not in any way affect Ibn Saud's ongoing relationship with Hitler." Higham, *Trading with the Enemy,* p. 81.
48. Confidential interviews, retired colonel U.S. Army, 1988–1990.
49. *Ibid.,* and confidential interviews, former colonel, U.S. MIS.
50. Lacey, *The Kingdom,* p. 263.
51. Engler, *The Politics of Oil,* p, 200.
52. Ibid.

53. Lacey, *The Kingdom*, p. 263.
54. J. B. Kelly, *Arabia, the Gulf and the West* (New York: Basic Books, 1980), p. 253; and Engler, *The Politics of Oil*, p. 201.
55. Kelly, *Arabia, the Gulf and the West*, pp. 255–256.
56. ". . . the help Britain gave to Zionism from 1917 onwards was the reason why [Ibn Saud] moved away from Britain towards the end of the 1930s and had, by the conclusion of the Second World War, effectively ended the special friendship with London which had been a cornerstone of his foreign policy for many years." Lacey, *The Kingdom*, p. 260.
57. The king's ". . . firmness disconcerted Roosevelt, who seems to have believed that a few hours' personal chichat and some lavish Lend-Lease assistance would win the King of Arabia to his purpose.

    "The president tried another tack. He was counting on the legendary hospitality of the Arab, he said, to help solve the problem of Zionism. But [the king] did not see why the Arabs of Palestine should feel especially hospitable towards the Jews.

    " 'Make the enemy and the oppressor pay,' he said; 'that is how we Arabs wage war.'

    "It was not the Arabs of Palestine who had massacred the Jews. It was the Germans and, as 'a simple bedouin,' the Sa'udi king could not understand why the president seemed so eager to save Germany from the consequences of its crimes. . . ." Ibid., pp. 271–272.
58. Returning to Washington, a chastened Roosevelt told Congress that "from Ibn Saud, of Arabia, I learned more of the whole problem of the Moslems and more about the Jewish problem in 5 minutes than I could have learned by the exchange of a dozen letters." Ibid., p. 272.
59. As previously discussed, the interview arose over Justice Goldberg's alarm regarding the author's revelations that the U.S. government had used former Nazis as intelligence agents. In Goldberg's opinion, those Americans who smuggled war criminals into the United States should be criminally prosecuted.
60. The report was shown to one of the authors by Tom O'Toole, the *Washington Post* reporter who discovered it in the National Archives.
61. Lev Bezymenskiy and Valentin Falin, "Who Unleashed the 'Cold War'—Documentary Evidence," *Pravda*, August 29, 1988, 2nd ed., translated in BBC Summary of World Broadcasts, September 1, 1988.
62. Confidential interviews, former NSA officer; former CIA agent; former officer, British Foreign and Commonwealth Office, 1982–1989.
63. The British had set up a similar dirty tricks shop in New York during World War I. According to top-secret U.S. debriefings of German scientists, British intelligence had sent a shipload of diseased horses from New York to Germany in an early form of biological warfare. The documents were retrieved under the Freedom of Information Act by Rachel Vernon, who graciously allowed the authors to read them. Vernon is currently compiling them in book form.
64. William Stevenson, *A Man Called Intrepid* (London: Sphere Books, 1977), p. 315.
65. Confidential interviews, former officer, NSA; former special agent, FBI, 1982–1989.
66. The classified files of U.S. congressmen who dealt with the Nazis are in the Top-secret vault, 6th floor, Main Justice Department, private files of the attorney general. One of the authors reviewed these records in 1980 during the course of his government employment.
67. Confidential interviews, former officer, NSA; confidential informant, identity of liaison agency withheld.
68. See the discussion, *infra*, on wiretapping of U.S. citizens by the NSA.
69. In an ironic twist, the ADL is under investigation in California in 1993 for doing exactly what the FBI asked it to do in 1941.
70. "Eleanor Roosevelt would complain in a memo to FDR that Allen, a recurring person-

age in 'Bill Donovan's outfit,' was 'closely tied up with the Schroeder Bank, that is likely to be a representative of the underground Nazi interests after the war . . ." Hersh, *The Old Boys*, p. 89.

71. Ibid., pp. 90–91.
72. It was ". . . a 'less glamorous post, but one where I felt my past experience would serve me in good stead.' Frankly, he would not work any longer 'with a lot of generals looking over my shoulder.' " Ibid., p. 93.
73. After the war Dulles requested the CIA to issue a pension to Admiral Canaris's widow, and it was done. Confidential interview, former officer, CIA, 1988.
74. "As late as October 1941, Gaevernitz listed his occupation in Switzerland as agent for Schildge Rumohr, Inc., a New York dummy corporation known as Transmares (the financing for which Dulles himself had expedited through J. Henry Schröder), and identified by the Department of Justice as a front for circumventing the British blockade with strategic materials for embattled Germany." Hersh, *The Old Boys*, pp. 98–99.
75. Confidential interviews, former officer, NSA; confidential informant, identity of liaison agency withheld.
76. Ibid.
77. Confidential interview, former senior U.S. counterintelligence agent.
78. Hersh, *The Old Boys*, p. 101.
79. Confidential interviews, former officer, the NSA, 1985–1988.
80. The key to retrieving the intercept reports from the vaults was the massive Operation Safehaven file index. We have confirmed that all copies of the index were destroyed by the State Department after Roosevelt died.
81. U.S. Department of Justice, Attorney Generals' Archive, Top Secret White House Correspondence File, War Crimes Dossier, 1943–1945.
82. The following quote from a letter sent to Morgenthau in May 1943 is indicative of the size of their targets: "(1) the business of the Ford subsidiaries in France substantially increased; (2) their production was solely for the benefit of Germany and the countries under its occupation; (3) the Germans have 'shown clearly their wish to protect the Ford interests' because of the attitude of strict neutrality maintained by Henry and Edsel Ford; and (4) the increased activity of the Ford subsidiaries on behalf of the Germans received the commendation of the Ford family in America." Letter of May 25, 1943, to Secretary Morgenthau, reprinted in Higham, *Trading with the Enemy*, p. 249.
83. Confidential interviews, retired colonel, U.S. Army, former officer, the NSA. See the discussion of Wallace in Hersh, *The Old Boys*, p. 101.
84. Confidential interviews, retired colonel U.S. Army; former officer, the NSA.
85. "The Germans enjoyed the advantage in this secret war on Swiss soil for some time because they had broken the codes used by Allied diplomats, even by Mr. Dulles himself. For years the Germans read their confidential correspondence. They also succeeded in penetrating the Swiss secret service, reputed to be the best in the world, by an obscure arrangement with Colonel Roger Masson, its chief, who thought it advisable to play the game with both teams." Ladislas Farago, *The Game of the Foxes*, (New York: McKay, 1971), pp. 345–347.
86. Higham, *Trading with the Enemy*, p. 44.
87. Confidential interview, retired colonel, U.S. Army; former officer, the NSA. See the discussion of Wallace in Hersh, *The Old Boys*, p. 101.
88. Ibid.
89. Bern Post Files, Diplomatic Records, U.S. National Archives, Safehaven Reports, Dulles and Gisevius files, 1945–1946.
90. Ibid. Although most of the Operation Safehaven reports have been shredded or shipped to the NSA, a copy of this investigative report was discovered by a graduate student, Mark Masurovsky, during his thesis research in the 1980s.

91. Confidential interviews, retired colonel U.S. Army; former officer, the NSA; former special agent, CIC.
92. Ian Sayer and Douglas Botting, *Nazi Gold* (New York: Congdon & Weed, 1984), p. 284 et seq. Although widely criticized by some members of the intelligence community, *Nazi Gold* should be recognized as a valiant effort to solve a complex puzzle.
93. Confidential interviews, retired colonel, U.S. Army; former officer, the NSA; and former special agent, CIC.

CHAPTER 4
THE MUTINEERS

1. In addition to Mr. Gowen, discussed extensively infra, we interviewed several former members of the OSS, the CIA, and the British diplomatic service, most of whom had personal knowledge of one or the other Angletons.
2. Tom Mangold, *Cold Warrior, James Jesus Angleton: The CIA's Master Spy Hunter* (New York: Touchstone, 1992).
3. *The Washington Post,* June 13, 1990, p. B1.
4. "As president of the U.S. Chamber of Commerce in Italy, Hugh Angleton grew very close to the American Ambassador in Rome, William Phillips, and to Thomas Watson, who had been a sales manager for NCR before founding IBM. By the late 1930s Hugh Angleton was probably the best known American in northern Italy.

   ". . . Angleton received visitors from all over Europe, friends he had made while Vice President of NCR, or members of the closely knit 'NCR family.' From these visitors he received information on arms manufacturing, especially in Germany, and statistics on the duration of running time of various models of German engines, on fuel capacities, and on flight distances between factories. Angleton also traveled to NCR factories in France, Germany, Poland and Rumania and Hungary, setting up what his son later described as 'an internal spy trade' which would be of benefit to the United States when war broke out." Robin Winks, *Cloak and Gown. Scholars in the Secret War* (New York: William Morrow, 1987), p. 329.
5. R. Harris Smith, *OSS. The Secret History of America's First Central Intelligence Agency* (Berkeley: University of California Press, 1972), p. 98.
6. For a fuller discussion of Sindona's financial scandals involving the Vatican, see Penny Lernoux, *In Banks We Trust* (New York: Doubleday, 1984).
7. "Hitler came one night to the holy residence of Archbishop Eugenio Pacelli. All others in the household were asleep by then, except Pascalina. The nun proceeded to let Hitler in and escorted him to the sitting room to await the archbishop. . . . Hitler told Pacelli that he was out to check the spread of atheistic communism in Munich and elsewhere. Through the door, which had been left ajar, Pascalina overheard the prelate say, 'Munich has been good to me, so has Germany. I pray almighty God that this land remain . . . free of communism . . .'

   "For that reason, and despite the Church's historical claim of strict neutrality, the prelate had made his goal the complete destruction of this 'insidious new threat to world freedom and brotherly love.' It did not come as a surprise to her, therefore, in light of Pacelli's hatred of the Reds, to see the prelate present Hitler with a large cache of Church money to aid the rising revolutionary and his small struggling band of anticommunists." Paul I. Murphy, *La Popessa* (New York: Warner Books, 1983), p. 52.
8. Confidential interview, former officer, CIA, 1989.
9. Confidential interviews, 1987–1988.
10. Rosters of church officials documenting Bishop Cikota's transfer were provided by a confidential source.
11. U.S. National Archives, Military Reference Branch, Third Army G-2 Intelligence Report, Interview of Stanislaw Hrynkievich, May 1945. Hrynkievich is an unimpeachable source as he was himself a senior member of the White Russian Nazi puppet

government that included one branch of the Radziwill family. Hrynkievich offered the resources of these Nazis in exile as an underground network for anti-Communist operations. His offer was later accepted by Allen Dulles as chief of covert operations of the CIA. There is no evidence that the other branch of the Radziwill family, which became in-laws to President John F. Kennedy, had any connection with Attorney General Robert Kennedy's subsequent release of German assets. One of the authors had access to the still-classified "Attorney General-Eyes Only" files of the Justice Department, which revealed no trace of any such connection. It also should be noted that Allen's brother, John Foster Dulles, volunteered to handle the settlement of postwar Japanese accounts for the State Department.

12. See the detailed history of Draganović's career presented in Mark Aarons and John Loftus, *Unholy Trinity* (New York: St. Martin's Press, 1992). See especially Chapters 4–7.
13. Ibid., chap. 6.
14. In 1982 one of the authors was walking down the street in Rockland, Massachusetts, when he was approached by a complete stranger who offered the following information. He described how his U.S. Army engineer company had been assigned to handle part of the smuggling. After being warned that the operation was of the highest security classification, they were led into a series of vaults under the autobahn. There they found a great deal of gold and silver jewelry, apparently taken from the inmates at Auschwitz, which had not been melted down by the Nazis in the final days of the war. The U.S. engineers spent several weeks packing the loot into crates, which was marked "costume jewelry." The final disposition of the crates was not known to the informant.
15. The author of the affidavit, who wishes his name withheld, was a major in the U.S. Army during the occupation of Germany. One of his intelligence sources, a Jew who posed as a fugitive German war criminal, uncovered the location of the buried vault. The major was present when its contents were inventoried by the U.S. government. He was stunned to learn that no trace of the find was ever reported to Washington.
16. U.S. National Archives, State Department Decimal Files, Appendix C to report by Vincent LaVista of May 15, 1947.
17. Winks, *Cloak and Gown*, pp. 329–330.
18. Ibid., p. 340.
19. Mangold, *Cold Warrior*, pp. 16–17.
20. Ibid., p. 21.
21. Confidential interviews, former officer, British Foreign and Commonwealth Office; colonel, U.S. MIS.
22. Ibid.
23. Charles Higham, *American Swastika* (New York: Doubleday, 1985), pp. 199–200. For a fuller account of Dulles's unauthorized secret surrender negotiations see Christopher Simpson, *The Splendid Blond Beast: Money, Law and Genocide in the Twentieth Century* (New York: Grove Press, 1993), pp. 199–205.
24. Anthony Cave Brown, *C: The Secret Life of Sir Stewart Menzies* (New York: Macmillan, 1987), p. 215*n*.
25. Higham, *American Swastika*, p. 186. Lindemann was a director of the Dresdener Bank and the HAPAG shipping combine and also "directed German-American Petroleum AG, a wholly owned subsidiary of Standard Oil of New Jersey and the principal source of the fuel for Lindemann's shipping companies. During the 1930s, Lindemann emerged as a leading supporter of the Nazi SS in German industrial circles." Simpson, *The Splendid Blond Beast*, p. 53. See also Higham, *American Swastika*, pp. 55, 155.
26. Higham, *American Swastika*, p. 190.
27. Smith, *OSS*, p. 214*n*.
28. Higham, *American Swastika*, p. 190.

29. Confidential interviews, colonel, U.S. MIS; retired CIA officer; former officer, British Foreign and Commonwealth Office. It is also the authors' opinion that Higham's integrity has been unfairly attacked on several points. As previously discussed, we took a lot of trouble to verify his sources or obtain another source corroborating his version, and author Burton Hersh reviewed much of Higham's documentation and found it to be extremely reliable. Interview with Hersh, 1992. The authenticity of the reports of Dulles's Hohenlohe conversations was confirmed by Christopher Simpson when he independently discovered the document in the U.S. National Archives among the captured German records in the microfilm collection, T-175, reel 458, frames 2975007–2975043. Simpson wrote: "A copy of Hohenlohe's reports was captured and eventually made public by the Soviets in an effort to discredit Dulles after the war, and for that reason it has been occasionally denounced in the West as a forgery. In fact, however, the Hohenlohe reports are authentic; the U.S. Army captured its own set of the same documents, and those papers are today available in U.S. archives at the citation above." Simpson, *The Splendid Blond Beast,* p. 346*n*, pp. 122–124.
30. Smith, *OSS,* p. 215.
31. Higham, *American Swastika,* pp. 190–191. According to Higham, the SS records also show that Dulles gave away vital information on Allied war plans.
32. Ibid., p. 191.
33. Cave Brown, *C: The Secret Life of Sir Stewart Menzies,* pp. 676–683.
34. Ibid.
35. The authors are grateful to Mr. John Taylor of the U.S. National Archives for an introduction to this source. He is currently compiling his research findings for publication.
36. Winks, *Cloak and Gown,* p. 355.
37. Confidential interviews, former officer, British Foreign and Commonwealth Office; colonel, U.S. MIS.
38. Ibid.
39. Confidential interview, former officer, British Foreign and Commonwealth Office. Some of the background for this section was contributed by a former employee of the NSA.
40. Winks, *Cloak and Gown,* p. 355.
41. Ibid., p. 353.
42. One of our sources, William E. Gowen, confirmed from the classified routing correspondence that Donovan presented the Vessel material directly to the White House liaison.
43. Copy in authors' possession.
44. David Martin, *Wilderness of Mirrors* (New York: Harper & Row, 1980), p. 183.
45. Winks, *Cloak and Gown,* p. 355.
46. Smith, *OSS,* p. 84.
47. Confidential interview, former officer, British Foreign and Commonwealth Office.
48. Mr. Gowen still has copies of his father's letter reporting the results of the suspiciously rapid Vatican investigation.
49. Confidential interviews, former officer, the NSA; retired agent, DIA.
50. There have been various histories of this event. See, for example, Winks, *Cloak and Gown,* pp. 386–389, which tells the story from Angleton's point of view.
51. Letter of November 18, 1992, from Gowen to the CIA. The letter goes on: "Scattolini served his sentence and then . . . 'disappeared.' He had never mentioned or compromised Angleton in any way."
52. Mr. Rocca did admit that all the JVX files were forgeries, although he refused to tell the authors how he knew this.
53. The phony JVX reports can be found in the U.S. National Archives, Record Group 226, E174, Box 1, folders 1 and 2.

54. Lacey, *The Kingdom*, p. 274.
55. This is one of those "misfiled" reports down in the Q cage, Vault 2, Suitland. One of the authors stumbled across it in 1980 at the same time that he discovered several dozens of boxes of "misfiled" CIA reports.
56. " 'I'm sorry, gentlemen,' said the president, summing up his position with the utmost candour, 'but I have to answer to hundreds of thousands who are anxious for the success of Zionism; I do not have hundreds of thousands of Arabs among my constituents.' " Lacey, *The Kingdom*, pp. 274–275.
57. The authors confirmed from several sources that shortly after the State Department assumed the Safehaven investigation, the Treasury Department's entire index was shredded and the investigators replaced by intelligence agents.
58. Confidential interviews, former CIC agent and German specialist.
59. Higham, *American Swastika*, pp. 67–68.
60. The *Fortune* magazine extract, circa 1985, was obtained from a computer search of the NEXIS database.
61. Wolff was sentenced to four years in prison in 1949 but served only one week. He was rearrested in 1962, sentenced to fifteen years in 1964, and served only six years, one year for every 50,000 people (mainly Jews) he murdered on the Eastern front.

CHAPTER 5
THE SEEDS OF BLACKMAIL

1. Cadogan diaries, extracts reprinted in Anthony Cave Brown, *C: The Secret Life of Sir Stewart Menzies*, (New York: Macmillan, 1987), p. 678.
2. As it happened, the U.S. Army occupied a villa where Windsor's German correspondent had been located. When the Windsor correspondence was discovered, U.S. Army Counter Intelligence notified its British counterparts. Our source was one of those who had access to the villa and read some of the letters before they disappeared into British custody.
3. One of the authors had access to the Windsor file during his government employment. It is stored in the attorney general's "Eyes Only" File collection, top-secret vault, 6th floor, Main Building, U.S. Department of Justice, Washington, D.C.
4. The top-secret Ribbentrop interview took place shortly before Ribbentrop was executed. He confirmed that Hitler personally favored an Anglo-Nazi alliance, and that Windsor and then–Prime Minister Ramsey MacDonald were not "entirely unsympathetic" to the Nazi philosophy. Interrogation file, U.S. National Archives, copy in authors' possession.
5. Confidential interviews, former officer, Foreign and Commonwealth Service; former officer, CIC; former staff member, British Field Intelligence.
6. Cave Brown, *C: The Secret Life of Sir Stewart Menzies*, p. 676.
7. Ellis's rather checkered career is discussed at length in Mark Aarons and John Loftus, *Unholy Trinity* (New York: St. Martin's Press, 1992). See pp. 158, 213, 216, 274.
8. Confidential interviews, former officer, Foreign and Commonwealth Service; former officer, CIC; former staff member of British Field Intelligence.
9. Ibid.
10. Confidential interviews, non-Western intelligence officers. (Nationalities withheld at sources' request.)
11. Confidential interviews, former officer, Foreign and Commonwealth Service; former officer, CIC; former staff member of British Field Intelligence.
12. John Costello, *Mask of Treachery* (New York: Morrow, 1988), p. 351.
13. The use of "Red Fascists" is discussed extensively in our previous work, *Unholy Trinity*. See Chapters 7–11.
14. The surfacing of the Scattolini papers in the Communist press coincided with Philby's selection as the new British intelligence liaison to the United States.

15. Peter Wright, *Spycatcher* (New York: Viking, 1987), describing Hollis's visits to the royal family.
16. Dulles's client lists were provided courtesy of Burton Hersh, who discovered them among the Dulles collection at Princeton University.
17. Confidential interviews, former White House aide; former agent, CIA.
18. Confidential interviews, colonel, U.S. MIS; former officer, British Foreign and Commonwealth Offices.
19. Harkins described how he made contact with his prewar German friends, who boasted that they had transferred their money to the United States before the collapse of the Third Reich.
20. For example, the "Himmler of Croatia," Pavelić's interior minister Andrija Artuković, settled in the United States. Eichmann's assistant Alois Brunner settled in Syria and helped plot the destruction of Israel.
21. Airgram from Cabot to Washington, June 12, 1947, U.S. National Archives, Record Group 59, 740.00116EW/6-1147.
22. Confidential interviews, former members, U.S. Foreign Service.
23. Later he was sent to the embassy in Belgrade, where he could put his Serbo-Croatian language skills to better use than hunting Nazis. Mudd later returned to Italy as first secretary at the U.S. embassy, a considerable improvement from his position as a CIC agent stuck in the backwaters.
24. Aarons and Loftus, *Unholy Trinity,* p. 83.
25. Ibid., p. 82.
26. To Agent Gowen, Vajta had disclosed that a man named Edward Page was his new patron in U.S. intelligence.
27. Confidential interviews, former agent, CIA; former members, U.S. Foreign Service.
28. Aarons and Loftus, *Unholy Trinity,* p. 68
29. GAO Report, "Widespread Conspiracy to Obstruct Probes of Alleged Nazi War Criminals Not Supported by Available Evidence," May 15, 1978.
30. Aarons and Loftus, *Unholy Trinity,* p. 68.
31. Confidential interviews, former officer, CIA; former members, U.S. Foreign Service.
32. After the JVX series was made available in the American archives, the authors discovered the blunder and, after carefully examining the originals, were able to reconstruct the rest of Angleton's censorship.
33. Instead of uncovering Angleton's code room fraud, Father Graham wrote a minor article for *The Washington Post* in 1980, which was still a bit unflattering about Angleton's work with Scattolini. Although Graham used the word "fraud," the Vatican historian still had not discovered the extent to which Angleton used the Vessel files in his con game.
34. Confidential interviews, former officers and agents, CIA, 1992–1993.
35. Letter from Australian Embassy, Washington, July 31, 1972.
36. Ibid.
37. One of the authors had access to this material during the course of his government employment. Historically, most new immigrants register as Democrats. Yet in the 1950s, while Allen Dulles was director of the Central Intelligence Agency, organizations such as the Byelorussian Republican Committee began to emerge. A surprising number of these ethnic campaign groups turned out to be dominated by the same Fascist leadership that received covert CIA subsidies to purchase printing presses. The subsidy program was eventually extinguished as a result of the Church committee's investigations into CIA abuses in the mid-1970s.
38. Monograph, Political Research Associates, "Old Nazis, the New Right, and the Reagan Administration" (Cambridge, Mass., 1988) p. 15 (The History of the Republican Heritage Groups Council).
39. Confidential interviews, former agent, OPC; former officers, CIA.
40. One source sent us the correspondence of a British-based Byelorussian organization

whose leader, a known war criminal Dimitri Kasmovich, boasted of his role in sending American arms to Angola.

41. When Bush later ran for president, the Republican campaign calendar listed April 10 as Croatian Independence Day, notwithstanding what the State Department thought. The man who organized the exodus of the Croatian Fascists through the Vatican, Father Draganović, would have been pleased. Not to mention Ante Pavelić, the bloody Nazi collaborator who had come to power on that day in 1941 and ushered in the Holocaust against the Jews, Serbs, and Gypsies.

CHAPTER 6
THE TRAP IS SPRUNG

1. Confidential interviews, former senior U.S. counterintelligence officer; former senior UK counterintelligence officer; former member, a Zionist intelligence service (pre-Mossad); former officer, CIA. Several former members of East Bloc intelligence services, while not providing direct corroboration, had heard similar stories from their Soviet counterparts and believed them credible. The authors obtained several volumes of declassified U.S. and British reports on this topic. They are described in part in our previous book: see Mark Aarons and John Loftus, *Unholy Trinity* (New York: St. Martin's Press, 1992).
2. Telephone interview with Rockler, 1992.
3. Confidential interview, former CIC officer assigned to internal security duties in Germany.
4. Confidential interviews, former member, Israeli military intelligence; former member, a Zionist foreign intelligence service (pre-Mossad); retired officer, CIA; former officer, OPC.
5. These "White" Russians were not from White Russia or what is today the independent nation of Belarus (formerly Byelorussia, or White Russia), but took their name from the White anticommunist forces who fought the "Reds" during the civil war after the Bolshevik Revolution. The largest and most important intelligence dossier declassified to date dealing with the whole "Jewish Fascist-White Russian Fascist" Max network is the CIC series of files on "Prince" Anton Turkul, IRR Series, U.S. National Archives, Record Group 319, Dossier Number XE001758.
6. Confidential interviews, agents and officers, former East Bloc intelligence services.
7. As discussed in our previous book, *Unholy Trinity,* the Vatican knew the Max organization as the "Black Orchestra" and used it to communicate with Dulles without knowledge of the Soviet connection. As bizarre as it may seem, Vatican intelligence also operated its own network of "Fascist spies" in the United States. Their leader was Monsignor Ivan Bučko, who worked directly with Nazi intelligence before being sent on a papal mission to negotiate better treatment for Catholics in Ukraine. Father Bučko's espionage career is described in chap. 10 of Charles Higham, *American Swastika* (New York: Doubleday, 1985), and in our previous book. Apart from the "Black Orchestra" penetration of the Vatican, it appears that the Max network had its tentacles in the United States as well. Bučko's Ukrainians were allied with a Russian Fascist, Count Anastase Vonsiatsky, who was convicted of Nazi espionage in the United States. Higham, *American Swastika,* pp. 120–121. Much of the "Catholic Fascist" spy network was revealed to the FBI by a defector, Father Alexei Pelypenko, who worked as an undercover informant. Ibid., pp. 125–133. However, the FBI ignored allegations that some of the Fascist "White" Russians were Communist agents in disguise. See, for example, correspondence from J. Edgar Hoover to Assistant Attorney General Tom C. Clark, circa 1944–1946, FBI Dossier: "White Russian Activities in the San Francisco Area," attorney general's top-secret files, 6th-floor vault, Main Justice Department. (The FBI dropped its Communist investigation of subjects on discovering their affiliation with a pro-Fascist White Russian network with connections to Allied intelligence.) Similarly, Higham did not realize that Vonsiatsky was also Turkul's

emissary in the United States. Turkul's Soviet connection is significant as the combined forces of Bučko and Vonsiatsky ran a far-flung espionage network for the Nazis in the Western hemisphere. Higham, *American Swastika* pp. 120–133. By the time Turkul was under suspicion as a Communist spy, Allen Dulles had become head of the CIA. Angleton blocked any further investigation, insisting that the Fascist networks were entirely anti-Communist. It was a crucial blunder, as the CIA eventually abandoned the networks as being "riddled with Soviet agents." Confidential interview, former officer, CIA.

8. See the CIA study, "German Intelligence in the Near East," part 2, p. 180, and part 4, pp. 23, 58. Modern Military Section, U.S. National Archives.
9. See Turkul dossier, IRR Series, U.S. National Archives, Record Group 319, Dossier Number XE001758; the CIA study, "German Intelligence in the Near East," part 2, p. 180, and part 4, pp. 23, 58; and Alexander Dallin, *German Rule in Russia: 1941–1945,* (New York: St. Martin's Press, 1957), pp. 133–137 and chap. 12.
10. Confidential interviews, former members, Israeli and East Bloc intelligence services.
11. Turkul dossier, IRR Series, U.S. National Archives.
12. Confidential interview, former East Bloc intelligence officer who claims to have had partial access to Soviet communications files.
13. See, for example, Higham, *American Swastika,* pp. 198–199.
14. The published books on the Battle of the Bulge confirm a complete absence of Ultra intelligence concerning the Nazi surprise attack. Several specialists in communications security, both British and American, told us in confidence that they believed there had been a leak to the Germans.
15. It has been suggested that the rise of Vladimir Zhirinovsky, a Russian Fascist Jew, is only the latest revival of the Max system by Russian intelligence. According to columnist William Safire, President Boris Yeltsin deliberately promoted Zhirinovsky's candidacy in order to unite the squabbling democratic factions under his leadership and then discredited Zhirinovsky among the Russian Fascists by leaking word that their anti-Semitic leader was himself a Jew. Safire published his conjecture as a speculative piece in *The New York Times* shortly after news of Zhirinovsky's Jewish antecedents were released in Moscow. There is a superficial similarity between the divide-and-conquer strategies of Yeltsin and the old Max network, but we think the "Jewish Fascist" connection is only a coincidence.
16. The reader is directed to our last book, *Unholy Trinity,* for a detailed analysis of the Max network's success in defeating Hitler during World War II and the CIA during the Cold War.
17. While by no means a consensus, these sources agree that it is the only way that Dulles could have gotten away with moving Nazi money across several continents without detection. Confidential interviews, former senior U.S. counterintelligence officer; former colonel, U.S. MIS; former officer, CIA; former members, a Zionist intelligence service (pre-Mossad).
18. Confidential interviews, former members, British Diplomatic Service; former officer, British Foreign and Commonwealth Office.
19. Confidential interviews, former Zionist intelligence officers (pre-Mossad).
20. The classified British documents reporting the British response appear as an appendix to Walter Laqueur's seminal work, *The Terrible Secret* (London: Weidenfeld & Nicholson, 1981).
21. A copy of that order is hanging in Yad Vashem, Israel's memorial to their 6 million dead.
22. A detailed contemporary account of this affair is given in a U.S. Military Intelligence report of June 19, 1944, American National Archives, Record Group 226, XL959. See also Robert John and Sami Hadawi, *The Palestine Diary 1945–1948,* vol. 2 (New York: New World Press, 1971), pp. 102–103.
23. Confidential interviews, former Zionist intelligence officers (pre-Mossad). According

to one Israeli source, several members of the wartime Red Orchestra and at least one survivor of the Max network later settled in Israel, where they were debriefed by Israeli intelligence. Copies of the debriefings allegedly exist in the private files of Ben-Gurion, which are still closed to the public.

24. Confidential interviews, former Zionist intelligence officers (pre-Mossad).
25. Confidential interviews, former senior U.S. counterintelligence officer; former senior UK counterintelligence officer; former member, a Zionist intelligence service (pre-Mossad); former officer, CIA.
26. One Canadian source has suggested that the real name for the currency smuggling was Operation Bernhard and that the main Nazi figure in the operation, Frederick Schwendt, used the name Sturmbannführer Wendig for himself, although he was never a member of the SS. Schwendt (alias Wendig) was only the "marketing manager" for Operation Bernhard and ended up in West Germany, "destitute, on welfare; before that, he lived in Asuncion, ran a 'greasy spoon joint' while his buddy Rauff sorted fish further South." According to this Canadian source, Wendig/Schwendt worked for a number of intelligence agencies in South America and became an informant for both the West and East Germans. Confidential letter, October 12, 1993. As American intelligence files consistently refer to the operation as "Wendig," so shall we.
27. The volumes were compiled by a special team of Vatican historians: Pierre Blet, Robert A. Graham, Angelo Martini, and Burkhart Schneider (eds.), *Les Actes et Documents du Saint Siège relatif à la Seconde Guerre Mondiale,* vols. 1–11 (Vatican City: Libreria Editrice Vaticana, 1966–81).
28. Top-secret CIC report, "Illegal Jewish Immigration in and Through Italy" (enclosure to the La Vista Report), U.S. National Archives, Record Group 59, FW800.0128/5-1547, Appendix C, page 4, para. 16.
29. See, for example, Gerald Posner and John Ware, *Mengele: The Complete Story* (New York: McGraw-Hill, 1986), pp. 247–248, describing Schwendt's relationship with various fugitive Nazis in South America; and Brendan Murphy, *The Butcher of Lyon* (New York: Empire Books, 1983), pp. 272, 279–80, 293.
30. Top-secret CIC Report, "Illegal Jewish Immigration in and Through Italy."
31. Ibid.
32. According to François-Poncet's entry in the 1950–51 edition of *Who's Who in America* (New York: Marquis, 1950), Addendum p. 3089, he was elected president of the Permanent Commission of the International Red Cross in 1949 to succeed Count Bernadotte.
33. Confidential interview, former member, British intelligence service. One of the authors had access to CIA archives during the course of his government employment and noted that virtually all of the U.S. foreign intelligence dossiers pertaining to World War II and the immediate postwar period had been "routinely destroyed" or misfiled. A small portion of OSS files has been turned over to the National Archives.
34. The original allegations of Angleton's recruitment came from Western sources but were confirmed by several Israeli sources who worked for Mossad's predecessor. A very senior Israeli source refused to either confirm or deny Angleton's work for Israel but insisted, without elaboration, that Angleton had never worked for the Soviets. All of our Western sources agree on this point.
35. Wilbur Crane Eveland, *Ropes of Sand* (New York: Norton, 1980), p. 95.
36. "Of all the sources Angleton tapped in Italy, perhaps the most valuable was the Jewish underground, which was organizing the exodus of survivors of the Holocaust through Italy to Palestine. Fighting for their very existence, the Jews had of necessity developed the most tenacious and most effective underground network in Eastern Europe. Angleton won their trust, establishing a bond that would give him special standing in the new state of Israel. One of Angleton's Israeli confidants, Teddy Kollek, who many years later would become mayor of Jerusalem, explained the bond in

an almost mystical way. 'I believe Jim saw in Israel a true ally at a time when belief in a mission had become a rare concept,' Kollek wrote." David Martin, *Wilderness of Mirrors* (New York: Harper & Row, 1980), p. 20.

37. Confidential interviews, former Zionist intelligence officers (pre-Mossad).
38. A more polite version of "co-opted Israeli agent" has appeared in other publications. See, for example, Burton Hersh, *The Old Boys: The American Elite and the Origins of the CIA* (New York: Scribners, 1992), p. 396.
39. Tom Mangold, *Cold Warrior. James Jesus Angleton: The CIA's Master Spy Hunter* (New York: Touchstone, 1992), pp. 49, 316, 429*n*.
40. Confidential interviews, former member, Israeli military intelligence; former member, a Zionist foreign intelligence service (pre-Mossad); retired officer, CIA; former officer, OPC.
41. Miles Copeland, *The Real Spy World* (London: Sphere, 1978), pp. 41–42.
42. Confidential interviews, former member, Israeli military intelligence; former member, a Zionist foreign intelligence service (pre-Mossad); retired officer, CIA; former officer, OPC.
43. Top-secret report, "Illegal Jewish Immigration in and Through Italy."
44. Confidential interview with a former agent, CIC, detailed to OPC to transport Nazi "agents" to Italy.
45. Top-secret report, "Illegal Immigration in and Through Italy," Vincent La Vista, US National Archives, Record Group 59, FW800.0128/5-1547, p. 6.
46. Ibid., p. 2, para. 7.
47. Ibid., p. 7.
48. Richard Deacon, *The Israeli Secret Service* (London: Sphere, 1979), pp. 29–30.
49. Ibid., p. 37.
50. Ibid., p. 30.
51. Gowen interview, 1993.
52. John and Hadawi, *The Palestine Diary,* p. 106.
53. Ibid., p. 103.
54. "In August 1946, the head of the consular section of the British embassy in Rumania, Mr. Kendall, visited the port of Constanza. His report on Zionist operations . . . included the names of men working on behalf of Jewish immigration headquarters which was centered in Budapest, with funds coming in through Switzerland. The Minister of the Interior was actively issuing emigration certificates and visas, with preference for younger people. The consul's information was that these had undergone military training and training in terrorist activities. 'I believe rumours that the Russians are sending to Palestine, together with the illegal immigrants, arms and explosives. I believe that a number of Russian Jews are included in each shipment. . . .' " Ibid., pp. 102–103.
55. Deacon, *The Israeli Secret Service,* p. 39.
56. Confidential interviews, former members, Israeli intelligence; former member, a Zionist foreign intelligence service (pre-Mossad).
57. See Turkul dossier, IRR Series, U.S. National Archives, Record Group 319, Dossier No. XE001758.
58. MISC CI Special Interrogation Report No. 1 of Klatt, April 8, 1946; SCI interrogation of Klatt, September 7, 1946, Turkul dossier, U.S. National Archives.
59. The circumstances of Baun's revolt against Gehlen are alluded to in Heinz Höhne and Hermann Zolling, *The General Was a Spy* (New York: Bantam, 1972), pp. 189–194.
60. Turkul dossier, U.S. National Archives.
61. During the Reagan and Bush administrations, the CIA asked one of the authors not to publish this casualty rate for fear that it would hurt recruitment in the future. During the Clinton administration, the objection was not renewed. The classified text of Bedell's speech is at the U.S. Army War College, Carlisle Barracks, Pennsylvania, confidential file collection.

62. Dulles succeeded Smith as director of the CIA in January 1953. For two years prior to that time, Dulles was the de facto head of OPC, the State Department's covert action shop that was in the process of being merged with the CIA. Smith's comments clearly were meant as a broadside against the kind of operations that Dulles had been running. Many historians have missed this early CIA period in Dulles's life and blamed his protégé, Frank Wisner, for instituting the Nazi "freedom fighters" program. An examination of CIA files shows that Wisner consulted with Dulles throughout and even stepped down to the number-two slot for several months to allow Dulles to take charge in anticipation of Eisenhower's election. It was Dulles who determined policy behind the scenes. See, for example, CIA queries to OPC on Nazi affiliations of Frantishek Kushel, routed directly to Dulles. CIA domestic contacts section, correspondence files, copy of memo to OPC, in Kushel dossier.
63. Readers interested in this history can find an account in our previous book, *Unholy Trinity,* p. 261.
64. Confidential interviews, former member, Israeli military intelligence; former member, a Zionist foreign intelligence service (pre-Mossad).
65. While this accusation originated with American sources, it was confirmed by several former Israeli intelligence officers and not denied by several others.
66. "When the Zionist movement, alongside its close ties with the money bags, sought also to develop sections which called themselves 'socialist' and applied on that basis to the old Socialist International, the International Socialist Bureau, representing at that time all sections of the socialist movement from the Fabians to the Bolsheviks, turned them down." R. Palme Dutt, "The Middle East—Explosion or Solution?" *Labour Monthly* (February 1970). "The claim of these elements to speak as Marxists is patently fraudulent. Hence it is not surprising that they have been repudiated by the world socialist movement, from the early days of Zionism up to the present." Hyam Lumer, *Zionism: Its Role in World Politics* (New York: International Publishers, 1973), pp. 26–27.
67. In 1920 Stalin was one of those who voted to keep even a left-wing Zionist splinter group out of the Communist International. In 1927 Stalin decreed that he would create his own Communist-Jewish homeland in Birobizhan. The "homeland" was a fig leaf for the labor camps, as many of the Jews who fled Hitler's persecution to find refuge in the "Socialist Motherland" discovered to their misery in the 1930s.
68. See discussion in Alfred M. Lilienthal, *The Zionist Connection,* (New York: Dodd, Mead, 1978), pp. 43–44.
69. Deacon, *The Israeli Secret Service,* pp. 28–29.

CHAPTER 7
"A JEWISH-COMMUNIST CONSPIRACY"

1. Charles Higham, *Trading with the Enemy* (New York: Delacorte Press, 1983), p. 212, describing the manner in which U.S. moves to break up Nazi cartels were blocked by the chief U.S. investigator in Germany: "Brigadier General William H. Draper, who was, along with James V. Forrestal, a vice-president of Dillon, Read, bankers who had financed Germany after World War I." See also Christopher Simpson, *The Splendid Blond Beast: Money, Law and Genocide in the Twentieth Century* (New York: Grove Press, 1993), pp. 48, 64, 248–253, 263–264.
2. Arnold A. Rogow, *James Forrestal. A Study of Personality, Politics and Policy* (New York: Macmillan, 1963), pp. 65–66, 82, 88, 90.
3. Ibid., pp. 178, 180.
4. Daniel Yergin, *The Prize: The Epic Quest for Oil, Money & Power* (New York: Touchstone, 1992), p. 407.
5. Rogow, *James Forrestal,* p. 192.
6. Ibid., p. 191.
7. Yergin, *The Prize,* p. 412.

8. Joe Stork, *Middle East Oil and the Energy Crisis* (New York: Monthly Review Press, 1975), p. 36.
9. Walter Millis (ed.), *The Forrestal Diaries. The Inner History of the Cold War* (London: Cassell, 1952), p. 312.
10. Higham, *Trading with the Enemy*, pp. 39, 80, 83, 135.
11. Charles Higham, *American Swastika* (New York: Doubleday, 1985), p. 188.
12. Richard Deacon, *The Israeli Secret Service*, (London, Sphere, 1979), p. 29.
13. In his diary in July 1946, Forrestal recorded a conversation with Admiral Stone, the U.S. chief of the Allied Control Commission for Italy: "He said the general opinion was that Ben Cohen [Benjamin V. Cohen, then Counsellor of the State Department] was the influence on Byrnes's staff which advocated surrendering everything to Russia in order to avoid war. . . . at the conference [on the Middle East] in Washington between Admiral Schuirmann, Matthews, Dean Acheson and Ben Cohen, Cohen had advocated giving Russia the Tripolitania trusteeship and permitting her to fortify the Dardenelles." Millis (ed.), *The Forrestal Diaries*, p. 183.
14. "We now know that Dr. Robert Soblen with his brother Jack Sobel, were members of a ring headed by Lavrenti P. Beria, Jewish head of the Soviet secret police under Stalin. Robert Soblen was a translator and consultant to UNRRA in 1944–1945, and in 1945–1946 was ostensibly adviser to UNRRA on specifications for medical instruments and equipment to be used in Europe. He was also assigned two contacts in New York with the Office of Strategic Services, in which the Russians had 'a group,' and numbers of O.S.S. personnel were active in and around Palestine." Robert John and Sami Hadawi, *the Palestine Diary 1945–1948*; vol. 2 (New York: New World Press, 1971), pp. 104–105.
15. Millis (ed.), *The Forrestal Diaries*, p. 330.
16. Stork, *Middle East Oil and the Energy Crisis*, p. 44.
17. Millis (ed.), *The Forrestal Diaries*, p. 341.
18. Ed Shaffer, *The United States and the Control of World Oil* (London: Croom Helm, 1983), p. 143.
19. Millis (ed.), *The Forrestal Diaries*, p. 327. For an earlier example of Forrestal's campaign to depoliticize the Palestine issue, see ibid., p. 311.
20. John and Hadawi, *The Palestine Diary*, pp. 260–261.
21. Millis (ed.), *The Forrestal Diaries*, p. 328.
22. David McCullough, *Truman* (New York: Simon & Schuster, 1992), p. 600.
23. Millis (ed.), *The Forrestal Diaries*, p. 474.
24. John Ranelagh, *The Agency: The Rise and Decline of the CIA* (New York: Simon and Schuster, 1986), p. 117.
25. McCullough, *Truman*, p. 597.
26. Ranelagh, *The Agency*, p. 179.
27. John and Hadawi, *The Palestine Diary*, pp. 247–248.
28. Millis (ed.), *The Forrestal Diaries*, p. 330.
29. McGrath emphasized that "Jewish sources were responsible for a substantial part of the contributions to the Democratic National Committee, and many of these contributions were made 'with a distinct idea on the part of the givers that they will have an opportunity to express their views and have them seriously considered on such problems as the Palestine question.' " John and Hadawi, *The Palestine Diary*, p. 248.
30. Millis (ed.), *The Forrestal Diaries*, p. 330.
31. "McGrath said that . . . 'the Jews would expect the United States to do its utmost to implement the partition decision if it is voted by the U.N., through force if necessary'; and that he was considering suggesting to the President that, in the event of partition, the President should invite a group of leading Jewish citizens to form a committee to go to Palestine 'and work out a peaceful and effective arrangement with the Arabs.' As to the use of force, McGrath thought 'it might be worth while

to have the Gallup Poll or some other opinion-reporting agency make a spot check' as to whether American opinion would favour supporting a partition decision with American troops, either alone or as part of a U.N. force." Ibid., pp. 330–331.

32. John and Hadawi, *The Palestine Diary,* p. 243.
33. The first resolution provided "for the reference to the International Court of Justice for an advisory opinion concerning eight legal questions connected with or arising out of the Palestine problem." The second resolution asked the court to determine "the competence of the United Nations to enforce any plan of partition contrary to the wishes, or adopted without the consent of, the inhabitants of Palestine."
34. John and Hadawi, *The Palestine Diary,* pp. 243, 266.
35. Those who voted against the Israeli position on the second resolution were: Argentina, Brazil, Colombia, Cuba, El Salvador, and Haiti. Those in favor of Israel: Chile, Costa Rica, the Dominican Republic, Guatemala, Panama, Peru, Uruguay, and Venezuela. Abstentions: Bolivia, Ecuador, Honduras, Mexico, and Nicaragua.
36. John and Hadawi, *The Palestine Diary,* p. 247.
37. Ibid., p. 262.
38. Among the Central and South American countries targeted were Argentina (eventually abstained, but previously thought by the Zionists to be not "susceptible to influence by the United States"), Colombia (abstained), El Salvador (abstained), Honduras (abstained), Mexico (abstained), and Paraguay (eventually voted in favor).
39. John and Hadawi, *The Palestine Diary,* p. 267.
40. Ibid., as quoted on p. 262.
41. On July 8, 1940, "Nelson [Rockefeller] was celebrating his thirty-second birthday with his family and close friends when the telephone rang with a long-distance call from Washington. It was James Forrestal, special assistant to President Roosevelt. An intense, suspicious man, Forrestal had already made a name for himself as the 'boy wonder' of Wall Street by pulling off the merger of Chrysler Automobiles and the Dodge Corporation. Years earlier, under subpoena by the Pecora [U.S. Senate] Committee, he had admitted to self-dealing in millions' worth of foreign securities during the boom days of the twenties, but like many whom the President had denounced as 'economic royalists,' Forrestal had since done penance by grudgingly supporting Roosevelt's reforms and had thus become eligible for national duty in the country's hour of need.

    "Now he was on the phone to Nelson asking about a job: Could Nelson come to Washington to talk further? The following evening Nelson dined with Forrestal in the garden of the F Club. When offered the newly created post of Coordinator of Inter-American Affairs, Rockefeller asked for a few days to think it over. Then he immediately boarded a plane for Salt Lake City to ask permission from the Republican standard-bearer, Wendell Wilkie, who was on the campaign trail in a candidacy Nelson's Uncle Winthrop had helped create and whose effort the Rockefeller family was heavily backing. But he knew before he hung up what his answer would be—not only because (as Wilkie would tell him) accepting the post was his patriotic duty, but because he himself had proposed the idea of creating such a position in his talk with Harry Hopkins barely a month earlier." Peter Collier and David Horowitz, *The Rockefellers: An American Dynasty* (New York: Holt, Rinehart and Winston, 1976), pp. 213–214.
42. "On the evening of June 14, 1940, Nelson appeared at the White House with the three-page memorandum and delivered it to Roosevelt's right-hand man, Harry Hopkins. At Hopkins's request, Rockefeller read aloud what began more like a manifesto than a mere policy recommendation: 'Regardless of whether the outcome of the war is a German or Allied victory, the United States must protect its international position through the use of economic measures that are competitively effective against totalitarian techniques.' " Ibid., p. 213.

43. As might be expected, British intelligence officials were the most adamantly anti-Rockefeller. Confidential interviews, former official British Foreign and Commonwealth Office; former members, British diplomatic corps. In addition, we had several helpful interviews with relatives of deceased members of MI6 and MI5 who had unusual insight into these affairs. The British intelligence community is not alone in disparaging the Rockefellers. Nelson's wartime activities attracted considerable adverse attention from the American side as well. Confidential interviews, former colonel, U.S. MIS; former officer, CIA.
44. Rockefeller "knew that the European war was creating new opportunities. As a result of the British blockade, one-third of Latin America's markets were cut off, and the situation was ripe. . . . A major objective . . . Rockefeller explained in an official memorandum, 'is to lessen the dependency of Latin America upon Europe as a market for raw materials. . . .' This, he added, was important as 'a hemisphere defense measure.' " Collier and Horowitz, *The Rockefellers,* pp. 229–230.
45. Rockefeller's office "came up with a complex plan to compel the British allies to put up some of the most valuable holdings in Chile and Argentina as collateral for food supplies in the war effort." His policy was to pick up the "good properties in the British portfolio," leaving only "a lot of trash which Britain should be allowed to keep." Ibid., p. 230 and note.
46. The Latin American press complained loudly about the tactics: "The war has further impoverished the poor and enriched the wealthy. It has increased the army's power, both politically and militarily. . . . The large exporting concerns of Latin America . . . are making fat profits." Ibid., p. 233.
47. "The Latin American republics had taken a backseat position in the struggle against the Axis powers. Only two of the twenty republics had even sent token forces to the war zone. Seven others, led by Argentina, had failed to declare war at all. As the conflict drew to a close, Rockefeller and the State Department pressed for a tighter anti-Axis front in the hemisphere. The Latin American nations that had not yet declared war on Germany and Japan were put on notice to do so before February 1 [1945] in order to qualify for admission to the new United Nations." Ibid., p. 235.
48. At the time, Rockefeller's pro-Axis tilt in South America was too much to stomach, even for some in the State Department: "Nicolo Tucci, then head of the Bureau of Latin American Research in the State Department resigned and asked Secretary Hull to abolish his bureau because—as he later put it—'my bureau was supposed to undo the Nazi and fascist propaganda in South America and Rockefeller was inviting the worst fascists and Nazis to Washington.' When Tucci took his complaints to Nelson, he was told: 'Everybody is useful and we're going to convert these people to friendliness to the United States.' And then Rockefeller's lawyer, Larry Levy, said to me, 'Don't worry, we'll buy those people.' " Ibid., p. 236.
49. Nelson's role was "as a sort of Parliamentary whip for the Latin American nations. . . . he was like a ward politician gathering votes and maneuvering with an almost reckless regard for the consequences. As one State Department official complained, 'Sometimes he acts as if he were a separate delegation.' " Ibid., p. 237.
50. "Roosevelt had promised Stalin twice at Yalta that the United States, because of Argentina's fascist record, would not support that nation's bid to enter the world organization. Yet such considerations did not restrain Rockefeller in his determination to ram the admission of Argentina through, no matter what opposition he encountered." Ibid., p. 238.
51. Ibid., p. 243.
52. Confidential interviews, former officer, Army Security Agency (forerunner of the NSA); former colonel, U.S. MIS; former CIA officer assigned to the Middle East; former technical intelligence consultant, British government.
53. Confidential interviews, former official, British Foreign and Commonwealth Office; former technical intelligence consultant, British government; former signals officer, Israeli Defense Forces; former military liaison, Government of Israel.

54. Confidential interview, former communications security specialist, Government of Israel.
55. Confidential interviews, former official, British Foreign and Commonwealth Office; former members, British diplomatic corps. The British intelligence services have always been connected with, if not dominated by, international bankers with long memories. We are grateful that some of the younger ones shared their recollections of their parents' operations.
56. Confidential interviews, former officer, Army Security Agency (forerunner of the NSA); former colonel, U.S. MIS; former CIA officer assigned to the Middle East.
57. Confidential interview, former U.S. intelligence officer assigned to liaison duty with the NSA.
58. Confidential interviews, former officers and agents of various NATO intelligence services who had access to some but not all of the Safehaven reports. With various differences, they all allege that copies of damaging files had been squirreled away long before Morgenthau's resignation as secretary of the treasury. We have confirmed that some of the Safeheaven reports had been distributed to other U.S. agencies in the immediate postwar period and may have been circulated through foreign liaison channels.
59. For a full discussion of the Schröder Bank, see Higham, *Trading with the Enemy*, pp. 32–62.
60. Ibid., p. 62.
61. Ibid., pp. 39–42.
62. In 1945 the Safehaven investigation was taken away from the Treasury Department and run by the Department of State. Predictably, the leads into pro-Nazi American businessmen were never followed up. The Safehaven index was destroyed, and Dulles replaced the Safehaven investigators with his own slate of intelligence officers. Ironically, the Nazi hunting unit became a cover for the recruitment of Nazis for anti-Communist intelligence operations. Confidential interviews, former members of OPC who served abroad under cover of State Department Safehaven Researchers.
63. Confidential interviews, former officer, Army Security Agency (forerunner of the NSA); former colonel, U.S. MIS; former CIA officer assigned to the Middle East; former U.S. intelligence officer assigned to liaison duty with the NSA.
64. Confidential interview, former Zionist intelligence officer who served under Reuven Shiloah.
65. Confidential interviews, former Zionist intelligence officers (pre-Mossad); former diplomat, Government of Israel. It should be emphasized that the accounts of these events came first from Western intelligence sources and was confirmed, only reluctantly, by the Israelis. Several Israeli sources asked us not to reveal the UN episode, but we believe that it is an important part of history.
66. Confidential interview, former Zionist intelligence officer under Reuven Shiloah. His use of the term "Israel" appears anachronistic as the name had not yet been decided. However, this is how he recalled the conversation when last interviewed in the mid-1980s. Something about the intensity of his speech left the impression that this conversation had made an indelible mark upon his memory.
67. Confidential interviews, former officer, Army Security Agency (forerunner of the NSA); former colonel, U.S. MIS; former CIA officer assigned to the Middle East; former U.S. intelligence officer assigned to liaison duty with the NSA. Corroboration came from former Zionist intelligence officers (pre-Mossad); former diplomat, Government of Israel.
68. The London correspondent of *The New York Times* reported Britain's reaction: "the U.N. decision was received there with no surprise, for 'British officials felt that the postponement of the vote on Friday had made partition a certainty.'" Quoted in John and Hadawi, *The Palestine Diary*, pp. 266–267.
69. Confidential interviews, former officer, Army Security Agency (forerunner of the

NSA); former colonel, U.S. MIS; former CIA officer assigned to the Middle East; former U.S. intelligence officer assigned to liaison duty with the NSA. Corroboration came from former Zionist intelligence officers (pre-Mossad); former diplomat, Government of Israel.

70. In 1979 one of the authors was among the first attorneys hired for the U.S. Justice Department's Nazi war crimes unit, the Office of Special Investigations. At that time, the Government of Israel still did not have a single prosecutor assigned to hunting Nazi war criminals.
71. Forty years after World II, Ivan Demjanjuk became the first, and only, alleged Nazi war criminal extradited from the United States to Israel. It was too late, and he was ultimately found not guilty, due largely to the lapse of time and because American investigators had withheld vital information in the original extradition proceedings. Other war criminals in Australia and Canada shared Demjanjuk's good fortune and were found not guilty due to doubts about fifty-year-old evidence. The Jews paid a high price to have their country: The murderers of their people went largely unpunished. In all fairness, hunting Nazis is not the concern of Israel, and should not be. It is the concern of countries such as Argentina, the United States, Australia, Britain, and Canada, which took the Nazis in and deliberately hid them.
72. Lovett "reported the result of the United Nations action on Palestine over the week end. He said he had never in his life been subject to as much pressure as he had been in the three days, beginning Thursday morning and ending Saturday night. . . . [Forrestal] remarked that many thoughtful people of the Jewish faith had deep misgivings about the wisdom of the Zionists' pressures for a Jewish state in Palestine. . . . [Forrestal] said [he] thought the decision was fraught with great danger for the future security of this country." Millis (ed.), *The Forrestal Diaries*, pp. 331–332.
73. John and Hadawi, *The Palestine Diary*, p. 306.
74. Ibid., p. 305.
75. At the end of December 1947, the Soviet deputy foreign minister, Andrei Gromyko, attended a mass Jewish rally in the United States and: "emphasized the importance of the agreement between his country and the United States on the subject of Palestine. This was echoed in an address by Dr. Emanuel Neumann, president of the Zionist Organization of America, and in a statement read on behalf of Moshe Shertok [Sharett] of the Jewish Agency. . . . Dr. Neumann harshly criticized Mr. Bevin's treatment of Jewish aspirations, and 'praised Gromyko's role, first in getting the Jewish Agency a voice in the U.N. councils and then in achieving partition itself.' " John and Hadawi, *The Palestine Diary*, pp. 306–307.
76. Confidential interviews, former officer, Army Security Agency (forerunner of the NSA); former colonel, U.S. MIS; former CIA officer assigned to the Middle East; former U.S. intelligence officer assigned to liaison duty with the NSA. It should be recalled that Harry Truman had just used the threat of the atomic bomb to force the Soviets out of Iran. Now it appeared that the Jews would invite them back in to the Middle East.
77. Mills (ed.), *the Forrestal Diaries*, pp. 343–344.
78. Forrestal's view was that, unfortunately, there was "a consciousness that a substantial part of Democratic funds came from Zionist sources inclined to ask in return for 'a lien upon this part of our national policy.' " Forrestal thought it was high time that Secretary of State Marshall should "take the matter up with the President. . . . Forrestal foresaw two dangerous issues that might arise before the political conventions in June, as [a] result of pressures to give or sell arms to the Jews in Palestine, or (in the very probable event that [the] U.N. would be unable to implement its decision) to force the United States to implement it unilaterally: He had discussed the question . . . 'with a number of people of the Jewish faith who hold the view that the present zeal of the Zionists can have most dangerous consequences, not merely in their divisive effects in American life, but in the long run on the position

of the Jews throughout the world.' " Lovett set the planning staff of the State Department to work on a paper, which "concluded that the U.N. partition plan was 'not workable,' adding that the United States was under no commitment to support the plan if it could not be made to work without resort to force; that it was against American interest to supply arms to the Jews while we were embargoing arms to the Arabs, or to accept unilateral responsibility for carrying out the U.N. decision, and that the United States should take steps as soon as possible to secure withdrawal of the proposal." Ibid., p. 344.

79. Ibid., pp. 346–347.
80. John and Hadawi, *The Palestine Diary,* pp. 311–312.
81. Ibid., pp. 312–313.
82. The "American Christian Palestine Committee—a subsidiary organization of the Zionist Organization of America—scorned the U.S. stand as a surrender to Wall Street and oil interests and also urged the lifting of the arms embargo." Press commentary on Austin's speech at the council was nearly unanimous in its condemnation of the U.S. position. Ibid., pp. 317–318.
83. The Soviet representative at the UN "accused the United States of yielding in Palestine to the 'pressures' of American oil interests." Ibid., pp. 318–319.
84. Ibid.
85. See the excellent discussion of the events leading up to the recognition of Israel in McCullough, *Truman,* p. 600 et seq.
86. Millis (ed.), *The Forrestal Diaries,* p. 346.
87. John and Hadawi, *The Palestine Diary,* p. 320.
88. "The day after the President's interview with Weizmann, the Security Council debate at the United Nations reached a new phase. On 19 March Warren R. Austin outlined the United States' understanding of the Palestine situation in regard to the implementation of the partition plan, and submitted the three following conclusions:

    (1) The partition plan was an integral plan which could not be implemented except as a whole, and there was general agreement that this could not be done by peaceful means.

    (2) In order to maintain peace and afford a further opportunity to promote agreement, the Council should call for an immediate special session of the Assembly to consider the establishment of a temporary trusteeship which would be without prejudice to the rights, claims or position of the parties concerned and without prejudice to the character of the eventual political settlement.

    (3) Pending the meeting of the proposed special session of the Assembly, the Council should instruct the Palestine Commission to suspend its efforts to implement partition." Ibid., p. 322.
89. McCullough, *Truman,* pp. 610–611.
90. Confidential interviews, former officer, Army Security Agency (forerunner of the NSA); former colonel, U.S. MIS; former CIA officer assigned to the Middle East; former U.S. intelligence officer assigned to liaison duty with the NSA. Dulles was coordinating more than the campaign strategy. One source told how he was called to Dewey's New York campaign headquarters to be interviewed by Allen Dulles for an intelligence position in the new Dewey Administration. At the time, all the polls showed that Dewey had a commanding lead. Confidential interview, former member, OPC.
91. Rogow, *James Forrestal,* p. 290.
92. Like many of his friends in the government, Forrestal was at best indifferent to the fate of European Jewry and was even opposed to more than a handful being allowed to immigrate to the United States.
93. While there is no evidence that Stalin was reminded of the Max blackmail at this time, the topic could not have been very far from the minds of those in Soviet intelligence.

94. John and Hadawi, *The Palestine Diary,* p. 353.
95. Millis (ed.), *The Forrestal Diaries,* p. 388.
96. McCullough, *Truman,* p. 614.
97. Ibid., pp. 616–617.
98. Senator Chavez told the crowd that: " 'The Hebrews have forged a nation for themselves. This is a fact, whether the British like it or not; whether the oil companies like it or not, and whether the anti-semites like it or not,' thundered the senator to 'roof-raising applause.' " John and Hadawi, *The Palestine Diary,* p. 370.
99. Ibid., p. 373.
100. McCullough, *Truman,* p. 618.
101. Robert Engler, *The Politics of Oil. A Study of Private Power and Democratic Directions* (Chicago: University of Chicago Press, 1967), p. 256.

CHAPTER 8

SPYING ON ŻION

1. Confidential interviews, former special agent, FBI; former liaison to the NSA; former officials and employees, the NSA; former consultants on communications security (U.S. and UK); former officers, Army Security Agency.
2. Confidential interviews, former officer, the NSA; former special agent, FBI, 1982–1989.
3. " 'In July 1919 . . . when British censorship ceased, we were ordered by the British government to turn over to them all messages passing between our own offices, 10 days after they were sent. . . . they wanted these messages only for such supervision as might give them an inkling of pending disorders within Great Britain, I assume having to do with Irish unrest, and also to do with Bolshevik propaganda.'

   "Asked by Senator Kellogg whether the messages turned over to British intelligence included United States government communications, the cable chief buckled. 'If you don't mind, I would not like to answer that,' he pleaded. 'It puts my company in a very embarrassing position with the British Government.' " James Bamford, *The Puzzle Palace* (New York: Houghton Mifflin, 1982), pp. 329–330.
4. Ibid., p. 40. As one our sources, an expert on NSA history, pointed out, Stimson did not make that remark at the time. It first appeared in a post–World War II biography.
5. Confidential interviews, former NSA officer; former Special Agent, FBI, 1982–1989.
6. Bamford, *The Puzzle Palace,* p. 312.
7. Confidential interview, further identifying data withheld at source's request.
8. Ibid., p. 313.
9. Confidential interviews, former officer, Army Security Agency; former liaison to the NSA.
10. "Hoover's racism . . . is now too well established to require elaboration. Not only were Jews shunned as agent material, but anti-Semitism flourished, especially in the core of functionaries surrounding Hoover. A true Archie Bunker, Hoover's bigotry was so deep-rooted that he barely felt the need to conceal it. (A 'Lebanese Jew' was his contemptuous put-down of Robert Mardian of the Nixon Justice Department when Mardian attempted to assert departmental authority over the bureau.) Fifty years earlier, he had ordered an investigation of Eamon de Valera, President of the Irish Republic—then in the United States to raise money for the cause of Irish independence—to check on reports that de Valera was a 'Spanish Jew.' " Frank J. Donner, *The Age of Surveillance* (New York: Knopf, 1980), p. 121.
11. The early wiretap programs against Jews have been independently corroborated by former members of a Zionist intelligence service (pre-Mossad). The American branch of the far-left Mapam party of Israel has recently asserted that it was the subject of illegal FBI surveillance during this period.
12. Reference to National Archives citation available on request. The authors are still in the process of copying these files and do not wish them reclassified.

13. According to our sources, Forrestal, at the behest of the Dulles brothers and the Dewey campaign, used the British wiretaps to undercut Truman's efforts to establish a Jewish state and, after May 1948, to prevent the shipment of American arms to Israel. Confidential interviews, former officer, Army Security Agency; former liaison to the NSA. The earliest documentary evidence of this is a memo from the State Department to Truman warning him that he must never allow the Jews to have their own country, because it would become a Communist puppet state within three years. Top-secret State Department files, Palestine, Q cage, Vault 2, Suitland storage vaults.
14. Robert John and Sami Hadawi, *The Palestine Diary, 1945–1948,* vol. 2 (New York: New World Press, 1971), pp. 307–308, 309*n*, 305.
15. "On December 5, 1947, less than a week after partition had been approved by the United Nations General Assembly, the United States Government, suddenly and inexplicably, had announced an embargo on the sale of all arms to the Middle East. The embargo extended to the Arabs as well as the Jews, but the Arab armies were already well equipped. They had bought more than $37 million worth of surplus American arms abroad through the Office of Foreign Liquidations Commission. They long had been supplied by Britain and would continue to be. The British had explained that they would not follow the U.S. lead and impose an embargo, because they had 'contractual obligations' to the Arab states." Leonard Slater, *The Pledge,* (New York: Pocket Books, 1971), p. 124.
16. U.S. National Archives, declassified documents in authors' possession.
17. Ironically, the ADL in California was under FBI investigation in 1993 for doing exactly the same thing Hoover had requested it to do during World War II.
18. Confidential interviews, former special agent, FBI; former liaison to the NSA; former officials and employees, the NSA; former consultants on communication security (U.S. and UK); former officers, Army Security Agency.
19. Bamford, *The Puzzle Palace,* p. 236.
20. "To ease their concerns, Secretary of Defense Forrestal asked them to meet with him . . . and requested their continued assistance, 'because the intelligence constituted a matter of great importance to the national security' . . . One official was still unclear as to Shamrock's level of authorization, however, and asked Forrestal if he was speaking not just for the Office of Secretary of Defense, but in the name of the President of the United States. Mr. Forrestal replied that he was." Ibid., p. 241–242.
21. NSCID 9, cited in *ibid.,* pp. 45–46.
22. "The significance of the pact was monumental. It established for the first time intimate cooperation on COMINT of the highest level. It provided for the exchange of personnel, joint regulations for the handling of the supersensitive material, and methods of distribution." Ibid., p. 314. "Among the most critical elements of cooperation between the two nations, especially with regard to the United States, was the right to establish listening posts on each other's territory." Ibid., p. 318.
23. The shell-game arrangement with the British, which had been an ad hoc practice, became institutionalized during the 1947 UK-U.S. discussions on Communications intelligence. Confidential interviews, former officers and employees, the NSA; former officers, Army Security Agency.
24. Bamford, *The Puzzle Palace,* p. 46, quotes the full text of this remarkable agreement.
25. Confidential interviews, former special agent, FBI, former liaison to the NSA; former officials and employees, the NSA; former consultants on communications security (U.S. and UK); former officers, Army Security Agency.
26. See, for example, David McCullough, *Truman,* (New York: Simon & Schuster, 1992), p. 990. Dulles leaked his version of the exchange to the press. Truman never published his.
27. Bamford, *The Puzzle Palace,* pp. 47 and 1.
28. Confidential interviews, former special agent, FBI; former liaison to the NSA; former officials and employees, the NSA; former consultants on communications security (U.S. and UK); former officers, Army Security Agency.

29. David Kahn, *The Codebreakers* (New York: Macmillan, 1966).
30. Here is an example of what the American government told Kahn to censor: "Another agency outside the US Government with which NSA maintains close contact is the Government Communications Headquarters—the cryptanalytic agency of Great Britain. NSA's United Kingdom Liaison Office exchanges cryptanalyzed material, techniques of solution, and so on, with GCHG. The two agencies sometimes divide the work of solution, one agency taking one country and another the other, and trade their results to save duplication of effort; but more often both work independently. *In addition, they exchange personnel on a temporary basis.*" Bamford, *The Puzzle Palace,* p. 129, emphasis added.
31. Confidential interviews, former officers and employees, the NSA; former officers, Army Security Agency. See note 22 supra.
32. Bamford, *The Puzzle Palace,* pp. 331–332.
33. Confidential interviews, former special agent, FBI; former liaison to the NSA; former officials and employees, the NSA; former consultants on communications security (U.S. and UK); former officers, Army Security Agency.
34. Bamford, *The Puzzle Palace,* p. 306.
35. Government Operations Committee, draft report, "Interception of International Telecommunications by the National Security Agency," quoted in ibid., pp. 305–306.
36. See the discussion of Inman's career in ibid., pp. 80–85 and 353–360.
37. Task Force 157 was a CIA-funded, navy-initiated, NSA-controlled hybrid that became involved in several scandals, including the sale of weapons to Libya in a foolish attempt to woo Gadhafi away from his Soviet suppliers. After the weapons deal was canceled, Inman fired the head of the task force, Edwin Wilson, who then defected to Gadhafi. Confidential interviews, former CIA officer assigned to the Wilson case. Apparently Wilson discovered that one of the authors (John Loftus) was one of the few who knew the background of Task Force 157. Wilson called from prison and asked Loftus to be his lawyer. Loftus declined.
38. This very point was made in a little-known passage from James Bamford's *The Puzzle Palace,* p. 306. Our sources say that Bamford never realized the importance of the connection that he had made. Bamford (and Congress) thought that incidental *American* targeting might still be taking place under the foreign espionage rationale. Ibid. They never suspected that the NSA was getting the domestic information handed to it on a silver platter as a result of the deliberate and widespread British targeting. Confidential interviews, former officers and employees, the NSA.
39. Confidential interviews, former special agent, FBI; former liaison to the NSA; former officials and employess, the NSA; former consultants on communications security (U.S. and UK); former officers Army Security Agency.
40. Bamford, *The Puzzle Palace,* p. 331.
41. Legal electronic surveillance of American citizens is permitted by application to a special panel of federal judges, who meet in the secure vault room inside the Justice Department. See discussion of FISA statute, infra, and in Bamford, *The Puzzle Palace,* pp. 367–373, 378.
42. October 23, 1974, testimony of General Allen, NSA director, before the Church committee. See extracts of testimony in Bamford, *The Puzzle Palace,* pp. 301–302.
43. Ibid., p. 297 (citing military files).
44. "The foreign influence thesis became a courtroom issue in the Spring of 1977 with the Kearney wiretapping and mail interception indictment [charges later dropped] based on FBI efforts to locate and apprehend the Weather Underground fugitives. A 400-page 'top secret' report . . . was prepared by FBI researchers and leaked to the press to establish that no crimes were committed because [of] inherent executive power, unrestrained by legal or constitutional requirements. The taps and mail interceptions, the report argued, were legitimate counter-intelligence practices sanctioned by a reservation in the Keith case, excluding targets with 'significant connections'

with a foreign power. . . . In June 1975, the vague language of *Keith* was sharpened by an appellate court ruling (*Zweiborn v. Mitchell*) that mere influence or support of a foreign power did not deprive a domestic group of the protection of warrant requirements in the absence of a showing of an actual agency relationship or collaboration." Donner, *The Age of Surveillance*, p. 279.

45. ". . . with rumors that he would be forced to retire. . . . Most prominently mentioned as a prospective successor was an aide to Secretary of Defense Robert S. McNamara, Adam Yarmolinsky, whose original appointments in 1961 Hoover tried to block with the support of the ultras. The rumor that Yarmolinsky (a Jew!) might replace the Director himself leaked through a friendly newsman, was like a trumpet blast summoning the faithful to battle." Ibid., p. 119.
46. "By carefully inserting the words 'by the National Security Agency,' the Agency has skillfully excluded from the coverage of the FISA statute . . . all interceptions received from the British GCHQ. . . . Thus it is possible for GCHG to monitor the necessary domestic . . . circuits of interest and pass them on to NSA through the UKUSA agreement." Bamford, *The Puzzle Palace*, p. 372.
47. Records of the censorship are in the archives of the Publication Review Committee, CIA, which at that time circulated the manuscript for comment to other intelligence agencies, including the NSA. The censored passages of the proposed postscript were to be added to the British edition of John Loftus's first book, *The Belarus Secret* (New York: Alfred A. Knopf, 1982).
48. See the written submission of Attorney John J. Loftus to the House Judiciary Subcommittee on Immigration and Naturalizatioan. The hearing was called to examine a GAO report on the recruitment of Nazis by U.S. intelligence. The author presented three declassified documents that flatly rebutted the GAO's findings. None of the documents was included in the committee's published report, nor was there any follow-up on the list of topics that were requested for executive session. Loftus also approached a staff member of the Senate Select Intelligence Committee who stated flatly that "the Committee is not interested in events pre-1975."
49. Andrew and Leslie Cockburn, *Dangerous Liaison* (New York: HarperCollins, 1991), p. 36.
50. The FBI's offices for the "Jew room" were at 218 Pennsylvania Avenue, where their code-breaking staff was housed for many years. This office allegedly served as the collection point for wiretaps on the Capitol and congressional office buildings. Although the British liaison office is still housed in the main NSA building at Fort Meade, the "Jew room" has purportedly been moved to a suite of offices in one of the new annexes. Confidential interviews, former special agent, FBI; former liaison to the NSA; former NSA officals and employees; former consultants on communications security (U.S. and UK); former officers, Army Security Agency.
51. Ibid.
52. It wasn't just the fact of Pollard's espionage on behalf of the extreme right-wing cabal of Israeli officials that alarmed Bush and his supporters, it was the sheer scope of what he had gotten away with, stealing and copying thousands of files in an operation that was bound to end in his detection and arrest.
53. Confidential interviews, former special agent, FBI; former liaison to the NSA.
54. Confidential source letter, January 7, 1993, p. 3.
55. Confidential interview, agency withheld to prevent identification.
56. Confidential interviews, current and former officers in several government agencies that liaise with the FBI, including but not limited to Defense, State, and Justice departments.
57. Confidential interview, former official, the NSA, 1990.
58. Confidential interviews, former senior U.S. counterintelligence officer; former special agent, FBI.
59. Confidential interview, former liaison to the NSA.

CHAPTER 9

ROBERT MAXWELL'S CZECH GUNS

1. "Discreet diplomacy . . . had ensured a sympathetic hearing for Israel's cause from the Italian as well as the French authorities. Secret transmitters were set up in Bari, Naples and elsewhere in Italy, which was made a centre for Mossad operations. Their headquarters was established in 1945 in the back room of a Jewish servicemen's club in Milan. Meanwhile another network was set up in France . . . [which] controlled a whole network of secret bases on the French Mediterranean coast from Marseilles." Richard Deacon, *The Israeli Secret Service* (London: Sphere, 1979), pp. 36–37, 40.
2. "Arazi turned up in Italy wearing the uniform of a Polish airman and made his headquarters at a farm outside Milan, using the code name of 'Alon.' He obtained false papers, set up a bogus military camp of his own and even managed to obtain Army petrol for his secret organisation. Arazi . . . who maintained radio contact with Palestine via some roundabout routes, arranged that each Palestinian Jewish unit stationed in Italy should deliver to him a fixed levy of petrol and other fuels and enable him to take over any Jeeps or trucks which they left behind when being demobilised." Ibid., pp. 40–41.
3. "It was estimated that by the end of that year 193 Bren guns, 1,500 rifles, 378 submachine guns and more than a million rounds of ammunition had been received by agents of Haganah and Irgun Zvai Leumi." Ibid., p. 37.
4. Ibid., p. 43.
5. "The British charged that the ships were full of potential Red 'fifth columnists' and others associated with the F.F.I. (Stern Gang), and linked Moshe Sneh's quarrel specifically with them. Presumably on representations of the British Government on the financing of the venture with dollars, the U.S. State Department asked for an inquiry into the use of relief agency funds for illegal Palestine immigration. . . .

   "Having escorted the ships to Cyprus and examined their passengers, the British repeated the charge that there were many communist agents among them. They said that the U.S.S.R. encouraged large-scale Jewish immigration to Palestine and reported the discovery among the immigrants of documents showing membership in Left-wing groups. . . . The Palestine Arab Higher Command backed the British charge, saying that Zionism was the secret ally of communism." Robert John and Sami Hadawi, *The Palestine Diary, 1945–1948,* vol. 2 (New York: New World Press, 1971), p. 309.
6. Deacon, *The Israeli Secret Service,* p. 38.
7. "Early in 1948 there had been evidence that Russia was manipulating some Jewish fanatics and that this had led to temporary hesitations in the USA about the administration's pro-Jewish policy in the Middle East. Somebody in the Pentagon had overreacted to this information and had decided that to back the Jews was to play into the hands of the Russians. James V. Forrestal, the US Secretary of Defense, had hinted in private conversations that it might be necessary to abandon support for the Jews to concentrate all efforts against the Russians. In public he expressed this somewhat differently, telling a Senate Committee that partition [of Palestine] would endanger American oil resources." Ibid., p. 48.
8. Confidential interviews, former East Bloc intelligence officers; former members, British Diplomatic corps; former agents, U.S. Counter Intelligence Corps; former senior official, OPC (State Department intelligence group, predecessor to the CIA).
9. Joe Haines, *Maxwell* (Boston: Houghton Mifflin, 1988), p. 5.
10. Ibid., p. 38.
11. "Politically, he was intervening in Zionist meetings in Solotvino when he was only 12. He joined the Betar, a religious movement but also a para-military organization which went on training exercises and made preparations for going to Israel. . . . In Maxwell's family, both his parents, his grandfather, three sisters and a brother, as

well as numerous aunts, uncles, cousins and boyhood friends were to die either by the bullet or in the gas chamber." Ibid., p. 54.

12. Ibid., chap. 2, pp. 37–63.
13. "The fate of those left behind was dire. The German High Command had issued a directive that Czechs captured while fighting for the allies were to be shot. Any identified as Jews were to be handed over to the Gestapo for execution . . . which is why Private Hoch adopted British pseudonyms several times before finally settling upon Maxwell." Ibid., p. 64.
14. Ibid., p. 73.
15. Confidential interviews, former East Bloc intelligence officers; former members, British Diplomatic corps; former agents, U.S. Counter Intelligence Corps; former senior official, OPC.
16. Confidential interviews, former members, British Diplomatic corps; former senior official, OPC.
17. Maxwell "became adjutant to the Military Government with offices in Berlin's Spandau prison." Haines, *Maxwell,* p. 113.
18. Ibid., pp. 117–118.
19. At this point in his career, Maxwell was little more than an interpreter. There is no indication, for example, that he discovered Schacht's financial links to Dulles. Confidential interviews, former agents, U.S. Counter Intelligence Corps; former senior official, OPC.
20. Haines, *Maxwell,* p. 120.
21. Confidential interviews, former members, British Diplomatic corps with previous service in wartime and postwar intelligence.
22. Haines, *Maxwell,* p. 121.
23. Confidential interviews, former members, British Diplomatic corps with previous service in wartime and postwar intelligence.
24. Haines, *Maxwell,* p. 125. What the British did not know was that Maxwell was quietly aiding the Social Democrats (his mother's party), which defeated both the British-backed Christian Democrats and the Communist party by an overwhelming margin. It was a portent of things to come. Ibid., p. 126.
25. Ibid., pp. 128–129.
26. "Many doctors, dentists, scientists, technologists, researchers and academics who served the Reich had only one thing to offer their conquerors in return for money, or a security clearance, or a job—their scientific documents.

    "Maxwell quickly organised a private trade in these highly valuable research papers, many of them eagerly sought in the West. He commandeered vehicles to return them to London where they were privately published in limited editions and sold for considerable profit." Alex Mitchell, "Maxwell Mystery Deepens," *The Sun-Herald,* November 24, 1991.
27. Ibid.
28. Confidential interviews, former East Bloc intelligence officers; former members, British Diplomatic corps; former agents, U.S. Counter Intelligence Corps; former senior official, OPC.
29. Haines, *Maxwell,* p. 131.
30. Ibid., pp. 134–135. Confidential interviews, former members British Diplomatic corps; former senior officer, OPC.
31. Confidential interviews, former East Bloc intelligence officers; former members British Diplomatic corps; former agents, U.S. Counter Intelligence Corps; former senior official, OPC.
32. Ibid.
33. Haines, *Maxwell,* pp. 134–135.
34. Confidential interviews, former members, British Diplomatic corps; former senior official, OPC.

35. Haines, *Maxwell*, p. 137.
36. Confidential interviews, former members, British Diplomatic corps; former senior official, OPC.
37. Confidential interviews, former East Bloc intelligence officers; former members, British Diplomatic corps; former agents, U.S. Counter Intelligence Corps; former senior official, OPC.
38. An extensive discussion of the Czech coup is contained in our previous book, *Unholy Trinity* (New York: St. Martin's Press, 1992).
39. Ibid., pp. 217–223.
40. Confidential interviews, former East Bloc intelligence officers; former agents, U.S. Counter Intelligence Corps.
41. Haines, *Maxwell*, p. 73.
42. Confidential interviews, former East Bloc intelligence officers; former members, British Diplomatic corps; former agents, U.S. Counter Intelligence Corps; former senior official, OPC.
43. Confidential interviews, former East Bloc intelligence officers.
44. One version records these extraordinary events in this way: "In the early stages Czechoslovakia was earmarked as the most promising source of supply for arms, not only because it was an arms-producing country, but because at that time it was freer from Soviet domination than any of the other Soviet bloc countries of Eastern Europe. Nevertheless it still required Secret Service style activities to plan the purchase of such arms. The Palestinian Jews were helped by a former German Jew who had been one of a number of such Jews specially recruited by Admiral Canaris as agents for his *Abwehr* (German Secret Service). . . . A team of four men was also sent from Palestine to Prague in December 1947, with the express purpose of negotiating arms purchases. Leader of this group was Ehud Avriel, who was given a forged identity document showing that he was Herr Ueberall, an agent of the Swiss Government. In Prague Avriel made contact with two Haganah resident agents. . . . Together they approached the Czechoslovakian Ministries of Defence and Supply and within two months had concluded the first major arms deal." Deacon, *The Israeli Secret Service*, pp. 38–39.
45. "But what surprised the Jews was that the Russians gave tacit approval to the undercover deal. It was the first sign that the Russians, who had always been indifferent if not actually hostile to the idea of a Jewish national home, were prepared to support the clamour for independence in Palestine." Ibid., p. 39.
46. According to Deacon, Mardor organized "the long and hazardous pipeline for smuggling the arms out of Czechoslovakia, then via the American zone of Germany into Belgium, whence they went by sea to Palestine," running the British naval blockade. Deacon's version is quite at odds with the Israeli version. Ibid.
47. "The [Czech] chief of staff explained that the Air Force could not release the additional fifteen Me-109's. Everything suddenly had become very difficult; the Russians had not delivered Czechoslovakia's new jets; there were diplomatic problems." Leonard Slater, *The Pledge* (New York: Pocket Books, 1971), p. 301.
48. Ibid., p. 291.
49. The accused were said to be working " 'in accordance with the plans and directives of the Western Imperialists for the severance of Czechoslovakia from her alliance with the USSR.' On November 21, the court was told, 'the conspirators were interested in connections with hostile Zionist organisations' . . . [One of the conspirators] Dr. Felix holds the rare distinction of being condemned as a western agent by the communists, who saw Zionism as an instrument of western imperialism, and later as a communist agent by some Western sources anxious to link Israel with communists." Ibid., p. 260*n*.
50. Ibid., p. 260.
51. Ibid., pp. 303–304.

52. "But later in the day came a new report. The Egyptians, sobered at the sight of Israeli fighter planes, were digging in at Ashdod, apparently for a prolonged stay. They had not been destroyed. But they would not be in Tel Aviv 'in forty-eight hours' either. . . . The Egyptians had been stopped. They would never get any farther. The danger had passed of a quick victory that would rally the other Arab states with the smell of blood, weaken the will of the Jews to resist, and shake the confidence of Israel's wavering sympathizers in the world." Ibid., p. 304.
53. "Huge motor convoys from the coast carrying all kinds of supplies, from Portuguese sardines to Czech guns and 'walkie-talkies' for the build-up in Jerusalem, had to run the Arab gauntlet. They were increasingly supported by 'surplus' light (Auster) airplanes and arms bought by the Jewish Agency, some from the British Government, but to a much greater extent from Czechoslovakia. The pounds and dollars needed were contributed by British and American Jews. . . .

    "An operation called *Nachshon,* 'to save Jerusalem,' had been planned as part of the general offensive to commence at the end of the month, and Ben Gurion cabled Hagana headquarters in Prague ordering his agents to load as many rifles and machine-guns as possible in a *Dakota* and fly them to Palestine immediately. These were needed 'to add bite and as a morale booster' for the offensive. The weapons arrived 48 hours before the attack and, still in their original Czech packing, were rushed to some of the support units." John and Hadawi, *The Palestine Diary,* pp. 325–326.
54. "For the Jews it was Passover. The Zionists turned it into a victory feast. Said Ben Gurion in Jerusalem, 'We stand on the eve of a Jewish state . . . heartened by the victories of our army. We have not retreated from any position. . . . We have broken open the road to Jerusalem, captured numerous villages . . . fully liberated Tiberias and Haifa. . . . We have just begun to buckle on the sword.' " Ibid., p. 337.
55. "The arms bought in Czechoslovakia, which started to arrive in April 1948 and continued until 1950, included tens of thousands of old-fashioned rifles, and light and medium machine guns, many of which had been produced for the Germans during World War II. The deal also included 12 German Messerschmitt 109 planes, which were flown to Israel in parts, assembled and used against the invading Egyptian forces . . . and 20 British made Spitfires which arrived later on. Israeli personnel were trained by the Czechs to fly and maintain the aircraft. The Czech arms were brought to Israel in Israeli transport planes, flown by Israeli and foreign volunteer pilots." Susan Hattis Rolef (ed.) *Political Dictionary of the State of Israel* (New York: Macmillan, 1987), p. 46.
56. "Beaufighters from Britain, three Flying Fortresses from the United States, Spitfires 'from a certain European country [Czechoslovakia],' dismantled Messerschmitt fighters, Dakota transports, were on their way or had reached Palestine. But not until 20 May was a military airfield in Czechoslovakia turned over to the Hagana, when 'it became the Hagana's main base in Europe for the shuttle-service of arms and planes to Israel." John and Hadawi, *The Palestine Diary,* p. 348*n*.
57. Slater, *The Pledge,* pp. 299–300.
58. Confidential interviews, former members, British Diplomatic corps.
59. Solomon Grayzel, *A History of the Jews* (New York: Mentor, 1968), p. 687.
60. "Ben-Gurion himself loathed Mapam, whom he regarded as much too close ideologically to the Soviet Union. One of his supporters in the government put the matter in terms that President Truman's Jewish advisers might have found uncomfortably blunt. 'In our relations with the U.S.A. we have in that country a fifth column, whereas in our dealings with the Soviet Union they have a fifth column here.' " Andrew and Leslie Cockburn, *Dangerous Liaison* (New York: HarperCollins, 1991), p. 30.
61. Ibid., p. 27.
62. See discussion in Chapter 8. Confidential interview, former member of Zionist intelligence service under Reuven Shiloah.

63. "Soon after the end of World War II, in a secret report prepared for Ben-Gurion, he had recommended that a Jewish state ally itself with the Americans. . . . Ultimately, he argued, Israel should aim for a strategic military alliance with the United States. As a first step toward this goal, he said, the Mossad should forge a connection with American intelligence." Cockburn and Cockburn, *Dangerous Liaison*, p. 35.
64. It was at this point, our sources suggest, that Angleton began to go mad. Confidential interviews, former agents, US Counter Intelligence Corps; former senior official, OPC.
65. Arnold A. Rogow, *James Forrestal. A Study of Personality, Politics and Policy* (New York: Macmillan, 1963), pp. 313–314.
66. Walter Millis (ed.), *The Forrestal Diaries. The Inner History of the Cold War* (London: Cassell, 1952), pp. 485–486.
67. Truman "had learned that Forrestal had been talking to Republicans at a time when it looked as if they might win the 1948 presidential election." John Ranelagh, *The Agency: The Rise and Decline of the CIA* (New York: Simon and Schuster, 1986), p. 131*n*.
68. Millis (ed.), *The Forrestal Diaries*, p. 514.
69. Rogow, *James Forrestal*, p. 1.
70. ". . . during his last months in office, [Forrestal] harbored a conviction that he was under day-and-night surveillance by Zionist agents; and when he resigned as Secretary of Defense in March, 1949, he was convinced that his resignation was not unrelated to pressures brought to bear on the Administration by American Jewish organizations." Ibid., p. 181.
71. Ibid., pp. 307, 4.
72. Confidential interviews, former agents, U.S. Counter Intelligence Corps; former senior official, OPC. For a detailed discussion of the Nazi smuggling, see our previous book, *Unholy Trinity*.
73. Rogow, *James Forrestal*, p. 307.
74. Confidential interviews, former member of Zionist intelligence under Reuven Shiloah; former members, Israeli military intelligence.
75. "Once, walking along the beach, he pointed to a row of metal sun-umbrella sockets in the sand and said to his companion, 'We had better not discuss anything here. Those things are wired and everything we say is being recorded.' He frequently declared that the communists were planning to invade the United States and was deeply anxious about communist infiltration and influence." Rogow, *James Forrestal*, p. 307.
76. Charles Higham, *Trading with the Enemy* (New York: Delacorte Press, 1983), pp. 210–212.
77. There are several similar versions of Forrestal's suicide. See James Bamford, *The Puzzle Palace* (New York: Houghton Mifflin, 1982), pp. 241–243; Ranelagh, *The Agency*, p. 132; and Rogow, *James Forrestal*, pp. 17–18. Another version has it that Forrestal slipped while attempting to hang himself. See Thomas Powers, *The Man Who Kept The Secrets: Richard Helms and the CIA* (New York: Alfred A. Knopf, 1979), pp. 312–313.
78. Confidential interviews, former members, British Diplomatic corps; former agents, U.S. Counter Intelligence Corps; former senior official, OPC.
79. Memo to File, State Department Decimal File 800.43 International of Liberty/6-1549 and 1649, USNA, RG 59, Secret Files.
80. John Loftus, *The Belarus Secret* (New York: Alfred A. Knopf, 1992), p. 108.
81. Heinz Höhne and Hermann Zolling, *The General Was a Spy* (New York: Bantam, 1972), p. 78.
82. "As early as 1949 an informer in one of the émigré organizations had warned Gehlen: 'The Russians are spreading false information of a military nature on a vast scale. They expect your agents to demand payment for these false reports from their masters. Source K. considers that ninety per cent of all intelligence reaching the Americans as a fake.' " Ibid., pp. 179–180.

83. Kim Philby, *My Silent War* (London: Grafton, 1989), p. 157.
84. Aarons and Loftus, *Unholy Trinity,* p. 259.
85. "One of [Gehlen's] Pullach investigators came to the conclusion that in a certain émigré organization known as 'NTS, people working directly for the Soviet Union are recklessly given cover and support.' " Höhne and Zolling, *The General Was a Spy,* p. 180.
86. Confidential interviews, former East Bloc intelligence officers; former agents, U.S. Counter Intelligence Corps; former senior official, OPC.
87. Confidential interview, former senior officer, OPC. A former Israeli military attaché confirmed the sensitivity of the West German connection.
88. Confidential interviews, former officer, CIA; former agent, CIC.
89. Confidential interviews, former East Bloc intelligence officers; former members, British Diplomatic Corps; former agents, U.S. Counter Intelligence Corps; former senior official, OPC.
90. Confidential interviews, former members of Zionist intelligence services (pre-Mossad).
91. Interview with Franklin Lindsay.
92. Confidential interview, former agent, CIA.
93. Confidential interviews, former agents, U.S. Counter Intelligence Corps; former senior official, OPC; former agents, CIA.

CHAPTER 10
THE REVOLVING DOOR

1. Confidential interviews, former agents, U.S. CIC; former officers, U.S. MIS; former officers and agents, SSU, CIG, and OPC (predecessors of CIA).
2. "The Nazi Connection," produced by Ira Rosen, *60 Minutes,* May 16, 1982. The CIA Publication Review Committee had cleared the material in connection with John Loftus's first book: *The Belarus Street* (New York: Alfred A. Knopf, 1982).
3. See, for example, various articles by Ralph Blumenthal that appeared in *The New York Times* in 1982 and 1983.
4. GAO Report to the House Judiciary Committee, Subcommittee on Immigration and Naturalization, "Nazis and Axis Collaborators Were Used to Further US Anti-Communist Objectives in Europe—Some Immigrated to the United States," June 28, 1985. In his testimony before Congress, GAO investigator John Tipton confirmed that the author was the person who identified the files for the GAO.
5. Higham's work, unfortunately, lacks footnotes, which makes independent corroboration difficult.
6. The attack on Hersh came not only from the book review but also from an extremely harsh letter to the editor that was subsequently published.
7. Christopher Simpson, *The Splendid Blond Beast: Money, Law and Genocide in the Twentieth Century* (New York: Grove Press, 1993).
8. The *Times Book Review* had prepared a lengthy review of Simpson's book, but the article was "spiked" without explanation. Interview with Christopher Simpson, January 1994.
9. Simpson, *The Splendid Blond Beast,* p. 33.
10. Allen Dulles to Mark Bristol, April 21, 1922, Bristol Papers, RG 45, USNA, quoted in ibid., p. 34.
11. Ibid., note, p. 218.
12. "With Allen Dulles's help, Karl Blessing cultivated a reputation after the war as an anti-Nazi who had once resigned a seat on the board . . . rather than cooperate with SS efforts to take over the company. Following this purported act of bravery, Blessing later told *The New York Times,* he was reassigned by Hitler to be a 'lowly functionary in the Ministry of Mineral Oil Industry [*sic*],' where he spent the war years

hiding out from the Gestapo. This claim was remarkable, both in that Blessing should make it and in that the *Times* would swallow it." Ibid., pp. 223–225.

13. Confidential interviews, former agents, U.S. CIC; former officers, U.S. MIS; former officers and agents, SSU, CIG, and OPC.
14. Ibid. Several of Nixon's biographers have noted his postwar assignment in the United States reviewing records. None of them attached any significance to this, as Nixon's primary assignment was reviewing contract documents. See, for example, Stephen E. Ambrose, *Nixon* (New York: Simon & Schuster, 1987), p. 115; Earl Mazo, *Richard Nixon* (New York, Harper, 1959), p. 44.
15. Confidential interviews, former agents, U.S. CIC; former officers, U.S. MIS; former officers and agents, SSU, CIG, and OPC.
16. Ibid. The source of Nixon's early money has been a subject of controversy over the years, with some speculation that his first campaign was bankrolled by California oil interests. Nixon may have first met the Dulles brothers in 1936 when he applied unsuccessfully for a job at Sullivan & Cromwell. Ambrose, *Nixon,* p. 81. Shortly before Nixon went off to Germany in 1947, the freshman congressman had a private meeting concerning the Hiss-Chambers affair with both Dulles brothers and New York banker C. Douglas Dillon at the Dewey Campaign Headquarters in New York. Mazo, *Richard Nixon*, p. 58. See also Ambrose, *Nixon,* p. 155 (Nixon as part of delegation to visit Berlin).
17. Confidential interviews, former agents, U.S. CIC; former officers, U.S. MIS; former officers and agents, SSU, CIG, and OPC.
18. The internecine CIA-OPC warfare is discussed in detail in our previous book, *Unholy Trinity* (New York: St. Martin's Press, 1992).
19. Confidential interviews, former Israeli military attachés; former members, Mossad; former members, Israeli diplomatic corps; former members, Zionist intelligence (pre-Mossad).
20. In 1952 "the Republican National Committee formed an Ethnic Division. Displaced fascists, hoping to be returned to power by an Eisenhower-Nixon 'liberation policy,' were among those who signed on. This would become the embryo for the formation of the Republican Heritage Groups Council in 1969.

    "In a sense, however, the foundation of the Republican Heritage Groups Council lay in Hitler's networks into East Europe before World War II. In each of those Eastern European countries, the German SS set up or funded political action organizations." Monograph, Russ Bellant, "Old Nazis, the New Right and the Reagan Administration: The Role of Domestic Fascist Networks in the Republican Party and Their Effect on U.S. Cold War Politics," Political Research Associates, Cambridge, MA, September 1988, p. 14; see also Charles Allen, Jr., "The Real Nazis Behind Every Bush," *The Village Voice,* November 1, 1988. For an account of a similar Fascist penetration of a Western political party, in this case the Liberals of Australia, see Mark Aarons, *Sanctuary! Nazi Fugitives in Australia* (Melbourne: Heinemann, 1989).
21. In other words, the Nazis helped get the ethnic vote out for Eisenhower and Nixon in their electoral victory over Adlai Stevenson in the 1952 election. In 1969, in the wake of Nixon's victory over Hubert Humphrey, in which the émigré Nazis played a similar role, the Ethnic Division became the basis for the Republican Heritage Groups Council. The fact is that the Fascist political organizations that had been set up by the SS during World War II were revised in the United States for the Republican party. Russ Bellant, "Old Nazis, the New Right and the Reagan Administration."
22. See, for example, press reports of Fascists in Bush's Ethnic Outreach staff, discussed infra.
23. Confidential interview, CIA. Soobzokov had been an officer in the ethnic Caucasian SS Division, which committed numerous atrocities. After the war Dulles sent him

on a parachute mission behind the Iron Curtain. In 1980, when the Justice Department charged Soobzokov with concealing his SS membership on his visa application, someone placed an amended visa form in his CIA file. The CIA's surprise document completely blocked the Justice Department's attempt to have Soobzokov stripped of his citizenship. His murder by a Jewish extremist group prevented any further investigation.

24. Confidential interviews, former officers, SSU, CIG, OPC, and CIA. The records of covert intelligence funding of ethnic factions in the 1950s suggest an unusually high correlation between Dulles's ethnic freedom fighters and local units of the Republican party. A cursory glance at the *Encyclopedia of Ethnic Organizations* for the 1950s will reveal an astonishingly large number of Eastern European Fascists in charge of ethnic organizations in the United States. See, for example, the discussion in Loftus, *The Belarus Secret* for Byelorussian Fascists, and in Christopher Simpson, *Blowback: America's Recruitment of Nazis and Its Effects on the Cold War* (New York: Weidenfeld & Nicolson, 1988), for an overview of the political-intelligence links.

25. "Malaxa's first step was to claim millions of dollars which had been deposited before the war in the Chase National Bank in the name of one of his corporations. These funds had been frozen as enemy assets during the war by John Pehle of the Treasury Department. . . . Pehle had since returned to private practice and Malaxa shrewdly hired the law firm of Pehle and Loesser to argue his case. . . . Pehle and Malaxa won." Howard Blum, *Wanted! The Search for Nazis in America* (New York: Quadrangle/The New York Times Book Company, 1977), p. 119.

26. "Similarly, Ugo Carusi was United States Immigration commissioner when Malaxa first attempted to enter as a displaced person. When Carusi resigned his job, Malaxa hired him. Other former government officials and their associates were recruited—and compensated—to assist in Malaxa's legal suits: Secretary of State John Foster Dulles's law firm of Sullivan and Cromwell; former Air Force Secretary Thomas K. Finletter's law firm; and the firm of former Undersecretary of State Adolph A. Berle, who personally testified on Malaxa's behalf before a Congressional Subcommittee on Immigration." Ibid.

27. "At Malaxa's urging, the junior senator from California, Richard Nixon, introduced a private bill in 1951 which would allow Malaxa to remain permanently in the United States. . . .

"The bill was defeated, but it was not the end of Nixon's involvement with Malaxa." Ibid.

28. Ibid., p. 120.

29. "On May 17, 1951, the Western Tube Corporation filed for a 'certificate of necessity' to give top war-time priority to its materials and personnel. Also, the company filed a petition seeking a 'first preference quota' for its treasurer, Nicolae Malaxa, on the grounds that he was indispensable to the operation of Western Tube.

"These two applications were personally promoted by Senator Nixon. Nixon telephoned the executive assistant to INS Commissioner James Hennessy to plead for Malaxa's permanent entry. And a letter sent by Nixon to the Defense Production Administrator marked 'Urgent' insisted, 'It is important strategically and economically, both for California and the entire United States, that a plant for the manufacture of seamless tubing for oil wells be erected . . . urge that every consideration it may merit be given to the pending application.'

"Both appeals were successful. The application for Western Tube was quickly approved and on September 26, 1953, Malaxa was admitted from Canada under a special first-preference petition as a permanent resident.

"Yet, once Malaxa obtained permanent residence in the United States, nothing further was ever done to make Western Tube a reality. Neither Malaxa nor Nixon nor any of the corporation's other sponsors ever again concerned themselves with Western Tube." Ibid., pp. 120–121.

30. "It was repeated in congressional debate that Western Tube was a dummy corporation and a front, because it did not build a single plant or issue a single instrument of war and was dissolved as soon as it had achieved its purpose and obtained its tax deductions.

"In fact, it has been stated on the Hill by no less an authority than former California congressman John F. Shelley that Mr. Nixon obtained for Malaxa a Certificate of Tax Necessity which brought about a tax write-off of several million dollars on a factory that did not exist." Charles Higham, *American Swastika* (New York: Doubleday, 1985), p. 219.

31. "Malaxa appealed the decision and won. Another Nixon friend, U.S. Attorney General William Rogers, affirmed the Immigration Appeals Board's ruling.

" 'How interesting,' Congressman Shelley noted with judicious understatement, 'that this man . . . found sanctuary in the United States thanks to the special favors accorded him by Mr. Nixon and Mr. Rogers. This was at a time when thousands of deserving displaced persons, victims of Mr. Malaxa's Nazis, Iron Guardists, and Communists, were unable to obtain admission. Maybe they would have done better if they transported plunder and been friendly enough with Richard Nixon to obtain his personal intervention in their behalf.' " Blum, *Wanted!* p. 121.

32. Ibid., pp. 115–116.

33. Confidential interview, former member, CIA. In fact, this source insists, it was Allen Dulles's assistant in the OPC, Frank Wisner, who had recruited both Malaxa and Trifa in Romania and smuggled them to the United States.

34. William Corson, *The Armies of Ignorance,* (New York: Dial Press, 1977), pp. 36–39. Aarons and Loftus, *Unholy Trinity,* p. 270.

35. See, for example, criticism of Nixon in Scott Anderson and Jon Lee Anderson, *Inside the League* (New York: Dodd, Mead, 1986) and in the authors' previous book, *Unholy Trinity.* Nixon's office also refused to comment on "The Nazi Connection" on *60 Minutes* in 1982 and offered no rebuttal to Ballant's allegations in PRA that he later used émigré Fascists in his political campaigns.

36. Confidential interviews, former members, Israeli diplomat corps; former agents, CIA.

37. Daniel Yergin, *The Prize: The Epic Quest for Oil, Money & Power* (New York: Touchstone, 1992), p. 481.

38. The French-Vatican relationship was discussed in our previous book, *Unholy Trinity,* Chap. 3.

39. Office of the Army Chief of Staff of Intelligence (OACSI), Project No. 4693, February 1, 1949, 2nd Quarter Report, para. G, obtained by Rachel Vernon under the Freedom of Information Act and shared with the authors.

40. Ibid., p. 6.

41. Confidential interviews, former member, CIA; former members, a Zionist intelligence service; former members, Israeli Military Intelligence.

42. Confidential interviews, former members, CIC, CIA.

43. Richard Deacon, *The Israeli Secret Service,* (London: Sphere, 1979), p. 125.

44. Suddenly, in mid-1956, just as the Suez Crisis was starting to boil over, the British agent was arrested "after a tip-off to the Czechs by a double-agent in the Czech Intelligence Office, a London-based émigré group financed by MI6 with extensive contacts throughout the Czech communist government." Jonathan Bloch and Patrick Fitzgerald, *British Intelligence and Covert Action* (London: Junction Books, 1983), p. 117.

45. Anthony Verrier, *Through the Looking Glass: British Policy in the Age of Illusions* (London: Jonathan Cape, 1983), pp. 131–132.

46. Bloch and Fitzgerald, *British Intelligence and Covert Action,* p. 118.

47. Confidential interviews, former agents, U.S. CIC; former officers, U.S. MIS; former officers and agents, SSU, CIG, and OPC.

48. Neither of the Dulles boys wanted "to be rid of Nasser." They did want London to believe that they agreed that Nasser should be curbed, because he could harm Western interests in the Middle East by assisting Soviet policy. In this way, the Dulles brothers lulled the Foreign Office and British prime minister Anthony Eden, into the false belief that their policies were in accord. In fact, "The Dulles brothers wanted Nasser 'in place' because, on the basis of intelligence acquired by the CIA in Cairo, he was thought in no way to threaten the one overriding US interest in the Middle East—access to cheap crude from Iran and Saudi Arabia. US Middle East oil policy from at least the 1930s had been to offer concessions to nationalist demands; Britain's to wihhold or deny them. In effect, US policy encouraged nationalism in the area, Britain's opposed it. Nasser was the rock on which a purely notional Anglo-American accord was shattered." Anthony Verrier's review of *Divided We Stand: Britain, The US and the Suez Crisis*, by W. Scott Lucas, in *The Financial Times*, October 12, 1991.
49. "Eisenhower was intent on his forthcoming election campaign, determined to become a peace-making President for a second term . . . 'hasten slowly' was a good motto in election year. In deference to the far more powerful oil lobby, Eisenhower hastened with extreme slowness in supplying Israel with weapons: he supplied none." Verrier, *Through the Looking Glass*, p. 130.
50. R. Harris Smith, *OSS. The Secret History of America's First Central Intelligence Agency* (Berkeley: University of California Press, 1972), p. 15.
51. Ibid., pp. 16, 42.
52. Ibid., p. 125, and "Famous U.S. Middlemen for Arab Money," *Business Week*, January 23, 1978.
53. Smith, *OSS*, pp. 166, 309, 325.
54. Richard Harwood and J. P. Smith, "CIA Oil Figures Raise Some Eyebrows," *The Washington Post*, April 23, 1978.
55. Confidential interviews, former agents, U.S. CIC; former officers, U.S. MIS, former officers and agents, SSU, CIG, and OPC.
56. Confidential interview, former officer, CIA.
57. Confidential interview, former officer, OPC.
58. "Miles Copland," *The Times*, January 16, 1991.
59. Miles Copeland, *The Game Player: Confessions of the CIA's Original Political Operative* (London: Aurum Press, 1989), pp. 129–130.
60. Miles Copeland, *The Game of Nations: The Amorality of Power Politics* (London: Weidenfeld and Nicolson, 1969), pp. 193–194.
61. Copeland, *The Game Player*, p. 140.
62. Ibid., p. 158.
63. Ibid.
64. "Miles Copeland," *The Times*, January 16, 1991.
65. Confidential interviews, former agents, U.S. CIC; former officers, U.S. MIS; former officers and agents, SSU, CIG, and OPC.
66. Copeland, *The Game Player*, p. 198.
67. Confidential interviews, former agents, U.S. CIC; former officers, U.S. MIS; former officers and agents, SSU, CIG, and OPC.
68. "Miles Copeland," *The Times*, January 16, 1991.
69. Copeland, *The Game Player*, p. 198.
70. Confidential interviews, former agents, U.S. CIC; former officers, U.S. MIS; former officers and agents, SSU, CIG, and OPC.
71. As Copeland himself wrote: "when someone had to hop on an aeroplane and go to Iran, Egypt, Jordan, or Saudia Arabia to talk to the Shah, Nasser, King Hussein or King Saud, the Dulles brothers would think either of Kim or myself, sometimes together, sometimes singly." Copeland, *The Game Player*, p. 197.
72. Copeland, *The Game of Nations*, pp, 193–194.

73. Verrier, *Through the Looking Glass,* p. 84.
74. Ibid., p. 97.
75. Confidential interviews, former officers and agents, OPC.
76. "I first met Maurice Oldfield in Cairo in the summer of 1946. He was a plump and owl-faced lieutenant colonel with untidy hair and a rumpled khaki uniform. He wore spectacles and one sock dangerously lower than the other." Later Oldfield was best man at Davendish's wedding. *Granta Magazine* (Summer 1988), p. 74. "Oldfield's section was mainly devoted to Jewish terrorism and, in particular overseeing the activities of the three illegal organizations in Palestine that were operating against the British. . . . The atrocity of the King David Hotel stiffened the attitude of the military, which was to a large extent, already pro-Arab and anti-Semitic. Lieutenant General Evelyn Barker, the Army Commander, whose office was in the old city, published an order blaming the Jewish public for its passive support of the terrorists. . . . He ordered the cessation of social intercourse between the British soldiers and the Jews." Ibid., p. 22.
77. Confidential interview, former member British diplomatic corps.
78. "In 1947, the Arabs also began using German prisoners-of-war who were still held in Egypt; the Germans had experience with explosives, they knew military weaponry; and they were sympathetic to the Arab cause, if not actually anti-Semitic. The Arabs would organize the escape of the Germans from their prison camps and channel them along various underground routes to the Arab groups operating in Palestine. The stolen weapons, carried by camel across the desert, would end up in the Sinai, where the escaped prisoners-of-war would be set up as instructors, training Arab units." *Granta Magazine* (Summer 1988), p. 24.
79. "Anti-Semitic disorders broke out in England, and in Palestine some members of the police and army took the law into their own hands and beat or killed Jews. . . . The killings increased, and it became clear that the problem was insoluble. At the end of 1947 Ernest Bevin's policy of non-participation was again approved, and it was decided that British rule would end." Ibid., pp. 28–29.
80. Verrier, *Through the Looking Glass*, p. 97.
81. Confidential interviews, former officers and agents, OPC.
82. Confidential interviews, former agents, U.S. CIC; former officers, U.S. MIS; former officers and agents, SSU, CIG, and OPC.
83. Confidential interviews, former analysts for CIA and DIA; former liaison to the NSA.
84. Yaacov Caroz, *The Arab Secret Services* (London: Corgi, 1978), p. 20.
85. Ibid., pp. 21–22.
86. Ibid., pp. 24.
87. Ibid., p. 13.
88. Foster Dulles "knew that another round in the Arab-Israeli war was likely. CIA aircraft and reports from the United Nations Truce Supervisory Organisation provided reliable intelligence of Egyptian and Israeli preparations for armoured offensives. UNTSO was an excellent intelligence source: the military observers moved with relative freedom through areas of likely conflict; their reports were coded and classified; predominantly American membership of the UN Secretariat's upper echelons guaranteed that the reports were on Dulles's desk before Secretary-General Dag Hammarskjöld saw them." Verrier, *Through the Looking Glass*, p. 146.
89. Caroz, *The Arab Secret Services,* p. 12.
90. Confidential interview, former officer, the NSA.
91. Caroz, *The Arab Secret Services*, p. 45.
92. Ibid.
93. Verrier, *Through the Looking Glass*, p. 151.
94. Confidential interview, former agent, CIA.
95. Young "said that Egypt, Saudi Arabia, and Syria threatened Britain's survival. Their

governments would have to be subverted or overthrown. . . . Since Nasser, dedicated to the destruction of Israel and now an out-and-out Soviet instrument, could not be stopped immediately, priority must be given to Syria, which was about to become a Soviet satellite. Because adverse Saudi reaction to what would be done in Syria was sure to follow, the overthrow of King Saud would have to come next. Then, before Nasser could use Soviet bombers to eradicate Israel, he would have to be eliminated. The fates of Jordan and Lebanon depended upon prompt action to overthrow Syria's government, Young warned." Wilbur Crane Eveland, *Ropes of Sand* (New York: Norton, 1980), pp. 169–170.

96. Confidential interviews, former officers and agents, OPC.
97. "An uncovenanted bonus resulted [to the British]. Intelligence from reconnaissance of Egypt and Israel by CIA aircraft was distributed to SIS. But Foster Dulles was the real beneficiary of this unusual form of liaison between SIS and his brother's CIA. Dulles knew that any 'ultimatum' which the British government might issue as Egypt and Israel went to war would merely be a smokescreen behind which Eden could use *Musketeer* for his own ends." Verrier, *Through the Looking Glass*, p. 151.
98. "Yet despite the hostility of the Eisenhower administration to the 'Suez adventure', the CIA secretly sympathised with Israel at this time, especially those among them who had had first-hand experience of the appalling leakages and trail of treachery in the ranks of British Intelligence—the SIS, and especially Naval Intelligence." Deacon, *The Israeli Secret Service*, p. 126.
99. The report noted that one of the Israeli drivers working for the Americans had been called for active duty with the Israeli army. The driver just happened to have lost an arm and a leg in a previous war, and was blind in one eye, said the report, and could have been called up only for a military emergency. Amory knew it meant that war was imminent, and said so to Dulles, who had then called the meeting.
100. Leonard Mosley, *Dulles: A Biography of Eleanor, Allen, and John Foster Dulles and Their Family Network* (New York: Dial Press, 1979), p. 414.
101. Ian Black and Benny Morris, *Israel's Secret Wars. The Untold History of Israeli Intelligence* (London: Hamish Hamilton, 1991), p. 132; and Mosley, *Dulles*, p. 415.
102. Confidential interviews, former officers and agents, OPC. (By 1956 OPC and the CIA had effectively merged, but the old nomenclature continued as a means to distinguish the various factions.)
103. It should be recalled that Angleton was by then head of the CIA's Counter-Intelligence section and held the Israeli account only as a result of his insistence that he continue to be in charge of operations in which he was "indispensable." The Middle Eastern desk thought that the Israeli account belonged under its wing, and could never understand why Dulles let Angleton get away with it. Our sources say that Dulles had no choice, as he needed Angleton to protect his flanks. Confidential interviews, former officers and agents, OPC.
104. Confidential interviews, former members, OPC and CIA; former official, British Foreign and Commonwealth Office; former liaison to the NSA.

CHAPTER 11
THE REVENGE OF THE PHILBYS

1. "Philby was the more voluble because the idol whom he had for so long thought fit to lead the whole Arab world now disappointed him by 'keeping quiet,' and tending to rubber-stamp whatever the Arab League in Cairo decided. As this body made its successive overbids and mistakes, he began to admire 'the courage and fanaticism of the Jews as much as I deplore the futility of the Arabs.' " Elizabeth Monroe, *Philby of Arabia* (London: Faber and Faber, 1973), pp. 237–238.
2. Ibid., p. 238.
3. "His disgust for the younger generation's lust for Western consumer durables drew rebukes from him which carried a strong flavour of anti-semitism. He was fond of

saying that the Arabs and the Jews were both Semites and therefore traders, and that the only difference lay in the fact that the Jews were honest traders and the Arabs were not." Bruce Page, David Leitch, and Phillip Knightley, *Philby: The Spy Who Betrayed a Generation* (London: André Deutsch, 1968), p. 41.

4. "The Arabia which once trafficked in spices and perfumes, for the service of the gods and dead of the ancient world, has risen at last from her long sleep to serve man and Mammon from the newfound sources of her hidden wealth," Jack wrote in 1951. Anthony Sampson, *The Seven Sisters* (London: Coronet, 1988), p. 103.
5. Robert Lacey, *The Kingdom: Arabia and the House of Sa'ud* (New York: Avon Books, 1983), p. 47.
6. Confidential interviews, former agents, CIA; former analysts, DIA; former liaison to the NSA; former member, British Foreign and Commonwealth Office; former members, British Diplomatic Corps; former members, East Bloc intelligence services.
7. As Philby's biographer wrote: "friends that he had made in the Arabian-American Oil Company . . . helped him to get on with other books. Senior specialists like Tom Barger, a president of the company who had come up through the ranks in Arabia, Bill Mulligan, interested in the modern history of the whole Middle East, and George Rentz, who had written on . . . the rise of Wahhabism, were concerned about his failure to find an English publisher for his books. Through them, and their influence on the Middle East Institute in Washington, he got an American university publisher. . . . In addition . . . Aramco supplied him with photostats of histories in Arabic that he did not possess, and with one unique manuscript." Monroe, *Philby of Arabia*, p. 275.
8. Lacey, *The Kingdom*, pp. 246–247.
9. Confidential interviews, former agents, CIA; former analysts, DIA.
10. "That such ideas should enjoy the currency they did was eloquent testimony to the success of the propaganda campaign ARAMCO had been conducting for many years on its own behalf and that of its Saudi patrons . . . because there were no other sources of information about that country open to the American public, ARAMCO could put across its version of recent Arabian history and politics with almost insolent ease.

    "Its propaganda was framed in a manner likely to strike a sympathetic response in the American people. . . . Naturally, little prominence was accorded in ARAMCO's publicity to the fanatical nature of Wahhabism, or to its dark and bloody excesses." J. B. Kelly, *Arabia, the Gulf and the West* (New York: Basic Books, 1980), pp. 257–258.
11. "Philby was a man of highly unpleasant character—mercenary, arrogant, irascible and untrustworthy. . . . That ARAMCO should have seen fit to cultivate the intimate acquaintance of such a man places its own corporate character in an interesting light . . .

    "From Philby ARAMCO initially learned a great deal about Arabia, past and present, while Philby was able to profit in later years from the mass of information about the peninsula which ARAMCO gradually accumulated in its research division at Dhahran. The fruits of their collaboration are visible in Philby's last major work, *Saudi Arabia*, published in 1955 when he was seventy. . . . To set out a list of the distortions, suppressions and falsifications of the historical record for which the Philby-ARAMCO school of Arabian history is responsible would require a chapter in itself." Ibid., pp. 258–260.
12. According to one account, following Jack Philby's release from a British prison as a suspected Nazi sympathizer in World War II, he "became a Communist and returned to Saudi Arabia, where, working on yet another secret retainer, he attempted to undermine Bechtel's interests in favor of British companies." Laton McCartney, *Friends in High Places: The Bechtel Story* (New York: Ballantine, 1989), p. 82.
13. "Another petroleum project that died abourning was a refinery Bechtel was to have built for British Petroleum in Haifa, Palestine, in 1948. Thirty days after the contract

for the job was signed, Israel declared itself a state and war commenced with the Arabs. As a result, the refinery was never built. The loss was a bitter one for Bechtel, which had to forego millions in potential profits, and according to several company executives it was a major factor in the company's growing anti-Semitism." Ibid., pp. 79*n*–114, 122.

14. Simpson was first introduced to John Foster Dulles in the mid–1930s. The Dulles connection "proved so helpful that he and his brother, a rather owlish fellow named Allen, were subsequently awarded all of Schröder's legal work. Schröder, in turn, began arranging financing for a growing number of Sullivan & Cromwell clients. It was a mutually beneficial relationship, and during the course of it the brothers Dulles became fast friends with the bank's rising young executive vice-president, John L. Simpson." Ibid., p. 74.
15. Steve Bechtel was "a frequent and familiar face in Washington, including at the White House," where Eisenhower took to him in a big way. Ibid., pp. 108, 112. For example, at a meeting in New York in September 1953, Simpson and Steve Bechtel met with Allen's brother, Secretary of State John Foster Dulles. They discussed U.S. problems "in securing reliable information in areas like the Middle East." A few weeks later Simpson wrote to Dulles: "In talking over our meeting afterward, both Steve and I had a thought which I would like to mention. Our organization has, as you know, rather far-flung activities in engineering and construction throughout the world. . . .

    "It might just happen that in this connection, or with regard to some particular matter, we could furnish information or be of assistance to your organization. Occasionally a private concern can perform a function or develop certain aspects of a problem with greater facility than a government agency." It was a good illustration of the symbiotic relationship between the spy world and big business. Of course, Dulles was only too willing to accept their kind offer. Ibid., pp. 117–118.
16. Ibid., pp. 118–119, 120–121.
17. Ibid., pp. 121–124.
18. Confidential interviews, former member, British Foreign and Commonwealth Office; former members, British Diplomatic Corps.
19. Lacey, *The Kingdom*, p. 309.
20. As discussed earlier, the king had made statements such as: "Our hatred for the Jews dates from God's condemnation of them for their persecution and rejection of 'Isa [Jesus Christ] and their subsequent rejection later of His chosen Prophet [Muhammad]." Ibid., p. 259.
21. H. StJ.B.Philby, *Arabian Jubilee* (London: Robert Hale, 1952), p. 204.
22. Ibid., p. 205.
23. Ibid., p. 209.
24. Ibid., p. 219.
25. Ibid., p. 211.
26. "Ordered by the *Times* to cover an out-of-town story, Brewer wanted me to accompany Eleanor to the Saint Georges to keep an appointment Sam had made to welcome to Beirut a fellow newsman with whom he'd worked during the Spanish Civil War—Harold Adrian Russell ('Kim') Philby. . . .

    "Now employed by the London weeklies the *Economist* and the *Observer*, Philby arrived in the midst of the Suez crisis to make his Middle East headquarters in Beirut. With him, as Eleanor Brewer introduced herself, was St. John Philby." Wilbur Crane Eveland, *Ropes of Sand* (New York: Norton, 1980), p. 259.
27. Confidential interviews, former agents, CIA; former analysts, DIA; former liaison to NSA; former member, British Foreign and Commonwealth Office; former members, British Diplomatic Corps; former members, East Bloc intelligence services.
28. "St John seemed delighted to have Kim with him and for the first time in years father and son had time for each other. They would sit on the verandah of the house,

enjoying the crisp mountain air, and talk until an approaching chill in the atmosphere made St John, who was now seventy-one, throw a bedouin cloak over his short-sleeved shirt. . . . Sometimes they would go off alone to Beirut where, conscious that his son had to earn a living, St John made a point of presenting Kim to everyone who might be a source of news or influence." Phillip Knightley, *Philby: The Life and Views of the KGB Masterspy* (London: Pan Books, 1989), p. 200.

29. "He was not taken back on the SIS books or properly integrated into the organization; rather his role was to be that of an outside informant on a retainer. Before he left London he was briefed by two senior SIS officers who explained to him that he was being re-engaged for reasons of simple justice as his friends were genuinely sorry for him. But because of the shadow over his name, because his total innocence had not been irrefutably established, he would be given no Communist targets. . . . Warned off Communist targets, he was directed to Arab matters, specifically to President Nasser's interventions outside Egypt and to internal developments in Saudi Arabia. . . . it was thought that his family connections with Arabia would yield intelligence dividends." Patrick Seale and Maureen McConville, *Philby: The Long Road to Moscow* (London: Hamish Hamilton, 1973), p. 237.
30. Knightley, *KGB Masterspy*, p. 204; and Seale and McConville, *Philby*, p. 241.
31. Confidential interviews, former agents, CIA; former analysts, DIA; former liaison to the NSA; former member, British Foreign and Commonwealth Office; former members, British Diplomatic Corps; former members, East Bloc intelligence services.
32. Ibid.
33. Confidential interviews, former member, British Foreign and Commonwealth Office; former members, British Diplomatic Corps.
34. "The Lebanon was a ringside seat for these events, and, to Philby, Nasser's acts in the name of Egyptian dignity and pride were a tonic. He snatched up his pen and deluged the Egyptian, Lebanese and British press with letters and articles. . . . Tucked away in his verbiage were the arguments that he had sustained all through his life about imperialism and the Arabs' right to run their own affairs. The Users' Conference held in London in August 1946 was a 'neat piece of international chicanery' aimed at depriving Egypt of a right:

    "The East does not trust the West, and there is no means of inducing it to do so until every vestige of the old Western imperialism is removed from its lands." Monroe, *Philby of Arabia*, p. 288.
35. Page, Leitch, and Knightley, *Philby*, p. 275.
36. Alfred Lilienthal, *The Zionist Connection* (New York: Dodd, Mead, 1978), p. 537.
37. Daniel Yergin, *The Prize: The Epic Quest for Oil, Money & Power* (New York: Touchstone, 1992), p. 491.
38. Anthony Verrier, *Through the Looking Glass: British Policy in the Age of Illusions* (London: Jonathan Cape, 1983), p. 156.
39. "On November 9, Eisenhower met with the National Security Council to begin considering help for the Europeans. He talked about getting the oil companies to cooperate on a major supply program. 'Despite my stiff-necked Attorney General,' he said with a smile, he would provide the companies with a certificate that they were operating in the interests of national security, thus protecting them from antitrust action. But what would happen if the heads of the oil companies landed in jail anyway for participating in such a program? Why, said the President, laughing, he would pardon them." Yergin, *The Prize*, p. 492.
40. Christopher Simpson, *Blowback: America's Recruitment of Nazis and Its Effects on the Cold War* (New York: Weidenfeld & Nicholson, 1988), p. 265.
41. Ibid.
42. Interview, Wendy Wisner, Rockland, Massachusetts.
43. Confidential interviews, former agents CIA; former analysts, DIA; former liaison to the NSA.

44. Verrier, *Through the Looking Glass*, p. 180.
45. In his book on the oil business, veteran American journalist Jack Anderson explained it this way: "According to Miles Copeland . . . Oil and allied business interests effectively turned around both the executive branch and Congress. Copeland and other experts credit their campaign with emasculating the pro-Nasser influence in the State Department, weakening congressional support for aid to Egypt, influencing Eisenhower to use American naval and marine forces to contain the 1958 wave of Nasserite uprisings, and helping persuade the Kennedy-Johnson administrations to strengthen Saudi internal security against Nasserites and to aid the Saudis in staving off Nasser's 1962–67 60,000-man invasion of the southern Arabian Peninsula—the high water mark of Nasser's drive to gain control of Middle Eastern oil." Jack Anderson with James Boyd, *Oil: The Real Story Behind the World Energy Crisis* (London: Sidgwick & Jackson, 1984), p. 171.
46. Miles Copeland, *The Game Player: Confessions of the CIA's Original Political Operative* (London: Aurum Press, 1989), p. 209.
47. Ibid., pp. 209–211.
48. Ibid., pp. 211–213.
49. Ibid., p. 218.
50. McCartney, *Friends in High Places*, pp. 122–124.
51. Copeland, *The Game Player*, pp. 211–212.
52. Knightley wrote that "according to documents obtained under the Freedom of Information Act, the CIA believed that Philby had a top-level source within the Agency who revealed to him in Beirut some of its covert actions. According to the documents, the CIA was convinced that one of its own officers, Wilbur Crane Eveland, told Philby about the Agency's operations in the Middle East and Africa, including plans to bring down the Syrian government in late 1956 and its efforts to rig the 1957 Lebanese election in favour of the pro-Western Chamoun regime. . . .

    "Eveland . . . had been employed directly by the CIA's director, Allen Dulles, as a trouble-shooter in the Middle East and Africa. He has denied the accuracy of the CIA documents, insists that he was never indiscreet with Philby, and says that the mere fact that he *knew* Philby in Beirut ruined his career in the Agency." Knightley, *KGB Masterspy*, p. 211.
53. As with the Vessel affair, Angleton had been on both sides of the Philby controversy at the same time. Confidential interviews, former members, CIA.
54. Confidential interviews, former Israeli military attachés; former members, Israeli diplomatic corps; former Western intelligence liaison to Israel; former members, East Bloc intelligence services.
55. Confidential interviews, former agents, CIA; former analysts, DIA; former liaison to the NSA.
56. Ibid.
57. Confidential interviews, former special agents, FBI. Hoover's notice of cancellation of émigré security checks can be found in the top-secret dossier, International Rescue Committee, attorney general's private files, 6th-floor vault, Department of Justice. For a brief discussion of the FBI's previous role in screening Nazi émigrés, see John Loftus, *The Belarus Secret* (New York: Alfred A. Knopf, 1982), pp. 95–96.
58. "During the Suez crisis he had been the Eisenhower instrumentality at the U.N. who had carried out the 'stop-Israel' action. A widely distributed piece of Democratic campaign literature quoted columnist Drew Pearson to the effect that: 'There is no one in American diplomacy who is considered by the Zionists more anti-Israel than Henry Cabot Lodge.' Lodge was further alleged to have 'championed Nasser and favored punitive measures against Israel to halt the invasion'—a charge Cleveland's Rabbi Abba Hillel Silver, endorsing the Nixon-Lodge ticket, attempted to refute." Lilienthal, *The Zionist Connection*, p. 538.
59. "The Israeli press intervened openly and—singularly enough—attacked the Demo-

cratic presidential nominee. *Herut,* the organ of Menachem Begin's . . . party . . . claimed that Senator Kennedy's father 'never loved the Jews and therefore there is a question whether the father did not inject some poisonous drops of anti-semitism in the minds of his children, including his son, John's.'" Ibid., p. 540.

60. Confidential interviews, former agents CIA; former analysts, DIA; former liaison to the NSA.
61. Confidential interviews, former Israeli military attachés; former members of Israeli diplomatic corps; former Western intelligence liaison to Israel; former members, East Bloc intelligence services; former agents, CIA; former analysts, DIA; former liaison to the NSA.
62. "Skorzeny used CIA money to recruit for the Egyptian security services about 100 German advisers, many of whom he reached through neo-Nazi organizations and SS escape networks. . . . Buensch, Gehlen's resident chief in Cairo, was a veteran of Eichmann's SS 'Jewish Affairs' office." Simpson, *Blowback,* pp. 250–251.
63. ". . . early in the Egyptian-American relationship, we began to suspect that Nasser was employing experts other than those we provided, his trust in us being less than 100 per cent. . . . Our suspicions were confirmed when former SS Colonel Otto Skorzeny dropped in on our station chief in Madrid to inform him that he had been approached by the Military Attaché in the Egyptian Embassy there to request his assistance in recruiting German army officers who might find Egypt a convenient place to hide out from the Nazi hunters. Could the CIA help? Indeed we could. With Otto's help, the CIA officer working with General Gehlen in Pullach chose some German generals, colonels and majors who were so stupid that they could be counted upon to screw up the Egyptian army so thoroughly that it wouldn't be able to find its way from Cairo to Ismailia, let alone fight the British after arriving there.

    "The idea of planting on Middle Eastern governments Germans suspected of war crimes had a lot to say for it, because they were generally both anti-American and anti-Soviet, and presumed to be anti-Semitic and therefore anti-Israel. Most of them were also anti-Arab, although they had the wit to conceal that fact. Anyhow, *all* of them were opportunists, willing to work for anyone who paid them, and they happily passed on to their Middle Eastern employers any advice we prescribed for them. Naturally, we had some trouble in getting clearance for projects involving the use of Nazis and ex-Nazis, but our difficulties disappeared when our friends in Israel's Mossad admitted that they, too, were using ex-Nazis for a number of nefarious purposes, and for the same reasons that they were attractive to us." Copeland, *The Game Player,* p. 181.
64. Richard Deacon, *The Israeli Secret Service* (London: Sphere, 1979), p. 142.
65. ". . . a first assessment on the development of ground-to-ground missiles in Egypt. A second intelligence Branch evaluation . . . predicted that about 100 rockets could be operational within a year to eighteen months . . ." Ian Black and Benny Morris, *Israel's Secret Wars. The Untold History of Israeli Intelligence* (London: Hamish Hamilton, 1991), p. 194.
66. Ibid., pp. 193–194.
67. "On September 26, 1962, the U.S. announced that it had agreed to sell Israel short-range defensive ground-to-air Hawk missiles. 'US to Sell Israel Hawk Missiles to Meet Arab Threat,' sang out the *Washington Post.* The tanks, jet-fighters, and long-range bombers received [by Egypt and Iraq from the Soviets] in the previous months allegedly had tipped the balance of military power to the Arabs and were the justification, according to the statement attributed to 'State Department officials' confirming the action. This marked the first time that the U.S. had departed from its policy of permitting Britain and France to serve as military suppliers for the Middle East." Lilienthal, *The Zionist Connection,* p. 546.
68. Confidential interviews, former agents CIA; former analysts, DIA; former liaison to the NSA.

CHAPTER 12

THE *LIBERTY* INCIDENT

1. Israel Film Service, *Follow Me: The Story of the Six Day War,* Doko Communications.
2. Seymour M. Hersh, *The Sampson Option* (New York: Random House, 1991).
3. Confidential interview, former officer, CIA.
4. Confidential interview, former agents CIA; former analysts, DIA. In rebuttal, former liaison to the NSA.
5. Israel's foreign minister, Abba Eban, later wrote that "I categorically assert that the *Liberty* tragedy was not deliberate," and conceded that the ship's mission was a "legitimate purpose." Abba Eban, *Personal Witness: Israel Through My Eyes* (London: Jonathan Cape, 1993), p. 422.
6. *The New York Times,* July 7, 1967, p. 3, and May 29, 1968, p. 8.
7. Ibid., June 9, 1967, p. 1.
8. "The Israeli plea that the incident was an accident of mistaken identity was accepted. Officially, the Israeli version was that the *Liberty* resembled an Egyptian supply ship, the *El Ksair,* and subsequently the US Government seemed reluctant to question these assumptions." Richard Deacon, *The Israeli Secret Service* (London: Sphere, 1979), p. 198.
9. James M. Ennes, *Assault on the* Liberty (New York: Random, 1979).
10. "Inside the NSA," *Ramparts* magazine (August 1972), Noah's Ark Publications, Berkeley, California, p. 48.
11. Anthony Pearson, *Conspiracy of Silence: The Attack on the U.S.S.* Liberty (London: Quartet Books, 1978), chap. 5.
12. Ibid., p. 62.
13. Eveland's version of the Angleton-Evron conspiracy is this: "The government-to-government channel between these two permitted Angleton to deal with top officials of Israel's ministry of defense and intelligence services, without involving Foreign Minister Abba Eban or the U.S. Departments of State and Defense. Evron arranged that Angleton meet with the heads of Israel's military and intelligence services, former General Moshe Dayan, and key Israeli politicians to discuss the feasibility of an attack on Egypt with the objective of toppling Nasser. The Israelis were interested but unwilling to carry the conversations further without evidence that Angleton was acting with White House approval." Wilbur Crane Eveland, *Ropes of Sand* (New York: Norton, 1980), p. 323.
14. ". . . top officials in the Pentagon had been briefed on the Angleton discussions with Israel. Long concerned over the possibility of Russian intervention in Vietnam, the military now worried about Soviet reactions to renewed fighting in the Middle East. Under orders from the Joint Chiefs of Staff, the U.S.S. *Liberty* was rushed to the waters off Israel's shore to permit this sophisticated communications-monitoring vessel to follow the fighting should the Israelis attack Egypt. The *Liberty* wasn't sent alone, for an even more important reason. Stationed below her was the Polaris nuclear submarine *Andrew Jackson,* for the Pentagon knew that the CIA had aided Israel in acquiring a nuclear capability. Moreover, the U.S. had provided the Israelis with missiles, to which atomic warheads could be attached. Thus, in case a bogged-down Israeli army decided to use ballistic missiles to win a war against the Soviet-equipped Egyptian army, the U.S. was in a position to warn both Israel and Russia that the introduction of nuclear warfare would produce instantaneous retaliation." Ibid., pp. 324–325.
15. "Defense Minister Dayan had stated his government's position bluntly: unless the United States wished the Russians and Arabs to learn of joint CIA-Mossad covert operations in the Middle East and Angleton's discussions before the 1967 fighting started, the questions of the lost American ship and how the war originated should be dropped. That ended the U.S. protestations!" Ibid., p. 325.
16. Deacon, *The Israeli Secret Service,* pp. 192–193.

17. "Each side—the United States and Israel—feared being double-crossed by the other. . . . The Israelis were concerned that at the last moment their secret agreement with the CIA might be compromised in some way by the State Department. . . .

"But while the Israelis had been suspicious of changes of face by the State Department, they had overlooked the possibility of the CIA trying to safeguard themselves against any Israeli changes of plan. The CIA had all along to consider the risks of Soviet involvement in a Middle East war if Israel allowed the conflict to spill over into Jordan and Syria. True, there was a tacit understanding that this would not be so, but the CIA wanted to be in a position to be abreast of every Israeli move. It was for this reason that the spy ship, the USS *Liberty,* bristling with electronic equipment, was ordered to sail to the eastern Mediterranean close to the Sinai Peninsula to listen to Israeli signals, as well, of course, as those of the Arabs. The *Liberty*'s assignment was to supply detailed intelligence on both Arab and Israeli movements on land, sea and air and signals traffic to the National Security Agency in Washington. But the Israelis were not informed of this." Ibid., p. 194.
18. Ibid., p. 196. Deacon's version seems to have been accepted by many historians. John Ranelagh wrote that: "The *Liberty* was on an intelligence-gathering mission off the Israeli coast, and the subsequent accumulation of evidence suggests that the attack was at the instigation of Israeli Intelligence, frightened that the Americans might use information collected by the *Liberty* to force Israel into an unsatisfactory peace." Ranelagh, *The Agency: The Rise and Decline of the CIA* (New York: Simon and Schuster, 1988), p. 253.
19. As Deacon concluded: "From the Israeli point of view the *Liberty* had to be put out of action." Deacon, *The Israeli Secret Service,* pp. 196–197.
20. Confidential interviews, former officers, CIA; former employees, the NSA; former liaison to the NSA; former analyst, Naval Intelligence. Partial corroboration from former officer, British Military Intelligence.
21. Confidential interviews, former Israeli military attaché; former Israeli military intelligence officers; former members of Israeli intelligence. Several of our Israeli sources had been briefed by the same general officer (now deceased) who had participated in the planning for the assault on the *Liberty.*
22. Confidential interviews, former officers, CIA; former employees, the NSA; former liaison to the NSA, former analyst, Naval Intelligence; former Israeli military attaché; former Israeli military intelligence officers; former members, Israeli intelligence. Partial corroboration from former officer, British Military Intelligence.
23. Confidential interviews, former CIA officers; former employees, the NSA; former liaison to the NSA; former analyst, Naval Intelligence; former Israeli military attaché; former Israeli military intelligence officers; former members, Israeli intelligence.
24. Ibid.
25. Ibid.
26. Confidential interviews, former liaison to the NSA; former analyst, Naval Intelligence.
27. Confidential interviews, former officers, CIA; former employees, the NSA; former liaison to the NSA; former analyst, Naval Intelligence; former Israeli military attaché; former Israeli military intelligence officers; former members, Israeli intelligence.
28. Ibid.
29. Ibid.
30. Andrew and Leslie Cockburn, *Dangerous Liaison* (New York: HarperCollins, 1991), p. 149.
31. " 'Didn't you tell me that Israel was not going to attack Jordan?' Hussein reportedly asked. The CIA man agreed that this was so. 'Have they not taken over half my country?' Again, the American agreed. 'Well,' said the shattered monarch, 'what the fuck do I do now?' " Ibid., p. 151.
32. Confidential interviews, former officers, CIA; former employees, the NSA; former

liaison to the NSA; former analyst, Naval Intelligence; former Israeli military attaché; former Israeli military intelligence officers; former members of Israeli intelligence.

33. Ibid.
34. Ibid.
35. Ibid.
36. Confidential interview, former employee, the NSA.
37. Confidential interviews, former officers, CIA; former liaison to the NSA; former analyst, Naval Intelligence; former Israeli military attaché; former Israeli military intelligence officers; former members, Israeli intelligence.
38. Confidential interview, former CIA officer with particular expertise on the *Liberty* incident.
39. Eban, *Personal Witness,* p. 422.
40. Ibid. See also Susan Hattas Rolef (ed.), *Political Dictionary of the State of Israel* (New York: Macmillan, 1987), p. 280, confirming that the Egyptians had resisted a ceasefire until after the *Liberty* was attacked on June 8.
41. Insight Team of *The Sunday Times, Insight on the Middle East War* (Sydney: Angus and Robertson, 1974), p. 117.
42. Confidential interviews, former officers, CIA; former employees, the NSA; former liaison to the NSA; former analyst, Naval Intelligence; former Israeli military attaché; former Israeli military intelligence officers; former members, Israeli intelligence. The allusion to an Israeli mole inside British intelligence was raised by a former communications security consultant to the British government and repeated by other former members of the British Foreign Office.
43. Confidential interviews, former officers, CIA; former employees, the NSA; former liaison to the NSA; former analyst, Naval Intelligence; former Israeli military attaché; former Israeli military intelligence officers; former members, Israeli intelligence.
44. Confidential interviews, former Israeli military intelligence officers; former members, Israeli intelligence.
45. Confidential interview, former Israeli military attaché. A phone leak cannot be ruled out. Arab communications security was notoriously lax in those days, a mistake that was not repeated in the 1973 war.
46. Confidential interviews, former Israeli military attaché; former Israeli military intelligence officers; former members, Israeli intelligence.
47. Our American sources are adamant that the Israelis could not have used electronic emissions to pinpoint the exact compartment holding the computer. The Israelis must have had inside information on this point. Confidential interviews, former officers, CIA; former employees, the NSA; former liaison to the NSA; former analyst, Naval Intelligence. Our Israeli sources are unable (or unwilling) to shed additional light on this point.
48. Confidential interviews, former Israeli military attaché; former Israeli military intelligence officers; former members, Israeli intelligence.
49. Ibid.
50. Confidential interview, former Israeli military attaché.
51. Confidential interviews, former officers, CIA; former employees, the NSA; former liaison to the NSA; former analyst, Naval Intelligence.
52. Deacon, *The Israeli Secret Service,* p. 198.
53. Confidential interviews, former officers, CIA; former employees, the NSA; former liaison to the NSA; former analyst, Naval Intelligence.
54. Confidential interviews, former officers, CIA; former employees, the NSA; former liaison to the NSA; former analyst, Naval Intelligence; former Israeli military attaché; former Israeli military intelligence officers; former members, Israeli intelligence.
55. Confidential interviews, former officers, CIA.
56. *The New York Times* reported each of the rumors as they surfaced during June and July of 1967. Neither the Pentagon nor the White House ever explained how or why

the various cover stories were initiated. Several people have pointed their finger at one of Lyndon Johnson's aides at National Security Affairs. See, for example, Anthony Pearson, *Conspiracy of Silence,* p. 70.

57. *The New York Times,* July 25, 1967, p. 10, June 29, 1967, p. 15, and June 9, 1967, p. 19.
58. Ibid., June 9, 1967, p. 19, June 12, 1967, p. 11, and June 11, 1967, p. 27.
59. Alfred M. Lilienthal, *The Zionist Connection* (New York: Dodd, Mead, 1978), p. 563.
60. Ibid.
61. "No explanation of this appalling muddle over top secret orders of great urgency ever seems to have been given. Did the Israelis have an agent inside the CIA who was able to cause the signal to be lost? Improbable, perhaps, but it is not an impossible solution to the mystery." Deacon, *The Israeli Secret Service,* p. 197.
62. Confidential interviews, former officers, CIA; former employees, the NSA; former liaison to the NSA; former analyst, Naval Intelligence.
63. Lilienthal, *The Zionist Connection,* pp. 562–563.
64. *The New York Times,* July 1, 1967, p. 22.
65. Lilienthal, *The Zionist Connection,* p. 563.
66. "The communications areas below decks—which housed intricate computers, decoding and listening devices manned by linguistic experts and other personnel who could be changed according to the ship's mission—were off limits to the crew, including the officer in charge, Commander (later Captain) William L. McGonagle. The communications areas were under direct control of a National Security Agency technician, known to the crew simply as 'the Major,' who had joined the ship with two other civilians at Rota, in Spain." Ibid.
67. Confidential interviews, former officers, CIA; former employees, the NSA; former liaison to the NSA; former analyst, Naval Intelligence.
68. *Ramparts* (August 1972), p. 48.
69. "The whole idea of sending the *Liberty* in was that at that point, the US simply did not know what was going on. We sent it in really close so that we could find out hard information about what the Israelis' intentions were. What it found out, among other things, was that [Israeli Commander Moshe] Dayan's intentions were to push on to Cairo and Damascus. The Israelis shot at the *Liberty,* damaged it pretty badly and killed some of the crew, and told it to stay away. It became pretty clear that the White House got caught with its pants down." Ibid., p. 43.
70. *The New York Times,* July 16, 1972, p. 19.
71. Ian Black and Benny Morris, *Israel's Secret Wars. The Untold History of Israeli Intelligence* (London: Hamish Hamilton, 1991), pp. 225–226.
72. Lilienthal, *The Zionist Connection,* pp. 568–569.
73. See, for example, *The New York Times,* which ran several articles during June and July 1967, including a transcript of the actual conversations.
74. Confidential interviews, former Israeli military attaché; former Israeli military intelligence officers; former members, Israeli intelligence.
75. Cockburn and Cockburn, *Dangerous Liaison,* p. 149.
76. Lilienthal, *The Zionist Connection,* p. 563.
77. Rowland Evans and Robert Novak, "Remembering The Liberty," *The Washington Post,* November 6, 1991. A. M. Rosenthal wrote in *The New York Times* (November 8, 1991) that Evans and Novak "are among the harshest and most persistent journalistic critics of Israel."
78. Letter to the editor, *The Washington Post,* original copy in authors' possession, dated November 14, 1991.
79. Hirsh Goodman, "Messrs. Errors and No Facts," *The Jerusalem Report,* November 21, 1991.
80. Confidential interviews, former Israeli military intelligence officers; former members, Israeli intelligence.

81. As discussed below, the fighter pilot's message said nothing about attacking an American ship. That information was discussed only in the coded message from the reconnaissance plane.
82. Confidential interviews, former Israeli military attaché; former employees of the NSA.
83. "Seaman Casper said that he was at his battle station as a gunner on the stern when the first salvo of rockets raked the 1,100 ton *Liberty* . . . 'We didn't even have a chance to load the guns because the rockets hit us so fast,' said Seaman Eugene W. Casper, 18 years old, of Carbondale, Pa. 'It was incredible how fast they hit us' . . . Philip M. Armstrong . . . the *Liberty*'s executive officer apparently had noticed [the planes] at the last moment . . . and sounded the call to battle stations, or general quarters . . ." *The New York Times,* June 11, 1967, p. 27.
84. Confidential interviews, former officers, CIA; former employees, the NSA; former liaison to the NSA; former analyst, Naval Intelligence.
85. *The Tampa Tribune,* June 8, 1992.
86. Confidential interviews, former employees, the NSA; former liaison to the NSA.
87. "At war's end, [First Secretary] Bill Dale was summoned by Barbour and told of a change in policy regarding the collection of intelligence . . . they were no longer to report on Dimona [the Israeli nuclear reactor] and no longer to undercut the Israelis by conducting operations with their British or Canadian counterparts. 'Israel is going to be our main ally,' Barbour told Dale, 'and we can't dilute it by working with others.' There was a second message, Dale recalled: 'Barbour said, "Arab oil is not as important as Israel to us. . . ."' " Hersh, *The Sampson Option,* p. 168.
88. Bruce Brill, "One Man's Agony After the Fact," *The Jerusalem Post,* Forum, October 31, 1992.
89. *The New York Times,* June 8, 1967, p. 19.
90. Ibid., June 17, 1967, p. 10.
91. Ibid., Editorial, p. 30.

CHAPTER 13
THE FINAL SOLUTION REVISITED

1. Confidential interviews, former agents, CIA; former agents, CIC; former officer, U.S. MIS.
2. Seymour M. Hersh, *The Sampson Option* (New York: Random House, 1991), p. 168.
3. Confidential interviews, former agents, CIA; former agents, CIC; former officer, U.S. MIS.
4. Readers interested in an account of this are directed to our previous book, *Unholy Trinity* (New York: St. Martin's Press, 1992), chap. 3.
5. Confidential interviews, former agents, CIA.
6. Confidential interviews, former agents, CIA; former officer, U.S. MIS.
7. Confidential interviews, former agents, CIA; former consultant to Fort Dietrich, Maryland.
8. We are indebted to Rachel Verdon for providing us with documents obtained under the Freedom of Information Act detailing French advances in chemical and biological warfare.
9. Confidential interviews, former members of Israeli military intelligence.
10. Confidential interviews, former agents, CIA; former agents, CIC; former officer, U.S. MIS.
11. Ibid.
12. Among them was General Gehlen's brother, a physician who used the pseudonym Doc Winters. He was wanted for alleged atrocities committed in the name of military research. Confidential interview, member of Pullach staff. According to this source, a man bearing a startling resemblance to Dr. Joseph Mengele was occasionally seen lounging at the pool beside Doc Winter's Pullach residence. Most people associate

Mengele with the cruel experiments on Jewish twins or recall his role as the "Angel of Death" in selecting "useless eaters" for the gas chambers at Auschwitz. In fact, these were sidelines to his major research work for the German military, virtually all of which continued to be classified by the Allied governments after the war. Confidential interviews, former agents, CIA; former agents, CIC; former officer, U.S. MIS.

13. Confidential informant, CIC. The CIC has a large collection of files on the Kaiser Wilhelm Institute, which are now being declassified. We are grateful to Ms. Verdon for sharing these records with us.
14. Confidential interview, German physician resident in the United States. According to him, several exposés of the medical atrocities were published after the war in Germany, but all copies were quickly suppressed.
15. Most of the German research on human beings was useless. For example, a confidential source in a U.S. military service sent us a copy of the navy's file on Dachau experiments. According to the postwar survey, the Jewish inmates altered the test procedures and faked the results in an attempt to save as many lives as possible.
16. Rachel Verdon, private collection of documents obtained under the U.S. Freedom of Information Act. Copies in authors' possession.
17. Ibid.
18. Mengele's brother Karl appears on a list of German scientists interrogated by British intelligence after World War II. Our sources say that Joseph used his brother to negotiate a trade: his freedom in return for documents on Nazi testing of nerve gas on human beings. Confidential interviews, former agents, CIC; former officer, U.S. MIS.
19. Confidential interviews, former Pullach staff members.
20. Confidential interview, former member of Argentine diplomatic corps who reviewed records of the German nuclear development protocol.
21. Richard Deacon, *The Israeli Secret Service* (London: Sphere, 1979), p. 145.
22. Confidential interview, former member West German intelligence service.
23. "I was dumbfounded when I saw this material. It means that someone working for Israel was—and no doubt still is—in a position to intercept letters passing between Egypt and the German Federal Republic—two states with which Israel has no diplomatic relations [today Israel has an embassy in Bonn]—photograph whatever correspondence interested him, and then pass on the letters to their destination without the correspondents being any the wiser." Denis Sefton Delmer, "The Secret Service Nasser Fears," *The Sunday Telegraph*, January 14, 1962, as quoted in Deacon, *The Israeli Secret Service*, p. 144.
24. Confidential interviews, former Pullach staff members; former agents, CIA; former agents, CIC; former officer, U.S. MIS.
25. Confidential interviews, former agents, CIC; former officer, U.S. MIS.
26. Rachel Verdon, private collection of documents obtained under the U.S. Freedom of Information Act. Copies in authors' possession.
27. Ibid.
28. "German chemists in Egypt are working on gas and germ warfare projects, according to reliable sources in Teheran and in other Middle Eastern capitals.

    "These Germans are said to be operating in strict secrecy under the direct orders of President Nasser's Cabinet. It appears they are experimenting with gas and bacteriological weapons that can be delivered either by bombs from aircraft or in rocket warheads.

    "The Saudi Arabian Government and Yemeni Royalists are preparing full reports on several recent cases when Egyptian Air Force planes were said to have dropped gas bombs on pro-royalist Yemeni tribesmen." *The Sunday Telegraph*, June 16, 1963, as quoted in John Cookson and Judith Nottingham, *A Survey of Chemical and Biological Warfare* (New York: Monthly Review Press, 1969), p. 6.
29. Ibid., pp. 6–14.

30. The nerve gases Soman, Sarin, and Tabun (known in NATO as the G Series) all had their origins with I. G. Farben's toxic research for the Third Reich. Before the end of World War II, the Nazis had perfected each of the formulas, down to the microscopic amount needed to kill one human being by skin contact. A confidential source in the U.S. Army intelligence service has confirmed that for ten years prior to disclosures in the press, the U.S. government protested to the West German government to no avail concerning its tolerance of the export of genocidal gas factories to the Middle East. The Bonn government explained lamely that it had little constitutional power to restrict exports, and the matter was out of its hands. According to one Israeli source, Pollard's discovery of this subterfuge led him to leak information to Israel. Confidential interview, member Israeli military intelligence.
31. Confidential interviews, former agents, CIA; former agents, CIC; former officer, U.S. MIS.
32. Rachel Verdon, private collection of documents obtained under the U.S. Freedom of Information Act. Copies in authors' possession.
33. Ibid.
34. Confidential interviews, former agents, CIA; former agents, CIC; former officer, U.S. MIS. Rachel Verdon has been collecting declassified records of Soviet research on Nazi toxins. She has compiled a frightening and formidable amount of documentation. Although the evidence is still incomplete, there is reason to believe that the Soviet military discovered that ticks, fleas, and lice could be systematically infected and then secretly dispersed throughout an enemy population. There are some indications that the Soviets used the "insect vector" on their own dissident Moslem populations.

    According to our sources, they tried it on an American population as well. Vernon has found some intriguing circumstantial evidence to support this claim. In the late 1940s, the Soviet ship *Elberus* delivered a load of furs and skins to the port of New York. Shortly afterward an epidemic of an unknown disease similar to rickettsial pox broke out in New York City. It was traced to a form of insect rarely seen in the United States but common in the Soviet Union.

    According to our sources, the U.S. government threw a top-secret classification over the entire episode and immediately began to study the Soviet insect vectors on Plum Island off the coast of Connecticut. That, the old spies say, is how Lyme disease began to spread. The government quietly commissioned a study of the New England population, using the unwitting Muscular Sclerosis Society as a cover. When no indications of epidemic infections in humans or animals were found, the whole study was quietly scrapped.

    What the government did not know was that Lyme disease can be dormant for several years and later may have reacted with common vaccines in a most unfortunate manner. While the Lyme disease story cannot be corroborated, Vernon has confirmed that a top-secret U.S. study labeled "Clandestine Attacks on Crops and Animals" once existed, but all copies have been destroyed. One of the participants in the study, Leo Alexander, has been identified as a U.S. intelligence expert on Nazi medical experiments on human beings. To this day, the Department of Agriculture Research Station on Plum Island is closed to human visitors. Still, it may all be a coincidence.

    Other accidents in toxic research, however, can be documented. Several thousand sheep in Utah were accidentally sprayed with nerve gas. One researcher inside the "Dome" at Fort Dietrich, Maryland, was killed when accidentally exposed to a virulent biological warfare experiment. The Soviets have admitted that they lost a large number of lives in an anthrax experiment that went wrong.
35. Ben Hills, "Japan's Wartime Plan for Australia: Plague Rats," *The Sydney Morning Herald*, August 17, 1993, p. 1.
36. Rachel Verdon, private collection of documents obtained under the U.S. Freedom of Information Act. Copies in authors' possession.

37. Confidential interview, former agents, CIA; former agents, CIC; former officer, U.S. MIS.
38. For an account of the history of Nazis in Australia and their intelligence connections, see Mark Aarons, *Sanctuary! Nazi Fugitives in Australia* (Melbourne: Heinemann, 1989).
39. Confidential interview, former Argentine diplomat who has subsequently fled the country. Corroboration was obtained from historian Paul Manning, who conducted his own independent research.
40. Ibid.
41. The illegal diversion was done "allegedly on behalf of an Italian chemical company in Milan. The sale was approved by Euratom in October, and the uranium was shipped out of Antwerp aboard a vessel renamed the *Scheersberg A*. The *Scheersberg A* had been purchased, with Mossad funds, by another Israeli agent-in-place in Turkey. Once at sea, according to published accounts that were confirmed by Israeli officials, the uranium ore was transferred to an Israeli freighter guarded by gunboats and taken to Israel. The disappearance of the huge shipment of uranium ore was known, of course, within months to Euratom; it wasn't much longer before U.S. and European intelligence agencies were reporting internally that the Israelis were involved." Hersh, *The Sampson Option*, p. 181.
42. "His message . . . was electrifying: the United States would not 'lift a finger for Israel' if the Soviets chose directly to intervene by, 'say, a Soviet missile attack against the Israeli Air Force bases in Sinai. . . . The main aim of any American President is to prevent World War III. Second, that no American President would risk World War III because of territories occupied by Israel. Three, the Russians know this.' " Ibid., p. 177.
43. Confidential interviews, former agents, CIA.
44. "In World War II Pasztor was a member of the youth group of the Arrow Cross, the Hungarian equivalent of the German Nazi party. . . . The Arrow Cross took power in Hungary, with Hitler's aid, to help defend Germany. Pasztor was sent to Berlin as part of the new diplomatic mission to Hitler until the war's end." Monograph, Russ Bellant, "Old Nazis, the New Right and the Reagan Administration: The Role of Domestic Fascist Networks in the Republican Party and Their Effect on U.S. Cold War Politics," Political Research Associates, Cambridge, MA, September 1988, p. 15.
45. This was accomplished not by Congress, but by administrative fiat of the director of the U.S. Immigration and Naturalization Service.
46. "One of the leaders of the 1968 Nixon-Agnew campaign's ethnic unit, Pasztor says that Nixon promised him that if he won the election, he would form a permanent ethnic council within the GOP, as the Ethnic Division was only active during presidential campaigns." Bellant, "Old Nazis, the New Right and the Reagan Administration," p. 15.
47. Ibid.
48. Ibid.
49. It also was Kim Philby's favorite Nazi front and had more than the usual share of Communist double agents in leadership positions. Confidential interviews, former members, CIA.
50. "The GOP nationalities council has provided an entry into the White House for several self-styled immigrant leaders with records as pro-Nazi extremists. Bulgarian-American Republican party notable Ivan Docheff, for example, who has served as an officer of the Republican party's ethnic council for years, has acknowledged that he was once a leader of the National Legion of Bulgaria, a group that the more moderate Bulgarian National Committee in the United States has described as 'Fascist' . . . Docheff . . . was once invited to share a Captive Nations prayer breakfast with President Richard Nixon." Christopher Simpson, *Blowback: America's Recruitment of Nazis and Its Effects on the Cold War* (New York: Weidenfeld & Nicholson, 1988),

pp. 273–274. The Docheff invitation was a bit much and caused a publicity backlash: "Docheff's picture at the White House with Nixon and Agnew, printed in the Bulgarian-language paper Borba, raised cries of outrage from moderate Bulgarian-Americans." Jack Anderson, "Nixon Appears a Little Soft on Nazis," *The Washington Post,* November 10, 1971, p. B17.

51. Anderson, "Nixon Appears a Little Soft on Nazis."
52. Anderson had previously presented evidence that Pauco "still worships the memory of the Nazi puppet in Slovakia, Joseph Tiso," the disgraced monsignor who had helped the Nazis kill the country's Jews. The Anti-Defamation League had confirmed and amplified upon Pauco's pro-Nazi record, and the "Republican National Committee quickly accepted Pauco's resignation" as "one of four controllers of the National Republican Heritage Groups Council." Despite this, Pauco still continued to hold an honorary position as adviser to Small Business Administrator Tom Kleppe, including the influential role of advising on loans to small entrepreneurs. Ibid., and *The Washington Post,* November 8, 1971, p. A2.
53. Anderson, "Nixon Appears a Little Soft on Nazis."
54. Pasztor told the meeting that "President Nixon . . . has promised an 'open door' for ethnic Americans tired of Democratic 'ultra-liberals' who had forgotten them.

    "Laszlo Pasztor . . . went on to report that 'as the Democrat Party has shifted further to the left, revived Republican 'heritage' groups have enrolled close to 100,000 members of German, Polish, Hungarian and other 'ethnic' minorities.

    ". . . Phillip Sanchez, director of the Office of Economic Opportunity, Elliot L. Richardson, Secretary of Health, Education and Welfare, and other administration figures promised the GOP Heritage Conference at the opening session Friday that, under Mr. Nixon, more federal aid would go to the ethnic groups.

    ". . . Indeed, the 'open door' was wide open." Peter Baestrup, "GOP's 'Open Door': Who's Coming In?" *The Washington Post,* November 21, 1971, pp. A1, A13.
55. Ibid.
56. The Waffen SS was a purely military unit and included some draftees, as opposed to the all-volunteer Algemeine SS, which ran the death camps. However, many of the Waffen SS divisions were composed of former police executioners who played a major role in the Holocaust. See discussion of 30th Waffen SS Division in John Loftus, *The Belarus Secret* (New York: Alfred A. Knopf, 1982).
57. Also among the featured speakers at the convention were a senior FBI official, the head of the General Services Administration, and Representatives William Scherle and Tom Gettys. The executive director of the group was Dr. Karol Sitko, "a rotund Polish-German émigré who has maintained close ties with the Republican Party as an adviser to the GOP National Committee's Heritage (Nationalities) Division." Sitko's own German organization had recently been extremely active in lobbying against any extension of the West German Government's statute of limitations on World War II war crimes.

    One of the leaders at the convention was Austin J. App, "noted Nazi apologist and historical revisionist." In "his prolific writings, he has contended that Jews were responsible for triggering World War II and that the Allies treated the defeated Germans brutally after the war." Paul Valentine, "German-Americans Relive Heritage in 'Obscure' Meeting," *The Washington Post,* November 21, 1971, p. A12.
58. In the spring of 1971, Deac's so-called extremist opponents started to get active in trying to take over his front group, the National Confederation of American Ethnic Groups (the NCAEG), in the form of Sitko, Docheff, App, and Ibrahim Dzinich, president of the Croatian National Union. Deac accused them of forming unconstitutional chapters and having themselves appointed to top positions, while they in turn accused Deac of being a dictator and keeping the power tightly in his own hands: "Meanwhile, even as they became active in NCAEG, Sitko, Docheff and friends offered themselves as allies to Laszlo Pasztor and his burgeoning GOP National Com-

mittee Heritage (Nationalities) Division. They were not only 'ethnic' leaders, but also 'Ethnic Republican leaders.' " Baestrup, "GOP's 'Open Door': Who's Coming In?"

59. In May 1971, for example, Pasztor made a trip to Scranton, Pennsylvania, accompanied by Anne Armstrong, co-chairman of the Republican National Committee. They met with one of the "extremist" faction's prime financial backers and several of the key members of the "extremist faction." The local newspaper called the extremist faction the "principals" of the Republican party's northeast Pennsylvania Heritage Group. Ibid.
60. "Each formed a Republican federation, with local clubs around the country. These local clubs of the various federations then formed state multi-ethnic councils. Today there are 34 nationality federations and 25 state councils that constitute the National Republican Heritage Groups (Nationalities) Council." Bellant, "Old Nazis, the New Right and the Reagan Administration," p. 15.
61. Confidential interviews, former members, CIA; former staffers, NSC.
62. ". . . two groups are missing at the Republican Heritage Groups Council. There are no Black or Jewish Republican federations. Remarks by a number of delegates . . . made it clear that there was no desire to have either community represented on the council. . . . Given the background of the Council's leadership, it is difficult not to conclude that elements of racism and anti-Semitism may play a role in the decision to exclude Black and Jewish constituencies." Bellant, "Old Nazis, the New Right and the Reagan Administration," p. 24.
63. Confidential interviews, former agents, CIA; former staff members, Radio Liberty/ Radio Free Europe.
64. Radio Liberty files, Foreign Affairs Information Management Center, U.S. State Department.
65. Ibid. See discussion of Stankievich's crimes and the cover-up in Loftus, *The Belarus Secret,* pp. 20, 25–28, 65–66, 119.
66. U.S. Department of Justice, Attorney General's Files, National Security Council, subdossier for IRC.
67. Confidential interviews, former agents, CIA.
68. See, for example, declassified CIA dossier, "German Intelligence Agents in the Middle East," USNA, Military Reference Branch, which gives a wildly erroneous background for the Organization of Ukrainian Nationalists and the Russian Fascist organization NTS. The amount of misinformation passed on to other government agencies is simply staggering. See, for example, Frank Wisner's letter to the U.S. Immigration Service, quoted in Loftus, *The Belarus Secret.*
69. Confidential interviews, former special agents, FBI.
70. Ibid. See, for example, FBI dossiers for Frantishek Kushel. Kushel was a police executioner for the SS who kept the FBI informed of Dulles's use of Nazis for covert operations.
71. U.S. National Archives, President Richard Nixon, tape collection.
72. Scott Anderson and Jon Lee Anderson, *Inside the League* (New York: Dodd, Mead, 1986).
73. Ibid., p. 61.
74. Ibid., p. 55. WACL began with John Foster Dulles's efforts to "revive" the Japanese economy after World War II. With the connivance of Douglas MacArthur, they recruited Japanese war criminals as anti-Communist organizers. One of them was Ryoichi Sasakawa, who later boasted "I am the world's wealthiest fascist."

    His protégé, Yoshio Kodama, was one of the financial backers for the U.S.-sponsored right-wing politicians, who made his fortune from the brutal Japanese occupation of China. He was also a leader of the black shirt terrorists called the Yakuza, the Japanese version of the mafia, which ran goon squads for the ruling Liberal Democrats. John Halliday and Gavan McCormack, *Japanese Imperialism Today* (London: Penguin, 1973), p. 92; and Jon Halliday, *A Political History of Japanese Capitalism*

(New York: Monthly Review Press, 1975), p. 265. Still, they were good anti-Communists, and of no use to the Dulles brothers sitting in jail: "Sasakawa, Kodama, and other prominent war criminals were quietly released from prison in 1948 and became some of the prime movers, organizers and funders of the Japanese Liberal Democratic party, a conservative pro-American party that has controlled the political life of Japan ever since. Through this maneuver, the old ruling circles of Japan, the men who had allied with Nazi Germany . . . were resurrected and brought back into leadership roles." Anderson and Anderson, *Inside the League,* pp. 62–63.

Sasakawa's cellmate was another Class A war criminal named Kishi Nobosuke, who in 1959 became the prime minister of Japan. Kishi was the "prime mover" in the establishment of the Asian People's Anti-Communist League, which became the World Anti-Communist League in the 1960s, with Kishi as chairman of the Planning Committee in 1970. Ibid., p. 63*n*.

75. In the early days, WACL was a joint venture of the Korean CIA and Japanese Fascists. It was purely an intelligence/propaganda operation. In July 1967 Sasakawa arranged a secret meeting with his new Korean front man, Reverend Sun Myung Moon, founder of the Unification Church, whose members were better known as the "Moonies." According to the "old spies," the Moonies became the bagmen for a Japanese propaganda effort in the United States. Apart from alleged under-the-table contributions to WACL, the Reverend Moon's propaganda team "also spends $1,500,000 a year on a conservative Washington think tank; has sunk $15,000,000 into national distribution for the unsuccessful *Washington Times;* has given a half-million dollars to the National Conservative Political Action Committee (NCPAC)." Ibid., pp. 128–129.

In addition, the Moonies have spent $100 million on South American newspapers, printing companies, and banks. Money means nothing to Moon's organization: "It lost an estimated $150,000 in the first two years of its publication of the *Washington Times* and many millions more through its New York–based *The News World,* the Spanish-language *Noticias del Mundo,* and *The Middle East Times* in Cyprus. At the same time, its membership declined dramatically." Ibid., p. 127.

The Reverend Moon did not raise that kind of money selling flowers in airports. According to several intelligence sources, it was coming from Sasakawa and his friends. Sasakawa denies funding Moon. However, "two former high officials of the Unification Church . . . have disclosed that as much as $800,000,000 was funneled into the United States from Japan over a nine-year period, often by disciples carrying cash in their luggage." Ibid., p. 129. The Japanese electorate may be surprised to learn that their tax payments were laundered through the Yakuza to the Moonies to finance an ultra–right-wing lobby in the United States. By 1993 the Japanese were so thoroughly sick and tired of the whole corrupt system created by Dulles and his allies that they defected in droves from the Liberal Democrats and forced them out of power for the first time in over four decades. But the real scandal, say the "old spies," is that while the Moonies' money came from the Japanese government, the distribution of funds was overseen by Dulles's cronies in the CIA. Confidential interviews, former agents, CIA; former members, CIC.

76. One version has it that the propaganda actually originated back in the 1950s with Allen Dulles's CIA station chief in Korea, who continued his association with WACL over the next several decades. A more plausible version, provided by some of our sources in the intelligence community, is that Dulles established a dormant front group in the 1950s, which Japanese Fascists then revived and used for their own ends in the 1960s and 1970s. Confidential interviews, former agents, CIA; former agents,CIC; former officer, U.S. MIS.

77. "Starting with the 1979 League conference, militant Arabs, under the banner of the Middle East Security Council, became a major force and financial backer of the League. Their chief 'anti' was not communism but Israel. This explains why govern-

ment officials from Arab nations that are closely allied with the Soviet Union, such as Syria, have found a platform in the World Anti Communist League.

"It is quite easy to see the Arabs' interest in the League. Here in one fell swoop they tapped into bitter enemies of Israel in the United States, Latin America and Europe. Certainly some of their new allies had different reasons for their anti-Israeli stance—they hated Israel because they hated Jews—but the result was the same: dedicated and unwavering enemies of the 'Zionist state.'" Anderson and Anderson, *Inside the League,* pp. 108–109.

CHAPTER 14

THE REAL HERO OF YOM KIPPUR

1. "Anwar Sadat was, in the view of Prime Minister Golda Meir and her cabinet, nothing more than yet another unyielding threat to the Jews. The new Egyptian leader had been jailed by the British authorities during much of World War II because of his openly pro-German stance and his public endorsement of Hitler." Seymour Hersh, *The Sampson Option* (New York: Random House, 1991), p. 221.
2. "Why didn't Kissinger join Rogers . . . in trying to increase the possibility of a breakthrough? 'I have a hard time believing that the balance wasn't tilted by personal feelings,' says one former [National Security Council] aide who was directly involved in Middle East affairs. 'It's such an unflattering thing to say, but I think there was a lot of not wanting State to do it—rationalized, to be sure, by Henry. If Henry would have had a shot at it, he might have attempted it. It was the one genuine missed opportunity in that period. It was a step that would have prevented the '73 war from taking place.'" Seymour Hersh, *The Price of Power* (New York: Summit Books, 1983), p. 407.
3. Confidential interviews, former East Bloc intelligence officers.
4. Ibid.
5. Ibid. For an insider's account of Soviet technical espionage, see Viktor Suvorov, *Inside the Aquarium* (New York: Macmillan, 1986).
6. As one historian has recorded: "The desert kingdom was now the swing producer for the entire world. The United States would no longer be able to increase production to supply its allies in the event of a crisis, and the United States itself was now, finally, vulnerable. The supply-demand balance was working to make Saudi Arabia even more powerful. Its share of world exports had risen rapidly, from 13 percent in 1970 to 21 percent in 1973, and was continuing to rise." Daniel Yergin, *The Prize: The Epic Quest for Oil, Money & Power* (New York: Touchstone, 1992), p. 594.
7. "By the spring of 1973, Sadat was strongly pressing Faisal to consider using the oil weapon to support Egypt in a confrontation with Israel and, perhaps, the West. King Faisal also felt growing pressure from many elements within his own kingdom and throughout the Arab world. He could not afford to be seen as anything other than forthright in his support both for the 'front-line' Arab states and the Palestinians. . . .

   "Thus, politics and economics had come together to change Faisal's mind. Thereupon the Saudis began a campaign to make their views known, warning they would not increase their oil production capacity to meet rising demand, and that the Arab oil weapon would be used, in some fashion, unless the United States moved closer to the Arab viewpoint and away from Israel. In early May 1973, the King himself met with Aramco executives. Yes, he was a staunch friend of the United States, he said. But it was 'absolutely mandatory' that the United States 'do something to change the direction that events were taking in the Middle East today.'

   "'He barely touched on the usual conspiracy idea but emphasized that Zionism and along with it the Communists were on the verge of having American interests thrown out of the area,' the president of Aramco reported afterward. . . . 'He stated that it was up to those Americans and American enterprises who were friends of the

Arabs and who had interests in the area to urgently do something to change the posture' of the United States government. 'A simple disavowal of Israeli policies and actions' would 'go a long way toward overcoming the current anti-American feeling,' the Aramco president said, adding there was 'extreme urgency' to the King's remarks." Ibid., pp. 595–596.

8. " 'You will lose everything,' he told the oil men" at this meeting. Ibid., p. 596.
9. " 'We have no wish to restrict our oil exports to the United States in any way,' he told American television viewers, but 'America's complete support for Zionism and against the Arabs makes it extremely difficult for us to continue to supply the United States with oil, or even to remain friends with the United States,' " Ibid., pp. 596–597.
10. The straight-talking sheik made the position crystal clear. The King was "one hundred percent determined to effect a change in U.S. policy and to use oil for that purpose." Ibid., pp. 597–598.
11. " 'While our interests in many respects are parallel to the interests of Israel,' Joseph Sisco, the American Assistant Secretary of State, told Israeli television, 'they are not synonymous with the state of Israel. The interests of the U.S. go beyond any one nation in the area. . . . There is increasing concern in our country, for example, over the energy question, and I think it is foolhardy to believe that this is not a factor in the situation. . . .'

    "The American 'disavowals' also came from even higher levels. At a press conference, President Nixon . . . went on to blame both sides, including Israel, for the impasse. 'Israel simply can't wait for the dust to settle and the Arabs can't wait for the dust to settle in the Mid-East. Both sides are at fault. Both sides need to start negotiating. That is our position. . . . One of the dividends of having a successful negotiation will be to reduce the oil pressure.' " Ibid., p. 598.
12. They "would once again have to obtain a business review letter from the Justice Department, giving them assurance that they were not in violation of antitrust laws." Ibid., pp. 599–600. "At one heated meeting with Justice, McCloy invoked the names of former attorney generals, going back to Robert Kennedy, who had permitted the companies to work out joint strategies on difficult matters involving foreign affairs. 'If Justice failed to give clearance,' he said, 'Justice would be responsible for the companies being picked off one by one. . . .' Justice Department attorneys . . . insisted that oil prices were going up because of the machinations of large integrated oil companies, not because of market conditions and OPEC's move to capitalize on them. . . . But . . . three days before the Vienna meeting was scheduled to begin, the Antitrust Division reluctantly gave McCloy's clients the clearance they needed to negotiate jointly." Ibid., p. 600.
13. Confidential interviews, former officers, CIA. See also Ian Black and Benny Morris, *Israel's Secret Wars. The Untold History of Israeli Intelligence* (London: Hamish Hamilton, 1991), p. 300.
14. Black and Morris, *Israel's Secret Wars,* pp. 296–297.
15. Ibid., p. 298.
16. "On 3 October, [Egyptian] war minister Ismail Ali flew again to Damascus and informed the Syrians of Egypt's final agreement to the date. . . . The Soviet ambassador in Cairo was apparently told by the Egyptians on 3 October of Egypt's intentions to 'violate the ceasefire.' The following day Assad informed the Soviet ambassador in Damascus of H-hour." Ibid., pp. 300–301. Our sources say that the Soviet consulate's cables to Moscow were immediately deciphered by the NSA. Confidential interviews, former employees, the NSA; former liaison to the NSA.
17. Confidential interviews, former White House staffer; former employees, the NSA; former liaison to the NSA.
18. Confidential interview, former White House staffer.
19. Two British authors confirm that the NSA had advance warning and imply that Kissinger was personally responsible for the delay in informing the Israelis. Andrew and Leslie Cockburn, *Dangerous Liaison* (New York: HarperCollins, 1991), pp. 172–173.

20. Bruce Brill, "One Man's Agony After the Fact," *The Jerusalem Post*, Forum, October 31, 1992.
21. Black and Morris, *Israel's Secret Wars*, p. 311.
22. Confidential interviews, former White House staffer; former employees, NSA; former liaison to the NSA.
23. Ibid.
24. "Bush adviser Fred Malek, a former White House personnel chief, resigned from a senior position at the Republican National Committee after admitting he had counted Jewish officials at the Bureau of Labor Statistics for Richard Nixon who railed against a 'Jewish cabal,' two of the officials were demoted." Holly Sklar, "Who's Who and What's What," Z magazine (1988).
25. As Kissinger recalled: "the President was convinced that most leaders of the Jewish community had opposed him throughout his political career. The small percentage of Jews who voted for him, he would joke, had to be so crazy that they would probably stick with him even if he turned on Israel." Hersh, *The Price of Power*, p. 213.
26. Confidential interviews, former members, Israeli intelligence.
27. As one historian has recorded, "no call for general mobilization was issued. In defense of this failure, the Israeli establishment later contended that they had bowed to the repeated warnings from Secretary Kissinger that under no circumstances were they to 'start the war—don't ever preempt. . . .' It was Meir who was said to have overruled [General] Dayan and his Chief of Staff in maintaining the posture demanded by Kissinger." Alfred M. Lilienthal, *The Zionist Connection* (New York: Dodd, Mead, 1978), p. 614.
28. Ibid.
29. Confidential interviews, former White House staffer; former employees, the NSA; former liaison to the NSA; former officers, Israeli military intelligence; former members, Israeli diplomatic corps.
30. "Neither Big Power seemed anxious to bring about an immediate cease-fire as they had in the earlier war, each sensing some advantage in keeping the fighting going. For the Soviets, their wards—or former wards—were making progress. The U.S. perhaps saw in the initial gain of the Arabs an opportunity to exercise leverage on Israel to comply with the withdrawal provisions of Resolution 242." Lilienthal, *The Zionist Connection*, p. 615.
31. Ibid., p. 616.
32. Anthony Sampson, *The Seven Sisters* (London: Coronet, 1988), p. 264.
33. "If the United States increased its military support for Israel, there could be a 'snowballing effect' in terms of retaliation 'that would produce a major petroleum supply crisis.' There was a further warning. 'The whole position of the United States in the Middle East is on the way to being seriously impaired, with Japanese, European, and perhaps Russian interests largely supplanting United States presence in the area, to the detriment of both our economy and our security.' " Yergin, *The Prize*, p. 604.
34. Lilienthal, *The Zionist Connection*, p. 616.
35. Hersh, *The Sampson Option*, p. 223.
36. Dan Raviv and Yossi Melman, *Every Spy a Prince: The Complete History of Israel's Intelligence Community* (Boston: Houghton Mifflin, 1989), p. 211.
37. Yergin, *The Prize*, p. 603.
38. "Kissinger made no secret of his initial strategy in the war, telling James R. Schlesinger, the secretary of defense that his goal was to 'let Israel come out ahead, but bleed.' Kissinger's goal was defended by some of his fellow diplomats as business as usual. 'Trying to take advantage of the situation?' rhetorically asked Nicholas Veliotes. 'We always do this.' " Hersh, *The Sampson Option*, p. 227.
39. Yergin, *The Prize*, p. 604.
40. Confidential interviews, former White House staffer; former employees, the NSA;

former liaison to the NSA; former officers, Israeli military intelligence; former members, Israeli diplomatic corps.

41. He was the educated son of a relatively comfortable, middle-class German family. Although his father was only an elementary school teacher, the family had decidedly elitist aspirations, especially for Henry. Kissinger emigrated to America in the late 1930s, and became a model of assimilation. After World War II, young Sergeant Kissinger tried to put as much distance as possible between himself and the Jewish refugees in the U.S. zone of Germany. See also Hersh, *The Price of Power,* p. 27.
42. John McIntyre, one of our sources, also was recruited from CIC and assigned to the EUCOM school while working for OPC. See also Hersh, *The Price of Power,* pp. 26–28.
43. Confidential interviews, former officer, U.S. MIS; former agents, OPC.
44. Confidential interview, former agent, OPC.
45. Declassified excerpts from this document can be found in John Loftus, *The Belarus Secret* (New York: Alfred A. Knopf, 1982), pp. 74, 92, 105, 149.
46. Hersh, *The Price of Power,* pp. 26–27.
47. Ibid.
48. Confidential interviews, former officers, CIA; former members, OPC.
49. Hersh, *The Price of Power,* p. 27.
50. See Loftus, *The Belarus Secret,* p. 133, for a discussion of Nixon's role as supervisor of clandestine operations. While Kissinger served as a consultant for operations in 1955, there is no evidence that he was involved with the White House betrayal of Israel's Suez plans in 1956.
51. Hersh, *The Price of Power,* pp. 27–28.
52. "Proving his loyalty remained an obsession for Kissinger in the Nixon White House . . . There were days when Nixon would directly castigate liberal Jews in front of Kissinger.

    " 'Nixon would talk about Jewish traitors, and the Eastern Jewish Establishment—Jews at Harvard,' John Ehrlichman recalls, 'And he'd play off Kissinger. "Isn't that right, Henry, Don't you agree?" . . .' "

    On the Halperin issue, Hersh writes: " 'I can't have you there,' Kissinger said. 'I've told the other people not to bring staff and I can't show up with three people from the NSC—two of them Jewish.'

    "Halperin said nothing to Kissinger, but he was strongly tempted to ask: 'Henry, who's the second Jew?' " Hersh, *The Price of Power,* pp. 84–86.
53. Interview with Seymour Hersh.
54. Confidential interviews, former Israeli military attachés; former members, Israeli intelligence.
55. "There was widespread rage inside the Israeli cabinet at the Nixon White House—aimed especially at Henry Kissinger—over what was correctly perceived in Israel as an American strategy of delaying the resupply in an attempt to let the Arabs win some territory, and some self-respect, and thus set up the possibility of serious land-for-peace bargaining. Kissinger, just sworn in as secretary of state, would direct the negotiation." Hersh, *The Sampson Option,* p. 227.
56. Ibid.
57. Ibid.
58. Black and Morris, *Israel's Secret Wars,* p. 314.
59. Sampson, *The Seven Sisters,* p. 264.
60. Confidential interviews, former White House staffer; former employees, the NSA; former liaison to the NSA; former officers, Israeli military intelligence; former members, Israeli diplomatic corps.
61. Confidential interviews, former White House staffer; former officers, Israeli military intelligence.
62. Briefing given to Lieutenant Loftus, Battalion Duty Officer, 5th Battalion, the School Brigade, U.S. Army Infantry School, Fort Benning, Georgia.

63. A few weeks later, word of the secret Israeli TOW training was leaked to *Time* magazine as proof of the Nixon Administration's support for Israel.
64. Confidential interviews, U.S. Army officers.
65. Hersh, *The Sampson Option*, pp. 231–238.
66. Confidential interviews, former White House staffer; former officers, Israeli military intelligence.
67. Ibid.
68. Confidential interviews, U.S. Army officers.
69. Ibid.
70. For years Agent John McIntyre hinted that one of his Pullach comrades later served in the National Security Council. When McIntyre added that his friend was later a candidate for president, the identification was complete. McIntyre died before he could add definitive details about Haig's role in the Gehlen base. Other sources added corroboration and vouched for Haig's disgust at the Nazis. Ironically, it was Haig's service in Germany that later helped him become commander of U.S. forces in Europe. Confidential interviews, former U.S. Army officers.
71. Len Colodny, *Silent Coup* (New York: St. Martin's Press, 1991). In fairness to General Haig, we wish to point out that he was not one of our confidential sources.
72. Hersh, *The Sampson Option*, pp. 232–235.
73. Ibid., p. 230.
74. On October 17 Nixon "expressed his concern to his senior advisers on national security. 'No one is more keenly aware of the stakes: oil and our strategic position.' " Yergin, *The Prize*, pp. 605–606.
75. A letter from King Faisal was given to the president "stating that if the United States did not stop supplying Israel within two days, there would be an embargo. But Nixon explained that he was committed to Israel; and on the same day the Senate voted, two to one, to send reinforcements." Sampson, *The Seven Sisters*, p. 265.
76. The Arabs also secretly decided "that the United States be subjected to the most severe cuts" with the aim that "this progressive reduction lead to the total halt of oil supplies to the United States from every individual country party to the resolution." Yergin, *The Prize*, pp. 607–608.
77. Ibid., p. 608; and Sampson, *The Seven Sisters*, p. 265.
78. Yamani commented ominously that the "next step would not just be more of the same." Yergin, *The Prize*, p. 611.
79. "Exxon and the others were now wide open to the charge that had so often been made against them in the past—that they put profits before patriotism." The media portrayed the oil companies as being "in league with an alien sovereign state," while Aramco "saw themselves as persecuted and encircled." Public opinion increasingly branded them as "the oil traitors." On the U.S. ambassador to Saudi Arabia: "Aramco was now closely in touch with Jim Akins, who had just become the Ambassador to Saudi Arabia. On October 25 Akins sent a confidential message to Aramco, to ask the oil tycoons in America to hammer home to their friends in government that oil restrictions would not be lifted 'unless the political struggle is settled in a manner satisfactory to the Arabs.' There were 'some communications problems,' Akins pointed out, with considerable understatement, between the industry and the government. The oil companies must put their views in an unequivocal way. Akins' message was duly transmitted the next day to the four Aramco partners in New York and San Francisco. It was an odd reversal of the diplomatic process. Was it the companies who were the instruments of the State Department, or vice versa?" Sampson, *The Seven Sisters*, pp. 266–268.
80. "Two days later, Egyptian and Israeli military representatives met for direct talks for the first time in a quarter of a century. Egypt and the United States, meanwhile, opened a new dialogue. Both had been objectives of Sadat when he first conceived his gamble a year earlier. The nuclear weapons were sheathed. But the Arabs contin-

ued to wield the oil weapon. The oil embargo remained in place, with consequences that would extend far beyond the October War." Yergin, *The Prize,* p. 612.

81. There was a lot of finger-pointing in Washington afterward. How had the State Department, and the whole intelligence establishment, so badly underestimated the threat of an Arab oil embargo? Why had the intelligence community been so incompetent in giving timely advice to the National Security Council? When the NSA's electronic intelligence had been so clear-cut, why had Kissinger not warned Israel that an attack was coming?
82. Confidential interviews, former officers, CIA; former employees, the NSA; former liaison to the NSA; former members of Israeli intelligence.
83. Tom Mangold, *Cold Warrior. James Jesus Angleton: The CIA's Master Spy Hunter* (New York: Touchstone, 1991), p. 309.
84. "In the spring of 1974 . . . he took the first step toward removing the Israeli Account from Angleton's control by rerouting all communications from Israel through the [deputy director for operations] and Near East Division, instead of through Angleton's office. This change had been Schlesinger's wish, but he had not had the time to follow through.

    "On Colby's first introductory trip to Israel, he discovered to his astonishment that Angleton had imposed a tight restriction that prohibited the CIA station in Tel Aviv from communicating directly with the CIA station in Cairo (or any other Middle East capital). All information or messages had to be sent first through Angleton's office in Washington." Ibid., 314.
85. Confidential interviews, former officers, CIA.
86. Colby "believed the [Deputy Director for Operations] and Near East Division needed to see the cable traffic much faster to be able to make timely decisions, and that Israel had become far too important a component of U.S. foreign policy to continue to handle intelligence distribution this way.

    " 'That situation was absolute nonsense,' Colby says now. 'It was a silly way for an intelligence service to operate. I started the process of change of the Israeli Account right then.' Angleton's only defense of his old system was to argue that 'our Israeli relations are too sensitive to change.' " Mangold, *Cold Warriors,* p. 314.
87. William Colby, *Honorable Men. My Life in the CIA* (London: Hutchinson, 1978), p. 365.
88. Ibid.
89. Mangold, *Cold Warrior,* pp. 429*n,* 316–317.
90. "Angleton's closest professional friends overseas, then and subsequently, came from the Mossad . . . and . . . he was held in immense esteem by Israeli colleagues and by the state of Israel, which was to award him profound honors after his death." Ibid., p. 362.
91. "Admiration for the Jewish state became an obsession with Angleton, who fell captive to the magic of Israeli intelligence. He zealously insisted on being the sole handler of the account. . . .

    "Israelis who worked with Angleton admit he had an unusual or even 'kooky' personality, but they appreciate him for shattering the American wall of suspicion about Israel while paving the way for vital strategic cooperation. In November 1987, a year after Angleton died, Israel dedicated a 'memorial corner' to its valued American friend. Within sight of the luxurious King David Hotel, where he loved to stay during his dozens of visits to Jerusalem, an inscription on a large stone was carved in Hebrew, English, and Arabic: IN MEMORY OF A DEAR FRIEND, JAMES (JIM) ANGLETON. It was unveiled at a gathering attended by present and former heads of the Israeli intelligence community." Raviv and Melman, *Every Spy a Prince,* p. 91.
92. "He was a master of backchannel and 'eyes only' reports, and his increasing inability to deal with the real world eventually led to his firing in late 1974, but his glaring faults in counterintelligence apparently did not spill over to Israel. Former Agency

officials, who, in prior interviews with me, had been unsparing in their criticism of Angleton's bizarre methods in counterintelligence, acknowledged he had performed correctly and proficiently in his handling of Israel." Hersh, *The Sampson Option,* p. 144.

93. Confidential interviews, former members of Israeli intelligence.
94. After he was retired, "intelligence community investigators were surprised to discover . . . a cache of Angleton's personal files, secured with black tape, that revealed what obviously had been a long-running—and highly questionable—study of American Jews in the government. The files showed that Angleton had constructed what amounted to a matrix of the position and Jewishness of senior officials in the CIA and elsewhere who had access to classified information of use to Israel. Someone in a sensitive position who was very active in Jewish affairs in his personal life, or perhaps had family members who were Zionists, scored high on what amounted to a Jewishness index.

    ". . . The Angleton matrix suggested that at some point a suspect who measured high enough on the Jewishness scale was subjected to a full-bore field investigation." Hersh, *The Sampson Option,* pp. 145–146.
95. Ibid., p. 146.
96. Confidential interviews, former White House staffer; former agents, CIA.

CHAPTER 15

THE DISAPPEARING OIL MYSTERY

1. Confidential interviews, former agents, CIA; former officer, air force intelligence; former officers, U.S. Army; former analyst, Defense Intelligence Agency; former members, Israeli military intelligence; former Israeli military attaché.
2. Ibid.
3. Daniel Yergin, *The Prize: The Epic Quest for Oil, Money & Power* (New York: Touchstone, 1992), p. 661.
4. Confidential interviews, former agents, CIA; former analyst, Defense Intelligence Agency. "Carter read a CIA report, prepared in late 1976, predicting future oil shortages; he found it compelling and persuasive, and it was important in motivating him to proceed the way he did. Schlesinger, like Carter, was convinced that hydrocarbons would be under growing pressure, which posed major economic and political dangers for the United States. . . . Both men shared a deep concern about the foreign policy implications of a tight oil market." Yergin, *The Prize,* p. 662.
5. Robert H. Williams, "Tough Stuff," *The Washington Post,* September 12, 1977, p. A3, *The Washington Post,* April 23, 1978.
6. Associated Press, April 18, 1977.
7. Confidential interviews, former agents, CIA; former officer, air force intelligence; former officers, U.S. Army; former analyst, Defense Intelligence Agency; former members, Israeli military intelligence; former Israeli military attaché.
8. Confidential interviews, former agents, CIA; former officers, U.S. Army; former analyst, Defense Intelligence Agency.
9. Confidential interview, former officer, air force intelligence.
10. Confidential interviews, former officers, U.S. Army.
11. Confidential interviews, former officers, U.S. Army; former analyst, Defense Intelligence Agency.
12. Confidential interviews, former agents, CIA.
13. George Bush with Victor Gold, *Looking Forward, An Autobiography* (London: The Bodley Head, 1988), p. 178.
14. Confidential interviews, former agents, CIA; former analyst, Defense Intelligence Agency.
15. "The oil people, inspired by their 'free booter' heritage, tend to believe that the dynamic of their industrial past will carry us successfully into the future, unlocking

new pools of energy when the price is right, if only the government will remove the constraints of price control and other regulations.

"The apostles of conservation, led by the Carter administration, insist that mankind is at a different crossroads now. . . . someday the energy delivery system will be overwhelmed unless the government convinces consumers and producers to reduce their appetites now. This warning does not include the other threat—the possibility of another oil embargo from the Middle East." *The Washington Post,* July 24, 1977, p. A1.

16. *The Washington Post,* April 23, 1978.
17. This expert was Vincent McKelvey, the director of the U.S. Geological Survey. Williams, "Tough Stuff," *The Washington Post,* September 12, 1977.
18. Confidential interviews, former agents, CIA; former officer, air force intelligence; former analyst, Defense Intelligence Agency.
19. Ironically, Congress saw Carter's conservation move very differently, as a way to make Americans pay more for their gas and thereby increase the oil companies' profits. Anthony Sampson, *The Seven Sisters* (London: Coronet, 1988), p. 331.
20. Jimmy Carter, *Keeping Faith. Memoirs of a President* (New York: Bantam, 1982), p. 92.
21. William Greider and J. P. Smith, "Fuels Crisis a Matter of Perception," *The Washington Post,* July 24, 1977, p. A1.
22. In essence, it was: "about the system of private enterprise and public regulation which governs the delivery of energy to consumers. There are fundamental conflicts between the private interests of the energy companies and [the] national goals of the Carter administration." Ibid.
23. Schlesinger said that it was only when the Carter policy prevented price increases that the companies then suddenly suggested: "We don't have an emergency, after all," and opportunistically told the electorate that the "world has vast resources in oil and natural gas and other hydrocarbons which the American people can enjoy—if only the government will get off the industry's back." Ibid.
24. The intense media scrutiny of the CIA's "revisionist" figures is exemplified by *The Washington Post*'s article of April 23, 1978, which examined "the unexplained gyrations that began appearing in December [1977] in the CIA's biweekly reports on world oil supplies." The newspaper pointed out that in November 1977, the CIA's estimates of "the productive capacity of the Saudi fields" was 11.5 million barrels a day, but that by December, the estimate had dropped to 10.5 million barrels, and in January fell to 8.8 million barrels. "These vanishing millions of barrels of oil baffled consumers of the CIA's intelligence reports. They were further baffled in February, when the CIA again shifted gears and reported Saudi capacity at 10.5 million barrels." *The Washington Post* quoted Schlesinger, as saying that the upward revision was "a result of certain articles in *The Washington Post,*" which had reported these fluctuations in the CIA's estimates, and "had further reported that between November and February the CIA had lopped 5 million barrels a day off the 'surplus production' capability of the 13 members of OPEC (Organization of Petroleum Exporting Countries)." Richard Harwood and J. P. Smith, "CIA Oil Figures Raise Eyebrows Among Experts," *The Washington Post,* April 23, 1978.
25. Ibid.
26. This was Walter McDonald, who had been appointed as Schlesinger's deputy assistant secretary of energy for international affairs. Another ex-CIA expert on Schlesinger's staff was Frank Pagnotta, who had previously worked for the CIA's deputy director. Ibid.
27. The GAO official was Philip Woodside, who had "spent more than a decade with the CIA as an oil analyst in the Middle East and Latin America." Ibid.
28. Ibid.
29. The oil companies and the Saudis had access to similar intelligence experts. George W. Cave, then the CIA station chief in Saudi Arabia, was a former Aramco employee,

while Raymond Close had retired from the same post in 1977 "and now works for the Saudis." It was typical of the revolving door between the oil companies and the espionage world discussed in previous chapters. As *The Washington Post* pointed out: "There are, in addition, scores of known or suspected CIA operatives, alumni and cooperators with an abiding interest in oil.

"Two of the best known and most respected in international oil circles are Mike Ameen of the London office of the Mobil Oil Corp., and Jack Bridges, a former congressional aide who now works for the Saudis as director of the King Faisal Foundation with offices in Northern Virginia.

"They ritually deny CIA ties, but there is no doubt that they have CIA contacts and intimate relationship with the Saudis.

"This web of relationships is nothing new in the oil business. For years, the CIA and the international oil companies have worked closely together out of a community of interest.

"Frank Jungers, board chairman of Aramco until last year, is candid on that point: 'For years out there [in Saudi Arabia] we had a good relationship with the agency, partly because I thought it would make things easier.'

"He said the industry-wide practice was to maintain 'liaison' with the CIA. But involvements sometimes were more direct. Ashland Oil, for example, said it was surprised to find some years ago that the CIA was using the company as a cover for an agent operating abroad." Ibid.

30. Ibid.
31. Confidential interviews, former agents, CIA; former officer, air force intelligence; former officers, U.S. Army; former analyst, Defense Intelligence Agency; former members, Israeli military intelligence; former Israeli military attaché.
32. Ibid.
33. Ibid.
34. Ibid.
35. As previously discussed, the Saudis were also sending over $3 billion a year to Israel's most feared enemy, Anwar Sadat, the man who had succeeded the hated Nasser as Egypt's president. Although he had cut himself off from the Soviets, the Communists had made significant headway in other parts of the region, including taking over Aden after the departure of the British and sending thousands of Cuban proxies to the Horn of Africa. Traumatized by Watergate and Vietnam, the United States seemed powerless to respond to the Soviet threat.
36. Confidential interviews, former officers, U.S. Army; former analyst, Defense Intelligence Agency.
37. Confidential interviews, former agents, CIA; former officer, air force intelligence; former officers, U.S. Army; former analyst, Defense Intelligence Agency; former members, Israeli military intelligence; former Israeli military attaché.
38. The Israeli intelligence advisers told Weizmann that: "It doesn't matter what the Egyptians say, we have to assume that they're preparing for war, and we will not know when. Their actions can serve as a smokescreen for war. Sadat will argue that he was prepared to go all the way and that Israel didn't respond. The decision to go to war depends on five or six people, and we can't depend on a date." Ian Black and Benny Morris, *Israel's Secret Wars. The Untold History of Israeli Intelligence* (London: Hamish Hamilton, 1991), p. 326.
39. Walter Laqueur and Barry Rubin (eds.). *The Arab-Israeli Reader* (New York: Penguin, 1976), pp. 592–595.
40. Black and Morris, *Israel's Secret Wars*, p. 327.
41. Confidential interviews, former agents, CIA; former officer, air force intelligence; former officers, U.S. Army; former analyst, Defense Intelligence Agency.
42. Alfred M. Lilienthal, *The Zionist Connection* (New York: Dodd, Mead, 1978), pp. 684, 686.

43. "Begin declared he would not accept a West Bank enclave under Jordanian sovereignty, a formula that the Rabin-Peres government had been prepared to accept . . ." Ibid., p. 688. Begin's election platform in March 1977 had stated that: "The PLO is no national liberation organization but an organization of assassins." Laqueur and Rubin (eds.), *The Arab-Israeli Reader,* p. 592.
44. Saudi Arabia was "Yasser Arafat's principal financial supporter. Increasing Sa'udi subsidies to the PLO since 1973 have given the organization currency reserves estimated at over a billion dollars—larger than those of many Third World countries—and most inhabitants of the Kingdom are proud that Sa'udi oil revenues should be supporting the cause of their Palestinian brothers." Robert Lacey, *The Kingdom: Arabia and the House of Sa'ud* (New York: Avon Books, 1983), p. 446.
45. Ibid., p. 449; Laqueur and Rubin (eds.), *The Arab-Israeli Reader,* pp. 601–602.
46. To most Moslems, the "Egyptian leader was preparing . . . for a sell-out on Jerusalem that the Al Sa'ud [Saudi royal family] were too scared to acknowledge themselves—and Riyadh became the object of as much Arab opprobrium as Cairo." Lacey, *The Kingdom,* p. 449.
47. Laqueur and Rubin (eds.), *The Arab-Israeli Reader,* pp. 608–609.
48. Lilienthal, *The Zionist Connection,* pp. 705–712.
49. Even Carter recognized the imbalance and later agreed to give Israel a larger number of F-16s to compensate. Confidential interview, former analyst, Defense Intelligence Agency.
50. "In the spring of 1978 the Carter administration paid tribute to . . . expanding Sa'udi power when they pushed through Congress, in defiance of fierce Israeli protests, the sale to Sa'udi Arabia of sixty F15 fighter-bombers, the most sophisticated warplanes in the world, and President Carter welcomed Crown Prince Fahad to Washington in a state of emotion that appeared close to ecstasy.

    " 'I don't think,' enthused the president in a statement which raised eyebrows in London, Bonn and Teheran, not to mention Tel Aviv, 'that there is any other nation with whom we've had better friendship and a deeper sense of cooperation that we've found in Sa'udi Arabia!' " Lacey, *The Kingdom,* p. 449.
51. "The Arab consensus was that Sadat had sold out the general cause to get back his own land, for though Egypt regained Sinai at Camp David, Israel kept Jerusalem—within two years the Knesset was to incorporate the city as Israel's 'complete and united capital'—while all that the Palestinians were offered on the West Bank was a poor apology for a Bantustan, dotted with fortified Israeli settlements, which Begin was determined to expand." Ibid., p. 450.
52. As we have seen, the president felt quite strongly that the United States should not be "jerked around by a few desert states." Carter, *Keeping Faith,* p. 92.
53. "Carter had staked his presidential prestige on bringing home an agreement from a dramatic last-minute shuttle between Cairo and Jerusalem. He wanted to get off Air Force 1 waving his arms in triumph, not explaining how a crew of Third World diplomats with robes and worry beads were coming to stir the pot further." Lacey, *The Kingdom,* pp. 452–453.
54. Carter, *Keeping Faith,* pp. 113, 282, 290.
55. "The disgruntled State Department began leaking to the media tales of the disagreements that had occurred as Fahad and his brothers argued over policy. The Al Sa'ud, it was suddenly suggested, were no more reliable than the Shah had proved. . . . Sa'udi Arabia had a new image . . . no longer a bulwark of the West, the Kingdom became the crumbling coping stone in a 'Crescent of Crisis' now perceived as stretching from the Horn of Africa to Pakistan, all of it about to fall victim to the marauding Russian bear in the north." Lacey, *The Kingdom,* p. 454.
56. The Saudi king didn't deviate from his commitment to Arab rights in Palestine, at least not on paper. The Saudi position was well summarized by one of the younger princes: "Of course, if God granted us a wish, we would like the Palestinians to

vanish off the face of the earth. We know they are only nice to us because they want our money. They are dangerous men with Marxist tendencies. But their disappearance would be a second wish. The first wish is the disappearance of Israel." Ibid.

57. Confidential interviews, former agents, CIA; former officer, air force intelligence; former officers, U.S. Army; former analyst, Defense Intelligence Agency; former members, Israeli military intelligence; former Israeli military attaché.
58. Confidential interview, former officer, U.S. Army.
59. Interview with Ari Ben-Menashe, November 19, 1991.
60. Confidential interviews, former agents, CIA; former officer, air force intelligence; former officers, U.S. Army; former analyst, Defense Intelligence Agency; former members, Israeli military intelligence; former Israeli military attaché.
61. Interview with Ari Ben-Menashe, November 19, 1991.
62. Confidential interviews, former agents, CIA; former officer, air force intelligence; former officers, U.S. Army; former analyst, Defense Intelligence Agency.
63. Ibid., and confidential interviews, former members, Israeli military intelligence, former Israeli military attaché.
64. Lacey, *The Kingdom*, p. 454.
65. Confidential interviews, former agents, CIA; former officer, air force intelligence; former officers, U.S. Army; former analyst, Defense Intelligence Agency.
66. Confidential interviews, former agents, CIA; former officer, air force intelligence.
67. Confidential interviews, former officers, U.S. Army, former analyst, Defense Intelligence Agency; former members, Israeli military intelligence; former Israeli military attaché.
68. By the mid-1980s Schlesinger was a powerful advocate for the Reagan-Bush policy of promoting Saudi military strength: "Speaking on separate television programmes, three former Central Intelligence Agency Directors—Richard Helms, James Schlesinger and Stansfield Turner—endorsed the Reagan Administration position that Saudi Arabia should take the lead in protecting gulf oil shipments." Reuters North European Service, May 27, 1984.
69. Associated Press, August 17, 1979.
70. Ibid.
71. "This year the Soviet Union will produce 593 million tons of crude and condensate to become the world's first country to come close to the 600-million-ton mark. Last year the U.S.S.R. produced 572 million tons of crude and condensate—more than Saudi Arabia and 36% more than the U.S.

    "In 1976–78 Soviet oil output increased by 81 million tons.

    "In the past 20 years no other country has shown such stable and high rates of oil production as the Soviet Union.

    "Severe frosts last winter and unprecedented high spring waters on the river of western Siberia, the main Soviet oil-producing area, did complicate the work of oil fields.

    "However, Soviet oil output did not fall, as the CIA predicted. In January–August it went up by 10 million tons from the corresponding figure for 1978 and continues to grow." Boris Rachtov, Master of Economics, Moscow, "How Soviet Union views future oil production, exports," *Oil & Gas Journal*, December 3, 1979.
72. Ibid.
73. Reuters, February 19, 1980.
74. Associated Press, April 22, 1980.
75. "Turner painted an extremely pessimistic picture of world energy reserves in the next decade.

    ". . . Among Middle Eastern producers, Turner said Saudi Arabia, America's most dependable supplier, could potentially increase its capacity by a million barrels over current production of 9.5 million barrels daily.

    "But instead of an increase, Turner said, 'we expect by this summer that the

Saudis may reduce actual output to 8.5 million barrels a day or lower' . . .

"The Soviet Union is the world's biggest oil producer, pumping 11.7 million barrels daily in 1979, Turner said. Production will 'probably peak this year at less than 12 million barrels daily and begin falling next year.'

"That means the Soviet Union and its dependent Eastern European nations will begin competing on world markets for oil, already in short supply. . . .

" 'It also is likely that the Soviets will be increasingly active in the diplomatic arena in the Middle East,' Turner said, 'holding out as a carrot the glimmer of a stable political atmosphere if the Gulf states become more cooperative on oil and political matters." Ibid.

76. Confidential interviews, former agents, CIA.
77. Turner announced that "Moscow is already making the point that Middle Eastern oil is not the exclusive preserve of the West. . . . 'The cardinal issue is how vicious the struggle for energy supplies will become.' " Associated Press, April 22, 1980. However, nothing that the administration said seemed to make much difference to the Western oil experts. Turner had to look wider afield for supporters. The Chinese Communists conveniently stepped in to stir the pot against their ideological foes in Moscow, telling the West that "the Soviet Union was carrying out a 'pincer movement' toward the Middle East and its oil reserves. . . . the Soviet Union was keen on controlling the Middle East . . . to gain leverage over Europe and Japan." If the Western oil experts wouldn't back Turner, the neo-Stalinists in Beijing would. British Broadcasting Corporation, "Summary of World Broadcasts," September 22, 1980.
78. Confidential interview, former analyst, Defense Intelligence Agency.
79. Reuters, March 20, 1981.
80. Ibid.
81. Associated Press, May 20, 1981; and *Newsweek,* August 10, 1981, pp. 19–20.
82. Ibid.
83. John M. Berry, "CIA Expands Forecast of Soviets' Oil Output," *The Washington Post,* May 20, 1981. "James Noren, one of the CIA officials who made the higher prediction, was quoted as saying the revision was based on substantial increases in drilling in Western Siberia, where the number of feet drilled has more than doubled since 1977." The Associated Press, May 20, 1981.
84. Ibid.
85. Confidential interviews, former agents, CIA.
86. *National Journal,* May 23, 1981, p. 944.
87. Confidential interviews, former members, Israeli military intelligence; former Israeli military attaché.
88. Confidential interview, former analyst, Defense Intelligence Agency.
89. Confidential interviews, refinery employees, St. Croix.
90. Confidential interviews, former agents, CIA; former officer, air force intelligence; former officers, U.S. Army; former analyst, Defense Intelligence Agency; former members, Israeli military intelligence; former Israeli military attaché.
91. Reuters, July 5, 1981.
92. Confidential interviews, former White House staffer; former analyst, Defense Intelligence Agency.
93. Reuters, July 5, 1981.
94. Hobart Rowen, "Oil Price Drop Signifies End of OPEC's Power," *Washington Post,* February 6, 1983, p. K1.
95. One Communist propagandist rubbed the CIA's noses in it. In April 1983 Valentin Zorin snickered "that the CIA forecast about Soviet oil was among the biggest mistakes made in recent years by the CIA.

"... I have told you all this today not only to try to show what shaky ground and flouting of real facts the Washington administration is using to base its policies on, but also that you could see how unrealistic are the plans of the Reagan administration to blackmail the Soviet Union with a threat of all sorts of economic sanctions.

". . . The Reagan administration has no more chances to influence . . . Soviet policy with economic sanctions than it can change at its will the ocean tides." "CIA's 'Big Mistake' over Soviet Oil Resources," British Broadcasting Corporation, "Summary of World Broadcasts," April 26, 1983.

96. Confidential interviews, former officer, air force intelligence; former analyst, Defense Intelligence Agency; former members, Israeli military intelligence.

CHAPTER 16
THE MEXICAN CONNECTION

1. Confidential interviews, former officers and agents, CIA; former special agent, FBI; former White House staffer.
2. Alan Friedman, *Spider's Web* (New York: Bantam, 1993), pp. 5–40.
3. Ibid., p. 164.
4. Ibid., p. 4.
5. Confidential interviews, former members, Israeli intelligence; officers, Israeli Defense Forces; former Israeli military attaché.
6. Confidential interviews, former analysts, Defense Intelligence Agency; former agents, CIA.
7. Confidential interviews, former officers and agents, CIA; former special agent, FBI, former White House staffer.
8. Confidential interviews, former OPC agents; former agents and officers, CIA; former officer, U.S. Army MIS.
9. *The New York Times*, June 25, 1953, p. 27.
10. George Bush, with Victor Gold, *Looking Forward. An Autobiography* (London: Bodley Head, 1988), pp. 27–29.
11. Christopher Simpson, *The Splendid Blond Beast: Money, Law and Genocide in the Twentieth Century* (New York: Grove Press, 1993), pp. 49–50.
12. "Another Wall Street firm that specialized in U.S.-German trade was Brown Brothers, Harriman, a private investment bank dominated by W. Averell Harriman, whose family fortune rivaled that of the Rockefellers. Harriman went on to become one of the most influential figures in U.S. foreign affairs over the next fifty years. His key political allies who also served as senior executives of the bank included Robert Lovett (later U.S. secretary of defense) and Prescott Bush (prominent legislator and father of the U.S. President)." Ibid., p. 48.
13. Ibid., pp. 49–50.
14. "Formally established in 1924, the Union Banking Corp. originally operated out of the offices of what was then W. A. Harriman & Co., Averell Harriman's investment firm located at 39 Broadway in Manhattan. The President of W. A. Harriman & Co. was George Herbert 'Bert' Walker, Prescott Bush's father in law, George Bush's grandfather." David Armstrong, "Banking on Hitler: Sins of the Fathers," original manuscript in authors' possession.
15. Confidential interviews, former agents, OPC; former agents and officers, CIA; former officer, U.S. Army MIS.
16. Ibid.
17. Interview with Daniel Harkins, U.S. intelligence agent inside Hamburg-Amerika.
18. "The Harriman group's stock in American Shipping and Commerce was controlled by the Harriman Fifteen Corp., a holding company run out of the offices of G. H. Walker & Co. The directors of the Harriman Fifteen Corp. were Averell Harriman, Bert Walker and Prescott Bush. The Harriman Fifteen Corp. also held a sizable stake in the Silesian-American Corp., a holding company with substantial investments in German and Polish steelmaking, zinc and copper-mining operations." Armstrong, "Banking on Hitler: Sins of the Fathers," p. 3.
19. Smedley Butler, *Common Sense Magazine* (New York, November 1935).

20. Armstrong, "Banking on Hitler: Sins of the Fathers," p. 3.
21. Interview, Daniel Harkins, U.S. Intelligence agent inside Hamburg-Amerika.
22. Copies of the client list were graciously loaned to the authors by Burton Hersh.
23. Ibid.
24. Armstrong, "Banking on Hitler: Sins of the Fathers," p. 1.
25. Confidential interviews, former agents, OPC; former agents and officers, CIA; former officer, MIS.
26. "In the fall of 1942, just eight months after Bush took over as chair of the USO fund drive, the Union Banking Corp., an affiliate of Brown Brothers, Harriman, was seized by the U.S. Government as a front for German nationals who had helped bankroll Hitler since the early 1920s.

    "Under authority of the Trading with the Enemy Act, on Oct. 20, 1942, the U.S. Office of Alien Property Custodian issued Vesting Order Number 248, confiscating all 4,000 shares of capital stock in the Union Banking Corp. The order states that the stock was held 'for the benefit of nationals' of 'a designated enemy country.' Identified as stockholders in the Union Banking Corp. were . . . Prescott Bush, who managed the Harriman brothers' personal investments." Armstrong, "Banking on Hitler: Sins of the Fathers," pp. 1–2.
27. "A report issued by the Office of Alien Property Custodian in 1942 states that, 'Since 1939, these [steel and mining] properties have been in possession of and have been operated by the German government and have undoubtedly been of considerable assistance to that country in its war effort.' In separate actions taken during the latter half of 1942, the U.S. government seized both the Hamburg-Amerika Line and the Silesian-American Corp. under the Trading with the Enemy Act." Ibid., pp. 2–3.
28. Confidential interviews, former agents, OPC; former agents and officers, CIA; former officer, U.S. Army MIS.
29. Ibid.
30. Confidential interview, former faculty member, Yale University.
31. Confidential interviews, Skull and Bones members.
32. Ibid. For example, while Prescott was a young soldier at Fort Sill, Oklahoma, he purchased the skull of Geronimo, the great Apache chief, from a gravedigger and sent the relic to Skull and Bones. In 1988 a spokesperson for the White Mountain Apache Tribe of Santa Clara, Arizona, cited a 1933 Skull and Bones Club history crediting George Bush's father as the person who actually stole the skull from the grave. According to the archivist at Fort Sill, Oklahoma, Prescott may have been conned into buying the wrong Indian's skull. Geronimo's family had quietly moved his grave to an unmarked site several years earlier. There was a substantial black market in Indian grave artifacts at the time, for those insensitive enough to purchase them.
33. Confidential interviews, former agents, OPC; former agents and officers, CIA; former officer, U.S. Army MIS.
34. In fact, there is reason to believe that George Bush's first association with intelligence operations came through his own circle of friends and not from his father. The Skull and Bones Club was one of the principal recruiting sources for Dulles's Office of Policy Coordination and later the CIA. Two of the thirteen members of George Bush's Skull and Bones class joined Dulles's intelligence fronts.

    According to extensive research by Peggy Robohm, one of George Bush's Skull and Bones classmates was Howard Weaver, the European desk chief for the Free Europe Press Offices in Munich, Germany, which praised Dulles's "freedom fighters." Weaver's boss was another of Bush's Skull and Bones classmates, Samuel Sloan Walker, Jr. From 1951 to 1959 Walker was the director of the Free Europe Press as well as vice president of the parent body, the Free Europe Committee.

    The Free Europe Committee, better known as Radio Free Europe, was the principal financial conduit for laundering money to Dulles's Nazi protégés. It was exposed as an intelligence front by the U.S. Senate in 1971. The Free Europe Committee was firmly under the control of the Dulles brothers' State Department clique. When Allen Dulles became head of the CIA, he brought Radio Free Europe into the organization and pretended to do a little house cleaning. A 1953 CIA investigation resulted in the firing of several of the more notorious Nazis on the committee, but most of them stayed on the payroll or switched to different organizations.

Bill Casey, who later became CIA director and played a key role in the Iran-Contra Affair, had worked in Germany on the Nazi "freedom fighters" program. When he returned to New York, he headed up the International Rescue Committee, which sponsored the immigration of Fascist "freedom fighters" to the United States. The front man for Crusade for Freedom, the money-laundering organization for Radio Liberty, was a young movie actor by the name of Ronald Reagan. Dulles could certainly spot talent. Confidential interviews, former agents, OPC; former agents and officers, CIA; former officer, MIS.

35. Pauley was a self-made multimillionaire who became president of the Petrol Corporation of Los Angeles in 1928, "a modest-sized firm engaged in the various phases of the industry, and he was also a minor stockholder in Standard of California." He also was an executive of several other major enterprises, including a bank and a construction company. Robert Engler, *The Politics of Oil. A Study of Private Power and Democratic Directions* (Chicago: University of Chicago Press, 1967), p. 341.
36. Janet Podell (ed), *The Annual Obituary 1981* (New York: St. Martin's Press, 1982), pp. 475–476.
37. "A generous contributor to Democratic causes, he was also a successful money raiser among oil and other corporate interests on the West Coast. (For example, President Collier of Standard of California made a contribution of $1,000 to the Democrats through Pauley. 'I am a Republican, and my contributions have always gone the other way, except . . . in 1940,' he explained.) Pauley was credited with erasing his party's deficit while serving as secretary, assistant treasurer, and then treasurer of the Democratic National Committee from the end of 1941 to 1945. He had been a leader in the movement to block the renomination of Henry A. Wallace as vice president in 1944, and had actively campaigned for his replacement by Senator Harry S. Truman." Engler, *The Politics of Oil*, pp. 342–343.
38. Ibid., p. 287.
39. Ickes's hostile attitude to the oil business was well known from the 1930s, when as a Republican he joined Roosevelt's first cabinet in 1933. Engler, *The Politics of Oil*, p. 286. The best policy was to have them working nearby, where Ickes could keep a close eye on them. For this reason, the upper echelons of the Petroleum Administration were drawn from the oil companies, but Ickes vehemently "denied that its policies were dominated by the big oil companies." He thought he had them where he wanted them. The left-wingers in the New Deal team would isolate, and publicly route the right. Ibid., p. 287.
40. From "1941 to 1945 Pauley oversaw the distribution of oil supplies to Russia and the United Kingdom through the Lend-Lease program." Podell (ed.), *The Annual Obituary 1981*, p. 475.
41. Ickes also was "strongly critical of the State Department's employment of the Universal Oil Products Company as a consultant in the State Department's Mexican negotiations, since this process-engineering firm was controlled by the expropriated majors." A few years later Pauley "charged that the State Department adviser blocked a contract he was arranging for a refinery in Mexico. When Mr. Thornburg said the project was in conflict with State Department policy, explained Pauley, Thornburg 'meant that no group of independent oil men could do business in Mexico, even if that business would have been of direct aid to our war program. He meant that his interests—the interests of the expropriated major oil companies by whom he was employed—came first. . . .' " Engler, *The Politics of Oil*, p. 196.

42. Podell (ed.), *The Annual Obituary*, pp. 475–476, and Engler, *The Politics of Oil*, p. 311. According to one of Pauley's 1981 obituaries: "Acting on instructions from Truman, Pauley convinced the representatives of the other Allied nations to accept a percentage settlement, rather than a dollar amount, of war damages collected from Germany. (The original plan . . . had been to de-industrialize Germany by extracting from it $20 billion in reparations fines; had this plan been carried out, Truman feared, the Soviet Union might have been able to take advantage of Germany's weakness to establish itself as the main power in Central Europe.)" Podell (ed.), *The Annual Obituary 1981*, p. 475.
43. There were, in fact, two major problems for Pauley to sort out. At Yalta the Soviets had been promised half the $20 billion reparations, which if they got it would immeasurably assist their economic recovery at a time when the West wanted to retard Moscow's progress. Further: "At Potsdam, Pauley estimated that removable direct war potential in the Western zones amounted to a scant $1.7 billion—the Russian estimate was four to five times higher—and since 'the mere mention of this figure at this time would preclude any agreement being made at all,' Pauley advised [Secretary of State] Byrnes to avoid figures altogether and persist only with percentages of unknown quantities." Gabriel Kolko, *The Politics of War. The World and United States Foreign Policy 1943–1945* (New York: Vintage, 1970), p. 572. For further details of Pauley's role in the reparations issue, see also ibid., pp. 519–521.
44. As already noted, the Dulles clique was then recruiting Japan's war criminals and their massive, illegally acquired assets as a bulwark against Soviet expansion into Asia. Pauley's inside knowledge undoubtedly helped to target recruits with suitable right-wing (Fascist) credentials and the money to buy Japan's postwar government. It would pay to keep Pauley in such influential posts.

    President Truman obliged. After writing his special report for the State Department on Japanese war reparations, Pauley was assigned to yet another influential post, one that gave him one more opportunity to assist the Dulles boys. As consolation for missing out on the position of James Forrestal's deputy as undersecretary of the navy, Truman made Pauley a special adviser on reparations to the secretary of state from 1947 to 1948. At least he got to keep an eye on things until Dewey could take over the White House, but it was a bitter consolation prize for Ed Pauley. See Podell (ed.), *The Annual Obituary 1981*, p. 475.
45. Confidential interviews, former agents, OPC; former agents and officers, CIA; former officer, MIS.
46. Engler, *The Politics of Oil*, p. 341.
47. "Pauley's relations with Congress and the Truman Administration were not smooth. On several occasions it was hinted in the press that Pauley had been named to his government positions as a payoff for political favors. When Truman nominated Pauley for the office of undersecretary of the Navy in 1946, critics pointed out that Pauley's petroleum holdings placed him in a conflict of interests, since the post for which he was nominated would give him control over the Navy's oil supplies." Podell (ed.), *The Annual Obituary 1981*, p. 476. One of the leading critics was Senator Charles Tobey, a Republican who led the case against Pauley in the confirmation hearings. Tobey had a much wider agenda, aimed at bringing "out all the evidence pertaining to 'the permeability of oil' " into key government posts. Tobey was one of the first U.S. legislators to take a serious look at the emerging "revolving door" between the oil companies and the government. Like all the others who tried to expose it, the senator came up against a powerful and well-organized counteroffensive.

    Indeed, the Pauley hearings threatened to expose all the scandals that the oil companies thought they had covered up forever. One of the many items aired at the hearings was the debate, then raging, between the major oil companies and the independent producers, over "state 'conservation' measures to control production."

At the time there were allegations that Pauley's Petroleum Corporation had received payments from Standard of California, which had helped switch his company from the independent's anti-conservation stance to the pro-conservation position of the majors. Engler, *The Politics of Oil,* p. 342.

48. From December 1945 Ickes had become concerned at widespread press speculation that the president might actually replace navy secretary Forrestal with his fellow Dulles agent, Edwin Pauley. When he resigned in mid-February 1946, Ickes stated that he had immediately intervened with Truman, hoping to stop it. Ickes came up against a brick wall in the White House. Arnold A. Rogow, *James Forrestal. A Study of Personality, Politics and Policy* (New York: Macmillan, 1963), p. 236*n;* and Ickes's resignation letter, *The New York Times,* February 14, 1946, p. 21.

49. "Senator Tobey's journey into oil politics led him far beyond any possible original intent to lambaste his Democratic opponents. . . . Never before in his entire thirty-year political career, Tobey declared, had he been subjected to such intense pressures, all directed against holding the hearings. 'This pressure comes from the West and from the East; it represents large capital interests . . . of tremendous influence and importance in the country.' " They had a telling effect, although the stubborn Senator Tobey would not be bullied into total submission. In fact, he won the point at issue, at least in principle: "Many of the charges and countercharges were never sorted out or pinned down. And despite the readiness with which the Congress generally assigns its own prose to posterity, the hearings were never published. They remain in the storeroom of the Senate Armed Services Committee in the transcript form received from the stenotypist." Engler, *The Politics of Oil,* p. 342. Before the draft transcripts were consigned to their dusty shelves, many tantalizing clues had emerged about Pauley's role in trying to buy the Democratic party for the oil companies. The oil Democrats apparently knew they had to counter the generosity of Jewish donors, and several instances of large oil donations were aired at the hearings. In one case gossip had it that in 1941, eighteen oil companies had given $50,000 each in return for a settlement in some tricky litigation. Ibid., p. 343.

50. Ickes had a reputation as a frank, overbearing man and was never one to do things by half measures. The feisty Interior secretary appeared on February 13, 1946, at a packed press conference to announce his departure, after serving continuously since the first days of FDR's presidency, almost thirteen years earlier. Ickes came to the point in a most abrupt and direct manner: "I don't care to stay in an Administration where I am expected to commit perjury for the sake of the party." For that matter, Ickes wasn't even a Democrat. *The New York Times* predicted that his resignation was "practically a death blow to Mr. Pauley's chances of confirmation by the Senate." His long-winded letter was a devastating assault, which implicated the president himself in a sleazy cover-up. It lost Ickes quite a few friends among the Democrats, even some who had previously been his strong supporters.

Ickes, who also had the reputation of an honest, if extremely difficult politician, pulled few punches at the press conference. He stated point blank that: "on Feb. 1, a few minutes before he testified before the Senate Naval Affairs Committee, the President told him: 'You must tell the truth, of course, but try to be as gentle as you can with Ed Pauley' . . . To which Mr. Ickes said he replied: 'I will.' " *The New York Times,* February 14, 1946, pp. 1, 21. In point of fact, Ickes did not seem to know the meaning of Truman's words. He was anything but gentle with Ed Pauley. In his testimony, he "recalled his warning to President Roosevelt against allowing an oilman to become party treasurer, for sooner or later 'you are going to have a scandal on your hands.' " Engler, *The Politics of Oil,* p. 343.

51. Ickes "recounted his version of 'the rawest proposition that has ever been made to me'—Pauley's reputed statement in 1944 that he could raise $300,000 for the party from oilmen if the federal government would not press its offshore oil suit designed to establish whether title was with the state of California or the United States. A

firm believer in state control of the offshore lands of California, Pauley apparently had explored the issue with everyone he could reach, from Franklin D. Roosevelt on down." Engler, *The Politics of Oil*, p. 343.

52. "Norman Littell, who had been Assistant Attorney General in charge of the Lands Division and . . . recommended that the federal government take legal action . . . to test title to the lands, described Pauley as a 'veritable jack-in-the-box' . . . who discussed offshore oil with Littell at every occasion. He cited one meeting with Harry J. March, vice president and general counsel of Signal Oil and Gas, who was sharing a hotel suite with Pauley. Littell testified that Pauley prefaced the introduction by saying that while he wouldn't want anything improper done, oil people had contributed to the campaign and 'they expected something for their money.' Known among some California politicians as 'the man with the black bag,' March raised money from West Coast oil interests and was actively lobbying for congressional quitclaim legislation rather than for any court determination." The embarrassing dirt just kept coming out. Pauley had arranged for his own personal attorney to have a position at Democratic party headquarters, and while there he also acted for the front committee pushing for quitclaim legislation. He just happened to use party resources for the oil companies' campaign. The lawyer, Welburn Mayock, was highly skilled at "the intricate political art of raising money and hopes without direct verbal commitments by either recipient or donor." Mayock was not the only Pauley crony on the Democrat payroll. Pauley seemed to have a habit of "buying" allies. On one occasion a reporter was surprised to find that a phone number for Pauley's Petroleum Corporation was actually on the desk of the Democratic National Committee's vice chairman, William Roach, who had been given a job in Pauley's company in 1943. Worse still, the seamier side of the tactics of both the oil majors and the independents were given quite an airing at the hearings. Two California legislators, "one of whom became a congressman, received retainers from Pauley's Petroleum Corporation, paid through the latter's advertising firm. According to [Senator] Tobey, vice president T. S. Petersen of California Standard admitted to him that 'we did things that no man should ever ask a man to do.' " Pauley tried to defend himself, as best he could. He told the hearings that "he was the victim of vicious and dishonest slugging. . . . 'I have never in my life solicited, suggested, or accepted a contingent contribution . . .' Most oil money, he ventured, was then going to the Republicans who may have offered oilmen inducements." Ibid., pp. 343–347.

53. Ickes quoted from numerous memos and records of conversation, and cited other witnesses who could corroborate, and expand on, his own testimony. The president had personally asked Ickes to stay on in his administration, but "when he got too big for his breeches and opposed me openly on my appointment of Pauley, I could not, as President, tolerate that." *The New York Times*, February 14, 1946, p. 21, and Engler, *The Politics of Oil*, p. 347.

54. In fact, Truman forced Ickes straight from his office, whereas Ickes had wanted to stay to finish some important business, finalizing the major Petroleum Agreement he had negotiated in London the previous September. To Truman, Ickes's resignation letter "was the kind of letter sent by a man who is sure that he can have his way if he threatens to quit." Daniel Yergin, *The Prize: The Epic Quest for Oil, Money & Power* (New York: Touchstone, 1992), p. 406. On the other hand, Ickes believed it was very simple: The President believed either his version or Pauley's. One of them was lying. Truman had "definitely aligned" himself with "Pauley against me, thus making my position as a member of your Cabinet untenable," he wrote in his resignation letter. *The New York Times*, February 14, 1946, p. 21, and Engler, *The Politics of Oil*, p. 347. At his standing-room-only press conference, the old warhorse was asked to list his objections to Pauley's nomination. For once, the usually loquacious Ickes was crisp and to the point. It was a telling summary:

"No. 1, he is in the active oil business and nominated for a position where he has a great deal to do with oil on the Government side.

"No. 2, he made me a proposition which disqualified him from holding high office, in my judgment.

"No. 3, when he testified under oath he didn't tell the truth. I have no more reasons." *The New York Times*, February 14, 1946, p. 21.

55. Engler, *The Politics of Oil*, p. 348. Truman was quietly furious, and although he later said he was fond of Ickes, he was very glad to see the back of him. The president didn't give up, though. He kept trying to get his friend Ed Pauley a good government job. Despite considerable plotting, he didn't pull it off. The smell of scandal was too strong, and Truman failed in his attempt to make Pauley the special assistant to the secretary of the army. Podell (ed.), *The Annual Obituary 1981*, p. 476.
56. There may well have been a touch of partisan politics involved, as the man who leveled the charges was Republican presidential candidate, Harold Stassen, "who accused him of profiteering in food commodities. Pauley admitted to having speculated in food and clothes, but refused to concede that these were anything more than cautious financial investments." Podell (ed.), *The Annual Obituary 1981*, p. 476.
57. Wolfgang Saxon, "Edwin Wendell Pauley Sr., 78," *The New York Times*, July 29, 1981, p. A19. Although he was an "independent" oil man, Pauley also was heavily involved in Middle Eastern oil. His stocks in Standard of California may have been minor by some standards, but then the returns from Saudi Arabia were very gratifying. Later he became a major stockholder in the American Independent Oil Company (Aminoil), which had first gained a Kuwaiti concession in the late 1940s, as a half share in the Saudi-Kuwaiti "Neutral Zone." Mira Wilkins, *The Maturing of Multinational Enterprise. American Business Abroad from 1914 to 1970* (Cambridge, MA: Harvard University Press, 1974), p. 321. Huge profits were involved. Pauley was in on two of the most lucrative oil deals in the Middle East. The Neutral Zone turned out to be one of the biggest discoveries ever. After Aminoil finally struck oil in 1953, it was described by *Fortune* magazine as "somewhere between colossal and history-making." The man who procured the Saudi half was J. Paul Getty. It transformed him from an extremely wealthy man into the richest man in the world. Pauley had good reasons to keep expanding his oil interests. Yergin, *The Prize*, pp. 443–444.
58. Confidential interviews, former agents, OPC; former agents and officers, CIA; former officer, MIS.
59. Ibid.
60. Mark Perry, "The Lonely Spy," *Regardie's* magazine (February 1989).
61. Confidential interviews, former agents, OPC; former agents and officers, CIA; former officer, MIS.
62. Perhaps it was not such a unique development. Many conservative Democrats, especially from the West, turn to the Republicans in their old age. But in light of the very prominent role that Pauley had played in Democrat party affairs over many decades, it does seem a major reversal of a supposedly lifelong commitment. Robert Engler, *The Brotherhood of Oil, Energy, Policy and the Public Interest* (Chicago: University of Chicago Press, 1977), p. 62. Pauley was a very right-wing Democrat, and his "wealth and influence drew him into a number of party battles, particularly in California in the preparations for the 1960 National Convention in Los Angeles. He was a conservative who supported Lyndon B. Johnson when the trend was toward John F. Kennedy." Like most of the minority of oil men who worked through the Democrats, Pauley most definitely preferred a Texas oil man to an Eastern liberal. Saxon, "Edwin Wendell Pauley Sr., 78." It didn't make any difference. Even the victor took him on board when he defeated Nixon in the 1960 ballot. Pauley "later served as a consultant on petroleum policy to Presidents Kennedy and Johnson." Podell (ed.), *The Annual Obituary 1981*, p. 476.

63. Confidential interviews, former agents, OPC; former agents and officers, CIA; former officer, MIS.
64. "Bush was an Easterner, with what some would have called a patrician background, but he was not entirely atypical. There was a noble tradition of Easterners coming to seek their fortunes in Texas oil . . . continuing through what *Fortune* magazine once called the 'swarm of young Ivy Leaguers' who, Bush among them, in the post World War II years had 'descended on an isolated west Texas oil town'—Midland—'and created a most unlikely outpost of the working rich' as well as 'a union between the cactus and the Ivy.' " Yergin, *The Prize,* p. 753.
65. Bush with Gold, *Looking Forward,* p. 65.
66. "The Mexican Connection of George Bush," *Barron's,* September 19, 1988, p. 8.
67. Confidential interviews, former agents, OPC; former agents and officers, CIA; former officer, MIS.
68. Serrano, it should be noted, was the Mexican representative of Dresser Industries, a close friend of Mexico's president, later head of Pemex, and then Mexican ambassador to the Soviet Union. Until he was convicted of embezzlement from the oil industry, Diaz Serrano was slated to become president of Mexico himself. "The Mexican Connection of George Bush," *Barron's,* p. 8.
69. According to Diaz Serrano: " 'It was mighty generous of Bush to sell us the rig, because we were taking his place,' he states. 'We replaced Zapata.'

    "There is no evidence that Zapata shareholders were ever told about Bush's apparent generosity. Instead, Bush, in the signed President's letter printed in Zapata's 1964 annual report, announced that the Nola 1 was sold 'to a subsidiary of a Mexican drilling company' (not identified) . . . because it had become a 'marginal operation.' " Ibid.
70. Ibid.
71. Confidential interviews, former agents and officers, CIA.
72. Ibid.
73. Researcher interviews with Fletcher Prouty, 1987–1988. While Colonel Prouty's credibility suffered greatly because of his consultancy on Oliver Stone's film *JFK,* his recollections about the CIA supply mission have been confirmed by other sources.
74. Joseph McBride, "The Man Who Wasn't There," *The Nation,* July 16–23, 1988.
75. "Last week, however, C.I.A. spokeswoman Sharon Basso told the Associated Press that, yes, there had been a George *William* Bush in the agency, who was apparently not the George H. W. Bush who is running for the President. The other George, she said, left the C.I.A. in 1964 to join the Defense Intelligence Agency, and his present whereabouts are unknown." *The Nation,* July 30–August 6, 1988.
76. In fact, George William Bush had only just arrived in the CIA as a lowly GS-5 analyst of coastlines in 1963. He studied maps and documents and never attended interagency meetings. *The Nation,* August 13–20, 1988.
77. Confidential interviews, former agents, OPC; former agents and officers, CIA; former officer, MIS.
78. George de Mohrenschildt had worked the Mexican oil connection for the Nazis before defecting to Allied intelligence at the beginning of World War II. His father, under the name of von Mohrenschildt, was the manager of the Nobel Oil Fields in Russia before the Bolshevik Revolution and, according to our source, was one of Dulles's recruits from the Nazi intelligence services. Confidential interview, former agent, OPC.
79. Researcher and journalist Peggy Robohm discovered a copy of de Mohrenschildt's notebook in the Kennedy Assassination Archives and sent a copy to the one of the authors. Bush's entry in the address book was later crossed out and written above it appears a barely legible entry "Wash. Col. Howard L. Bush w d.c. 5-9008." An arrow drawn to "Col. Bush" lists his office address as the RCA building, 1725 K Street North West, Washington, 20000. Because the writing is hard to decipher, it

is unclear whether the name is Bush or Bussu. Perhaps it is only a coincidence, but that address was also the home of one of Dulles's Office of Policy Coordination branches. It also should be noted that Bush inherited the nickname "Poppy" from his grandfather, but in his autobiography, he claimed that the nickname didn't stick. Bush with Gold, *Looking Forward,* p. 28. The nickname did, however, follow him as far as de Mohrenschildt's address book, many years later in the 1960s.

80. After the listing for George "Poppy" Bush, the very next page of de Mohrenschildt's book lists another CIA agent, "Buckley, W.F." Next to one of de Mohrenschildt's entries, "Amer. Sec. Bldg, Washington 5 D.C." appears the handwritten entry: "Em. Cia tel: 34203." Although there were several emergency telephone lines for the CIA at the time, we have not been able to confirm that this was one of them. Still, the number of CIA connections is intriguing.
81. Confidential interviews, former agents, CIA.
82. Bush with Gold, *Looking Forward,* pp. 88, 90–91.
83. Confidential letter, congressional staffer, enclosing undated article from *The Realist.*
84. Bush with Gold, *Looking Forward,* pp. 120–121.
85. In "setting up the Council, Pasztor went to various collaborationist and fascist-minded émigré groups and asked them to form GOP federations. It eventually became clear that it wasn't an accident or a fluke that people with Nazi associations were in the Republican Heritage Groups Council. In some cases more mainstream ethnic organizations were passed over in favor of smaller but more extremist groups. And it seems clear that the Republican National Committee knows with whom they are dealing." Russ Bellant, "Old Nazis, the New Right and the Reagan Administration: The Role of Domestic Fascist Networks in the Republican Party and Their Effect on U.S. Cold War Politics," Political Research Associates, Cambridge, MA, September, 1988, pp. 15–16.
86. Ibid.
87. Confidential interviews, former agents, CIA; former analyst, Defense Intelligence Agency, former White House staffer. On the other hand, several senior CIA agents say that Bush's greatest value to Nixon was his unquestioning gullibility.
88. Charles Allen, Jr., "The Real Nazis Behind Every Bush," *The Village Voice,* November 1, 1988.
89. Letter from Australian Embassy, Washington, July 31, 1972.
90. Confidential interviews, former agents, CIA; former White House staffer.
91. Bush with Gold, *Looking Forward,* p. 122.
92. Reagan's name is listed among the Rockefeller Commission members, although he has claimed that he attended very few meetings. In the U.S. National Archives there is 1950s newsreel footage of a young Ronald Reagan asking for donations to the Crusade for Freedom. This organization was later acknowledged as a covert front for the distribution of funds to the OPC's network of émigré Fascists. See John Loftus, *The Belarus Secret* (New York: Alfred A. Knopf, 1982), pp. 107, 141. In essence, Reagan's public "Crusade" raised less than 1 percent of the funds; the rest came from CIA covert accounts that had been laundered through the State Department. The money was distributed to Radio Liberty, Radio Free Europe, and the "Institute of Russian Research" in Germany. All three organizations had Nazi war criminals on the payroll, as CBS' *60 Minutes* program documented in 1982. The covert funding was first exposed in the 1970s in the U.S. Senate and later acknowledged by the radios themselves. See, for example, Radio Liberty brochures and pamphlets on file at the Library of Congress.
93. As previously discussed, the CIA was using Pemex, the Mexican oil corporation, as cover for its operations. At the same time, Bush's business associate Ed Pauley was allegedly using Pemex as the secret bagman for the oil companies in funding Richard Nixon in all of his presidential campaigns, not just in 1972. In 1960, while working within his own party to defeat JFK and make Texas oil man LBJ the Demo-

cratic candidate, Pauley was secretly funding the Republican candidate. After serving with both Kennedy and Johnson as an oil adviser, ostensibly as a Democrat, Pauley again secretly funded Nixon in both 1968 and 1972. Confidential interviews, former agents, CIA; former White House staffer.

94. Bush himself did nothing illegal, but he may have learned from Pauley how campaign contributions could be laundered with the help of a few friendly foreign politicians. Pauley's slush fund for Nixon's campaigns was buried under a layer of Mexican corporations, some of which occasionally worked for the CIA. When the Senate began to investigate Nixon's campaign financing as part of the Watergate affair, Nixon tried to coerce the CIA into throwing a shroud of "national security" over the scandal. Confidential interviews, former agents, CIA; former White House staffer.
95. Confidential interviews, former agents, CIA.
96. Two members of Congress, Joshua Eilberg and Elizabeth Holtzman, had begun to ask embarrassing questions about the presence of Nazi war criminals in the United States.
97. Confidential interviews, former agents, CIA.
98. Ibid. One of the authors interviewed a CIA officer precisely on this point. She candidly admitted that the OPC files can be accessed only through project cryptonyms. The cross-index for individual names cannot be located. The CIA was extremely embarrassed to discover that several OPC agents had been known Nazi war criminals, several of whom were suspected as Communist double agents by Army counterintelligence. See, for example, Loftus, *The Belarus Secret,* pp. 93, 99–101, 112–115.
99. Confidential interviews, former agents, OPC; former agents, CIA.
100. Confidential interview, former U.S. intelligence agent. (Further identification withheld at request of source.)
101. Former U.S. intelligence agent, confidential letter to authors.
102. Confidential interviews, former members, CIA; former U.S. intelligence agent.
103. Former U.S. intelligence agent, confidential letter to authors, p. 3.
104. Confidential interview, former officer, CIA.
105. Confidential interview, former agent, CIA.
106. Confidential interview, former officer and agent, CIA.
107. Former U.S. intelligence agent, confidential letter to authors.
108. Ibid.
109. Confidential interviews, former agents, CIC; former agents, CIA; former U.S. intelligence agent.
110. To be fair, the FBI had jurisdiction over the hijack investigation, although the CIA was requested to provide intelligence support. Confidential interviews, former agents, CIA. According to a former FBI special agent, the Bureau's Croatian files make very interesting reading. The FBI agreed to let the Croatians distribute propaganda leaflets in return for leaving the passengers behind in the United States. The terrorists were arrested in Europe.
111. Interview with Elizabeth Holtzmann.
112. CIA correspondence to House Judiciary Committee, Subcommittee on Immigration and Naturalization.
113. Confidential interviews, former officers, CIA.
114. Christopher Simpson, *Blowback: America's Recruitment of Nazis and Its Effects on the Cold War* (New York: Weidenfeld & Nicholson, 1988), pp. 282–283.
115. Kasmovich's correspondence from his World Anti-Communist League period was provided to the authors by a donor who wishes to remain anonymous.
116. Confidential interview, former agent, CIA.

CHAPTER 17
REHEARSAL IN ANGOLA

1. Confidential interviews, former agents and officers, CIA; former analysts, DIA; former officers, U.S. Army, U.S. Air Force; employees and officers, the NSA; former U.S. intelligence agent. (Further identification withheld at request of source.)
2. Confidential interview, former U.S. Air Force intelligence officer.
3. Confidential interviews, former agents and officers, CIA; former analysts, DIA; former officers, U.S. Army, U.S. Air Force; employees and officers, the NSA; former U.S. intelligence agent. (Further identification withheld at request of source.)
4. Ibid.
5. Confidential interviews, members of American-Jewish lobbying organizations.
6. Confidential interviews, members of Israeli intelligence; former officers, Israeli military intelligence; members, Israeli political parties.
7. Mrs. Robohm received the documents from a member of the Aspin family who found them after Leslie's death.
8. Leslie Aspin with Trevor Aspinall, *I, Kovaks* (London: Everest Books, 1975), frontispiece.
9. Often "restless ex-SAS men join one of a plethora of security firms which provide bodyguards, training units or mercenaries. The mercenary business is often misinterpreted as a purely commercial exercise, albeit rather seedy. In fact it is subject to relatively tight political scrutiny and operations which run contrary to [British] foreign policy are blocked. Some initiatives are discreetly promoted by Whitehall because, in the event of some mishap, they are completely deniable." Jonathan Bloch and Patrick Fitzgerald, *British Intelligence and Covert Action* (London: Junction Books, 1983), p. 46.
10. Interviews with Aspin family members and former business associates. Leslie's view of these events appears in his autobiography, *I, Kovacks.*
11. For details on the Assad brothers, see Daniel Pipes, *Greater Syria. The History of Ambition* (Oxford: Oxford University Press, 1990), and *Who's Who in the Arab World* (Beirut and London: Publitec and Bowker, 1987).
12. Confidential interviews, former agents and officers, CIA; former analysts, DIA; former Aspin family members and business associates. Leslie's view of these events appears in his autobiography, *I, Kovacks.*
13. Aspin with Aspinall, *I, Kovacks,* pp. 25–26.
14. Ibid., pp. 90–105.
15. Ibid., p. 90.
16. Ibid., p. 104.
17. "The guy then came back with an offer I couldn't refuse, so to speak. He said: 'Well, Leslie, much as I hate saying this, we think that having your help is so important that we are prepared to blackmail you.' " Ibid., p. 106.
18. According to Aspin's biography, he told the British about the "key names in my dealings with the Arabs over the past year. I told him of the [Libyan] Colonel and his side-kick Major and gave him the addresses and telephone numbers for the pair and their associates throughout Europe. I gave him details on . . . the [Swiss] Bank and its managers and of the Irishmen I had helped into Libya. I also gave him the names of skippers and boats I knew to be involved with shipping Arab arms throughout Europe." Ibid., p. 107.
19. Ibid., pp. 109–111.
20. "His first success was to learn of the *Claudia* arms shipment from Libya for the Provisonals. Aspin contacted 'Homer', and an air and sea watch was mounted to chart the progress of the *Claudia* from Tripoli to the Irish Republic. When the boat reached Irish territorial waters, Irish security officers seized the boat, but only after

most of its cargo had been jettisoned." Bloch and Fitzgerald, *British Intelligence and Covert Action,* pp. 222–223.

21. Here is an account of Aspin's very next operation: "After a series of meetings between Malta, Amsterdam, and Dublin, Aspin arranged the shipment of six Soviet rocket launchers and seven tons of automatic weapons. The *Sea Fox* picked up the consignment from Malta. . . . Through 'Homer,' the Irish security forces were informed and a patrol boat prepared to intercept the *Sea Fox* before the exchange was made. The patrol boat missed the incoming vessel, and by the time it was found, the greater part of the consignment was in the possession of the fishing boats. As before, Aspin was not affected by the mishap: he was paid by both MI6 and in a commission from the Libyan dealer." Ibid., p. 223.
22. Aspin with Aspinall, *I, Kovacks,* pp. 146–147.
23. The father's drug-smuggling career began in 1946, the year the British and French armies pulled out of Syria. From the little town of Yabroud, just across the Lebanese border, Mohammed smuggled hashish out of the Bekaa Valley to Damascus. Manfred Morstein, *The Godfather of Terror: The Murderous Link Between Terrorism, Drugs and Arms Dealing* (LN016-91). Page citations are given to a U.S. government translation from the German manuscript, in this case p. 28. The book was published in Germany circa 1989–90 and translated by the U.S. government in 1991. A copy of the translated manuscript was provided by a source who wishes to remain anonymous. The Morstein book is by far the best reference for the history of the Al-Kassar family.
24. Ibid., pp. 16–29.
25. Ibid., p. 29.
26. Ibid. The British increased their surveillance on the boys' father, who seemed to have prepared the groundwork in each country. As a Syrian diplomat, Mohammed had traveled to Canada, England, Italy, and Austria before becoming ambassador to India in 1970. The Indian authorities were tipped off and discovered 100 kilograms of hashish in the diplomat's luggage. The incident was quietly hushed up. Ibid., pp. 29–30.
27. Confidential interviews, former agents, a Western intelligence service.
28. Morstein, *The Godfather of Terror,* pp. 30–31.
29. Confidential interviews, members of Aspin family and former business associates; former agents, a Western intelligence service.
30. Confidential interviews, former agents, a Western intelligence service.
31. Ibid.
32. Aspin with Aspinall, *I, Kovaks,* pp. 222–228.
33. This assassination was aimed at Kenneth Littlejohn, a rogue agent provocateur for MI6 who was beginning to talk to the press about some of "Homer's" dirty tricks, such as robbing Irish banks and blaming it on the IRA. See discussion of Littlejohn in Bloch and Fitzgerald, *British Intelligence and Covert Intelligence,* pp. 37, 40, 217–220; 222–225 and in Aspin with Aspinall, *I, Kovaks,* pp. 229–234.
34. Aspin, *I, Kovaks,* pp. 236–239.
35. Ibid., pp. 169–171.
36. Since the narcotics were going to New York rather than London, MI6 could not have cared less, as it was only American kids who were taking the drugs. American readers will probably be shocked that the British government would permit its own agent, Monzer Al-Kassar, to smuggle heroin to the United States, but that was nothing when compared to the terrorist operations hidden from the Americans. According to Aspin, hiding information from its American ally is one of the hallmarks of British intelligence. Confidential interviews, family members and former Aspin associates.
37. Aspin with Aspinall, *I, Kovacks,* pp. 180–181.
38. The particular arms shipment involved the *Claudia,* while the provocateur was Littlejohn. Ibid., pp. 237–239.

39. Ibid., p. 239.
40. Confidential interviews, former agents, CIA; former agents, a Western intelligence service.
41. Confidential interviews, members of Aspin family and former business associates.
42. Confidential interviews, former agents, CIA; former agents, a Western intelligence service.
43. Ibid.
44. John Stockwell, *In Search of Enemies: A CIA Story* (New York: Norton, 1978), p. 21.
45. Ibid., pp. 19–23.
46. Stockwell recalls the debate: "Mercenaries seemed to be the answer, preferably Europeans with the requisite military skills and perhaps experience in Africa. As long as they were not Americans, the 40 Committee approved. We began an exhaustive search for suitable candidates, a search which brought me into conflict with my bosses and kept me at odds with them even into March 1976, months after the Senate had ordered a halt to the Angola program. The conduct of European and South African mercenaries in previous African civil wars had left them with a murderous reputation, and the use of white mercenaries at the crest of the era of black nationalism was a blunder, I felt, which could only damage United States credibility in the Third World." Ibid., p. 182.
47. Confidential interviews, former members, CIA; former members, a Western intelligence service.
48. According to Stockwell, the British, who had the largest source of non-American mercenaries, refused to help. Stockwell, *In Search of Enemies,* p. 182. What the liberal Stockwell did not know was that his own superiors in the CIA were keeping him in the dark. According to an Irish history, published after Stockwell's: "Britain became involved in the war around this time because American support was meeting with opposition from Congress. . . . Washington made at least two formal approaches to the Foreign Office via the CIA's London station. They desperately wanted the British to send rockets, which from America would have required the acquiescence of Congress." Bloch and Fitzgerald, *British Intelligence and Covert Action,* p. 192. "Mercenaries are preferred if the British government wishes to support an insurgency, for it is sensitive to allegations of subversion and careful to preserve its international reputation." Ibid., p. 46.
49. Ibid., p. 50.
50. Confidential interviews, former agents, CIA; former agents, a Western intelligence service. See also Bloch and Fitzgerald, *British Intelligence and Covert Action* pp. 189–195 (naming British agents in Angola), and compare it with Morstein's account of Al-Kassar's associates.
51. Shortly after Bush was installed at the CIA, Stockwell was told that the whole thing had been organized by one of the rebel leaders, the FNLA's Holden Roberto: "a mercenary force of about 150 British and Americans was being assembled by Roberto himself. No memos were written about this program at CIA headquarters and no cables went out approving it. Since it overlapped extensively with our other activities, we became increasingly concerned at headquarters. . . . Two Englishmen . . . had been recruiting for Roberto in England. . . . In January, over one hundred Englishmen were fighting for the FNLA in northern Angola. Their quality was exceptionally low, some had no previous military training. In two cases London street sweepers were recruited directly from their jobs and dispatched to Angola. . . . Were the mercenaries on the CIA payroll? . . . it was confirmed that the Englishmen were being paid new hundred-dollar bills, just like those we were using to fund Roberto." Stockwell, *In Search of Enemies,* pp. 223–224.
52. Confidential interviews, former members, CIA; former members, a Western intelligence service.
53. Bloch and Fitzgerald, *British Intelligence and Covert Action,* p. 223.

54. "The CIA received the go-ahead from the British government to recruit mercenaries for the FNLA with American and Zairean money. . . . The main recruiter was John Banks, who had served a spell with the Parachute Regiment which ended with a dishonourable discharge. Using a firm named Security Advisory Services as a front, he recruited a total of 120 mercenaries. Their departure was heavily publicized and badly organized. Of the second group of twenty, which left Heathrow in January 1976, eleven were without passports or on bail." Ibid., p. 194.
55. Ibid., pp. 194–195.
56. "On February 11 the CIA spokesman promised Savimbi another million dollars in arms and money. On February 8, 1976, Secretary Kissinger sent the American chargé in Kinshasa a cable, instructing him to tell UNITA leaders that the United States would continue to support UNITA as long as it demonstrated the capacity for effective resistance. . . . In his last meeting with a CIA officer, on February 1, 1976, Savimbi vowed never to leave the Angolan Bush alive." Stockwell, *In Search of Enemies,* p. 235.
57. Confidential interviews, members of Aspin family and associates.
58. Confidential interviews, former members, CIA.
59. The South African mercenaries "continued to support the movement which now claims armed forces of 15,000. 1,200 of the FNLA guerrillas were regrouped into the South African army's '32 Battalion' with mercenary officers and instructors. Western governments have supported such plans but have been careful to avoid direct involvement, especially in America where a statute known as the Clark Amendment prohibits aid to Angolan opposition movements. A British army officer attended a series of meetings held in the last two months of 1977 in Western European capitals at which further mercenary recruiting was discussed. Among the other participants were . . . an executive from an unidentified oil company." Bloch and Fitzgerald, *British Intelligence and Covert Action,* p. 195.
60. Confidential interviews, former members, CIA; former members, a Western intelligence service.
61. Ibid.
62. Ibid.
63. Ibid.
64. The fishing boats, for example, carried radiation counters to detect the presence of nuclear weapons on Soviet ships. Confidential interview, former employee, the NSA.
65. Joseph C. Goulden, *The Death Merchants* (New York: Simon & Schuster, 1984), p. 57.
66. "The West treated Quaddafi with wary respect in his first years. The United States accepted his expulsion of the American and British military as inevitable acts of a Third World strongman. The oil companies, which were not unaccustomed to strange bedfellows, continued to do business with the new revolutionary government, even as they were shoved into an increasingly narrower corner. . . . The United States' great fear was that Libya would cut the flow of its oil to Western Europe. Henry Kissinger, President Nixon's national security adviser, quoted in his memoirs a governmental memorandum which summarized the administration's decision that the only choice was to 'try to get along with Quaddafi.' " Ibid., p. 89.
67. Bloch and Fitzgerald, *British Intelligence and Covert Action,* pp. 48–49.
68. "The Central Intelligence Agency, encouraged by Quaddafi's anti-Communist and anti-Soviet stance, warned him of several coup attempts by domestic foes." Goulden, *The Death Merchants,* p. 89.
69. Ibid., p. 135.
70. "Report of the Congressional Committees Investigating the Iran-Contra Affair," Appendix B, vol. 13, Depositions of Albert Hakim, p. 56.
71. Confidential interviews, former business associates of Aspin. Correspondence with one of GIA's bankers was found among Aspin's papers after his death.

72. "Report of the Congressional Committees Investigating the Iran-Contra Affair," p. 332 et seq.
73. Pizzo, Fricker, and Muolo, *Inside Job*, McGraw-Hill, New York, p. 89; Confidential letter, congressional staffer, enclosing undated articles from *The Kansas City Star*.
74. Hakim fired Wilson in 1976, which coincidentally was the year that Admiral Inman fired Wilson.
75. Confidential interviews, former agents, CIA; former congressional staffer.
76. Ibid.
77. Ibid.
78. "Admiral Bobby Ray Inman, who reviewed the 1976 investigation five years later when he became deputy director of Central Intelligence, [said] 'It's hard to dignify what happened with the word "investigation." The people running it seemed more interested in drawing the wagons in a tight circle . . . than in getting at the truth. I found it all most disquieting.' For one thing, Inman noted, the probe relied almost entirely on personal interviews. 'Little or no attempt was made to try and put together supporting documentary evidence.' " Goulden, *The Death Merchants*, p. 137.
79. Confidential interviews, former members, CIA; former members, a Western intelligence service.
80. The contents of this report were described to the authors by a source who wishes to remain anonymous.
81. Peggy Robohm, "Hakim's Connection," *Covert Action* No. 30, Summer 1988, pp. 35–37.
82. Confidential interviews, former officer and members, CIA; former members, a Western intelligence service.
83. As a young movie actor in the early 1950s, Reagan was employed as the public spokesperson for an OPC front named the "Crusade for Freedom." Reagan may not have known it, but 99 percent of the Crusade's funds came from clandestine accounts, which were then laundered through the Crusade to various organizations such as Radio Liberty, which employed Dulles's Fascists. Bill Casey, who later became CIA director under Ronald Reagan, also worked in Germany after World War II on Dulles's Nazi "freedom fighters" program. When he returned to New York Casey headed up another OPC front, the International Rescue Committee, which sponsored the immigration of these Fascists to the United States. Casey's committee replaced the International Red Cross as the sponsor for Dulles's recruits. Confidental interviews, former members, OPC; former members, British Foreign and Commonwealth Office.
84. Confidential interviews, former agents, CIA; former members, a Western intelligence service.
85. Ibid.
86. Ibid.
87. One of Nugan-Hand's con men fleeced Aramco and Bechtel employees of hundreds of thousands, perhaps millions of dollars. See Jonathan Kwitney, *The Crimes of Patriots* (New York: Touchstone, 1988), pp. 261–271.
88. "In yet another coincidence, Nugan Hand and BCCI used the same law firm in the Cayman Islands: Bruce Campbell & Company. The firm acted as the registered agent for Nugan Hand. In 1976, it set up BCCI's most secretive unit: International Credit & Investment Company, Ltd. (ICIC). Bruce Campbell, which shared the same office building as ICIC, also organized and managed several other corporate entities related to BCCI." Peter Truell and Larry Gurwin, *False Profits* (New York: Houghton Mifflin, 1992), p. 125.
89. Confidential interviews, former agents, CIA; former members, a Western intelligence service.
90. Ibid.
91. Ibid.

92. Ibid.
93. Ibid.
94. Arnold Fine, "Maybe This Is Why George Bush Is So Pro-Arab," *The Jewish Press*, March 6, 1992. That items such as this were Israeli-inspired was confirmed in confidential interviews with a former Israeli military attaché and former members of Israeli intelligence.
95. Truell and Gurwin, *False Profits*, p. 123.
96. Confidential interviews, former agents, CIA; former members, a Western intelligence service.
97. Truell and Gurwin, *False Profits*, p. 120 et seq.
98. Bloch and Fitzgerald, *British Intelligence and Covert Action*, pp. 135–138.
99. "The British . . . advised the Saudis on internal security during the early 1960s. A former British intelligence officer who lived in Jiddah . . . spoke frequently with Adham. . . . Saudi-British relations were marred by periodic disputes over the border between Saudi Arabia and Abu Dhabi, a British protectorate. Nevertheless, Adham was well connected in Britain. One of his friends was Julian Amery, a Conservative member of Parliament who served for a time as minister of air. Amery . . . later supplemented his salary by acting as a paid adviser to BCCI." Truell and Gurwin, *False Profits*, p. 120.
100. The "CIA strengthened its relationships with so-called friendly Arab intelligence agencies. One of the most important of these was Saudi Arabia's intelligence service, run by Kamal Adham, Prince Turki, and Abdul-Raouf Khalil, all of whom were BCCI insiders." Ibid., p. 130.
101. "That interest should not have come as a surprise. Bush's Zapata Oil had won the contract in the mid-1960s to build Kuwait's first offshore oil rig, and Bush himself was at ease with Arab businessmen. 'He understood that part of the world very well,' one Bush friend notes simply." Mark Perry, *Eclipse: The Last Days of the CIA*, p. 139.
102. "Also included in Bush's [1976] requests was a top secret signals project that called for the construction of four overseas ground stations to intercept foreign communications. Bush's interest in high-tech spying later paid huge dividends, agency officials say." Ibid. Our sources say that the "dividend" pun was not an intentional allusion to the BCCI's commercial intelligence. Most of the CIA had no idea that British agents were using an American listening post in the Gulf to tap an Arab bank. Confidential interviews, former officers and agents, CIA; former employees, the NSA.
103. Ibid.
104. Truell and Gurwin, *False Profits*, pp. 128–129.
105. Confidential interviews, former officers and agents, CIA; former employees, the NSA.
106. The beret is still in the possession of the Aspin family in England, along with copies of his Special Forces orders.
107. "Dear Mr. Aspin,

    We are pleased to inform you that you have been tentatively selected for a position with us on a contractual basis and we have now initiated the processing of your application.

    A firm offer of employment can be made only after the satisfactory completion of intensive background investigations. . . . As you can well understand, this is a confidential transaction, and we would appreciate your telling no one other than your spouse of our interest in you."

    Letter from R. S. Wattles, CIA Director of Personnel, April 25, 1978, to Leslie Aspin, copy in authors' possession.
108. Confidential interviews, Aspin family members.

109. Ibid.
110. The photos are in the possession of the Aspin family.
111. This man was Gaith Pharaon. Truell and Gurwin, *False Profits,* p. 131*n*.
112. One example of what Leslie was up to in the late 1970s is contained in a letter from Colonel Ralph Warren, of Ralph Warren & Partners, dated June 20, 1978, found in Leslie's files. The letter is addressed to Transworld Commodities in Georgetown, Grand Cayman in the British West Indies, and is an order for "20,000 rounds British .303 ball ammunition post 1970 manufacture at $142 per 1000 rounds." Warren said that he was purchasing the ammunition "on behalf of the Crown Agents who will be responsible for all export and licensing arrangements," that it was destined "for the Royal Swaziland Police" and would be routed through Durban in South Africa.
113. Confidential interviews, Aspin family members.
114. According to Aspin's relatives, Leslie and his brother were involved with several hostage release negotiations as well as South African and Thai arms deals. Confidential interviews, Aspin family members.
115. Confidential interviews, U.S. government officials with access to BCCI archives.
116. National Security Archive, *The Chronology* (New York: Warner, 1987), p. 1.
117. Confidential interviews, former agents, CIA.
118. Ibid.
119. Confidential interviews, former members, a Western intelligence service.
120. Confidential interviews, U.S. government source with access to BCCI archives; Aspin family members.
121. Ibid.
122. Interview with Michael Aspin; confidential interviews, former members of a Western intelligence service.
123. Undated press clippings provided by Michael Aspin.
124. Confidential interviews, former members, a Western intelligence service.
125. For a discussion of the Interpol conference, see Morstein, *Godfather of Terror.*

CHAPTER 18
THE IRAN–CONTRA DEBACLE

1. Confidential interview, former Israeli officer.
2. Confidential interview, former U.S. Army chemical warfare officer. According to this source, the U.S. government had protested to the Germans for ten years about the sales, to no avail.
3. Confidential interviews, former agents, CIA; former officers, U.S. Army; U.S. State Department analysts; members of Israeli intelligence.
4. Confidential interview, former officer, CIA. In 1992 an American contractor publicly confirmed that he had obtained the Osirak construction blueprints and passed them to the Israelis.
5. Confidential interviews, former agents, CIA; former officers, U.S. Army; U.S. State Department analysts; members, Israeli intelligence.
6. Confidential interview, former officers, CIA; former naval investigators.
7. Confidential interviews, former agents, CIA; former officers, U.S. Army; U.S. State Department analysts; members of Israeli intelligence.
8. Confidential interview, U.S. military security officer with access to Pollard investigative files.
9. Many of our American sources are staunch Republicans, politically conservative, and have spent their entire careers in the intelligence community. They include military officers, civilian analysts, and professional agents from the DIA, CIA, and FBI. Most of them were excluded from Bush's covert planning and were greatly disappointed when they began postmortem investigations of the Iran-Contra debacle.

10. Confidential interviews, U.S. Army officers specializing in hostage rescue.
11. Miles Copeland, *The Game Player: Confessions of the CIA's Original Political Operative* (London: Aurum, 1989), p. 256.
12. Confidential interviews, U.S. Army officers specializing in hostage rescue.
13. Confidential letter, former congressional staffer, enclosing undated news clipping.
14. Ibid.
15. Confidential interviews, former members, Israeli intelligence.
16. Ibid.
17. Confidential interviews, U.S. Army officers specializing in hostage rescue.
18. See the discussion of the Bush-British connection in Chapter 19.
19. See Manfred Morstein, *Godfather of Terror: The Murderous Link Between Terrorism, Drugs, and Arms Dealing* (U.S. government translation), for citations to Interpol records on Monzer's terrorist activities, pp. 60–85.
20. Confidential interviews, former members, a Western intelligence service.
21. Confidential interviews, former members, CIA; former members, a Western intelligence service.
22. Confidential interviews, former officers, U.S. Army.
23. Confidential interviews, former White House staffer; former members, CIA.
24. Letter of Miles Copeland, July 22, 1987, from CIA Political Action files, copy provided by a source who wishes to remain anonymous.
25. Ibid.
26. Memorandum of William P. Clark, May 14, 1982, The White House, Top Secret, p. 1, declassified version provided by a congressional staffer.
27. Confidential interviews, former White House staffer; former members, CIA.
28. Memorandum of William P. Clark, p. 2.
29. Oliver North, CNN *Crossfire,* November 1991.
30. Confidential interviews, former White House staffer; former members, CIA.
31. Copy of Shultz's memo and Reagan's response provided by a congressional staffer.
32. Confidential interviews, former White House staffer; former members, CIA.
33. Ibid.
34. Confidential interviews, former members, a Western intelligence service.
35. "CSF holds its bank account at the Republic National Bank in New York. Edmund Safra, known for his extensive Saudi and other Middle East ties, is the president of Republic. The majority of CSF Investments Ltd. Bermuda stock is owned by CSF (Compagnie de Services Fiduciaries) S.A. with offices in Geneva." National Security Archive, *The Chronology* (New York: Warner, 1987), p. 15.
36. Ibid, p. 16.
37. Confidential interviews, Aspin family members and business associates; former members, CIA; former members, a Western intelligence service.
38. Ibid.
39. Unedited transcript, Aspin statement, copy in authors' possession.
40. Confidential interviews, Aspin family members and business associates; former members, CIA; former members, a Western intelligence service.
41. Ibid.
42. Interview with Vince Cannistraro; confidential interviews, former White House staffer; former U.S. military specialists in hostage rescue.
43. Confidential interviews, former members, CIA; former U.S. military specialists in hostage rescue.
44. Ibid. Confidential interviews, Aspin family members and former business associates.
45. Leslie Aspin, second statement to barristers, copy in authors' possession.
46. McMahon reprimanded North "for proposing in a classified document that Reagan authorize planning to 'neutralize' terrorists. North's recommendation comes at a time when the Administration is putting together a pro-active policy against terror-

ism in the wake of the bombing of the Marine barracks in Beirut in October 1983. The outburst reflects sharp differences within the bureaucracy over the new policy. It is unclear whether North's wording is ever changed as a result of McMahon's objections, but officials report later that the final directive clearly states that the President does not condone assassination as part of the program." National Security Archive, *The Chronology*, p. 48.

47. Ibid., p. 42.
48. Testimony of Lt. Col. Robert Earl, Appendix B, Depositions, taken by congressional Iran-Contra investigators.
49. ABC news report, quoted in National Security Archive, *The Chronology*, p. 31.
50. Ibid.
51. Unedited transcript, Aspin statement, copy in authors' possession.
52. "The North Diary," pp. AMX002021, AMX002065, AMX002067, AMX002069, AMX002076.
53. Ibid., pp. AMX00288, AMX00296, AMX002101–2103.
54. Ibid., pp. AMX00212, AMX002116, AMX002138.
55. Ibid., p. AMX002140.
56. National Security Archive, *The Chronology*, p. 54.
57. "The North Diary," pp. AMX00215, AMX002133, AMX002153.
58. Ibid., p. AMX002154.
59. A U.S. "team had been deployed to Beirut, we were told. Ambassador Bartholomew has been alerted directly by the NSC and would assist." National Security Archive, *The Chronology*, p. 153.
60. Confidential interviews, former members, CIA; former U.S. military specialists in hostage rescue.
61. "The North Diary," p. AMX002156.
62. Ibid., pp. AMX002159–2162, AMX002130.
63. Ibid., p. AMX002209.
64. Ibid., pp. AMX002209–2211.
65. Ibid., p. AMX002211.
66. Ibid.
67. Ibid.
68. Ibid., p. AMX002212.
69. Ibid., p. AMX002214.
70. Ibid.
71. Ibid., p. AMX002230–2232.
72. See the discussion of Buckley's work for Bush in Angola in Chapter 17.
73. Confidential interviews, former members, a Western intelligence service.
74. Ibid.
75. Telephone interview, Michael Aspin.
76. W. H. Jeffrey, Letter of April 27, 1979.
77. The phone book is in the custody of a member of Aspin's family.
78. Before his death, Leslie told several of his close associates that Ian Gow was his direct contact for the hostage deals. Confidential interviews, Aspin family members and former business associates.
79. There are numerous references to "Thatcher cables" in North's notebook as well as references to his meetings with British government agents.
80. Confidential interviews, former members, CIA; former U.S. military specialists in hostage rescue; former members, a Western intelligence service; Aspin family members and former business associates.
81. Ibid.
82. Ibid.
83. Hirtenberger Proforma Invoice No. 84/1834, dated 03-24-84.
84. Confidential interviews, former members, CIA; former U.S. military specialists in hostage rescue; former members, a Western intelligence service.

85. Hirtenberger Proforma Invoice.
86. "The Al-Kassars have been involved in the smuggling of arms and large amounts of narcotics for years. They are strongly suspected of being among the 'major international narcotics traffickers.'" Morstein, *The Godfather of Terror,* p. 48.
87. ". . . in March 1984, the CIA learned that Monzer Al-Kassar had contacted the Texas aircraft producer, Gates Learjet Corporation, Tucson Arizona . . . cost 1.8 million US dollars, according to the contract, 'payable upon delivery from Tucson. . . .'" Ibid.
88. Confidential interviews, former members, CIA; former U.S. military specialists in hostage rescue; former members, a Western intelligence service; Aspin family members and business associates.
89. The text of the telegram was as follows: "Several members of the Al Kassar family have been trying for several weeks via various embassies in the Near East to obtain entry visa for England. They are using passports in various names of different origin. As of this time the Al Kassars are in possession of travel documents of the People's Republic of North Yemen (diplomatic passports), Syrian 'Passeport Speciale' for members of the diplomatic corps, and Syrian travel documents for Palestinian refugees. The family has outstanding connections with high-level offices in the Syrian government and has presented diplomatic letters of reference from the Syrian Foreign Ministry and high-ranking military officers." Morstein, *The Godfather of Terror,* p. 47.
90. Ibid., p. 53, citing BKA report, June 20, 1986, pp. 2–8.
91. Hirtenberger Invoice, "on condition that End-User-Certificate of Greek Authorities . . . obtained."
92. Unedited transcript of Leslie Aspin's sworn statement to his British attorney, May 1, 1987, p. 3.
93. Confidential interviews, former members, Israeli intelligence.
94. Morstein, *The Godfather of Terror,* p. 49.
95. Ibid., p. 55.
96. Confidential interviews, former members, CIA; former U.S. military specialists in hostage rescue; former members, a Western intelligence service; Aspin family members and business associates.
97. Unedited transcript of Leslie Aspin's sworn statement to his British attorney, May 1, 1987, p. 7.
98. "The Astra pistols, caliber 7.65mm, No. A 0108, Model Falcon, seized in Greece strangely enough had no proof marks. As it turned out, they had been copied in the East Bloc. . . . The Ceska pistols found in Greece also came from the CSR [Czechoslovakian Socialist Republic]." Morstein, *The Godfather of Terror,* p. 55.
99. Confidential interviews, former members, CIA; former U.S. military specialists in hostage rescue; former members, a Western intelligence service; Aspin family members and business associates.
100. "The North Diary," p. AMX002257.
101. Ibid., p. AMX002259.
102. Ibid., pp. AMX002273–2275, censor codes A, B, E, F, S.
103. Ibid., pp. AMX002295, AMX00297, AMX002303.
104. Confidential interviews, former members, CIA; former U.S. military specialists in hostage rescue; former members, a Western intelligence service.
105. National Security Archive, *The Chronology,* p. 55.
106. Confidential interviews, former members, Israeli intelligence.
107. The Israeli supply of Communist weapons was part of an overall weapons procurement program called Operation Tipped Kettle. Confidential interviews, former members, CIA; former U.S. military specialists in hostage rescue.
108. McFarlane told Congress that "We were aware that . . . [the Contras] would in May 1984 find themselve without funds. For this reason, we asked the help of country

number one [Israel]. . . . I asked my interlocutor [David Kimche] if his country would be willing to supply the Contras with arms and training. He promised to find out. Not long afterwards he notified me that his country could not fulfill that request." Samuel Segev, *The Iron Triangle: The Untold Story of Israel's Role in the Iran-Contra Affair* (New York: Free Press, Macmillan, 1988), p. 150.

109. "Officials speculate that the U.S. may be trying to get Israel to take over covert support for the Contras, whose funding sources are nearly exhausted since CIA funding ended in March. Contra leaders say that they have been receiving Soviet-made arms from Israel, but Israel denies the charges. Intelligence sources say that the U.S. could repay Israel for its aid through defense aid and intelligence sharing, which CIA Director William Casey has greatly stepped up, for example, by giving Israel reconnaissance photos taken by U.S. spy satellites, which former Director Stansfield Turner, refused to do." National Security Archive, *The Chronology*, p. 56.
110. Confidential interviews, former members, Israeli intelligence.
111. "In a note to the National Security Adviser, Casey suggested telling Israel that, if the Contras succeeded in toppling the Sandinista regime, the new government would establish normal diplomatic ties with Israel and end Nicaraguan support of the PLO. . . . He suggested that Israel supply the rebels with arms and military advisers, and emphasized that, should Israel again reject the request, it would cause the President great disappointment. Kimche's reply was negative again." Segev, *The Iron Triangle*, p. 150.
112. Confidential interviews, former members, CIA.
113. Ibid.
114. "The North Diary," p. AMX00264.
115. Testimony of General Secord, Appendix B, Depositions, Iran-Contra Investigation.
116. Hakim produced the bank records for payments to Al-Kassar. Testimony of Albert Hakim, Appendix B, Depositions, Iran-Contra Investigation.
117. The Soviet generals quickly confirmed that their Chinese rivals were pulling the same scam, selling to the Contras for dollars, paying with slave labor arms, and financing their own terrorist operations with the exchange difference.
118. Confidential interviews, former members, CIA; former U.S. military specialists in hostage rescue; former members, a Western intelligence service.
119. This insidious scheme was the brain child of Boris Ponamarev, the intelligence chief of the International Liaison division of the General Secretariat of the Communist party. Even Boris Yeltsin has yet to locate his files. Our sources say the GRU is sitting on them until the day they come back into power. Confidential interviews, former members, CIA; former members, a Western intelligence service.
120. Ibid.
121. Confidential interviews, former members, CIA; former U.S. military specialists in hostage rescue; former members, a Western intelligence service.
122. Ibid.
123. Confidential interviews, former members, a Western intelligence service.
124. Confidential interviews, former members, CIA; former U.S. military specialists in hostage rescue; former members, a Western intelligence service.
125. Ibid.
126. Confidential interview, former agent, CIA.
127. Morstein, *The Godfather of Terror.*
128. Confidential interview, congressional staffer.
129. "Syria, President Bush, and Drugs—The Administration's Next Irangate," Staff Report issued on November 23, 1992, by the Subcommittee on Crime and Criminal Justice of the Committee on the Judiciary, 102nd Congress, 2nd Session (Washington, D.C.: U.S. Government Printing Office, 1993).
130. Ibid., pp. 10–11.
131. Confidential interviews, former members, CIA; former U.S. military specialists in hostage rescue; former members, a Western intelligence service.

132. Ibid.
133. Confidential interviews, former members, CIA; former U.S. military specialists in hostage rescue.
134. "The North Diary," p. AMX002304–2305.
135. Confidential interviews, former members, CIA; former U.S. military specialists in hostage rescue.
136. Segev, *The Iron Triangle,* pp. 154–165, 305.
137. Confidential interviews, former members, CIA; former U.S. military specialists in hostage rescue.

CHAPTER 19
BUSH'S INNER SANCTUM

1. Confidential interviews, former members, CIA, DIA, and Military Intelligence; former members, Western intelligence services; former White House staffers.
2. Confidential interviews, former members, CIA; former Pentagon and White House staffers.
3. For an example of international reaction to the publication by the Special Prosecutor of sections of the Weinberger diaries, see M. R. Lehman, "Bush Done in by Iraqgate & Irangate", Allgemeiner Journal, Friday, November 13, 1992, p. B4. In addition to the 1,700 pages of Weinberger's diary, Secretary of State George Shultz dictated his own notes of top-level meetings with Reagan, Bush, and Weinberger. When Weinberger informed Reagan that the arms sales were illegal, the president replied "They can impeach me if they want: visiting days are Wednesday." Weinberger replied "you will not be alone." Malcolm Byrne & Peter Kornbluh, "Iran-Contra: The Press Indicts The Prosecutor," *Columbia Journalism Review,* March/April 1994, p. 44, col. 2. Weinberger, it should be noted, was investigated himself by the special prosecutor and then was pardoned by President George Bush. Shultz's comments on Bush's role were confirmed by confidential interviews, U.S. government employees. Further identification withheld at sources' request.
4. "Bush had been a key advocate for the CIA's Cambodian program in the White House. In 1982, he was one of William Casey's chief allies in convincing President Reagan of its worth. In many ways, when it came to his program, Bush's personal reputation was at stake." Mark Perry, *Eclipse: The Last Days of the CIA* (New York: William Morrow, 1992), pp. 143–147.
5. Ibid., p. 375.
6. Alan Friedman, *The Secret History of How the White House Armed Iraq* (New York: Bantam, 1993), pp. 24–34.
7. Confidential interviews, former White House staffer; congressional staffer; former members, CIA and DIA; U.S. military officers and employees; former members, a Western intelligence service.
8. Ibid.
9. Ibid.
10. Ibid.
11. North wrote that the anti-Israel bias "is the result of an ingrained streak of anti-Semitism in our government. Many mid-level officials—and not only at the State Department—are the sons and grandsons of the great elite American families, where a genteel, discreet anti-Jewish prejudice was often taken for granted. . . . I noticed a distinct anti-Israel bias in some circles." Oliver North, *Under Fire* (New York: Harper Paperbacks, 1992), p. 183.
12. Ibid., pp. 154–155.
13. "With the departure of George P. Shultz, who was nominated yesterday . . . as Secretary of State, Bechtel has lost two of its most senior executives to the Reagan Administration. . . . Mr. Shultz, president of the Bechtel Group Inc. . . . has been widely regarded as second in command of the San Francisco based company, be-

hind Bechtel's chairman, Stephen D. Bechtel. Secretary of Defense Caspar W. Weinberger had been Bechtel's general counsel until his appointment to the Reagan Cabinet. He, like Mr. Shultz, also served in a Cabinet post under President Nixon." *The New York Times,* June 25, 1982. In fact, Shultz had been Richard Nixon's Treasury secretary and the man who had offered George Bush a job after the 1972 election. Instead, Bush took President Nixon's offer and became chairman of the Republican National Committee. At the time Weinberger had served under Shultz in the Treasury Department. Bechtel played musical chairs with the White House. It had been going on for a long, long time. The history of Bechtel is, in many ways, a metaphor for the incestuous system established by the pirates of Wall Street way back in the 1920s. That Bechtel provided so many influential officials during the Reagan-Bush era is testimony to the endurance of the system. Laton McCartney, *Friends in High Places: The Bechtel Story* (New York: Ballantine, 1989), pp. 54, 72*n*, 73.

14. Ibid., pp. 175, 178.
15. "Established in 1948, by Saudi Arabia and the other members of the Arab League, in response to the partitioning of Palestine and the creation of Israel, the boycott prohibited Arabs from trading with Israel directly or from doing business with firms which themselves dealt with Israel or were owned or controlled by Jewish interests."

    "Until the middle 1970s, complying with the boycott had never caused Bechtel any notable trouble—nor had Bechtel ever complained about its discriminatory provisions. The company, in the words of its former personnel manager, 'ran deep with Aryan blood,' and according to its critics, just as deep with country-club-style antiSemitism. Steve senior, for one, habitually identified friends and associates who were Jewish—'he's a Jewish fellow, you know,' he would say, as if they required special categorization—while the company employed few Jews generally and even fewer in supervisory positions. Not wanting to offend Arab clients like Saudi King Faisal, who repeatedly harangued Steve senior about the alleged perfidy of 'Zionists,' the Bechtel Corporation had also resisted numerous invitations to do business in Israel. Its stated reason for doing so was Israel's 'unstable conditions'—a stricture that did not apply to countries like Libya." Ibid., pp. 183–184*n*, 186*n*.
16. This was exemplified by a 1974 contract with Egypt: "Bechtel International does not possess any plant, firm or branch in Israel . . . does not have any agreement for manufacturing, assembly, license or technical assistance with any firm or person or resident of Israel . . . has never participated in the boosting of Israeli products . . . does not use David's Star in connection with its products or trademark . . . has no board members [who are] members of the Joint American-Israeli Chamber of Commerce." Ibid., p. 185. Bechtel defended itself by issuing a press statement in which it pointed out that since 1965, the U.S. Army Corps of Engineers had operated in Saudi Arabia under the boycott's terms, a deal arranged by former U.S. ambassador to Saudi Arabia, Pete Hart, who later not only became a senior State Department officer but also Bechtel's representative to Saudi Arabia and North Africa. Ibid., pp. 188–190. While the details were being worked out, Steve Bechtel, Jr., and Shultz went to the Middle East "to secure the approval of the Arabs. They did not come away empty-handed. 'They urged the Arabs to ease the boycott restrictions,' said Aramco's former chairman Frank Jungers of their mission. 'And with the exception of Iraq and Syria, neither of which did any real trading with the West, most of the Arab League nations were agreeable to it. After all, they needed us as much as we needed them.' " Ibid., pp. 192–193.
17. Congress wanted to go even further and impose criminal penalties against companies and their executives who heeded the boycott, cutting off their tax credits, foreign tax deferrals, and export subsidies. It would have closed down most U.S. business in the Arab world. "Alarmed that antiboycott sentiment was getting out of hand, the administration dispatched Kissinger and [Treasury Secretary] Simon to

Capitol Hill to cool tempers and head off passage of either measure." Harking back to James Forrestal's propaganda, Kissinger "predicted that enactment of either measure would wreak incalculable harm on U.S. foreign relations and assist the Soviets in creating mischief in the area." Ibid., pp. 193–194.

18. "As far as the Bechtels were concerned, Connally had a number of things to recommend him, not least of them his position on the Middle East. Connally spelled out that position on October 13 [1979], a month before Reagan's declaration of candidacy, in a forceful speech at the National Press Club in Washington. Raising the specter of 'the economic upheaval that would ensue if the flow of Arab oil, the lifeblood of Western civilization for decades' were disrupted, Connally called on Israel to abandon the West Bank, return the strategic Golan Heights to Syria and give up its exclusive sovereignty to Jerusalem. The Bechtels, who had been lobbying in behalf of the Arabs for decades, were delighted—so much so that they hired the speech's ghostwriter, a former CIA analyst and National Security Council staffer named Samuel Hoskinson." Ibid., pp. 214–215.
19. "The incident that spelled Haig's downfall—his public anger at the White House's criticism of Israeli moves on Beirut—came as the climax of a long-simmering war between Haig and Caspar Weinberger over U.S. policy vis-à-vis the Middle East." Ibid., p. 221n.
20. "As it happened, Shultz also played a role in Haig's demise, when, in an effort to head off a threatened Haig trip to demonstrate U.S. support [for Israel], he recommended to the State Department the appointment of retired diplomat Philip Habib as a special presidential emissary. The fact that Habib, not Haig, went to Israel, was among the numerous straws that, for Haig, finally broke the camel's back. Shultz was gratified on two counts: not only did he win the government post he sought, but Philip Habib was, then as now, a consultant to Bechtel." Ibid., p. 221*n*. Like the oil companies, Bechtel had perfected the art of the Washington "revolving door." In addition to Nixon administration men such as Shultz and Weinberger, Bechtel had "also recruited others with experience at high levels of government. Richard Helms, a former director of Central Intelligence in the Nixon Administration, is employed by Bechtel as an outside consultant on the Middle East and international affairs. Bechtel's roster of consultants also includes Francis Jungers, a former chairman of the Arabian American Oil Company, who is also a consultant on Middle Eastern affairs." *The New York Times,* June 26, 1982.
21. Confidential interviews, former White House staffer; congressional staffer; former members, CIA and DIA; U.S. military officers and employees; former members, a Western intelligence service.
22. McCartney, *Friends in High Places,* pp. 222, 222–223*n*.
23. This project was the construction of the city of Jubail. *The New York Times,* June 26, 1982, and McCartney, *Friends in High Places,* pp. 12, 208.
24. "Israel's arguments about Iraqi intentions held sway in the State Department and the White House, but only because then-Secretary of State Alexander Haig pushed Israel's position. He persuaded Reagan to allow Israel to ship high-tech weapons to the Iranian port of Bandar Abbas, knowing full well that they would end up on the battlefield of the Iran-Iraq war. Haig's influence also was responsible for the United States' muted response to Israel's June 1981 strike at Iraq's nuclear reactor at Osirak." Perry, *Eclipse,* p. 379.
25. North "viewed Iraq as an unreconstructed terrorist state that would stop at nothing to humiliate the United States. North viewed Israel as a bulwark against Iraqi autocracy and extolled its virtues to anyone who would listen. His admiration for the Israelis was deepened by his close cooperation with them in planning a number of counter-terrorism initiatives. . . . By early 1982, as Iraq's military position deteriorated. . . . North's views on Iraq were ignored in the Reagan White House." Ibid., p. 378.

26. Confidential interviews, former members, CIA, DIA, and Military Intelligence agencies; former members, Western intelligence services; former White House staffers.
27. Ibid. See also Perry, *Eclipse,* pp. 375, 380–384.
28. "Bush knew about the covert operations, and Casey felt he could trust him, with his intelligence orientation and all that. . . . I attended meetings where Bush made it clear he wanted to help Iraq." Alan Friedman, *Spider's Web: The Secret History of How the White House Armed Iraq* (New York: Bantam, 1993), p. 25.
29. Ibid., pp. 5–7, 28–30, 106–107. Shultz shut down the poison gas project in 1989 after he returned to Bechtel from the Reagan administration. Ibid., pp. 117–118.
30. "When I left the White House, I had expected that of all the people who might have defended me from the absurd allegation that I had been off on my own, Bud was the most likely to step forward and say, 'That's ridiculous, Ollie always told me what he was doing. . . .'

    "But the Bud McFarlane who testified at the hearings, and again at my trial, was a different man from the one I thought I knew. . . . Bud's statements were so muddled and incoherent that the judge called the lawyers up to the bench. 'This man has told so many different stories since he has been on direct [examination],' said the judge, 'that there isn't any way to know what he believes or what he knows. He is an intensely unreliable witness in almost every aspect of his testimony.' Judge Gesell added, 'I'm not at all sure that it's intentional on his part.' " North, *Under Fire,* p. 225.
31. Confidential interviews, former members, CIA, DIA, and Military Intelligence agencies; former members, Western intelligence services; former White House staffers.
32. The story of the Reagan-Clinton meeting was spread by several White House sources who subsequently leaked it to the press. Confidential interviews, congressional staff.
33. "During one briefing Casey had vehemently argued that [terrorist bomb-maker Mohammed] Rashid should be kidnapped. . . . Casey became increasingly enraged by his inability to persuade key clandestine service officers to take extreme steps to deal with the 15 May [terrorist] Group. By early 1984 he had convinced himself that his assistants were more concerned with saving their own careers than with defending national security. . . . His face was beet red, and the veins on his neck stood out against his starched white collar. . . . Finally he mastered his anger and barked out a series of orders to his top aides . . . come up with a plan to kidnap Rashid." Perry, *Eclipse,* p. 43.
34. Ibid., p. 44.
35. Confidential interview, former agent, CIA.
36. Perry, *Eclipse,* p. 44.
37. Confidential interviews, former members, CIA, DIA, and Military Intelligence agencies, former members, Western intelligence services; former White House staffers.
38. See Chapter 18 for cites to North's diary on meetings with British intelligence.
39. Confidential interviews, former members, CIA; former members, Western intelligence services.
40. The Trading with the Enemy Act made it a felony to assist a Nazi in emigrating to America. It was still in force during the 1950s when Casey was running the International Rescue Committee in New York. Confidential interviews, former members of CIA, DIA, and Military Intelligence agencies, former members of Western intelligence services, former White House staffers.
41. "Casey announced that he had talked about the kidnapping [of Rashid] with . . . the French overseas intelligence service.

    "The CIA's leading counter-terrorism officers were horrified. . . . the French weren't as interested in kidnapping Rashid as they were in killing him. . . . This was going to be a tough and dangerous operation, the French said; you never knew what would happen—Rashid might even be accidentally shot. The trigger-happy

French appeared unconcerned by the trouble this might cause for the CIA, whose nightmare was that unnecessary gunplay could result in the death of innocent . . . citizens." Perry, *Eclipse*, p. 45.

42. Ibid.
43. Confidential interviews, former members, Western intelligence services.
44. National Security Archives, *The Chronology*, (New York: Warner, 1987), p. 409.
45. Unedited transcript of Leslie Aspin's sworn statement to his British attorney, May 1, 1987, p. 1.
46. Ibid., pp. 1–6.
47. Ibid., p. 1.
48. Second Aspin statement, unedited transcript, copy in authors' possession.
49. Their joint terrorist operations began in 1978, when Monzer and Abbas tried their first kidnap operation, but unfortunately grabbed the wrong man who turned out to be a cousin of the Saudi royal family. President Assad of Syria told Monzer to let him go and apologize. Monzer's brother Ghassan was a member of George Habash's PFLP-SC (People's Front for the Liberation of Palestine/Special Command). Manfred Morstein, *The Godfather of Terror: The Murderous Link Between Terrorism, Drugs and Arms Dealing* (U.S. government translation), pp. 39–40.
50. Ibid., pp. 50, 52, 38.
51. The two arms dealers the Al-Kassars met were Simon Neal Main of Great Britain, and a Frenchman, Philip Joseph Lethier. "In Septemher 1983, a few weeks after the meeting with the arms dealers in Vienna, the Israeli Mossad agent Ephraim Halpern was shot to death on a street in Hamburg. A then unknown terrorist group, 'Black September-Sabra and Shatila,' a killer clique that is related to the Palestinian Liberation Front of Abul Abbas, admitted to the deed." Ibid., p. 39.
52. "In the spring of 1984 Monzer and his brother Haitham had met in . . . Budapest for a 'strategy conference' [including] Abu Mohammed . . . Chief of the PFLP, Zaki el-Helou (a military leader of the PFLP-SC), Dr. George Habash (leader of the PFLP-SC), Marwan Al Khatib (chief of the PFLP bureau in Kuwait), Zediki Hatari (chief of the PFLP bureau in Baghdad/Iraq)." Ibid., p. 45.
53. Confidential interviews, former members, CIA, DIA, and Military Intelligence agencies; former members of Western intelligence services; former White House staffers.
54. Ibid.
55. Scotland Yard had discovered that Al-Kassar had ordered "1000 time fuzes for the type of bomb preferably used by terrorists." Morstein, *The Godfather of Terror*, pp. 74–75.
56. Confidential interviews, former members, Western intelligence services.
57. Al-Kassar flew to London in May 1983, prepared to testify in Berry's defense, but a public trial was the last thing MI6 wanted. MI5 was not amused at Berry's "escape," and placed a lifetime ban on Monzer entering England. Morstein, *The Godfather of Terror*, p. 75.
58. Ibid.
59. Ibid., pp. 71–72.
60. Ibid., citing copies of CIA files provided to Interpol.
61. Ibid., pp. 73, 47.
62. Al-Kassar visited England in 1984, 1986, 1987, and again in 1988, when he attempted to coordinate a major arms transaction through the BCCI. MI5 allegedly tipped off the press about the last transaction. Confidential interviews, former members, CIA; former members, Western intelligence services.
63. Morstein, *The Godfather of Terror*, p. 47.
64. Confidential interviews, former members, CIA, DIA, and Military Intelligence agencies; former members of Western intelligence services; former White House staffers.
65. Ibid.
66. Confidential interviews, former members, Western intelligence services.

67. Ibid.
68. Text of cable in Aspin files, copy in authors' possession.
69. June 29, 1984, message to Leslie Aspin, with handwritten notes referencing June 12, 1984, arms offer.
70. Delta Investments Invoice No. 004150-SA-EBP-MLA, July 7, 1984. Confidential interviews, former members, Western intelligence services.
71. BR&W Industries Ltd., Agreement, July 28, 1984.
72. Confidential interviews, former members, Western intelligence services.
73. Ibid.
74. Ibid.
75. Aspin was intimately involved with Libyan shipments to the IRA and ETA for years and confirmed that neither group was ever charged a penny by Gadhafi.
76. "The level of Soviet-Libyan cooperation tended to decline in the early 1980s as Qaddafi himself became increasingly discredited. Qaddafi's first visit to Moscow, in 1981, left much Soviet resentment in its wake." Christopher Andrew and Oleg Gordievsky, *KGB: The Inside Story* (New York: HarperCollins, 1990), p. 551. At one point during the late 1960s and early 1970s, the KGB and GRU had run joint operations involving narcotics and terrorists. According to the minutes of the 1967 Moscow meeting of all Warsaw Pact intelligence chiefs, it was agreed to provide "active support of international drug traffickers with the goal of forcing the social disintegration of Western nations." In a follow-up meeting in Sofia on July 16, 1970, it was agreed to establish a Europe-wide trucking firm, Kintex, owned by Bulgaria to handle the drug trade. "Monzer Al Kassar's firm Alkastronic in Austria was a partner of Kintex." Morstein, *The Godfather of Terror*, p. 58.
77. Claire Sterling, *The Terror Network* (New York: Berkeley Books, 1982), p. 218.
78. Andrew and Gordievsky, *KGB*, p. 548.
79. Confidential interviews, former members of CIA, DIA, and Military Intelligence agencies, former members of Western intelligence services.
80. The Abu Nidal network, for example. Confidential interviews, former members, CIA; former members, Western intelligence services.
81. The CIA even "presented evidence that the USSR attempted to dissuade certain Palestinian terrorist groups from taking violent actions against American targets. These official conclusions didn't bother Casey, however, he continued to support the claims in the Sterling book." Perry, *Eclipse*, p. 47.
82. Confidential interviews, former members of CIA, DIA, and Military Intelligence agencies, former members of Western intelligence services.
83. Morstein, *The Godfather of Terror*, citing CIA reports given to Interpol.
84. Ibid., p. 62.
85. Delta Investments letterhead, July 25, 1984.
86. Confidential interviews, former members, NSA, CIA, Western intelligence services.
87. Confidential interviews, former members of CIA, DIA, and Military Intelligence agencies, former members of Western intelligence services.
88. Pentagon shipping records for TOWS (declassified to show countries but not quantities) were provided to the Iran-Contra Investigators, and reprinted with General Secord's deposition transcript, Appendix B, Iran-Contra report.
89. Sworn statement of Horace Lok Fu Hsu, denying TOW deal but admitting work for Oman.
90. Invoice PE 66/84 referencing Purchase Order 118/84 S.Aq.
91. Unedited transcript of Leslie Aspin's sworn statement to his British attorney, May 1, 1987, p. 2.
92. Ibid., p. 8.
93. October 23, 1984, EUC, Nigeria. Aspin's files also contain correspondence with a London law firm, establishing a bank account for their client, a Nigerian diplomat. According to Aspin, his Nigerian friend would get a commission of 10 percent in

return for the end-user certificate. Aspin's family has a photo of the Nigerian official with a big smile on his face.

94. Confidential interviews, Aspin family members and business associates.
95. The French arms dealer was identified in Aspin's correspondence as well connected with French intelligence.
96. Confidential interviews, Aspin family members and former business associates.
97. Confidential interviews, U.S. government employees who wish to remain anonymous.
98. Ibid.
99. Confidential interviews, former White House staff.
100. "The North Diary," declassified under U.S. Freedom of Information Act, p. AMX002316.
101. Sam Hall, *Counter Terrorist* (New York: Donald Fine, 1987), pp. 196–245.
102. North received word that a suitcase bomb had been found by a "Brit girl—very sophisticated—worked w/Brit. Services." Investigators had not been able to find the bomb at first, but their source was able to tell only certain details. North was not told that the British source was Monzer Al-Kassar. All he knew was that a connection was made to Abu Ibrahaim and a bomb factory in the Bekaa Valley. North made sure that El-Al headquarters in Tel Aviv was protected and that the FAA had been alerted. "The North Diary," June 14, 1984.
103. Ibid., p. AMX002321.
104. Ibid., p. AMX002327.
105. Natural Security Archive, *The Chronology*, p. 52.
106. "The North Diary," June 26, 1984.
107. Ibid., p. AMX002337.
108. Confidential interviews, former agents, CIA.
109. Records of the 1984 Jonathan Institute published in Benjamin Netanyahu, ed., *Terrorism: How the West Can Win* (New York: Farrar Straus Giroux, 1986).
110. When Bush was director of the CIA, Clarridge was his personal deputy. The two men stayed very close over the years. Confidential interviews, former agents, CIA.
111. "The North Diary," p. AMX002340.
112. Ibid.
113. Ibid., pp. AMX002341, AMX002336.
114. Ibid., p. AMX002342 et seq.
115. Ibid., pp. AMX002343, AMX002355.
116. Ibid., pp. AMX002345, AMX002347.
117. Ibid., p. AMX002355.
118. Ibid., p. AMX002360.
119. Ibid., p. AMX002371.
120. Ibid., pp. AMX002375, AMX002383.
121. Ibid., p. AMX002384.
122. Ibid., p. AMX002386.
123. Ibid., pp. AMX002412–2413, AMX002416, AMX002418.
124. Ibid., pp. AMX002419–2420, AMX002429–2438.
125. Ibid., p. AMX002444. The vice president was himself a little preoccupied. He was preparing to go on a trip with Bill Middendorf, who had been promoted from banker to ambassador. Middendorf, of course, was the former Nixon appointee who had sold his bank to the BCCI, and then issued a press release that scandalized Lance and the Carter administration. Ibid., p. AMX002446, and Peter Truell and Larry Gurwin, *False Profits* (New York: Houghton Mifflin, 1992), pp. 42–43.
126. On August 1, 1984, North noted that there had been a "call to . . . Stielhamer" at his number in London, 04-32-5228. "The North Diary," pp. AMX002460, AMX002474, AMX002476, AMX002494, AMX002500.
127. Confidential interviews, Aspin family members and former business associates. Gow's private phone number was discovered among Aspin's files after his death.

128. "The North Diary," pp. AMX002508, AMX002522, AMX002524.
129. The man who told North was Hugh Montgomery, a senior member of the Thatcher administration. Ibid., pp. AMX002576, AMX002591.
130. Ibid., p. AMX002610.
131. Ibid., p. AMX002611–2612. Later on in the month President Reagan fumed, "why the hell can't we tell the Syrians to send the Iranians home?" The cynical reply was that Murphy was in Damascus right now and that this might be a "good chance to split Syrians/Iranians." In point of fact, the Syrian intelligence service already exercised de facto control over the Iranian kidnappers in Lebanon, while Syrian diplomats pretended to be honest mediators for the hostages. Ibid., p. AMX002005. Because the British data was being held closely by Bush's inner circle, U.S. intelligence did not have a clue what was going on. The CIA and the Defense Intelligence Agency were still squabbling over the authenticity of the photos of Buckley in captivity. Each agency blamed the other for not doing enough to get Buckley back. Ibid., p. AMX001995.
132. Ibid., p. AMX002008.
133. Al-Kassar made a number of other covert arms deals for foreign governments at the time. See discussion in Morstein, *Godfather of Terror*, Chapter 1.
134. "The North Diary," pp. AMX000033–0034, AMX000035.
135. Ibid., pp. AMX000023, AMX002501, AMX002504.
136. Ibid., pp. AMX000042–0043, AMX000064. North had more than a few problems convincing people that the same word had different meanings in the two documents. To resolve the controversy, North's buddy Dewey Clarridge was made the scapegoat for the Contra manual.
137. Ibid., p. AMX000048.
138. Ibid., p. AMX000053.
139. Ibid., pp. AMX000070, AMX000077. To be fair, North's diary shows that Admiral John Poindexter had strong reservations about becoming overly dependent on the British. He reminded Bush's CPPG members that they also should look at options developed independently of the British government, unconstrained by the new intelligence alliance. Still, the planning with the British went on. While most of the pages are censored, there is a note to "keep mouth shut—never mention North." It is ironic that North wrote a note to himself to remind himself never to mention himself. Ibid., pp. AMX0000116, AMX0000130–133.
140. According to one of our sources, John McIntyre, the British government wanted to stop the flow of arms as well as money from IRA supporters in the United States. McIntyre's son had been arrested by the U.S. Customs Service in October 1984 in connection with an aborted arms shipment aboard the SS *Valhalla* out of Boston. Shortly afterward North made some phone calls to the Customs Service. Customs commissioner Von Raab briefed Ambassador Price about a possible new source on the *Valhalla*. Price has admitted that he then passed the information to British intelligence in London.

    Almost immediately thereafter McIntyre's son disappeared, but his description appeared in the London press. British intelligence had planted a lurid series of articles that falsely portrayed young McIntyre as a longtime top American informant inside the IRA and blamed him for the betrayal of the *Valhalla* arms shipment. As one of the authors reported in a previous book, *Valhalla's Wake*, John McIntyre was a retired U.S. intelligence agent. He arranged to burglarize British intelligence files and discovered the truth. The British secret service had a supermole at the very top level of the IRA. It was this mole, not McIntyre's son, who had betrayed the *Valhalla* in 1984.

    According to the British files, McIntyre's son had been kidnapped and murdered in Boston by an MI6 team from Bermuda. The execution of an American citizen and the subsequent press disinformation campaign had been arranged by

British intelligence to distract the IRA's attention from the real British source. John McIntyre blamed the U.S. government for betraying his son, but his accusations were dismissed even after a number of sources from the Customs Service came forward to corroborate them. Still, the U.S. government scoffed at the notion that the British would murder an American citizen to protect some unnamed supermole in Ireland.

We knew that our source really had burglarized British files. McIntyre was telling the truth, and, sooner or later, someone in British intelligence would confirm it. In 1993 it happened. MI6's supermole quit working for the secret service. He made a public confession to the Irish press that he was, in fact, the informant who betrayed the *Valhalla* while he was working for the British service service. In view of this startling confession and the recent corroboration of the British quid pro quo in North's diaries, it appears beyond doubt that McIntyre did indeed burglarize British intelligence files and that Bush's inner circle unwittingly sacrificed the life of an American citizen upon the altar of British cooperation. In 1984 the British got their quid pro quo, but they took more than North and the naive Americans knew. See John Loftus and Emily McIntyre, *Valhalla's Wake: The IRA, MI6, and the Assassination of a Young American* (New York: The Atlantic Monthly Press, 1989).

141. Ibid., p. AMX000137.
142. "There was only one point in the apparatus [*sic*] who was functioning and who seemed to be able and was interested in working the process, and that was Ollie North. And it was Ollie North who moved into that void and was the focal point for the administration on Central American policy during that time-frame." National Security Archive, *The Chronology*, p. 65.
143. Confidential interviews, former agents, CIA; former members, White House staff.
144. "The North Diary," pp. AMX0000139–170.
145. Copy of travel voucher in authors' possession.
146. Aspin wrote that "it was agreed that I would go to Zurich and meet with a Mr. Ghorbanifar who would act on behalf of the Iranians. . . . I went to Zurich on the 14th of November, 1984, with Ben Bannerjee where we booked into the Opera Hotel. . . . [One of my agents] arrived, who in fact lives quite near the hotel, along with . . . an ex-U.S. Army officer, although he is a German and is also a [former] member of the CIA. . . . He was also at that time acting as Mr. Ghorbanifar's aide-de-camp and escorting him everywhere. They had in fact, just come from Hamburg where Mr. Ghorbanifar had been conducting meetings with the Mullahs. That is to say, the [Iranian] religious leaders who were overseeing this affair, live in a villa outside Hamburg." Unedited transcript of Leslie Aspin's sworn statement to his British attorney, May 1, 1987, p. 5. We reached the ex-U.S. Army officer at the telephone number Aspin gave, but he declined to be interviewed. It has been independently confirmed that Ghorbanifar was in fact in contact with Iranian representatives in Hamburg at this time, exactly as Aspin alleged. National Security Archive, *The Chronology*, p. 72.
147. Unedited transcript of Leslie Aspin's sworn statement to his British attorney, May 1, 1987, pp. 4–5.
148. Ibid., p. 4.
149. Copies of these documents are in authors' possession.
150. Confidential interviews, two U.S. government employees who wish to remain anonymous.
151. An investigator for the Iran-Contra Committee has admitted that he had come across some evidence of an attempted arms-for-hostage deal, "but the Committee did not want to embarrass the French Government."
152. Testimony of Albert Hakim, Congressional Deposition, Appendix B, Iran-Contra report.
153. Ibid., pp. 4–5.

154. "The accounts that were opened were: number one account, 10 243 8625, into which $5 million U.S. dollars was placed. #2 account was 10 243 9725, the interest account. #3 was 10 24 400 25, that account only had the signatures of North and Bannerjee, on all the others, I was a co-signatory along with Bannerjee and Ghorbanifar." Ibid., p. 5.
155. Transcript excerpts provided courtesy of Senator Kerry's staff.
156. Hakim's records of transfers from the BCCI can be found in his deposition transcript, Appendix B, Iran Contra report.
157. One of Aspin's business associates explained to us why the French deal collapsed. "The problem was that the Iranians didn't want the frog missiles, 'cause they had too short a range. They weren't in any rush to go to Allah. When an Iraqi tank is coming at you, you want as much distance as possible." Shortly after North landed back in America, the Iranians had told Ghorbanifar to forget the STRIM missiles, they wanted good old American TOWs.
158. "One of the most important meetings was on the eve of the 5th of December, at the Frankfurt Sheraton. . . . on the morning of the 6th, a car arrived from the Iranian Embassy in Bonn. I went in the car to Bonn with a letter given to me by Mr. Ghorbanifar. I gave this letter to the Ambassador, Mr. Mohammad Javad Salari. He asked me to wait for possibly one or two hours for the paperwork to be completed. I went to a Chinese restaurant just next door to the Embassy and had a meal. When I returned to the Iranian Embassy, I was given a letter for Ben Bannerjee and three [arms purchase] certificates." Unedited transcript Leslie Aspin's sworn statement to his British attorney, May 1, 1987, pp. 6–7.
159. Letter of December 6, 1984, Ambassador, Islamic Republic of Iran.
160. "The North Diary," pp. AMX000225–227, AMX000231.
161. The immunity offer was made by the prosecutor, Lawrence Barcella, in a letter from Calvin White to Michael Aspin, copy in authors' possession.
162. Affidavit of Calvin White, January 13, 1986, given to British prosecutors.
163. Ibid., p. 2.
164. Confidential interview, former members, CIA; former members, a Western intelligence service.
165. Ibid., and interviews with Aspin family members and former business associates. Leslie's version of these events was often different from Michael's.
166. Ibid.
167. Michael's contact gave the following information to U.S. Customs Agents: "Howard stated that the country of Iran was attempting to purchase approximately 5,000 TOW Anti-Tank missiles, first generation 1980 date of manufacture. Howard stated that a British arms broker identified as a Michael Aspin of Delta investments . . . was arranging the sale. . . . According to Howard, Aspin was supposedly interested in stopping the transaction because some of the missiles were intended for allegedly terrorist groups. Aspin was reportedly willing to co-operate with United States authorities in return for the securing of the $1,500,000 performance bond. . . . [He is] willing to co-operate in thwarting the shipment of missiles." U.S. Customs dossier, statement of informant Howard, pp. 29–30.
168. Ibid.
169. Confidential interviews, former White House staff; former members, a Western intelligence service.
170. Statement of Rodney Allan Hale, U.S. Customs, to British prosecutor.
171. Interview with John Taylor; confidential interview, former Aspin business associate.
172. Confidential interviews, former members, CIA.

CHAPTER 20
BLACKMAILING THE PRESIDENT?

1. "Iran-Contra: The Press Indicts the Prosecutor," *Columbia Journalism Review* (March–April 1994), citing *Times-Mirror* survey of December 1992.

2. Confidential interviews, former members, CIA; former agents, U.S. military intelligence; members, Western intelligence services; Senate and House staff; former members, White House staff.
3. Earl Transcript, Iran-Contra Depositions, Appendix B, Volume 9, p. 1055.
4. "The North Diary," p. AMX000876.
5. "While CIA officers who became entangled in the Iran-Contra scandal disagree about many of its details, they are convinced Casey used Oliver North in order to circumvent the agency's unwillingness to participate in high-risk activities. North became Casey's unofficial director for operations and the acknowledged inheritor of his activist dream; in Casey's eyes, North was a hero. Despite Casey's growing friendship with the young lieutenant colonel, only a small group of agency officers knew that North was running a mini-CIA inside the White House." Mark Perry, *Eclipse: The Last Days of the CIA* (New York: William Morrow, 1992), p. 48.
6. Confidential interviews, former members, CIA; former agents, U.S. military intelligence; members, Western intelligence services; Senate and House staff, former members, White House staff.
7. Ibid.
8. "The North Diary," declassified under U.S. Freedom of Information Act, 1993, p. AMX000239.
9. During the Vietnam War, Earl and North worked on special operations, including hostage rescue. Only a few days before North's unit was sent in "to rescue the American crew of the *Mayaguez,* a freighter hijacked off the coast of Colombia," Earl convinced North to go back to the United States to try to save his mental health and his marriage. Shortly afterwards North collapsed and spent the next several weeks in a psychiatric hospital for severe depression. Earl may have saved North's life. See discussion in North's autobiography, *Under Fire* (New York: Harper Paperbacks, 1992), and Earl's testimony about his relationship with Gregg and North. Earl Deposition, Appendix B, Iran-Contra Investigation.
10. Earl Deposition, Appendix B, Iran-Contra Investigation.
11. Confidential interviews, former members, CIA; former agents, U.S. military intelligence; members, Western intelligence services.
12. On December 10, 1984, North made a note "Newport—Counterterrorism." On February 27 Admiral Moreau informed North the next "seminar" would be held in Newport on April 12. These were not normal seminars, as McFarlane himself would be attending. On April 10 North was informed that "Shultz signed out action for terrorism at summit." Newport was good cover for a covert meeting site, as the April 22 war games were also scheduled for the Naval War College. North's diary showed plans for a February 1985 trip to London for Steve Bryan and "Pearl." (North sometimes called his colleague "Earl the Pearl"). Shortly before the London counterterrorism summit, North called Bob Earl in Newport to discuss the Joint Special Operations Force, the Pentagon's hostage rescue team. It should be noted that one week after this phone call, Aspin reported that he met with North and Earl in London to discuss the arms-for-hostage deal. On April 1 North made a note that he would see Bob Earl on Easter Sunday night. On April 8 North called Bob Earl again. On June 19, a Sunday, Bob Earl dropped by North's house at night. Earl called again on July 30. It was not until September 3, 1985, that Earl had a White House phone number, 395-4950 and had gone to work for the vice president. See generally North's diary for December 1984 to September 1985.
13. The congressional investigation focused primarily on the post-October 1985 time frame and, during the three short months allowed for its work, generally ignored the 1984 documents. Confidential interviews, former congressional staff.
14. "The North Diary," p. AMX000266.
15. Telexes: December 20, 1985, BCCI to Westminister Bank, December 20, 1985, West Bank to Iranians, December 27, 1985, BCCI to Switzerland, copies found in Leslie Aspin's files.

16. In early December General Secord was in the hospital for a gall bladder operation, and North took over some of the arms shipments, including the provision for a "small Danish ship (700 tons)." This turned out to be the famous *Erria,* which shuttled arms to the Contras.

The ship is famous for narcotics smuggling as well. According to Interpol records, the *Erria* was one of Monzer Al-Kassar's chartered vessels. North paid for the vessel through Albert Hakim's Dolmy Corporation, which Morstein, relying on Interpol sources also confirms was used as a front for Monzer's shipping enterprise. "The North Diary," pp. AMX000273, AMX000289, AMX000306, AMX000215. In the summer of 1985 Al-Kassar briefly borrowed the *Erria* back for a massive arms shipment from Spain to Sierra Leone. What Interpol does not know is that Al-Kassar was helping the British secret service mount a countercoup in the little African nation. The Communists had just ousted President Siaka Stevens, who had always depended on SAS mercenaries for his bodyguards. Interpol knew that Al-Kassar was meeting in Spain with ex-President Stevens but did not understand that Al-Kassar was aiding a joint British-Spanish effort to put him back in power. Jonathan Bloch and Patrick Fitzgerald, *British Intelligence and Covert Action* (London: Junction Books, 1983), p. 48.

17. The company's representative reported that General Secord had "5 launchers, one training device, 13 missiles-on order." A former Special Forces expert would handle the training. "The North Diary," entry circa December 26, 1984.

18. Confidential interviews, former agents, CIA; former members, Western intelligence services.

19. On December 27, 1984, North had a call from Andrew Green concerning another British mercenary, David Walker. North was told that Walker would be responsible for coordination but must have no official connection with the British government. Clair George, who had replaced Dewey Clarridge after the Contra assassination manual scandal, ended up working with the British liaison for Central America. Clarridge kept his hand in from overseas, reporting on January 5, 1985, that 200 tons of arms were en route from South Africa to Costa Rica. On January 10 General Secord, who usually handled Contra supplies, called North to say that there was some red tape on the movement of the vessel, and it would not move until the twenty-seventh at the earliest. There were "conditions on payment/forms, etc." and to check with "Bob, who used to be in my place." This coincides with the period that North took over from Bob McFarlane as Bush's liaison to the British. "The North Diary," entries for December 27, 1984, through January 10, 1985.

20. North's contact added later that the Blowpipes would be free, but that the Contras would "have to infer" that they were a gift not from the Chileans but from the British. The Chileans also offered to sell five thousand light antitank weapons (LAWS), useful for blowing up Sandinista gun emplacements. The Blowpipe deal later collapsed because of the high Chilean prices for these other armaments. On January 11 North was informed that one of the Republican senators was "against lethal covert action," "wants everything in writing," and does "not understand IC or process of tasking." "IC" stands for the Intelligence Consortium, and "tasking" means asking the British end of the consortium to do that which Congress has prohibited. Confidential interview, former agent, CIA; "The North Diary," entries for January 10–11, 1985.

21. On March 12 North noted the "fundamental decision. Do we pay ransom? [It is] considered that Levin was paid [for]." "The North Diary," pp. AMX000494, AMX000510. For example, North was involved in a discussion with the German Interior Minister's Group on U.S.-German cooperation on combating terrorism. Ibid., p. AMX000432. On March 6 North reported that the Republic of China had agreed to purchase $70 million worth of U.S. torpedoes from Israel. According to our sources, these torpedoes were actually ship-to-ship Harpoon missiles, which as

we shall see were later delivered by the Azimas' aircraft to Iran, along with the Phoenix missiles. The Iranians confirmed that they indeed received both. Ibid., p. AMX000505.

22. Unfortunately, word of another Chinese arms sale, the one with the "Canadian Arms Dealer working with Secord" seemed to have leaked out. Similarly, the CIA was getting information that there were two British advisers working with the Contras. At this time, John Negroponte dropped back in to town for a "Very good visit with V.P." Ibid., p. AMX000539.
23. Ibid., p. AMX000541.
24. While it is beyond the scope of this book, Manfred Morstein's survey of Interpol records confirms that the Al-Kassar family was expanding their drug empire into South America. Morstein flatly accuses Al-Kassar of working with the Medellin cocaine cartel and has ample sources to back it up. The most intriguing claim is that the Al-Kassars engineered the betrayal of a minor Colombian drug lord, Carlos Lehder, to the Americans, so that Vice President George Bush could claim a public relations victory in the war against drugs. At the same time, Interpol confirms that the Al-Kassar family and the Ochoa family were merging their narcotics empires, expanding the Medellin cartel into European markets. Manfred Morstein, *The Godfather of Terror: The Murderous Link Between Terrorism, Drugs and Arms Dealing* (U.S. government translation), last two chapters.
25. Confidential interviews, former members, CIA; former White House staffers.
26. Telephone interview, Vincent Cannistraro, 1992.
27. Confidential interview, former White House staffer.
28. Confidential interviews, former members, CIA; former agents, U.S. military intelligence; members, Western intelligence services.
29. Confidential interviews, former members, CIA; members, a Western intelligence service; interview with Michael Aspin.
30. Ibid.
31. "In return for dropping charges against him, for having violated U.S. laws in May 1984 in trying to export arms to Iran, Hashemi continued to work [in London] as a 'double agent' for the American Customs authority. His name would surface again on April 22, 1986, when he turned in several arms dealers, including retired Israeli Brigadier General Avraham Baram.They were all arrested in the U.S. and accused of secretly trying to sell $2.5 billion worth of arms to Iran. [The charges were later dismissed when it was revealed that the White House itself had authorized arms sales to Iran.] Hashemi died in London in July 1986 under mysterious circumstances. His death certificate recorded a natural death, but according to various sources Hashemi was murdered by Iranian intelligence agents on charges of treason." Samuel Segev, *The Iron Triangle: The Untold Story of Israel's Role in the Iran-Contra Affair* (New York: Macmillan, 1988), p. 141.
32. Confidential interviews, former members, CIA; members, a Western intelligence service; interview with Michael Aspin.
33. William J. Casey, memorandum, reprinted in Earl transcript, pp. 1128–1130.
34. Confidential interviews, former members, CIA; members, a Western intelligence service.
35. Interview with John Taylor.
36. In this case four Irishmen were falsely convicted of an IRA pub bombing. It was later discovered that the prosecution had concealed a witness statement that confirmed their alibi.
37. Interviews with Michael Aspin and John Taylor.
38. Ibid.
39. Affidavit of William Harper, with supporting affidavits from his physicians and family.
40. Interviews with Michael Aspin, John Taylor, William Harper. Confidential interview, Aspin business associate.

41. An Israeli defector claimed that Prime Minister Shamir had ordered an intelligence investigation of Nir's death and that it was "a well-executed CIA operation." Ari Ben-Menashe, *Profits of War* (Sydney: Allen and Unwin, 1992), p. 290.
42. "The North Diary," pp. AMX000321, AMX000328.
43. On December 12 North had a call from General Yariv, former director of Israeli Military Intelligence. Apparently there had been a leak to Israel. Confidential source.
44. On January 23, 1985, Claire George advised North to brief Bush about the growing concerns. "The North Diary," pp. AMX000332, AMX000333, AMX000336.
45. Among the information received from the British was the hiring of a British SAS agent and his mercenary company. North later reported that the agent was completely useless. His replacement was Major David Walker, formerly of the SAS. His London office was right next door to Aspin's. It was so very convenient. Ibid., pp. AMX000400, AMX000549. Walker was associated with KMS security, a firm that specialized in "kidnap and ransom insurance" in the Middle East. KMS had their offices at "Saladin Security at 13 Sloane Street . . . close to SAS Regimental Headquarters." Aspin's offices were at 14 Sloane Street, and he is believed to have worked with Walker on several operations.
46. Ibid., pp. AMX000427, AMX000437, AMX000439. North reported that the British government was providing yet another SAS mercenary company to protect the hostages who were expected to be released.
47. Ibid., pp. AMX000394, AMX000449.
48. Ibid., pp. AMX000468, AMX000471.
49. Clair George called North to tell him. Ibid., p. AMX000472.
50. Ibid., pp. AMX000473, AMX000475.
51. Aspin records, copy in authors' possession.
52. "The North Diary," p. AMX000543.
53. Ibid., entries for March 15 et seq.
54. Ibid., p. AMX000558.
55. Ibid., pp. AMX000559, AMX000551.
56. General Secord telephoned North to report that the Portuguese Defense Ministry was fully aware of "transactions for DEFEX to support" the Contras. "The North Diary," p. AMX000638. Everything was fine in Lisbon until General Singlaub started a cat fight with General Secord over who could buy "commie" guns the cheapest. On May 17, Secord told North that Singlaub had been dealing with a German dealer in purchasing AK-47s from the Soviet Union. The DEFEX people would not work with them. This is not surprising since Interpol records show that Al-Kassar favored DEFEX, and the German dealer was one of his rivals. Morstein, *Godfather of Terror,* pp. 113–125.
57. On April 19 Clarridge advised that if MI "5 hears of secret of whole house—Cruz will be blown." Cruz was the Contra liaison for the White House and the recipient of British funding after the congressional arms ban. The British anxiety seems to have dissipated quickly. On May 1 David Walker called North and said that his friend was keen to set up some specific deliveries. "The North Diaries," entries for April 19–May 1, 1985.
58. In the second week of April, North had another meeting with Mike Ledeen to discuss his terms of reference for dealing with the Iranian kidnappers. The plan to open an Israeli channel had begun. North met with Don Gregg the following day; the topic of the meeting is not stated in the diary. On April 9 North called Dewey Clarridge to get the latest information. Five minutes later he spoke to General Singlaub about the "exclusivity of Israeli offer" and the Israeli request for reciprocity. Once again North was asked to help draft a cable for the vice president. Ibid., April 8–22, 1985.
59. On May 13 Ledeen reported on his first meeting with the Israelis in Zurich. Ibid., p. AMX000664.

60. Ibid., pp. AMX000606, AMX000629.
61. Confidential interviews, members, a Western intelligence service.
62. Segev, *The Iron Triangle,* pp. 137, 139.
63. Ibid., p. 141.
64. Confidential interviews, former members, Israeli intelligence.
65. Ibid.
66. Our sources say that things have calmed down now and Pollard could be released in a few years. Everyone knows that the U.S. spies on Israel from Jordan and the Israelis spy on the United States from Canada. The Israelis have already released the American agent who was their Pollard, and things are getting back to normal. The real problem is that the Mossad does not want Pollard out, for fear that he will emigrate to Israel and write a book. This would cause still more damage to an already weakened relationship with U.S. intelligence. Our sources say that several American politicians are also afraid of Pollard's future literary career. Confidential interviews, former members, Israeli intelligence; former members, CIA.
67. Hakim testimony, Congressional depositions, volume B, Iran-Contra Report.
68. Confidential interviews, former members, a Western intelligence service; former members, CIA.
69. As previously discussed, Gregg had prepared the contingency plans for third-country funding of the Contras in 1983. McFarlane and Casey started the British arms-for-hostages exchange in 1984. North's diary shows that he was reporting to Gregg and Bush throughout 1984 and early 1985.
70. Secretary of State Shultz was a constant opponent of sending arms to Iran and was kept out of the loop well into 1986. Confidential interviews, former White House staffers.
71. As far back as December 1984, North knew that the vice president was the one who would get the credit for any hostage release. On December 11 North noted that the "Acting Secretary Defense would meet bodies," but "would prefer V.P.—Germany now." "The North Diary," entry for December 11, 1984.
72. "The North Diary," p. AMX000732.
73. Segev, *The Iron Triangle,* p. 281.
74. "According to the Belgian agents, Monzer Al Kassar, quite obviously on orders from the PLF of Abul Abbas, was preparing murder and bombing attacks against Israeli persons and facilities throughout Europe. The attacks were aimed at, among other things, two Israeli MOSSAD agents who, acting as arms dealers, were trying to infiltrate the PLF. The Belgian intelligence agents had also learned that in addition Monzer was interested in the [Paris] offices of the [Israeli-backed] Christian Militia of the Lebanese. . . . Planned for the same time, according to the secret service agents, was an attack on Jewish institutions in Vienna." Morstein, *The Godfather of Terror,* p. 67.
75. Confidential interviews, former members, Western intelligence services.
76. Confidential interviews, former members, CIA; former members, Western intelligence services.
77. "The agency penetrated the organization by recruiting defectors and by establishing a number of front companies that did business with Abu Nidal agents in Europe and North Africa. The corporations the CIA established sold a variety of military equipment to the Palestinian fringe group—boots, hats, and knapsacks. Other CIA proprietaries sold the [Abu Nidal Organization] electronic equipment." Perry, *Eclipse,* pp. 191–192.
78. Confidential interviews, former members, CIA; former members, Western intelligence services.
79. "One of the best-kept secrets during this anti-[Abu Nidal Organization] campaign was the agency's close cooperation with the Tunis-based PLO, which helped provide intelligence for dismembering Abu Nidal's European and North African terror-

ist networks. The CIA contacted PLO officials through intermediaries in Beirut, Morocco and Tunis. Their most senior PLO contact was . . . Abu Iyad, who served as Yassir Arafat's chief intelligence aide. At the height of the operation, Iyad privately confirmed to a reporter that the CIA-PLO links had been vital to the success of the operation." Ibid., p. 192.

80. Confidential source letter, April 13, 1992, p. 3.
81. Ibid., p. 5.
82. Confidential interview, former agent, CIA.
83. "A number of these companies, the CIA discovered, were front groups for the Mossad, the Israeli intelligence service, that were also attempting to penetrate the terrorist groups using the same tactics as the CIA. Agency officials were gleeful about the treasure trove of information they were able to uncover about Mossad front companies operating in the United States and took particular pleasure in shutting them down. Several of these Israeli-backed companies were broken up, their executives put on trial, convicted and jailed." Perry, *Eclipse*, p. 192.
84. Confidential interview, former U.S. Army intelligence officer.
85. Perry, *Eclipse*, p. 73.
86. "The Iranian student said he had been dispatched as an escort for his employer, the high-level Iranian government official, on a tour to inspect Iran's military installations. . . . While standing on the tarmac of the Tabriz Air Base, the FBI agent said, the Iranian student spotted what looked like an unmarked U.S. aircraft unloading sophisticated weapons. . . . The CIA officer's answer was curt: the agency had no knowledge of any U.S. arms shipments to Iran. He added that such shipments violated established American policy. Iran was branded a terrorist state, so the Iranian student *must* be mistaken." Ibid., pp. 73–74.
87. "When the CIA learned of the meeting in Geneva on the AAMs [Anti Aircraft Missiles] they greeted the news with a smile—impossible! The people in Washington were certain that no one in the world would be able to procure these F-14 missiles, guarded as a state secret, illegally. When nine months later the first Iraqi fighter-bombers were shot down with Phoenix missiles, Monzer Al-Kassar . . . advanced in the USA to one of the 'most wanted arms-traffickers of the world.' In view of the Syrian's incredible contacts, however, it was very difficult to prosecute him." Morstein, *The Godfather of Terror*, p. 47.
88. "The North Diary," p. AMX001836.
89. Ibid., p. AMX000440. At first there was some concern that Michael may have leaked word about the Azima brothers' work for Leslie. Fortunately, Michael was a terrible speller and told U.S. Customs that it was the "Azarnia brothers" and gave their base as New York instead of Kansas City. It was safe to continue using the Azimas' unmarked airplane. See affidavit of U.S. Customs Official previously discussed.
90. Confidential interviews, former members, CIA; former members, Western intelligence services.
91. "The North Diary," p. AMX000443.
92. Speech cited in transcript of Elizabeth Colton, Foreign Affairs Correspondent, November 13, 1986, Morning Edition, National Public Radio.
93. "The North Diary," p. AMX000988.
94. Segev, *The Iron Triangle*, pp. 296–301.
95. Colton, National Public Radio, November 13, 1986.
96. Telephone interviews, Azima brothers and family members, 1991–1992.
97. Unedited transcript of Leslie Aspin's sworn statement to his British attorney, May 1, 1987, pp. 10–11.
98. Telephone interviews, Kansas City Attorney William Chambers, 1991–1992. Copies of papers where Leslie practiced signing his Frengold signature were discovered after his death. Copy in authors' possession.
99. Aspin file, copy in authors' possession.

100. Nir reported his conversation with Ghorbanifar to North, who made extensive notes set forth in the following notes.
101. "The North Diary," pp. AMX001518, AMX001530, AMX001523, AMX001521.
102. Confidential interviews, former members, CIA, DIA, and Western intelligence services.
103. Ibid.
104. Ibid.
105. Official transcript before the United States Department of Justice, Office of Professional Responsibility, Interview of Kris Kolesnik, Washington, D.C., April 14, 1992, pp. 44–45.
106. "The most prominent of the hostages was William Buckley, a 57-year-old bachelor and head of the CIA station in Lebanon. Tall, black-haired, with a deep voice and a broad smile, Buckley's external appearance was quite imposing. Behind his quiet facade hid a strong and adventurous personality. Buckley's cover as a CIA agent had been broken in a book about the CIA. Ignoring the risk, Casey posted him to Lebanon. As a result, when he was kidnapped, his pro-Iranian captors knew exactly who they had. They used cruel and horrendous tortures to wring every crumb of information about his actions and about American Middle East policy from him. His confession spread over 400 pages, and was sent to Tehran and Damascus—and by Syrian intelligence to the Soviet Union and it allies." Segev, *The Iron Triangle,* p. 129.
107. Confidential interviews, former members, CIA, DIA, and Western intelligence services.
108. Ibid.
109. "The North Diary," pp. AMX000743, AMX000745.
110. Ibid., pp. AMX000703, AMX001260, AMX000813, AMX000842.
111. Ibid., pp. AMX000845–846.
112. Ibid., pp. AMX001235, AMX001738.
113. Ibid., p. AMX001314.
114. Ibid., p. AMX001850.
115. Ibid., entry for December 6, 1985.
116. Ibid., entry for March 31, 1986.
117. Ibid., pp. AMX001114, AMX001123.
118. Ibid., p. AMX001153.
119. Ibid., p. AMX001199.
120. Kolesnik transcript, p. 45, declassified copy provided by a source who wishes to remain anonymous.
121. "Bush met with Prime Minister Peres, as well as with Foreign Minister Shamir and Defense Minister Rabin. After a preliminary conversation with Israel's Chief of Staff . . . he went by helicopter to an air force base in the south of Israel and watched combat and paratrooper maneuvers." Segev, *The Iron Triangle,* p. 291.
122. Confidential interviews, Israeli pilots and base employees, 1991.
123. R290, dated 12/8/86, "Subject: American official holding talks over the hostages issue in Syria."
124. Confidential interviews, former members, CIA, DIA, and Western intelligence services.
125. "The North Diary," pp. AMX001356, AMX001366.
126. Ibid., pp. AMX001394, AMX001426, AMX001425.
127. Ibid., pp. AMX001437, AMX001490.
128. Confidential interview, former Pentagon official (further identifying data withheld at source's request).
129. Ibid.
130. Confidential interviews, former members, CIA, DIA, and Western intelligence services.

131. Confidential interviews, associates of Lilly Boustanny.
132. Kolesnik transcript, p. 8.
133. Confidential interview, associate of Jean Kirkpatrick.
134. Confidential interviews, former members, CIA, DIA, and Western intelligence services.
135. Ibid. Copies of correspondence in authors' possession.
136. Confidential interview, former Pentagon official.
137. Confidential interviews, former members, Western intelligence services.
138. See discussion of international politicians associated with Monzer Al-Kassar in Morstein, *Godfather of Terror.*

CHAPTER 21
THE VICTORS AND THE VICTIMS

1. Confidential interviews, former members, CIA; U.S. military advisers; and former members, Western intelligence services.
2. Ibid., citing conversations with their oil company liaisons.
3. "The CIA utilized the assistance of an American oil service company that transported its workers on helicopters from the Saudi base of Dhahran to oil platforms in the Persian Gulf. During the day, Agency operatives flew in the company's civilian helicopters; at night, they used their own aircraft to patrol, and eventually engaged in secret bombing runs." Alan Friedman, *Spider's Web: The Secret History of How the White House Armed Iraq* (New York: Bantam, 1993), p. 42.
4. Confidential interviews, former members, CIA.
5. Confidential interviews, former members, CIA; U.S. military advisers; former members, Western intelligence services.
6. Ibid.
7. Confidential interviews, former Israeli liaison to allied forces in Operation Desert Storm.
8. Paula Dwyer et al., "Bechtel's Iraqi Pipe Dream Could Land It In Hot Water," *Business Week,* February 22, 1988, p. 33.
9. Ibid., and Ari Ben-Menashe, *Profits of War* (Sydney: Allen and Unwin, 1992), p. 172.
10. Dwyer et al., "Bechtel's Iraqi Pipe Dream."
11. By "early 1985 it appeared that Iraq would opt for a competing pipeline through Saudi Arabia to be built by Brown & Root Inc. Iraq was also placing nearly impossible conditions on Bechtel's plan. The Baghdad government feared Israel would bomb the pipeline and wanted ironclad financial protection. Bechtel responded with a global lobbying blitz to save the project. That's where the intrigue began." Dwyer et al., "Bechtel's Iraqi Pipe Dream."
12. Ben-Menashe, *Profits of War,* pp. 172, 181.
13. "Independent counsel James C. McKay has uncovered a memo from Wallach to Meese that allegedly outlines a plan for paying the then-ruling Israeli Labor Party for a guarantee not to attack the pipeline." Dwyer et al., "Bechtel's Pipe Dream." "Initially, the pipeline seemed to benefit everyone. Iraq needed petrodollars to buy weapons for its long-running war with Iran. Israel, through Rappaport, might be able to get much-needed oil. Jordanian officials saw the pipeline as a windfall. And for the U.S., getting these three parties together could provide the basis of a Middle East peace accord. Indeed, sources say William Casey, the director of the Central Intelligence Agency, backed the proposal when he was briefed on it in January, 1984, about the time Bechtel got involved." Ibid.
14. It should be noted that extensive U.S. investigations failed to corroborate many of the allegations made by Ben Menashe. See Ben-Menashe, *Profits of War,* p. 173.
15. Dwyer et al. "Bechtel's Iraqi Pipe Dream."
16. Friedman, *Spider's Web,* pp. 30, 132–137, 163.
17. Ibid., pp. 167, 172.

18. The deal had begun to fall apart when Yitzhak Shamir, the Israeli coalition and Likud leader, found out about the bribe. "Shamir, in a very stormy cabinet meeting in 1985, called Peres a traitor and threatened to leave the coalition. The pipeline deal was called off." Ben-Menashe, *Profits of War,* p. 173. Shamir's hostile stance threatened huge profits, so Bechtel tried to resurrect the deal anyway it could: "Enter OPIC—the Overseas Private Investment Corp., a small U.S. agency that insures companies against political risks such as expropriation of assets. The agency turned down Bechtel's first request for $360 million in risk insurance. But Wallach called Meese about the matter, and the Attorney General referred him to National Security Adviser Robert C. McFarlane. As a result, OPIC in the fall of 1985 agreed to form a syndicate of insurers, including Citicorp and Lloyd's of London. Meanwhile, others working for Bechtel lined up support from Jordan's Hussein." Dwyer et al., "Bechtel's Iraqi Pipe Dream."
19. The quotations by Sol Shnadow are from a transcript of a videotape interview, Solomon Shnadow, copy in authors' possession.
20. Living in bombed-out shacks in Lomjew, his younger brother became desperately ill. Sol was asked to smuggle him across the Lithuanian border for medical treatment. Sol's older brother lived in Vilna and would take care of him. But the Lithuanians were hardly more sympathetic than the Nazis. They robbed Sol and his sick brother of their money and waited until nightfall to throw them back across an unfamiliar part of the border.

    Sol realized why the Lithuanian crooks had picked this particular spot, when he saw the green glow from the eyes of the approaching wolves. Sol dropped his brother and tried to get his matches to light in the heavy wind and snow. They were saved, temporarily, when a Russian soldier arrived on skis. He placed them under arrest for illegal entry. It took seven days to convince the Soviets that they already were residents. In those seven days, Sol and his brother were imprisoned with thirty-four other people in a cell built for eight. The cold dampness made his brother even more ill. He died in Sol's arms, five days after they were released.
21. "The Nazi Connection," produced by Ira Rosen, *60 Minutes,* May 16, 1982.
22. For example, *60 Minutes* had interviewed Anton Adamovitch, a former Nazi propagandist who was then working for Radio Liberty as a staff writer. Adamovitch admitted on camera his contacts with U.S. intelligence, including with the FBI, to whom he had confessed his Nazi background.
23. Confidential interview, former member, CIA.
24. Confidential interviews, former members, CIA, DIA, Western intelligence services.

SELECTED BIBLIOGRAPHY

Aarons, Mark. *Sanctuary! Nazi Fugitives in Australia.* Melbourne: Heinemann, 1989.

Aarons, Mark, and John Loftus. *Ratlines: How the Vatican's Nazi Networks Betrayed Western Intelligence to the Soviets.* London: Heinemann, 1991. Published as *Unholy Trinity* in the United States. New York: St. Martin's Press, 1992.

Anderson, Jack, with James Boyd. *Oil: The Real Story Behind the World Energy Crisis.* London: Sidgwick & Jackson, 1984.

Anderson, Scott, and Jon Lee Anderson. *Inside the League.* New York: Dodd, Mead, 1986.

Andrew, Christopher, and Oleg Gordievsky. *KGB: The Inside Story.* New York: HarperCollins, 1990.

Aspin, Leslie, with Trevor Aspinall. *I, Kovaks.* London: Everest Books, 1975.

Bamford, James. *The Puzzle Palace.* New York: Houghton Mifflin, 1982.

Ben-Menashe, Ari. *Profits of War.* Sydney: Allen and Unwin, 1992.

Black, Ian, and Benny Morris. *Israel's Secret Wars. The Untold History of Israeli Intelligence.* London: Hamish Hamilton, 1991.

Blair, John M. *The Control of Oil.* New York: Vintage, 1978.

Blandford, Linda. *Oil Sheiks.* London: Star, 1977.

Blet, Pierre, et al. (eds.). *Les Actes et Documents du Saint Siège relatif à la Seconde Guerre Mondiale,* vols. 1–11. Libreria Editrice Vaticana, Vatican City: 1966–81.

Bloch, Jonathan, and Patrick Fitzgerald. *British Intelligence and Covert Action.* London: Junction Books, 1983.

Blum, Howard. *Wanted! The Search for Nazis in America.* New York: Quadrangle/The New York Times Book Company, 1977.

Borkin, Joseph. *The Crime and Punishment of I. G. Farben.* New York: Free Press, 1978.

Bower, Tom. *The Pledge Betrayed.* New York: Doubleday, 1982.

Cave Brown, Anthony. *C: The Secret Life of Sir Stewart Menzies.* New York: Macmillan, 1987.

Bush, George, with Victor Gold. *Looking Forward. An Autobiography.* London: The Bodley Head, 1988.

Caroz, Yaacov. *The Arab Secret Services*. London: Corgi, 1978.

Carter, Jimmy. *Keeping Faith. Memoirs of a President*. New York: Bantam, 1982.

Cockburn, Andrew and Leslie Cockburn. *Dangerous Liaison*. New York: HarperCollins, 1991.

Collier, Peter, and David Horowitz. *The Rockefellers: An American Dynasty*. New York: Holt, Rinehart and Winston, 1976.

Cookson, John, and Judith Nottingham. *A Survey of Chemical and Biological Warfare*. New York: Monthly Review Press, 1969.

Colodny, Len and Robert Gettlin. *Silent Coup*. New York: St. Martin's Press, 1991.

Colby, William. *Honorable Men. My Life in the CIA*. London: Hutchinson, 1978.

Copeland, Miles. *The Game of Nations: The Amorality of Power Politics*. London: Weidenfeld and Nicolson, 1969.

———. *The Real Spy World*. London: Sphere, 1978.

———. *The Game Player: Confessions of the CIA's Original Political Operative*. London: Aurum Press, 1989.

Corson, William. *The Armies of Ignorance*. New York: Dial Press, 1977.

Costello, John. *Mask of Treachery*. New York: Morrow, 1988.

Costello, John, and Oleg Tsarev. *Deadly Illusions—The First Book from the KGB Archives*. London: Century, 1993.

Davis, Uri, Andrew Mack, and Nira Yuval-Davis (eds.). *Israel & the Palestinians*. London: Ithaca Press, 1975.

Deacon, Richard. *The Israeli Secret Service*. London: Sphere, 1979.

———. *British Secret Service*. London: Grafton, 1991.

Donner, Frank J. *The Age of Surveillance*. New York: Knopf, 1980.

Eban, Abba. *Personal Witness: Israel Through My Eyes*. London: Jonathan Cape, 1993.

Engler, Robert. *The Politics of Oil. A Study of Private Power and Democratic Directions*. Chicago: University of Chicago Press, 1967.

———. *The Brotherhood of Oil, Energy, Policy and the Public Interest*. Chicago: University of Chicago Press, 1977.

Ennes, James M. *Assault on the Liberty*. New York: Random, 1979.

Evans, Rowland, Jr., and Robert D. Novak. *Nixon in the White House*. New York: Vintage, 1972.

Eveland, Wilbur Crane. *Ropes of Sand*. New York: Norton, 1980.

Farago, Ladislas. *The Game of the Foxes*. New York: McKay, 1971.

Friedman, Alan. *Spider's Web: The Secret History of How the White House Armed Iraq*. New York: Bantam, 1993.

Gilbert, Martin. *Auschwitz and the Allies*. London: Michael Joseph/Rainbird, 1981.

Goulden, Joseph C. *The Death Merchants*. New York: Simon & Schuster, 1984.

Grayzel, Solomon. *A History of the Jews*. New York: Mentor, 1968.

Haines, Joe. *Maxwell*. Boston: Houghton Mifflin, 1988.

Hall, Sam. *Counter Terrorist*. New York: Donald Fine, 1987.

Halliday, Jon. *A Political History of Japanese Capitalism*. New York: Monthly Review Press, 1975.

Halliday, Jon, and Gavan McCormack. *Japanese Imperialism Today*. London: Penguin, 1973.

Hersh, Burton. *The Old Boys: The American Elite and the Origins of the CIA*. New York: Scribners, 1992.

Hersh, Seymour M. *The Price of Power*. New York: Summit Books, 1983.

———. *The Sampson Option*. New York: Random House, 1991.

Herzog, Chaim. *Heroes of Israel: Profiles of Jewish Courage*. London: Weidenfeld and Nicolson, 1989.

Higham, Charles. *Trading with the Enemy*. New York: Delacorte Press, 1983.

———. *American Swastika*. New York: Doubleday, 1985.

Höhne, Heinz, and Hermann Zolling. *The General Was a Spy*. New York: Bantam, 1972.

John, Robert, and Sami Hadawi. *The Palestine Diary 1945–1948*, vol. 2. New York: New World Press, 1971.

Kahn, David. *The Codebreakers*. New York: Macmillan, 1966.

Kaplan, Robert. *The Arabists: The Romance of an American Elite*. New York: Free Press, 1993.

Kelly, J. B. *Arabia, the Gulf and the West*. New York: Basic Books, 1980.

Knightley, Phillip. *Philby: The Life and Views of the KGB Masterspy*. London: Pan Books, 1989.

Kolko, Gabriel. *The Politics of War. The World and United States Foreign Policy 1943–1945*. New York: Vintage, 1970.

Kwitney, Jonathan. *The Crimes of Patriots*. New York: Touchstone, 1988.

Lacey, Robert. *The Kingdom: Arabia and the House of Sa'ud*. New York: Avon Books, 1983.

Laffin, John. *The P.L.O. Connections*. London: Corgi, 1983.

Laqueur, Walter. *The Terrible Secret*. London: Weidenfeld & Nicolson, 1981.

Laqueur, Walter, and Barry Rubin (eds.). *The Arab-Israeli Reader*. New York: Penguin, 1976.

Lernoux, Penny. *In Banks We Trust*. New York: Doubleday, 1984.

Lilienthal, Alfred M. *The Zionist Connection.* New York: Dodd, Mead, 1978.

Loftus, John. *The Belarus Secret.* New York: Alfred A. Knopf, 1982; reprinted New York, Paragon Press, 1990.

Loftus, John, and Emily McIntyre. *Valhalla's Wake: The IRA, MI6, and the Assassination of a Young American.* New York: Atlantic Monthly Press, 1989.

Lumer, Hyam. *Zionism: Its Role in World Politics.* New York: International Publishers, 1973.

McCartney, Laton. *Friends in High Places: The Bechtel Story.* New York: Ballantine, 1989.

McCullough, David. *Truman.* New York: Simon & Schuster, 1992.

Mangold, Tom. *Cold Warrior. James Jesus Angleton: The CIA's Master Spy Hunter.* New York: Touchstone, 1992.

Manning, Paul. *Martin Bormann.* Secaucus, NJ: Lyle Stuart, 1981.

Martin, David. *Wilderness of Mirrors.* New York: Harper & Row, 1980.

Millis, Walter (ed.). *The Forrestal Diaries. The Inner History of the Cold War.* London: Cassell, 1952.

Monroe, Elizabeth. *Philby of Arabia.* London: Faber and Faber, 1973.

Morstein, Manfred. *The Godfather of Terror: The Murderous Link Between Terrorism, Drugs and Arms Dealing.* U.S. government translation.

Mosley, Leonard. *Dulles: A Biography of Eleanor, Allen, and John Foster Dulles and Their Family Network.* New York: Dial Press, 1979.

Murphy, Brendan. *The Butcher of Lyon.* New York: Empire Books, 1983.

Murphy, Paul I. *La Popessa.* New York: Warner Books, 1983.

Nakdimon, Shlomo. *First Strike: The Exclusive Story of How Israel Foiled Iraq's Attempt to Get the Bomb.* New York: Summit Books, 1987.

National Security Archive. *The Chronology.* New York: Warner, 1987.

Netanyahu, Benjamin (ed.). *Terrorism: How the West Can Win.* Proceedings of the Jonathan Institute, 1984; New York: Farrar Straus Giroux, 1986.

Nixon, Richard. *The Memoirs of Richard Nixon.* New York: Grosset & Dunlap, 1978.

North, Oliver, *The North Diary,* declassified under U.S. Freedom of Information Act, 1993.

———. *Under Fire.* New York: Harper Paperbacks, 1992.

Odell, Peter R. *Oil and World Power.* Harmondsworth: Pelican, 1972.

Ostrovsky, Victor, and Claire Hoy. *By Way of Deception: The Making and Unmaking of a Mossad Officer.* New York: St. Martin's Press, 1990.

Oudes Bruce (ed.). *From the President: Richard Nixon's Secret Files.* London: André Deutsch, 1989.

Padfield, Peter. *Himmler: Reichsführer SS*. New York: Macmillan, 1972.

Page, Bruce, David Leitch, and Phillip Knightley. *Philby: The Spy Who Betrayed a Generation*. London: André Deutsch, 1968.

Pearson, Anthony. *Conspiracy of Silence: The Attack on the U.S.S. Liberty*. London: Quartet Books, 1978.

Perry, Mark. *Eclipse: The Last Days of the CIA*. New York: William Morrow, 1992.

Pipes, Daniel. *Greater Syria. The History of Ambition*. Oxford: Oxford University Press, 1990.

Philby, Harry St. John Bridger. *Arabian Days: An Autobiography*. London: Robert Hale, 1948.

———. *Arabian Jubilee*. London: Robert Hale, 1952.

———. *Arabian Oil Ventures*. Washington, D.C.: The Middle East Institute, 1964.

Philby, Kim. *My Silent War*. London: Grafton, 1989.

Podell, Janet (ed.). *The Annual Obituary 1981*. New York: St. Martin's Press, 1982.

Posner, Gerald, and John Ware. *Mengele: The Complete Story*. New York: McGraw-Hill, 1986.

Powers, Thomas. *The Man Who Kept the Secrets: Richard Helms and the CIA*. New York: Alfred A. Knopf, 1979.

Ranelagh, John. *The Agency: The Rise and Decline of the CIA*. New York: Simon & Schuster, 1986.

Raviv, Dan, and Yossi Melman. *Every Spy a Prince: The Complete History of Israel's Intelligence Community*. Boston: Houghton Mifflin, 1989.

Richelson, Jeffrey T., and Desmond Ball. *The Ties that Bind: Intelligence Cooperation between the UKUSA Countries—the United Kingdom, the United States of America, Canada, Australia and New Zealand*. Boston: Unwin Hyman, 1990.

Roberts, Glyn. *The Most Powerful Man in the World: The Life of Sir Henri Deterding*. New York: Covici Friede, 1938.

Robinson, Jeffrey. *Yamani: The Inside Story*. London: Simon & Schuster, 1988.

Rogow, Arnold A. *James Forrestal. A Study of Personality, Politics and Policy*. New York: Macmillan, 1963.

Rolef, Susan Hattis (ed.). *Political Dictionary of the State of Israel*. New York: Macmillan, 1987.

Roosevelt, Kermit. *Countercoup: The Struggle for the Control of Iran*. New York: McGraw-Hill, 1979.

Said, Edward. *Orientalism*. London: Peregrine, 1985.

Sampson, Anthony. *The Seven Sisters*. London: Coronet, 1988.

Sayer, Ian, and Douglas Botting. *Nazi Gold*. New York: Congdon & Weed, 1984.

Seale, Patrick. *Abu Nidal: A Gun for Hire*. New York: Random House, 1992.

Seale, Patrick, and Maureen McConville. *Philby: The Long Road to Moscow.* London: Hamish Hamilton, 1973.

Segev, Samuel. *The Iron Triangle: The Untold Story of Israel's Role in the Iran-Contra Affair.* New York: Free Press/Macmillan, 1988.

Shaffer, Ed. *The United States and the Control of World Oil.* London: Croom Helm, 1983.

Simpson, Christopher. *Blowback: America's Recruitment of Nazis and Its Effects on the Cold War.* New York: Weidenfeld & Nicolson, 1988.

———. *The Splendid Blond Beast: Money, Law and Genocide in the Twentieth Century.* New York: Grove Press, 1993.

Slater, Leonard. *The Pledge.* New York: Pocket Books, 1971.

Smith, R. Harris. *OSS. The Secret History of America's First Central Intelligence Agency.* Berkeley: University of California Press, 1972.

Sterling, Claire. *The Terror Network.* New York: Berkley Books, 1982.

Stevenson, William. *A Man Called Intrepid.* London: Sphere Books, 1977.

———. *Intrepid's Last Case.* London: Sphere, 1985.

Stockwell, John. *In Search of Enemies: A CIA Story.* New York: Norton, 1978.

Stork, Joe. *Middle East Oil and the Energy Crisis.* New York: Monthly Review Press, 1975.

Sunday Times Insight Team. *Insight on the Middle East War.* Sydney: Angus and Robertson, 1974.

Suvorov, Viktor. *Inside the Aquarium.* New York: Macmillan, 1986.

Truell, Peter, and Larry Gurwin. *False Profits.* New York: Houghton Mifflin, 1992.

Verrier, Anthony. *Through the Looking Glass: British Policy in the Age of Illusions.* London: Jonathan Cape, 1983.

von Klass, Gert. *Krupps: The Story of an Industrial Empire.* London: Sidgwick and Jackson, 1963.

Who's Who in the Arab World. Beirut and London: Publitec and Bowker, 1987.

Wilkins, Mira. *The Maturing of Multinational Enterprise. American Business Abroad from 1914 to 1970.* Cambridge, MA: Harvard University Press, 1974.

Wilson, Jeremy. *Lawrence of Arabia: The Authorized Biography of T. E. Lawrence.* New York: Athenaeum, 1990.

Winks, Robin. *Cloak and Gown. Scholars in the Secret War.* New York: William Morrow, 1987.

Wright, Peter. *Spycatcher.* New York: Viking, 1987.

Wyman, David. *The Abandonment of the Jews.* New York: Pantheon, 1984.

Yergin, Daniel. *The Prize: The Epic Quest for Oil, Money & Power.* New York: Touchstone, 1992.

INDEX

ABOUT THE AUTHORS

JOHN LOFTUS, an attorney, was born in Boston to an Irish Catholic family, and now lives in St. Petersburg, Florida. After service as an army officer, he completed his legal studies and, in 1977, joined the U.S. Justice Department in Washington, D.C. He was one of the first lawyers appointed to the Office of Special Investigations, responsible for prosecuting Nazi war criminals who had entered the United States illegally after World War II.

Mr. Loftus left government service in 1981 and obtained CIA permission to expose the intelligence scandals he had uncovered. In 1982 he helped *60 Minutes* to produce an Emmy-award winning documentary about the recruitment of Nazis by Western intelligence, and the assistance given them by U.S. spy agencies to settle in the United States. He then wrote a book called *The Belarus Secret*, which was the first detailed account of Western complicity in protecting Nazi mass murderers from justice after the war.

Mr. Loftus makes regular contributions to newspaper, radio, and television investigations on intelligence and related matters, and speaks widely throughout the United States on a wide range of topics. He is also the coauthor of *Valhalla's Wake* (with Emily McIntyre), which recounts the story of the assassination of a young American citizen by British intelligence as a result of his involvement with the Irish Republican Army.

Mr. Loftus's last book, *Unholy Trinity: The Vatican, The Nazis and Soviet Intelligence* was coauthored with Mark Aarons. *Unholy Trinity* is the first definitive history of the Vatican's intelligence service, and tells the story of how Pope Pius XII authorized the smuggling of Nazi war criminals out of Europe to the United States, Canada, Australia, Britain, and South America in cooperation with U.S., French and British intelligence, and how Soviet intelligence penetrated the operation and subverted it for Stalin's purposes. *The Secret War Against The Jews* is the second major collaboration between Mr. Aarons and Mr. Loftus.

MARK AARONS lives in Sydney, Australia, where he spent 20 years working as a broadcaster and investigative reporter for the Australian Broadcasting Corporation. In the mid–1970s he began to investigate the large

Nazi émigré community in Australia, and produced a series of documentaries which were debated hotly in the Australian parliament. After Mr. Loftus's first book, *The Belarus Secret,* was published in 1983, Mr. Aarons began to collaborate with him on a series of documentary projects. The first was about Klaus Barbie, the "butcher of Lyons," and the second was a series of documentaries called *Investigating the Vatican,* which won the prestigious Armstrong Award in 1986.

In 1986, with the help of Mr. Loftus, Mr. Aarons produced a series of documentaries, which examined the war crimes of several prominent Nazis living in Australia. As a result of these broadcasts, the Australian government established an official inquiry which confirmed that Nazis were living in Australia, and recommended legal sanctions against them. The government then amended the War Crimes Act to make it possible to prosecute Nazi war criminals, and established the Special Investigations Unit to gather evidence against them, resulting in several criminal trials in Australian courts.

Mr. Aarons is the author of *Sanctuary: Nazi Fugitives in Australia* which recounts how Nazis were settled "down under" with the help of Western intelligence, and how the Australian government protected them after they had emigrated. He is also the coauthor of *East Timor: A Western Made Tragedy* (with Robert Domm), which tells the story of the ongoing genocide by the Indonesian government against the people of East Timor, a Portuguese colony just north of Australia, which Indonesia illegally occupied in 1975. Mr. Aarons now writes fulltime, having left the ABC in 1993, and makes regular appearances on Australian television and radio. He has contributed to several major newspapers and magazines, and speaks widely on intelligence and related subjects.